Guthrie Memorial Library
Hanover's Public Library
Hanover, PA 17331-2283

WITHDRAWN
By
Guthrie Memorial Library
Hanover's Public Library

HANOVER
PUBLIC
LIBRARY

PERPETUAL MEMORIAL

Gift of

CO-OWNER EMPLOYEES,
THE SHERIDAN PRESS

In Memory of

JAMES T. HUSTON, JR.

Bernard Shaw

Florida A&M University, Tallahassee
Florida Atlantic University, Boca Raton
Florida Gulf Coast University, Ft. Myers
Florida International University, Miami
Florida State University, Tallahassee
University of Central Florida, Orlando
University of Florida, Gainesville
University of North Florida, Jacksonville
University of South Florida, Tampa
University of West Florida, Pensacola

University Press of Florida
Gainesville
Tallahassee
Tampa
Boca Raton
Pensacola
Orlando
Miami
Jacksonville
Ft. Myers

Bernard Shaw

A Life

A. M. Gibbs

Guthrie Memorial Library
Hanover's Public Library
Hanover, PA 17331-2283

B SHAW

Copyright 2005 by A. M. Gibbs
Printed in the United States of America on acid-free paper
All rights reserved

10 09 08 07 06 05 6 5 4 3 2 1

A record of cataloging-in-publication data is available from the Library of Congress.
ISBN 0-8130-2859-0

The University Press of Florida is the scholarly publishing agency for the State University System of Florida, comprising Florida A&M University, Florida Atlantic University, Florida Gulf Coast University, Florida International University, Florida State University, University of Central Florida, University of Florida, University of North Florida, University of South Florida, and University of West Florida.

University Press of Florida
15 Northwest 15th Street
Gainesville, Fl 32611-2079
http://www.upf.com

To Donna

I rejoice in life for its own sake. Life is no "brief candle" to me. It is a sort of splendid torch which I have got hold of for the moment; and I want to make it burn as brightly as possible before handing it on to future generations.

Shaw, in a speech delivered at Brighton, Eng., 1907

As institution, the author is dead: his civil status, his biographical person have disappeared; dispossessed, they no longer exercise over his work the formidable paternity whose account literary history, teaching, and public opinion had the responsibility of establishing and renewing; but in the text, in a way, I *desire* the author: I need his figure (which is neither his representation nor his projection), as he needs mine.

Roland Barthes, *Mythologies*

If a man is a deep writer all his works are confessions.

Shaw, *Sixteen Self Sketches*

Funding to assist in publication of this book
was generously provided by the
David and Rachel Howie Foundation

Contents

Illustrations xi

A Note on Quotations from Shaw's Writings xv

Introduction 1

1. "A Family of Pooh-Bahs": Shaw's Irish Origins 5
2. The Family Skeletons 19
3. Growing Up in Dublin 37
4. The Townshend Connections 57
5. Self-Searching: London and the Novels 77
6. A Fabian Don Juan 103
7. Rival Attractions 123
8. "The Coming Man": Critic and "Platform Spellbinder" 137
9. On Stage 152
10. A Taste of Success 170
11. Wars of the Theaters, Mothers and Bicycles 177
12. An Irish Courtship 195
13. Marriage 210
14. New Century, "New Religion" 231
15. Eternal Irishman 245
16. Edwardian Summers 267
17. Votes for Women 293
18. Enter Critics, Stage Right 307
19. A Love Affair, a Death, and a Triumph 314
20. Armageddon, and the "Ruthless Light of Laughter" 343
21. Sages, Saints, and Flappers 364
22. The Road to Baveno: Dangerous Flirtations 382
23. World Traveler and Village Squire 400
24. Last Flourishes and the Call of the Silver Screen 431
25. "A man all light": Last Years 440

Abbreviations and Notes 459

Acknowledgments 521

Index 525

Illustrations

BL	British Library
BLPES	British Library of Political and Economic Science
BSTC	F. E. Loewenstein, *Bernard Shaw Through the Camera*, 1948
Guelph	Dan H. Laurence Collection, University of Guelph Library
Getty	Getty Images
PTBA	Photo Taken by Author
Tas	Private Collection, Tasmania

Illustration Location

Between Chapters 4 and 5
Bernard Shaw of Kilkenny—Tas
Frances Shaw—Tas
Sir Frederick Shaw, 1872—Tas
Frederick Shaw—BSTC
Lucinda Elizabeth Shaw—BLPES
Lucinda Elizabeth and George Carr Shaw—BSTC
Walter John Gurly—BLPES
33 Synge Street—PTBA
Drawing Room—PTBA
Shaw's Bedroom—PTBA
Derry House Rosscarbery—National Library of Ireland
Bushy Park House—PTBA
Lucinda Frances Shaw—BLPES
Elinor Agnes Shaw—BLPES
Matthew Edward McNulty and Shaw—BSTC
Shaw as Mephistopheles—Guelph
Shaw with Robert Moore Fishbourne—BLPES
Shaw with his sister Lucy—BSTC
Juvenile Sketches by Shaw—BL
Shaw at Ventnor—BLPES

Townshend Family—BLPES
Edward Carr Shaw—Tas
Charles MacMahon Shaw—Tas
Bernard Shaw of Hobart, Chief of Police—Tas

Between Chapters 13 and 14
Shaw in 1898—BLPES
Beatrice Webb—BLPES
Sidney Webb—National Portrait Gallery, London
Graham Wallas—BLPES
William Archer—BSTC
Alice Lockett—Guelph
May Morris—Christie's Images
Mrs. Jane Patterson—Guelph
Florence Farr—University of London Library
Ellen Terry—Getty
Janet Achurch—Guelph
Annie Besant—Getty
Eleanor Marx—Marx-Engels Photo Gallery
Sir Arthur Wing Pinero and Shaw—*Vanity Fair*, Jan. 1897
"The Platform Spellbinder"—BLPES

Between Chapters 19 and 20
Charlotte Shaw on Beach—BLPES
Shaw as Beggar—BLPES
Charlotte in early 1900s—BLPES
Shaw in 1906—BLPES
Charlotte Shaw, 24 January 1904—BLPES
Harley Granville-Barker—Guelph
Lillah MacCarthy as Ann Whitefield,—Theatre Museum, Covent Garden
Erica May Cotterill—Guelph
Mrs. Patrick (Stella) Campbell—BLPES
Shaw at Lady Gregory's Estate, 1915—Guelph
Augustus John Portrait of Shaw—Fitzwilliam Museum, Cambridge, UK

Between Chapters 23 and 24
Shaw at Burren Pier, Galway Bay—Guelph
Shaw in AC Motor Car—BLPES
Shaw on diving platform, Antibes—BLPES
Shaw at Pompeii—BL

Shaw diving at Madeira—BLPES
Shaw in the Strand, London, May 1927—Getty
Shaw at work in hut, 1929—BLPES
Sir Edward Elgar conducting—Getty
Maggie Cashin receiving mail at Ayot—*Shaw the Villager and Human Being,* ed. Allan Chappelow, 1961
Villa leased by Molly Tompkins, Lake Maggiore—PTBA
Molly Tompkins at her exhibition, 1934—*Shaw and Molly Tompkins,* ed. Peter Tompkins, 1961
Shaw, aged eighty-nine, in garden at Ayot—Getty
The house, viewed from the garden at Ayot—Welwyn Garden City Library
Shaw with Danny Kaye, 1949—BLPES
Shaw with Robert Morley and Gabriel Pascal—Guelph
Shaw at 94—BLPES

A Note on Quotations from Shaw's Writings

In quotations from Shaw's writings in the present work, his preferences regarding spelling and punctuation have been preserved. These include the omission of apostrophes in words such as "don't," "you've," and "didn't," where no ambiguity results. Quotations from Shaw's novels are from the Constable standard editions. Quotations from the plays are from the Penguin Classics editions, except as indicated in the discussion of *Pygmalion*.

Introduction

The writing of this new life of Shaw was largely inspired by a compulsive curiosity and fascination similar to that which drives the central characters in A. S. Byatt's novel *Possession: A Romance,* which deals with a biographical quest. Having been familiar with Shaw's work since schooldays, and having written about various aspects of his life and career in other books and essays, I became obsessed with the idea of trying to come to grips with the man and his inner life and personality in a biographical study. The materials for such a study are dauntingly numerous and very widely scattered. During the course of his long life, Shaw wrote over fifty plays and playlets, five novels, and several short stories. He is estimated to have written more than a quarter of a million letters, many of which are still being published in special editions that supplement the four-volume collection edited by Dan H. Laurence. The prefaces he wrote to his own works and those of others, his music and theater criticism, book reviews, and his autobiographical writings are published in multiple volumes. His other nondramatic writings—such as political tracts and polemical works like *Common Sense About the War* (1914)—also fill many volumes. His contributions to periodical literature number in the thousands—enough to fill the CVs of dozens of academics. Apart from Shaw's published writings, there are large collections of unpublished materials relevant to biographical study in various institutions in the United Kingdom, North America, and Canada. Small caches of Shaviana have a way of turning up in almost every corner of the world. Some of the material used in the present work was found in a private house belonging to descendants of one of Shaw's uncles in Tasmania, an island state of Australia lying off the southern coast of the mainland—the next stop being the South Pole.

The vast size of the subject is not the only problem in the field of Shaw biography. In William Golding's classic tale *The Lord of the Flies*—to invoke another novelist—the group of schoolboys who are cast up on a desert island without any adults work out a way of controlling their early discussions about their situation and plans by passing round a large seashell, which they call "the conch." The person who holds the conch has a right to speak without interruption. As far as the story of his own life was concerned, Shaw went to great lengths during his lifetime to ensure that the biographical conch remained firmly in his own hands. Even in his collection of autobiographical essays called *Sixteen Self Sketches* (1949), published in his ninety-third year, he was still tenaciously in control of his story. One of the last chapters in the book is called "Biographers' Blunders Corrected." The Shavian stamp on his life story began to be asserted in the 1890s and early twentieth century, when he was gradually becoming a well-known figure in literary and intellectual circles, with the writing of autobiographical articles about himself with catchy titles such as "Who I Am, and What I Think." The early biographies of Shaw by Archibald Henderson and Hesketh Pearson were in many ways forms of surrogate autobiography in that Shaw fed both writers with large quantities of material that became the staple of their works. "The best authority on Shaw is Shaw,"[1] the playwright told Archibald Henderson; but even Henderson, influenced as he was by Shaw, came to realize that his hero's word was not always to be trusted. The Shavian account of his life, particularly of its early years, has been uncritically adopted and lavishly embroidered by all of his major biographers. One of the aims of this book has been to pass the conch around and let other voices from the past relate the story of Shaw's life and associations.

The subjects of Shaw's long life and extraordinarily productive career lend themselves to a wide range of biographical approaches. Like all other forms of human knowledge, biography does not stand still. New information continually comes to light, as it has during the writing of this book, both through my own research and that of others. With changes in intellectual, cultural, and social history, new ways of looking at existing sites of biographical study naturally emerge. The present study interprets Shaw's life and defines its major themes in ways that differ from those found in the earlier biographies by Archibald Henderson, Hesketh Pearson, St. John Ervine, and Michael Holroyd.[2] Drawing extensively on previously unpublished and overlooked material, this book radically challenges existing views of Shaw, creating a portrait of the man that is new in both its factual and conceptual foundations.

Bernard Shaw: A Life presents a completely revised account of Shaw's family background and upbringing—especially regarding the characters of his parents and the early days of their marriage—and newly identifies a number of key influences on Shaw's development during his Dublin childhood. His attitudes toward sex and his own sexuality are reexamined, and fresh perspectives are presented on those subjects, and more generally on Shaw's emotional life and psychological makeup are presented. His relations with the numerous women in his life—with both his close relatives and his numerous female friends and lovers—and their influence on his creative writing are more fully explored here than in previous biographies. His contribution to changing attitudes toward gender roles in Victorian society, and his creative involvement in the formation of new paradigms of male-female relations, and new theatrical values, liberated from the constraints and delusions of nineteenth-century ideals and conventions, are among other subjects that are freshly explored in this book. His politics and his "religion," as he called it, of Creative Evolution are closely examined in the context of other aspects of Shaw's life, as are his attitudes toward Ireland and his Irish background and identity.

The numerous unpublished materials that are drawn upon in this study include: the only surviving piece of autobiographical writing by Shaw's mother, Lucinda Elizabeth Shaw; correspondence from Shaw's father, George Carr Shaw, to Lucinda Elizabeth in the early years of their marriage; letters from his father to Shaw himself during the latter's early years as a struggling novelist and journalist in London; letters to Shaw from his uncle, Richard Frederick Shaw; diaries and correspondence of Shaw's wife, Charlotte; correspondence written by various women friends of Shaw and his lover, Mrs. Jane Patterson, during the early London years; letters to Shaw from his friend William Archer; autobiographical material Shaw supplied in response to questionnaires from an Irish American scholar, Thomas Demetrius O'Bolger; and correspondence from Shaw to Janet Achurch, Pakenham and Ida Beatty, Sir Arthur Wing Pinero, Denis Johnston, Lady Stanley (wife of the British explorer), Rachel Mahaffy, and various Australian relatives. The present study also draws upon extensive research carried out in connection with my previous publications, including *Shaw: Interviews and Recollections* (1990) and *A Bernard Shaw Chronology* (2001). A number of illustrations—including reproductions of juvenile sketches by Shaw and portraits by an unknown artist of his paternal grandparents—are published here for the first time.

* * *

In one of his letters to Archibald Henderson, Shaw described himself as a man "up to the chin in the life of his own time."[3] Earlier he had boldly declared in a letter to a friend that "my business is to incarnate the zeitgeist."[4] Shaw's engagement with his epoch was indeed remarkably full; he was, in manifold ways, a herald and creator of cultural and social change. Thus, a biography of Shaw has to trace his career in relation to a wide spectrum of factors that shaped the spirit of the age in which he lived. There was, however, another side of Shaw that I hope this biography will bring out. In the final scene of Shaw's play *Captain Brassbound's Conversion* (1899), the brooding, Byronic rebel Captain Brassbound pays a fine compliment to the heroine, Lady Cicely Waynflete, by saying:

> Since you saw me for the first time in that garden, youve heard me say nothing clever. And I've heard you say nothing that didnt make me laugh, or make me feel friendly, as well as telling me what to think and what to do. Thats what I mean by real cleverness.

The special kind of "cleverness" celebrated here—an intelligence of the heart characterized not by mental pyrotechnics or logic but by sensitivity, warmth, and friendliness of feeling, coupled with psychological shrewdness—is a recurrent theme in the Shavian comic universe. In his comedies, instinctive life, feeling, and passion repeatedly triumph over reason and system. The disorderly Life Force—whose embodiment in Shaw's creative imagination is more often female than male—sweeps away the pretensions of rationality. The present study is dedicated to a greater understanding not only of Shaw the controversialist and social critic but also of the man who celebrates, and often exemplifies in his many friendships, the intelligent heart.

1

"A Family of Pooh-Bahs"

Shaw's Irish Origins

George Bernard Shaw came into the world as he was destined to live in it—unconventionally. He arrived on Saturday, 26 July 1856, after a difficult breech birth, as the third child and only son of George Carr Shaw Esq., gentleman corn merchant, and Lucinda Elizabeth ("Bessie"), a leading amateur soprano and (later) professional music teacher. The boy was delivered by Dr. John Ringland, Master of the Coombe Lying-In Hospital, Dublin, and an announcement of the birth appeared the following Monday in *Saunders's News-Letter and Daily Advertiser*.[1] Both mother and son were physically robust. Bessie Shaw lived till she was eighty-three, with hardly a day's illness until she suffered several strokes toward the end of her life. Her son also enjoyed mostly very good health; he had already celebrated his ninety-fourth birthday when he died at his home in the tiny village of Ayot St Lawrence, in Hertfordshire, England. Shaw disliked his first given name of George and habitually signed his name in formal contexts as G. Bernard Shaw. In 1890 he began signing his music criticism for *The World* with the initials GBS; with his growing fame as playwright and social critic, the initials became an instantly recognizable name for him worldwide.

The birthplace was the Shaw family home, 3 Upper Synge Street, Dublin, which was renamed 33 Synge Street after the authorities decided to do away with the distinction between the upper, middle, and lower sections of the street. The three-storey dwelling in a row of terrace houses had been built not long before the Carr Shaws came to live there following their marriage in 1852.* Though it was then located at the edge of the city and formed part of a recent housing development, the house is about a fifteen-minute walk from the center of Dublin, providing easy access to such landmarks as St. Stephen's Green, Trinity College, Parliament, and the National Library and Art Gallery.

* Skillfully and meticulously restored so as to resemble its appearance in the mid nineteenth century, the house is now a Shaw Museum.

The gallery was opened in 1854 to great fanfare, in time for it to become one of Shaw's favorite haunts while growing up in Dublin. Unlike Merrion Square, where Shaw's fellow countryman Oscar Wilde was raised (since the mid eighteenth century it had become an attractive residential area for members of Dublin's social elite), Synge Street was not a very fashionable address. The architectural elegance of some pockets of eighteenth-century Dublin had not been repeated in this fairly ordinary street of semi-detached houses built in the middle of the following century. Here is how Shaw described his birthplace in a letter written in 1930 to Frank Harris: "The house had in the basement, a kitchen, a servant's bedroom and a pantry. On the *rez de chaussée* [ground floor] a parlor (a *salle à manger*), a nursery, and a 'return room' which served as a dressing room for my father, and subsequently as also a bedroom for me when I grew out of sleeping in the nursery with my two sisters. Upstairs was the drawing room and the best bedroom; and that was all."[2]

The Ireland into which Shaw was born in the second half of the nineteenth century was economically backward, ridden with denominational and political strife, and cursed with an extraordinarily rigid and socially divisive class system. Poverty and squalor were everywhere to be seen, not least in the slums of the overcrowded city of Dublin. Shaw has one of the characters in his early novel *Immaturity* declare: "I hate Ireland. It is the slowest, furthest behind its time, dowdiest, and most detestably snobbish place on the surface of the earth." That is not the only opinion about the country expressed in the novel, but it does touch on some of the key problems of nineteenth-century Ireland; moreover, it is in tune with some of Shaw's own complex views about his native land. A few years before Shaw's birth, the Great Exhibition was held in London under the patronage of Queen Victoria's consort, Prince Albert. On show was a sampling of the marvels of invention and symbols of progress developed as a result of the Industrial Revolution. It was an impressive display of power by a country that was becoming the center of a vast empire. The Industrial Revolution of course brought with it a huge toll of human misery, but it was also the engine of economic and political power. With only limited participation in the Industrial Revolution, Ireland was left behind; in some ways it was rather like a neglected outpost of empire, with some of the characteristics of subaltern, garrison states similar to those of the British colonies.

Ireland was a cultural as well as economic and political backwater, so it was almost miraculous that within as many decades in the second half of the nineteenth century the small country gave birth to four writers who were to become towering figures in the history of modern literature and drama. Oscar Wilde was born two years before Shaw, in 1854; W. B. Yeats, who was to become a Nobel laureate two years before Shaw received his award, was born a decade later; and in 1882 the transformer of the novel as a literary form, James Joyce, was born in the city a character in one of his short stories described as "dear, dirty Dublin."[3] The word "dear," however, would never have been included in any of Shaw's descriptions of his native city. All four writers were, in fact, Dublin-born, though Yeats had stronger early associations with the lovely rural scenes of Sligo, the memories of which remained for him, as he put it in a well-known early poem, "in the deep heart's core."[4] Shaw's first experience of the enchantment of Ireland's scenery was not to occur until he was ten years old, when his family moved for a time to the seaside area of Dalkey, outside Dublin.

Ireland left an indelible imprint on the outlook and work of each of the four writers. Yet it was also true of each of them that they held hostile and critical opinions about the country, and that in order to bring their literary ambitions to fulfillment they had to leave Ireland for the broader cultural streams of London and Europe. Even Yeats, who retained stronger ties with Ireland than the other three, came to maturity and wrote some of his most distinctively Irish poems in London. The drive toward self-exile from Ireland as a path to self-realization was vividly expressed by the Irish novelist George Moore in his autobiographical work *Hail and Farewell* (1911–14), where he wrote that while writing "The Wild Goose," it occurred to him that "it being impossible to enjoy independence of the body and soul in Ireland, the thought of every brave-hearted boy is to cry, Now, off with my coat so that I may earn five pounds to take me out of the country." Shaw anticipated this in an 1896 letter to his future Irish wife-to-be, where he wrote that "as long as Ireland produces men who have the sense to leave her, she does not exist in vain."[5]

* * *

As with many catchall phrases imposed on the fabric of Irish history, "Protestant Ascendancy" has its limitations. Nevertheless, ever since the successful invasions of Ireland in the late seventeenth century by King William III of England (William of Orange) and his defeat of the Irish and European Catholic forces (which had rallied to the cause of the deposed and exiled James II), Protestants did have the ascendancy in the political and social dispensation of affairs in Ireland for over two centuries. They were also the largest property holders. The Irish Shaws had been associated with the Protestant Ascendancy since its foundation.

In a summary description of his Irish relatives in a 1912 postcard to his Socialist friend Henry Hyde Champion, Shaw wrote: "We are a family of Pooh Bahs–snobs to the backbone. Drink and lunacy are minor specialties." Unlike the pompous character in Gilbert and Sullivan's *Mikado* whose name gave us the term *Pooh-Bah*, Shaw's own father, George Carr Shaw, was not the holder of multiple positions of high public office. The nearest he came to being a Pooh-Bah was an early period of employment as a (presumably minor) civil servant in the Dublin Four Courts.[6] However, the larger clan of Irish Shaws, to which the comparatively impecunious George Carr was related, did answer well to the playwright's description. In the great denominational, political, and social divide that had remained one of the defining characteristics of the Irish nation since the Reformation—the hostile relationship of Protestants and Catholics—the Shaws belonged to the class of the top dogs and played prominent roles in the Protestant Ascendancy. The Irish Shaws saw themselves as akin to the great family dynasties of Europe. According to the irreverent playwright, "the Shaws" thought and spoke of themselves as being on the same social plane as families such as the Bourbons and the Hapsburgs, "and their world conceded their point to them."[7] The mere fact of being related to this Irish "house" of Shaws was seen as conferring high social status.

Evidently fired by the same anti-Catholic feeling that drove the new king of England, William III, in his campaigns in Ireland, on 7 August 1689 a certain Captain William Shaw delivered to a Committee of the House of Lords in London his written "Proposals for subduing those in rebellion in Ireland." The Shaws were originally a Scottish clan, but by this time the branch of the family represented by the author of this document had moved to Hampshire. The prejudiced yet decisive Captain Shaw outlined a detailed plan of action involving the dispatch of "seven or eight nimble frigates" and "some good ships of war, with 8,000 or 9,000 arms," to deal with the "infatuated" Papists whose activities were presenting an unprecedented threat of revolt in Ireland.[8] Thanks to his subsequent involvement in William III's Irish campaigns, Captain William Shaw was to become the founder of the line of Irish Shaws from which the playwright is descended. After the Battle of the Boyne, he was rewarded with a grant of land at Sandpits, an area adjacent to the Earl of Bessborough's Demesne at Piltown, near Carrick-on-Suir, County Kilkenny. Eighteenth-century gravestones at St. Nicholas's Church of Ireland* at Carrick-on-Suir confirm that Shaw families were established in that region from the early years of the century. GBS's grandfather and namesake, Bernard Shaw of Kilkenny, was directly descended from Captain William Shaw.

During the eighteenth and nineteenth centuries several members of the Irish branch of the Shaw clan rose to positions of great prominence in the social, political, and judicial systems of the Ascendancy regime. Among them

---

* The church is now a Heritage Museum.

was Robert Shaw, cofounder of "Shaw's Bank," which later became the Royal Bank of Ireland. He held the office of Accountant General of the Post Office and purchased Terenure Manor in Dublin. This side of the family was raised to the baronetage when, on 17 August 1821 Sir Robert Shaw was created 1st Baronet of Bushy Park by George IV. In 1796 he had acquired the large estate and imposing residence of Bushy Park House, Terenure, as part of his marriage dowry from Abraham Wilkinson. In the playwright's lifetime the Pooh-Bah in residence at Bushy Park was the 3rd Baronet, the Right Honorable Sir Frederick Shaw, Recorder of Dublin, MP, and privy councillor. Sir Frederick was the epitome of the strongly pro-British, church-and-state establishment in the Protestant Ascendancy regime. Queen Victoria thought him extremely handsome.[9]

Although Shaw says he visited it on only one occasion,[10] Bushy Park House holds a symbolic place in his reconstructions of his childhood. The prosperous and powerful Bushy Park Shaws were the point of contrast in his famous description of his immediate family's position in the social hierarchy as belonging to "the Shabby Genteel, the Poor Relations, the Gentlemen who are No Gentlemen."[11] Alluding to his father's and his own situation in relation to the more fortunate Shaws, the playwright comically referred to himself as a social "downstart."[12]

The Carr Shaws of Synge Street were not in line to inherit any of the wealth enjoyed by their rich relations. Nevertheless the future playwright was brought up in relatively comfortable surroundings in a household staffed with servants. In the beguiling narratives about his family background found in his numerous and scattered autobiographical writings, Shaw exaggerated the poverty of the Carr Shaws; he also told other tales about them that can be shown to be highly questionable. He was not one to spoil a good story with the truth, as will be seen in an examination of the family skeletons in the next chapter.

* * *

Catholics did not have a monopoly on the production of large families in the nineteenth century. Shaw's paternal grandfather, Bernard Shaw of Kilkenny, and his wife, Frances Carr Shaw, daughter of the Reverend Edward Carr, rector of Kilmacow (near Waterford), brought forth a family of fifteen children, of which the last was stillborn. Bernard Shaw of Kilkenny combined activities as a public notary and stockbroker with holding office as High Sheriff of Kilkenny. As represented in an anonymous portrait of him (now in Tasmania), his features could be those of a romantic poet or a musician, although very little is known about him. He died in 1826 while still in his early fifties, allegedly having suffered a loss of some fifty thousand pounds through fraudulent behavior on the part of a Dublin business partner.

Left in dire financial straits and saddled with the care of eleven of the children, Shaw's grandmother, Frances, was rescued by Sir Robert Shaw, the 2nd Baronet of Bushy Park, who, according to Shaw's Australian cousin Charles MacMahon Shaw, was in love with her and unsuccessfully sought her hand in marriage. Sir Robert provided the family with rent-free accommodations in a "quaint cottage, with Gothically pointed windows" located on the grounds of the Bushy Park estate. Shaw remembers the cottage as running "picturesquely along its little walled garden near the tram terminus." The brass helmet and sword of grandfather Bernard, obtained during his service "in the Yeomanry or Militia as a gentleman amateur soldier," hung in the hallway.[13]

The adult Shaw frequently entertained listeners in conversation (and amused readers) with stories about his father's family. He remembered their having between them a remarkable number of squints, to such an extent that a squint became so familiar a phenomenon to him that he came to notice it "no more than a pair of spectacles or even a pair of boots."[14] Oscar Wilde's father, the famous eye surgeon Sir William Robert Wilde, is said to have attempted to correct the squint of Shaw's father with an operation, but he only succeeded in making the squint go in the other direction.[15] (Although Shaw said his father had a "stupendous squint,"[16] it is barely discernible in one of several surviving photographs.)

All members of the family played some type of musical instrument. Shaw's father played the trombone and could render "Home, Sweet Home" on the pennywhistle or flute.[17] The aunts could all "pick out tunes" on the piano. His eldest uncle, Barney (William Bernard Shaw), played a wind instrument called the ophicleide, a giant forerunner of the tuba, which Berlioz described as "a chromatic bullock" and which Barney was able to make "moo and bellow very melodiously." Aunt Emily played the violoncello and Aunt Charlotte the harp and tambourine. Evenings were spent at Bushy Park "with the bachelor Sir Robert and his clan seated round an ottoman on which . . . uncle Barney stood, solemnly playing Annie Laurie on the ophicleide."[18] George Carr Shaw and Barney had also been members of a brass band that gave open-air concerts at the Ely Gate on the River Dodder. When their welcome at Bushy Park ran out (according to Shaw, it was because of their drinking habits, but more probably because of the Carr Shaws' associations with Catholics),[19] they enlisted two others and formed a brass quartet that traveled around the country "playing all the popular tunes by ear,"[20] depositing the pennies they collected in the charity box at the Mercers Hospital.

Uncle Barney figures prominently in Shaw's stories as an example of the family's specialization in "drink and lunacy." Though "a most amiable man," as Shaw describes him, Barney evidently combined his ophicleide playing with a large consumption of alcohol and was hardly ever sober in his younger days. After many years of bachelorhood, however, he suddenly renounced his drinking and smoking and married "a lady of distinguished social position and great piety." He then became fervently religious, though the old Adam showed through in his practice of sitting "with a Bible on his knees, and an opera glass to his eyes, watching the ladies' bathing place in Dalkey." (According to Shaw, his sister Lucy, a swimmer, corroborated this story, at least as far as the opera glass was concerned.) Uncle Barney's mind deteriorated in old age, and after suffering from various religious delusions—including the idea that he was the Holy Ghost—he was eventually committed to a lunatic asylum in the north of Dublin, where he came to an unusual end. Shaw recalls that his "custodians" in this institution, fearing the possibility of suicide, thought they had removed every possible weapon but had "reckoned without the Shavian originality." Uncle Barney attempted to take his life by strangling himself in a carpet bag that had somehow been left within his reach, dying of heart failure in the process.[21]

Some members of the family became part of the great nineteenth-century Irish diaspora. Four of the children migrated to Australia, where two of them settled permanently. One of the daughters, Frances ("Fanny") Shaw, emigrated to Western Australia in 1830 with her husband, Arthur Greene, and her younger brother, Edward Carr Shaw. After several adventures, including a shipboard fire, *The Rockingham* was wrecked in a storm on the coast of Western Australia at the place now named after it. The three then traveled on the schooner *Eagle* to Tasmania, where they began farming at Campania. The Greenes having returned to Ireland, Edward Carr Shaw moved to the eastern coast of Tasmania, where he established a property (still in Shaw family hands) at Swansea called "Red Banks." Edward Carr Shaw prospered in Tasmania and became an important local dignitary—Shaw compared his Australian immigrant uncles to Mr. Micawber in *David Copperfield* who succeeded in mending his broken fortunes by migrating to Australia. One of the Edward Carr Shaw family, another Bernard Shaw, became chief of police in Hobart, prompting GBS to dub him "the Supercop." A daughter of this Tasmanian side of the family, "Patty" Shaw, who was later to become Lady Lyne, would have been the wife of the first prime minister of Australia at Federation had her husband, Sir William Lyne, been able to form a ministry when invited to do so. The ninth child of the family, Robert, migrated to Australia but returned and settled in England. The last migrant was the thirteenth child,

Walter Stephen, who settled in Melbourne and worked as a clerk in a government auditing office. One of his sons was Charles MacMahon Shaw, the author of a Shaw family history called *Bernard's Brethren.*[22]

Shaw's father and the non-emigrating aunts and uncles all remained in Dublin. One of the uncles, Richard Frederick Shaw, became another of the Shaw family Pooh-Bahs, serving as chief of staff of the Irish Valuation Office. It was through Uncle Frederick's influence that the future playwright gained his first employment in 1871 as a clerk (and, later, chief cashier) at the respectable land agent's office of Uniacke Townshend. Aunt Charlotte had a daughter who was to become the first celebrity in the family, the prolific novelist and journalist Mrs. Cashel Hoey. Mrs. Hoey introduced Shaw to Arnold White, who offered him a job with the Edison Telephone Company in 1879. Her second husband, John Cashel Hoey, was agent-general in London for the State of Victoria, Australia.

* * *

GBS's attitude toward the Shaw clan was highly critical. He disliked the family snobbery and laughed at its pretensions. He also reacted strongly against the narrowness and prim censoriousness of the Protestant churchgoers the family's affiliations brought him into contact with. As he grew up, he developed strong sympathies with English radical Protestantism—with the republicans Cromwell and Milton; with Bunyan and the Quaker-born Tom Paine; and, of course, with the whole tradition of revolutionary nonconformism in England, as represented by figures such as Blake and Shelley. However, he detested the institutionalized Protestantism, with all its social trappings, of his youth in Ireland. In a well-known statement first published in 1898, Shaw described Irish Protestantism as "not . . . a religion" but "a side in political faction, a class prejudice, a conviction that Roman Catholics are socially inferior persons who will go to hell when they die and leave Heaven in the exclusive possession of Protestant ladies and gentlemen."[23]

Despite his stated hostility toward his "Family of Pooh-Bahs" and undoubtedly sincere dislike of their prejudices, Shaw's own social manners (and eventual social position as a kind of squire of the village of Ayot St Lawrence, employer of chauffeurs, housekeepers, and other servants, and first-class traveler), his accent, circle of friends and acquaintances, and his marriage to the wealthy daughter of an Irish landowning family, complicate the account of his relationship to his family background. The integrity of his lifelong dedication to attacking social inequalities and class prejudice is unquestionable. He was always ideologically and spiritually a friend of working-class people, and there is much evidence to show that he was completely without snobbishness in his personal dealings with them. Yet even in his office-boy days in Dublin, he never became closely associated with people at the lower end of the socioeconomic scale. His own social background contributed in a variety of ways to the shaping of the Shavian career and his complex persona—more so, perhaps, than he himself would have wanted to admit.

* * *

Shaw's mother, Lucinda Elizabeth ("Bessie") Shaw, came from a family named Gurly that belonged to the hunting, shooting, and fishing representatives of Protestant Ascendancy society. It is not altogether clear whether her father, Walter Bagnall Gurly, followed any other pursuits, apart from collecting rent from the odd assortment of properties that he owned. The Gurlys were members of the Irish squirearchy, landowners in County Carlow and the west of Ireland, and attorneys-at-law. In the chancel of St. Mary's Church of Ireland, Carlow, is an elaborate monument in late-eighteenth-century neoclassical style erected by "THO.S GURLY ESQ.RE,/ as an affectionate Tribute to the Memory of his Brother/BAGNEL GURLY Esq.RE, /and to Commemorate his many Virtues." After enumerating his many qualities and his "Social Virtue that sweetens and adorns private Life," the tablet goes on to record that Bagnel Gurly died on 25 February 1796 in his twenty-fifth year. The gentleman who commissioned this monument was Shaw's great-grandfather, Thomas Gurly, solicitor and registrar of Leighlin diocese. The Gurlys were a leading family in the Carlow district, descended from James Gourlay (or Gourly) of Wexford, who originally hailed from Cumberland and Chester. The Gurly family, like the Shaws, were clearly prominent lay members of the Church of Ireland.

In a Carlow town valuation of tenements taken around 1853, Walter B. Gurley [*sic*] is named as the lessor of twelve properties in Carlow and one in the parish of Ballinacarrig. A number of these Carlow properties were inherited—reluctantly—by GBS on the death of his uncle Walter John Gurly in 1899. The properties were mostly small tenement houses and yards, used as dwellings and offices, but they also included an impressive building known as The Assembly Rooms, which was originally used for social gatherings and entertainments, such as balls and concerts, by the local gentry.[24] In 1945 Shaw brought to fruition a plan he had conceived long before of making a gift to Carlow town of his properties there, a special act of the Irish Republican parliament (the Dáil) being required to effect the unusual procedure of municipalizing privately owned property.

Walter Bagnall Gurly married twice. On 29 December 1829 he first married Shaw's maternal grandmother-to-be, Lucinda Whitcroft, daughter of Squire John Hamilton Whitcroft of Highfield Manor, Whitchurch, Rathfarnam, a cotton manufacturer, landowner, and pawnbroker, and Lucinda Davis of Dublin. On 25 May 1852 he married his second wife, Elizabeth Anne Clarke. By his first marriage Walter Bagnall Gurly had two children. The first was Shaw's mother-to-be, Lucinda Elizabeth Gurly, who was born on 6 October 1830. The second child was Walter John Gurly, who was educated at Kilkenny College and later enrolled at Trinity College, Dublin. He entered medical school and became a licentiate of the Royal College of Surgeons.[25] On 14 July 1881, following several years of service as a ship's doctor on the Inman Line, he set up practice as a physician at 200 High Road, Leyton, Essex, on the border of Epping Forest. He married Emily Jane Walton, but the marriage was without issue. Shaw described Walter in *Sixteen Self Sketches* as his "Rabelaisian uncle," a rich source of ribald jokes and "unprintable limericks." Along with George Carr Shaw and the musical entrepreneur Vandeleur Lee—with whom, from early 1867, the Shaw family shared houses in Dublin and Dalkey—GBS regarded him as one of his three "fathers."[26] During his early days in London, Shaw occasionally visited his uncle and Emily Gurly in Leyton; the Gurly house was his refuge when he was ill with smallpox in the summer of 1881.

By his second marriage Walter Bagnall Gurly had seven children, six daughters and a son who died in infancy. Those who had a special connection with Shaw included Arabella ("Moila"), who, after being widowed young from her husband, John Gillmore, resided with GBS's mother (her half-sister) Bessie Shaw from 1898 until the latter's death in 1913. She later became a companion to Mrs. Jane ("Jenny") Patterson, Shaw's lover in the 1880s and early 1890s. Arabella's daughter, Georgina ("Judy"), who married Harold Chaworth Musters in 1912, served as Shaw's first full-time secretary from 1907 to 1912. Another of Walter Bagnall's daughters by his second marriage, Georgina ("young Georgie"), was Shaw's favorite aunt.[27]

* * *

GBS's father, George Carr Shaw, was eleven years old when his father, Bernard Shaw of Kilkenny, died in 1826. In 1838 he occupied a clerical position at the merchant firm of Todhunters, where he remained for seven years.[28] Probably through the potent influence of the Right Honorable Sir Frederick Shaw, Recorder of Dublin, around 1845 he obtained his post as a civil servant in the Four Courts. (The position was apparently some sort of sinecure; the duties it entailed are not known.) When the post was abolished in 1851, Shaw received a pension of forty-four pounds per annum. After brief periods of employment in ironmongery and corn merchant firms, he sold his pension to a Mr. Joseph Henry O'Brien for the sum of five hundred pounds. With this capital he was able to enter into a partnership with one George Clibborn in an established wholesale corn, flour, and cereals firm. Clibborn and Shaw had an office and warehouse located at 67 Jervis Street and a mill (purchased in 1857) "on the country side of the canal, at the end of a rather pretty little village street called Rutland Avenue"[29] in Dolphin's Barn, where GBS was sometimes taken by his father to play as a child.

After the death of Walter Bagnall Gurly's first wife in 1839, Shaw's future mother, Lucinda Elizabeth Gurly, was placed in the care of her maiden aunt, Ellen Whitcroft, who was aided in this task by John Hamilton Whitcroft, Ellen's brother. Aunt Ellen lived in Palmerston Place, Dublin, and under her care Bessie received an education in French, music, and all the ladylike virtues. From 1839 to 1846 she studied piano at the music-teaching establishment of Johann Bernhard Logier; she has left a lively account of the Logier teaching methods.[30] Bessie had a mezzo-soprano voice that Shaw describes as being "of extraordinary purity of tone."[31] Following her marriage, she became a leading amateur concert and opera singer in Dublin. She composed songs and, as a devotee of spiritualism and seances, produced some remarkable "spirit" drawings.[32]

* * *

The marriage of Shaw's parents took place on 17 June 1852 at St. Peter's Church, Dublin. The bridegroom is described in the church register as a bachelor residing at 17 Lennox Street, Dublin, and the bride as a spinster from Stillorgan. The minister officiating at the ceremony was the Reverend William George Carroll, the husband of George Carr Shaw's sister, Emily. The marriage was witnessed by the bride's father and a gentleman named George H. MacMullen.[33] According to GBS—the only source of information about the matter—the honeymoon was spent at Liverpool. George Carr and Lucinda Elizabeth Shaw had three children, Lucinda Frances ("Lucy"), Elinor Agnes ("Yuppy"), and George Bernard. The latter was nicknamed "Bob" or "Bobza" as an infant and "Sonny" as a young boy.

Like her mother, Lucy Shaw had a fine mezzo-soprano voice and enjoyed a successful career as a star performer in musical comedy and light opera until she was forced into retirement after contracting tuberculosis around 1898–99. She had a working knowledge of several languages, wrote translations of plays by Strindberg for the Adelphi Stage Society, and tried her hand at translations of works by Ibsen and Bjørnson. Lucy worked initially in amateur productions under the direction of Vandeleur Lee, whom she came to dislike intensely. According to Shaw, Lee developed "a certain sexual sentimentality" in his London days and made unwelcome amorous advances toward Lucy, who was by this time "very attractive." Lucy found his attentions "odious."[34] She made her professional theatrical debut as "Frances Carr" on Christmas Eve 1879 in the pantomime *Beauty and the Beast* at the Royal Park, Camden Town, and subsequently worked with the Carl Rosa and D'Oyly Carte Opera companies. From the mid 1880s Lucy was frequently on tour, leaving Shaw alone with his mother. She married fellow actor Charles Robert Butterfield in 1887 and, following a long separation, divorced him in 1909. Shaw's lifelong friend Matthew Edward McNulty (known as Edward) had a close friendship with Lucy that lasted long after she had refused his marriage offer in the late 1870s. Regarding their personal correspondence as "sacred," McNulty burned it all on her death, keeping in his Dublin home only the Bechstein piano she had bequeathed him, which Shaw arranged to be sent to him.

By all accounts, as well as being physically attractive Lucy was confident without being overbearing, clever, and personable, outshining her shy brother in their early years. She is recalled in the characterization of two women in Shaw's early novels: Lalage Virtue in *The Irrational Knot* and Madge Brailsford in *Love Among the Artists*. From the time of his marriage, Shaw gave financial assistance to Lucy, who was gradually reduced to invalid status by her tuberculosis.

The second daughter of the family, Agnes, was described by Shaw's friend McNulty as "a lovely, sweet-tempered girl with large hazel eyes and superb, reddish-gold hair which could be combed almost to her heels."[35] Other than a fine photographic portrait taken in 1874, which still survives, little is known about this sister. She contracted tuberculosis, as her sister was later to do, and died at the age of twenty-one in the Hospital Saint Lawrence at Ventnor, on the Isle of Wight. She is buried in a churchyard at Ventnor beneath a tombstone that bears the following text from St. Paul's Epistle to the Philippians: "To be with Christ which is far better" (1:23).

* * *

The speculation—enthusiastically endorsed by Thomas Demetrius O'Bolger, B. C. Rosset, and others—that Shaw was the product of an adulterous relationship between Vandeleur Lee and Bessie Shaw is based on very slight "evidence." While it is not possible to make categorical statements about the matter, on balance it seems highly unlikely to have any foundation in fact.[36] Particularly in his old age, the playwright showed a strong family resemblance to male relatives in the Shaw clan. In a 1947 postcard written after receiving photographs of his grandparents' portraits from Tasmania, Shaw exclaimed about his grandmother: "What a change the Carr nose and ears made!"[37] In a 1942 letter to Grace Goodliffe he declared that "the Carr nose is now all over Australia."[38] Both Shaw himself and his paternal uncle, Edward Carr Shaw, the immigrant to Tasmania, bear clear traces of those Carr features, and their general family likeness is apparent in photographs taken in old age. There is also a striking resemblance in some photographs between GBS and his Tasmanian first cousin, another Bernard Shaw, the eldest son of Uncle Edward. Various comments by Shaw and others suggest that his mother had a very strong sense of propriety. In a 1916 letter to O'Bolger, Shaw wrote that his mother was "one of those women who could act as matron of a cavalry barracks from eighteen to forty and emerge without a stain on her character."[39]

* * *

In his autobiographical writings Shaw wrote a good deal about his immediate family. However, like that of many people, his interest in his more distant ancestry was spasmodic and his knowledge patchy. At times certain possibilities of connections between himself and famous historical figures would catch his imagination. He liked to think that his lineage could possibly be traced to the Scottish thane Macduff, the slayer of Macbeth and a suitable role model for a quixotic world betterer. He also entertained the theory that his family was related by marriage to Oliver Cromwell ("old Noll," as Shaw called him), a connection that many other Irishmen would not care to trumpet. The Cromwell connection rested on the dual assumptions that a certain Mary Markham (who became one of Shaw's great-great-grandmothers) was the sister of Bishop William Markham, archbishop of York from 1777–1807, and that this Markham family was descended from Oliver Cromwell. Neither of these assumptions turned out to be correct. Bishop Markham had only one sister, Elizabeth, who died unmarried and childless. Moreover, the idea that this Markham family ancestry could be traced back to Cromwell was shown to be erroneous by a family member, Sir Clements Markham. The Irish Mary Markham in the Shaw ancestry was a daughter of Bernard Markham of Fanningstown, County Kilkenny: this was most likely the way in which the name Bernard was introduced into the Shaw family pool of Christian names.[40]

One of Shaw's summaries of his Irish ancestry, which appeared in a letter written in 1936 to his future biographer St. John Ervine, is a factually flawed but—as usual when writing about his family—entertaining statement. After declaring his descent from "Macduff the Unborn, through his third son Shaigh," Shaw continues in sweeping style: "I am also descended from everybody who was alive and fertile in these islands in the XVII century and earlier; but old Noll and Macduff are my selections."[41] Who could argue with such poetic genealogical licence? When discussing his ancestry and family, Shaw did not often fall into what Oscar Wilde, in *The Decay of Lying*, deplores as "careless habits of accuracy."

2 The Family Skeletons

In all his accounts of his family background and childhood in Dublin, Shaw seems to have been governed by a strong—perhaps unconscious—urge to present himself as a self-created phenomenon, a man who rose to fame out of very unpromising and adverse circumstances, a process in which his biological parents did little to help and, in the case of his father, much to hinder. He does acknowledge certain legacies from his parents. From his father, he asserts, came his fondness for comic anticlimax and a spirit of skepticism about the stories in the Bible. Shaw also acknowledges the supreme importance in his early life of his mother's musical interests and career and the influence on him of her mentor, Vandeleur Lee. On the whole, however, Shaw's self-portraits involved the creation of extremely negative views of his parents that have greatly influenced subsequent accounts and interpretations of his life.[1] With a father ruined by drink and hopelessly incompetent in business, so his story goes, and a mother who, whatever other admirable qualities she may have possessed, lacked "the specific maternal passion" except as it was rather feebly displayed in the case of her daughter Agnes,[2] Shaw was thrown entirely onto his own resources. He was fond of boasting that he was lucky in having three fathers: his biological one, Vandeleur Lee, and his blasphemous uncle, Walter Gurly. One by one, however, each of these fathers was discredited, leaving the impression that he virtually had to become his own father. He presented himself almost as a product of autogenesis and amusing autobiography was one of his instruments of self-creation. Unlike the trustworthy Houyhnhnms in Swift's *Gulliver's Travels*, however, Shaw was frequently apt to say "*the thing which was not*" in telling his life story, a set of narratives over which, as has been noted, he tried to maintain the tightest authorial control. While his own accounts of his life must be respected, their veracity is often thrown into doubt by information drawn from other sources.

The story of the early years of marriage of Shaw's parents and the impressions that have been handed down concerning their character and behavior toward their son have been almost entirely shaped by the accounts in Shaw's autobiographical writings. A substantial amount of evidence suggesting that these accounts may be unreliable has been largely overlooked. Important documents have remained unpublished. Although he had scathing things to say about biography as a literary form, from the 1890s to just before his death in 1950 Shaw continually regaled his readers with often hilarious—and frequently misleading—accounts of his family background and upbringing; his advice to T. P. O'Connor (contained in an autobiographical sketch first published in 1898) that "all autobiographies are lies"[3] has not been as closely heeded by subsequent commentators as it deserves to be in his case. He described himself as having to an "abnormal degree" the Shaw family "power of derisive dramatisation that made the bones of the Shavian skeletons rattle."[4] Apart from his sister Agnes, who died at twenty-one, no member of Shaw's immediate family escaped the fate of being immortalized in his cartoonlike portrayals of their characters and mannerisms. As Archibald Henderson justly remarked, Shaw "was incapable both professionally and temperamentally of drawing a true portrait of any member of his family or relative."[5]

The salient feature of most existing accounts of the family, the essential outlines of which have their roots in Shaw's autobiographical writings, is that his parents' marriage was instantaneously discovered to be a disaster by Mrs. Shaw while on their honeymoon in Liverpool, and that she became permanently estranged from her husband from that moment. It is true that after some twenty-one years of marriage, Shaw's mother decided to leave her husband and Dublin and to set up practice as a music teacher in London. What happened within the marriage in the intervening years, however, is a more complicated matter than Shaw and later commentators have allowed us to see.

* * *

Shaw's account of the marriage and its immediate aftermath is a Victorian melodrama in comic form. In preparation for the climax of the story in his late collection of autobiographical writings, *Sixteen Self Sketches* (1949), he describes his father at this time as an "apparently harmless gentleman of forty."[6] (George Carr Shaw was thirty-seven when he married the twenty-two year-old Bessie on 17 June 1852.) According to Shaw, Bessie's Aunt Ellen, with whom she was still living in Dublin at the time of her entry into society and courtship by George Shaw, intended to bestow a large dowry on her niece. In one of his accounts (provided to Thomas O'Bolger) Shaw unequivocally states that his father's motive in proposing marriage to Bessie was "to make a bid for [the] property" of her aunt.[7] Although this allegation was substantially toned down in *Sixteen Self Sketches*, there remains in the later account a clear insinuation that his father was behaving as an "adventurer."[8]

Shaw relates that Bessie's announcement of her engagement brought vehement opposition from her family. Not only was this George Carr Shaw impecunious, he was also a drunkard. When Bessie confronted her fiancé with the latter charge, he replied that he was "a convinced and lifelong teetotaller."[9] The "adventurer" was also a deceiver, however, since he failed to explain that although he was a teetotaller in principle, he was not so in practice. The pair were duly married, and Bessie was cut off without a penny by her aunt. They traveled to Liverpool on honeymoon, and it was there that the young bride discovered the horrid truth. Opening her bridegroom's wardrobe, she found it "full of empty bottles."[10] While attempting to run away to sea to become a stewardess, she was molested by rough Liverpool dockyard workers. Resigning herself to her "tragedy,"[11] she returned to Dublin and to a "hell" of "shabby-genteel poverty with a drunken husband."[12]

Inconveniently for the plot of Shaw's account of his parents' honeymoon, his elder sister, Lucy, was born on 26 March 1853, exactly nine months and nine days after the marriage of George Carr and Lucinda Elizabeth. The Wronged Innocent had clearly yielded to the embraces of The Deceiver on at least one occasion at about the time of the marriage and, in all likelihood, on the fateful honeymoon.

Shaw's biographers have largely followed—and elaborated upon with their own touches of melodrama—the Shaw account of the marriage. In forensic style B. C. Rosset declares: "I believe that when George Carr stood exposed as a drunkard and a liar, Bessie Elizabeth had been driven beyond the breaking point, and the little that held them together was permanently breached. I finally suggest that Mrs. Shaw detached herself from her husband, rejecting him in every sense, including, possibly, the sexual sense.[13] Other biographers are unanimous in declaring the marriage to have been a loveless affair, entered into for mercenary reasons on George Carr Shaw's part, and on Bessie's part because she wanted to escape from an intolerable domestic situation.[14]

* * *

In the summer of 1857—as Bernard Shaw was reaching his first birthday (26 July) and almost nipping a long career in the bud by falling backward through a kitchen window—his mother, in the company of her eldest daughter, Lucy, traveled to the west of Ireland on a month's visit to her father. She left behind her in the Shaw house at Synge Street her husband and the two other children, Agnes and George Bernard ("Yuppy" and "Bob"—or "Bobza"—as they were currently nicknamed), a nurse, and a cook-maidservant.

Fifteen letters written by George Carr Shaw to his wife while she was staying with her father provide a uniquely revealing glimpse into the life of the family at this time. Shaw kept these letters, together with a few others written to him by his father during his early years in London as a struggling journalist and novelist. Several quotations from the 1857 letters were included by Bernard Shaw in the first chapter of *Sixteen Self Sketches*. Because of his father's references to himself as a baby, Shaw entitled the chapter "My First Biographer." (George Carr Shaw *was* the first biographer of GBS. Unfortunately for the future reputation of the former, his son became practically the only biographer of his father.) Numerous passages—which raise profound doubts about the truth of his tales about the beginning of his parents' marriage and could even be said to make nonsense of them—were omitted by Shaw. The letters his father wrote to him in London, which show a keen and intelligent interest in Shaw's early writings, are never mentioned by Shaw and have been overlooked in biographical accounts. In his letters the playwright's father appears as an amiable, sweet-natured man, with a quirky sense of humor (he loved puns), an inquiring mind, and a great deal of patience.

Written shortly after the fifth anniversary of the Shaw marriage, the letters of George Carr to Bessie Shaw, which were apparently exchanged on an almost daily basis, contradict suggestions that the relationship between the two had broken down from the time of their honeymoon.[15] The letters are loving and good-humored in spirit. Bessie is addressed variously as "my darling one," "my honey," "my beloved Bess." A letter dated 18 August begins: "I like your signature this morning better than any I have had from you yet. You *are* my own Bessie and may you long continue to be so."[16] Absence may have made the heart grow fonder, but to sign herself his "own Bessie" hardly suggests a state of emotional estrangement on her part. Bessie's replies were eagerly awaited, being brought in by "Bob" in his first attempts at walking: "You are better than goodness for writing so regularly. . . . Whatever the motive power . . . that impels you write away my honey or I will feel disappointed every morning that Bob does not stagger into me with a letter from you and desperate fighting there is to get it from him."[17]

That the relationship included a good deal of banter and teasing, especially on the young wife's part, is suggested in more than one passage. In a letter of 20 July he issues the following reproach: "You are a coward to take advantage of the distance you are from me to indulge in sauciness and impertinence but I shall take a memorandum of it in the Tablets of my memory and have it in reckoning for you when you come back."[18] When she sent the children kisses—apparently with orders that he was to have none for himself—he replied: "I delivered your kisses to Yup and Bob but contrary to your instructions I fobbed a few for myself. You know how sweet a stolen kiss is!"[19]

The correspondence shows that as a father George Carr did not conform to the type of the remote patriarch having little contact with children that gentlemen of his class tended to be in the Victorian era. His one-year-old son—and future proponent of theories about the Life Force—was apparently charged with a great deal of vitality at this time. The father variously reports that "Bob is growing very unruly,"[20] adding "I left him this morning roaring and tearing like a bull."[21] These reports issued forth from a father who was clearly delighting in his parental role:

> We are all getting on famously here—Yup and I generally spend the morning together between my dressing room and the parlor—Bobza also honors me with his company and we have walking matches together. His exploits in that way have not yet extended beyond a couple of yards which he performs in a plunge from Nurse to me and back again to Nurse or Brabazon. . . .
>
> I brought the 2 youngsters out yesterday morning and gave them a drive in the pambulator [*sic*] which they, indeed I too enjoyed greatly. . . .
>
> Bob spent some time in bed with me this morning. . . . I was at home in the middle of the day, and had a great ½ hours [*sic*] fun with Yup and Bob.[22]

At around this time Bessie was apparently recovering from a bout of ill health and suffering from an aching face. For the latter George Carr prescribed gin: "I think you ought to try the Gin again if you get back. There are some people . . . with whom such a remedy might prove worse than the disease but I am not afraid of you, and as to its being a nasty dose that is only little childrens [*sic*] talk."[23]

Clearly alcohol was not a taboo subject at this time; the fact that George Carr Shaw was able to speak quite openly about it inevitably raises doubts concerning the legends created by his son about this aspect of the family background. Nevertheless, his father's drinking was a subject to which Shaw returned more than once; from his point of view it was the major skeleton in the cupboard of the family history.

Shaw first began to write about the subject in 1879 in a pseudoclinical note addressed to Dr. James Kingston Barton, a medical friend at St. Bartholomew's Hospital, London.[24] At the time the twenty-three year-old Shaw was researching the subject of dipsomania for his new novel *The Irrational Knot*. He apparently chose to present Kingston Barton with a type of case history in which, under the rubric "Instance of involuntary abandonment of brandy drinking," he presented a survey of the drinking habits of his father's family. According to this account, the main drinkers were three of the brothers, including his father. On one or two occasions, Shaw reported, his father went on binges and disappeared for a few days before coming home "with every symptom of an uncontrolled excess," although "ordinarily he came home in the evening, fuddled, ate his dinner, had a nap, and then kept going out for drams [shots of brandy] until he went to bed." The case history goes on to record that "his appetite was good, but he suffered from diarrhea at intervals." The account presents George Carr Shaw, before he gave up alcohol altogether, as mostly a steady tippler: "Although he was never sober, he was seldom utterly drunk." The term *unconvivial* is applied by Shaw to his father not as a description of his social character as a whole but more specifically in relation to his drinking habits: he and his brothers were "alike in being unconvivial dramdrinkers. They avoided observation while drinking."[25] In this note Shaw says that his father had abandoned drinking altogether (following some kind of fit)[26] for "more than ten years" before the date the note was written, after a previous period of abstinence that had lasted sixteen months. This means that by the time the playwright had reached his teens—and several years before the parental separation—his father was a complete teetotaller.

Although his teetotaller son may have exaggerated George Carr Shaw's drinking problem, it seems unlikely that his stories were without some basis in fact. Whatever the extent of his father's drinking, it clearly played a highly significant role in Shaw's reconstruction of his childhood and his accounts of the formative shaping of his outlook on life. But Shaw's foregrounding of his father's weakness in various autobiographical writings has tended to overshadow other aspects of George Carr Shaw's character, especially the nature of the father-son relationship during Shaw's childhood and early manhood, which have been neglected by Shaw himself and his previous biographers.

The father's interest in his son's development continued during this period. Shaw recalls that although his father was not a great reader, "he had read Sir Walter Scott and other popular classics; and he always encouraged me to do the same, and to frequent the National Gallery, and to go to the theatre and the opera when I could afford it."[27] His first experience of reading aloud occurred while he was sitting on his father's knee.[28] George Carr Shaw gave his son his first swimming lessons at Killiney Bay, solemnly telling him that it had been his own ability to swim that enabled him, at the age of fourteen, to save the life of his brother Robert. Seeing that the young Shaw was very impressed by this, the father leaned down and said confidentially: "And to tell you the truth, I never was so sorry for anything in my life afterwards," following which he "plunged into the ocean, enjoyed a thoroughly refreshing swim, and chuckled all the way home."[29] Swimming was to become one of Bernard Shaw's favorite recreations in later life.

Shaw's journeys round his father in his autobiographical writings peter out after the period of his early childhood and teenage years. The letters that George Carr Shaw wrote to his son in the late 1870s and early 1880s (after the latter had moved to London) show that he took a keen interest in Shaw's early creative activities. Along with presents of postal notes in amounts ranging from 10 to 30 shillings and complaints about the "ill-natured cur"[30] for not writing would come encouraging and shrewd comments on various writings that Shaw appears to have been sending to him in installments. A particular favorite of his father's among Shaw's character creations in the early novels was Sidney Trefusis in *An Unsocial Socialist.*

Trefusis is a wealthy young man who drops out of fashionable society to carry out subversive Socialist activities among the rural gentry, adopting the guise of a servile yokel called Smilash. In a letter dated 15 August 1884 containing a postal order for one pound and the message "sending the same to your Mar," George Carr wrote: "I am very fond of friend 'Slimash' [*sic*] altho' I don't altogether agree with him as I cannot see how his ideas can be carried out even supposing he is right."[31] Evidently in response to a complaint about the misspelling of Smilash, he wrote again a fortnight later:

> 15/- [shillings] enclosed. Hope it will keep you from starving.
>
> Thanks for your letters. If I spelled your hero "Slymash," as you say I did, it was altogether a slip of the pen. I know and like the name too well to make any mistake about it. I agree in a great measure or in fact altogether with him (which of course means you) as to the working people not receiving a fair share of the produce of their labor, but as I said before how is the evil to be remedied? Without Capital it strickes [*sic*] me that the work cannot be carried on, which is to give either the Employer or employed the needful![32]

The same father who forbade his son to play with a schoolfellow whose father was in trade as a shopkeeping ironmonger[33] was still able to respond sympathetically and intelligently to the young man's fictional portrait of an unsocial Socialist busily and outrageously engaged in verbally tearing apart the whole fabric of the class system.

In a 1937 letter Shaw did admit to feelings of remorse about being "inconsiderate" toward his father when the latter was still alive. A revised version of this letter was published in *Sixteen Self Sketches*, where the relevant sentence reads: "When I recall certain occasions on which I was inconsiderate to [my father] I understand how Dr. Johnson stood in the rain to expiate the same remorse."[34] However, the remorse was not sufficient to prevent Shaw from making some very damaging remarks about his father in his autobiographical writings, the justice of which is open to question. Shaw's telescoping of events and subsequent distortion of his father's moral identity is reminiscent of Pirandello's exploration of such issues in the portrayal of the Father in *Six Characters in Search of an Author*. Like the poet James Clarence Mangan and other nineteenth- century Irishmen, Shaw seems to have been driven by some desire to commit a form of rhetorical parricide, to "slay his da," as Shawn Keogh puts it in Synge's *Playboy of the Western World*.

* * *

Although Shaw was generous enough in his acknowledgment of his mother's musical talents and the vital part she played in his early musical education, he was also the sole source for images of her as a cold and emotionally reserved woman, and for the idea that she had "no comedic impulses."[35] The latter statement is called into question by the accounts of more than one eyewitness. Archibald Henderson recalled that "her eyes danced with suppressed mirth as she talked, and it is quite easy to see from whom her son derived his sense of humour."[36] When Katharine Tynan had tea with May Morris and Bessie Shaw in the garden of Kelmscott House in September 1889, she found that, "like her son, she was very witty, very satirical, and yet neither wit nor satire left anything painful behind." Mrs. Shaw, she remembered, "expressed strong Irish Protestant sentiments."[37] Sydney Haldane Olivier (later Baron Olivier), an early Fabian friend and associate, recalls that his acquaintance with Shaw's mother, whom he frequently met at her home at 29 Fitzroy Square in London, was "as delightful and invigorating" as that of Shaw himself."[38] Her social and political opinions are pungently suggested in Shaw's report of her comment in response to his pointing out R. B. Cunninghame Graham to her in Regent Street: "Nonsense! Cunninghame Graham is one of your Socialists: that man is a gentleman."[39]

The only surviving piece of autobiographical writing by Bessie Shaw is a brief account, written for Bernard, of her childhood piano lessons from 1839 to 1846 under the direction of the Logier family. Graphic images of the constraints under which the Logiers placed their piano pupil are followed by an engagingly self-deprecatory assessment of her success in this branch of music:

> I . . . have often played with various coins of the realm on the backs of my hands, also with my hair which I wore in two long plaits down my back tied to the back of the chair, also with a square of pasteboard hung on my neck by a string pretty much as pictures are hung on the wall now-a-days, in order to prevent me looking at my hands. . . . I remember perfectly that one of the battle cries was "keep your wrists down & keep de fingers on de keys[.]" I think the highest flight attempted in that academy was Mose in Egitto arranged by Thalberg & now that I look back it was generally a disgraceful scramble[.] I got it as a reward of merit at the last & I humbly beg to apologise to all on whom I inflicted my performance of it or indeed anything else[.] But in those days I had quite a reputation as a splendid "performer" & no doubt I accepted the verdict as my just due & continued to believe in it until not long after my marriage I went to hear Thalberg—he played his "Mose" arrangement. After which I said to myself "Never again" & gave up the piano thenceforth & for ever.[40]

The impression one gains is that of a spirited lady with a sense of fun.

One cannot simply deny Shaw his perceptions that he grew up in a loveless household, that his mother was deficient in maternal feeling, and that she deprived him of maternal love. Nevertheless, like a great deal of the information about his family in the "derisive dramatisations" he created about them, the veracity of his claims remains open to question.

Someone who knew both Shaw and his mother and who touched on the subject of the "loveless household" in a later recollection was Grace Chappelow, second cousin of photographer and author Allan Chappelow, who edited collections of biographical materials about Shaw that were published in the 1960s. In the 1890s Grace Chappelow attended the North London Collegiate School for Girls, where by this time Bessie Shaw had gained public recognition as an outstandingly successful music teacher. (Lucy Shaw reported of her mother's teaching at the school that "she delighted in the work and was most successful, her College taking the highest honours at an examination in the Albert Hall of six hundred schools.")[41] In what appears to be the only surviving memoir of Shaw's mother from one of her pupils at the school, Grace Chappelow recalled that she visited the Shaw house at Fitzroy Square for private singing lessons on a weekly basis while Shaw was still living there, and that she was always asked to stay for tea. She remembered being served delicious, thinly sliced homemade bread, and being dubbed by Mrs. Shaw "the bread-and-butter girl." (Mrs. Shaw would instruct Mrs. Harris, the housekeeper, that "the bread-and-butter girl is coming for tea.") Shaw was frequently present at these afternoon teas and Grace had what she described as "some degree of 'crush' on him."[42] Sometimes Grace would find Mrs. Shaw knitting unusual "Japanese-style" socks for her son, with "separate compartments or 'thumbs' for big toes." This was a service Bessie Shaw continued to provide for her son even after his marriage. In a 1903 letter to Ida Beatty, wife of his friend Pakenham Beatty, in which he was discussing the subject of clothing for her son Bert, Shaw advised against buying Jaeger socks as being too expensive and not as good as home-knitted ones. "All my socks," he wrote, "are made by my mother, who has learnt in her old age how to knit rights and lefts instead of the usual same for both feet."[43]

Grace Chappelow admired her teacher and friend Mrs. Shaw, recalling that "her voice was soft and rich. She was a most charming, gentle, and kind woman. I was very fond of her, and she of me." She was also puzzled by the "loveless household" idea, which had been circulating by the time she wrote her recollection for publication in 1961. This seemed very much at odds with her impressions of the household at Fitzroy Square:

> I have read in some books that the Shaw household was supposed to be loveless. I don't know if there was any truth in this as regards their earlier life in Dublin, but it certainly wasn't true of the household I knew. She had, of course, separated from her husband long before I first met her. I never saw Mrs. Carr Shaw kiss her son, or vice versa, but in any case, such intimacies were not considered proper before guests in those days, so that doesn't prove anything. She used to call her son "G.B." The atmosphere of her home was a friendly and hospitable one. There was plenty of affection, even if not of a demonstrative kind.

The writer, of course, had no way of knowing, except by inference, what things were like in the "earlier life in Dublin," but what she says does supply an important perspective on Shaw's mother and her relations with her son.

Grace Chappelow also wrote in her recollections about Mrs. Shaw's spiritualism and her claim that she often received messages from her deceased daughter Agnes. After Shaw had married and left Fitzroy Square, Grace remembered the excitement at one of Mrs. Shaw's afternoon teas about his having finished writing *Man and Superman.* Knitting socks for a grown-up son and taking a keen interest in his work, in addition to seeking conversations in the spirit world with a much-grieved-for daughter, do not seem to be the marks of a woman who lacked maternal affection.

After his arrival in London in 1876, Shaw lived companionably and (apparently) harmoniously with his mother for twenty-two years until his marriage in 1898. They attended plays and concerts together, and Shaw recalls lively comments his mother made on some of these occasions. His diary records her coming in one day with a present of the score of Wagner's *Parsifal,* which made the future author of *The Perfect Wagnerite* "spend a good deal of [his] time at the piano in consequence."[44] Music must have been a major subject of mutual interest for these two very knowledgeable experts. Shaw's mother closely followed all the activities of both of her surviving children. In the extensive correspondence of Lucy Shaw—who, as her letters repeatedly show, adored her mother—there is not a word about Bessie Shaw being an unloving parent. Following his mother's death in 1913, Shaw wrote in a letter to Mrs. Patrick Campbell: "My sister found among my mother's belongings the cap I used to wear as a baby. Had anyone suggested such a possibility I should have laughed him (or her) to scorn. We never know anything about our parents."[45]

Considering the highly suspect accounts of his parents Shaw created in his autobiographical writings, the last sentence in this passage takes on a peculiar resonance. In his apparent determination to present his life story as having begun in circumstances that were both materially and psychologically adverse, the reputations of both his parents became casualties in ways that seem unjust in the light of information other than that provided by Shaw himself.

* * *

One biographer who took Shaw to task over his portrayals of his family during his lifetime was his Australian first cousin, Charles MacMahon Shaw, in his 1939 book *Bernard's Brethren.*[46] The tone of MacMahon Shaw's treatment of his distinguished cousin in this book is generally genial and respectful, but one of his stated motives for writing his family history of the Shaws was his feeling that in various autobiographical statements GBS had misrepresented his family—especially his father. He was touching on a tender nerve. When GBS reviewed the typescript of his cousin's book, a red pen was brought out to set right a large number of statements that Charles had made about the family. The book was finally published with most of Shaw's inked-in comments included as marginal commentary. The comments were generally good-humored and, of course, proved a major selling point for the book. Many of the marginal corrections were well justified. But when the narrative began to deal with Shaw's immediate family, the red ink seemed to become redder, with expostulations such as "Oh! these Australians," "Charles: you are a liar," "For shame, Charles!," and—perhaps most memorably—"Rubbish! I was . . . a Freethinker before I knew how to think."[47]

From a biographical point of view, Charles MacMahon Shaw's challenge—based on evidence from other members of the family—to GBS's accounts of his father is the crux of the Australian cousin's critical case in *Bernard's Breth-*

ren. Charles could not help feeling that Shaw's depiction of his father as "a miserable drunkard" was a vast exaggeration of the truth. It clashed with other family members' recollections of George Carr Shaw ("a dear old courteous and charming gentleman")[48] and may have had some psychological origins of which GBS was not fully aware. "I can't help wondering," the Australian cousin ventured boldly, "if the egotism that must be the basis of all genius does not spur a great man on to repudiating his father."[49] Shaw took some pains to set Charles straight about his father's drinking habits. However, for some reason—possibly because it made him sound too defensive—his rebuttal of the charge of repudiating his father was omitted from the published text. The unpublished interlinear comment reads: "I never repudiated my father. I have done everything I could to bring out his amiable side, and to show that my comedic genius is inherited from his humorous delight in anti-climax. But it is useless to deny that he wrecked his marriage and ruined his career by drinking. I have made as little of it as I can. Don't try to make it worse by putting speeches into my mouth which quite belie my feelings."[50]

* * *

In his autobiographical writings Shaw frequently reverts to the subject he once referred to as his family's "ridiculous poverty."[51] He pronounced his father "impecunious and unsuccessful," and says that he himself grew up with a hatred of poverty.[52] Frequent reverberations can be heard in the dramatic works. Undershaft in *Major Barbara* declares poverty a crime committed by society against some of its unfortunate members and wants it abolished. Ellie Dunn in *Heartbreak House* contemplates marriage with the unprepossessing capitalist Boss Mangan in order, she tells Captain Shotover, "to save my soul from the poverty that is damning me by inches."

Strictly speaking, however, the poverty of the Shaw family could hardly be described as severe, especially in comparison with conditions elsewhere in Ireland. In the years when George Carr held his post at the Dublin law courts, Ireland was suffering from one of the most disastrous famines in history. Triggered by successive failures through disease of the Irish potato crop in the years 1845–49, the Great Famine constituted a catastrophic blow to an economy that was already markedly backward in comparison with those of Great Britain and comparable European countries.[53] Even without the disaster of the famine, a large proportion of Irish people lived in wretched and impoverished circumstances, and nearly half of the population was completely illiterate.[54] In 1841 over a third of Irish houses were one-room cabins, which in rural areas were often without any floor and shared with domestic animals such as pigs. In Dublin—a city in decline in the nineteenth century as its more prosperous citizens moved to the Protestant-dominated suburbs—multiple-family occupancy of houses was the norm, and much of the housing was of poor quality. The city sewage, drainage, water supply, and sanitation systems were inadequate, and disease was rife. In the words of one of the city's historians, Dublin in the nineteenth century was "a markedly unhealthy place to live."[55]

In the context of mid-nineteenth-century Ireland and Dublin, it is impossible to think of the Carr Shaws as suffering from poverty in anything but a rhetorical sense. They lived, as Shaw himself occasionally acknowledged, in genteel rather than real poverty. It is true that in comparison with some of the other members of the Shaw clan, George Carr was not a wealthy man. He entered the grain industry at an inauspicious time. The repeal of the Corn Laws in 1846 led to a collapse in prices. The industry was in such a state of decline in Ireland during the latter half of the nineteenth century that by the late 1880s it had become "about the most depressed of all the trades in the country," with mills closing down daily.[56] Yet there are many indications that the Shaw family lived in reasonably comfortable circumstances.

While their number would have varied from time to time, the Carr Shaws employed several servants, including a cook, a nurse, a maid, and (in Shaw's early childhood) a governess. In *Sixteen Self Sketches* Shaw writes that in the house at Synge Street there was "always at least one 'thorough-servant,' paid £8 a year in cash, and lodged in the basement."[57] When the year-old Shaw "flittered his hat to pieces," it had to be replaced with "nothing short of Tuscan," an Italian straw hat costing ten shillings, which would have been more than three times the weekly wage of the servant instructed to purchase it.[58] When the Shaws decided to pool their resources with Vandeleur Lee (probably in early 1867), they moved from Synge Street into his more commodious residence at 1 Hatch Street, a house situated on a corner that boasted "eight rooms besides the spacious basement and pantry accommodation."[59] The contributions George Carr Shaw made to the family upkeep following the marital separation—some of which, as was previously noted, are mentioned in his correspondence with his son—were substantial and regular.

* * *

Shaw's parents separated in June 1873, when he was seventeen—and not, as he stated in his 1935 preface to *London Music in 1888–89*, when he was fifteen.[60] The reasons for the separation can only be speculated upon. On 4 June 1873 Vandeleur Lee abandoned his career in Dublin, sailed for England, and set up house at 13 Park Lane, London, from which he conducted new musical enterprises. His departure may have been precipitated by an attack against him as an impostor by his Dublin rival Sir Robert Prescott Stewart, then professor of music at Trinity College.[61] On 17 June, accompanied by her younger daughter Agnes, Bessie Shaw also left Dublin and settled in lodgings at 13 Victoria Grove, in southwest London.

The idea that Bessie left her husband in order to join Lee as her lover in London has scant evidence to support it, and there is much to suggest it was unlikely. The two did not cohabit in London, and although some collaboration in musical enterprises continued for a short time, there are indications in Shaw's correspondence and autobiographical comments that relations between Lee and the female members of the Shaw family deteriorated. One of Shaw's earliest letters testifies to his mother's and sister's annoyance at the exasperatingly "unbusinesslike" way in which Lee managed his musical productions. Lee had further lost favor by his unwelcome attentions to Lucy. Nevertheless, it does seem likely that with Lee's departure from Dublin, the musical careers and prospects of both Bessie and Lucy would have been drastically altered, and that removal to London would have opened up more potential for employment for both, as turned out to be the case. In London the musical association between Bessie and Lee, according to Shaw's account, gradually dwindled: "She dropped Lee very gently: at first he came and went at Victoria Grove, Fulham Road; and she went and came at 13 Park Lane, helping with the music there at his At Homes."[62] Lucy's increasing dislike of him in London—Shaw says she had already quarreled with him as a child—was likely to have been one of the main causes of the eventual complete rift between Lee and the family. By the time of his death, in November 1886, the Shaws had not seen him for "some years."[63]

As for the spirit in which the separation of Shaw's parents occurred, Shaw recalled that they parted "in the friendliest fashion."[64] His friend McNulty supplied a description that supports this view and probably has validity since he clearly kept in touch with George Carr Shaw during the latter's post-1873 existence in lodgings (first in company with his son and later alone) at 61 Harcourt Street, Dublin. McNulty wrote that "Mrs Shaw decided to live in London with her children, leaving her husband to manage or mismanage his affairs in Dublin. But, as a matter of fact, wife and husband parted good friends and remained so until he died."[65]

His parents' separation during his late teens may have colored Shaw's entire view of their marriage and may explain why his account of the early years of the marriage seems so melodramatic and negative. No doubt Shaw felt that he suffered as a child from a lack of maternal affection and warmth. However, to translate this into a single psychoanalytical theory about Shaw's adult behavior and, moreover, to account for his career in terms of a search for the maternal love supposedly missing in his childhood is to load the tenuous evidence with more weight than it can reasonably bear.[66] What is clear is that mother figures of various kinds abound in his plays, and that their treatment in his creative work, which is both complex and ambiguous, points to a deep preoccupation with ideas about maternal influence and power.

The mother figures in the plays range from the benign, good-humored, and quietly persuasive Lady Ciceley in *Captain Brassbound's Conversion* (partly modeled on Ellen Terry, who became a kind of "mother confessor" for Shaw, as reflected in his extensive—and often remarkably candid—correspondence with her) to the alluring but callous and manipulative sirens in *Heartbreak House*, exercising their "mothering tyranny" in such a way as to infantilize and subordinate their menfolk. In all his treatments of this theme, there are qualities of playfulness and artistic authority that make the theory that Shaw was emotionally crippled by a lack of maternal affection seem unsatisfactory.[67] His wide-ranging, witty, and subtly penetrating explorations of maternalistic behavior in the plays and early novels point to someone who was much more in command of the range of psychological experience involved in the mother-child relationship than he is sometimes given credit for. In my view Shaw had a remarkably robust psychological makeup, even if his behavior in emotionally charged areas of human experience was often surprisingly—and sometimes disturbingly—unconventional. At the very least, his reflections on the mother-son relationship became an extraordinarily fertile source of playful creativity in his works.

* * *

Another family figure of great importance in Shaw's life who is sometimes given short shrift and less than fair treatment in Shavian biography was his elder sister Lucy. From the quite extensive correspondence (addressed mostly to close women friends) that has survived, and from several detailed reminiscences of her, she emerges as a person of great warmth, vivacity, charm, wit, and courage. She had a teasing, conspiratorial, affectionate sisterly relationship with Shaw, following his career with the keenest interest and with great pride in his achievements. Her nicknames for him (in letters to others) included "Der Berühmte" (the famous one) and "the Super One." "He and I" she wrote to her friend Jane "Janey" Crichton Drysdale in the early 1900s, following what she described as a delightful talk with her brother, "are always two thorough blackguards when we get together alone."[68]

An indication of the bantering relationship between Shaw and his sister Lucy is provided in the earliest surviving letter written by Shaw, dated 4 March 1874 and addressed to her in London from 1 Hatch Street, Dublin, where he and his father were still living. Lucy had evidently been making rude remarks about her brother's nose, to which he responds vigorously. The letter begins with the Italianate flourish "Cara Lucia" and continues: "I am sorry to say that I have read your letter. I shall take especial care not to do so again for you are really worthy of your parent in the matter of verbosity and far more personal. Your remarks are most offensive. Let my nose alone, better a bottle than a peony. Did the Mar mention that the cat has got mange as well as Paddy. It has no hair at all on its head which adds to its already prepossessing appearance."[69]

An early letter from Lucy to her brother in Dublin, undated but probably written around 1876, shows her sense of humor and her affectionate feelings about her family. She was sending GBS a comically sentimental poem (apparently her own) that had been set to music, rapturously thanking her "Par" for a new pair of boots, and confessing to having sent another of her stories ("The lady help") off to a publisher: "My dear Swit.Voila la poeme!!! It has been set to music sufficiently touching. Tell Par the boots have just come. they [*sic*] are delightful, enchanting, ravishing to a degree. I have got them on and am in heaven in consequence."[70] She expects the story, which she describes as "exceedingly commonplace and occasionally vulgar," to bring her between two and three pounds, with which she wishes to buy "Mar" a new dress. Her brother annotated the poem with the words: "I have taken the liberty, pleasure and trouble of revising this effort of genius as regards punctuation."[71]

Lucy had the family sense of class, though not, according to Shaw, its pretentiousness.[72] When asked by Mabel Dolmetsch why she married Charles Robert Butterfield, a fellow actor and member of a touring theater company, she replied: "Because he was the only gentleman in the company." According to Mrs. Dolmetsch, he had "pleasing manners" and was good company, but he was irresponsible about money, of which he spent a great deal on drink.[73] Lucy divorced him in 1909 after discovering that he had been having a longstanding affair with another woman.

* * *

A notable feature of Shaw's rattling of the family skeletons was his mockery of their class pretensions. It is not surprising that class issues should figure so prominently in Shaw's writings. He had been brought up in a society based on one of the most rigid class systems in the world, and in a family highly conscious of its position in that system. It was one in which religious denomination and social rank were inseparable—and mutually reinforcing—cultural formations. When Shaw moved from Dublin to London at the age of nineteen, he not only found a similarly rigid stratification of the classes but also developed a powerful understanding of and hostility toward the networks of class, culture, economics, and power in late-nineteenth-century England.

Shaw's exuberant satirical assault on the English class system and his deftly managed, repeated fictional collapsing of class barriers in comic theatrical coups of various kinds can be seen, in part, as an extended reaction against the oppressive class system of the Ireland of his childhood and his own family's class assumptions and pretensions. However, Shaw's association with and treatment of the class systems of his time are more complex than such an account might suggest.

The complexity of Shaw's treatment of class difference in his creative work can be illustrated by the case of *Pygmalion.* In some ways the play is a subversive work. Eliza Doolittle's metamorphosis from flower girl to duchess is not a transformation of an inner self or moral nature. It is effected through entirely superficial means. A new accent and vocabulary and a fresh set of clothes do the trick of transferring her from one social grouping to another. The instability of the linguistic system that forms such an essential part of the class hierarchy is suggested in Freddy Eynsford Hill's assumption that Eliza's odd way of speaking at Mrs. Higgins's at home is some new form of funny society "small talk." Yet the play can also be seen as an exploitation of class differences. Eliza (in her untutored state) and Doolittle are funny because of their drastic and unconscious transgressions of upper-class linguistic codes. Shaw's unerring sense of those codes and his knowledge of his largely middle-class audience's sharing of that sense situate the creator and spectators of the Doolittles in a position of superior power. Higgins's class-oriented rudeness and callousness toward "the squashed cabbage leaf" Eliza gives the comedy of the play a distinct edge of cruelty.

One of the reasons for the ambiguities in Shaw's treatment of class issues is that he himself was a member of the class he so often attacked. Although he describes the family in which he was brought up as "snobs to the backbone," Shaw himself was not one in the ordinary senses of the term. He was a critic and would-be subverter of class systems. His subversions, however, were not carried out from the disadvantaged viewpoint of querulous underdogs such as Peter Shirley in *Major Barbara* or the young Socialist burglar discovered in Mr. Tarleton's private Turkish bath in *Misalliance.*

Horrendous as the proposition would have sounded to many of his John Bullish contemporaries—for many of whom the phrase "Irish gentleman" would seem a contradiction in terms—Shaw exemplified the social type of which he was a constant and scathing opponent: a gentleman, with the accent ("Rathmines")[74] and manners of the Protestant ascendancy, of which his immediate family was a somewhat down-at-the-heels representative. Sir Ralph Richardson remembered Shaw as "perhaps the most polite man" he had ever met in his life.[75] W. H. Auden commented on how much "nicer" Shaw's manners were than those of his younger British contemporaries.[76] An interesting edge is given to these descriptions in Hilaire Belloc's aperçu that "Shaw was a gentleman pretending to be a cad."[77]

Shaw's understanding of class and his own class background were to prove of major importance in his roles as social critic and political activist. As a born controversialist and iconoclast, his intellectual stance was frequently pugnacious and antagonistic. His tone and manner, by contrast, were generally courteous, amusing, and disarming. In political debate his unfailing politeness could be a deadly weapon, as it was, for example, in his Fabian Society encounters with the blustering H. G. Wells. This politeness, however, was not a contrived strategy: comments about it from so many people in different social contexts clearly indicate that it was a natural part of his character.

Shaw's class background very likely influenced the paths he followed in his political life. In the mid 1880s he turned away from the doctrinaire and raucously Marxist Social Democratic Federation, led by Henry Mayers Hyndman, to the more congenial circle of the Fabian Society, many of whose members came from a social background not unlike his own. The latter was essentially made up of middle-class intellectuals, some of whom later attained very high social rank. Two members of its first executive, Sidney Webb and Sydney Olivier, were elevated to the baronetage in the following century. It was an organization that could not easily be dismissed as socially beyond the pale. Giving the wicked wolf of the new Socialism such respectable clothing was probably the most effective way of introducing it into the fold of Victorian England. The Fabian Society became one of the political nurseries of the first Labour prime minister of England, Ramsay MacDonald. Bernard Shaw was its most eloquent and lively public voice. He was, of course, one of a kind, a unique figure on the stage of late Victorian and early modern social and cultural history who defies simple description in terms of class or family. Shaw, however, owed more to the Dublin family about which he enjoyed creating "derisive dramatisations"—and not least to the father his Australian cousin referred to as a "courteous and charming gentleman"—than he perhaps was willing to acknowledge.

3 Growing Up in Dublin

"I hated school, and learnt nothing there of what it professed to teach," Shaw wrote in a work published in 1944.[1] He was sent to several schools in Dublin, all of which he found disagreeable and virtually useless. The pattern of discreditation evident in his account of his parents repeated itself in his description of his schools—though in this case probably with greater justification. He saw schools as a form of imprisonment. When, at the age of fifteen, he "escaped" from the last one he attended—"my last school prison," as he called it[2]—he found himself "condemned to five years penal servitude in another sort of prison called an office."[3] There is evidence that he was a quite able pupil, especially in Latin and English. Had the Shaw family finances permitted this as an option, he could conceivably have gone on from school to Trinity College. Whether he would have followed that path if it had been open to him—or enjoyed treading it if he did—is uncertain. In his later years he railed against universities and what he saw as their pernicious effect on the mind, this despite the fact that he formed some very close friendships with academics as well as with numerous university graduates.

Shaw's education began at home with instruction from a governess, a Miss Caroline Hill, who was employed by the family to teach Shaw "to read and write and do a few sums in simple arithmetic,"[4] a task she performed very well, according to Shaw. She was ladylike, needy, and moralistic. Of her disciplinary measures Shaw recalled that "she punished me with little strokes with her fingers that would not have discomposed a fly, and even persuaded me that I ought to cry and feel disgraced on such occasions."[5] The next mentor was his clerical uncle-by-marriage, the Reverend William George Carroll, who included Shaw in early-morning lessons he gave to his own two boys at his house located at 21 Harrington Street. Shaw says that as a result of these lessons, by the time he was sent to school he "knew more Latin grammar than any other boy in the First Latin Junior."[6]

The syllabus at his first school, the Wesleyan Connexional (later Wesley College), which he attended sporadically from 1865 to 1868, was dominated by Latin and Greek: "Education meant Caesar, Virgil, and Homer."[7] Apart from the study of classical languages and literature, the curriculum at the Wesleyan Connexional also comprised, according to Shaw, "a pretence of mathematics (Euclidean), of English history (mostly false and scurrilous) and some nominal geography of which I have no recollection." He added that "the classes were too large, and the teachers untrained in pedagogy, mostly picking up a living on their way to becoming Wesleyan ministers."[8] Wesley College records indicate that for fees of two guineas for tuition, three shillings and sixpence for books and stationery, and two shillings and sixpence for elocution, G. B. Shaw attended the school during the quarter ending 31 July 1865. His formal schooling thus began as he was approaching his ninth birthday.[9]

In the course of only seven years of schooling (1865–71), Shaw attended no fewer than four different institutions. During this time, the family stayed for lengthy periods at Torca Cottage in Dalkey, and while they were there, the young Shaw was sent to a "very private" preparatory school run by one James Frederick Halpin at 23–24 Sandycove Road, Glasthule.[10] He returned to the Wesleyan Connexional for a period of time in 1868. It was then decided that he should be enrolled in the Central Model Boys' School in Marlborough Street, on the advice given to Vandeleur Lee by a drawing master there. A whole chapter of Shaw's *Sixteen Self Sketches*, entitled "Shame and Wounded Snobbery," was prompted by this dramatic and, in Shaw's eyes, disastrous development in his school education.

The adult Shaw was able to laugh at the absurd religious and social caste system, which meant that going to the Central Model Boys' School could be a cause of "shame and wounded snobbery." At the time, however, having been brought up to think that the system was part of the natural order of things, he felt that being sent to this school involved a great loss of face. The problem was that although in theory the school was "undenominational and classless," it was "in fact Roman Catholic." The boys there were sons of shopkeepers and lower-middle-class Catholics. As a pupil at the school, he "at once lost caste outside it and became a boy with whom no Protestant young gentleman would speak or play."[11] The physical appearance of the school did not help. There were times when the grim portraits of English schools in the novels of his favorite novelist, Charles Dickens, seem to have been close at hand in Shaw's imagination when he described some of his personal experiences. Judging by his own account, the grimmest of all Shaw's schools, as regards both its physical ambience and the feelings of shame it aroused in him, was this school in Marlborough Street. It was a huge place with "unscaleable railings" and gates on which Shaw thought should have been inscribed the motto Dante placed over the entrance to Hell in *The Inferno*: "All hope abandon, ye who enter here."[12]

After eight months there, he rebelled and flatly refused to continue attending the school. At the "last school prison," which carried the unwieldy name of the Dublin English Scientific and Commercial Day School, he was a more contented inmate. Indeed, he rose to become joint head boy there, together with a schoolfellow named Frank Dunne, a boy of whom Shaw said that "at sixteen or thereabouts he had the bearing and moral weight of a bishop." Shaw recalls that he himself had developed "a new moral dignity as a head boy."[13] It was also at this last school that he met Edward McNulty, the closest and most significant friend of his Dublin childhood, one with whom he shared the secrets of his dreams and ambitions.

Despite Shaw's declared antipathy toward the Dublin schools of his childhood, he himself was a gifted and well regarded student. The *Irish Evangelist* for January 1868 recorded that he had achieved "a first place in English, in writing" in the Christmas 1867 examination at the Wesleyan Connexional School. In August 1867 the same periodical had reported that he had received certificates of good conduct from the school. At the Wesleyan Connexional School, apart from rising "to the head of the First Latin Junior" thanks to the Reverend Carroll's instructions, in essay writing he "got a first class for a very florid description of the Liffey pool below bridges."[14]

At the age of fifteen Shaw's formal education was over. On 1 November 1871 he commenced employment as an office boy with the "highly genteel firm of Irish estate agents"[15] Uniacke Townshend and Co., located at 15 Molesworth Street, Dublin.

* * *

Some of the most powerful and significant influences on Shaw during his childhood derived not from real people or his schooling but from the realm of the imagination, from literature, music, opera, and art. He was particularly struck in his youth by two contrasting figures from this realm, a fiend and a pilgrim. In his 1930 preface to his novel *Immaturity* (1879) Shaw recalled his early acquaintance, during his childhood in Dublin, with Mephistopheles, the demon in the Faust legend who persuades the latter to sell his soul to him. This legendary figure captured his imagination and had a profound influence on the development of his own self-image and his career as a creative writer. Mephistopheles first entered Shaw's consciousness in the form in which he appears in Charles Gounod's opera *Faust*. There were several ways in which

Gounod's mocking, cynical conjuror would have become a familiar figure in the Shaw households in Dublin and Dalkey. *Faust* was one of the operas presented by Vandeleur Lee in Dublin's Antient Concert Rooms, where the leading soprano role of Marguerite was played by Shaw's mother, Bessie.[16] Edward McNulty reported in his "Memoirs of G.B.S." that *Faust* was Shaw's favorite opera, and that he knew every note of the work before he could play a five-finger exercise on the piano. He and Shaw, McNulty recalls, "made of Mephistopheles a familiar and almost living character."[17] On the whitewashed walls of his room at Torca Cottage Shaw painted watercolor frescoes of Mephistopheles "as the patron saint of sceptics and deriders," explaining to O'Bolger that at this time "for the most part my intellectual attitude & affectation was Mephistophelean."[18]

In later years, in his music criticism and other writings, Shaw frequently returned to the subject of Gounod's *Faust*—often in scathingly critical terms. In a review published in August 1885, he justly and succinctly described Gounod's enormously popular work as "giving us Faust with all Goethe's thought left out."[19] In December of the same year he described the "mountebank" Mephistopheles as "perhaps the most childish and ridiculous travesty of a serious conception that the public has ever disgraced itself by taking in earnest."[20] Nevertheless, the mountebank cast an extraordinarily powerful spell over the young Shaw, who in the 1930 preface to *Immaturity* claimed that he was so bewitched by the legendary figure that his whole physical appearance became a reflection of this influence: "When Nature completed my countenance in 1880 or thereabouts (I had only the tenderest sprouting of hair on my face until I was 24), I found myself equipped with the upgrowing moustaches and eyebrows, and the sarcastic nostrils of the operatic fiend whose airs (by Gounod) I had sung as a child, and whose attitudes I had affected in my boyhood."[21]

The resemblance was not lost on others. A pretty girl called Geraldine Spooner—whom Shaw met in 1888 and with whom he fell "rather in love" (as he put it in his diary entry for 21 April 1890)—has left us a memorable description of Shaw's physical appearance at this time, as "different to everybody" because "one side of his face was Christlike, although the other was Mephistophelian."[22] Shaw is presented explicitly as "Mephistopheles" in one of the many cartoons of him produced by Max Beerbohm.[23] His appearance was apparently matched by his behavior at meetings of the various literary and political societies that Shaw joined as a young man in London. "He was often the Mephistopheles of the debate," said his friend Henry S. Salt of Shaw's performances at meetings of the Shelley Society, the Fellowship of the New Life, the Fabian Society, and other organizations.[24]

Like the Good Angel ranged against the Mephistophelean Bad in a medieval morality play, another influence played a powerful part in the shaping of the young Shaw's imagination. The earliest childhood recollection was that of reading John Bunyan's *The Pilgrim's Progress* to his father and being corrected for pronouncing the word "grievous" as "grievious."[25] Bunyan's allegory and its presentation of life as a courageous pilgrimage of faith pursued in opposition to the idleness, the sins and follies, the moral cowardice and hypocrisies, and the pride and bigotry of Vanity Fair haunted Shaw's imagination for the rest of his career. It was fitting that at the funeral ceremony for Shaw held at Golders Green crematorium on 6 November 1950, he was symbolically identified with a courageous figure from Bunyan's work. His friend Sidney Cockerell read from the valedictory speech of Mr. Valiant-for-Truth as he is about to cross the River of Death at the end of the Second Part of *The Pilgrim's Progress*,[26] a passage beginning with the famous sentence: "My sword, I give to him that shall succeed me in my pilgrimage, and my courage and skill, to him that can get it." Shaw once wrote of this passage that "the heart vibrates like a bell to such an utterance as this."[27] Almost a half century before his death, in the Epistle Dedicatory to *Man and Superman* (1903), Shaw had quoted these words from Bunyan immediately before a statement often viewed as a summary of the Shavian credo: "This is the true joy in life, the being used for a purpose recognized by yourself as a mighty one; the being thoroughly worn out before you are thrown on the scrap heap; the being a force of Nature instead of a feverish selfish little clod of ailments and grievances complaining that the world will not devote itself to making you happy."[28]

Shaw was not a slavish admirer of Bunyan, once referring to his (and Sir Isaac Newton's) astonishing "credulity and Bible fetichism."[29] Nevertheless, Bunyan's allegory and social criticism were deeply ingrained in Shaw's consciousness. What particularly seized his imagination and greatly influenced his stance as a critic of society was the way in which the seventeenth-century nonconformist and outsider attacked the outwardly righteous and respectable pillars of his own society: "Mr. Legality in the village of Morality." Bunyan's villains were not ordinary criminals but rather the people in power in late-seventeenth-century England. This left a lasting impression on the way in which Shaw viewed the world of capitalism in the late nineteenth and early twentieth centuries.[30] As a writer with a passionate moral and social vision, Bunyan heads a short list of authors whom Shaw called "artist-philosophers," creative thinkers whose "peculiar sense of the world" he recognized as akin to his own.[31]

The seeds of a singular combination of mocking iconoclast and self-dedicated world-betterer that characterized the mature Shaw can be seen in these early musical and literary experiences of Gounod and Bunyan, in which a jesting devil and a Christian idealist and moralist were equally potent imaginative presences. They set him on a life course as what might be described as a Mephistophelean pilgrim, a satirical idealist. The influence of these early bedfellows in Shaw's psyche, namely, Mephistopheles and Bunyan, can be seen throughout the course of his career as a creative writer. The impression created by their dual presence in his makeup was reflected in a summary comment on Shaw by the actress Lena Ashwell in her 1936 autobiographical work *Myself a Player*: "The best description of him is: 'An angel masquerading as Mephistopheles.'"[32] Recurring like strange specters in a recurrent dream, figures of the archskeptic and the courageous pilgrim appear in multiple metamorphoses in the plays, usually in paradoxically antagonistic but amiable relations.

In *Major Barbara* (1905) Andrew Undershaft, the ruthless but charismatic millionaire arms manufacturer, a majestic derider of conventional morality, threatens to undermine the Christian idealism of his daughter, Barbara, a Salvation Army major, with witty skepticism and the force majeure of his immense wealth and power, by means of which he strives to tempt her away from her faith. Barbara's fiancé, Cusins, repeatedly calls Undershaft "Mephistopheles." In *Androcles and the Lion* the handsome Roman Captain uses sophisticated arguments in comparative religion as a kind of Mephistophelean temptation for the beautiful and courageous Christian prisoner Lavinia to save herself from being thrown to the lions by sacrificing incense to the Roman gods. The "Don Juan in Hell" scene, which occurs as a dream in the third act of *Man and Superman*, brings the old duo into full play in the opposition between the cynical Devil and the optimistic Life Force evangelist Don Juan Tenorio. A stage direction calls for The Devil to appear "*very Mephistophelean*," and Shaw has his character approach to the accompaniment of music from Gounod's *Faust*, which Shaw intended to recall the opening bars of Mephistopheles' song "The Golden Calf."[33] The theme reappears in *Saint Joan* (1923), with the Bunyanesque heroine, a Shavian Ms Valiant-for-Truth, staunchly rejecting the Mephistophelean temptations to save herself from the stake by renouncing her personal faith.

* * *

For a budding creative artist and radical thinker, the Shaw household and mid-nineteenth-century Dublin provided an extraordinarily fertile background of religious, cultural, social, and intellectual influences. The Shaw clan included powerful and prominent upholders of the proprieties in religion. Sir Frederick Shaw, the Recorder of Dublin, was an early supporter of the Sunday School Society for Ireland. The other leading figure in the clan during Shaw's childhood, Uncle Richard Frederick Shaw, was clearly a staunch conservative in religious matters. Shaw's mother was brought up with "ruthless strictness," according to Shaw, by the Whitcrofts in Palmerston Place, and this regime presumably included proper religious observances.[34] George Carr and Bessie Shaw were certainly not renegades from the faith. Katharine Tynan, following her visit in 1889, remembers Shaw's mother expressing "strong Irish Protestant opinions,"[35] and George Carr Shaw urged his wife to keep up her churchgoing in the letters he wrote her in the summer of 1857.

The George Carr Shaw family ties to orthodoxy, however, were comparatively weak, and there was clearly a considerable strain of humorous freethinking in the conversations about religion between George Carr and his son, aided and abetted by the Rabelaisian uncle Walter Gurly. Shaw recalls his father's way of concluding a serious eulogy of the Bible by saying anticlimactically—and with prolonged laughter—that "even the worst enemy of religion could say no worse of the Bible than that it was the damndest parcel of lies ever written."[36] George Carr's "religious instruction" to the young Shaw also included an outrageously frivolous account of the meaning of Unitarianism.[37] In another autobiographical recollection Shaw recounted the theory propounded by Walter Gurly that the biblical story of Lazarus could be explained by the fact that Lazarus was persuaded by Jesus to pretend he was dead so that the persuasive "miracle" of his resurrection could be performed.[38] Such talk would, of course, have been anathema to Richard Frederick Shaw, who wrote to his nephew in 1885: "Your Father was in the habit of reading some of your Socialistic and Atheistic views, as expressed in your letters to him, to many intimate friends, and such of them as hold views similar to Mr Phillips and myself are a good deal shocked at the views you have adopted. . . . You have given expression to sentiments that would justify Mr Phillips or any one else in thinking you an unparalleled rascal."[39]

In an 1896 essay entitled "On Going to Church," Shaw left a graphic recollection of his loathing of churchgoing as a young boy in a "genteel suburban Irish Protestant church," with the "unnaturally motionless figures of the congregation in their Sunday clothes and bonnets, and their set faces, pale with the malignant rigidity produced by the suppression of all expression."[40] His release from this particular form of imprisonment occurred at about the age of ten, when the family began their stays at Torca Cottage on Dalkey Hill and abandoned their Sunday churchgoing—probably not without regret on the part of George Carr Shaw. (His son was never confirmed.)

* * *

Apart from Gounod's fiend, Bunyan's pilgrims, and Protestant churchgoing, numerous other manifestations of religious and spiritual experience and practices jostled together in the fictional and nonfictional worlds of Shaw's childhood in Dublin. Roman Catholicism impinged on his childhood life in a number of ways. One of his nurses was a Catholic, and Shaw recalled her instructions about prayers and her "sprinkling me with holy water occasionally."[41] Quite possibly it was the same nurse who took him to the (probably mainly Catholic) "slums" of Dublin tenement houses to visit her friends when she was supposed to be exercising her young charge in the park.[42] In 1869, when Shaw was twelve, came the episode of his being sent to the Central Model Boys' School, which involved mixing with Catholic children.

Other influences from beyond the social pale in Dublin came through Bessie Shaw's career as a singer and helper with Vandeleur Lee's productions in the Antient Concert Rooms. Music in Dublin had a way of crossing social and denominational barriers, the inescapable truth being that some of the best musicians and singers were Catholics. Through her musical interests Bessie Shaw was drawn into social circles that would otherwise have remained closed to her. As Shaw eloquently explained in one of his autobiographical writings: "My first childish doubts as to whether God could really be a good Protestant was suggested by my observation of the incongruous fact that the best voices available for combination with my mother's in the works of the great composers had been unaccountably vouchsafed to Roman Catholics. Even the Divine gentility was called in question; for some of these vocalists were undeniably connected with retail trade."[43]

Most of the singers in Lee's concerts were Catholics, and since the Shaw house was the venue for rehearsals, it must have frequently been full of "invaders" from the opposite side of the Dublin religious and political divide. Shaw found them charming, "more cultivated and much kinder and better mannered than the Protestant [bourgeoisie]."[44] Not only did Bessie join forces with Catholics in the concert hall, but she was sometimes approached by Roman Catholic priests and drawn into the "house of Belial," the Roman Catholic chapel, to take part in masses of Haydn and Mozart.[45] Through these contacts Shaw was led to the discovery that the Dublin Protestant assumption concerning the natural superiority of Protestants over Catholics was far from infallible.

Bessie Shaw was the source of Shaw's introduction to another form of spiritual experience through her interest in the occult and her practice of holding séances. Shaw's claim that his mother was the owner of the first planchette (a device for receiving from and writing messages to the spirit world) in Ireland should probably be viewed with some skepticism. But Bessie's "spirit" drawings and Shaw's recollections of her séances and use of a planchette and Ouija board testify to her more than passing interest in a pursuit that was coming into its heyday as Bessie Shaw was growing up. Shaw himself maintained "sturdy doubts"[46] (to borrow Sir Thomas Browne's phrase) about spiritualism, recalling how he once cheated at one of his mother's séances. In a late preface he describes spiritualists as one of England's numerous sects of "Peculiar People." Yet in the same preface he celebrates inexplicable experiences of humans, mysterious moments of happiness and acts of creativity that science can't explain.[47] Psychic powers are characteristic of some of his later dramatis personae, such as Captain Shotover in *Heartbreak House* (1916–17) and several of the figures in the *Back to Methuselah* cycle of plays.

* * *

Shaw recalled that when his mother told him that the family was going to live in Dalkey, "I felt an intense joy that I have never felt since."[48] At the time of Shaw's childhood, Dalkey was a largely rural area, with furze-covered hills and dramatic seascapes. Torca Cottage, the house the Shaws shared with Vandeleur Lee, commands views of Dublin and Killiney Bays, and "a vast and ever changing expanse of sea and sky far below and far above."[49] Shaw intensely disliked the urban scene of Dublin in his day, with its tenement slums, poverty, and grim Protestant churches. Dalkey was a great moment of liberation for him and the source, as he declared in a late interview, of his permanent sense of bonding with Ireland: "It is the beauty of Ireland that has made us what we are. I am a product of Dalkey's outlook."[50]

Another great liberating and educational influence in Shaw's childhood was provided by the National Gallery of Ireland. He described Dalkey, the National Gallery, and Lee's musical activities as the three "universities" of his youth. As though in preparation for its future frequent visitor and later munificent benefactor, the National Gallery of Ireland was established by an act of Parliament in August 1854, two years before Shaw's birth. He was seven years of age when the National Gallery was opened in a grand ceremony by the Lord Lieutenant, the earl of Carlisle, in January 1864. At the opening (in what is now the Shaw Room) there were 106 plaster casts taken from classical sculptures, while in other rooms there were 69 Italian Renaissance and baroque paintings and about the same number of works from other European countries. There was also a large collection of Irish and British watercolors.[51] It is very fitting that a fine full-length statue of Shaw, by Prince Paul Troubetskoy, now stands in the Shaw Room, having been brought in from where it previously stood outside the building. Shaw has been returned to his rightful place in one of his spiritual homes.

European Counter-Reformation painting was strongly represented in the early collection. The young Shaw would have been able to see such works as Marco Palmezzano's *Virgin and Child Enthroned with St. John the Baptist and Lucy*; Giovanni Lanfranco's *Last Supper*; Charles Poerson's soaring *Assumption of the Virgin Mary*; Giovanni Antonio Pellegrini's *Susanna and the Elders*, with its erotic, semidraped figure of the female subject; and many other baroque paintings of religious subjects. These works were mingled with a small but impressive collection of Renaissance and baroque paintings based on classical mythology, such as Rutilio Manetti's *Victorious Earthly Love*, a striking allegorical work with a dominant figure of Cupid as its central icon, and Carlo Maratta's *Rape of Europa*.

In the National Gallery the young Shaw encountered aesthetic, religious, and sensuous imaginative experiences that were a world apart from what he found in the puritanical fold of the Protestant church. The visits to the National Gallery were another part of Shaw's childhood experiences that brought him into contact with the world of European Catholicism. There was quite a strong vein of sympathy in Shaw for certain conceptions of Catholicism. But the complexity of his religious outlook—as a sort of skeptical and heretical covert Christian, who sometimes described himself as an atheist—can be judged from the following paradoxical declaration in the essay "On Going to Church": "My own faith is clear: I am a resolute Protestant; I believe in the Holy Catholic Church; in the Holy Trinity of Father, Son (or Mother, Daughter) and Spirit; in the Communion of Saints, the Life to Come, the Immaculate Conception, and the everyday reality of Godhead and the Kingdom of Heaven. Also I believe that salvation depends on redemption from belief in miracles. . . ."[52]

Among many signs in his work and career that seem to reflect Shaw's early contacts with Catholicism are such things as his choice of a Catholic icon, the main figure from Titian's *Assumption of the Virgin*, as a prominent feature of the setting of *Candida* (1894); his portrayal of the defrocked Catholic priest Father Keegan in *John Bull's Other Island* (1904), and his remarkable late friendship with Margaret (known first as Sister and later as Dame Laurentia) McLachlan, abbess of Stanbrook Abbey. In October 1924 Shaw presented a copy of *Saint Joan* to the abbess with the following inscription: "To Sister Laurentia from Brother Bernard."[53]

Just as Shaw's early experiences encouraged him to see beyond narrow denominational orthodoxies and prejudices in religion, so his early political sympathies were unusual for a person of his class. In writing of history lessons at the Central Model School, which "ignored Ireland and glorified England," Shaw relates that he substituted Ireland for England in "such dithyrambs," and "was, in fact a young Fenian in my political sympathies, such as they were."[54] Shaw's later voluminous commentary on Ireland and its problems took him far beyond naïve Fenianism, but his way of seeing the world—especially that of John Bullish Englishmen—from an Irish perspective never left him.

* * *

Shaw's earliest ambition was to become a great artist like Michelangelo. "When I was a small boy and by some chance got hold of sixpence I always bought a box of paints with it," he told Charles MacMahon Shaw in 1937.[55] From the autumn of 1870, when he was fourteen, until about February of the following year he attended evening freehand classes at the Royal Dublin Society School of Art, and for three years (1871–73) he had season tickets to art exhibitions at the Hibernian Academy and the Dublin Exhibition. Several examples of juvenile sketches by Shaw (which probably belong to the period of the freehand classes) are preserved in the British Library. They include sketches of religious subjects entitled *Assumption, St. Sebastian, Prophet, St. John the Baptist*; elegant studies of *Hunting Gent with Rifle, Youth,* and *Catharine of Alexandria*; and a drawing, entitled *Calypso,* depicting a recumbent nude female figure by the sea.[56]

Calypso, the nymph in classical legend who held Ulysses captive on her island for seven years, also makes an appearance in an early poem by Shaw about an unknown woman with whom he had a romantic relationship in the 1870s. In 1872 he purchased a copy of Browne's *Large Pocket Diary and Almanack* for 1873 and a notebook that lists the name of the supplier as "J. L. Dixon, Stationer, Engraver and Bookbinder, 136 Stephen's Green, Dublin." These became repositories of Shaw's earliest collections of memoranda, notes about his family, autobiographical jottings, and essays in creative writing, including the "Calypso" poem, which opens with the lines "Hail, Folly! and flourish, Delusion." The notebook includes a section headed "The L*** [Love?] Episode" about "The Calypso infatuation." Together with evidence in the poem, Shaw's notes indicate that Calypso was an attractive, dark-haired woman whom he first met in 1871 at Dalkey. A relationship with an obviously strong sexual dimension developed in 1875. In the poem Calypso is referred to as a "blackeyed enslaver" who is "prone to each impulse of passion / That she gasps for a breath of romance." She has also "succumbed to the cruel old fashion" and become married "in an exquisite gaol by the sea." The "gaol" was Dalkey:

To her weary sense stagnant and rotten
  But Elysium to me
Four years of my childhood I spent there
  Their danger was veiled to me then
Four years more elapsed, and I went there
  And saw her again
But she proved a too perilous plaything
  . . .
I thought her of women the rarest
  With strange power to seduce and alarm
One Beside whose black tresses the finest
  Seemed barren of charm
The wisest men sometimes get smitten
  And I fear I was so in those days.

The "Calypso" poem was completed after Shaw emigrated to London ("my fate brought me shortly to Britain"); the temptress was farewelled with a clangorous rhyme on her legendary name and a resolution about writing poetry on romantic themes: "Then farewell, oh bewitching Calypso / Thou didst shake my philosophy well / But believe me the next time I trip so / No poem shall tell."[57] In the same notebook he experimented with comic rhymes ("enchantment / My aunt meant") that give a foretaste of the amusing verses he occasionally wrote to girlfriends in London.

* * *

The young Shaw shared his interest in art and literature with his school friend, Matthew Edward McNulty, whom he later described as "a corpulent youth with curly black hair."[58] The close attachment they formed at school was the foundation of a lifelong friendship. After leaving school, McNulty went on to a career in banking, but his early literary ambitions were carried out through the writing of novels of Irish life (including *Misther O'Ryan* and *The Son of a Peasant*), poetry, and three plays (two of which, *The Lord Mayor* and *The Courting of Mary Doyle*, were successfully produced at the Abbey Theatre). Announcing to Shaw in 1883 that he had secretly married Alice Maude Brennan in Dublin (with Shaw's father, George Carr Shaw, as witness), McNulty urged his friend to follow his example. "Go and get married," McNulty counseled, and find "the sensation of Rest, Eternal Rest from the Eternal Parade." But he also added: "There was another dream—a cottage in seclusion with

G. B. Shaw & Edward McNulty, recluses, bookworms & philosophers alone."[59] The closeness of the friendship was earlier attested to by the nineteen-year-old Shaw in a letter to McNulty dated 3 June 1876, where he wrote: "You are the only person in the world to whom I am a person with an identity and a soul. That is why I cling to you."[60] When, in the years 1871–74, McNulty was transferred to the Newry branch of the Bank of Ireland, the two conducted a regular correspondence, which Shaw referred to in a chapter of *Sixteen Self Sketches* as "unreserved soul histories." By mutual agreement, according to Shaw, the letters were destroyed as soon as they had been answered.[61]

McNulty's recollections of Shaw's childhood exist in two main documents. On 6 July 1901 *The Candid Friend* (London) published McNulty's reminiscences under the title "George Bernard Shaw as a Boy." A more extended account, entitled "Memoirs of G.B.S.," was assembled from holograph notes into a typescript by members of McNulty's family circle following his death on 12 May 1943. Both sets of memoirs need to be approached with caution. Shaw added marginal annotations to a personal copy of *The Candid Friend* article, pointing out a number of errors. Though the "corrections" themselves may be too sweeping, confidence in McNulty's reminiscences is somewhat undermined at the outset by Shaw's terse marginal comment ("4 mistakes") on the brief, sixteen-word opening sentence describing his attire when McNulty first met him. Since the only subject of the sentence is the four wrongly remembered items of dress, the recollection seems to be left completely bare of useful information, if Shaw's comment can be relied upon. Confusion, obvious errors, and doubtfully authentic anecdotes are present in the longer "Memoirs of G.B.S." Nevertheless, in the main there emerges from McNulty's recollections a convincing portrait of a friendship between two boys with unusually mature artistic and intellectual interests.

McNulty's accounts of Shaw's early theatrical activities are among those upon which the latter casts doubt. It would be pleasant to think that the future critic of Shakespeare worship and inventor of the word "bardolatry" did indeed play the part of Ophelia in a school production of *Hamlet*, "walking about on his toes and delivering his lines in a shrill falsetto which changed the play from tragedy to farce." However, "all invented" was Shaw's comment on this and other stories of juvenile theatricals. Another story concerning Shaw's proposal, made in his bedroom at 1 Hatch Street, that he and McNulty further their endeavors in art by posing naked for one another as models in an extended "study of the nude" seems plausible enough. McNulty excused himself from this experiment on the grounds that he did not want to incur a relapse of a recent attack of bronchitis in the drafty room.

* * *

Other first-hand glimpses of Shaw's Dublin boyhood were provided by some of the speakers at a BBC symposium broadcast in September 1954 and included in a 1972 volume entitled *Irish Literary Portraits*.[62] The speakers included Lady Constance Geraldine Hanson, patroness of the arts and friend of the Shaw family, who held a literary salon in the days of Oliver St. John Gogarty; her mother, Mrs. Ada Tyrrell, poet and wife of a Regius professor of Greek at Trinity College, Dublin; Joseph Foy, who "as a boy ran the streets of Dublin with Shaw"; and William Meegan of Dalkey, who was also a playfellow of Shaw's as a boy. Mrs. Tyrrell had earlier supplied a fuller version of her recollection to Frank Harris. The Tyrrells remembered Shaw as a "very nice-looking," serious, polite, and dignified young man, with an air of superiority. Mrs. Tyrrell recalled: "My first memory of 'George' is a little boy in a Holland overall sitting at a table constructing a toy theatre. 'Sonny' the other Shaws called him, then. . . . George was about ten—he had a superior manner to his sisters and me, a sort of dignity withal, and I remember feeling rather flattered when he condescended to explain anything that I asked him; though we girls were a year or two older."[63]

The image of Shaw as a rather remote child that this recollection creates is qualified by the Meegan and Foy recollections. Between them, Shaw's former Dublin playfellows conjure up an image of a physically vigorous and robust child who enjoyed the rough-and-tumble and ordinary games of boyhood. William Meegan recalled scuffles with him over birds they had captured and described the slightly older Shaw as "a strong lump of a fellow with a red face."[64] Joseph Foy recalled: "I shot marbles with him, I lashed tops with him, I boxed the fox with him, I robbed the orchard with him." He remembered Shaw as "a stern lad . . . and a good sport."[65] In the late 1940s Shaw corroborated the marbles story and located the venues of the games as being "from Synge Street, up the Pottle into the Coombe and back by the 'Barn' past my father's mill at Rutland House."[66] Replying to a question about his favorite games at school in an interview published in 1927, Shaw recalled: "We played rough, *unorganised* games, like Police and Robbers; and I enjoyed roaring and rushing about and struggling."[67] These recollections tend to counter the image that is sometimes created of the young Shaw as a lonely and isolated child—with interests only in a private world of art, literature, and dreams—as does his memory of playing at the Rutland Avenue mill with "two boon companions, the sons of my father's partner [George Clibborn]."[68]

* * *

Outside the grim walls of the schools he attended, the Dublin years furnished Shaw with an extraordinarily rich education in literature, music, theater, and art. Whatever skeletons may have lurked in the cupboards, the Shaw households in Dublin and Dalkey must have constantly been filled with music and—judging from the family correspondence that has survived—lively banter. Preparation for Lee's concerts provided "a string of musical masterpieces [performed] right up to the point of full choral & orchestral rehearsals."[69] Before he could read music, he could sing many of the "musical masterpieces" he heard in the house from beginning to end: "I really hated and despised Strauss's waltzes as vulgar trash, and could sing you Beethoven's Mass in C, Mozart's Twelfth Mass, Mendelssohn's Athalie, Handel's Messiah, Verdi's Trovatore, Donizetti's Lucrezia, Gounod's Faust & (above all) Mozart's Don Giovanni from cover to cover, besides a heap of separate numbers from other works before I could read a note of music."[70] The foundations of Shaw's superb equipment as a music critic had been firmly laid by the time he left school.

If the Shaw household was filled with music, it was also filled with musical theory, owing to the presence of Vandeleur Lee in the family circle during much of Shaw's childhood. The sobriquet "charlatan genius" applied to Lee by the Dublin author John O'Donovan seems to capture his spirit well.[71] The man who shared living quarters with the Shaws from 1866 to 1873 was an eccentric, charismatic, talented, and energetic individual who indeed seemed to combine real genius and originality with a good deal of quackery. He was born about 1830, the son of Robert Lee (variously described as "clerk" and "coal merchant" in contemporary Dublin records) and his wife, Eliza. From 1871 he assumed the name George Vandeleur Lee, which, O'Donovan argues, was an assertion of his claim to be the natural son of a wealthy member of the landed gentry, a certain Colonel Crofton Moore Vandeleur, M.P., J.P., D.L., of Kilrush House, Kilrush, County Clare, and 4 Rutland Square, Dublin.[72]

As the founder (in 1852) of the Dublin Amateur Musical Society, Lee enjoyed extraordinary success as a musical entrepreneur; his evenings of operatic and other musical entertainments in the Antient Concert Rooms, with Mrs. Shaw as his leading soprano and the young Lucy Shaw as another of his stars, were attended by members of the highest echelons of Dublin society. He developed a theory of voice production (Shaw dubbed it "The Method") that was expounded—with illustrations like those found in a medical treatise on the ear, nose, and throat—in a work entitled *The Voice: Its Artistic Production, Development, and Preservation,* which was first published in December

1869.[73] In 1960 the theories about voice production in *The Voice* were found to be "quite sensible" by a professor in the School of Anatomy at Trinity College, Dublin.[74] The idea that the work was ghostwritten for Lee by someone with anatomical knowledge was first suggested by Shaw. O'Donovan conjectures that the supposed collaborator was a next-door neighbor of Lee's, Malachi J. Kilgarriff, an eminent surgeon who, because of illness, was unable to attend work during the time when Lee's book was in preparation. When a second edition of *The Voice* appeared the following year, it was prefaced by enthusiastic press notices from *The Irish Times* and *Freeman's Journal.*

The example of a self-made man challenging the professionals from an "outsider" perspective—Lee despised, and was despised by, musical academics—must have been an empowering example for Shaw. Lee was an original figure, and he obviously gave early inspiration to what was to become a much more original mind. The talents of "the charlatan genius" did not extend to literary skills, and it is not surprising that he farmed out to the young Shaw in his London days the writing of musical notices that were published under Lee's name. By this time, though they still remained on friendly terms, Shaw's admiration for Lee had cooled, as the acolyte was beginning to become the master, and Lee fell out of favor with the family. Some of Lee's notes to Shaw in the early London days, written in a large florid hand, as though the writer were conducting a concert, with requests for articles, suggestions about contacts for possible literary employment, and help with piano playing at rehearsals, survive amongst the Shaw papers at the British Library. They show a kindly, avuncular spirit, not rewarded by Shaw's incorrect statement that after Lee's death at his house in Park Lane in November 1886, "the postmortem and inquest revealed the fact that his brain was diseased and had been so for a long time." Medical evidence shows that Lee died of heart disease.[75]

* * *

The young Shaw's extraordinary musical education was matched by his early exposure to a wide range of reading material. "I read everything I could lay hands on," he told Thomas Demetrius O'Bolger in one of the most detailed accounts we have of Shaw's reading habits in Dublin.[76] Apart from *The Pilgrim's Progress*, the very different text of *The Arabian Nights* figures prominently in his childhood recollections. (These two childhood favorites are amusingly brought together in the scene in Shaw's play *Too True to Be Good* (1932) where, within an Eastern setting, the Sergeant is discovered reading Bunyan in a pink grotto called The Abode of Love.) Shaw's early reading of *The Arabian Nights* may have helped to form the playwright's taste for exotic settings, such as that in *Captain Brassbound's Conversion* and in many of the later plays. Perhaps they also played a part in the development of Shaw's sexual imagination and attitudes, as they were known to do for many a Victorian. In his 1901 preface to *Three Plays for Puritans* (1896–99), Shaw pointed to the "frankly indecent" stories of *The Arabian Nights* as an instructive and welcome contrast, in their treatment of sex, to the combination of prurience and prudery, and the narrow range of fictional resources, of Victorian romance.[77] Thomas Moore's series of tales in *Lalla Rookh* provided another early contact for Shaw with nineteenth-century orientalism, Shavian developments of which became a prominent feature of such late plays as *The Simpleton of the Unexpected Isles* and *Buoyant Billions*.

Shakespeare and Dickens were childhood favorites, and Shaw had a profound and intimate knowledge of both writers. Among the novelists, he also read Scott, Dumas père, George Eliot, Thackeray (but "tittle-tattle, however well done, remains tittle-tattle"), and Trollope ("always surprised to find him so readable"). He read Byron "very early and all through," Coleridge's *The Rime of the Ancient Mariner* and William Cowper's "John Gilpin." He read G. H. Lewes's *Life of Goethe* and "every translation of Faust [he] could get hold of."[78]

Among nonfictional works, he read Tyndall's lectures "religiously," Emerson and Carlyle, John Stuart Mill's *Autobiography* as well as some of his shorter essays, Robertson's histories, Hume, and—a special favorite—the *Maximes* of La Rochefoucauld. (The latter provided an early model for the pithy, epigrammatic style that Shaw deploys brilliantly in the "Maxims for Revolutionists" attached to the published text of *Man and Superman*, in sallies such as "He who can, does. He who cannot, teaches.") Shelley, Blake, Ruskin, Morris, Ibsen, Wagner, Schopenhauer, Comte, Henry George, and Marx were soon to become further influences of major significance in his early London days.

One of Shaw's extended replies to O'Bolger's questions about his early reading provides valuable insights into the ways in which he acquired his self-education in literature, music, and art. O'Bolger had asked him if there was any "system" in his early reading, to which he replied:

> No system whatever. I didn't know what system was. I had no access to any library, and didn't know anything about libraries. I had no money to buy books with. Literally I read what I could lay my hands on. Nobody directed me; and nobody interfered with me. Lee, who tried to read himself to sleep for many years with Tyndall on Sound, never read anything

else. He was astonished to hear that Carlyle was an author, believing him to be the Lord Lieutenant (The Earl of Carlisle) who came to his concerts, and woke up with an oath at the bang in Haydn's Surprise Symphony.[79]

Of all the writers he read in the Dublin days, Charles Dickens may be singled out as having had the most direct and pervasive influence on Shaw's early development as a playwright. His first play, *Widowers' Houses* (1892), is full of Dickensian echoes. The rack-renter landlord Sartorius and his scruffy rent collector Lickcheese are clearly modeled on the smooth "Patriarch" Casby and his rent squeezer in Bleeding Heart Yard, Mr. Pancks in *Little Dorrit*. The scene in which Sartorius reviles Lickcheese for his soft treatment of the tenants directly recalls a similar scene in Dickens's novel when Mr. Casby berates Pancks for "a very bad day's work." Cokane, the obsequious upholder of proprieties and Harry Trench's chaperone in Shaw's play, fills a role very similar to that of Mrs. General in *Little Dorrit*; both characters underscore the importance of surface appearances and ceremony in the social system they help to uphold. Harry Trench's realization of his own involvement in the corrupt social and economic system portrayed in *Widowers' Houses* recalls a similar development in *Little Dorrit* concerning the career of Arthur Clennam. *Little Dorrit* continued to be a fruitful influence in Shaw's later plays, providing in Mrs. Clennam a model for Mrs. Dudgeon in *The Devil's Disciple* (1896). The pathetically commonplace business entrepreneur Mr. Merdle, whose vast financial empire is discovered to rest on nothing, served as a model for Boss Mangan in *Heartbreak House* (1916–17). The early play, *You Never Can Tell* (1896), draws substantially on *Bleak House* and *Great Expectations* for its characterizations.

Shaw was not an uncritical reader of Dickens, but the presence of this writer in his own work can be seen both in details and in the larger contours of his social vision and comic manner. In his capacity for appealing both to highbrow and popular taste, his social range, his skill in the creation of sharply individualized personae who yet have significance as social types, his passionately felt concern about the injustices and inequities of his society, and in the searching quality of his social satire, Shaw is the direct heir of Dickens in the tradition of English critical comedy.

* * *

Visits to the Theatre Royal served to complete the armory of cultural experience and knowledge with which the Dublin years equipped the future novelist, critic, and playwright. The Royal was Dublin's principal theater at the time of Shaw's childhood, and its varied offerings furnished the young Shaw with a strong grounding in the nineteenth-century theatrical tradition. In his own work as a playwright Shaw drew upon all of the major genres of the Victorian theater in various (mostly parodic) ways.[80] Melodrama, pantomime, historical costume drama, the pièce-bien-faite, romantic comedy, and farce were among the forms of a lively if intellectually threadbare popular tradition that Shaw inherited and transformed when he began his career as a playwright for the public theater in the 1890s. By the time he left Dublin, approaching his twentieth birthday, Shaw had encountered many examples of these genres.

Before he reached the age of fifteen and earned enough to afford theater tickets, his visits appear to have been infrequent. He has, however, left lively accounts of the few occasions when he did attend the theater as a child. Shaw first visited the theater in January 1864 at the age of seven and a half (accompanied either by his father or Vandeleur Lee), when he saw Tom Taylor's *Plot and Passion*, which was followed by the pantomime *Harlequin Puss in Boots, or, the Fairies of the Gossamer Grove*, featuring "a real policeman deliciously shot into several pieces by the clown." He was so entranced by *Plot and Passion* that he had to be "removed forcibly from the theatre," refusing to believe that after three falls of the curtain at the end it would not go up again. In March 1868 he went by himself to see Dion Boucicault's *The Corsican Brothers*, on this occasion with a more sophisticated understanding of how the magic of the theater works. Boucicault's play employed a device ("The Corsican Trap") that enabled a ghost to appear and slide across the stage, illuminated by a green lantern. Shaw knew how the ghost was managed, and that the villain Chateau-Renaud, though killed in a duel, was not really dead at the end of the play; Shaw "enjoyed the fight all the more" because of this knowledge.[81] During his last five years in Dublin—when his wages from his employment at the firm of Uniacke Townshend enabled him to afford it—Shaw visited the theater almost every week; by the time he emigrated to London, he had seen "every major touring performer."[82]

* * *

Looking back on his childhood in the 1930 preface to *Immaturity*, Shaw perceived how much ideas of the theater and role-playing affected his own self-fashioning and behavior as he was growing up. In the passage preceding the one where he describes his childhood fascination with Mephistopheles, he tells us that he did not experience remorse in telling lies, but rather reveled in "the exercise of dramatic invention involved." He writes that "even when I was a good boy I was so only theatrically, because, as actors say, I saw myself in the character; and this occurred very seldom, my taste running so strongly on stage villains and stage demons."[83]

Earlier, in one of his replies to O'Bolger in 1916 about his Dublin childhood, he had said: "In fact the real Shaw is the actor, the imaginary Shaw the real one."[84] Images of the theater and role-playing are an underlying thread in several other self-descriptions by Shaw. Toward the end of his preface to *Immaturity* he explains that as a young man he felt himself a stranger in the real world: "I was at home only in the realm of my imagination, and at my ease only with the mighty dead. Therefore I had to become an actor, and create for myself a fantastic personality, fit and apt for dealing with men, and adaptable to the various parts I had to play as author, journalist, orator, politician, committee man, man of the world, and so forth."[85] These comments are consistent with an image of himself that Shaw volunteered in an autobiographical letter written to Frank Harris in 1930: "I am the true Shakespearean type: I understand everything and everyone, and am nobody and nothing."[86]

Shaw's recognition of his role-playing disposition does not negate the sincerity and integrity of his self-transcending idealism, the idea of "being used for a purpose recognized by yourself as a mighty one," or his lifelong dedication to a meliorist social and philosophical vision, even though the expressions of that vision, as will be seen, were almost invariably accompanied by skepticism and pessimism. He had an extraordinary ability to enter with imaginative sympathy and gusto into very different points of view from that of idealistic world betterers, in ways that sometimes—as, for example, in *Major Barbara*—create a baffling complexity in the distribution of sympathies in his plays. The idealism of his Mr. Valiants-for-Truth or Faustian dreamers always tended to be accompanied by the mocking voices of Mephistophelean skeptics and realists. Shaw's Dublin childhood laid the foundations of a complex, plural self, in which contradictory ideas were freely entertained and works of the imagination shaped his outlook quite as powerfully as his real-life experiences.

4 The Townshend Connections

By coincidence the family name Townshend links two important events in Shaw's life. On 20 January 1857, about six months after Shaw's birth in Dublin, a baby daughter, Charlotte Frances, was born into the well-to-do family of Mr. Horace Payne-Townshend of Derry House, Rosscarbery, County Cork. Forty-one years later, Charlotte Frances was to become—to the consternation of some members of her family circle—the bride of the amusingly unconventional music and theater critic, avant-garde Socialist, and budding playwright George Bernard Shaw. On 1 September 1871 the fifteen-year-old Shaw had established an earlier Townshend connection when he obtained his employment as office boy at the firm of estate agents belonging to Charles Uniacke Townshend. Charlotte's father, Horace Payne-Townshend, and Shaw's employer were distant relatives, belonging to different branches of a group of Irish Townshend families who traced their common descent to Richard Townsend (also spelled Townesende or Townshend), an officer in the Parliamentary army during the English Civil War who handed the keys of Cork to Cromwell after the Commonwealth was proclaimed and acquired Castle Townshend in 1666.[1]

The upbringing of Charlotte Frances Payne-Townshend, though probably based on a range of social attitudes and assumptions similar to those of the Shaw clan, was very different from that of her future husband. Built at the end of the eighteenth century by Charlotte's great-grandfather Horatio Townsend, Derry House, Rosscarbery, was the large, rambling residence of a substantial country estate. The house is situated in an elevated position on the southern coast of Ireland, with a small lake in immediate view and, beyond that, some fields running down to the Celtic Sea. Lying between Clonakilty and Skibbereen, Rosscarbery is within fairly easy reach by car of Parknasilla, on the southern side of the Ring of Kerry, where Charlotte and Bernard Shaw were to spend several long summer holidays from 1917 to 1923. The main house was severely damaged during the troubles of 1922: "[Michael] Collins burnt the chateaux (including the one in which my wife was born)," Shaw told Lord Alfred Douglas in 1940. The present house is considerably reduced in size as a result of subsequent demolition of derelict sections.[2] Still standing to the rear of the house—and probably in much its original state—is an attractive block of stone-built farm offices and stables. These would have won the approval of the magnificently dogmatic Lady Utterword in Shaw's *Heartbreak House,* who says near the end of the play: "Go anywhere in England where there are natural, wholesome, contented, and really nice English people; and what do you always find? That the stables are the real centre of the household."

Horse riding was one of the many accomplishments included in the young Charlotte Payne-Townshend's upbringing at Rosscarbery. On 28 December 1876 she recorded in her faithfully kept diary a "splendid ride on the sand in the morning." In the days leading up to Christmas of that year she had been making progress with guitar playing and acquiring some "books of Guitar Songs." On 21 December she records that her father (whom she was later to describe as "gentle & affectionate, well-educated & well read") gave her a Latin lesson in the morning.[3] In addition to Latin, she studied French, Italian, and German, and, like her father, developed a wide range of reading interests. Charlotte (known in the family as "Lottie") was the eldest of two daughters, her younger sister being Mary Stewart ("Sissy") Payne-Townshend. The girls' upbringing was very much like that of young women from well-to-do families in the England of Jane Austen. Their mother was Mary Susanna, a daughter of Lieutenant Colonel Thomas Kirby, who married Horace Townshend on 25 October 1855. An Englishwoman, apparently with strong social pretensions and Mrs. Bennett-like "ambitions" for her daughters, she was the driving force behind the family's regular migrations to Dublin and London to attend the social seasons of parties, balls, and receptions. The family assumed the additional surname of Payne and adopted the spelling Townshend (formerly Townsend) by royal license in 1863 under the will of Thomas Payne of Edstaston, Susanna being a devisee of Thomas Payne's will.[4]

Unfortunately, the stables at Derry House proved insufficient to ensure the type of "contented" inhabitants guaranteed by Lady Utterword in *Heartbreak House.* On 17 May 1927 Charlotte revealed much about her childhood experiences in a lengthy autobiographical letter written to T. E. Lawrence (Lawrence of Arabia), with whom she enjoyed a close friendship.[5] "I had a perfectly hellish childhood & youth," she told Lawrence. The main reason for her discontent was her intense dislike of her "managing and domineering" mother, which cast a long shadow over her entire life and profoundly influenced her attitudes toward marriage and family. Charlotte described the relationship between her father and mother in terms of her analysis of the difference between the Irish and English class systems before the transforming political events of the 1920s. Her father was a member of the Irish gentry, her mother, Charlotte says, was a snobbish member of the English provincial middle class:

> In Ireland we have had, up to now, no *middle class*. It came partly from having in the country two races & two religions. We had The Gentry and The People: nothing else. You will say "But the in-betweeners?" They belonged to the people. Michael Collins' father was a "ssthrong farmer,"—he had a relative who kept a shop in Clonakilty, but he would have been the first to tell you he belonged to The People.[6] We had none of the infamous snobbery of "the Nobility" & "the upper middle class." The Duke of Leinster & Provost Mahaffy of Trinity & myself & the doctor's daughter were all equally The Gentry. . . .
>
> My mother was middle-class, my father was . . . gentry.[7]

According to Charlotte, Mary Susanna constantly used emotional blackmail against her husband and daughters with tearful remonstrations about their lack of proper love and respect for her, subjecting them to a tyrannical regime of obedience to her wishes and to her schemes for the social advancement of the family. In her letter to Lawrence Charlotte also recalls that Horace loved his home, where his real interests lay, whereas Mary Susanna "constantly railed about 'exile' + 'this accursed country [of Ireland].'" Charlotte tried to resist her sway, and took her father's side in arguments, but she was weighed down by "a fearful streak of conscience, & sense of duty" and felt that she had been crushed by her mother's authority. Her own experience of the mother-daughter relationship made her determined never to bear children: "I don't believe, as far as I can remember, that I was born with a dislike for children—perhaps I was. But, anyway, my own home life made me fairly resolve never to be the mother of a child who might suffer as I had suffered."[8]

Charlotte felt as strongly about the stifling effects of middle-class morality on natural human impulses as did her future husband, who treated the theme hilariously in one of his greatest comic creations, Alfred Doolittle, Cockney dustman and father of Eliza in *Pygmalion* (1912), who, after a sudden and unexpected access of wealth, sees himself ruined and his happiness destroyed by his being "tied . . . up and delivered . . . into the hands of middle class morality."

In a curious echo of the clash between Shaw's accounts of his father and George Carr Shaw's self-presentation in letters to his wife and son, Charlotte's description of her parents and their relationship is at odds with the affectionate references to his wife in a notebook of financial memoranda that Horace Payne-Townshend began to keep in 1856. On 9 November 1872, his forty-eighth birthday, he embarked on the writing of an extensive memorandum about his financial affairs, intended as a supplement to and explanation of matters set down in his will, or, as he described it, "a few observations which may be of use to my dear wife and children chiefly with regard to the property with which God has blessed me and which my will disposes of."[9] References to "my dear wife" recur in the memorandum. Particularly noteworthy is the language he employs to refer to their relationship as husband and wife in giving directions about where he wants to be buried: "I wish to be buried in such place whether in England or Ireland as my dear wife may select for her own place of interment, that as we have lived many years together in great happiness and harmony, we may not be separated in death."[10]

Charlotte was fifteen when this was written. She was deeply devoted to her father, shared his interests, and enjoyed extensive travels with him. It may be that a certain amount of jealousy of her mother lay behind the caustic remarks about her in the letter to Lawrence. It is also quite possible, of course, that Horace was glossing over some of the family tensions when he wrote so warmly about Mary Susanna in the memorandum. Whatever the cause or truth of Charlotte's assertions, a negative view of her parents' relations was something she would share with her future husband; it remained a factor that influenced her own aversion to the idea of having children.

Horace Payne-Townshend was indeed blessed in the matter of worldly possessions. He inherited extensive properties in Ireland, including Derry House and its surrounding farms, and a share of houses situated in King Street, Cheapside, London. Having graduated from Trinity College, Dublin, and qualified as a barrister at Lincoln's Inn in 1851, he went on to become an exceptionally capable estate owner and a shrewd investor. A great part of his wealth derived from shares in the National Provincial Bank of England; he also held shares in various railway, gas, and waterworks companies. He owned land (valued at £30,000 in 1884) in Shropshire and Gloucestershire, this in addition to his properties in Ireland. In his financial memorandum he estimated the value of his personal property in December 1884 at £200,572 (the equivalent of more than twenty million US dollars in 2005). Charlotte's combined family inheritances were to make her an extremely wealthy woman. After being introduced to the Fabian circle by Beatrice and Sydney

Webb, she was to provide substantial financial support to their causes, and became a major contributor to the foundation of the London School of Economics.

* * *

While the young Charlotte was acquiring the accomplishments necessary for her debut in fashionable society on the family estate in County Cork, her future husband was embarking on his life as a clerk in Charles Uniacke Townshend's firm in Dublin. In *Sixteen Self Sketches* Shaw described his employer as "a pillar of the Church, of the Royal Dublin Society, and of everything else pillarable in Dublin."[11] Land agency was a respectable and sought-after profession at that time in Ireland, and the staff of the Townshend office included a number of young men from well-to-do families who had "paid big premiums to be taught a genteel profession."[12] The social milieu of the firm and its employees is conveyed in the following summary: "In some ways I had a better time of it than most clerks. My associates in the office were apprentices of good social standing, mostly University men. I was not precluded from giving myself certain airs of being in the same position; and when, making a journey on the firm's business, I travelled first-class, my expenses were not challenged."[13]

Shaw's companions in the office included Humphrey Lloyd, son of the provost of Trinity College, who, as Shaw commented to McNulty, was "clearly a gentleman of decent stock."[14] Even at this stage of his career, however, Shaw was no tame conformist with the gentlemanly mores of Protestant Ascendancy Ireland. His skepticism in religious matters was in evidence here, as it was in his Mephistophelean fantasies and discussions with McNulty at home. Shaw recalls being "severely battered" during arguments that arose in the Townshend office. It was Humphrey Lloyd who said to the young Shaw: "What is the use of arguing . . . when you don't know what a syllogism is?"[15] On April 3 1875 Shaw's first publication, in the form of an open letter, appeared in the London weekly news digest *Public Opinion*. In it he denounced revivalist meetings held in Dublin by American evangelists Dwight Lyman Moody and Ira D. Sankey and publicly declared his own atheism.

Apart from debates about religion—with or without syllogisms—the gentlemen in Townshend's office engaged in other forms of entertainment. The young Shaw taught his fellow employees "scraps of opera." He recounts the story of how one of their number once turned the office washstand and its screen into the tower dungeon in which the troubador Manrico is imprisoned in the third act of Verdi's *Il Trovatore*. The young man was so passionately engaged in his rendition of Manrico's aria "Ah, che la morte"—perching on the washstand and peering over his dungeon wall—that he was unaware of the arrival on the scene of the senior partner in the firm, Charles Uniacke Townshend, "who stared stupended at the bleating countenance above the screen, and finally fled upstairs, completely beaten by the situation."[16] Despite being such a pillar of all things "pillarable," Townshend was evidently a reasonably tolerant employer. When he learned of Shaw's heterodox religious opinions, he "respected [his] freedom of conscience" and simply extracted a promise not to discuss the subject in the office.[17]

Shaw detested his work as office boy and, later, chief cashier at Uniacke Townshend's firm, saying that he "never made a payment without a hope that I should never have to make it again."[18] Nevertheless, he proved to be an exceptionally proficient employee; his work at this office left an imprint on his outlook and work as a creative writer in more ways than one. He was never so much as "a farthing out" in the office accounts, which he kept in a neat and compact hand. In his later career Shaw was generous with money. Even before he became wealthy himself, he was constantly helping out friends in need. At the same time, throughout his life he remained a careful keeper of accounts and shrewdly protective of his rights and interests in his business dealings as an author. As a public speaker, he never accepted fees.

Apart from making him a careful and experienced account keeper, his involvement in the estate-agency business was important in another way. It brought him into early direct contact with a sphere of social and economic life in capitalist societies—the landlord-tenant relationship—which was to become a major preoccupation of his political thinking and creative activity.

The mid nineteenth century was a period marked by increasing agitation over land ownership and the landlord-tenant relationship in Ireland. According to the radical land reformer James Fintan Lalor, the soil of Ireland belonged to the people, and the system of landlordism alienated the people from their sovereign rights. With Michael Doheny he founded the Tenant League in 1845, and in 1847 he "advocated peasant proprietorship through rent strike and joint resistance to eviction."[19] This early form of Irish communism was closely linked with the emergence of the Young Ireland movement, Fenianism, and the rise of romantic nationalism. Concerning the Tenant Right movement, Roy Foster comments that, "like other agrarian issues of nineteenth-century Irish politics, it knitted together a number of incompatible grievances by identifying the landlord as the enemy."[20] In the years immediately following Shaw's period of employment at Uniacke Townshend's estate agency, renewed land agitation led to the formation in 1879 of the Land League, with its slogan "The Land for the People" and with Charles Stewart Parnell, the future nationalist leader, as its president.

As an adult, Shaw came to detest nationalism. However, it seems unlikely that the intelligent teenager—who, by his own account, substituted "Ireland" for "England" in the recitation of patriotic dithyrambs about the latter in history lessons at school, and declared himself to have been at that time "a young Fenian in my political sympathies"[21]—would have been unaware of the tensions surrounding the profession in which he became a minor employee in 1871. His critical thoughts about private land ownership crystallized after his arrival in London, stimulated by his contact with Marxist and other Socialist thought, such as that of Henry George and Pierre-Joseph Proudhon (whose dictum "Property . . . is theft" is frequently quoted by Shaw). These later influences must have chimed with much that was happening in the land wars during his early years in Ireland. By 1884 Shaw had begun collaborating on the play that was to become his first full-length composition for the stage, *Widowers' Houses,* a central theme of which is slum landlordism. No playwright could have known about the subject at closer hand than Charles Uniacke Townshend's former chief cashier. In the third part of his five-play cycle *Back to Methuselah* (1918–20), which is set in Ireland in the year A.D. 3000, a young woman called Zoo explains to The Elderly Gentleman, who has strayed from a previous civilization, that the word *landlord* is the name of a primitive animal that used to be hunted and shot but has now become extinct.

* * *

Shaw's connection with the firm of Uniacke Townshend ended abruptly. It is quite likely that his dislike of Dublin and his job, together with the prospect of wider intellectual horizons in the London metropolis, had earlier prompted thoughts about joining his mother and sisters in their emigration from Ireland. In the 1930 preface to *Immaturity* Shaw recalled his decision concerning what he called "my abandonment of Dublin for which many young Irishmen of today find it impossible to forgive me":

> My business in life could not be transacted in Dublin out of an experience confined to Ireland. I had to go to London just as my father had to go to the Corn Exchange. London was the literary centre for the English language, and for such artistic culture as the realm of the English language (in which I promised to be king) could afford. There was no Gaelic League in those days, nor any sense that Ireland had in herself the seed

> of culture. Every Irishman who felt that his business in life was on the higher planes of the cultural professions felt that he must have a metropolitan domicile and an international culture: that is, he felt that his first business was to get out of Ireland.[22]

Shaw's self-image as essentially and permanently an Irishman, with Irish loyalties, remained with him throughout his life. However, this statement about his "business in life" having to be conducted in England probably does supply a large part of the reason behind his leaving the country in 1876. He was certainly not alone among the early modern Irish writers in feeling the need for "a metropolitan domicile and an international culture" in which to develop his vocation.

There were, however, two more immediate precipitating causes of his departure. One, which he referred to in his later correspondence, was that the Uniacke Townshend firm had decided to install a Townshend relative in the position of cashier, offering Shaw the position of "general clerk," with an increased salary. As he explained in his letter of resignation, Shaw felt that he did not have enough useful employment to justify his salary once the cashier's job was no longer his.[23] In a letter dated 3 June 1876 he answers what had apparently been a suggestion by McNulty concerning his reason for leaving Dublin: "I did not burn my boats for the sake of a flame. My prospects in Dublin were stupendous. The employer's daughter would have been mine for the asking and partnership in the firm assured. The only obstacle to the fortune was that I cared neither for the post nor for the daughter, not insuperable, I admit."[24]

A testimonial provided to Shaw by the firm, dated 9 August 1878, confirms that he was held in high regard there, and that he left on good terms with his employer.[25] Charles Uniacke Townshend had several daughters; Shaw's letter to McNulty contains the only reference we have to the idea that his prospects at the Townshend firm included the possibility of marriage into the family. Destiny, however, had another Townshend connection in store for him.

A more pressing reason for Shaw's departure from Ireland—not mentioned in autobiographical writings when dealing with the subject of his emigration—was the fact that his sister Agnes was in the last stages of her illness from tuberculosis. Shaw wrote his letter of resignation on 29 February 1876 from the lodgings he shared with his father at 61 Harcourt Street, Dublin. The resignation was to take effect at the end of March. Although there is no surviving correspondence about Agnes's terminal illness, it seems unlikely that by the time Shaw wrote his letter of resignation he had not heard of his sister's plight. Presumably in the hope that the milder climate would help, on 3

March Bessie Shaw moved with Agnes to Balmoral House, a guest house on the esplanade at Ventnor, on the Isle of Wight, a small and attractive island off the southern coast of England. On 27 March Agnes died and was buried at Ventnor three days later. Shaw completed his month of service at Uniacke Townshend's office on Friday, 31 March, and the following day he boarded a ferry at North Wall Quay on the Liffey, bound for England. Nearly three decades were to pass before he returned to Ireland, as a forty-eight-year-old man, in July 1905.

1.1. Bernard Shaw of Kilkenny, grandfather of GBS. Oil on canvas by unknown artist.

1.2. Frances Shaw, grandmother of GBS. Oil on canvas by unknown artist.

1.3. Sir Frederick Shaw, Bart. of Bushy Park, Recorder of Dublin, 1872.

1.4. Frederick Shaw, Chief Valuation Officer of Dublin, paternal uncle of GBS, 1863.

1.5. Lucinda Elizabeth Shaw, mother of GBS.

1.6. Lucinda Elizabeth and George Carr Shaw, parents of GBS.

1.7. Walter John Gurly, maternal uncle of GBS.

Above: 1.8. Shaw's birthplace, 33 Synge Street, Dublin. (It was opened in 1993 as a Shaw Museum, with interior restored to resemble its probable appearance when the Shaws lived there from 1852 to 1867.)

Left: 1.9. The drawing room.

Below: 1.10. Shaw's bedroom.

1.11. Derry House, Rosscarbery, County Cork, Ireland; Charlotte Shaw's birthplace.

1.12. Bushy Park House, Dublin, seat of Shaw's wealthy relatives and visited by him as a child.

1.13. Shaw's sister Lucinda Frances Shaw, c. 1890.

1.14. Shaw's sister Elinor Agnes Shaw, in 1874.

1.15. Matthew Edward McNulty (*left*), close friend of Shaw's from his schooldays; photographed with Shaw in 1874.

1.16. Shaw as Mephistopheles, detail of Max Beerbohm cartoon. (In his teens Shaw painted watercolor frescoes of Mephistopheles as 'the patron saint of skeptics and deriders' on his bedroom wall at Torca Cottage, Dalkey.)

1.17. Shaw seated at the piano, with Robert Moore Fishbourne, an apprentice at the Uniacke Townshend Estate Agency where Shaw was employed. This photo was taken in Dublin shortly before Shaw's departure for London in 1876.

1.18. Shaw with his sister Lucy at Ventnor, Isle of Wight, in 1876, at the time when their sister Elinor Agnes died.

"Juvenile Sketches by Shaw"

1.19. "Calypso."

1.20. "Prophet."

1.21. Shaw at Ventnor, Isle of Wight, in 1876, aged nineteen.

1.22. Charlotte Frances Payne-Townshend, Shaw's future wife, as a schoolgirl in fancy dress, taken in 1874.

1.23. Horace Payne-Townshend, Charlotte's father.

1.24. Mary Stewart Payne-Townshend, Charlotte's sister, who later married Col. Hugh Cholmondeley. Shaw wrote his book *The Intelligent Woman's Guide to Socialism* for her.

1.25. Edward Carr Shaw (1813–1866), paternal uncle of GBS. He migrated to Australia from Roundtown, Dublin, in 1830 and established the property "Red Banks" at Swansea, on the eastern coast of Tasmania. Shaw described him as "my uncle Edward, whom I never saw, and who was therefore my most impressive uncle."

1.26. Charles MacMahon Shaw, Melbourne cousin of GBS and author of *Bernard's Brethren*.

1.27. (to far right of group) Bernard Shaw, cousin of GBS, chief of police in Hobart, Tasmania, with constabulary. He was nicknamed "The Supercop" by GBS.

5 Self-Searching

London and the Novels

On Sunday, 2 April 1876, Shaw arrived by train at Euston Station in London from the ferry port at Holyhead and took a "growler" (a type of four-wheeled cab) through "streets whose names Dickens had made familiar to me"[1] to the lodgings in a small, semi-detached villa his mother had taken at 13 Victoria Grove, West Brompton. (This was the first of three dwellings the family occupied until they finally moved [5 March 1887] to a handsome house at 29 Fitzroy Square in Bloomsbury, which was later to become one of the London homes of Virginia and Leonard Woolf.)[2] After settling in at Victoria Grove, on 4 April Shaw proceeded to Ventnor. The family, which by this time had also been joined by Lucy, remained in Ventnor till the beginning of May, when they returned to London.

* * *

When Shaw arrived in London, the Mephistophelean metamorphosis in his appearance had not yet taken place. The young Irishman had a wispy beard and his reddish hair was parted in the middle and pasted down. On advice from Richard Deck, an opera singer and one of Shaw's early London associates, he was soon to adopt a different hairstyle modeled on Greek statues. Shaw recalled: "When I was in my twenties an old Alsatian opera singer pointed out to me that in Greek statues the hair was always brushed up from the brow so as to form a sort of natural coronet, and asked me why I pasted my hair down, like a Victorian matron. I experimented with my brushes and comb, and found that the Greek plan was feasible and much more picturesque; so I adopted it."[3] The Victorian matron style is evident in several photographs of the time, one of which was to be reproduced in *Sixteen Self Sketches*, where Shaw gives it the caption "Immature, and apparently an arrant prig."[4]

Shaw spent the late spring and summer of 1876 taking singing lessons from his mother and developing his skills on the piano by playing duets with Lucy. In May he saw Ellen Terry, with whom he was later to have a famous epistolary love affair, and Marie Bancroft playing in a revival of Tom Robertson's play *Ours*. By September he began studying for entry by examination into the excise division of the Civil Service, a path that would have been similar to that followed by his father before he became a corn merchant. By November, however, his excise studies had been abandoned. Shaw's professional career as a writer began through the agency of Vandeleur Lee, who, having obtained an appointment as music critic for the satirical weekly *The Hornet*, paid his young protégé a guinea apiece to ghostwrite the articles.

In his early London days Shaw suffered a common fate of young people with his kind of interests, namely, that reading, thinking, and writing tend not to be regarded as real work. He engaged in a prodigious amount of activity in all three categories, but this did not silence his critics in the family, who were understandably concerned about the family economy. "I have a notion hazy that mother thinks me crazy and Lucy thinks me lazy," Shaw rhymed to Matthew Edward McNulty in the first letter (3 June 1876) written from his new quarters. "Here I am, in London," he wrote in the same letter, "without the credentials of a peasant immigrant and I still bear traces of the Shaw snobbery which considers manual work contemptible, and on no account will I enter an office again."[5] In December 1882 the rarely complaining and still affectionate George Carr Shaw was writing to his son: "There is no use expressing my opinion that it would be well if you get something to do to earn some money—It is much wanted by all of us."[6] The letter came with an enclosed postal order for ten shillings.

In his 1905 preface to the first publication in book form of his second novel *The Irrational Knot* (written between June and December 1880) Shaw included a droll retrospective account of what he described as a monstrously parasitical dependence on his mother and father during his time as a struggling novelist in London: "I did not throw myself into the struggle for life: I threw my mother into it. I was not a staff to my father's old age: I hung on to his coat tails. . . . Callous as Comus to moral babble, I steadily wrote my five pages a day and made a man of myself (at my mother's expense) instead of a slave."[7] A less flippant reference to the children's dependency, during the family's early years in London, on the income derived from Bessie Shaw's teaching was supplied by Lucy Shaw, who, in a letter to Janey Drysdale, wrote that the money was "most direfully" necessary.[8]

The frugal life led by Shaw in his early London days is revealed in the extraordinarily detailed account of daily expenses he kept in his diaries from February 1880. The records of his spending—on railway, bus, and tram tickets; stamps; bread, custard, and confectionery; newspapers and gallery catalogues; the theater (the Alhambra, which figures in his first novel, cost 2 shillings entry and threepence for the program); the lavatory man (1 shilling) and washing in public wash places (twopence)—are juxtaposed with notes of his eclectic (and voracious) reading. The entry for Saturday, 13 March 1880, is typical: "Custard &c for lunch 6d. Bus to Holborn 3d. B[ritish] Museum. Score *Wm. Tell. Fidelio.* [Moritz] Retsch's [illustrations to] *Faust. Coriolanus* Ov[erture]. Selous's [illustrated] *Pilgrim's Progress.* Berlioz *Instrumentation.*"[9]

A large outlay totaling four shillings and sixpence was made on 15 March 1880 for "Hair cut, singed, shampooed," perhaps part of the new hairstyle plan suggested by Richard Deck. On the same day he bought *La Semaine Française* for threepence. The reddish-brown ("kino") suit of clothes he bought in May 1880 for £3.10.0 may have had to last him until George Carr Shaw's death in 1885, when money from an insurance policy enabled Shaw to buy the first of his famous Jaeger suits. Although the diary records are a fairly poor man's ledger, they include frequent items of discretionary spending on such things as theater, galleries, newspapers, and periodicals.

The witticisms in the preface to *The Irrational Knot* concerning his dependence on his parents, though containing a large grain of truth, overlook the fact that Shaw did make a number of attempts to secure regular employment during this early period in London; his small income from columns published in *The Hornet* began a few months after he turned twenty. Having avoided the dreaded prospect of office work by discontinuing his civil service studies, he wrote weekly columns (first entitled "Musical Notes" and later "Musical Buzzings") for *The Hornet* from 29 November 1876 to 26 September 1877.

The following year was largely devoted to various forms of self-improvement (studies of French, harmony, and counterpoint) and attempts at literary composition. In February 1878 he embarked on the writing in blank verse of a distinctly heterodox "Passion Play" entitled *The Household of Joseph.* (Jesus, a rebellious child, is the illegitimate son of Mary, Lazarus a drunkard, and Judas a cynical atheist.) This project was abandoned, as was the writing in autumn of a first novel entitled *The Legg Papers.* In November he was introduced to a representative of the Imperial Bank in South Kensington, presumably with the idea of possible employment, but "without result."[10] Early in 1879 he began what was to become his first completed novel, *Immaturity.* By the end of the year a "real" job appeared on the horizon in the form of a position in a recently established telephone company.

Shaw's early years in London coincided with the first years of successful commercialization of the inventions—by Alexander Graham Bell, Thomas Alva Edison, and others—that led to the telephone. Shaw was later to make fine comic use of the telephone in the writing of the final scene of his one-act play *Press Cuttings* (1909), in which an Irish charwoman, Mrs. Farrell, makes an onstage phone call to her daughter to discuss a marriage proposal she has just received from her employer, General Mitchener, while he listens apprehensively. A cordless voice-communication instrument—used by one of the characters in the future age projected in Part IV of *Back to Methuselah,* the pentalogy Shaw completed in September 1920—is a remarkable fictional anticipation of mobile phones and walkie-talkies.

Following Mrs. Cashel Hoey's introduction of him, in October 1879, to Arnold White, manager and secretary of the Edison Telephone Company of London, Shaw began on 14 November of that year, a period of employment in the Way-leave department of the company. At the same meeting Shaw was introduced to his future medical friend (the first of several friends in a profession he liked to satirize) Dr. James Kingston Barton, with whom he was to spend many of his Saturday evenings in the early London days.

His job at the Edison Telephone Company was to persuade property owners to allow the company to erect structures for supporting telephone wires on their rooftops. At first Shaw worked on commission, but after obtaining only one agreement in the first six weeks, with a total payment of two shillings and sixpence, he wrote a letter of resignation to the company, which responded by putting him on a salary of forty-eight pounds per annum. By the following February he had been promoted to head of the Way-leave department, with an office and a salary of eighty pounds plus commissions. However, when the Edison Telephone Company merged with its rival, the Bell, in June 1880 to become the United Telephone Company of London, Shaw took the opportunity of resigning.

* * *

What Shaw no doubt wanted to do most was to get back to his true vocation as a writer, reader, and thinker. After leaving the telephone company, he began his second novel, *The Irrational Knot,* in 1880. This was also the year in which he began to occupy a sort of second home in the great circular Reading Room at the British Museum, where a good deal of his writing and most of his reading was done. In October he took his first plunge into the public intellectual life of London by joining a debating society called the Zetetical, which had been formed two years earlier "to furnish opportunities for the unrestricted discussion of Social, Political, and Philosophical subjects."[11] Shaw did make some efforts—mostly unsuccessfully—during the next few years to gain employment where he could make use of his literary skills, answering various advertisements for secretaries, paragraphers, editorial advisers, and the like. However, it was not until 1885 that he returned to any sort of regular employment. He recorded succinctly in his diary notes for that year: "My father died in April, and paid journalism became inevitable."[12]

At the center of his literary activities in the intervening years—before the "inevitable" arrived—was the writing (after *Immaturity*) of the next four of his five full-length novels: *The Irrational Knot, Love Among the Artists, Cashel Byron's Profession*, and *An Unsocial Socialist*.[13] Taken together, the novels provide a fascinating map of Shaw's preoccupations and development in his early twenties; in many ways they provide the best available access to his inner life at this time. Shaw's diaries—though vastly informative concerning his daily activities, meetings, and reading—do not contain discursive passages of self-scrutiny or reflections about his life in general. Only a few letters of a personal nature survive from the very early London days.

The five novels he wrote from 1879 to the end of 1883 show that the young Shaw was engaged in a remarkable program of creative, imaginative, and morally centered—though not morally conventional—thinking about a wide range of subjects relating to the life and society of his time: about the concept of maturity; about love, romance, and the "irrational knot" of marriage; about the class system, politics, and religion; about the status of women; about art and the life of artists. The novels provide a unique view both of the way in which Shaw was reacting (as an Irish outsider) to his new social environment in England and of the internal dialogues he was conducting about his own character and destiny.

The novels are obviously the product of an extraordinary and unusual intelligence: "too clever for the 'general'" was the verdict of a publisher's reader to indicate the unsuitability of one of them for general readership, a judgment that was echoed in other readers' comments on the novels.[14] Nevertheless, the works also provide a self-reflexive critique of the cleverness they display. Cleverness is one side of a continuing dialogue in these works, in which the "big instincts," as Marian calls them in *The Irrational Knot*, were the other. Often this dialogue is in the form of a male-female opposition. But males do not by any means have a monopoly on cleverness. One of the most formidably intelligent characters in the novels is Lydia Carew, the heroine of *Cashel Byron's Profession* (1883), a young woman with a George Eliot-like range of intellectual interests and abilities (she shares with Eliot a detailed knowledge of Spinoza and Goethe), who is rivaled by Agatha Wylie, her astute fictional successor in *An Unsocial Socialist* (1883). The novels show the young Shaw's fascination with, and sensitive observation of, female behavior. Perceptive descriptions of the nuances conveyed by the way women dress, their physical movement, their ways of dealing with ideas, their handling of emotional challenges, their acuity in penetrating male pomposity, and the whole range of feminine strategies in dealing with relations between both sexes are a striking feature of all the novels.

Despite their merits, the novels did not find favor with any of the major publishers to which Shaw patiently submitted them over a period of several years. With monotonous regularity, the brown-paper parcels containing the manuscripts came back to the author accompanied by letters of refusal. The parcel containing the manuscript of the rejected first novel *Immaturity* began to be nibbled by mice; even they, Shaw later joked to Archibald Henderson, could not finish it.[15] Shaw's resilience and persistence in the face of repeated rejection by publishers of his first novels was remarkable. *Immaturity* was rejected by ten publishers in 1880–81, and an eleventh declined to read it. (Shaw even suggested "putting this unlucky book into the fire" to Richard Bentley & Son after they had advised him of the fourth rejection.)[16] It was not until 1930, when it became the first volume of the first collected edition of Shaw's works (published by Constable) that *Immaturity* was made available in print in silently revised form. The last written of the novels was the first to appear in print. *An Unsocial Socialist*, which brought Shaw to the attention of William Morris and other important future friends, was published serially in Henry Hyde Champion's Socialist periodical *To-Day* (March–December 1884). Serial publication of *Cashel Byron's Profession* followed soon after in the same periodical (April 1885–March 1886). These were the only two of Shaw's novels also to appear in book form during the 1880s.

In his first three novels Shaw undertook the commercially impossible task of writing what hindsight suggests were a type of Victorian antinovel.[17] Both in their narrative structures and themes the three works went completely against the grain of Victorian romantic fiction, while still invoking some of its situations and expectations, and—even more objectionable from some contemporary viewpoints—against that of the prevailing ideological, moral, and class assumptions of the age. Some publishers' readers recognized a very unusual talent and comic gift, while others reacted with predictable indignation.

The Macmillan reader of *Immaturity* found the novel "undoubtedly clever," the "work of a humourist and a realist," with a "piquant oddity" about some of the situations, but such that "most readers would find it dry, unattractive, and too devoid of any sort of emotion." Responding to this reader's thoughtful report in a letter to the publisher, Shaw wrote that his design was "to write a novel scrupulously true to nature . . . yet which should constantly provoke in [a] reader full of the emotional ethics of the conventional novel, a sense of oddity and unexpectedness."[18]

The unusual phrase "emotional ethics" provides an insight into Shaw's thinking at this time. He was viewing emotions not as stable essences of human nature but as forms of behavior and reaction influenced and constructed by cultural contexts and value systems. Shaw challenged Victorian prescriptions about how people should behave in circumstances where emotions are called into play. However, his experiment in deliberately contravening the "emotional ethics of the conventional novel" was not one in which the publisher wished to become involved. Two days later Macmillan rejected the "very long" manuscript.

Beginning with the novels of Jane Austen, one of the dominant paradigms of narrative in mainstream prose fiction in the nineteenth century had as its telos, or desired and governing form of closure, a marriage between two people seen—either early or late in the story—as preeminently suited to one another. "It is a truth universally acknowledged, that a single man in possession of a good fortune must be in want of a wife," wrote Austen, crisply and satirically, in the famous opening sentence of *Pride and Prejudice.* What was true of the telos of fiction was also true of the expectations placed on men and women in Victorian life. Cultural and biological imperatives marched in step.

In *Immaturity* the principal male character, Robert Smith, remains throughout the novel in an almost Beckettian state of inertia with regard to romantic entanglements, and eventually happily free from them. When nothing comes of a final challenge to his single state, he "looks forward to a long respite from further lovemaking." This occurs after the collapse of a flirtatious relationship with the beguiling brunette Isabella Woodward, a relationship that may well reflect Shaw's affair with the "blackeyed enslaver" referred to in his autobiographical poem "Calypso." Earlier in the novel Smith has become attracted to a fellow boarder at his Dickensian lodgings in Islington, the vibrant, independent-minded, and powerfully attractive yet limited and conventional Harriet Russell, who is described by one character as having "a strange grace in her action and in the carriage of her finely shaped head" simultaneously reminiscent of "a panther and of the Venus of Milo."

Harriet is in some ways an early example of the nineteenth-century New Woman, the first in a splendid gallery of female portraits Shaw was to create in his novels and plays. But when her disappointing naïveté as a reader and her intellectual limitations become painfully apparent while Smith is acting as her unpaid tutor, his ardent admiration and romantic feelings begin to "relax." In the middle of the novel (instead of at the end, where the event normally takes place in romance) Harriet marries the artist Cyril Scott, to whom she becomes a second mother, thus inaugurating a persistent theme in Shaw's treatment of female-male relations in marriage, in which the female infantilizes the male. For Harriet "immaturity" means not engaging in the necessary pursuits of "pushing" oneself in the world of commerce, getting married, and settling down—a view of growing up that amusingly reflects the contrary situation of her authorial creator.

The portrayal of Smith is part of an ambitious critical exploration by the young Shaw of Victorian society and its staple values, its symbolic order. The novel engages in an extended play on the idea of "immaturity." The very society in which Smith is viewed by others as "immature" is itself full of different forms of immaturity that in many ways are much more problematic and reprehensible than his—and the pressure of Shaw's personal experience is felt in all this. The novel makes frequent allusions to Shakespeare's *Hamlet*: one of the characters, an Irish manservant with an almost incomprehensible brogue who might have stepped straight out of the pages of a novel by Maria Edgeworth, is called Cornelius Hamlet; there is a gravedigger scene in which Hamlet is directly recalled; and the question as to whether Hamlet is really mad is raised but not answered in connection with a proposed public reading of the play. The allusions prompt speculation that Smith is partly to be viewed—with comic incongruity since he is not even an attendant lord in social rank—as a latter-day Hamlet surveying the rotten state of *his* as well as his young author's "Denmark" in mid-Victorian England: a world full of failed marriages, dilettantish and affected triflers, decadent art and effete aestheticism, class snobbery, gentlemen who are not gentlemen, bullying parents, drunkenness and domestic violence, religious cranks and hypocrites, and spoiled, predatory women.

Like his Shakespearean counterpart, Smith is much given to private reflection and soliloquy; his capacity for action, especially as regards the opposite sex, is overshadowed by the "pale cast of thought"; he has an exceptionally strong conscience; and he rejects marriage. He is a social misfit, discontented with and alienated from his surrounding society. Mrs. Daly (an Irish housekeeper who also speaks with a brogue that Smith detests) describes him as "a bit of a sawney," a dialectal word meaning simpleton or fool. As in Shakespeare's play, what the audience/reader might view as sanity in the protagonist those within the narrative view as madness.

The novel provides a multifaceted view of Smith, as well as a partly self-mocking view of the young Shaw. He is precociously knowledgeable about literature, art, and music. He is bookish, pedantic, and sententious, while at the same time being engagingly self-critical and honest. In the eyes of the female characters he is "the pale scholar of Islington, whose thoughts were like bloodless shadows of conscience and logic" (Harriet) and "a monster of propriety" (Isabella). For a character in a mid-Victorian novel, he is remarkably self-conscious and self-analytical. He is often seen alone, gazing at himself in the mirror, behaving ridiculously, engaging in internal conversations with and about himself, and singing. It is impossible not to suspect some comic self-portraiture on the part of Shaw in these descriptions.

In conception and in much of its execution *Immaturity* is an extraordinarily original and powerful first novel. A salient feature of the work is its inconclusiveness, the lack of narrative closure in the story of its protagonist. It is this that makes it difficult to fit *Immaturity* into the category of bildungsroman such as Joyce's *Portrait of the Artist as a Young Man* or Goethe's *Wilhelm Meister's Apprenticeship*. Smith scarcely develops at all. At the end of the novel he remains the same quizzical, critical, uncommitted and free self that he was at the beginning. In revisions made before publication of the novel in 1930, Shaw made both deletions and additions that underscored the idea of an essentially unchanged character. As Richard Dietrich has remarked with reference to these revisions, "Shaw significantly emphasises Smith's lack of positive growth."[19] The revisions are consistent with the overall pattern of Smith's characterization. The conclusion of *Immaturity*, like that of some of Shaw's early plays, is wry and open-ended: "As Smith recrossed the bridge, he stopped and stood in one of the recesses to meditate on his immaturity, and to look upon the beauty of the still expanses of white moonlight and black shadow which lay before him. At last he shook his head negatively, and went home."

* * *

"I don't like Smith. You may think he is like you but one never knows one's self, and I am sure he is not. He behaves like a prig. He only *half* cares about anything or anybody." So wrote Shaw's novelist friend Elinor Huddart, who had just read and admired *Immaturity*, to the author in March 1881.[20] She was making a perceptive distinction between Shaw and his character, of which she perhaps wrongly assumes Shaw himself was not aware. Smith's characterization clearly contains some autobiographical touches. Like Shaw, Smith hates being a clerk (his occupation at the beginning of the novel) and delivers a long internal monologue against that calling. In its literary references the novel includes a virtual checklist of Shaw's early reading, with the addition of the new figure of Shelley, who displaces Byron in Smith's interests. Like Shaw, Smith writes some not very good poetry in his early manhood. However, the presentation of Smith as a sometimes ridiculously priggish character who has forceful and amusing female critics in the novel argues against a too easy biographical equation between Shaw and his fictional creation. Rather than simply representing the author's immature state, Smith's characterization challenges the reader by presenting a searching view of society's definitions of maturity and immaturity. The novel is as much a portrait of society as a self-portrait.

Immaturity reflects Shaw's early interest in pictorial art and presents a critical view of the contemporary Aesthetic movement. On 1 May 1877 Oscar Wilde attended the opening of the lavishly decorated new Grosvenor Gallery attired in a fittingly spectacular costume, the salient feature of which was a coat, the back of which was tailored in the shape of a cello, designed so that "in some lights it looked bronze, in others red." The Aesthetic movement was in its heyday, and by 1881 Gilbert and Sullivan had produced *Patience, or Bunthorne's Bride,* their topical comic opera on the affectations associated with it, Oscar Wilde being the chief butt of their satire.[21]

Shaw was almost certainly alluding to the new Grosvenor Gallery (his diary records the purchase of a Grosvenor Gallery catalogue—presumably during a visit—in March 1880)[22] in "Book the Second" of *Immaturity,* subtitled "Aesthetics." "Book the Second" opens with a description of a Mr. Halket Grosvenor, patron of the arts and owner of a large and elaborately decorated mansion called Perspective, which includes in its features an art gallery and a music room. Off-puttingly described as a man of "moist eye and spongy flesh," Grosvenor leads a life devoted to "luxurious indolence." His elaborate entertainments, attended by poets, musicians, artists, critics, and dilettantes, together with the receptions held at her house in Wilton Place by Lady Geraldine Porter—another, more likable patron of the arts—are the focal points of a largely satirical view of contemporary art and culture in England that the novel embraces.

A leading figure in the novel's artistic world is the pretentious poet Patrick Hawkshaw, who appears in an Oscar Wilde-like costume at Wilton Place for a recital of his new translation of a Greek tragedy. He is attired "in a long black coat, dove-coloured trousers, primrose gloves, and a bronze-hued scarf, fastened by a brooch representing a small green beetle with red eyes." Shaw was later to see Wilde as an ally in his struggle against British philistinism, and strongly supported him at the time of the trial. The two probably met sometime after early November 1879, when Shaw's diary records his first visit to Lady Wilde's London house, shortly after he finished the writing of *Immaturity.*[23] Both Oscar and his brother, Willie, were attracted to Lucy Shaw. It is likely that Shaw had heard of Wilde's visit to the new Grosvenor Gallery, and that Hawkshaw recalls Oscar's ostentatious first entry into the London artistic world. Although Hawkshaw displays some Wilde-like wit, he is without Oscar Wilde's charm. The poet in the novel is an unpleasant doppelgänger of Smith: the two find one another mutually "disconcerting." Shaw obviously admired Wilde's work, but the portrayal of Hawkshaw may well reflect ambivalent feelings on Shaw's part toward his fellow-countryman. Certainly the second part of *Immaturity* displays a good deal of hostility toward the type of aesthete-poseur lampooned in *Patience* as "a greenery-yallery, Grosvenor-Gallery, foot-in-the-grave young man."

* * *

Elinor L. Huddart, who met Shaw when she was taking singing lessons from Mrs. Shaw at 13 Victoria Grove in 1878, took a keen interest in his early literary career and was among the first to recognize his unusual abilities. Her novels were published anonymously or under various noms de plume (Elinor Aitch, Elinor Hume, Louisa Ronile). An extensive correspondence ensued (only her letters survive), lasting until 1894. During the time of their friendship, what Shaw later described as her "fervidly-imaginative novels"—including *Cheer or Kill* (1878), *Via Crucis* (1882), *My Heart and I* (1883), *Commonplace Sinners* (1885), *Leslie* (1891), and *A Modern Milkmaid* (1892)—rolled off the presses of respectable publishing houses, sometimes going into second editions (apparently with some financial backing from a rich aunt). *My Heart and I* was published by Richard Bentley & Son, one of the publishing firms that were regularly rejecting Shaw's novels at this time. Elinor was approaching forty when the correspondence began. Beginning with advice (apparently requested by her) on *Cheer or Kill*, Shaw adopted toward Elinor the mentoring role reflected in the characterization of Smith in *Immaturity*, as well as in several of the characters in the plays. This was to become characteristic of his relations with numerous women. In the case of Elinor Huddart, there was some irony in the fact that it was the pupil who was having her novels published while the mentor was receiving rejection letters.

Elinor was well read, intelligent, and modest about her own attainments. Although her early letters are deferential and humble, she gained confidence as the correspondence developed; her tone frequently becomes mocking, witty, and boldly critical. Underlying all her comments, however, is a profound respect for Shaw's potential as a writer: "Someday the world will acknowledge you a genius," she wrote to Shaw in May 1881, and "the bloom of an unobtrusive originality is over all your work" in the following year.[24] These compliments gain strength from the fact that her criticisms could sometimes be quite scathing. "What an abominable set they are," she remarks of the characters in *The Irrational Knot*. "Their discussions are absurdly lengthy and tedious. . . . All the same it is a marvelous piece of work."[25]

They discussed books, plays, ideas, spiritualist experiences, families, writing, childhood, friendship, love, reason, and irrationality. He evidently made the mistake of saying that women are like flowers. She replied that there are a great variety of flowers and that some, when trampled on, "yield poison instead of fragrance." Anyway, she added, "you cannot generalise in that August fashion about so subtle a creation as woman."[26] In one letter she describes a portrait of her seafaring grandfather, Captain Huddart, "sitting at a table whereon is a chart. He holds a pair of compasses in his hand over the map."[27] The image lodged in Shaw's mind to become one of many that contributed to his portrait of Captain Shotover and his table of instruments in the play *Heartbreak House* (1916–17).

Elinor and Shaw met only occasionally, and there is a suggestion in the letters that the meetings were rather unsatisfactory. In what she called "our very innocent epistles"[28] sexual flirtation was held at bay, but the letters reveal an extraordinary degree of intimacy in the friendship. Both were clearly using the letters as a form of self-exploration. Elinor remained unmarried despite Shaw's frequent urging—not on his own behalf—that she should. Sadly, the correspondence dwindled to a close in the early 1890s, with some quarrels and recriminations from Elinor about Shaw's neglect of her. On 8 July 1894, following a misunderstanding, she bade farewell to him with a learned salute and gentle reproach, quoting St. Paul's response to the Roman procurator Porcius Festus: "I am not mad most noble Festus."[29]

* * *

Another friend of Shaw's in the early years in London who paid tribute to his literary gifts was a young Irish poet named Pakenham Thomas Beatty. Beatty was the son of Pakenham William Beatty, a merchant from Mount Pleasant, near Dundalk, County Louth. He was a pupil at Harrow School for three years and, following what appears to have been a brief enrollment at Trinity College, Cambridge, was admitted to the Middle Temple on 16 March 1875 at the age of eighteen. Although his first letter to Shaw on 29 October 1878 was written from the stately family home in County Louth, their London friendship began in 1880, by which time Beatty had married and was living in Philbeach Gardens, Earl's Court.[30] "George Balzac Shaw Esq" was one of the many humorous forms of address employed on the envelopes of the letters written from 1878 to 1889 by Beatty to his "Honoured & beloved Pal," and novelist Shaw.[31] In one of the letters Beatty added a Hibernian touch to his allusion by calling his friend—whose novels reflected the traditions of nineteenth-century French realism, of which Balzac was a major exemplar—"O'Balzac Shaw."[32] An engaging delight in extravagant fun is a hallmark of the Beatty letters to Shaw. In one invitation to lunch, he commands that Shaw be set on "eight white she asses" and transported to "our palace of Philbeach." Another letter sends "from the mighty Caliph Haroun . . . to his Vizier Ben Shaw greeting." [33] In another communication Beatty casts himself in the role of Virgil, quoting from the opening line of the *Aeneid*: "Arma virumque cano."[34] Although Shaw was probably familiar with the line, his friend's use of it may have stuck in his mind to become the basis of the title of his 1894 play *Arms and the Man*, in which the character of Sergius has some affinities with Beatty.

Long after this early correspondence Shaw told Beatty: "Lord bless you, my plays are full of your jokes. I waste nothing. What you drop goes into my shop window next day."[35] Shaw lamented the fact that his friend's gift for comedy and lively language was absent from Beatty's own writing: "The way in which you elect to deliberately suppress all your humour, your experience, your command of comic situation and living language the moment you write for the public, and fall back on a factitious and idiotic mechanism of blank verse and literary shop, drives me to despair." The advice to Beatty throws light on Shaw's attitude toward the writer's craft. His friend needed to cast off the "filthy rags of academic tradition" and give up his preoccupation with following literary models. "You must be preoccupied most intensely with life," he told him.[36]

It is not, of course, possible to trace the Beatty "jokes" in Shavian drama, but Shaw's works contain several echoes of the friendship. Shaw used Beatty's nickname "Paquito" for his main character in *Captain Brassbound's Conversion*. The Beattys' naming of one of their sons Mazzini, after the Italian revolutionary, is reflected in the name of Mazzini Dunn in *Heartbreak House*. "Tavy," the shortened version of the name Octavius in *Man and Superman*, is the same as that used in the Beatty family for a younger brother of Pakenham, Octavius Holmes Beatty; Shaw probably had that in mind, as well as Kipling's Ricky Ticky Tavy, when he was writing the play.[37] The not very complimentary portrait of a minor poet, Chester Erskine, in *An Unsocial Socialist* was partly modeled on Beatty.

Beatty wrote and published love poems—he sent Shaw his first volume, *To My Lady, and Other Poems*, in 1878—and a poetic drama—*Marcia*, very loosely based on Russian history, in 1880—which Shaw reviewed mostly unfavorably in August 1884.[38] Although Beatty's dash and humor were not well reflected in his writings, his wit, literary interests, and revolutionary zeal made him a good companion. Shaw made regular visits to the Beatty house on Sunday evenings and got on well with Beatty's wife, Ida, with whom he practiced French. It was Beatty who introduced Shaw to Ned Donnelly, professor of boxing at the London Athletic Club, who became one of the models for Shaw's novel *Cashel Byron's Profession*, which concerns a professional boxer. Under the professor's "scientific" tutelage in the noble art of self-defense, Shaw and

Beatty became regular sparring partners and made frequent visits to championship bouts.

There were, alas, downsides to Beatty's high spirits. He lived extravagantly on an inheritance that ran out during the course of his friendship with Shaw. He drank to excess and was once rescued by Shaw in a state of delirium tremens.[39] He also got into trouble with the Shaw family by flirting with Lucy. Over the years, Shaw became a generous benefactor of the Beattys and assisted them with advice and financial support in the education of their children. The Beatty family, in turn, remained loyal to Shaw. One of Ida and Pakenham's daughters, Cecilia Olivia, was reported to have been the last to leave the chapel at Golders Green Crematorium following Shaw's funeral ceremony in 1950.[40]

* * *

A diary note indicates that on 5 January 1879 Shaw first made the acquaintance of the Lawson family, who lived at Carlton House, Cheyne Walk, on the Chelsea Embankment, an area inhabited by many artists in the Victorian period and a center of the Pre-Raphaelite movement. He was subsequently invited to Sunday evening at homes with this artistic and musical family. His hostess, Mrs. Elizabeth Lawson, was the mother of the landscape painter Cecil Lawson and the musician and conductor Malcolm Lawson. The character of Cyril Scott in *Immaturity* was partly modeled on Cecil Lawson, though Shaw provided a caveat about this biographical equation that can be applied more generally to his use of real-life models. He warned the reader not to take Cyril Scott as "an authentic portrait" of Lawson, whom he knew only slightly: "He set my imagination to work: that was all."[41] The Lawson family at homes are recalled not only in *Immaturity* but (decades later) in the third act of *Pygmalion*, where Mrs. Higgins's at home in her flat on the Chelsea Embankment (in which, according to a stage direction, hangs a large landscape by Cecil Lawson) is the scene of Eliza Doolittle's sensational social debut.

Despite the fact that Shaw liked the Lawsons and found the house and its "artistic atmosphere" most congenial, he records in the preface to *Immaturity* that he suffered "agonies of shyness" before making his visits there. As he had not yet "tuned the Shavian note to any sort of harmony" he thought the Lawsons must have found him "discordant, crudely self-assertive, and insufferable."[42] An invitation from Mrs. Lawson to a dance at her home evoked a sweet, self-deprecatory note of refusal that remains one of the earliest surviving letters of Shaw's London days. Although he had another engagement, he explained that he would have been afraid to accept anyway since he was a "dispiriting object in a drawing room" and did not know how to dance: "I could not accomplish a waltz for the sake of the most attractive partner you could offer me, and this, for one who has the privilege of knowing the resources you have at hand, is saying everything. I should be an envious and gloomy wallflower, and in your house an unhappy guest would be an anomaly."[43] Shaw's visits to the Lawsons are echoed and transformed in the dramatic presentation of an all too self-confident Eliza Doolittle, who at this stage of her training makes her famous exclamation "Not bloody likely" at Mrs. Higgins's house.

* * *

"O'Balzac" Shaw's ruthless dissection of marriage and society in his second novel, *The Irrational Knot*, was even less calculated to be relished by the general reader than its predecessor. "A novel of the most disagreeable kind," declared the publisher's reader for Macmillan. While recognizing in the work "a certain originality, and courage of mind," and the unconventionality of the novel's style and structure, the reader went on to say that "the thought of the book is all wrong; the whole idea of it is odd, perverse and crude. . . . publication . . . is out of the question. There is too much of adultery and the like matters."[44] The comments were echoed by readers for other publishers.

The revolutionary thrust of the book had been recognized by Elinor Huddart, who wrote to Shaw on 27 March 1881: "The title itself is . . . a challenge flung in the face of society, heralding, no doubt, a raid against its dearest prejudices."[45] Elinor disclaimed any likeness—apart from the quality of "unswerving faithfulness"[46]—to her namesake, Elinor McQuinch, in Shaw's new work. Nevertheless, the fictional Elinor also writes novels, has forthright and down-to-earth opinions, and does seem to reflect Shaw's friend in some ways. Elinor McQuinch and her friend Marian, another leading female character in *The Irrational Knot*, also echo—both in their names and thematic associations—the characters of Elinor and Marianne in Jane Austen's *Sense and Sensibility*.[47] Dialogues between sense and sensibility, reason and romantic passion, respectability and instinct run throughout the novel and dictate the course of its action. Against the wishes of her family, Marian enters into a registry-office marriage with the ultra-rational American electrical engineer and inventor Ned Conolly. The latter is not only a gifted scientist but an accomplished musician, linguist, and formidable intellectual with atheistic views. Conolly has an equally independent-minded sister, Susanna, who under the stage name of Virtue Lalage is a successful performer in musical burlesque—like Shaw's sister Lucy, on whom the character is partly based.

With the creation of Conolly, Shaw continued the process of oblique self-questioning and self-parody displayed in the characterization of Smith. With his superhuman control of emotions and imperturbable reasonableness, Conolly resembles his own highly successful invention, the Conolly Electromotor. Elinor McQuinch nails him with some telling phrases, accusing him of being "a calculating machine . . . a stone full of brains," and describing him to Marian as "monotonously amiable." The first two novels both convey a sense of half-humorously, half-anxiously perhaps posed questions in the young author's mind as to whether he is himself becoming like Smith, the bloodless "pale scholar of Islington," or the "calculating machine" Conolly.

Shaw amusingly acknowledged some of the defects of his second novel in a prefatory letter to the reader he wrote for the book publication in 1900 of *Love Among the Artists*: "If you have read my *Irrational Knot* to the bitter end, you will not accuse me of mock modesty when I admit that it was very long; that it did not introduce you to a single person you could conceivably have been glad to know; and . . . that no satisfactory ending was possible."[48]

The Irrational Knot did, however, mark an important phase in Shaw's development both as man and artist. The early influence on his thought of nineteenth-century scientific rational materialism and religious radicalism[49] —transmitted through the writings of Thomas Henry Huxley and John Tyndall, radical essays published in John Chapman and George Eliot's *Westminster Review*, and other sources—continues to be strongly present in the first two novels. *The Irrational Knot* can be seen as a partial exorcism of this influence. In a typescript preface he added to the manuscript when he presented it to the National Library of Ireland in 1946, Shaw wrote of the novel: "It is interesting to me as marking a crisis in my progress as a thinker. It carried me as far as I could go in Rationalism and Materialism." Earlier, in one of his replies to Thomas O'Bolger, he wrote in the same vein: "The Irrational Knot . . . really gives the summing up of my Dublin culture. After that I deliberately threw over my intellectual integrity, so to speak, and took the unreasonable instinctive man for my theme. I finished with rationalism (except as a butt) in my second book, just as I had finished with operatic romance (now cinematographic romance) before my first."[50]

Although Shaw exaggerates in saying that he "finished with rationalism" in this novel, *The Irrational Knot* displays tensions that are of fundamental importance both in Shaw's creative writing and in his self-development. In mature Shavian comedy the (usually male) exponents of reason and theory, like Professor Higgins in *Pygmalion* and Jack Tanner in *Man and Superman*, meet more than their match in their encounters with "unreasonable instinctive" women who puncture their pretensions with laughter-provoking guile, resourcefulness, and human vitality. The creative dialogue in the early novels between sense and sensibility, reason and passion, was to grow into as rich a source of dramatic conflict in Shavian comedy as that between Mephistophelean skepticism and Bunyanesque idealism. Although Shaw never quite divested himself of the traces of Ned Conolly in his own makeup, his engagement, both as artist and man, with the complexities of human life and society became far more subtle and flexible. In *The Irrational Knot* he had not yet discovered the secret of what Captain Brassbound was to call "real cleverness."

* * *

While he was attempting to place *The Irrational Knot* with publishers, Shaw began to experiment with vegetarianism: "Became a vegetarian, and remained so until June,"[51] he recorded in his diary in January 1881. His adoption of vegetarianism—he resumed the diet in October 1881 and remained a lifelong devotee and advocate—reflects the powerful influence exerted on the young Shaw by Percy Bysshe Shelley.[52] Works by Shelley such as *Queen Mab* and its appended "Notes," consisting of a series of explosive revolutionary essays ("against Jesus Christ, & God the Father, & the King, & the Bishops, & marriage, & the Devil knows what"); *Prometheus Unbound*, which looks forward to the overthrow of cosmic and human tyrannies and the liberation of man into a state "Sceptreless, free . . . / Equal, unclassed, tribeless and nationless"; and the *Revolt of Islam*, with its eloquent complaints against the position of woman as "the bond-slave"[53] of man—all provided a treasure trove of ideas that Shaw plundered in his writings, both in the early novels and beyond.

The "Notes on Queen Mab" included the theory—derived by Shelley from John Newton's book *The Return to Nature; or, A Defence of the Vegetable Regimen* (1811)—that when Prometheus stole fire from the gods, he brought down on mankind all the ills that are associated with the Fall in the Christian religion. Through its use in cooking, fire provided the means of screening from humans a natural disgust at consuming flesh, "the horrors of the shambles." To the consuming of flesh and spirituous liquors are attributed all the ills of the human postlapsarian state: disease, suffering, crime, vice, warfare, tyranny, and all the rest of the contents of Pandora's box. Shaw took a great deal of this to heart, declaring his aversion to "the enormity of eating the scorched corpses of animals"[54] and echoing Shelley's idea about the ability of a vegetable diet to "restore to the mind that cheerfulness and elasticity which not one in fifty possesses on the present system."[55]

Shaw was to become a shining example of the virtues of vegetarianism. In his forties he could leave men half his age panting behind him as he strode effortlessly and at high speed on country walks. In his eighties, during one of his stays at the Astors' palatial residence, Cliveden, Joyce Grenfell described his physical appearance as "incredible . . . wonderfully pink and white and fresh and beautifully dandified."[56] In an 1898 essay Shaw joked that he had provided in his will that his funeral would be followed "not by mourning coaches, but by herds of oxen, sheep, swine, flocks of poultry, and a small travelling aquarium of live fish, all wearing white scarves, in honour of the man who perished rather than eat his fellow creatures."[57]

In the "Notes on Queen Mab" the young Shaw found not only a lengthy advocacy of vegetarianism (published separately in 1813 as *A Vindication of Natural Diet*) but also a number of other ideas that were to become part of his mental furniture. Glossing the line in his poem "Even love is sold," Shelley linked marriage with prostitution, a notion echoed by Susanna Conolly in *The Irrational Knot* and the title character in *Mrs. Warren's Profession*. The idea that wedlock should be indissoluble is countered by Shelley's arguments that "husband and wife ought to continue so long united as they love each other. . . . Love is free: to promise for ever to love the same woman is not less absurd than to promise to believe the same creed." The loosening and untying of various knots involving relationships between men and women, and the very critical view of marriage expressed in Shaw's early novels reflect this Shelleyan view. In the "Notes to Queen Mab" Shelley also adumbrated an important feature of Shaw's religious outlook when he glossed the line "There is no God" by saying: "This negation must be understood solely to affect a creative Deity. The hypothesis of a pervading Spirit co-eternal with the universe remains unshaken." Both the rejection of the personal deities of orthodox religions and the idea of a "pervading Spirit" in the universe are echoed in the Shavian theory of the Life Force.

Identification with the revolutionary romantic Shelley—especially in his political, social, and religious views—became part of Shaw's self-definition in his twenties. His declaration, made at a meeting of the Shelley Society in March 1886, that he was, "like Shelley, a Socialist, Atheist and Vegetarian" was an important moment of self-fashioning.[58] Henry Arthur Jones, the conservative playwright with whom Shaw was later both to joust as critic and to form a friendship, was heard to say after Shaw's famous introduction of himself to the Shelley Society: "Three damned good reasons why he ought to be chucked out."[59] Another hostile witness, the poet Philip Bourke Marston, was infuriated by Shaw's pronouncement at the meeting that *Queen Mab* was a more important work than *The Cenci*. He later vented his frustration in a letter by writing: "I wanted to get up and murder him [Shaw], and could not even hiss." Following the meeting, Marston and a friend ate tripe and onions because it "needed something pretty strong to take the taste of Shaw out of one's mouth."[60]

During the summer of 1881, the new vegetarian diet had to be abandoned temporarily when Shaw became seriously ill with smallpox in May.[61] Following solitary confinement in his room at 27 Fitzroy Street for three weeks, he underwent a long period of recuperation in the care of his uncle, Dr. Walter Gurly, and Walter's wife, Emily, at their home at Leyton, on the eastern outskirts of London.[62] At Leyton—probably because the smallpox prevented him from shaving—he began to grow the beard that "to the world at large," as Blanche Patch, his secretary for thirty years has said, "was probably his most distinctive feature."[63] During his convalescence he also wrote a substantial part of a new novel, *Love Among the Artists*. Shaw attributed the fact that the novel "exalts the wilful characters to the utter disparagement of the reasonable ones" to his enfeebled state at the time of writing it.[64]

Having condemned a Lucy Shaw-like figure to a melancholy death in New York as a dipsomaniac in *The Irrational Knot*, Shaw revived her in *Love Among the Artists* as Madge Brailsford, a willful and rebellious young woman from a good family who runs away from her father and becomes a highly successful actress under the stage name of Virtue Lalage. She is one of a group of artists in the novel, which includes Owen Jack, her mentor in elocution—a spectacularly unreasonable, socially disagreeable, and curmudgeonly music composer (an early prototype of the character of Professor Higgins in *Pygmalion*)—and a beautiful and brilliant pianist named Aurélie Szczympliça. The "artists" present a form of alternative upper class to that determined by birth and family. "I hold that an artist is above all ladies," declares Aurélie roundly to her mother-in-law, the haute bourgeoise Mrs. Herbert; such comparisons between the meritocracy of the artists and the moribund aristocracy of their surrounding society abound in the novel.

Love Among the Artists continues, in a different key, Shaw's project in his early fiction of forging a new and decidedly, for the time, utopian view of the social order. The true superiors in the social groups projected in the novels are patently not the titled dignitaries and ladies and gentlemen but people of energy and talent—professionals, who in the existing scheme of things are looked upon as outré, bohemian, or simply vulgar. Many of the superior outsiders in the novels are differentiated from the English by race. Harriet Russell is from Scotland, Ned Conolly is American, Owen Jack is Welsh, and Aurélie Szczympliça is Polish. Cashel Byron (in Shaw's fourth novel) has learned his profession and gained some of his speech habits in Australia. It is as though Shaw were projecting onto these figures his own sense of alienation and revolt as an Irishman in England, while at the same time obliquely asserting a sense of superiority that had not yet been justified or confirmed by public recognition. As for the Irish and Ireland, they are treated very ambiguously in the novels—an early reflection of the love-hate relationship with his country of origin that Shaw displayed throughout his life.

* * *

A feeling of restless alienation from London society on Shaw's part is suggested by his project—conceived around September 1881 and probably suggested by the Bell family—of emigrating to America.[65] Apart from a very brief reference in his diary, there is no other information concerning this project. However, there were other signs of Shaw's interest in America in the early 1880s. While working at the Edison Telephone Company, for instance, he had met a number of Americans who "sang obsolete sentimental songs with genuine emotion" and whose "language was frightful even to an Irishman." But they were "free-souled creatures, excellent company . . . with an air of making slow old England hum."[66] The plan of emigrating to the homeland of these companions was never carried out; Shaw did not visit America until 1933—and then only briefly.

* * *

Just as the young Irish novelist was resolutely avoiding the *cursus honorum* of becoming an English gentleman, so his sister Lucy was entering the still distinctly unladylike profession of the theater. As the novels—especially *Love Among the Artists*—remind us, a stage career was generally looked down upon and regarded as a somewhat unsuitable calling for a woman in mid-Victorian England, as it still is in some circles today. Lucy had embarked on her professional theatrical career as a singer and actress soon after her brother made his first submission to publishers of the manuscript of *Immaturity*. Like Madge Brailsford in *Love Among the Artists*, she adopted the stage name Frances Carr (both a salute to and concealment of her family) when she made her debut on Christmas Eve 1879 as Primrose in the pantomime *Beauty and the Beast*. Thereafter she "came out," as it were, and adopted the professional name Lucy Carr Shaw in her career as a musical-comedy star. Having joined the Carla Rosa Opera Company, she performed the part of the heroine Arline in Michael Balfe's *Bohemian Girl*, one of the most popular operas of the day, at the Royal Theatre, Huddersfield, in September 1881. Shaw drew on his sister's experiences as well as his own theatergoing in Dublin and London in a virtuoso portrayal of the mid-nineteenth-century theater world in *Love Among the Artists*.

Shaw was careful to distinguish Lucy, the star of *The Bohemian Girl*, from the bohemian ways often associated with theatrical people.[67] He told Charles McMahon Shaw that although Lucy "had no use for the Shaw pretensions, nor for the country-gentility of her maternal stock . . . she hated Bohemianism and was ashamed of it."[68] Yet it was the bohemian worlds of the theater and artists to which Shaw and Lucy were attracted, while still retaining the good manners and sense of social decorum that derived from their family background.

The brother and sister had a great deal in common. Lucy placed a certain satirical distance between herself and her brother's later tub-thumping political career, when he was "hurling anarchy from street corners and Hyde Park pitches," as she put it in a 1908 letter to Janey Drysdale.[69] Nevertheless, she shared her brother's Mephistophelean skepticism concerning religious matters and a humorously irreverent attitude toward many of the sacred cows of Victorian society, including, for example, respect for one's parents. The critical treatment of child-parent relations in Shaw's novels is epitomized in the extravagant statement about himself and his mother by Adrian Herbert in *Love Among the Artists*: "Our natures are antagonistic, our views of life and duty incompatible: we have nothing in common."

A similar spirit of revolt against conventions is evident in two little satirical volumes about children and parents written by Lucy Shaw, *Five Letters of the House of Kildonnel* (1905) and *The Last of the Kildonnel Letters* (1908). The satire takes the form of subversive letters of advice purporting to be from Lady Theodosia Alexandra Kildonnel from her castle in County Kerry to her infant goddaughter-grandniece, who is also called Theodosia. The letters warn the infant about "certain bogus Ethics that will be brought into operation for the enslavement of your person and the undoing of your individuality, commonly known as 'Bringing up.'" The child is advised never to do what she is told purely as an act of obedience—only if it is something she'd like to do anyway—and that "it is you, Theodosia, You Yourself, who must begin by training and educating your Parents."[70]

Edward McNulty thought the Kildonnel letters showed a "scathing irony and a literary style as masterful as Shaw's own" and wanted Shaw to promote them.[71] McNulty, however, exaggerated their literary merit and Shaw was wise in turning down this suggestion. Nevertheless, the Kildonnel letters do show strong thematic similarities with Shavian ideas in the novels, and later in such works as *You Never Can Tell* and *Misalliance*. In fact, the letters seem rather heavily indebted to Shaw's own subversive advice to a young lady in his 1878 sketch *My Dear Dorothea: A Practical System of Moral Education for Females Embodied in a Letter to a Young Person of That Sex*, which was published posthumously in 1956.

Bessie Shaw would probably have been simply amused at the cheekiness of her two offspring on the subject of parents. After all, if Shaw's account is to be believed, she may herself have rebelled against her family's wishes in terms of her marriage; moreover, she later cut the "irrational knot" and became an independent professional in much the same way as some of the women in Shaw's novels.

* * *

Despite what he said about his abandonment of rationalism and materialism in *Love Among the Artists,* the real watershed in Shaw's career as a novelist came not with that work but with his penultimate novel *Cashel Byron's Profession,* which was written between April 1882 and February 1883. The lively preface that Shaw wrote for a revised edition of the novel begins with the sentence: "I never think of Cashel Byron's Profession without a shudder at the narrowness of my escape from becoming a successful novelist at the age of twenty-six."[72]

The work was and remains the most marketable of the novels. It has a piquant central narrative in which a prizefighter meets and eventually marries a highly intelligent and well-educated lady with an enormous fortune. The novel is considerably shorter than the previous three and has a fast-moving plot, scenes of violence, a strong undertow of erotic interest, and a structure that basically conforms to the conventions of romantic comedy. A marriage between hero and heroine occurs in the usual place for romance—at or near the end of the narrative—after a number of obstacles have been overcome. The uses Shaw made of romance conventions in this work are similar to those he was to make in his fourth play *Arms and the Man,* which marked a turning point in his career as a dramatist comparable to that effected by *Cashel Byron's Profession* in his career as a novelist. In this novel Shaw even adopted the perennial romance device (deployed in Shakespeare's play *The Winter's Tale* and in Balfe's opera *The Bohemian Girl*) of a final revelation of the high birth of a seemingly lowborn hero or heroine. Cashel Byron, far from being a common prizefighter, is revealed at the end to be descended from one of the oldest county families in England.

"I say, Archer, my God, what women!" exclaimed Robert Louis Stevenson of the female characters in *Cashel Byron's Profession* after William Archer had sent him a copy in 1886. Stevenson found the work replete with "strength, spirit, capacity, sufficient vision and sufficient self-sacrifice, which last is the chief point in a narrator. It is all mad, mad and deliriously delightful. . . . It is *horrid* fun. All I ask is more of it."[73] Shaw's excellent portraits of women in the new novel included his heroine Lydia Carew, her young lady companion Alice Goff, and Cashel's mother, a successful actress with the stage name of Adelaide Gisborne. There is also a skillfully written comic cameo of Mrs. Skene, the wife of Cashel's mentor in the profession of boxing.

In some ways *Cashel Byron's Profession* is a fictional forecast of Shaw's later meeting with and marriage to Charlotte Payne-Townshend. Like Lydia Carew, Charlotte is enormously wealthy, devoted to her father, with whom she travels widely and who encourages her acquisition of foreign languages and learning, and makes a marriage, initially regarded by her family and friends as a disastrous mésalliance, with a street corner Socialist (also formerly an amateur pugilist) who is really a gentleman.

For a novel written in the early 1880s *Cashel Byron's Profession* is remarkably advanced in its treatment of sexual themes. The relationship between Cashel and Lydia is charged with sexual tension from the outset. Having returned to England from Australia, where he has learned his profession of boxing, Cashel has become a tenant at a lodge on Lydia's estate. Before she has been introduced to him, Lydia discovers Cashel exercising—under the watchful eye of his attendant, Mellish—in a body-revealing boxing outfit in a forest clearing on a part of the estate unfamiliar to her. Thinking that the "vision of manly strength and beauty" she sees is some hallucination, a statue, "an antique god in his sylvan haunt," or perhaps the "Hermes of Praxiteles, suggested to her by Goethe's classical Sabbat," Lydia returns to the castle, alarmed at the feelings the experience has aroused in her normally composed self yet experiencing an "irrational glow of delight." Cashel himself is instantly smitten: "his lips parted; his color rose; and he stared at her with undisguised admiration and wonder." Suggestions of Lydia's disconcerting but pleasurable sexual feelings about Cashel recur in the novel, as when he expertly helps her to her feet from where she is sitting by a pool in her park, an "unexpected attention" that "gave her a shock, followed by a thrill that was not disagreeable," and a "faint mantling" in her cheeks.

The scene of Lydia's first encounter with Cashel conveys the impression of a Victorian prefiguring of a similar scene in D. H. Lawrence's *Lady Chatterley's Lover*, where Constance Chatterley finds the gamekeeper Mellors stripped to his waist and washing himself in a part of her husband's estate she has never visited before. Like Lydia, when she glimpses Cashel with his pectoral muscles "in their white covering . . . like slabs of marble," Connie is overwhelmed by the feelings that the sight of Mellors's "white torso" arouses in her, thinking it godlike. The treatment of this scene in the second version of *Lady Chatterley's Lover* shows remarkable parallels in imagery and detail with the Shavian text. Connie retreats from the scene as Lydia has done and dwells on the "beauty alive" of what she has seen: "That body was of the world of the gods." Then "a great soothing comes over her."[74] A similar electric collision between the worlds of mind and body, accompanied by a dramatic transgression of class barriers, occurs in both novels.

Toward the end of *Cashel Byron's Profession* Lydia Carew comes across a poem among her deceased father's papers. It opens with lines that again seem to be part of Shaw's oblique self-scrutiny in the novels: "What would I give for a heart of flesh to warm me through / Instead of this heart of stone ice-cold whatever I do!" The poem prompts Lydia to follow what she calls her "heart's business" and accept Cashel's proposal of marriage. The work continues the dialogue in the novels between head and heart, reason and passion, that was to be reflected in numerous romantic entanglements in which Shaw was shortly to become involved himself.

A very different kind of champion from Cashel in the novel is Alice Goff, a young woman who is introduced as having "a well-developed resilient figure" and is later discovered to be an outstanding competitor in lawn tennis, with a recent defeat of the top Australian player to her credit. Accustomed to much attention from men—one of her suitors has proposed to her six times—Alice displays a disdainful hauteur in her behavior toward them. She tosses her head "superbly" when told she is "awfully fetching" by the rather vulgar boxing enthusiast Lord Worthington.

Two months before he began writing *Cashel Byron's Profession*, Shaw had met a real-life Alice with whom he was to have what was probably his first serious love affair. She can well be imagined giving a superb toss of the head at such compliments from males, judging by a surviving photograph and her spirited letters. In January 1882 Shaw, having suffered what he described as "a light attack of scarlet fever," returned to Leyton to recuperate and to work on his novels. Introduced by her older sister, Jane, in February, Shaw met and instantly fell in love with the twenty-three-year-old Alice Mary Lockett, likewise a tennis player and a young lady of good looks and beautiful complexion, whose tempestuous love affair with Shaw was to last until 1885. It was to influence the writing of his last two novels, specifically the portrayals of Alice in *Cashel Byron's Profession* and Gertrude in *An Unsocial Socialist*.[75]

In the meantime, before he began work on *An Unsocial Socialist* Shaw had embarked on a reading of Karl Marx's *Das Kapital*. Even more momentous, as far as his future outlook was concerned, was a lecture he attended on 5 September 1882 given by the American economist Henry George, author of *Progress and Poverty*, on "Land Nationalization and Single Tax." Shaw wrote of the impact of this lecture: "He struck me dumb and shunted me from barren agnostic controversy to economics." He then proceeded to read *Progress and Poverty* and to join the Georgite Land Reform Union, where he met a number of important figures in his future career as a Socialist, including James Leigh

Joynes, Sydney Olivier, and Henry Hyde Champion.[76] Another man who was shortly to join Shaw's rapidly expanding circle of friends in London was the critic and Ibsen translator William Archer, also a frequenter of the British Museum's Reading Room. Probably in about February or March 1883 Archer noticed in the Reading Room a young man "with pallid skin and bright red hair and beard . . . day after day poring over Karl Marx's *Das Kapital* and an orchestral score of Wagner's *Tristan und Isolde*."[77] The young man was, of course, Shaw, with whom Archer was to form a lifelong friendship and with whom he would collaborate on early drafts of what was to become Shaw's first professionally performed play, *Widowers' Houses*.

* * *

The novels were a seedbed of innumerable ideas, situations, and characterizations that were later to flourish in Shaw's plays. *An Unsocial Socialist*, written from July to December 1883, when Shaw was twenty-seven, leads more directly into the thematic world of the early plays than any of the previous novels and obviously bears the marks—not always to its advantage—of his new contacts with Socialist, Georgeite thought. The unsocial Socialist is Sidney Trefusis, an inheritor of a huge fortune from his father's activities as a Manchester captain of industry. Having run away from his wife after only six weeks of marriage, he conceals himself in the country as an outlandish yokel called Smilash (the character much liked by Shaw's father) whose name is a combination of the words *smile* and *eyelash*. There he becomes a cat among the pigeons as he flirts with a group of nubile, upper-class schoolgirls at a ladies' college. Shaw records that the idea for the character of the most lively of the girls came to him in the British Museum as he was beginning to write the novel: "I saw a young lady with an attractive and arresting expression, bold, vivid, and very clever, working at one of the desks. On that glimpse of a face I instantly conceived the character and wrote the description of Agatha Wylie."[78]

"This is one of your clever novels. I wish the characters would not talk so much," says Agatha Wiley to Trefusis about a book he finds her reading in one of the later chapters of the novel. As Shaw no doubt realized, Agatha's remark was bound to strike a chord in the minds of some of the readers of *An Unsocial Socialist*. The novel begins with a wonderfully lively description of Agatha and two of her friends breaking the school's rules by joyously sliding down the bannister of its main staircase. Although there is much of the "mad and deliriously delightful" material of the kind Stevenson admired in *Cashel Byron's Profession*, the work conveys an uneasy sense that Shaw was trying to justify a part of himself as the heartless vivisector of love and ordinary "emotional ethics" that he sometimes could be. There is also a great deal of Socialist sermonizing from Trefusis, which differentiates the novel from Shavian comedy at its subtle best. In *Man and Superman* the gentleman-Socialist Trefusis is transformed into the more engaging and vulnerable Jack Tanner. In *Widowers' Houses* a young gentleman named Harry Trench finds himself in a situation like that of Trefusis: the origins of his inherited wealth are in brutal capitalistic exploitation. However, Trench is treated much more convincingly in Shaw's early play than is Trefusis in the novel.

An Unsocial Socialist contains an ending that brings the narrative into qualified conformity with romance conventions. The two brightest sparks in the novel, Trefusis (who has already seen one heartbroken bride to an early grave) and Agatha are to be married in a congenial, rational partnership, with "a consoling dash of romance" to please the sentimentalists, as Trefusis puts it, but no promises about absolute fidelity. Following various permutations of relationships and lovers' quarrels reminiscent of *A Midsummer Night's Dream*, the novel closes with the Puckish mischief maker Trefusis breezily quoting the verse with which Shakespeare has Puck close the third act, beginning: "Jack shall have Jill / Nought shall go ill."

The novel proved prophetic of Shaw's immediate future. Trefusis, the charismatic, rebellious, unconventional, and clever Socialist gentleman—with reddish beard and snuff-colored suits—is irresistible to young women and becomes a serial heartbreaker. In his portrayal of this character Shaw was foreshadowing the next phase of his own career as a Fabian Don Juan and creating a landmark in the evolution of the multifaceted Shavian self. Equally significant in the novels as a pointer to the future was the range of forces relating to the "big instincts" and the "heart's business" that come into conflict with Trefusis-like intellectuality. At twenty-seven, when Shaw finished writing *An Unsocial Socialist*, the "Shavian note" was still not harmoniously tuned, but the novels had nevertheless provided an important instrument both of self-development for Shaw as an artist and thinker and of self-scrutiny as a young man.

6 A Fabian Don Juan

Shaw made a major statement about the subject of sex in biography—and his own sexuality—in the sixteenth chapter of *Sixteen Self Sketches.* The sexual history of biographical subjects, he declares, does not tell us anything about the sort of people they are:

> First, O sex-obsessed Biographer, get it into your mind that you can learn nothing about your biographees from their sex histories. The sex relation is not a personal relation. It can be irresistibly desired and rapturously consummated between persons who could not endure one another for a day in any other relation. If I were to tell you every such adventure I have enjoyed you would be none the wiser as to the sort of man I am. You would know only what you already know: that I am a human being. If you have any doubts as to my normal virility, dismiss them from your mind. I was not impotent; I was not sterile; I was not homosexual; and I was extremely susceptible, though not promiscuously.[1]

The chapter in *Sixteen Self Sketches* was a slightly revised version of a letter Shaw addressed to Frank Harris, his fellow Irishman and former employer on the *Saturday Review,* in 1930.[2] At the time, Harris, the author of *My Life and Loves,* a notorious account of his own sexual adventures, was questioning Shaw about his sex life while preparing his *Bernard Shaw: An Unauthorised Biography.* Shaw's statement, the personal details of which are largely corroborated by other evidence, is of great biographical interest—as well as being a caution to other biographers, apart from the addressee. It contains Shaw's most direct declaration of his *enjoyment* of sex and acknowledgment of "its power of producing a celestial flood of emotion and exaltation"—even though he added to this the rider that the experience gave him "a sample of the ecstasy that may one day be the normal condition of conscious intellectual activity."[3]

However, the seventy-four-year-old Shaw's disengagement of sexual relations from personal relations in the prose of a letter to Harris was not so easy to maintain in the real world of his relations with women in the 1880s and 1890s, where sexual attraction and personal intimacy of other kinds were combined in emotionally complex ways. The story of Shaw's relations with members of the opposite sex during this period is further complicated by the ways in which it intersects with the larger history of changes in attitude toward sexual difference and gender roles, and toward romance and marriage, during the same period.

Shaw clearly felt some degree of self-identification with the legendary Don Juan. A short story he wrote in 1887 under the title "The Truth About Don Giovanni" (published in 1932 as *Don Giovanni Explains*) has obvious autobiographical reference; the figure of Don Juan, like that of Mephistopheles, continued to hold sway over his imagination, as his appearance as a principal figure in the preface and play of *Man and Superman* attests. Shaw was not, like the legendary compulsive seducer or the sexually boastful Harris, a roué or sexual conquistador. In one of his pieces of music criticism published in *The World*, Shaw said that Don Juan's problem was his failure to discriminate among the objects of his amorous pursuits: "Don Juan did not love anybody: he was an Indifferentist." If Shaw himself had been the Commander standing in judgment over Don Juan, he would have "offered to let him off if he could rise for a moment to a preference for some woman above another."[4]

In a letter addressed to a Frenchman in 1890 Shaw wrote that opinion about him with regard to "les séductions de la femme" tended to be divided between those who thought of him "as a saint or a statue" and those who suspected him of being "an Irish Don Juan" with the potential to "compromise Socialism by some outrageous scandal of the Parnell sort." In the same letter he said "the truth" was that he had "an Irishman's habit of treating women with a certain gallantry" of a kind understood in Ireland to be harmless, but which was "apt to be taken seriously in matter-of-fact British circles."[5] In 1939 the eighty-three-year-old Shaw gave the same explanation of his behavior to H. G. Wells, after the two of them had been flirting outrageously with the recently crowned Miss Hungary, the twenty-two-year-old Zsa Zsa Gabor, at a luncheon at the Shaws' London home. When Wells told Shaw he was much too old for philandering, Zsa Zsa recalls that Shaw replied: "A man is never too old. But anyway, you're mistaking gallantry for philandering."[6]

Shaw was, however, a relatively innocent Don Juan—often more the quarry than the pursuer in the field of love and romance, and was not undiscriminating in his amorous affairs. Nevertheless, he was certainly—as he said in the 1930 letter to Harris—"an incorrigible philanderer." When he said (in the same letter) that in the fourteen years before his marriage there was "always some lady in the case," he might more accurately have set the period at sixteen years and written, instead of "some lady," "at least one lady."

* * *

The first of the ladies "in the case," Alice Mary Lockett, was brought up in a middle-class family, of which the father, Walford Charles Lockett, was an engineer by profession.[7] Alice and her sister, Jane, attended a ladies' college, Cambridge House, in Leyton, similar to the one portrayed by Shaw in *An Unsocial Socialist*. At the time of Alice's meeting with Shaw in February 1882, the family's circumstances were affected by a number of recent adversities. They had moved from the family home of Rawstorne House to a smaller residence at 5 Pembroke Place, Walthamstow, the address from which most of Alice's letters to Shaw were sent. In order not to be a burden on their grandmother, who had undertaken their support, the girls embarked on careers. Jane began her training as a teacher and Alice enrolled in a nursing course at St. Mary's Hospital, Paddington. Alice also began taking lessons in singing from Bessie Shaw, which created the opportunity for meetings at least once a week with Shaw. At this time Alice was twenty-three and Shaw twenty-five.

An early reference to the budding romance occurs in a letter to Shaw dated 19 March 1882 from his aunt-by-marriage Emily Gurly, who reported that Alice had appeared "looking blooming for I fear you have . . . made a deep impression."[8] Shaw's enthrallment by the "tyrannical but irresistible" Alice is recorded in verses he wrote in his pocket notebook, in which Gilbertian variations on rhymes for the poetically difficult name of Locket ("knock it," "pocket," "mock it," "rocket")[9] mingled with expressions of rapture, including an outpouring of eighteen repetitions of "Alice!," culminating in "Darling Alice!"[10] Beginning in April 1882, Alice came for lessons each Thursday to 36 Osnaburgh Street. She and Shaw played the piano and sang duets; they walked together to the train at Liverpool Street for her journey back to Walthamstow.

The greater part of the surviving correspondence between the two belongs to the latter part of 1883 and 1884. By then the relationship had not only deepened but had also developed tensions and become quarrelsome. Accusations, reproaches, and repeated declarations that the correspondence and relationship between them was at an end flew back and forth from Osnaburgh Street to Walthamstow. At one point she informs him that he is "one of the weakest men I have ever met" and he tells her that she is an "incorrigible trifler."[11] Nevertheless, indications of a great deal of tender feeling for his "cherished Alice"[12] and of his attraction toward her remain in Shaw's letters.

Following one of her visits to Osnaburgh Street on 19 November 1883, he wrote a letter to say good night, quoting from some tune they had been playing. The letter was apparently making up for a quarrel. It included an acute observation about one of her mannerisms, her "eloquent checked revelations," and a confession about her seductive charm as a page turner at the piano:

> Dearest Alice
> Goodnight!
>
> You are dancing through my head to this tune [quotes the tune] and I cannot refrain from telling you so. Forgive me.
>
> This is a silly letter to replace the one you tore up and threw out of the window. Or else it is a sensible letter to replace the silly one you destroyed. I do not know which—I only know that when we were at the piano this evening, and you—No, I will not tell you. Is that not like yourself? I am catching the infection of your reserve—your eloquent checked revelations. . . . Oh the infinite mischief that a woman may do by stooping forward to turn over a sheet of music![13]

For the most part Alice played a part not unlike that of the disdainful Cruel Fair of Elizabethan sonnet sequences in response to Shaw's flattery. In a reproving letter of 6 November 1883 mockingly addressed "to the irresistible George Shaw," she tells him he is piqued because his "base flattery" has not worked. "Some genuineness and manliness would find a responsive chord in my heart,"[14] she advises her admirer, whom, despite his perceived faults, she nevertheless finds difficult to renounce, and who must obviously have presented an exciting contrast to the conventional social circle in which she was brought up. Yet she could be fiercely critical. They were still quarrelling, breaking up, and making up throughout the following year.

The two seemed locked in a pattern of attraction and rejection. In some ways life was imitating art. Alice had many of the qualities of the spirited and independent Harriet Russell in *Immaturity*, including some of her limitations. She was undoubtedly intelligent, but her letters, unlike those of Elinor Huddart, do not reflect wide-ranging reading and intellectual interests. In the latter part of 1884 she and her sister (of whom Shaw was also fond) both followed the monthly installments of *An Unsocial Socialist* in the pages of *To-Day*. In a letter dated December 1884 she reports "by the way" that she has finished the novel and has come to the conclusion that Sidney Trefusis is more knave than fool. She then teasingly asks: "Is he meant to represent yourself?"[15] However, this is one of the few references to literary matters in her correspondence, and it is probable that a lack of any prospect of a "marriage of true minds" contributed to the falling off of Shaw's ardor, just as Smith's recognition in *Immaturity* of Harriet Russell's limitations had caused his romantic feelings about her to "relax." Shaw probably didn't advance the cause of romance very much by telling Alice she was a "trifler" in comparison with his "serious friend" Elinor.[16]

Shaw diagnosed in Alice what he called a "dual entity," or double personality, comprised, on the one hand, of a prim and convention-bound "Miss Lockett" and, on the other, of a free-spirited, instinctive, and lovable "Alice." He wrote letters playfully begging "Alice" not to show them to her other self, the tyrannical "Miss Lockett." Shaw's idea about Alice is directly echoed in the fourteenth chapter of *An Unsocial Socialist*, when Trefusis tells Gertrude Lindsay of her conflicting "Miss Lindsay" and "Gertrude" selves. However, the Shaw-Lockett correspondence and relationship also reveal deep divisions in Shaw's own personality that reflect and develop the self-searching of the novels. In the same letter of 11 September 1883 in which he first expounded his idea about the two Alice Locketts, he also wrote: "Have I not also a dual self—an enemy within my gates—an egotistical George Shaw upon whose neck I have to keep a grinding foot . . .?" In this instance the "other" Shaw is defined as the conceited and dutiful "model of a righteous man" and self-appointed improver of others.[17] However, in the "good night" letter referred to earlier Shaw probed more deeply into another self: a kind of cynical and derisive, Mephistophelean Mr. Hyde-like persona* who mocked his romantic feelings even in the midst of their expression: "I am alone, and yet there is a detestable, hardheaded, heartless, cynical, cool devil seated in my chair telling me that all this is insincere lying affection."[18]

The fact that he could externalize—and detest—this "cool devil" suggests a degree of critical distance from this aspect of himself; yet Shaw's acknowledgment of the existence of the skeptical and disturbing "other" side of his personality testifies to the complexity of his feelings and attitudes in dealing with a love relation such as that with Alice Lockett. The affair was sexually unconsummated and was probably attended by a considerable amount of sexual frustration and repression, of which the "eloquent checked revelations" were perhaps partly symptomatic.

* * *

The year 1884 was a crowded one for Shaw: he formally joined the recently established Fabian Society in September and a fortnight later delivered Fabian

*Robert Louis Stevenson's classic tale about a dual personality, *Dr. Jekyll and Mr. Hyde*, was published three years later.

Tract No. 2, "A Manifesto"; new female charmers entered the scene even as the affair with Alice continued; he began to be active as a public lecturer on Socialist themes; he wrote book reviews for the *Christian Socialist* and *To-Day*, while the installments of *An Unsocial Socialist* appeared in the latter; and from August to November he was intermittently writing the first draft of *Widowers' Houses*, his first full-length play, developing plot material suggested to him by William Archer.

"Like kindred particles in a fluid" was the analogy Shaw's friend Sydney Haldane Olivier (later Baron Olivier) employed to describe the young men who were drawn together in the early 1880s to form the Fabian Society: "The only assortment of young middle-class men who were at that time thinking intelligently, in England, about social and economic conditions, gravitated into close contact with one another, like kindred particles in a fluid, and consolidated into an association out of whose propaganda . . . originated the British Parliamentary Socialist Labour Party."[19]

At various points in the history of the Fabian Society these intelligent young men were joined by a number of intelligent women, including: the children's writer, novelist, and poet Edith Nesbit; social activist and, later, Theosophist Annie Besant; sociologist and reformer Beatrice Webb; the famous suffragette Emmeline Pankhurst; and Shaw's wife, Charlotte.

The beginnings of the Socialist movement in England should not be judged by some of the later manifestations of Socialism internationally, which were often accompanied by even worse forms of oppression than those the movement was designed to oppose. Not only has Socialism been discredited by the totalitarian regimes it spawned in Communist Russia, China, and elsewhere, but it has also failed as the basis of economic systems. In the second half of the nineteenth-century, however, Socialism emerged as an essential force in the empowering of labor against the ruthlessly oppressive forces of industrial capitalism. Even now, at the beginning of the twenty-first century, while the comparative success of capitalism as an economic model has been proven, the evils associated with it—corporate greed and fraud, gross inequalities, unscrupulous exploitation of workforces, environmental degradation, and other forms of antisocial behavior—have by no means disappeared. Nor has the need for political and social compacts and legislative restraints to counter those evils.

The oppression of the poor in nineteenth-century England had its basis in many factors, principal among which were: the concentration of land ownership in the hands of a tiny, privileged minority; the class system and the barriers it created to hinder advancement for most except the well connected; the exploitation of labor in capital-based industrial, manufacturing, and mining enterprises; and the exclusion of women from the franchise, as well as their social, educational, and economic subordination. The Fabian Society was one of several radical groups formed in the 1880s to combat the forces of oppression, the poverty, and human and environmental degradation that attended the march of Victorian material progress and imperial expansion. The Fabian Society was contemporary with the Social Democratic Federation (SDF), whose leading spokesman was Henry Mayers Hyndman, an early disciple of Karl Marx, who was editor of the periodical *Justice* and the author of *England for All.* As an upper-class, Cambridge-educated radical, the impetuous Hyndman became one of the models—apart from Shaw himself—for the character of the gentleman-Socialist Jack Tanner in *Man and Superman*. Poet, artist, and craftsman William Morris had become a member of Hyndman's group before resigning to form a separate organization, the Socialist League. Shaw attended meetings of Hyndman's SDF before throwing in his lot with the Fabians. He also formed a close friendship with William Morris, frequently attended the famous Sunday-evening meetings in the coach house of Morris's Hammersmith home, Kelmscott House, and fell in love with Morris's daughter, May.

The Fabian Society had its birth in meetings held during 1882–83 by a group called the Fellowship of the New Life, one of whose main founders was Thomas Davidson, the Scottish-born philosopher and wandering scholar. Sydney Olivier recalls that Davidson exhorted those who attended meetings of the group "to espouse the New Life, and to emigrate to Southern California (the then projected colony of Topolobampo [in northwestern Mexico] was suggested) to found a new Colony to recreate the world." Instead, wrote Olivier, "we formed the Fabian Society."[20] The latter was founded and named at a meeting of the Fellowship of the New Life on 4 January 1884 held at the Osnaburgh Street home of Edward Reynolds Pease, opposite the Shaws' house. Pease was a London stockbroker who, inspired by William Morris and yearning for a simpler life, decided to shift to cabinetmaking. He served as the Fabian Society's secretary from 1890 to 1913 and wrote *The History of the Fabian Society* in 1916.

The platform of the Fabian Society was certainly radical. It proposed collective ownership of "the supply of the general necessities of life" and "the reorganisation of society by the emancipation of land and industrial capital from individual and class ownership, and the vesting of them in the community for the general benefit."[21] However, the Fabian Society took a much more gradualist, pragmatic, and outward-looking approach to reform than its Socialist rivals of the day. It derived its name from that of an early Roman general, Quintus Fabius Maximus Cunctator (Fabius the Delayer), whose strategy of delaying direct confrontation thwarted Hannibal's advance on Rome. The Fabian Society's methods were evolutionary rather than revolutionary: it aimed at "concrete reforms," its main strategy being that of "permeation" of existing political parties with reformist ideas. As a political think tank, it was a key organization in the building of the intellectual foundations of the British Labour Party and the welfare state. The Fabians—through the agency, in particular, of Sidney and Beatrice Webb and the support of Shaw's wife, Charlotte—were also primarily responsible for the founding of the London School of Economics. Shaw attended his first Fabian meeting on 16 May 1884 and formally joined the Fabian Society on 5 September that same year. He was elected to the executive committee in January 1885 and continued serving until 1911, when he resigned to make way for a new generation of Fabian leaders.

In addition to Shaw, who became its most famous spokesperson, the Fabian Society attracted some exceptionally talented and intelligent people. After graduating from Oxford University, Sydney Olivier topped the entrance examination for the British Civil Service, with his fellow Fabian Sidney Webb coming in second in the same examination. Graham Wallas—who joined the Fabian Society in 1886 and served on the executive committee as one of "the Big Four" (together with Shaw, Webb, and Olivier) from 1888 to 1895—was a distinguished political scientist and psychologist who became one of the early lecturers at the London School of Economics and professor of political science at London University. Olivier was described by Shaw as "an extraordinarily attractive figure . . . handsome and strongly sexed, looking like a Spanish grandee in any sort of clothes, however unconventional."[22] He became governor of Jamaica (where Shaw and Charlotte visited him in January 1911) and secretary of state for India.

Physically Sidney Webb was the opposite of Olivier. Before the courtship between the two began, his future wife Beatrice penned an extraordinarily derogatory description of Webb in her journal: "His tiny tadpole body, unhealthy skin, lack of manner, Cockney pronunciation, poverty, are all against him,"[23] she wrote. Beatrice's niece, Kitty Muggeridge, supplied an equally unflattering portrait: "Small, thick, his large head seemed all in one with his neck—only a reddish goatee beard marking the division between the two. His face was red, with a fleshy nose and bulging watery greenish eyes behind thick-lensed pince-nez. One felt rather than saw him to be intelligent. He always wore a very thick heavy serge suit which fitted him like a suit made for a teddy bear with his limbs protruding oddly. He perspired ('Sidney sweats you know' Aunt Bo [Beatrice] so often pointed out)."[24]

From the point of view of the upper-middle-class Potter family from which Beatrice came—she was brought up in a huge house in the Cotswolds, a picturesque rural area northwest of London, her father being a wealthy industrialist and a director of the Great Western Railway—Webb must have seemed a poor (in every sense of the term) substitute for the tall Liberal statesman Joseph Chamberlain, with whom she had previously had a romance that ended in heartbreaking disappointment. However, what Sidney Webb may have lacked in physical appeal he made up for in brains and ability—"the ablest man in England" was Shaw's description of him.[25] Beatrice Potter—a tall, willowy woman with attractive hair, a patrician face, and an income of a thousand pounds a year—was to grow very fond of the "tiny tadpole." Her marriage to him in 1892 was the beginning of a remarkable partnership that had a profound impact on British political and social history. Kitty Muggeridge's sharp-eyed account of her aunt included the comment that, "though beautiful, she gave the impression of some predatory bird, a golden eagle perhaps, soaring in search of prey."[26] The "golden eagle" was to take a very close and critical interest in Bernard Shaw.

Other bourgeois rebels and "kindred particles" drawn to the Fabian Society as part of a refashioning of their own lives and a way of channeling their protest against the social conditions of the day included: journalist and author Hubert Bland, husband of fellow Fabian Edith Nesbit (and father of two illegitimate children by Alice Hoatson, who served as the Fabian Society's secretary from 1885 to 1886); Henry Stephen Salt, a master at Eton until his resignation in 1884; and his wife, Catherine ("Kate"). Bland, who was elected to the Fabian Society in spite of his Tory and imperialist leanings, was editor—together with poet James Leigh Joynes and music critic Belfort Bax—of the periodical *To-Day*, which serialized Shaw's *An Unsocial Socialist* from March to December 1884. Both Edith Nesbit and Kate Salt were to become involved in the complex network of Shaw's relationships with women during the early Fabian days.

* * *

Political and amatory affairs often demanded almost equal amounts of Shaw's time and attention during his early years in the Fabian Society. In May 1884, while attending his first meeting, rehearsals were in progress at Vandeleur Lee's residence at 13 Park Lane for a production of Mozart's *Don Giovanni*, which, as Shaw noted in his diary, "came to nothing."[27] Earlier in the year Lee had given Shaw the task of finding a suitable Donna Anna. The person he proposed was an attractive young Jewish woman, with "dark hair, soulful eyes, sultry Mediterranean features, and ample bosom,"[28] named Katherine ("Katie") Samuel, daughter of Rabbi Isaac Samuel of the Bayswater Synagogue. Shaw added to his diary note about the production: "The Donna Anna was Katie Samuel, with whom I fell in love for a week or so."[29] In a letter written to Charlotte Payne-Townshend in 1897, Shaw referred to Katie as "an old flame."[30] The flame did not last long, and Shaw's flirtation with Katie does not seem to have been encouraged by her. Nevertheless, a lively correspondence between the two in May and June of 1884—which included some flattering doggerel verses from Shaw certainly indicate his interest in her. The music critic in the young man, however, doused any chances the lover might have had. Having shattered her "peace of mind," as Katie told him, by telling her that her voice would not last much longer, he hardly improved the situation by writing: "Do not be anxious about losing your voice. You have never found it. But you seem to be on the way to it at last." This letter concludes with a Mozartian flourish in the form of a quotation from *Don Giovanni*: "Io sono, 'bella Donn'Anna, / il crudele chi osò, la calma turbar del viver vostro'" (I am, lovely Donna Anna, the cruel one who has dared to trouble the tranquillity of your life). Katie apparently forgave the cruel one, kept all his letters, and, years later—following her marriage to a rabbi from Montreal—visited London and wrote a warm letter to Shaw to say how delighted she was with a performance of his play *You Never Can Tell.*

It was not only with his "bella Donn'Anna" that the still virginal Fabian Don Juan flirted while continuing his relationship with Alice Lockett. A letter from Elinor Huddart of 28 April 1884 implies that Shaw had by this time become attracted to Karl Marx's daughter Eleanor, the common-law wife of Marx's disciple and translator Edward Bibbins Aveling.[31] Beginning in January 1885 Shaw formed an intimate friendship with Eleanor Marx Aveling, as she styled herself. He frequently visited the Avelings' flat in Great Russell Street, opposite the British Museum, where—probably sometime in the second half of 1885—he played the part of Krogstad in a reading of Ibsen's *A Doll's House* (in Henrietta Frances Lord's translation of the play, which bore the title *Nora*), in which Eleanor played Nora.[32] Shaw wrote of his "off-stage" moments during this reading: "I chattered and ate caramels in the back drawing-room (our green-room) whilst Eleanor Marx, as Nora, brought Helmer to book at the other side of the folding doors."[33]

The Aveling marriage was to end even more disastrously than that of Nora and Helmer. Eleanor committed suicide in March 1898, following Aveling's revelation to her of his treacherous secret marriage—while still bound by his common-law marriage to Eleanor—to Eva Frye, a twenty-two-year-old actress. Aveling himself died shortly afterward. Shaw drew on several aspects of

Aveling's behavior—such as his numerous affairs with women, carelessness with money, and unreliability as a borrower—in his portrayal of the unscrupulous artist Louis Dubedat in *The Doctor's Dilemma.*

* * *

During a quarrel with Alice Lockett in July 1884, Shaw mentions that he took "for consolation a long walk with Mrs. Chatterbox."[34] This was a slighting nickname for Jenny Patterson, the lady who was to become—almost exactly one year later—the first woman with whom Shaw had a sexually consummated relationship. Jenny was an Irish widow who had moved to London after the death of her wealthy husband and who, like Alice Lockett, had come into Shaw's orbit by taking singing lessons with Bessie Shaw. She knew Shaw's mother's family, the Gurlys, in Ireland[35] and, having been introduced by them, was in contact with the Shaw family in London some time before 28 December 1882 (the date of her first surviving letter to Shaw). While only one of Shaw's letters to her has survived, two large volumes of her letters to him are held in the manuscripts collection of the British Library.[36] Jenny's letters—by turns passionate, tender, affectionate, adoring, humorous, self-pitying, critical, reproachful, and expressing ferocious jealousy—testify to a relationship involving powerful and complex emotions. For Shaw the relationship was to prove, on the one hand, a sexual and emotional release and education, on the other, a trap.

Of mixed Irish and Scottish descent, Jenny Patterson was a spirited, intelligent woman with a sense of humor and a volatile, highly emotional temperament. May Morris, who met her early in 1886, found her "fascinating," as well as "charming & amusing."[37] She could read French and Italian, enjoyed music, and sang with a mezzo-soprano voice. Among the effects left in her will was a Bluthner grand piano; Shaw frequently mentions playing and singing music as being among their pastimes during her visits to the Shaw households at 36 Osnaburgh Street and Fitzroy Square and his visits to her homes.[38] Jenny had town houses in the fashionable suburb of Knightsbridge, first at 5 Hans Place and then at 23 Brompton Square. During the period of her relationship with Shaw, she also had a seaside holiday residence "Chandos House" at Broadstairs, Kent, in southeast England. Her London houses could be reached by train or bus—or lengthy walks across Hyde Park—from the Shaw residences.

As a result of a large gap in the early holdings of the Jenny Patterson letters to Shaw in the British Library collection, the reader is confronted with a dramatic shift of tone from the first letter (28 December 1882) to the second (6 January 1886). During the Christmas season of 1882, on a day when she was evidently planning to meet Bessie Shaw for a concert or recital at St. James's Hall, Regent Street, she writes:

> Dear Mr Shaw
> Many thanks for all your trouble. . . . I hate Xmas time—but I always have a foolish hope that the New Year will bring something good. [Message at top of page] Tell Mrs Shaw if you please that I'll be out side the Regent St side of the [St James's] Hall at 8 o/c sharp. [Wishes him "the luckiest of New Years"]
> Yours very truly
> Jane Patterson

The letter of 6 January 1886 begins and ends:

> My dearest I shall not go away now. I am very well & I will be at home every evening from tonight. You are right "Life is too little to measure our care." Let me be happy I love you. My far seeing love. . . . When you come let it be fairly early so that I may get to sleep before 2 a.m.
> J[39]

Between the two letters lay the unfolding story of an intimacy, the record of which is mostly found in brief comments in Shaw's diary, and which began to develop early in 1885.

Beginning with a note on 10 February 1885 ("Mrs Patterson here [at 36 Osnaburgh Street] in the evening"), Shaw's diary records increasingly frequent meetings with Jenny Patterson during the early months of the year, either at the Shaws' house, where she had become a regular visitor, or at her home in Brompton Square. On 21 February, the day after delivering a lecture on "Money" to the Fabians, Shaw returned home from the Aveling house to find "Mrs Patterson," whereupon he "sat chatting and playing and singing until past 21 [9 p.m.], when [I] put her into a cab with her dog. . . ." Opportunities for intimate conversation arose—or were created—in various ways, as on 27 April, when Shaw left a concert before the end and "went on to Mrs. Patterson. Found her alone, and chatted until past midnight."[40]

* * *

The developing relationship with Jenny Patterson was accompanied by a flurry of other events and activities in Shaw's life during the first half of 1885. Following his election to the Fabian Society executive in January, he became heavily involved in political activities, lecturing and attending meetings several times a week. He lectured on such subjects as "Private Property, Capital and Competition" at William Morris's Thames-side Kelmscott House at 26 Upper Mall, Hammersmith, and developed his relationship with Morris's daughter May. He tramped up the hill from Regent's Park to Hampstead to attend meetings—organized by Mrs. Charlotte Wilson, "a Rossettian woman with dense hair"[41] and radical views—where Marx and economics were discussed.

He debated about Marx in the pages of *To-Day* with the Reverend Philip H. Wicksteed, whom he was later to dub "my father in economics."[42] (Wicksteed initiated Shaw into the mysteries of "Jevonian curves"—a concept related to the laws of supply and demand—employed by the neoclassical economic theorist William Stanley Jevons.) Shaw frequently visited the Avelings in Bloomsbury and played the role of Stratton Strawless in a production of Palgrave Simpson and Hermann Merivale's "third rate comedy" *Alone*, featuring a cast that also included Edward Aveling, May Morris, and Eleanor Marx Aveling.[43] Around this time he met Annie Besant, who had joined the Fabian Society in May. In February he began writing music criticism for the *Dramatic Review*—the position having been obtained for him by William Archer—and in May he became a regular book reviewer for the *Pall Mall Gazette*. He attended numerous musical programs included in the great International Inventions Exhibition, which had opened in South Kensington in May, and reviewed them in the *Dramatic Review* and elsewhere. He labored at the incongruous task (for him) of preparing an index to the work of the Elizabethan poet Thomas Lodge, an undertaking he came to curse as a waste of time and to relinquish unfinished. During this period he was working on proofs of *Cashel Byron's Profession* and *The Irrational Knot* for serial publication in, respectively, *To-Day* and in Annie Besant's Socialist magazine *Our Corner*. On 19 April 1885 he received news of the solitary death in Dublin of his father, George Carr Shaw.

Shaw had a particularly strong antipathy toward the Victorian way of death, with its dismal trappings of black clothes, veils, and extended periods of mourning, such as that indulged in by Queen Victoria following the death of Prince Albert. Outwardly he seemed impervious to grief and tended to view death with a kind of Ovidian detachment. "Why does a funeral always sharpen one's sense of humour and rouse one's spirits?," he asked Mrs. Patrick (Stella) Campbell (with whom he was having an amatory affair) in a remarkable letter he wrote to her on 22 February 1913 after attending his mother's funeral ceremony at Golders Green Crematorium. There are plenty of signs of Shaw's great affection for his mother in this letter, including memories of "the wasted little figure with the wonderful face" whom Shaw imagined "leaning over beside me, shaking with laughter" at the sight of the crematorium workers sifting through two piles of bones following the cremation and wondering: "Which . . . is me?" That night Shaw remarked to Desmond MacCarthy: "Don't think I am a man who forgets the dead." He had witnessed the actual burning of the coffin (which was draped in violet rather than black) and was able to write to Stella Campbell: "Then the violet coffin moved again and went in, feet first. And behold! The feet burst miraculously into streaming ribbons of garnet colored lovely flame, smokeless and eager, like pentecostal tongues, and as the whole coffin passed in it sprang into flame all over; and my mother became that beautiful fire."[44]

For Shaw death was the occasion for a renewed assertion of life, an idea that he had his artist-character Louis Dubedat express eloquently while on his deathbed in the play *The Doctor's Dilemma* (1906). He begs his beautiful wife, Genevieve, not to wear black and go into mourning but rather to wear "beautiful dresses and splendid magic jewels." Dubedat himself wishes to be cremated and become a flame of "garnet color."

The death of George Carr Shaw from congestion of the lungs at the age of seventy-one, which occurred in his Dublin lodging house at 21 Leeson Park Avenue, evoked much less comment and celebration of his memory from Shaw than that of his mother. His diary tersely records the event on 19 April 1885: "Telegram from J. C. Shaw announcing death of my father."[45] On the same day he wrote facetiously to J. Kingston Barton, to whom he had previously addressed his pseudoclinical analysis of his father's and uncles' drinking habits: "Telegram just received to say that the governor has left the universe on rather particular business and set me up as

An Orphan."[46]

In some ways the death was a precursor—perhaps even a psychological catalyst—to new developments in the Shavian persona, a blossoming. The regular postal money-order notes from Dublin ceased, but roughly £100 was owed the family in London from an insurance policy on George Carr's life. This allowed Shaw to acquire "the first new garments I have had for years."[47] By June he was able to order from the Jaeger shop in central London (whose clothes were made in accordance with "Dr. Jaeger's Sanitary Woollen System," which stipulated that nothing but animal fiber was to be used in order to permit the body to breathe) a splendid set of clothes—including a woolen suit, black coat and vest, collars, cravat, and pants—for a total of £11/1/0. This was his first set of the Jaeger apparel, which was to become a Shavian hallmark, as much identified with him, as G. K Chesterton later remarked, "as if it were a sort of reddish-brown fur . . . like the hair and eyebrows, a part of the animal."[48]

* * *

From 30 June 1885, when he collected his new clothes from Jaeger's, until the early hours of the morning of his twenty-ninth birthday on 26 July, events moved inexorably—but not without signs of resistance on Shaw's part—toward the sexual consummation of his affair with Jenny Patterson. On 4 July he visited her twice. Finding her at home on the second visit, he stayed until 1 a.m., later recording: "Vein of conversation decidedly gallant." On 10 July he found her at Osnaburgh Street when he came home, then "walked to her house by way of the park. Supper, music and curious conversation, and a declaration of passion. Left at 3. *Virgo intacta* still." He met her again on 17 July, having had a supper and a meeting with May Morris in the interim. The following day, on his way to the International Inventions afternoon concert, he purchased for five shillings "some f[rench] l[etters]." Following this purchase, he was obliged to interrupt a bus journey and return home after discovering that he had placed his ticket for the concert in another coat. This afforded him the opportunity for close inspection of what he had bought, which, according to his diary record, produced a strongly adverse reaction: "Came back here and examined my charges [the condoms], which extraordinarily revolted me." After the concert, he went to Jenny Patterson's and experienced "forced caresses." He then attended a reception at Lady Wilde's, and later visited his friend J. Kingston Barton to discuss Socialism. Late that night he called again at Jenny Patterson's house, but, finding her not at home, "did not wait." On 20 July, suggesting his repossession of a self he felt had been threatened by Jenny's advances, he wrote in his diary: "Myself again as to J. P. Wrote her a good letter in reply to hers." He received a "satisfactory letter from J.P." in response on 21 July.[49]

From Shaw's diary account of the denouement of this drama, which occurred on 25–26 July 1885, it is fairly obvious that Bessie Shaw would have had a good idea of what was likely to happen. Shaw had left his mother and Jenny at an evening session of the International Inventions program at South Kensington on Saturday, 25 July, and met them afterward at Brompton Square. Failing to find a bus in Brompton Road that was not full, Bessie Shaw went home by herself, whereupon Shaw and Jenny returned to Brompton Square:

> and stayed there until 3 o'clock on my 29th birthday which I celebrated by a new experience. Was watched by an old woman next door, whose evil interpretation of the lateness of my departure greatly alarmed us.

In the prefatory notes to his 1885 diary he wrote of this event: "I was an absolute novice. I did not take the initiative in the matter."[50] Shaw was at least fifteen years younger than Jenny Patterson. In the lead-up to the sexual consummation of their relationship—with his report of enduring "forced caresses" and other indications of unwillingness to surrender—Shaw is reminiscent of the coy young Adonis disdaining the advances of the voraciously amorous and experienced Venus in Shakespeare's poem *Venus and Adonis*. Both Adonis and Shaw are alike in seeing lovemaking as a distraction from their true vocation—in Adonis's case that of hunting, and in Shaw's case pursuing his career as writer and critic. However, whereas Shakespeare's Venus was disappointed in her lovemaking attempts with the young Adonis, Jenny Patterson had much more success with her young Irish friend. Part of Shaw's immediate reaction to his "new experience" seems to have been a puritanical attack of conscience. Having made love to her again on Sunday, 2 August, the following day he penned "a rather fierce letter to JP." On the fourth he "resolved to begin [the writing of] a new *Pilgrim's Progress* at once." The new *Pilgrim's Progress* was begun on the fifth, but nothing has survived of this project.[51]

Whatever feelings of remorse he may have had, Shaw did not remain a "novice" in sexual matters for long. Beginning with the occasion on Sunday, 2 August 1885, he maintained in his diary the practice of indicating with bracketed numerals—(0), (1), or (2)—the number of times sexual intercourse occurred during his meetings with "JP," as she was now referred to. The "expense of spirit," to quote the Shakespearean metonym for "lust in action" in the famous sonnet (no. 129), was recorded as punctiliously in Shaw's diary as his bus fares. He and Jenny became regular lovers, frequently making love more than once during their meetings. Little else is revealed about the relationship for the remainder of 1885 except for the fact that on one occasion (11 November), during a meeting at which they made love, Shaw records that "she gave me a pair of slippers she had worked for me."[52] She gave him another pair early in 1887, writing: "Your slippers are waiting for you. So come for them. . . . The slippers are quite too beautiful for any but saintly feet."[53]

Jenny's gifts may well have planted in Shaw's mind the idea of the slippers as a dramatic motif in the relations of the lordly Higgins and Eliza Doolittle in *Pygmalion*. In the fourth act, following Eliza's stunning success at passing herself off as a lady during the day—thereby winning his wager about turning a flower girl into a duchess—Higgins's lost slippers and Eliza's knowledge of their whereabouts become symbolic of her solicitous attention to his needs. This is in strong contrast to his self-engrossed failure to acknowledge her presence and offer her any word of congratulation on the eve of her triumph. Her final flinging of the slippers one by one at Higgins's head marks a major climax in their relations. Shaw had personal experience to draw on here as well. On the afternoon of 23 September 1888, he records in his diary: "JP came, raged, wept, flung a book at my head etc."[54]

With the commencement of the main sequence of the Patterson correspondence in 1886, a picture unfolds of an extraordinarily passionate, stormy (outdoing, in this respect, Shaw's relationship with Alice Lockett, which was still continuing), and complex affair, which lasted about eight years. It was only broken off permanently following a violent quarrel early in 1893. Jenny had an angry showdown with Shaw at the home of the actress Florence Emery Farr, with whom by this time Shaw was having another sexually consummated affair and who was becoming an important figure in his early career as a dramatist. Jenny's letters, obviously written at great speed and often with scant regard for punctuation, show her to have been an ardent, tender, adoring, generous, and lively yet extremely possessive lover. "I did for you what I have done for no other: loved you with all my soul and body," she wrote on 12 May 1886.[55] She fussed about his health and treated him hospitably during his visits: "Will you come to me before your lecture? I will feed you on brown bread, Cocoa, strawberrys & cream and any other fruit I can get."[56] Whatever inhibitions the novice Shaw may have had about lovemaking, they seem to have been decidedly conquered with experience. In one of her later letters Jenny wrote: "Be as ardent as you were last week . . . I adore to be made love to like that. It takes my breath away at the time & leaves oh such a memory behind!"[57]

In fact, as the relationship developed, it was Shaw who may possibly have been the more sexually demanding partner, an Adonis turning the tables on his Venus. In a letter dated 20 October 1888 Jenny accuses him of "only just thinking of me as a sucking baby does of its Mar when it is hungry!" On 12 May of the same year she had told him: "You will not believe me I know but it is absolutely true that often my body has been an unwilling minister to you."[58]

There is evidence that during the early phase of the long-lasting affair between Jenny Patterson and Shaw, the novelist and journalist T. Tighe Hopkins was trying to renew advances to Jenny, which he had begun making two years earlier and which she had rejected. In his diary Shaw recorded an evening visit to Jenny on 12 January 1886 when he found Hopkins already there: "He was bent on seduction, and we tried which should outstay the other. Eventually he had to go for his train (1). To bed late." The bracketed number—his customary record of lovemaking episodes—indicates Shaw's victory in this particular contest. A week earlier Jenny had written to tell Shaw that Hopkins was not successful in his overtures toward her: "I haven't turned over anything curiously in my mind regarding Hopkins[.] If I loved him I'd not stop to consider anything or any one. He will not be my friend. He would be my lover. That he tried to be two years ago & went off in a fine rage because I made (he says) a fool of him. He don't believe in platonics & saints. Nor do I."[59]

Jenny insisted on her loyalty to Shaw, even though, later in the year—probably to relieve the intensity of Jenny's demands on him—Shaw appears to have even encouraged relationships with others, including Hopkins. This is revealed in a letter of Jenny's dated 28 May 1886: "You tell me to love you to be good to be generous & then tell me to pick up men as I may please oh George this is not worthy of you—I do not regret the least bit in the world what I did. I did it all with my eyes open knowing the risks I ran I had nothing else to give, & I do not hold that gift so cheap that I can give to Hopkins & Co what I thought good for you."[60]

* * *

An early clue to the problems that were to develop within and continue throughout Shaw's relationship with Jenny Patterson is contained in the terse diary entry of 20 July, one week before they first made love: "Myself again as to J.P." While the relationship initiated Shaw into new experiences of sexual pleasure—and probably mutual love, although the extent of the latter sentiment on Shaw's part is hard to determine—it also presented a threat to his self-sovereignty and independence of spirit. As he put it later in his letter to Frank Harris, "I wanted to love, but not to be appropriated and lose my boundless Uranian liberty."[61] In this statement Shaw was drawing on the distinction (derived from Plato's *Symposium*) between the heavenly Venus, or *Venus Urania*, and the earthly Venus, goddess of sexual desire, or *Venus Pandemos / Vulgaris*, the figure most clearly represented in Shakespeare's poem. For Shaw *Venus Urania* presided over ideal forms of love and beauty that find expression in the world of the imagination, in works of art and poetry, and in the contemplation of such scenes as the "enchanting panorama of sea, sky and mountain" he surveyed in childhood from Dalkey Hill. In short, he wanted his spirit to remain free of the confinement that he felt the sexually sealed compact with one woman imposed upon his life. Not surprisingly, Shaw's assertion of his "Uranian liberty"—especially when it included unrestrained association with other women, such as Eleanor Marx Aveling, May Morris, Annie Besant, Janet Achurch, and Florence Farr in the midst of his relationship with Jenny Patterson—led to wounded feelings, reproaches, and tantrums on her part.

A related and problematic feature of the relationship between Shaw and Patterson arose from the conflicts that always seems to have arisen in Shaw's relations with women between ideals of free, disinterested friendship between people, on the one hand, and the claims of possession that sexual relationships naturally give rise to, on the other. This was also partly the subject of the first paper delivered by Karl Pearson at the new Men and Women's Club, which was established in London at the same time as the beginning of Shaw and Patterson's sexual relationship. In "The Woman's Question" Pearson asked:

> Is it or is it not possible for the sexes to mix freely in all the relations of life? The hitherto almost complete separation of the sexes in the business of life has led to what appears to me a very artificial relation between them. . . . Close friendship between single men and women is almost impossible. It may be due to something inherent in human nature, the existence of a sexual attraction produced by the struggle of a group in the battle of life, or it may be due to an artificial relation, the outcome of a false social system.[62]

Shaw was strongly drawn to the idea of friendly relations and comradeship between men and women that were free of the conventions created by the "false social system" and the rigid Victorian gender stereotypes to which Pearson was alluding in this paper, as well as of the ties imposed by sexual relations. This idea plays a vital part in his portrayal of male-female relations in the early plays, especially in *The Philanderer* (1893) and *Arms and the Man* (1894), for which the affairs of the 1880s and early 1890s were a form of rehearsal.

The conflict in *The Philanderer* between "advanced" ideals of obligation-free friendship and the demands for commitment and proprietorship that typically attend sexual relationships between men and women, was an echo of tensions in Shaw's own relationships with women. Charteris, the philanderer of the play's title asks at one point: "do I belong to Julia; or have I a right to belong to myself?" The question was almost certainly one that Shaw himself asked about his relationship with Jenny Patterson. To Shaw erotic entanglements tended to be viewed as constricting and oppressive. While he was highly susceptible to the attractions of the opposite sex, he was also exceptionally resistant to possessiveness and emotional coercion. The classical legend of Calypso, the ensnarer and lover of Odysseus remained an image in Shaw's language of love from his teenage years to old age. Some of his most intimate relationships with women were formed on the basis of a spoken or unspoken pact of celibacy. In the case of May Morris, some kind of compact on this subject had apparently been reached, as can be inferred from her letter to Shaw dated 5 May 1886:

I am "strongly moved" to answer of your letter just this: that your resolution when we became acquainted not to make love was most judicious and worthy of all praise, having, as you say, the most entirely satisfying results: I don't think our intercourse can have caused you more pleasure than it has me.

I have always been most impatient of the bourgeois vulgarity of thought and the attendant convention which almost entirely prevent young men and women from holding that frank and friendly intercourse without which life is nothing, to my mind.

Let us be comrades by all means—I salute you, friend Shaw! As you apparently still desire that absurdly sentimental photograph so petulantly withheld formerly, I will throw consistency to the winds and send it or a better one shortly.

Yours very sincerely
May Morris[63]

Irony is created around this charming letter when we learn from Lucy Shaw—who is likely to have been a reliable source of information in the matter—that May was madly in love with Shaw. "She always wore her heart upon her sleeve," Lucy told her friend Janey Drysdale, "and every one knew about her madness for G[eorge]." In the same letter she said of May—whom she described as "a beautiful damosel of the Rosetti [*sic*] and Burne Jones [*sic*] type"—that her only object in divorcing Henry Halliday Sparling in 1898, following eight years of marriage, was "to give G[eorge] the chance of marrying her."[64]

7 Rival Attractions

Shaw's various love affairs of the 1880s and 1890s coincided with a tide of profound change in the role of women in society and in attitudes toward sexual difference. A new cohort of often highly educated, independent-minded young women was beginning to make forays into the male bastions of business, politics, and economics—anticipating the fictional career of Shaw's Cambridge-educated actuarialist Vivie Warren in his play *Mrs. Warren's Profession* (1893). University College London began admitting women in 1870, and Lady Margaret Hall and Girton College were established at Oxford and Cambridge, respectively, during the 1870s. The New Woman had arrived.

Despite overwhelming resistance from conservative forces, both male and female, history was beginning to give birth to at least some of the rights for which Mary Wollstonecraft pleaded a century earlier in *A Vindication of the Rights of Women* (1792). Radical thinkers of the late nineteenth century, such as Edward Carpenter, author of *The Intermediate Sex*—whom Shaw met and heard lecture at Hammersmith in January 1886—and Havelock Ellis, champion of women's rights and author of *Man and Woman* (1894) and *Studies in the Psychology of Sex* (1897–1928)—who was known to Shaw from his days at the Fellowship of the New Life—were in the vanguard of males who were also providing a critique of the rigidities of Victorian gender stereotypes and the subordination of women in Victorian social, political, and economic life.

It was from the ranks of the "advanced" women of the day that Jenny Patterson's rivals for Shaw's attention were to come. In 1886 Eleanor Marx Aveling had publically shown her advanced credentials—and loyalty to her father Karl Marx's creed—in an essay entitled "The Woman Question," which she coauthored with her husband and which appeared in the *Westminster Review*. The essay argued, among other things, that "women are the creatures of an organised tyranny of men, as the workers are the creatures of an organised tyranny of idlers."[1] Annie Besant—having been banished from her home by her patriarchal and authoritarian clergyman husband, the Reverend Frank Besant, for refusing to take communion—became a leading secularist free-thinker, political activist, and advocate of birth control. May Morris helped organize the Socialist lectures at Kelmscott House. Florence Farr, who Shaw met in 1890 and about whom he later wrote that "she was in violent reaction against Victorian morals, especially sexual and domestic morals,"[2] was to become a leading figure as actress-producer in the avant-garde theater of the 1890s.

Jenny Patterson did take some interest in Socialism. On 8 February 1886 she wrote (rather unconvincingly) to Shaw: "I am just as good a Socialist as you or May Morris."[3] Her letters, however, suggest that politics did not rank very high in her range of interests. She was intensely focused on her relationship with Shaw and constantly taking its temperature. She was ready to meet all his demands, and if he wanted friendship rather than love, as in the compact between May Morris and Shaw, she was happy to comply. On 29 June 1886, she wrote:

> Goodnight my love. My friend & lover. I am content that there are no barriers betwixt us—that you have taken me back. I will try to make *you* content with *me*. Be my friend when you will my lover when you will, but let the friend be first.
> Always & ever yours
> Jenny[4]

Sadly, she was fighting a losing battle. She was a shrewd, vibrant woman, and perhaps broke down the barriers that Shaw set up around his emotions more successfully than any other woman, with the possible exception of Mrs. Patrick Campbell. Nevertheless, it is easy to imagine that Shaw, whose behavior toward her seems to have been quite callous at times, must have tired of her constant importunities and emotional demands. Her letters are full of reproaches and accusations: "You are a man of stone without either feelings or passions," she declared on 21 September 1886.[5] At times she displayed melodramatic—though probably justified—self-pity. She was "the most miserable woman in London," she told Shaw on Christmas Day 1887, following her discovery of some intimate letters from Annie Besant to Shaw that he had "incautiously" left on the table in his room.[6] As he himself admitted, Shaw the philanderer was indeed "incorrigible": "Very well my dear boy. You are beginning again the old games," the wounded Jenny wrote on 29 January 1888, making yet another complaint about his neglect of her.[7]

* * *

It was with May Morris, perhaps more than any other of his early women friends, that Shaw found the kind of friendly companionship with a member of the opposite sex that he cherished. Without being obsequious, May showed a real appreciation of his humor and intelligence, qualities that were evidently also being relished by his audiences at Kelmscott House. "I don't know," she wrote to him on 21 July 1885, "if you are aware that our audiences love you much: their faces always broaden with pleasure when we promise them that if they are good Bernard Shaw shall be their next teacher."[8] The previous month she had told him her intellect was "enfeebled this morning by too much laughing at you last night."[9] She appreciated his sardonic review of a tedious book about ghosts ("the tender but inexorable touch of which is unmistakeable") in the *Pall Mall Gazette* on 24 November 1886, saying: "Heaven save me from your irony if ever . . . I plunge into print."[10] She was not, however, an uncritical friend and took Shaw to task for what she called "insincere compliments" about her own intelligence and for scoffing at Jenny Patterson behind her back.[11]

Many years after the main phase of their friendship, Shaw wrote a romanticized account of what he called his "Mystic Betrothal" to May Morris. He claims that this "Betrothal" was indicated by a "gesture of assent" from May when their eyes met as he was rejoicing in her lovely appearance one day at the Morris's house in Hammersmith. Blithely assuming that the "Betrothal" was understood and registered in heaven, he made no effort at all to confirm the matter. Eventually—committing what he describes as "the most monstrous breach of faith in the history of romance" and to his "utter stupefaction"—May "married one of the comrades," namely, William Morris's assistant and protégé Henry Halliday Sparling.[12] Shaw's statement about his "utter stupefaction" at this turn of events, which occurred in 1890, is inconsistent with the fact that he had known about the Sparling–May Morris love affair since early 1886. It is another of the many examples of his not wanting to spoil a good story with the truth. In what must have been a slightly awkward conversation, Sparling himself told Shaw about the affair during a train journey from Hammersmith to St. James's Park on 4 April 1886. A few days later William Morris's neighbor and friend Emery Walker was "talking a good deal about May Morris and Sparling" in Shaw's presence at the Wheatsheaf Restaurant.[13]

May's marriage to Henry Sparling, which was contracted in 1890 and ended in divorce in 1898, by no means put an end to her close friendship with Shaw. Before the marriage Shaw had regular meetings with May not only at the Sunday-evening gatherings at Kelmscott House but also, pursuing shared interests, at various other venues. They acted in several plays together. In January 1885 May played the role of Maude Trevor in the Socialist League production of *Alone*, in which Shaw played Stratton Strawless. She also played Mrs. Linde (Krogstad's wife-to-be at the end of the play) to Shaw's Krogstad in the reading of *A Doll's House* at the Aveling home. On 12 February 1888 the two were rehearsing a "little play," in which Shaw acted the part of a photographer, that was performed at Kelmscott House on the twenty-fifth. They also sang duets and played chess together. May, Shaw, and Sparling went "rowing & sailing" on the Thames at Lechlade on 17 August 1888, during a stay at Morris's Oxfordshire home of Kelmscott Manor.[14]

May was very likely to have been present on 12 February 1888 when Shaw met "an Irishman named Yeats [who] talked about Socialism a good deal."[15] This was the first of many meetings with his fellow countryman W. B. Yeats, both of them having been drawn together, in different ways, by the genius of William Morris. It was in Yeats's account of this meeting, contained in a letter to Katharine Tynan, that he made the remark about Shaw, which is sometimes seized on by hostile critics that "he is certainly very witty. But like most people who have wit rather than humour, his mind is maybe somewhat wanting in depth."[16] The Shakespeare critic G. Wilson Knight was much nearer the mark when he wrote that "Shaw's humour is bright, kindly and exciting" and described an example of it from *John Bull's Other Island* (1904) as plumbing "depth beyond depth."[17]

For a time after her marriage, Shaw had meetings and outings with May almost as often and as freely as before—with and without Sparling in attendance. They continued to play and sing duets, they took long walks together, they skated, they lay down on the grass in Richmond Park one day, fell asleep, and got "frightfully sunburnt,"[18] they attended German classes in Hampstead, they dined at various vegetarian restaurants. At the beginning of the winter of 1892–93 repairs and redecoration were being carried out at 29 Fitzroy Square, which by this time had become the Shaw family home. On 1 November 1892 suffering from the "unbearable" smell of paint at Fitzroy Square and exhaustion from overwork, Shaw asked the Sparlings if he could stay at their house at 8 Hammersmith Terrace "for a few nights."[19] The visit lasted until mid January and was followed by additional stays at Hammersmith during 1893. The three had formed a ménage à trois that Shaw later described in his essay "William Morris as I Knew Him" as initially blissful but eventually producing intolerable strain:

> Everything went well for a time in that *ménage à trois*. She was glad to have me in the house; and he was glad to have me because I kept her in good humour and produced a cuisine that no mere husband could elicit. It was probably the happiest passage in our three lives.
>
> But the violated Betrothal was avenging itself. It made me from the first the centre of the household; and when I had quite recovered and there was no longer any excuse for staying unless I proposed to do so permanently and parasitically, her legal marriage had dissolved as all illusions do; and the mystic marriage asserted itself irresistibly. I had to consummate it or vanish.[20]

The "Mystic Betrothal" must have come perilously close to consummation in the late spring of 1893. Sparling was away in France and Shaw was alone in the Hammersmith house with May. At the time he was—appropriately enough—writing his play *The Philanderer*, parts of which he read to May. The previous February the two had "rather an emotional" conversation about old times. The atmosphere at 8 Hammersmith Terrace must, one imagines, have been highly charged. On 21 May 1893 Shaw records that with "May . . . at the Terrace alone, Sparling being in France," he entertained her with a piano rendition of the passion-filled music of Wagner's *Die Walküre*, with its powerful themes of brother and sister love and wild horsewomen who fly through the air. That night he "slept at the Terrace." On the twenty-third they "played Beethoven's Second Symphony as a duet. . . . Emery Walker came in whilst we were playing; but he did not stay long; and after he was gone May and I had a long and rather confidential conversation."[21]

It is quite likely that the "confidential conversation" included a discussion of the Sparling marriage, which, according to Shaw, was already foundering. Shaw's claim (in "William Morris as I Knew Him") that out of loyalty to Sparling he did not take advantage of the situation by physical lovemaking is almost certainly true. The facts—omitted from his 1936 account of the "Mystic Betrothal"—that he was already at this time involved in a sexually consummated relationship with Florence Farr (of which May Morris was aware), and that he had not yet completely ended his relationship with Jenny Patterson could have had a bearing on the decision not to complicate his life with a further sexual entanglement.

* * *

The stories of Shaw's love affairs during the late 1880s and 1890s resemble the multiple, separately developed yet interconnected plots of Victorian multi-decker novels. Since they are intimately connected with the early stages of Shaw's career as a dramatist, an account of the development of his affair with Florence Farr and the outcome of that with Jenny Patterson must be deferred. But what of the others?

In October 1885—by which time his sexual relationship with Jenny Patterson was in full swing—a fierce letter from Shaw to Alice Lockett indicates that she was still hoping to keep the romance alive by proposing a meeting. Shaw refused the proposal with a Macbeth-like cry of "Avaunt, sorceress." After saying "love-making grows tedious to me—the emotion has evaporated from it," he concluded the letter rhetorically with the statement, that when love has gone from him, he is remorseless: "I hurl the truth about like destroying lightning." However, in August of the following year he was writing quite an affectionate letter to her about her awful handwriting.[22] Nevertheless, the affair virtually came to an end in December 1885 when she wrote him a grumpy letter in which she refused to send him her photograph. On 29 September 1888 Alice spent the day at the Shaw house. When Shaw came home, he records that "I sang some of the old [*Marriage of*] *Figaro* bits with Alice, who presently went home, overcome, I think, by old associations."[23] "Home" for her now was St. Mary's Hospital, Paddington, where she was on the nursing staff and where she met the man who was to become her husband in 1890, Dr. William Salisbury Sharpe, a physician and surgeon. One wonders whether the famous aria "Now your days of philandering are over" (Non più andrai, farfallone amoroso) was one of the "*Figaro* bits" they sang on the twenty-ninth. The words of the aria were far from the truth in Shaw's case.

* * *

Apart from May Morris, Jenny Patterson's most significant rival for Shaw's affections during the 1880s was Annie Besant (her own pronunciation of the name rhymes with "pleasant"). Shaw described Annie as "the greatest orator in England"[24] of her time; she was certainly one of the most powerful, articulate, and effective late-nineteenth-century political activists. Besant's extraordinary career in many ways exemplifies the Victorian search for alternative "religions" in an age of doubt. Neatly summarizing her career, Shaw wrote that "she was successively a Pusyite Evangelical, an Atheist Bible-smasher, a Darwinian secularist, a Fabian Socialist, a Strike Leader, and finally a Theosophist." She was, Shaw declared, a "born actress" who successfully assumed these roles in her career in much the same way as the eighteenth-century actress Mrs. Siddons played the various roles for which she was famous opposite a series of "leading men."[25] This underrates Annie Besant's independence of mind and way of thinking through the various philosophical stages of her career, as well as her opposition to the ideas of some of the men with whom she collaborated. In her autobiography she described the "keynote" of her life as a "longing for sacrifice to something felt as greater than the self," which corresponds closely with Shaw's statement about "the true joy in life, the being used for a purpose recognized by yourself as a mighty one" in the Epistle Dedicatory to *Man and Superman*.[26]

An underlying and unifying theme in Annie Besant's career was her passionate concern for the victims of nineteenth-century systems of oppression, whether in the workforce or in the institution of marriage. A spirited advocate of birth control and sex education, she remained in the vanguard of feminist thought about women's rights. One of her triumphs as a political activist was her successful support, in collaboration with W. T. Stead, of a strike in 1888 by fourteen hundred female workers subjected to sweated labor—"White Slavery," as she and Stead dubbed it—and industrial diseases caused by contact with phosphorous at their work site in the Bryant & May matchstick firm. The box makers in the factory worked for pathetic wages ("twopence farthing per gross of boxes, and buy your own string and paste") and had no job security. No more graphic image of the abject condition of those at the bottom of the pile in the Victorian social hierarchy could be imagined than that evoked in Besant's description—like an echo in prose of William Blake's "London"—of the plight of the Bryant & May workers and their families: "When the work went more rapid starvation came. Oh, those trudges through the lanes and alleys around Bethnal Green Junction late at night when our day's work was over; children lying about on shavings, rags, anything; famine looking out of baby faces, out of women's eyes, out of the tremulous hands of men. Heart grew sick and eyes dim, and ever louder sounded the question, 'Where is the cure for sorrow, what the way of rescue for the world?'"[27]

The year before her intervention in the Bryant & May action, Besant had participated with Shaw in the "Bloody Sunday" protest demonstration of 13 November 1887 in Trafalgar Square, which resulted in violent action by police and troops against the protestors, with massive injuries among the latter.[28] Shaw reported that he and others had to beat a rapid retreat from the police charge. "Running hardly expresses our collective action," Shaw later wrote to William Morris. "We *skedaddled*." He subsequently returned to Trafalgar

Square and was admitted by the police "in consideration of my genteel appearance," as he told Morris, and then went off in search of Annie Besant, from whom he had been separated "in the scrimmage."[29]

Apart from their mutual concern over social injustice and the sense of a shared cause, probably part of the appeal of Shaw for Annie Besant was his Irishness. Although she was born in London, she declared in her autobiography that "three-quarters of my blood and all my heart are Irish," and that "the Irish tongue is musical in my ear, and the Irish nature dear to my heart."[30]

Shaw was surely correct in saying of Annie that "comedy was not her clue to life," although he added that "she had a healthy sense of fun."[31] Certainly she missed the irony when, in May 1884, she heard a speech by Shaw in which he described himself as "a loafer," and subsequently "gave an angry snarl at him" in the *National Reformer*. She was later embarrassed to discover that Shaw, "one of the most brilliant of Socialist writers and most provoking of men," was actually very poor and hard-working, and that the phrase "a loafer" was "only an amiable way of describing himself because he did not carry a hod." She apologized but "privately felt somewhat injured at having been trapped into such a blunder."[32]

Shaw first met Annie Besant on 21 January 1885. They dined at her house in St. John's Wood ten days later. By the following April Shaw's novel *The Irrational Knot* was being serialized by Annie in the radical periodical *Our Corner*, of which she was editor and financial backer and to which she soon invited Shaw to make paid contributions in a regular "Art Corner" column devoted to reviews of all the arts. In May Annie joined the Fabian Society. Shaw had thus entered into a professional association with her at the same time as the approaching consummation of the affair with Jenny Patterson, his other lady friend of Irish descent.

His intimacy with Annie Besant "gradually ripened," as Shaw put it in his diary notes for 1885. By January 1887 it had "threatened to become a vulgar intrigue, chiefly through my fault. But I roused myself in time and avoided this." On 27 January 1887 he recorded a walk with Annie from the British Museum to Fleet Street during which he had a "scene with her." Jenny Patterson had become extremely jealous of his attentions to "Mrs B." and even took to following them in the street, as Shaw discovered on 18 March 1887. On the previous day he had both made love to Jenny and contrived to write a letter to Annie in Jenny's house. In July 1887 Shaw received a telegram from Annie asking him to come and see her. After "eagerly" going across to her house, he found it was "sentimental nonsense only; no business of real importance." On 15 November he had a "tedious quarrel about Mrs. Besant" with Jenny and then made love to her. Matters came to a head on Saturday, 24 December 1887, when Jenny discovered and took possession of the letters from Shaw to Annie that the latter had returned to him the previous day. The following day Shaw was rudely awakened by a knock at the door from Jenny and a quarrel. He recovered the letters Jenny had taken and destroyed them—and with them probably a great deal of our knowledge of the nature of his personal intimacy with Annie Besant. On 31 December he saw the New Year in with lovemaking at the home of Jenny Patterson.[33]

Before returning his letters, Annie had presented Shaw with a document setting forth the conditions according to which she proposed they should live as common-law husband and wife, she having been refused a divorce by her husband Frank. Shaw rejected this proposal, later telling Hesketh Pearson that his reaction to it was to exclaim: "Good God! This is worse than all the vows of all the Churches on earth. I had rather be legally married to you ten times over."[34] They remained friends, but by the end of the decade Annie was won over to a new creed by Madame Blavatsky's *Secret Doctrine* and left the Fabian Society to become a Theosophist. "Gone to Theosophy" was the brief note written in red ink beside her name in the Fabian records kept by Edward Pease.

* * *

Shaw invented the category of "Sunday husband" to describe his role in relation to several married women with whom he associated with varying degrees of intimacy during the years before his marriage. (Extensive personal experience lay behind his creation of the triangular situation of husband, wife, and visiting creative writer in his play *Candida*.) The problem with this for some of the women in his nonfictional life, especially, for example, Edith Nesbit (Mrs. Hubert Bland), was that they very much wanted him to become a weekday husband as well.

Edith Nesbit became "passionately attached" to her fellow Fabian in 1886.[35] Shaw often visited the Bland house, and during the summer of 1886 Edith was tracking Shaw down in his haunt in the Reading Room at the British Museum on an almost daily basis. She had provided a vivid description of Shaw in a letter to a friend probably written in 1885, claiming (with an unconscious contradiction of W. B. Yeats's remark) that "GBS has a fund of dry Irish humour that is simply irresistible," that he was the "grossest flatterer . . . horribly untrustworthy as he repeats everything he hears and does not always stick to the truth, and is *very plain* like a long corpse with a dead white face—sandy sleek hair and a loathsome small straggly beard, and yet is one of the most fascinating men I have ever met."[36] She revealed her passionate feelings toward him during almost a whole day and evening they spent together on 26 June 1886. However, as with Annie Besant's pursuit of him, Shaw managed to prevent things from going further with Edith than a serious flirtation and an intimate friendship. According to Shaw, Edith complained about this unconsummated affair by telling him (when he refused to let her commit adultery with him): "You had no right to write the preface if you were not going to write the book."[37]

Another friend on the list of ladies for whom Shaw was a "Sunday husband" was Catherine ("Kate") Salt. Kate ("born Kate Joynes, and half German") was the wife of Henry Stephens Salt, who, after resigning his post at Eton, became a leading Socialist, humanitarian, and vegetarian, in addition to becoming a member of the Fabian Society. Shaw was very fond of the Salts and visited them often at their cottages in Surrey, where he played "endless pianoforte duets" with Kate. Her sexual preference was for women, and she was drawn to the teachings of Edward Carpenter, who championed the superiority of Urnings as the "chosen race." Carpenter, the sandal-wearing "Noble Savage" (as the group called him), would join Kate and Shaw in "making a fearful noise at the piano" with renditions of Wagner. Shaw recalled that "Kate (Mrs Salt) loved me as far as she could love any male creature."[38]

Minor stars in the galaxy of Fabian women who became amorously interested in Shaw included younger members of the Fabian Society, such as Grace Gilchrist, daughter of William Blake biographer Alexander Gilchrist, and Grace Black, a neighbor of Shaw's in Fitzroy Street. The two Graces both made declarations of love to him. On 4 June 1887 Shaw sang "The Wearing of the Green" at "Miss Gilchrist's" home, scene of the last meeting and supper of the Hampstead Historical Club. In 1887 and 1888 he was writing long letters to her (which have not survived), and on 8 February 1888 he "began composing music to Browning's 'I go to Find my Soul' for Grace Gilchrist, but did not get very far with it."[39] By March she had fallen in love with Shaw and was regretting her "childish jealousy of other women."[40] Shaw was taken to task about the "Gilchrist affair" by Emma Brooke, another young Fabian—she was a friend of Charlotte Wilson and a future member of the Fabian Executive—who, apparently considering he was trifling with Grace's affections, "heaped abuse" on Shaw when she called on him on 1 April. This storm in the Fabian teacup had to be calmed by Shaw through letters and a long "interview" with Emma Brooke over coffee at the British Museum on 12 April.[41]

Grace Black was also a disappointed lover. Shaw was seeing a good deal of her in 1887, further complicating his affairs with others. On 24 and 25 May 1887 she wrote several letters, in the second of which she confessed her love for him. On the twenty-fourth she had written: "You have a greater power of seeing truth than most people. . . . What I fear is that you do not care for nor believe in people sufficiently, and you won't be able to understand them unless you do, and your socialism must be warped if you don't understand human nature." On the following day, apparently in reply to a letter of Shaw's that has not survived, she wrote adroitly:

> I guessed you would think I am in love with you. So I am, but that has nothing to do with my letter and it is a pity if that thought has clouded my meaning. My personal happiness is certainly connected with your success as a teacher of socialism. . . . But apart from that I do love you, & why do you wish to dissuade me from that and from believing in you? No doubt you believe in & love yourself quite as much as I do and as you know more truth about yourself than any one else, it is not unreasonable of me to do so too. . . .[42]

Evidently Shaw's dissuasion worked, but it was not until 1889 that Grace Black found she was able to love somebody else. She wrote to Shaw on 31 March of that year, telling him of her recent engagement: "Long ago I saw that my love for you was a waste of force, because you were so different to me: but it is only lately that I have been able to love anyone else."[43] She had chosen a man with the right surname to describe the quality she said she was seeking in Shaw, Edwin Human, another Socialist.

* * *

By the end of the 1880s Shaw's Leporello list of conquered female hearts was impressively long. Until he met Florence Farr in the 1890s, Jenny Patterson was the only woman with whom he had a fully consummated sexual relationship. But the list of those who had fallen seriously in love with him included, at least: Alice Lockett, Jenny Patterson, May Morris, Annie Besant, Eleanor Marx Aveling, Edith Nesbit (Mrs. Bland), Grace Gilchrist, Grace Black, and—with the qualification recorded by Shaw—Kate Salt. Shaw's transformation from an acutely shy young Irishman of the late 1870s—hardly able to bring himself to attend Mrs. Lawson's at homes in Chelsea and feeling that he would be a wallflower at her dances—to the brilliant platform spellbinder and center of female attention and rivalry he had become in the late 1880s had about it an almost fablelike quality reminiscent of the career of Synge's hero Christy Mahon in *The Playboy of the Western World.*

The experiences of Shaw's various love affairs in the 1880s and 1890s were to resonate throughout the plays of his early and middle periods. However, the more immediate reflection of these experiences in his creative writing may be found in his less well known short story "Don Giovanni Explains," which was completed on 1 August 1887 as "The Truth about Don Giovanni" but not published until 1932.[44] In May 1887 Shaw had reviewed for the *Pall Mall Gazette* Samuel Butler's *Luck or Cunning?*, a polemical work opposing Darwin's theory of evolution that profoundly influenced Shaw's ideas about creative evolution.[45] Taken together, the review and short story make 1887 a very significant year in the genesis of Shaw's early-twentieth-century play *Man and Superman*.

Shaw's affairs with women in the 1880s involved innumerable train journeys in their company (for example, out to Walthamstow with Alice Lockett, down to Hammersmith with May Morris, and to South Kensington with Jenny Patterson). It was perhaps on one of these train journeys that he conceived the idea of his story "Don Giovanni Explains." There is also the possibility of a literary source for the germ of the idea in the 1813 tale *Don Juan* by Ernst Theodor Wilhelm (later Amadeus) Hoffmann, which also features a supernatural encounter with a character from Mozart's *Don Giovanni*. Apart from its considerable merit as a short story, Shaw's humorous fantasy, in which the ghost of Don Giovanni explains his history to a young woman during a train journey, is of interest both as an early draft of *Man and Superman* and for its autobiographical bearings. It is a mistake to view the story as a straightforward piece of autobiographical writing. Although it closely resembles Shaw's recent relations with women in several narrative details, it also presents a classic case of the way in which he impishly distorts his own past and that of others.[46] The story's critical—and quite cruel—reflection on his relationship with Jenny Patterson may explain why Shaw seems to have made no attempt to publish it until 1932, eight years after Jenny's death.

The narrator of "Don Giovanni Explains" is a bright twenty-four-year-old New Woman who unceremoniously introduces herself in the opening sentence as "very pretty." She dislikes the flirtatious nonsense her prettiness provokes in men, and the way in which "even the nicest of them seek my society to gloat over my face and figure, and not to exercise their minds." She has just attended a bad production of Mozart's *Don Giovanni* in a provincial capital and is returning home by train in a first-class compartment that she has all to herself. The train stops, being enveloped in a fog, and her attention is caught by a rush of rain against the carriage window. When she turns back, sitting opposite her is a gentleman with "a steadfast, tranquil, refined face" dressed in a splendid red cloak, kid boots, and a "superbly shaped cartwheel hat," with a sword at his side. It is, the story reveals, the ghost of Don Giovanni, who, after assuaging the young woman's alarm, provides an eloquent revisionary history of his life story.

The Don Giovanni of the ghost's story of complaint about his former life is a man much more sinned against than sinning. In Shaw's version of the legend he is cursed by the "infernal fascination" he inspires in members of the opposite sex, thus echoing the problem the young woman has with her prettiness. Rather than the notorious libertine, relentless sexual pursuer, and seducer of the traditional accounts, he is the one who is constantly being pursued. As a young man whose main interests are in "reading, travelling and adventure," this Don Giovanni loses his virginity to a "widow lady" who becomes desperate at his sexual naïveté and seduces him. After this, he enjoys "without scruple" the pleasure the lady gives him for "nearly a month," but he soon begins to tire of the associated game of romance: "I found the romantic side of our intercourse, which seemed never to pall on her, tedious, unreasonable, and even forced and insincere except at rare moments, when the power of love made her beautiful, body and soul."

Having overcome his timidity with women, Shaw's Don Giovanni finds that he "began to attract them irresistibly" and that he has become "the subject of fierce jealousies." He acquires a baseless reputation as a libertine, the majority of the names on the famous "list" of his alleged sexual conquests having been copied from the account books of the mischievous servant Leporello's father, a wine-shop keeper. Mesmerized by the majestic eloquence of the ghost in telling this story, the young woman has to pull herself up short in the act of making an involuntary declaration of her love for him. The story ends with salutations and hopes for a future meeting "within eternity" between the two.

The story's ingenious and playful rewriting of the plot of Mozart's *Don Giovanni*, its idea of the reverse love chase, and its excursion (near the end) into a very unconventional portrayal of the hell to which the Don is dispatched following his death all anticipate principal motifs in *Man and Superman*. Close parallels with Shaw's recent history in the narrative include the story of Don Giovanni's sexual initiation by a "widow lady" and the rivalries and jealousies among women that his "infernal fascination" provokes. One reason why this tale should not be taken too literarily as autobiography, however, is that the story conveys an impression that Shaw tired of *his* "widow lady," Jenny Patterson, after a very brief time. In fact he continued making love to her on a regular basis for some eight years after 1885. Whatever negative feelings Shaw may have had about the "romantic side" of the relationship, they seem to have been outweighed for a very considerable period of time by his enjoyment of a physical and personal intimacy that he did not find easy to relinquish.

Another reason for observing caution in reading "Don Giovanni Explains" as straight autobiography is that Shaw was, in fact, a less passive player in the games of courtship, flirtation, and love than the hero of his story. While he may have become "irresistible" to many women in an almost involuntary way thanks to his charismatic, unusual, and amusing personality, his diary entries and letters of the 1880s show that he often deliberately provoked and encouraged female interest and flirtation. Though he was not sexually promiscuous, the Fabian Don Juan was a conqueror of many hearts and an active player in the duel of sex. He acknowledged and was rather remorseful about his "incorrigible philandering." In a note about his love life and the exchange of letters with Annie Besant that he appended to the opening of his 1887 diary, Shaw wrote: "Reading over my letters [to Annie Besant] before destroying them rather disgusted me with the trifling of the last two years or so about women."[47] The days of his philandering, however, were far from over.

8 "The Coming Man"

Critic and "Platform Spellbinder"

On 13 April 1886 Jenny Patterson wrote to Shaw, in characteristically headlong style, from her seaside house in Broadstairs, to inquire about some new Jaeger clothes he had recently been trying on: "My dear Love. Are you over come by your new "Jager" filled with vanity. Of course I know you will be quite too beautiful & that you will run many dangers from my abandoned sex. You will be hardly safe—without *me*. . . . Now you are newly clothed will you not give us a treat & amaze the eyes of the Broadstairsites with a sight of 'the coming man'?"[1]

Her reference to Shaw as "the coming man" anticipates a biographical article about him entitled "Coming Men: Mr. G. Bernard Shaw," which appeared in the *London Figaro* in 1889.[2] This piece, spanning three columns in length and accompanied by a pen-and-ink drawing of its subject, appears to have been the first of the innumerable articles and personal interviews in periodicals and newspapers devoted to Shaw during his lifetime, which helped to make him one of the best-known literary figures of all time. Although the article contains factual inaccuracies for which Shaw is unlikely to have been responsible (such as giving 1871 instead of 1876 as the year when he left Dublin), at least some of the material is likely to have been supplied by Shaw himself.

By 1889, the year in which he turned thirty-three, Shaw had still not become a publicly performed dramatist. However, as the *London Figaro* article suggested, he had gained considerable celebrity in the political, intellectual, and cultural world of London. He had made over six hundred contributions to periodicals—in the form of book reviews; art, music, and theater criticism; and interventions in political debate—and was greatly in demand as a lecturer. "Tied, neck and heels, to stump and inkpot" was how he described his life of lecturing and reviewing in a letter to Mrs. T. P. O'Connor on 16 September 1888.[3]

When the *London Figaro* sketch appeared, he had recently invented the beguiling nom de plume and persona of "Corno di Bassetto" (Italian for bassett horn) over which exotic signature he was to pen his weekly "Musical Mems" columns in the *Star*, a newspaper recently founded by his compatriot T. P. O'Connor, whose deputy and eventual successor as editor was H. W. Massingham. In these "Musical Mems" (which ran from February 1889 to May 1890) and his subsequent weekly columns in Edmund Yates's *World* (28 May 1890 to August 1894), Shaw entertained London readers with music criticism, the freshness, vitality, and pungency of which makes it still very readable over a century later. By 1891 the *Sunday World* confidently declared: "Every-body in London knows Shaw."[4]

The *London Figaro* was pleased to hear that Shaw had changed his mind about giving up writing and devoting himself entirely to Socialism. A new edition of his "very clever and very original" novel *Cashel Byron's Profession* had just been published and had attracted "fresh attention. He has manifest gifts as an author," the article sagely concluded, "which justify the conviction that he might, by perseverance and industry, make a name." But Shaw the Socialist also figured prominently in this sketch: "He looks forward . . . to the transfer of . . . property from the few to the many; and he regards such measures as manhood suffrage, the abolition of all property disqualification, the abolition of the House of Lords, the public payment of members and election expenses, and annual Parliaments, as mere stepping stones to the Socialist ideal."[5]

In a rather ambiguous compliment, the young man's idealism is attributed to his nationality: "He is, of course, an Irishman—most idealists are." It scarcely needs saying that some of this Irishman's ideals of the late 1880s were to become standard practice in Western democracies in the next century.

By the beginning of the 1890s, Shaw had acquired unique skills in the art of self-presentation that, along with his writings and lectures, were to add to his burgeoning reputation. Early in 1891 the *Nottingham Daily Express* had requested Shaw to provide some personal information for a notice to coincide with his visit there on the weekend of 17 and 18 January to present two lectures at the Mechanics' Hall on "Evolution of Socialism" and "Alternatives to Social Democracy." A private letter Shaw dashed off to the newspaper was immediately turned into one of his first pieces of public autobiographical writing. The material he provided was simultaneously published on 17 January under the rubric "Notes of the Week" in the *Nottingham Daily Express* and as "A Sketch of Mr George Bernard Shaw: By Himself" in the *Pall Mall Gazette*. A portion of his letter read: "I am a bachelor, an Irishman, a vegetarian, an atheist, a teetotaller, a fanatic, a humourist, a fluent liar, a Social Democrat, a lecturer and debater, a lover of music, a fierce opponent of the present status of women, and an insister on the seriousness of art. If the *Express* cannot manufacture a little copy out of that—enough at any rate to make all the young ladies of Nottingham madly curious to see and hear so strange a bird—I cannot help it."[6] As a provider of lively material for "copy" such as this, Shaw was to become a journalist's dream.

* * *

Shaw's key patron during his early career as a journalist and dramatist was William Archer. It was Archer who obtained for Shaw the position of music critic for the *Dramatic Review*, thus enabling him to resume—beginning on 8 February 1885, when his first article in the newly established periodical appeared—the career he had begun as a ghostwriter for Vandeleur Lee in *The Hornet* during the 1870s. Shaw was also indebted to Archer for securing him a place on the book-review staff of the *Pall Mall Gazette*, in which his first contribution appeared on 16 May 1885, and for his appointment in the following year as art critic for the *World*, where his first piece appeared on 10 February 1886. Apart from obtaining these bread-and-butter posts for his friend, in 1884 Archer had already encouraged Shaw to embark on the writing of what would become his first play, *Widower's Houses*.

Almost exactly Shaw's contemporary, William Archer was born in Perth, Scotland, on 23 September 1856. He acquired a knowledge of Scandinavian languages—which served as the basis for his qualifications as a future translator of Ibsen—while on visits to his grandparents, who had immigrated to Norway in 1825. After graduating with a master's degree from Edinburgh University in 1876 (the year in which Shaw emigrated from Dublin to London), Archer traveled to Australia, where a stay with farming relations in Queensland gave him a taste of life in the outback, and San Francisco, where he worked briefly as a journalist. At the age of twenty-two he settled in London, where he became drama critic of the *London Figaro*. Archer was a tall, good-looking man who wore tight-fitting black suits and shirts with high, starched collars like a clergyman's—which, as Shaw remarked, gave him the appearance of having his head stuck in a pot of jam. His rather severe public persona was offset by the warmth and generosity of his personal relations. According to Shaw, in contrast to the dour self Archer projected in public, in his private life he displayed "an unsleeping and incorrigible sense of humour."[7]

Without knowing a great deal about stage technicalities, Archer shared with Shaw a passion for the theater and an ardent conviction of the importance of its social role. He himself had ambitions as a dramatist and wrote several plays, but he only achieved real success with *The Green Goddess*, a romantic melodrama that had successful seasons in both London and New York from 1921 to 1923 and was later made into a film. A matinee performance in December 1880 at the Gaiety Theatre, London, of Archer's freely adapted version of Ibsen's *The Pillars of Society,* under the title *Quicksands,* was the first production of an Ibsen play in Britain. Archer met Ibsen in December 1881, and his translations were published in twelve volumes as *The Collected Works of Henrik Ibsen* in 1906–7.

From the time of their first meeting—probably in the winter of 1883—Shaw and Archer remained close friends until Archer's untimely death in 1924 following surgery for a malignant tumor. Whereas Pakenham Beatty was Shaw's chief sparring partner with the boxing gloves, Archer became the equivalent in the fields of literature and drama. In the lively correspondence sustained throughout their friendship, they had quarrels of an intensity that might have wrecked any other literary relationship. Despite his championing of Ibsen and the relatively advanced views expressed in his book *The Old Drama and the New* (1923), Archer was in many ways a conservative thinker when it came to drama—and at times curiously imperceptive about the nature of Shaw's genius. Even after the triumphant success of Shaw's plays—including *Pygmalion*—in the years leading up to World War I, Archer was still expressing doubts about Shaw's abilities as a playwright and wanted him to develop into another kind of writer altogether. Archer was looking for Victorian high seriousness, while under his very eyes—and without his real appreciation of the phenomenon—his friend was becoming a master of serious comedy and the creator of genuinely "new" forms of English drama.

Writing to Shaw in 1921 after reading *Back to Methuselah,* Archer pleaded: "Why not prove once for all the reality of Creative Evolution by creatively evolving from the privileged lunatic all the world knows [into] a Leader of Men and a Saviour of Society? . . . The wisdom is *in* you, right enough; it has only to be liberated from the tyrannous, irrepressible idiosyncrasy."[8] Shaw's prodigious achievements in comic drama in the years before this was written were still not enough for the stern Scot. In 1903, following the completion of *Man and Superman,* Shaw had been similarly reprimanded by Archer: "You are not doing yourself justice or anything like it. I don't mean merely as a dramatist—I mean that in no way are you making the mark, either upon literature or upon life, that you have it in you to make. The years are slipping away . . . and you have done nothing really big, nothing original, solid, first-rate, enduring."[9] In 1893 Archer published in the *World* a very unfavorable review of *Widowers' Houses*—the play about slum landlordism that Shaw had embarked upon at Archer's own suggestion in 1884. In the review Archer advised the future Nobel Prize winner not to be "tempted to devote further time and energy to a form of production [writing plays] for which he has no special ability and some constitutional disabilities."[10] He was later to be equally disparaging about the seven works in Shaw's *Plays Pleasant and Unpleasant.*[11]

Although he wrote very generously about Archer in public, in private Shaw gave as good as he got from his friend. After reading the review in the *World,* which appeared on 14 December 1892, Shaw wrote a letter expressing his exasperation on the same day, concluding:

> A more amazing exposition of your Shaw theory even I have never encountered than that World article. Here am I, who have collected slum rents weekly with these hands, & for 4½ years been behind the scenes of the middle class landowner—who have philandered with women of all sorts and sizes—and I am gravely told by you to go to nature & give up apriorizing about such matters by you, you sentimental Sweet Lavendery recluse. Get out!
>
> GBS[12]

The friendship of the "privileged lunatic" and the "sentimental Sweet Lavendery recluse" miraculously survived these heavy punches, though further fierce exchanges about Shaw's plays were to occur, as in 1894, when Archer attacked *Arms and the Man.* This attack provoked not only an insult—"you have a perfect rag shop of old ideas in your head which prevent your getting a step ahead"[13]—but (as will be seen later) an important statement about Shaw's dramatic values. Whatever shortcomings Archer may have had as a public critic of Shaw, however, he had none as a steadfast friend, literary companion, and patron. The importance of his assistance in launching "the coming man" into his career as a journalist in the second half of the 1880s, and his introduction of Shaw to Ibsen, can hardly be overestimated as factors in the development of the playwright's career.

* * *

As a book reviewer Shaw had an abundance of material upon which to exercise his powers of ridicule. However, as Brian Tyson has remarked, Shaw had a gift as a reviewer for generally preserving a good-humored geniality of tone while at the same time making short shrift of the books under consideration—a characteristic more generally applicable to the style of his critical journalism.[14] The great majority of the works—comprising a roughly equal mixture of popular fiction and nonfiction, which came his way as the reviewer for W. T. Stead's *Pall Mall Gazette*—have been consigned to oblivion. Shaw's patience with respect to the great tide of Victorian ephemera he was obliged to review week after week—in return for which he was paid two guineas per thousand words—was remarkable.

The first work to fall into the hands of the friendly demolition expert of the *Pall Mall Gazette* was *Trajan: A Novel*, by Henry F. Keenan. Shaw describes the hero of the novel, Trajan Gray, as "an American artist with a Chinese taste in suicide" and generously remarks that the adventures of this hero are "by no means deficient in interest." However, in Shaw's description the absurdity of the adventures is finely conveyed: "A shipwreck, a man and bull fight, a war, the siege of Paris, and a revolt vary highly wrought domestic scenes, at the conclusion of which the gentlemen stagger, ghastly and despairing, from the premises, while the ladies are found prone on the carpet, with their hands clenched over the undone masses of their hair. Bouts of brain fever ensue; but all the characters are in good condition for the final massacre."

One of the first speeches of the novel's heroine is addressed to her brother, recently graduated from Harvard: "I am surprised that the dragons of impropriety permitted you into such disreputable dissipation." Upon which Shaw remarks: "A woman who can say this without stammering is evidently no ordinary person." Readers are advised that the novel's "exciting incidents and highly-colored scenes . . . will not wear out their thinking apparatus too rapidly." The review closes with a final sardonic warning: "It may be added that they [the readers] must be persons whose time is of comparatively small value."[15]

The book reviews skillfully expose the absurd mechanisms of Victorian popular romantic fiction. Similarly, the artificial devices of the Wilkie Collins detective novel *The Evil Genius* come in for withering comment: "Perhaps Mr Wilkie Collins innocently believes that it is in average human nature to like his cryptograms, his deciphering experts, his lawyers, his letters, his extracts from diaries, his agony-column advertisements, his detectives, his telegrams and his complicated railway and hotel arrangements. If so, he errs: these things are only tolerable for the sake of the stories they almost strangle."[16]

Occasionally works of more substance came Shaw's way. On 27 July 1885 a new edition of William Cobbett's *Rural Rides* produced a forceful Shavian essay-review and salute to that fearless early-nineteenth-century radical, whom Shaw compared to Swift and with whom he clearly felt an affinity of spirit. Other works influenced later developments in Shaw's intellectual and creative life. The review of Samuel Butler's *Luck or Cunning?*—referred to earlier as influencing the development of Shaw's theory of creative evolution—appeared on 31 May 1887.[17]

Shaw's career as a reviewer also brought to his notice the life and work of the Theosophist Madame Helena Petrovna Blavatsky. On 6 January 1887 he reviewed *Incidents in the Life of Madame Blavatsky*, which was compiled and edited by A. P. Sinnett. Two years later the *Star* newspaper sent him two volumes of Blavatsky's work *The Secret Doctrine,* which he passed on to Annie Besant for review. This proved to be a momentous event in Besant's life since it marked the beginning of her conversion to Theosophy. Blavatsky's ideas about the seven stages of spiritual development influenced Shaw's creation in *Heartbreak House,* of the Mahatma-like Captain Shotover and his quest for "the seventh degree of concentration." A novel by George Fleming (the pen name of Julia Constance Fletcher) called *Andromeda; or A Castle in the Air,* which dealt with a group of society idlers who have "nothing to do but fall in love," was another work Shaw encountered in his book-reviewing days that seems to find an echo decades later in *Heartbreak House.*[18] Shaw's play bore the earlier provisional titles *The Studio at the Clouds* and *The House in the Clouds*; and its idle inhabitants also have little else to do but engage in futile games of love.

* * *

In January 1888 Shaw briefly joined the *Star,* in the pages of which "Corno di Bassetto" was to shine. However, having unsuccessfully tried to change its political directions from Liberal to Socialist, he resigned the next month. O'Connor, an old-fashioned Fenian, supported Liberal politicians such as John Morley, who was a particular butt of Shaw's criticism. After his resignation, Shaw made occasional freelance contributions to the *Star* while reviewing books for the *Pall Mall Gazette* and writing art criticism for the *World.* His occasional contributions to the *Star* included second-stringing for its regular music critic, fellow Socialist E. Belfort Bax. By February 1889, he replaced Bax completely. But in May of the following year, after T. P O'Connor had made the "Himalayan mistake," as Shaw called it, of not agreeing to raise Corno's salary of three guineas a week, Shaw resigned and almost immediately took up the post he had negotiated with Yates as regular music critic for the *World.*[19]

Both O'Connor and Shaw later gave romanticized and factually inaccurate accounts of his career at the *Star,* Shaw's being the more entertaining and the more essentially true version. At the beginning of his 1894 essay "How to Become a Musical Critic," he wrote: "My own plan was a simple one. I joined the staff of a new daily paper as a leader writer. My exploits in this department spread such terror and confusion that my proposal to turn my attention to musical criticism was hailed with inexpressible relief, the subject being one in which lunacy is privileged. I was given a column to myself precisely as I might have been given a padded cell in an asylum."[20]

Archer wrote of Shaw's qualities as a music critic that "he had a peculiar genius for bringing day-by-day musical criticism into vital relation with aesthetics at large, and even with ethics and politics—in a word with life."[21] Shaw was superbly well equipped as a music critic. He was immensely knowledgeable—"as well try to prove the earth flat," he justifiably replied to a rash *Star* reader who had dared to suggest that the "captious frolic," as the reader dubbed Corno, was ignorant about music.[22] The "frolic," however, wore his learning well and had a gift for making musical technicalities interesting and accessible. An 1892 interviewer declared of Shaw's music criticism that he "makes diminished sevenths interesting. Throws positive halo round augmented ninths."[23] Shaw was a great mocker of the pretentious use of technical jargon in academic music criticism, on one occasion presenting a parody of it in the form of what he called his "celebrated 'analysis' of Hamlet's soliloquy on suicide": "Shakespeare, dispensing with the customary exordium, announces his subject at once in the infinitive, in which mood it is presently repeated after a short connecting passage in which, brief as it is, we recognize the alternative and negative forms on which so much of the significance of the repetition depends. Here we reach a colon; and a pointed pository phrase, in which the accent falls decisively on the relative pronoun, brings us to the first full stop."[24]

Shaw's claim, in reference to his criticism in the *World*, that he "could make deaf stockbrokers read my two pages on music"[25] has been vindicated by the fact that his writings on music have remained enjoyable to read for more than a century after they were first penned. He wrote as a good conversationalist, not hesitating to digress into snatches of autobiographical anecdote and nonmusical subject matter, constantly able to pluck apt quotations from the furthest recesses of Shakespeare, Dickens, Scott, and other authors, and always able to amuse as well as instruct. He frankly declared his prejudices and argued against the value or possibility of objective criticism: "Who am I that I should be just?," asked Corno di Bassetto disarmingly.[26] Reviewing a dull concert of elongated sonatas, Corno wrote: "The general feeling (I always speak of my own private sensations as the general feeling) was that of Christopher Sly at The Taming of the Shrew: 'Would 'twere done!'"[27]

Rank and fame provided no shelter from the merry barbs that continually accompanied Shaw's reporting of musical events. Sir Arthur Sullivan, of Gilbert and Sullivan fame, was one of Shaw's victims in a crisp account of his conducting of a Beethoven overture: "Sir Arthur Sullivan conducted. Under his *bâton* orchestras are never deficient in refinement. Coarseness, exaggeration and carelessness are unacquainted with him. So, unfortunately, are vigor and earnestness. The No. 1 Leonore overture, one of Beethoven's most impetuous compositions, would not have hurt a fly on Wednesday evening. It is well for Sir Arthur to be fastidious; but one cannot help thinking that he would get a firmer grip sometimes if he took his gloves off."[28]

On 23 March 1889, in a column headed "Richard Orchestrated," Shaw reported that Arthur Bingham Walkley, the drama critic of *Star*, had advised "the frolic Bassetto" to go to the Globe Theatre[29] to see the popular actor Richard Mansfield play the lead in Shakespeare's *Richard III*. Shaw followed his advice, taking along the sharp critical faculties and theatrical knowledge that were later to inform his theater criticism in the *Saturday Review*. This episode in Shaw's life involved two figures who were to play significant roles in his future career as a dramatist. A. B. Walkley, by then drama critic of *The Times*, was to become the addressee of a major Shavian preface, the 1903 "Epistle Dedicatory" of *Man and Superman*. Richard Mansfield was to be instrumental in introducing Shaw's plays to America, where he had become a successful actor-manager, with productions of *Arms and the Man* (1894) and *The Devil's Disciple* (1897).

Shaw's review of *Richard III* was the first of several sharp exchanges over theatrical matters that Shaw had with Mansfield, to whom he nevertheless became much indebted. Having waxed lyrical about the "splendor of sound, magic of romantic illusion, majesty of emphasis, ardor, elation, reverberation of haunting echoes, and every poetic quality that can waken the heart and the imaginative fire of early manhood" in Shakespeare's history plays, Corno di Bassetto went on to be far less than complimentary about Mansfield's handling of the cadences of Shakespearean blank verse. The passage is interesting for what it reveals about the intimacy of Shaw's knowledge of Shakespeare and the sensitivity of his ear to the musical qualities of his poetry:

> Mr Mansfield's execution of his opening *scena* was, I must say, deeply disappointing. When I heard his rendering of the mighty line—
>
> In the deep bosom of the ocean buried,
>
> which almost rivals "the multitudinous seas incarnadine" I perceived that Richard was not going to be a musical success. And when in that deliberate staccato—
>
> I am determinéd to be a villain,
>
> he actually missed half a bar by saying in modern prose fashion, "I am determin'd to be a villain," I gave him up as earless.[30]

Another notable visit to the theater by Shaw in his capacity as music critic occurred on 11 December 1893. Having found that he had mistaken the date of a concert he was to review at another venue, Shaw decided to drop in to St. James's Theatre to see a performance of Arthur Wing Pinero's celebrated new play *The Second Mrs. Tanqueray*, in which the role of Paula Tanqueray was being played by the captivating Mrs. Patrick (Stella) Campbell. Paula Tanqueray is a Victorian "Woman with a Past" who commits suicide at the end of the play because of her realization that she is permanently tainted in the eyes of herself, her husband, and society by her out-of-wedlock sexual liaisons and fast living in her previous life. But Corno di Bassetto, now "G.B.S.," the blithe music critic of the *World*, provides an entirely different explanation for the second Mrs. Tanqueray's suicide, mockingly referring in passing to Pinero's would-be tragic play as a "comedy":

> I was late, and only saw a scrap of the first act; but when the curtain rose on the second it revealed a pianoforte at which the chief lady in the piece—a very attractive person–presently sat down and began to play. To my surprise, she played not only with sufficient skill, but with such convincingly right expression and feeling and so sympathetic a hand that I immediately forgot all about the comedy, and prepared to enjoy Schubert.
>
> Will it be believed that the wretched people on the stage interrupted her after a few bars? The same thing happened at a subsequent and equally promising attempt. After that she never succeeded in even sitting down to the piano; and at last, worn out by repeated interruptions, she left the stage abruptly, and we were presently given to understand that she had committed suicide. No wonder![31]

Over a decade later—in June 1912—when he read his play *Pygmalion* to her, Shaw was to fall "violently and exquisitely in love"[32] with Stella Campbell and subsequently had what was perhaps his most serious extramarital affair with her. Pinero's plays were to become a principal target of Shaw's theater criticism shortly after the 1893 visit to *The Second Mrs. Tanqueray*, though he and Shaw enjoyed a cordial friendship.

* * *

From mid February to the end of March 1892 Shaw had several sittings for a portrait painted by Bertha Newcombe, the gifted artist, book and magazine illustrator, and Fabian. The portrait, the original of which is now lost, was given the caption "G.B.S., Platform Spellbinder" for its reproduction in Shaw's *Sixteen Self Sketches* at the beginning of the chapter entitled "How I Became a Public Speaker." The figure in this nearly full-length portrait stands in a relaxed, hands-on-hips pose that is strikingly offset by the intensity of the gaze with which he surveys his audience. Numerous firsthand accounts of Shaw as a "platform spellbinder" have survived. Contemporaries remember him as a cool, audacious, eloquent, and witty speaker. In debate he was quick-witted, disarmingly courteous, and powerfully persuasive. William Richard Titterton, theater critic, music-hall singer, Fabian, and author, has left us an account of Shaw's manner as a public speaker in the 1890s: "There he stands, slim, trim, alert and gallant . . . his hands veiled now in the pockets of his rough tweed jacket. His head is cocked sideways provocatively, his red beard juts out like a challenge. . . . his eyebrows—by art or by nature—have an archly diabolical lift. . . . The pose relaxes, the trim figure swaggers—jauntily, yet with sure restraint. . . . Out comes an epigram—a flock of epigrams—the hall roars. But the speaker himself remains calm and cool, supremely self-controlled."[33]

David J. O'Donoghue, journalist, biographer, and editor of numerous works on nineteenth-century Irish subjects, including a collection called *The Humour of Ireland* (1894), provides another account, this one of an occasion in 1886 when he heard Shaw addressing an outdoor meeting:

> He spoke for a full hour, and having heard a good many out-of-doors orators, I was struck with his absolute originality and curious refinement of speech. He then possessed a good deal of the "Rathmines accent," which he has never entirely lost, and his speech was a remarkably witty performance, mainly directed against certain Liberal politicians.
>
> As always, he was careful to explain that he was an Irishman, trying to make an impression on the thick wits of John Bull with only indifferent success. The crowd, which had swelled considerably, were agape with the audacity of the speaker, and interrupted barely at all. The cool assumption of the orator that the English were naturally stupid and inferior, and were, therefore, walked upon without protest by every exploiter, political and commercial, quite silenced the audience. . . . At the end one or two listeners questioned Shaw, who was even more insolent and amusing than in his address. In repartee he has always been at his best.[34]

The "Rathmines accent" mentioned here was also commented upon decades later when the American journalist, author, and critic Edmund Wilson wrote an account of Shaw's famous address at the Metropolitan Opera House in New York on 11 April 1933. He describes Shaw's "lovely cultivated voice" as having "the fine qualities of his prose": "With a charming accent, half-English, half-Irish—what the Irish call a Rathmines accent after the fashionable quarter of Dublin, an accent which says 'expawts' when his voice rises, 'exporrts' when it deepens, with a style from eighteenth-century Dublin in which phrases of the most commonplace modern slang start into vulgar relief, in a tone of old-fashioned courtesy which varies between the kindly and the sarcastic, he caresses and enchants the auditor with the music of a master of speech."[35]

In describing his path to success as a public speaker, Shaw relates that he had first to overcome agonizing experiences of "excessive nervousness," which he decided could only be cured by repeated exposure to the cause of his fear: "I infested public meetings like an officer afflicted with cowardice, who takes every opportunity of going under fire to get over it and learn his business." He gained practice by intervening at meetings of numerous societies, beginning with the Zetetical, and gradually became known and sought after as a Socialist orator.

Shaw's first public lecture, delivered on 4 May 1884 at the Woolwich Working Men's Club, was called "Thieves" and was described by Shaw as "a demonstration that the proprietor of an unearned income inflicted on the community exactly the same injury as a burglar does." Thereafter "for about twelve years" he "sermonized on Socialism at least three times a fortnight average" in a range of venues, from street corners and marketplaces to the Economic Section of the British Association for the Advancement of Science, where he lectured on 7 September 1888, introducing himself as "a live Socialist redhot 'from the streets.'" He also lectured at both Oxford and Cambridge universities. The audiences for his lectures ranged in size from "tens to thousands." He recalls that the audience at one of his best lectures, delivered in torrents of rain one day in Hyde Park, was entirely comprised of a group of six on-duty policemen: "I can still see their waterproof capes shining in the rain when I shut my eyes," Shaw recalled in *Sixteen Self Sketches*.[36]

The theme of "Thieves," which no doubt owed something to Proudhon's maxim "property is theft," was to recur in Shaw's lectures and other writings. It turns up in the pithy exchange between the gentleman-Socialist Jack Tanner, described as a Member of the Idle Rich Class (M.I.R.C.), and the brigand Mendoza in the Sierra Nevada in the third act of *Man and Superman*.[37] In response to Mendoza's proud introduction of himself as a brigand who lives by robbing the rich, Tanner promptly responds: "I am a gentleman: I live by robbing the poor." (The episode chimes with a passage in William Morris's prose tale "A King's Story," where a captain explains his "craft" to the king by saying: "As the potter lives by making pots, so we live by robbing the poor.")[38] Shaw went on to make further playful use of the theme of burglary in his plays, introducing hilarious and verbosely articulate representatives of the profession in *Misalliance* (1909), *Heartbreak House* (1916–17) and *Too True to Be Good* (1932).

Shaw's career as a "platform spellbinder" adds a remarkable dimension to his personality. It was as though the spirit of a seventeenth-century field preacher such as John Bunyan had been miraculously combined in one person with that of a late-nineteenth-century wit and "man of culture rare," like Oscar Wilde. It was a further stage of evolution in the progress of the Mephistophelean pilgrim. In his 1901 preface to *Three Plays for Puritans* Shaw declared that, "like all dramatists and mimes of genuine vocation," he was "a natural born mountebank," adding: "I leave the delicacies of retirement to those who are gentlemen first and literary workmen afterwards. The cart and trumpet for me."[39]

As far as his future reputation in academia was concerned, Shaw's linking of his mountebank "cart and trumpet" self with that of the dramatist was unwise. It sent out misleading signals about the character of his dramatic work. His self-description in the preface to *Three Plays for Puritans* is appealing in its spirited and defiant differentiation of himself from the gentlemanly belletrist. However, Shaw was creating weapons, here and elsewhere in discussions of his work, that would be used against him by hostile critics such as Raymond Williams. The lectures of the "platform spellbinder" carried clear political messages from a man fired with a mission to do something about the grotesque conditions of inequality, injustice, and suffering in his society. Although the plays engage with political and social ideas, they constantly show theory being upset by life and invariably end not with a message but with irreducible complexity. There is no straightforward progression from the Shavian platform/pulpit to the stage of Shavian comedy.

Attempts to "explain" Shaw's career as a proselytizing Socialist in psychoanalytical terms as his way of sublimating other emotional impulses tend to founder on some indisputable biographical facts. In the peak years of his career as a "platform spellbinder," spanning the late 1880s through 1898, Shaw's love life became even more involved and complicated than it had been in the early years of his affair with Alice Lockett. He was engaged in sexually consummated affairs with both Jenny Patterson and Florence Farr and had entered into numerous other relationships with women, characterized by varying degrees of intensity and romantic passion. In this period Bertha Newcombe, the artist who gave us the memorable visual image of Shaw as public speaker, became one in a long procession of Fabian women—like the troop of hapless, deserted wives who emerge at the gallows scene of the irresistible but faithless highwayman Captain Macheath at the end of John Gay's *Beggar's Opera*—who fell hopelessly in love with Shaw. An allusion to Bertha's succumbing to the charms of her subject is found in the subcaption added to the title "G.B.S., Platform Spellbinder" in *Sixteen Self Sketches*: "Portrait by Bertha Newcombe, spellbound." Far from running away from emotional entanglements in his career as a "platform spellbinder," Shaw entered into a new phase of philandering.

About a year and a half before he sat for his portrait by Newcombe, Shaw had his first meeting with Florence Farr (Mrs. Edward Emery), the actress, novelist, and (from 1894) manager of the Avenue Theatre, London. Farr was educated at Queen's College, London, and after an unsuccessful attempt at teaching (1880–82) she became interested in theater and creative writing. By the time of her meeting with Shaw, her brief and unhappy marriage with actor Edward Emery had ended in a separation. Shaw met the thirty-year-old Florence, whom he described as "a magnetic young woman,"[40] on 26 August 1890 at a picnic held at William Morris's factory in Merton Abbey, a village on the River Wandle in Surrey. Florence's presence at the picnic is probably explained by the fact that she was at this time taking embroidery lessons from May Morris and had become her friend. Shaw recalled that at the Merton Abbey meeting "Florence . . . astonished me by asking would I play the Stranger in [Ibsen's] the Lady from the Sea if she succeeded in getting up a performance. She said that as I had a red beard she thought I would look the part in a pea jacket. I pleaded ineptitude and declined."[41]

By November 1890 a love affair had begun between Shaw and Florence, a development that was to create an explosive situation in his relationship with Jenny Patterson. By this time Janet Achurch, outstanding Shakespearean actress and powerful interpreter of leading roles in plays by Ibsen, had entered Shaw's circle and become the recipient of extravagant letters of admiration and affection from him.

* * *

The emergence of "the coming man" in the late 1880s and early 1890s was accompanied by a considerable rise in the fortunes of the small Shaw family in London. By late 1885 Shaw's mother, Bessie, having thus far conducted private music lessons at her homes, began to find employment as a singing teacher in London high schools. In January 1886 she was appointed singing mistress at the North London Collegiate School for Ladies.[42] As has been noted above, "she delighted in the work and was most successful."[43] Lucy Shaw was by now well established as a professional singer and actress, the career she had embarked upon in December 1879. Corno di Bassetto saw her play the lead in the 789th performance of the musical comedy *Dorothy* on 7 September 1889. He thought her talents were wasted on this piece, which had the "silliest libretto in modern theatrical literature." Under the guise of his nom de plume, Shaw wrote about his sister in a complimentary but despairing vein for the *Star*: "Dorothy herself, a beauteous young lady of distinguished mien, with an immense variety of accents ranging from the finest Tunbridge Wells English (for genteel comedy) to the broadest Irish (for repartee and low comedy) sang without the slightest effort and without the slightest point, and was all the more desperately vapid because she suggested artistic gifts wasting in complacent abeyance."[44]

In *Sixteen Self Sketches* Shaw recorded that his earnings from journalism ranged from £117.0s.3d. in 1885 to "about £500" when his journalistic career ceased in 1898.[45] He earned £150 in 1888, £197 in 1889, £252 in 1890, and £310 in 1893.[46] These earnings, supplemented in a very minor way by those from the novels, did not make him a rich man, but they did provide a regular income. On 4 March 1887 the family moved from 36 Osnaburgh Street to the more elegant quarters at 29 Fitzroy Square in Bloomsbury, where they occupied the third and fourth floors.[47] This was to remain Shaw's home until his marriage in 1898.

9 On Stage

Shaw's career as a playwright was launched at the Royalty Theatre in Dean Street, Soho, London, on 9 December 1892 with the first performance of his play *Widowers' Houses,* in a production by Jacob Thomas Grein's Independent Theatre. Having been a rather late starter in the field of playwriting—he was thirty-six when *Widowers' Houses* was first performed—Shaw's output thereafter was rapid and prolific. By 1897 he had completed seven plays, comprising a group of three works he dubbed "unpleasant" (*Widowers' Houses, The Philanderer,* and *Mrs. Warren's Profession*) and four "pleasant" plays, (*Arms and the Man, Candida, The Man of Destiny,* and *You Never Can Tell*). In 1898 the seven plays were collected and published in two volumes as *Plays Pleasant and Unpleasant.*

By the end of the century Shaw had also completed all of the following group of plays, *The Devil's Disciple, Caesar and Cleopatra* and *Captain Brassbound's Conversion,* which were published in 1901 as *Three Plays for Puritans.* By the end of his career he had written fifty-one dramatic works, including twenty-eight full-length plays, nineteen playlets, and a puppet play. The puppet play *Shakes versus Shav,* which Shaw wrote for performance at the Malvern Festival in 1949, the year before his death, drew on the conventions of *Punch and Judy* to present a final pugilistic bout between Shaw and the figure whose influence pervaded his entire career as a creative writer, William Shakespeare.

At the same time as Shaw was forging a new kind of drama for the English stage, he became one of the most trenchant theater critics of his day, in the weekly columns he wrote from 1895 to 1898 for Frank Harris's periodical *Saturday Review.* In a letter to Tighe Hopkins dated 2 September 1889 Shaw briefly outlined what was to become his agenda for the next decade and beyond. He realized that a new kind of comedy needed an entirely new theatrical culture for its reception:

I have the instinct of an artist; and the impracticable is loathsome to me. But not only has the comedy to be made, but the actors, the manager, the theatre & the audience. Somebody must do these things—somebody whose prodigious conceit towers over all ordinary notions of success—somebody who would blush to win a 600 night run at a West End theatre as a duke would blush to win a goose at a public house raffle—some colossal egotist, in short, like

yrs in hot haste
GBS[1]

This was a remarkably prophetic letter. In the plays of the 1890s Shaw was laying the foundations of the unique contribution he would make to the tradition of comedy in the English theater. At the same time, his critical writings were making the general run of theatrical offerings of the late nineteenth century seem out of date and not in touch with the forward-looking social and intellectual movements of the day, and helping to create a climate of opinion sympathetic to his own aims and directions as a playwright. The bold project announced in the letter to Tighe Hopkins would come to fruition in the early years of the following century with the highly successful collaboration between Shaw, as principal playwright, the theater manager J. E. Vedrenne, and the actor-manager Harley Granville-Barker at the Court Theatre from 1904 to 1907. The dream theater conjured up "in hot haste" in the letter of 1889 became a reality at the Court.

* * *

The summer of 1889 marked the beginning of a reawakened interest on Shaw's part in becoming a playwright. It was not a coincidence that from 1889 until 1893, the dominant cultural influence in his life was Henrik Ibsen. The then highly controversial Norwegian playwright and his growing following in England represent a common thread in various strands of Shaw's professional and personal life at this time. During these years he wrote his major critical essay *The Quintessence of Ibsenism* and engaged in numerous skirmishes with critical opponents of Ibsen, such as the conservative theater critic Clement Scott (whom Shaw described as "the sentimentalist of the *Daily Telegraph*" and whom he caricatured in *The Philanderer* as Cuthbertson), the fashionable playwright Sydney Grundy, and the poet and novelist Robert Buchanan (who described Ibsen in a ferocious essay as "Zola with a wooden leg").[2] By 1893 the new "fashionable cult of Ibsenism,"[3] as Shaw later called it, had become a subject of comic and satirical treatment in *The Philanderer*, the second act of which is set in an imaginary "Ibsen Club" in London. Janet Achurch and Florence Farr, the two new alluring female stars who entered the firmament of the Fabian Don Juan during this period—the first of whom he met in the summer of 1889 and the second the following summer—were directly involved with Ibsen's arrival on the English theatrical scene.

The work that became *The Quintessence of Ibsenism* began its public life as a two-hour lecture to the Fabian Society delivered at St. James's Restaurant on 18 July 1890, with Annie Besant chairing the meeting. Edward Pease records of this "high-water mark in Fabian lectures" that "the effect on the audience was overwhelming. It was 'briefly discussed' by a number of speakers, but they seemed as out of place as a debate after an oratorio."[4] The lecture contained a political punch for Socialists, and not everybody in Socialist circles was as favorably impressed as some of the Fabians. Ibsen was not a Socialist, Shaw declared, and the way in which some of his plays showed the downfall of high-minded idealists carried an oblique message for hardline Socialists who refused to recognize political realities. *The Quintessence Of Ibsenism* was published in revised and expanded form the following year, after the production of *Ghosts* and the outcry it prompted, which Shaw was able to report and comment upon in the published version.

Shaw had first been attracted to Ibsen the dramatic poet rather than to Ibsen the "social" dramatist of the middle period who created such a stir in the 1890s in England and elsewhere with works such as *Ghosts* and *A Doll's House*. (His report of his chattering and eating of caramels "backstage" during the reading of a translation of *A Doll's House*, in which he took part in 1885, suggests less than riveted attention to that play in his first acquaintance with it.) His interest in Ibsen was more keenly awakened in 1889 when he was introduced to the poetic drama *Peer Gynt*. Shaw was intrigued by this work, perhaps seeing in its playful and fantastical hero—with his role-playing and kaleidoscopic changes of career in an unsuccessful search for the essential "Gyntian self"—some echoes of his own experiences and assumptions of different personae. He even embarked on a translation of the play, but this turned out to be an unfinished experiment. In a letter to Ellen Terry he likened himself to the madman in *Peer Gynt*, "who thought himself a pen and wanted someone to write with him. I want to be *used*, since use is life."[5]

In some ways Shaw's experiential response to Ibsen is better conveyed in some of the reviews he wrote of performances of the plays than in his exegetical essays in *The Quintessence of Ibsenism*. Of a performance of *The Wild Duck*, for example, he wrote, in a way that shows his recognition of the humorous and ironic dimensions in Ibsen's drama at a time when hostile critics were persistently characterizing Ibsen as the grim Norwegian: "Where shall I find an epithet magnificent enough for The Wild Duck! To sit there getting deeper and deeper into that Ekdal home, and getting deeper and deeper into your own life all the time, until you forget that you are in a theatre; to look on with horror and pity at a profound tragedy, shaking with laughter all the time at an irresistible comedy."[6]

In contrast to such a response, *The Quintessence of Ibsenism* seems rather too schematic and neglectful of the aesthetic properties of the plays, the latter omission being a deliberate and, of course, theoretically questionable choice on Shaw's part. However, critics of the essay tend to underestimate its worth and significance as an account of Ibsen's thematic preoccupations. The relevance of this essay both to Ibsen and Shaw is well expressed by J. L. Wisenthal's comment that "Ibsen's special message, the quintessence of Ibsenism for Shaw, is that morality is relative, not absolute. . . . What Shaw stresses in Ibsen's plays is that morality is not fixed but evolving."[7] This is an idea that chimed with Shavian themes in the early novels, which permeates his thinking about creative evolution, and is frequently reflected in his dramatic work.

Shaw entered the debate over Ibsen at a time when the Norwegian playwright's work had become a focal point of heated disputation not only about theatrical values and the social role of the theater but also about the moral and religious foundations of society itself. Ibsen's plays touched the nerve centers of major anxieties in late-nineteenth-century English society. They challenged sexual hierarchies and traditional gender boundaries. Moral and ethical values handed down by the church were being questioned by characters such as Nora in *A Doll's House*, who, like a Kierkegaardian existentialist, wanted to shape her own religion, to find out for herself what was good. The Christian virtues of socially prescribed ideals of duty, of unselfishness and sacrifice were seen in some of the plays—most powerfully in *Ghosts*—as destructive of human vitality and growth.

In Ibsen's plays an unruly Dionysian god was challenging the authority of Christian orthodoxy in the bourgeois doll's house. This was the Ibsen recognized and hailed by Shaw in *The Quintessence of Ibsenism*. He did not try to enroll Ibsen in the ranks of the Socialists, and he did not try to imitate Ibsen's style in his plays. What Ibsen presented to Shaw was not a stylistic model but the possibility of a type of drama that engaged seriously and imaginatively with moral and philosophical issues in ways that presented a sharp contrast to the great majority of the theatrical entertainments that made up the staple diet of the late-nineteenth-century theater.

Apart from his attempt at a translation of *Peer Gynt*, another sign of Shaw's interest in reviving his playwriting ambitions in 1889 was his beginning of a play called *The Cassone*, of which a fragmentary relic has survived in manuscript. The example of Ibsen may also have been at work here since Shaw began writing *The Cassone* two weeks after seeing *A Doll's House*. This work seems to have been planned as some form of drawing-room comedy, with extramarital flirtation and jealousy among its themes. A scrap of dialogue from the work, between Lady Sybil and Teddy, gives a foretaste of Lady Britomart's stern talk with her son Stephen at the beginning of Shaw's Edwardian play *Major Barbara*, and her remonstrance about his fiddling with his tie:

> Lady Sybil: Teddy, I want to speak to you rather particularly for a few minutes.
> Teddy: Oh bother! What is it? I've got some things to look after.
> Lady S: Yes: you have got something to look after; and I am going to tell you what it is. Sit down there; and stop fiddling with your hat.
> Teddy: (*sits*) Oh bother!
> Lady S: Your wife—
> Teddy: Oh damn![8]

The Cassone seems to have been partly inspired by tensions in Shaw's relations with William and Frances Archer. On 23 June Shaw recorded that in a meeting between him and Archer that morning they had "talked about Ibsen and some unlucky offense I had given Mrs. Archer by going on about Miss Achurch."[9] Shaw felt that Archer was losing his creative freedom in his marriage with Frances, whose conventional attitudes appear to have been, not surprisingly, upset by Shaw's frankly declared infatuation with the married actress.

* * *

On 7 June 1889 Shaw, accompanied by his mother and William Archer, attended the first performance of *A Doll's House* at the Novelty Theatre, produced by Charles Charrington (who played Torvald) opposite his wife, Janet Achurch, as Nora. In an unsigned review published in the *Manchester Guardian*, Shaw wrote that Janet Achurch brought "her charm, her magnetism, and her instinctive intelligence" to the role.[10] Having sat next to Janet at a celebration dinner in honor of the play at the Novelty Theatre on 16 June, he began writing extravagant letters of adoration to her. A short while before her departure on 5 July for an Australasian tour with her husband, Charles Charrington, Shaw rhapsodized about her effect on him and declared that her absence in the Antipodes could not destroy his "starry" love for her: "The world has vanished: the gardens of heaven surround me. . . . Away with you to Australia—for ever if you will."[11]

On the day after their meeting he wrote to her, enclosing a copy of his lecture "Acting, by one who does not believe in it," and passed on his mother's intuitive comment about the actress after seeing her play the part of Nora: "That one is a *divil.*"[12]

Whether or not it was a consummated relationship is uncertain, but Shaw's friendship with the charming "*divil*" became extraordinarily intimate. She was clever—"speaks German like a native, & writes capital English dialogue,"[13] Shaw remarked about her in a letter to T. Fisher Unwin—and an outstandingly gifted actress. However, as their relationship developed, Shaw became painfully aware of her struggles with alcohol and morphine addiction; his early raptures tended to give way to repeated laments about the wasting of her powers through these habits. In one of his letters he vividly described what he was seeing as a terrible progression in her days: "1, boredom, leading to whisky; 2, whisky, leading to maudlin hysteria; 3, maudlin hysteria, leading to morphia; 4, morphia, leading to vulgar abuse from me." He went on to remind her of an episode in her life she would probably have preferred to forget: "Do you remember once adventuring forth with a penny only in your purse, and finishing up in Kensington Gore by hurling a bus conductor from his perch into the mud, beating him with your gloves, jumping on him, and leaving him for dead because the fare had been raised in consequence of the illuminations?"[14]

In 1894 Shaw wrote Janet "a most private letter" in which he attempted to summarize his attitude toward her:

> I have two sorts of feeling for you, one valuable to you and the other worthless. The worthless one is an ordinary man-and-woman hankering after you—the word is not a nice one; but I do not want to give the feeling any fine airs just now. As you know, you are very handsome and clever, and rich in a fine sort of passionate ardor which I enjoy, in an entirely selfish way, like any other man. . . . But I have another feeling for you. As an artist and a trained critic, I have a very strong sense of artistic faculty and its value. I have, as you know, a high opinion of your power as an actress; and just as I want to have my own powers in action and to preserve them from waste or coarsening, so I have sympathetically a strong desire to see your powers in action, and a dislike to see them wasted or coarsened.[15]

Later in 1894 Shaw wrote *Candida*, the play in which Janet Achurch was to create the leading role.

Having seen the Charringtons off at the beginning of their tour to Australia at Charing Cross Station on 5 July 1889, Shaw himself, borrowing a suitcase from Jenny Patterson, traveled on the twenty-fifth to Bayreuth for the Wagner Festival, which he wrote enthusiastically about in the *Star*. His touring activities in Germany—which included a river journey on the Rhine and a visit to Nuremberg, where he saw a collection of instruments of torture ("an awful sight")[16]—provided ideas for the activities of the idle rich tourists visiting the Rhine in the first act of *Widowers' Houses*. In the opening speech of the play, the gentlemanly connoisseur Mr. Cokane recommends a visit to Nuremberg to see "the finest instruments of torture in the world," an image that foreshadows the play's portrayal of the underlying brutality of the elegant social world of the rack-renting landlord Mr. Sartorius and his family in Shaw's first publicly performed play.

* * *

In his summary diary of 1884, Shaw had written that he "set to work on a drama on a plot of W. Archer's, who was to collaborate. I wrote two acts and dropped it."[17] This was the play that, after several stops and starts during the passing of eight years, was to become *Widowers' Houses*. The germ of the plot was taken by Archer from an early play by Émile Augier entitled *Ceinture Dorée*. Judging by Archer's own account, the plot idea (which was radically transformed in Shaw's handling of it) was probably the extent of his contribution to the "collaboration." Archer recalled that,"having handed the scenario to Shaw, I heard no more about it for six weeks or two months," whereupon Shaw reappeared saying he had used up all the plot and asked for more. Archer thought this was impossible because the plot he had supplied was an organic whole: asking for more was like asking a sculptor to add more arms and legs to an already completed statue. "So I had to leave him," writes Archer, "as we say in Scotland, 'to make a kirk or a mill of it.'"[18]

When Archer saw a further draft of Shaw's play, which was neither kirk nor mill to his liking, he was amazed to find that "my sentimental heroine . . . was transmuted into a termagant who boxed the ears of her maidservant." Shaw had invested a character who in a conventional Victorian well-made play would have been the ingénue figure—the innocent young lady who eventually marries the handsome young man—with a forthright, cool intelligence, a manipulative use of sex appeal, and a ferocious temper that is occasionally combined with erotic feelings and intentions.

This was Shaw's first stage "heroine," Blanche Sartorius, whose role was first performed by Florence Farr, Jenny Patterson's archrival, from late in 1890, after Annie Besant had "gone to Theosophy." The cool self-possession and frank sexuality shown in the characterization of Blanche was clearly influenced by Florence; and the ferocious temper could have been based on firsthand experience with Jenny and Janet Achurch. Shaw also mentions a scene he had witnessed during a midnight walk through Wigmore Street, of one woman physically bullying another, as having influenced his creation of the notorious episode in which Blanche beats her maid in *Widowers' Houses*.[19] The "unladylike" behavior of Blanche was a central point of contemporary criticism of the play.

The events of the first part of Archer's story about the genesis of *Widowers' Houses*—his suggestion about the plot and the writing of the first two acts—took place from 18 August to 18 November 1884. Shaw resumed work on the play briefly in August 1885, and in the autumn of 1887, when it was again abandoned after Archer had ridiculed it.[20] Five years later, on 29 July 1892, Shaw reports that he had begun to get his papers in order (a task in which he was assisted later that day by Jenny Patterson, who made a collection of all his old articles in the *World* for him) and "came across the comedy which I began in 1885 [*sic* for 1884] and left aside."[21] He set to work to finish it the following day. The decision to give the play its biblical-sounding title *Widowers' Houses* was made by Shaw on 20 October 1892; previous working titles included *The Way to a Woman's Heart*, *Rheingold*, and *Rhinegold*.[22] One week later he met J. T. Grein to discuss casting for the forthcoming production. They had trouble finding a suitable actor for the part of Lickcheese, the scruffy rent collector whose role anticipates that of Doolittle in *Pygmalion*. In a serendipitous moment during one of the early rehearsals, the "wonderful comedian" James Welch popped his head in the door and asked, "Any actor wanted here?" He was immediately enlisted for the role, in which he made a great success.[23]

The play's premiere at the Royalty Theatre, Soho, on Friday, 9 December 1892, was followed by a second and final scheduled performance the following Tuesday. According to Grein (whose account is supported by others), the play had "an uproarious reception" at its opening. Shaw told Lady Gregory much later that he remembered "half the House applauding, half booing."[24] King's College Cambridge Fellow G. Lowes Dickinson, whom Shaw had met when he presented a lecture to the Cambridge Fabian Society on 18 February 1888, found the play "miserably dreary and unconvincing" and remembered "a great deal of noise and hissing" before the pale figure of Shaw himself appeared to make a defiant speech.[25]

Shaw may well have taken grim pleasure in the way in which newspaper reviews resembled the outcry over Ibsen's *Ghosts* the previous year. In their revelations of the dark underbelly of middle-class nineteenth-century society, both Shaw and Ibsen were seen as committing a form of indecent exposure on the stage. *Ghosts*, according to a leading article in the *Daily Telegraph*, was "an open drain; a loathsome sore unbandaged; a dirty act done publicly; a lazar house with all its doors and windows open."[26] Similarly the *Athenaeum* said of *Widowers' Houses* that "Mr Shaw's world has not rags enough to cover its nudity. He aims to show with Zolaesque exactitude that middle-class life is foul and leprous." The reviewer in the *Speaker* complained that "the mere word 'mortgage' suffices to turn hero into villain," and the *Sunday Sun* decided the whole play was a "revelation of a distorted and myopic outlook on society."[27] All this was hardly surprising in a world where standards of acceptable dramatic fare were set by journalists such as Clement Scott, one of the leading theater critics of the day, who contended that "the play you witness on the stage *after* dinner should never exceed the limits of decency you allow *at* dinner." There was no sympathy in Scott's mind for "nasty, dirty, impure" matter such as that portrayed in the new "Problem Plays."[28] Scott is likely to have been the author of the leading article on *Ghosts* referred to earlier.

* * *

Before his meeting, in August 1890, with the "magnetic young woman" Florence Farr, who was to become his leading lady in *Widowers' Houses*, Shaw had noticed her acting in a production at Bedford Park of a play called *A Sicilian Idyll* by the Dublin-born physician and playwright John Todhunter, son of the owner of Todhunter's ironworks in Dublin, where Shaw's father had been employed from 1838 to 1845.[29] In one of his last Corno di Bassetto columns in the *Star* (9 May 1890) Shaw commented on Florence's "striking and appropriate good looks" in the role of the shepherdess Amaryllis.[30] A beguiling 1890 photograph of Florence in her costume for this role, showing her reclining in a hammock, bore the inscription: "Do I inspire thee?" The answer for Shaw was definitely affirmative. During October Shaw was arousing Jenny Patterson's jealousy by his frequent meetings with Florence, with whom he was discussing Ibsen, and trying to persuade her to put together a production of *Rosmersholm* (in which she was to play the leading female role) instead of *The Lady from the Sea*.

On 15 November 1890 he had his "first really intimate conversation" with Florence, and thereafter the diary records numerous late-evening meetings with her, after which he either caught the last train home or "lost it" and had to walk.[31] Early in the following year Jenny Patterson went on a three-month tour to the Near East with Georgina Gurly, Bessie Shaw's half-sister, during which time Shaw's intimacy with Florence deepened. It was almost certainly during this time, the winter of 1890–91, that what Shaw was later to describe as his "Harrisian adventures" (experiences of sexual intercourse) with Florence began.[32] According to Shaw, she was not only "clever, good-natured and very goodlooking" but also unusually forthright and uninhibited about sex.[33]

She became a most significant figure in Shaw's early career as a playwright in several ways. Apart from her influence in shaping the personality and performing the role of Blanche Sartorius, her character is also reflected in the portrayal of Grace Tranfield in Shaw's second play *The Philanderer*. She was also the manager at the Avenue Theatre during the 1894 season that included the first production of Shaw's *Arms and the Man*, in which she played the spirited and sexy maidservant Louka.

When Jenny Patterson returned from her tour in the Near East, her "spies" had evidently made her aware of what was going on between Florence Farr and her wayward lover, and she made her feelings clear. The fury of a woman scorned was to become a very familiar experience for Shaw during the next phase of his love affairs. His situation in a new love triangle; his dialogues about love, sexuality, and friendship with May Morris (with whom he was continuing his very close relationship) and Jenny Patterson; and his involvement in the Ibsen debates—all supplied him with rich material for plot and theme in *The Philanderer*. In this play he also launched his first satirical attack on the medical profession and vivisection in his portrayal of the hapless Dr. Paramore, whose celebrated discovery, "Paramore's Disease," is conclusively shown by another researcher to be a nonexistent medical condition.

Strong signs of Shaw's fretfulness under the yoke of Jenny Patterson's importunate claims on his affections and loyalty appear in his diary and letters during 1891. After Jenny's return from her travels, a "fearful scene about FE" (Florence Farr was normally referred to in Shaw's diary by the initials of her married name, Florence Emery) occurred at Shaw's first reunion with her at Brompton Square on 27 April.[34] Four days later, on 1 May, he wrote to Florence, asserting his passionate commitment to his relationship with her and expressing "contemptuous fury" about Jenny:

> I shall get to bed now without staying to discuss that other relation [with Jenny Patterson]. At this moment I am in a contemptuous fury & vehemently assert that your Christmas estimate of it was the right one. Not for forty thousand such relations will I forego one forty thousandth part of my relation with you. . . . The silly triumph with which she takes, with the air of a conqueror, that which I have torn out of my own entrails for her almost brings the lightning down upon her. . . . You must give me back my peace. . . . The hart pants for cooling streams.[35]

But neither the "fearful scene" nor this May Day declaration from the overheated "hart" were sufficient to bring about the end of the affair with Jenny. The love triangle in which Shaw divided his attentions between Florence, the cooler, university-educated, advanced New Woman and Ibsenite, and her stormy rival, the abject but tempestuous and demanding Jenny, remained in place for more than two and a half years.

Shaw was quite critical of Florence Farr's acting, and eventually would tire of her increasing immersion in Eastern mysticism and the occult. Nevertheless, like her other admirers, such as W. B. Yeats, Shaw recognized and admired her distinctive genius and considerable yet never fully realized potential as an actress. In his letters to her during 1891–92, elaborate compliment ("my best and dearest love, the regenerator of my heart, the holiest joy of my soul")[36] alternated with castigation of her failure to commit herself to the hard work and patient refinement of technique necessary to make herself a serious actress. They both, he told her, belonged to a special order of genius in the evolutionary scheme of things, still "immature at thirty" and needing to work laboriously for excellence, but eventually superior to a second order of genius produced by "an accidental excess of some faculty—musical, muscular, sexual," the possessors of which achieve success without effort. If only she would work on *her* genius, the letter modestly suggests, they would be perfect mates. The same letter shows that it was her exchanges of opinion with Shaw about literary matters that elicited from him one of his most interesting early statements of self-definition as an artist, public figure, and future comic dramatist: "You are wrong to scorn farcical comedy. It is by jingling the bells of a jester's cap that I, like Heine, have made people listen to me. All genuine intellectual work is humorous."[37]

* * *

"*The Philanderer* began with a slice of life," Shaw told his biographer Archibald Henderson in 1925.[38] The "slice of life" that provided material for the first scene of the play—and also precipitated the beginning of the end of Shaw's relationship with Jenny Patterson—was this time "a most shocking scene" that occurred at Florence Farr's apartment on the evening of Saturday, 4 February 1893. Shaw had already had an eventful day. In the morning he had called on the attractive American-born actress, novelist, and playwright Elizabeth Robins to interview her concerning a production of Ibsen's *The Master Builder* in which she was involved. The interview (never published) did not go well, and Shaw recorded in his diary that "Miss Robins got rather alarmed about [it] and swore she would shoot me if I said anything she did not approve of." Late in the evening, evidently overcome by her feelings of jealousy and betrayal, Jenny Patterson burst in on a tête-à-tête between Shaw and Florence, and a violent quarrel ensued: "In the evening I went to FE; and JP burst in on us very late in the evening. There was a most shocking scene, JP being violent and using atrocious language. At last I sent FE out of the room, having to restrain JP by force from attacking her. I was two hours getting her out of the house and I did not get her home to Brompton Square until near 1, nor did I get away myself until 3."[39]

Following this incident—echoed in the opening scene of *The Philanderer*—which left Shaw "horribly tired and shocked and upset," he made Jenny write a letter to him expressing regret and "promising not to annoy FE again." The letter was delivered to Florence Farr by May Morris on the following day. The Shaw-Patterson affair was over, though Jenny still persevered with her claims on him and continued her association with the family. On 22 February Shaw burned a letter from her "at the first glance" and later in the year took to deliberately leaving the house at Fitzroy Square to avoid seeing her on her visits to the family.[40]

The quarrel between Shaw and Jenny Patterson was carried on in a curiously public manner in the course of a controversy about a trial relating to the so-called Wormwood Scrubbs Murder. In July 1893 Constable George Samuel Cooke was sentenced to death for the murder of Maud Smith, a prostitute with whom he had been frequently consorting. Cooke's unsuccessful defense was that Smith had provoked him with incessant nagging after he had wished to discontinue the relationship, which was threatening his career. Shaw contributed two letters to correspondence about the case that appeared in the *Star*. In the first, published on 18 July 1893, he conceded that "it is not good public policy to allow people to kill one another on 'provocation,' or on any ground but that of urgent defence of their own lives." On the other hand, he claimed, the case exposed the lack of defining rules about such cases: the murder was an instance of "lynch law produced by anarchy." There were laws against actual physical assault, but none about "unlimited privileges to infuriate."[41] Public sentiment led the heartbroken woman to make claims on Cooke that were regarded as natural for a wife. But what are the claims of a mistress on a man who had formerly loved her but now wishes to be free of her?

Shaw's first letter provoked several replies from "lady correspondents," one of whom (despite the fact that the letter is signed "E") was almost certainly Jenny Patterson. On 24 July 1893 Shaw's diary records that "he wrote a letter to *The Star* in reply to one written by JP about the murder case." The letter signed "E," published on 21 July, identified the writer as having been in a similar position to the spurned Maud Smith, saying, "I know too well the feeling when a girl knows she is no more loved by the one she has given her all to, but is only a thing to be cast aside like a toy which has been tired of."[42] In his second letter, published on 25 July, Shaw dissociatd himself from idle side taking in the case, insisting that "at the bottom of all the unreason, however, will be found the old theory that an act of sexual intercourse gives the parties a life-long claim on one another for better or worse."[43] Shaw was clearly using this occasion for a declaration of his independence from Jenny Patterson.

A decade before the breakup of the affair with Patterson, Shaw composed a musical setting to Shelley's poem "When the Lamp Is Shattered." The setting survives, with Shaw's handwritten copy of the poem from the Rossetti edition of Shelley's works.[44] Shaw must have known the poem very well; its third stanza has a sad relevance to the situation of the weaker party, Jenny, in the love affair that was shattered in 1893:

When hearts have once mingled
Love first leaves the well-built nest;
The weak one is singled
To endure what it once possessed.
O Love! Who bewailest
The frailty of all things here,
Why choose you the frailest
For your cradle, your home and your bier?

The theme of this stanza seems to have become part of the dialogue between Shaw and Jenny in 1886. With reference to herself in one of her letters, Jenny exclaimed: "Alas! It's the poor weak one that suffers all now."[45] Yet possession was precisely what Shaw resolutely refused to submit to in his relations with women. The cruelty of the fate that befalls the rejected "weak one" in a love relation is part of the emotional fabric of the final tableau of *The Philanderer*, in which the company gathers round Julia, the disappointed mistress of Leonard Charteris, the play's philanderer, feeling "*the presence of a keen sorrow.*"

On 14 March 1893, a little over a month after the "shocking scene" at Florence Farr's apartment, Shaw bought for one shilling a notebook "to begin new play in."[46] Later that month he traveled down to Oxted, in Surrey, to stay with the Salts, where, on 29 March, his diary records: "After breakfast went up to the Common by Rockfield Rd. and selected a spot on the West Heath, near the orphanage, where I lay down and got to work on the new play which I have resolved to call *The Philanderer*."[47] Shaw wrote quite a large amount of the play in various outdoor locations, including by the lake in Regent's Park under an umbrella in the rain, by the Thames at Richmond and Hammersmith, and in nearby Ravenscourt Park while in the company of Florence Farr. Florence must have known that she was, in a sense, *in* the work he was writing, serving as the inspiration for Grace Tranfield, Charteris's other mistress in the play. While he wrote, she passed the time looking at the peacocks in the park.

In the latter half of June 1893, the play was substantially revised on the advice of the Irish-born playwright, journalist, and art critic Lady Colin Campbell, whom Shaw had met in 1890. Lady Campbell had wisely seen that Shaw's original third act was really the beginning of a new play. Shaw wrote a much more satisfactory substitute act in a remarkably short space of time, completing *The Philanderer* on 27 June. It had to wait until 20 February 1905 for its first public performance and until 30 March 1898 for even a copyright performance. Despite Shaw's frequently expressed dislike of the play, the stageworthiness of his "extremely advanced farcical comedy," as he described it in a letter to Henry Arthur Jones in 1894, has been well proven ever since.[48]

Charteris, the breezy, amusing, clever yet heartless philanderer—and charismatic object of female attention and rivalry in the play—is clearly, in some respects, a self-portrait of Shaw. But he is also, like some of the characters in the novels, an instrument of self-examination and criticism. As the leading "philosopher" of the Ibsen Club, where the second act of *The Philanderer* is set, Charteris runs rings around everybody else in argument, joyously exposing the gaps between advanced "Ibsenite" principles and the actual behavior of club members. A main source of satirical comedy in the play arises from the clash between the Ibsen Club ideals of undemanding, rational comradeship and freedom in relations between the sexes, on the one hand, and ordinary human passions, jealousies, and demands for commitment and proprietorship in love, on the other. Yet Charteris is frequently seen in a very critical light in the play, especially in the speeches of Julia Craven, the character modeled on Jenny Patterson, who at one point calls him a "miserable little plaster saint" and draws on Dr. Paramore's profession as a medical researcher for a metaphor about Charteris's ruthlessly analytical, dissecting mind when she flings at him the accusation: "It is you who are the vivisector: a far crueller, more wanton vivisector than he." Shaw hated the practice of vivisection, and his use of it here forms a powerful trope in the critical rhetoric directed against Charteris.

The portrayal of Charteris, with its obvious echoes of Shaw's own experiences, seems another manifestation of his acknowledgment of the Dr. Jekyll and Mr. Hyde-like double persona he had discerned in himself in his relationship with Alice Lockett, in which he could see a cynical, critical self standing back and mocking another self engaged in love and romance. Through Charteris Shaw seems once again to be imaginatively scrutinizing the apparently heartless side of himself that was displayed in Trefusis in *An Unsocial Socialist* (which was originally entitled *The Heartless Man*). Conversely, through the highly emotional, jealous, and possessive Julia Craven he makes another protest about the importunate Jenny Patterson. Yet the critical animus generated against Charteris in the play continues to grow as Julia becomes an increasingly sympathetic character and the object of "*keen sorrow*" at the end. Shaw also gave Charteris's other mistress, Grace Tranfield, the following line, prominently placed near the complex end of the play: "Never make a hero of a philanderer." In autobiographical terms the play can be read as both a self-justifying and self-incriminating apologia.

* * *

Neither *The Philanderer* nor *Mrs. Warren's Profession,* its immediate successor in Shaw's dramatic works, succeeded in helping to establish a firm footing for Shaw in his career on the English stage in the early 1890s. *Widowers' Houses* had had its brief and controversial run of only two performances. In 1898, looking back at the fortunes of *Widowers' Houses* and the two following plays, Shaw wrote: "I had not achieved a success; but I had provoked an uproar; and the sensation was so agreeable that I resolved to try again."[49] He went on to explain that the "demands on the most expert sort of high comedy acting" that *The Philanderer* made were beyond the resources at J. T. Grein's disposal. The part of Charteris could have been done, Shaw said, by Charles Wyndham, a successful light comic actor of the day, but his overtures to Wyndham about the play were unsuccessful.

The next play, *Mrs. Warren's Profession,* with its provocative thematic mix of prostitution and incest, was too risky a venture for even Grein to undertake. In a letter to Grein dated 12 December 1893 in which he discusses the casting of the play, Shaw wrote: "I do not think there is the least chance of the play being licensed."[50] Grein apparently agreed and did not go ahead with any production. Even the copyright reading of 1898 was threatened by the censor, obliging Shaw to make extensive cuts in order to obtain a license for the play. It was first presented privately by the Stage Society at the New Lyric Club on 5 and 6 January 1902, with Fanny Brough as Mrs. Warren, Madge McIntosh as Vivie, and Harley Granville-Barker as Frank. At the first performance of the play in America, which took place on 27 October 1905 at the Hyperion Theater in New Haven, Connecticut, the mayor ordered police to close the theater because of the play's "indecency." The first licensed public production of the play in England occurred in 1925, when it was presented by the Macdona Players under the direction of Esmé Percy at the Prince of Wales Theatre, Birmingham, on 27 October. It has been frequently revived, an early twenty-first century production being that directed by Sir Peter Hall at the Strand Theatre, London, that opened on 2 October 2002.

The first act of *Mrs. Warren's Profession* was composed in a remarkable explosion of creative activity that occurred over ten days at the end of August 1893. In the first two weeks of the month, having recently dispatched his second letter to the *Star* about the Wormwood Scrubbs murder case (which refers to the subject of prostitution in its penultimate sentence) Shaw traveled to Switzerland, where he attended an International Socialist Congress in Zurich and experienced some undistinguished "Swiss art, musical and pictorial." On the fifteenth he returned to a week of what outwardly seemed rather "desultory" (the word appears twice in the diary entries for that week) activities in London. On the sixteenth he remarked on the weather as being "terribly hot," and much of the week was spent out of doors, twice in the company of Florence Farr.[51]

On the afternoon of the eighteenth, continuing during these August dog days the curious lull in activities before what was to be a creative storm, Shaw had a swim at the Hampstead Swimming Bath and, having bought some nuts, milk, and a pair of nutcrackers, went up to the Upper Heath, where he lay "idling and sleeping" till 3:30 p.m. Later he met Florence and they attended the Earl's Court Exhibition at St. James's Park, where they saw a water show and went down a water chute together. They then returned to Florence's apartment, from where he returned home on the last train but one. (Shaw had by this time relinquished his practice of recording sexual episodes by numbers in brackets; individual incidents of "Harrisian adventures" have thus become a subject of speculation.) The following day was passed in much the same way as its predecessor, with Shaw again returning to Florence's apartment after a lazy day on Hampstead Heath. On the twentieth Shaw felt giddy, possibly having been affected by the sun the day before. But on this day he records the beginning of the composition of *Mrs. Warren's Profession*: "At last succeeded in beginning a new play."[52]

Although the outward events of the week leading up to this new development in his creative career were unremarkable enough, the period included two significant acts of reading by Shaw. In Richmond Park on 17 August 1893 he read a copy printed for private circulation of Pinero's *The Second Mrs. Tanqueray*, which had been lent to him by William Archer. *The Second Mrs. Tanqueray* belongs to a flourishing literary, operatic, and dramatic tradition of works in the second half of the nineteenth century about fallen women, or the Woman with a Past, to which Shaw would give a revolutionary twist in *Mrs. Warren's Profession*. On the day in which he actually began the new play he had returned in his reading to his childhood favorite, *The Pilgrim's Progress*, which, as he wrote on 20 August 1893, "still retains its fascination for me."[53]

The rather prurient interest taken in the second half of the nineteenth century with the subject of the Fallen Woman, or the Woman with a Past, found expression in numerous cultural forms. The literary tradition associated with the theme was initiated by Alexandre Dumas fils with his 1848 novel *La Dame aux Camélias,* which tells the story of Marguerite Gautier, a beautiful Parisian courtesan who has an ill-fated romance with a young aristocrat named Armand. Dumas turned this novel into a successful play, *Camille,* which was first performed in 1852. By the following year Verdi had created his opera *La Traviata,* based on the story. In 1893, as Shaw was composing *Mrs. Warren's Profession,* Oscar Wilde and Arthur Wing Pinero had created variations on the theme with their plays *A Woman of No Importance* and *The Second Mrs. Tanqueray.*

Reporting his progress on *Mrs. Warren's Profession* to William Archer on 30 August 1893, Shaw breezily wrote: "I have finished the first act of my new play, in which I have skilfully blended the plot of The Second Mrs. Tanqueray with that of The Cenci. It will be just the thing for the I.T. [Independent Theatre]."[54] The truth, of course, was that it was impossible for the Independent or any other theater to produce the play at that time. In *Mrs. Warren's Profession* Shaw not only made explicit the subject of prostitution—which is glossed over and glamorized in most works belonging to the tradition to which the play bears a critical relation—but also followed Shelley's example in *The Cenci* of linking incest with corrupt patriarchal systems of wealth and power in general. In the early draft of the play, a passage of dialogue (later toned down and made more plausible by having its intention conveyed in a stage direction) refers very explicitly to the incest theme when Mrs. Warren expostulates with her old roué friend Sir George Crofts about his interest in marrying her daughter Vivie:

> Mrs W: . . . How do you know that the girl maynt be your own daughter, eh?
>
> Crofts: . . . How do *you* know that that maynt be one of the fascinations of the thing?

The play also contains a scene in which it is revealed that the two young lovers, Vivie and Frank, are possibly either full or half sister and brother.

The plot of *Mrs. Warren's Profession* had been suggested to Shaw by Janet Achurch, with whom he had resumed contact after her return from touring with her husband through Australia and New Zealand in the spring of 1892. Janet was writing a play called *Mrs. Daintree's Daughter,* based on a story by Guy de Maupassant called *Yvette.* Maupassant's tale belongs to the genre of works about fallen women, but with the added complication of giving the courtesan figure an innocent daughter, who, after attempting suicide upon learning about her mother's trade, eventually shows every sign of following the same path. Shaw carried out further work on the play during a three-week stay with the Webbs at a favorite retreat of theirs in the west of England, The

Argoed, a house near Tintern in the Wye Valley, acquired by Beatrice's father in 1865, a place described by Shaw as "amazingly beautiful in all directions." He sent Janet an account of the way he was handling the *Yvette* material:

> The play progresses bravely; but it has left the original lines. I have made the daughter the heroine, and the mother a most deplorable old rip (saving your presence). The great scene will be the crushing of the mother by the daughter. I retain the old roué, but keep him restrained by a continual doubt as to whether the heroine may not be his daughter. . . . The girl is quite an original character. The mother, uncertain who the girl's father is, keeps all the old men at bay by telling each one he is the parent. The second act is half finished and wholly planned. How does your version progress?[55]

A quest for Christian salvation is not a part of the future suggested for Vivie Warren at the end of *Mrs. Warren's Profession*. In fact, she settles down to actuarial work, conveyancing and law in city chambers, with an "eye on the Stock Exchange." However, Shaw's reading of *The Pilgrim's Progress* just as he began writing the play seems to have left a powerful, if obliquely expressed, imprint on the work. Vivie is turning her back on a tainted world just as Christian does in Bunyan's allegory, flying from his house and family with his fingers in his ears, crying, "Life, life, eternal life." Leading up to the end of Shaw's play is a series of renunciations on Vivie's part: she rejects the disgusting Sir George Crofts, partner with Mrs. Warren in the exploitation of young women in a European chain of high-class brothels; the romance with Frank, the "agreeable young spark, wholly good-for-nothing,"[56] as Shaw described him; the pleasures of art and culture, which the artistic family friend Praed urges her to enjoy; and, finally, after a harrowing quarrel, her own mother.

Shaw was drawing on deep impulses in his own personality in the writing of this play. The young woman who resolutely sits down to work at her desk in the final scene, with broken relationships but recovered integrity, can be seen as a self-portrait of the playwright, counterbalancing that of the fickle philanderer Charteris in the preceding play. Shaw's later statement that in creating Vivie Warren he was following a suggestion of Beatrice Webb's that he should "put on the stage a real modern lady of the governing class" seems to provide a rather artificial and oversimplified account of the genesis of this character, omitting as it does some potent autobiographical and literary ingredients.[57]

10 A Taste of Success

In 1894 Shaw had his first taste of substantial success as a playwright with the production of his play *Arms and the Man* at Florence Farr's Avenue Theatre. Both *The Philanderer* and *Mrs. Warren's Profession* had turned out to be like documents in a time capsule, to be opened under more propitious circumstances of social, cultural, and theatrical history. Revolutionary as it was in its themes, *Arms and the Man* was pervaded by an altogether more genial comic spirit. It contained no more obviously "nasty" themes to upset the likes of Clement Scott. Yet in its own way it was just as subversive as its three predecessors among Shaw's dramatic works, bringing satirical weapons to bear on cherished nineteenth-century ideals of love and war. The play attacked not only "the romantic idea of a soldier as a sort of knight in armour,"[1] as Shaw put it to the labor historian R. Page Arnot, but also the chivalric code underpinning relationships between men and women in nineteenth-century society.

Shaw began writing *Arms and the Man* on Sunday, 26 November 1893, a little over three weeks after he finished *Mrs. Warren's Profession.* Jenny Patterson had called at the Shaw house in Fitzroy Square, causing Shaw to go out in order to avoid her. When he returned, he "spent the evening in playing [the piano] and in beginning a new play—a romantic one—for FE [Florence (Emery) Farr]."[2] This is one of those diary entries by Shaw in which much is conveyed in a few words. The play is "romantic" in that it concludes happily with an ending that looks forward in its action to the marriages of the two main young couples. But Shaw achieved a rejuvenation of a typical romantic structure by attaching to well-tried dramatic situations an unconventional set of values. The real hero of the play is not the Byronic, dashing cavalry officer Sergius, who would fill the role in ordinary nineteenth-century romantic fiction, but the pragmatic Shavian soldier Bluntschli, who carries chocolate in his pocket instead of bullets as being of more practical use, and who scoffs at the romantic idealism of the young lady Raina, who eventually transfers her affections from Sergius to him. Shaw was skillfully insinuating his unique brand of antiromantic satire into a dramatic structure that conforms to basic narrative conventions of romantic comedy. He was writing an antiromantic romance.

The words "for FE" in the diary have a prosaic explanation. The wealthy heiress Annie Elizabeth Frederika Horniman, fellow member with W. B. Yeats and Florence Farr in the Order of the Golden Dawn hermetic society, was beginning her career as patroness of the arts that was to make her one of the major founders of the Abbey Theatre early in the next century. Having received a large legacy following the death of her grandfather, the founder of a tea company, in 1893 she gave Florence Farr a substantial sum to assist her in developing her theatrical career. Florence decided to use the money as backing for a season of plays by playwrights within her circle, including three Irishmen: W. B. Yeats, Dr. John Todhunter, and Shaw. The Avenue Theatre, by the Thames Embankment, was chosen as the venue. Although Shaw remained unaware of the identity of Florence's backer until 1905, Annie Horniman was Shaw's anonymous patroness in the production of his first theatrically successful play, *Arms and the Man*, written "for FE" and her Avenue Theatre venture.

The play can also be viewed as having been written "for" Florence Farr in other senses. Shaw's unconventional and candid friend was to create the part of Louka, an amusing Shavian rendering of the nineteenth-century comic character type of the soubrette, a pert and coquettish maidservant. From what we know about Florence, she would have been well suited for the role of the rebellious and attractive Louka, who rails against the hierarchical and patriarchal social system to which she is subordinated, and from which she escapes in the end by marrying Sergius. The play was a salute to the type of New Woman of which Florence Farr and May Morris were the principal representatives in Shaw's life at this time. In a letter to Harley Granville-Barker dated 17 November 1907 concerning the casting of a forthcoming revival of *Arms and the Man* at the Savoy Theatre, London, Shaw wrote: "To me the scenes between Sergius and Louka are so much more deeply felt than those between Bluntschli & Raina that I had myself rather play Sergius than Bluntschli, & rather have the strong woman of the cast as my Louka than as my Raina."[3]

In *Arms and the Man*—as he had done briefly in its immediate predecessor, *The Philanderer*—Shaw was fashioning a refreshingly unconventional style of dramatic dialogue between male and female characters that reflected not only the new voice of women—who were demanding a full and equal part with men in social, political, and intellectual discourse—but also the unusual degree of intimacy and candor that he himself had found in his own relationships with Florence Farr, May Morris, and Janet Achurch. In contemporary drama of the 1890s, only Oscar Wilde's dialogue—especially in scenes such as that between the racy Mrs. Allonby and Lord Illingworth at the end of the first act of *A Woman of No Importance*—offered any parallel to the new kind of frank and sexually egalitarian male-female discourse that Shaw was creating. An exchange of dialogue in *The Philanderer* between Julia's sister, Sylvia, and Charteris about the secret of the latter's success with women provides an early Shavian example:

> Sylvia [*thoughtfully*]: Do you know, Leonard, I really believe you. I don't think you care a bit more for one woman than for another.
> Charteris: You mean I don't care a bit less for one woman than another.
> Sylvia: That makes it worse. But what I mean is you never bother about their being only women: you talk to them just as you do to me or any other fellow. Thats the secret of your success. You cant think how sick they get of being treated with the respect due to their sex.

A conversational breakthrough in male-female discourse to the human beings concealed beneath the veils of artificial conventions and codes marks a turning point in the development of the relationship and romance between Raina and Bluntschli in *Arms and the Man* in a passage of dialogue similar to that between Sylvia and Charteris in *The Philanderer*. When Bluntschli mocks Raina for her habit of striking a "noble attitude" and using a "thrilling voice," his candor breaks down barriers and creates a new, easy familiarity between the two. In the exchange that follows his insults, "seriousness" in woman-to-man relationships is placed on a new footing, and a mood of chatty comradeship is established:

> Raina: How did you find me out? . . . [*wonderingly*] Do you know, you are the first man I ever met who did not take me seriously?
> Bluntschli: You mean, don't you, that I am the first man that has ever taken you quite seriously?
> Raina: Yes: I suppose I do mean that. [*Cosily, quite at her ease with him*] How strange it is to be talked to in such a way! You know I've always gone on like that.
> Bluntschli: You mean the—?

Raina: I mean the noble attitude and the thrilling voice. [*They laugh together*].[4]

History was being quietly reflected and forged in these examples of Shaw's creative engagement with late-nineteenth-century redefinitions of Victorian gender codes.

* * *

The opening night of *Arms and the Man* was a major landmark in Shaw's career as a dramatist and public figure. The play had not been completed in time for the opening of Florence Farr's season of plays at the Avenue Theatre, a fact that almost proved disastrous for her new venture. The theater opened on 29 March 1894, with John Todhunter's *Comedy of Sighs* and, as a curtain-raiser, W. B. Yeats's *The Land of Heart's Desire.* Shaw described the opening night as a "fiasco," John Todhunter's play having "failed rather badly," and the following day Shaw was summoned by telegram to the theater, where he found Florence and the acting manager Charles Helmsley with *Widowers' Houses* in front of them, "contemplating its production in despair."[5] He dissuaded them from that, and with the ready dispatch that characterizes his prosaic but "incurably romantic" hero Bluntschli, "took my new play out on to the Embankment and there and then put the last touches to it before leaving it to be typewritten."[6] By 11 April the play was in rehearsal and on the twenty-first it opened. Of the opening night Shaw wrote: "I had the experience of witnessing an apparently insane success, with the actors and actresses almost losing their heads with the intoxication of laugh after laugh, and of going before the curtain to tremendous applause."[7]

When Shaw appeared for a curtain call, a solitary voice from the gallery booed while the rest of the audience laughed and cheered. The booer was R. Golding Bright—later a drama critic and eventually one of Shaw's theatrical agents—to whom Shaw gave his famous response: "My dear fellow, I quite agree with you, but what are we two against so many." W. B. Yeats, who was present, gave an account of this electrifying night in his autobiographical work *The Trembling of the Veil.* After recording his version of Shaw's riposte to the booer, Yeats wrote: "And from that moment Bernard Shaw became the most formidable man in modern letters, and even the most drunken of medical students knew it."[8]

Shaw's satirical demolition of romantic idealizations of war in *Arms and the Man*—in a cultural context in which Tennyson's poem "The Charge of the Light Brigade" and the soldiers' chorus in Gounod's *Faust* reflected more usual attitudes—seemed extraordinarily eccentric to some. Yeats records a visit to the play by the Prince of Wales and the Duke of Edinburgh, during which, he was told, the latter "kept on repeating, 'The man is mad,' meaning Mr Shaw."[9] From the outset—and long before it became the title of Oscar Straus's opéra bouffe based on the play—the phrase "the chocolate soldier" had become firmly associated with Shaw's work. On a contemporary poster for the play people were invited to "Stop at Charing Cross for the Avenue Theatre where the Chocolate-Cream Soldier Is To Be Seen Nightly. He appears at Ten Minutes to Nine In Bernard Shaw's Excruciatingly Funny Play."[10] Such was the effect of the play's "excruciatingly funny" comedy that Shaw considered it had failed in its serious themes, and that he had been regarded merely as "a monstrously clever sparkler in the cynical line."[11] He was half serious in his agreement with Golding Bright's expression of dissatisfaction.

Arms and the Man had fifty performances at the Avenue Theatre, running until 7 July. Shaw had become, on a modest scale, a marketable playwright. By 24 April the Australian-born actor Charles Overton was negotiating with him for the American rights to the play on behalf of the American theater manager Albert Marshman Palmer. In June Shaw negotiated a self-drafted contract—a "Shylockian bond" as he called it—with the actor-manager Richard Mansfield, who played the part of Bluntschli in a production that opened at the Herald Square Theater in New York on 17 September 1894. Hailed by New York critics, the play initially ran for sixteen performances, returned to the bill later in the season, and remained in the Mansfield repertory for many years. Shaw's combined royalties from the London and New York productions in 1894 amounted to £341.15.2, enabling him, at age thirty-eight, to open his first bank account on 6 November. Although there were hills of difficulty to be overcome before the high plateau of the Court Theatre successes of 1904–7, *Arms and the Man* was an important point of ascent on Shaw's path to fame as a dramatist.

* * *

Shaw and Florence Farr had been seeing less of one another following the final performance of *Arms and the Man* in July 1894. Shaw's diary entry for 8 November of that year misleadingly suggests that the date marked a decisive moment of closure in their relationship. The diary shows that Shaw visited Florence's Dalling Road apartment at 8 p.m. that evening. The only other entry for the day is a single word in German, *Trennung*, meaning "parting." As Shaw probably remembered, the word was used by Brahms as the title for two of his lieder about the end of love affairs.[12]

The *Trennung* almost certainly indicated the end of the love affair and physical intimacy, but it was not as complete a breakup as Shaw's dramatic diary entry might suggest. The two had been extremely close companions, theatrical collaborators, and lovers. Shaw had found this attractive, emancipated, and intelligent woman an irresistible alternative companion to the demanding Jenny Patterson, and the idea of marriage had obviously arisen between them as a possibility. Florence herself appears to have found the relationship difficult to relinquish.

A rapid exchange of letters in October 1896 reveals both Florence's continuing interest in Shaw and some of the reasons why the affair had faltered. On the twelfth Shaw declared her a "lost wretch" for her self-immersion in "exoteric Egyptology" instead of "working at some reality every day."[13] Florence had just published a small book entitled *Egyptian Magic* under the pseudonym S.S.D.D. (Sapientia Sapienti Dono Data, meaning "wisdom is given to the wise as a gift"), the name by which she was known in the Order of the Golden Dawn society. He received what he described as a "nasty letter" in reply, which apparently included a complaint about his abandonment of her. "Do you want me *for ever*, greedy one?," he asked.[14] Her immediate response (which has not survived, but which must have been a protest against his message) elicited yet another letter from Shaw on the fourteenth, in which admiration and affection are mingled with denunciation. Florence's attractive gray eyes and semicircular eyebrows[15] are recalled in the general warning to mankind Shaw delivered to her in this letter:

> Serve you right!
> I hereby warn mankind to beware of women with large eyes, and crescent eyebrows, and a smile, and a love of miracles and moonshees. I warn them against all who like intellectual pastimes; who prefer liberty, happiness and irresponsibility to care, suffering and life; who live for and in themselves instead of for and in the world; who reject the deep universal material of human relationship and select only the luxuries of love, friendship, and amusing conversation.[16]

Farr's biographer, Josephine Johnson, remarks that this passage provides a singularly accurate description of Florence, "fathomed out of as generous perception as she would know."[17] Shaw and Florence were moving in different directions, and Shaw told her that the "true relation" between them had become that of polar opposites.[18] Although the meeting at Dalling Road in November 1894 marked the end of their close intimacy and physical relationship, their friendship continued and their paths would cross in several ways in the future. On 3 May 1895, six months after the *Trennung*, Shaw wrote a letter to Janet Achurch in America—where she was performing in Richard Mansfield's production of *Candida*—complaining about her not having written to him and saying that unless he received a letter by the following day, "F.F. [Florence Farr] shall be Mrs. Bernard Shaw at the earliest date thereafter permitted by statute."[19] No doubt he was joking, but the form of the jest is some indication of the extent to which the Shaw-Farr relationship had become seriously established and recognized.

11 Wars of the Theaters, Mothers and Bicycles

In the second half of the 1890s Shaw was involved in a two-pronged attack on the nineteenth-century theater through his critical writing and his own unconventional new plays. The plays and correspondence of this period also show an intense preoccupation on his part with mother figures and with the nature of the maternal role. On a lighter side, it was a time when he and his fellow Fabians took up the new craze of bicycle riding, which in Shaw's case would lead to some amusing incidents and become linked to his new friendship with Charlotte Payne-Townshend.

In November 1894, when his romance with Florence Farr came to a close, several changes were about to take place in Shaw's career as playwright and critic, as well as in his personal life. On 4 December he called on Frank Harris to settle his appointment as regular theater critic on the *Saturday Review* at six pounds per week. On the eighth he finished the writing of *Candida*, the second of his "Plays Pleasant," which he was to follow up in 1895 with *The Man of Destiny*, his "beautiful little one act play for Napoleon and a strange lady,"[1] and the beginning of *You Never Can Tell*, his comedy of family division and partial reunion, presided over by a splendidly benign waiter, William, who reminds people of Shakespeare. The year 1895 was also the one in which the claims of another potential candidate for the title of Mrs. Bernard Shaw, his 1892 "Platform Spellbinder" portrait painter Bertha Newcombe, were being strongly pressed by others but resisted by Shaw: "Everybody seems bent on recommending me to marry Bertha—a fact fatal to her hopes (if it is fair to accuse her of hopes)," he reported to Janet Achurch (alias Mrs. Charrington) on 24 August 1895. "She is only wasting her affections on me," he added, and "ought to marry someone else."[2]

Shaw corresponded extensively with the improvident Charringtons during 1895 and helped them out financially. Late in the year he was making overtures to Ellen Terry in an endeavor to win her over to the Shavian drama, hoping at first that she would play the role of the Strange Lady in *The Man of*

Destiny, with Henry Irving as Napoleon. This marked the beginning of the famous epistolary romance between Shaw and Terry, in the course of which he would freely comment on the progress of his relationship with the *woman* of destiny in his own life, the actual future Mrs. Bernard Shaw, Charlotte Payne Townshend.

* * *

Shaw's career as a theater critic, which came into full flower in the pages of the *Saturday Review* in the three and a half years (1895–mid 1898) leading up to his marriage, was closely linked with his project as a dramatist. Both the drama and the criticism were expressions of a passionate quarrel Shaw was engaged in with the nineteenth-century theater and the social and ideological values it upheld. Following the Restoration period—with the exception of occasional meteoric flashes such as those provided by John Gay in *The Beggar's Opera*, Richard Sheridan, and Henry Fielding—the British theatrical tradition had become virtually devoid of work that entered into any engagement, through satire or other means with serious social, moral, philosophical, and religious questions. In the nineteenth century the novel and poetry reigned supreme as the genres in which subjects that seriously engage the mind were reflected and explored.

The lively popular theater of the nineteenth century in England was principally devoted to various forms of more or less mindless entertainment. William Archer described the situation well when he wrote, in the introduction to his 1882 study *English Dramatists of To-day*, that the theatrical offerings of the time catered to a shallow and philistine British public that "will laugh always, cry sometimes, shudder now and then, but think—never." In the same passage, before Shaw had written any of his "Plays Unpleasant," Archer remarked of this public that "especially it will have nothing to do with a piece to whose theme the word 'unpleasant' can be applied."[3] Shaw could well have had this in mind when he gave his first three plays their defiant title.

In the preface to a collection of his theater reviews of the 1890s, Shaw described his "journalistic utterances" as a calculated military campaign: "I must honestly warn the reader that what he is about to study is not a series of judgements aiming at impartiality, but a siege laid to the theatre of the XIX century by an author who had to cut his way into it at the point of a pen, and throw some of its defenders into the moat."[4]

Very few, if any, of his contemporaries in the 1890s had a better idea than did Shaw of the nature of the forces he was attacking. His novel *Love Among the Artists* provides a disparaging list of the stereotypical forms of dramatic entertainment in vogue in England and the provinces in the last quarter of the nineteenth century. The round of offerings included: "comedy of contemporary life . . . Shakespeare, sensation drama, Irish melodrama, comic opera or pantomime, new comedy from London over again, with farce constantly." In London Henry Irving reigned supreme, acting in spectacle-filled melodramas such as Leopold Lewis's *The Bells* and mangled versions of Shakespeare—and, Shaw believed, keeping Ellen Terry as a beautiful slave to a decadent theatrical tradition in his "Ogre's castle," the Lyceum Theatre.[5] "He [Irving] is an ogre who has carried you off to his cave; and now Childe Roland is coming to the dark tower to rescue you," her would-be rescuer Shaw informed Ellen Terry in September 1896.[6]

Shaw's weekly columns in the *Saturday Review* constituted a devastating assault on the contemporary theater. As one commentator remarked, in the course of a review of James Agate's criticism in the London *Spectator* in 1944, Shaw's theater criticism "shook the English theater to its foundations."[7] Shaw wrote about the theater with superb vivacity, wit, and point, and was often generous in praise as well as sharply critical. His complimentary description of the acting of Johnston Forbes-Robertson as Hamlet and Mrs. Patrick Campbell as Ophelia in an October 1897 production of Shakespeare's play at the Lyceum Theatre—wonderfully evocative in its description of individual performances, as well as offering searching commentary on Shakespeare's dramatic art—could be cited as one among innumerable examples of Shaw's exemplary style as a theater critic.[8]

Two particular objects of attack in Shaw's theatrical criticism were the fashionable drawing-room drama—which he memorably summed up as "a tailor's advertisement making sentimental remarks to a milliner's advertisement in the middle of an upholsterer's and decorator's advertisement"[9]—and the *pièce bien faite*, or well-made play, deriving largely from French dramatists such as Scribe and Sardou. Punning on the latter's name, he coined the term *Sardoodledom* for the mechanical, formulaic, highly artificial plotting of the plays written according to the rules of the well-made play.[10]

Shaw had endless arguments with William Archer on the subjects of dramatic construction and plotting. In 1923, the year before his death, Archer wrote to Shaw complaining about his alleged perversity in these matters. By then Shaw had become one of the few champions of Chekhov in England, and Archer linked him with the Russian dramatist as creators of supposedly invertebrate, plotless plays. To illustrate his argument, Archer invented an imaginary dialogue between himself and Shaw, in which he represents Shaw as confusing a cat with a jellyfish and arguing for the existence of an anomalous invertebrate creature called "the Tchekho-Shavian cat." Shaw replied to the "perfect idiot" of a "professor of dramatic Constructionism" with a characteristic blend of good humor and sharpness:

> My dear W. A.
>
> You haven't got it yet. The alternatives are not a cat and a jellyfish, but a clockwork cat and a live cat. The clockwork cat is very ingenious and amusing (for five minutes); but the organisation of the live cat beats the construction of the mechanical one all to nothing; and it amuses you not for an age but for all time.[11]

Shaw's personal relations with some of the prime targets of his satirical barbs as a theater critic came to be surprisingly cordial, considering the withering attacks he made against them in the 1890s. The leading dramatist of the day in London during the 1890s was Arthur Wing Pinero, a playwright with a Portuguese-Jewish background who was born in London in 1855, a year before Shaw. Shaw wrote scathing reviews of several of Pinero's plays, criticizing them for both technical clumsiness and the exploitation of subjects such as the "New Woman" and the "Woman with a Past" in ways he felt simply endorsed conventional, old-fashioned attitudes. His most successful play, *The Second Mrs. Tanqueray* (1893), has real merits and remains stageworthy, but at times it betrays its good intentions of exposing the Victorian double standard in the matter of male and female sexual misconduct with an essentially conservative, gentleman's club view of the "Woman with a Past."

In his 1895 play *The Notorious Mrs. Ebbsmith* Pinero had taken advantage of the topical interest of another "daring" theme by attempting a portrayal of the "New Woman" in the creation of his heroine Agnes Ebbsmith, played by Shaw's future inamorata Mrs. Patrick Campbell, fresh from her success with "Mrs Tank," as Shaw indecorously described Mrs. Tanqueray in a letter.[12] A ludicrously melodramatic final tableau shows Agnes frantically changing her mind about her decision to hurl the Bible into a stove fire: *"The expression of her face has changed to a look of fright and horror. Uttering a loud cry, she hastens to the stove and thrusting her arm into the fire, drags out the book."*[13] One critic in the audience did not join in the applause at Mrs. Ebbsmith's return to the fold. Shaw wrote: "The Church is saved; and the curtain descends amid thunders of applause. In that applause I hope I need not say I did not join. A less sensible and less courageous stage effect I have never witnessed. . . . This, I submit, is a piece of claptrap so gross that it absolves me from all obligation to treat Mr Pinero's art as anything higher than the barest art of theatrical sensation." Shaw added that Pinero had "no idea beyond that of doing something daring and bringing down the house by running away from the consequences."[14]

By 1908, however, Shaw had entered into a good-humored and friendly correspondence with Pinero, centered on their common interest in the affairs of the Society of Authors and the Dramatists' Club. A striking 1906 Max Beerbohm cartoon depicts two figures walking in opposite directions from one another. On the left is Pinero as a top-hatted, stocky figure in a voluminous Victorian frock coat and with an enormous pointy nose, while on the right is the lanky Shaw in his casual Jaeger suit and soft felt hat. Beerbohm has brilliantly captured a historic moment in theater history, the contrasting attire and walking in different directions seeming to symbolize both the differences between the two dramatists and the fact that whereas Shaw was a man of a new age, Pinero belonged to the past. Nevertheless, Pinero still had further heights to scale in terms of his social standing, and Shaw played a major part in this respect.

On 3 July 1908 Shaw wrote to William Archer: "I have made up my mind to make Pinero a knight," a move that "would undoubtedly strengthen the theatre movement." Accordingly, Shaw reported, "I made the heroic sacrifice of going into Society. I went to Mrs Asquith's garden party, and told her flatly that A.W.P. must be made a knight."[15] Shaw's pursuit of this matter during 1908 with Margot Asquith, wife of the new prime minister, and Reginald Baliol Brett, 2nd Viscount Esher, a government official with interests in the theater, were successful. Through the efforts of the man who, as a theater critic in 1895, had described Pinero's plays as representing "the barest art of theatrical sensation" and the ending of one of them as "claptrap," Pinero was knighted in the Birthday Honours of 1909.[16]

Although Shaw wrote scathingly about much of the theatrical fare of the 1890s in his *Saturday Review* articles, Oscar Wilde and Henry Arthur Jones, the second-ranking playwright of the day after Pinero, were singled out for praise. Shaw paid a handsome tribute to his fellow countryman Wilde in his review of *An Ideal Husband* on 12 January 1895. He neatly countered the criticism made by others—namely, that Wilde's tricks of comedy were too obvious—with a tilt at the critics and an ironically phrased compliment to Wilde's unique touch: "As far as I can ascertain," he wrote, "I am the only person in London who cannot sit down and write an Oscar Wilde play at will." He then went on to provide a fine summary of Wilde's theatrical genius: "In a certain sense Mr Wilde is to me our only thorough playwright. He plays with everything: with wit, with philosophy, with drama, with actors and audience, with the whole theatre."[17] (In the same review, entitled "Two New Plays," Shaw was one of the few critics to write respectfully about Henry James's theatrically unsuccessful play *Guy Domville*.)

Shaw's compliment to Wilde was undercut, to some extent, by his review the following month of *The Importance of Being Earnest.* His remarks on that play now seem to do it far less than justice. He thought the play unworthy of the author, regarding its humor as being "adulterated by stock mechanical fun" and finding a lack of depth in the play's comedy: "I cannot say that I greatly care for The Importance of Being Earnest. It amused me, of course; but unless comedy touches me as well as amuses me, it leaves me with a sense of having wasted my evening."[18] Shaw had too much generosity of spirit and too great a respect for Wilde's genius for this to be seen as a case of professional jealousy.

Shaw overrated the plays of Henry Arthur Jones, who in a work such as *The Case of Rebellious Susan*—a specious exploitation of the contemporary struggle for female emancipation that ultimately endorses extremely conservative male opinions—deserved equally scathing criticism as was heaped upon Pinero for *The Notorious Mrs. Ebbsmith.* Shaw, however, discerned in Jones's other works a refreshing originality: "His qualities are creative imagination, curious observation, inventive humor, originality, sympathy, and sincerity," he wrote in May 1895.[19] Posterity has not endorsed these views. But Shaw was comparing Jones's work to a vast procession of mechanical and inferior plays that he reviewed with almost unfailing good humor and lively wit in the pages of the *Saturday Review* for over three years. He and Jones formed a "delightful and cordial friendship," as Jones's daughter, Doris, described it, which was to be irreparably shattered as a result of the views Shaw expressed at the outbreak of World War I in his essay *Common Sense About the War.*[20]

* * *

Shaw's strategy in his war against the theater of the 1890s was not always one of direct attack. In the case of another knight of the theater, Sir Henry Irving, his approach was to try to get the enemy over to his side, using Ellen Terry as his ambassador. Shaw sent Ellen Terry the typescript of *The Man of Destiny* on 28 November 1895, as she was touring with Irving in America. "Not one of my great plays . . . a commercial traveller's sample," he wrote slightingly of the work, but which he nevertheless hoped Irving might become interested in, with the impressive role of Napoleon as the bait.[21] Ellen found the play "delicious" and tried to persuade "His Immensity," as Shaw dubbed Irving, to take it on.[22]

Irving did not like Shaw, and in 1891 he had publically attacked *The Quintessence of Ibsenism* and its author. Shaw had not done much to foster a friendship with his insulting essay in the *Saturday Review* of 9 February 1895, entitled "Why Not Sir Henry Irving?," in which he openly suggested that a lecture by Irving at the Royal Institution about the need for more official public recognition of work in the theater was actually a thinly veiled plug for Irving's own advancement, the knighthood he was to receive later that year.[23] When Shaw finally came to meet Irving in 1896, he reported to Ellen Terry: "I liked Henry, though he is without exception absolutely the stupidest man I ever met—simply no brains—nothing but character and temperament." He modified this by going on to say: "Curious how little use mere brains are: I have a very fine set; and yet I learnt more from the first stupid woman who fell in love with me than ever they taught me."[24] The woman referred to was probably Alice Lockett.

Irving appears to have behaved in a rather duplicitous manner toward Shaw concerning *The Man of Destiny*, apparently having obtained the rights to the play without any serious intention of going ahead with it. Shaw wanted Ellen to play the Strange Lady and Irving to play Napoleon. It was exasperating to him that Irving was instead playing Napoleon and Ellen the Duchess-washerwoman in *Madame Sans-Gêne*, a historical drama by the prince of "Sardoodledom" himself, Victorien Sardou, in collaboration with Émile Moreau. Negotiations over *The Man of Destiny* dragged on into 1897. Matters were not helped by an unfavorable review by Shaw of Irving's performance in *Richard III* in December 1896, which hinted at the possibility that Irving was drunk while onstage. Shaw referred to some "odd slips in the text" in Irving's delivery and remarked that "once he inadvertently electrified the house by very unexpectedly asking Miss Milton to get further up the stage in the blank verse and penetrating tones of Richard." Further references in the review to Irving's "too genuine" exhaustion in the battle scenes, coupled with a slyly introduced allusion to the early-nineteenth-century actor Edmund Kean's well-known drunkenness during performances, left little doubt as to Shaw's inference.[25] In May 1897 the manuscript of Shaw's play was summarily returned to him by Bram Stoker, author of *Dracula*, who was Irving's manager and adviser. Shaw's attempt to bring a theatrical enemy into his own camp, along with his leading lady, had ended in failure.

* * *

Ellen Terry first came into contact with Shaw in June 1892, when he replied to a letter she had sent to the *World* asking that its music critic (Shaw) attend a recital by Miss Elvira Gambogi, a protégée of hers. The epistolary romance began in 1895: "We developed a perfect fury for writing to each," recalled Terry years later in her autobiography *The Story of My Life*.[26] Except for a brief encounter at a performance of Sir Arthur Sullivan's *Ivanhoe* in 1891—in which Terry did not recognize Shaw as the person to whom she had casually said: "Good evening, sir"—they did not meet in person until 16 December 1900 at the Stage Society premiere of *Captain Brassbound's Conversion*.[27] Terry served as the model for the skillfully diplomatic, motherly Lady Cicely Waynflete in this play and was finally persuaded to play the role herself at the Court Theatre in March 1906. Shaw described Terry as "heartwise,"[28] which was exactly the kind of quality he wanted to convey in the character of Lady Cicely, the "real cleverness" he makes his surly and rebellious captain acknowledge in the final scene. Together with Mrs. (later Lady) H. M Stanley (née Tennant), wife of the famous explorer, Terry was also one of his models for the role of Candida.[29] On 16 July 1897 Shaw told Ellen Terry: "I have always said that there are only two really sympathetic women in London—yourself & Dorothy Tennant (Mrs Stanley)."[30] It is likely that Shaw borrowed the shortened form of Dorothy Stanley's first name, Dolly, for that of one of the twins in his play *You Never Can Tell* (1897). He refers to Mrs. Stanley as Dolly in a letter to Sidney Webb dated 7 May 1898, where he also reports he had told her "she was the original of Candida and I adored her."[31]

Shaw's friendship with Dorothy Stanley is an almost lost chapter in his history. A small cache of five unpublished letters from Shaw to her, written between 17 November 1897 and 3 July 1905 provides a glimpse into their friendly relations, as well as displaying some nice touches of Shaw's wit and charm in social situations.[32] In November 1897 Shaw had been invited to dinner with Mrs. Stanley but was unable to attend due to the injuries sustained as a result of one of his many spectacular cycling mishaps. The injuries reminded Shaw of the fate of his fictional prizefighter Billy Paradise, who is left a battered wreck following his epic bout with Cashel in the 1883 novel *Cashel Byron's Profession*. Shaw wrote her as follows:

> My dear Mrs. Stanley
> All is lost: I have just taken my annual bicycle accident. Read the description of Paradise after his combat with Cashel Byron, and it will give you a notion of what I look like. You can't have a man at dinner with an appalling black eye, and his face knocked out of drawing. . . . Isn't it exasperating? Damn![33]

In 1903, the year before his death, Henry Morton Stanley had apparently suffered a minor stroke. Self-appointed medical adviser Shaw told Lady Stanley (as she was known by this time) not to be concerned. His own mother had suffered a collapse of that kind a couple of years ago, he told her in a letter dated 18 May 1903, and a doctor had given her some "digitalis, which upset the action of her heart for a whole night; and in the extremity of her indignation she recovered with such violence that she has been extraordinarily well ever since & takes mountain walks in Germany." The "counselor" went on to explain that "Stanley has been cerebrating too vigorously, and has cracked some trumpery little vein in his head probably; but the contents of it must be nearly absorbed by this time." The real doctors and sympathizing friends would be disappointed when Stanley got better, added the future author of *The Doctor's Dilemma*, a scathing satire on the medical profession.[34]

In a letter to Bertha Newcombe Shaw referred to the "blarneying audacities" of his correspondence with Ellen Terry. But the blarney was clearly accompanied by a great deal of genuine affection and admiration: "I really do love Ellen," he went on to say in the same letter.[35] He also had enormous respect for her gifts as an actress and became deeply absorbed in the details of her performance in such roles as that of Imogen in Shakespeare's *Cymbeline*. (His advice to her about the latter shows, again, his extraordinarily close knowledge of Shakespeare's work; he was later to produce a comic rewriting in blank verse of the end of the play entitled *Cymbeline Refinished* (1937), which exposes some of the absurdities of Shakespeare's ending, especially from a feminist viewpoint.) There nevertheless remains an air of theatrical artificiality about the disembodied romance; it clearly did not involve Shaw emotionally to the same extent as his later affair with Mrs. Patrick Campbell.

The blarney of Shaw's letters to Terry signals "approach with caution" as far as their autobiographical content is concerned. Shaw's oft-quoted theatrical cry concerning his early upbringing—"Oh, a devil of a childhood, Ellen, rich only in dreams, frightful & loveless in realities"—becomes suspect in the light of other evidence about his family background that has already been explored earlier in this book.[36] Nevertheless, Shaw often used his correspondence with Ellen Terry as a medium of autobiographical writing to which due notice must be paid. She was not only a lovely and gifted friend—adored safely from afar—but also a mother confessor. Shaw's letters to Terry contained confessions and pleas for advice regarding his love life as well as on professional subjects. They also display his natural gaiety of mind. For example, in one letter to Terry he wrote apologetically about his unusually large ears, which he claimed were a legacy of the Carr side of his father's family, and which were starkly revealed in a photograph taken in 1896: "I am really sorry about the ears. They are a Shaw speciality. They stick straight out like the doors of a triptych; and I was born with them full size, so that on windy days my nurse had to hold me by my waistband to prevent my being blown away when the wind caught them."[37]

Shaw's feelings of admiration and affection for Terry were reciprocated. When she finally came to see "Mr Shaw" regularly during preparations for the 1906 presentation of *Captain Brassbound's Conversion* at the Court Theatre—with her in the role of Lady Cicely—she found him "wonderfully patient at rehearsal." She looked upon Shaw as "a good, kind, gentle creature whose 'brain storms' are just due to the Irishman's love of a fight; they never spring from malice or anger." She concluded her reminiscence about their relationship with some shrewd comments about the playfulness of Shaw's mind and the elusiveness of his intellectual stances in the plays. She invokes the image of a cat, which was to appear again in the previously mentioned correspondence between Archer and Shaw: "It doesn't answer to take Bernard Shaw seriously. He is not a man of convictions. That is one of the charms of his plays—to me at least. One never knows how the cat is really jumping. But it *jumps.* Bernard Shaw is alive, with nine lives, like that cat!"[38]

* * *

Shaw was much preoccupied with mothers during his early years as a dramatist. In an April 1896 letter to Ellen Terry Shaw wrote that "from our birth to our death we are women's babies, always wanting something from them, never giving them anything except something to keep *for us.*"[39] The idea that husbands often become their wives' babies had already been treated by Shaw in his first novel, *Immaturity,* and runs through his work, culminating in the "mothering tyranny" of the Shotover daughters in *Heartbreak House.* In the plays, his first significant portrayal of a mother was that of his "deplorable old rip"[40] Kitty Warren in *Mrs. Warren's Profession,* who early on is presented as admirably independent and cheerfully contemptuous concerning respectability, whereas in the final quarrel with her daughter she becomes a wheedling, self-pitying, and emotionally manipulative mother before finally reasserting her self-possession.

In a letter to Ellen Terry dated August 1896 Shaw wrote about her playing of the role of a mother in *Madame Sans-Gêne*: "It is all very well for you to say that you want a Mother Play. . . . I *have* written THE Mother Play—'Candida.'"[41] The latter, which he had written with extraordinary rapidity between 2 October and 7 December 1894 (with Janet Achurch in mind for the leading female role), presents its mother figure in remarkably ambiguous terms—a cross between nurturing madonna and ruthless dominatrix who infantalizes and demeans her "big baby" husband, the Reverend James Mavor Morell, and flirts with his rival, the poet Eugene Marchbanks. This double view of Candida in the play itself (in some ways she recalls the women in Strindberg's play *The Father,* which appeared in 1887 but which Shaw had not yet seen or read) is echoed in comments Shaw made about Candida in his correspondence. Again addressing Ellen Terry, whom he also tried to interest in playing the title role, he confided: "Candida, between you and me, is the Virgin Mother and nobody else."[42] He emphasized this connection by calling for "*a large autotype of the chief figure in Titian's Assumption of the Virgin*" as part of the setting of the play. In another comment, however, he invoked a Wagnerian comparison: "Candida is as ruthless as Siegfried. . . . She seduces Eugene just exactly as far as it is worth her while to seduce him. She is a woman without 'character' in the conventional sense. Without brains and strength of mind she would be a wretched slattern or voluptuary."[43]

Shaw thus created in Candida a curiously ambiguous portrait of a mother: a baffling combination of the Virgin Mary and a power-hungry coquette. In the writing of *You Never Can Tell* and *Captain Brassbound's Conversion*, two more genial mother figures emerged from Shaw's imagination. Lady Cicely Waynflete, who tames the heart of the melodramatically rebellious Captain Brassbound, is a shrewd, gracious, and emotionally intelligent woman who—in the wilds of Morocco, where the play is set—counters aggression and danger with perfect manners and thoughtful acts of kindness, such as mending people's clothes for them. Mrs. Clandon in *You Never Can Tell*, who Shaw described as "a composite of the advanced woman of the George Eliot period, with certain personal traits of my mother,"[44] is another more gently portrayed maternal figure.

Shaw's preoccupation with mother figures in the plays written between 1894 and 1899 can be accounted for quite simply by the intrinsic interest of the subject and the way in which it engaged his creative imagination and skill. Yet it also prompts speculation about what might have been Shaw's inner state at this time and what he was seeking in his relations with women. The affair with Jenny Patterson—who in some ways had tried to be his mother (and supplier of cocoa, strawberries, and slippers) as well as his ardent lover—had come to a dramatic end with the "shocking scene" at Florence's Farr's apartment in February 1893. By the end of 1894, Florence herself, to whom he had turned rapturously from the overpossessive Jenny, had begun to disappoint him by her unfocused life and her lack of serious commitment either to her own career or to concern about the social causes he espoused. Like his poet Marchbanks, Shaw was averse to the idea of making happiness and fireside comforts the main objects of life's quest; he had decided that the possessiveness Jenny displayed—which even the more emancipated Florence had shown signs of—was too high a price to pay for sexual fulfillment. Rather than being in pursuit of love—in the romantic sense of complete and reciprocated devotion and commitment to another person—he was trying to escape it.

In the meantime he enjoyed his relationship with the delightful Ellen Terry, whom he could charm, consult, instruct, flatter and amuse without threat to his loss of self-ownership. It appears that he may have enjoyed a similar relationship with Dorothy Stanley, the other member of his elite circle (the "only two really sympathetic women in London"). At about this time (1895) another woman was making her appearance on the horizon, Charlotte Payne Townshend, who although she adamantly rejected the idea of biological motherhood for herself, would come to play a distinctly maternal role in Shaw's life.

* * *

In his critical writings for the *Saturday Review* Shaw's campaign against the nineteenth-century theater could be counted a sparkling success. On the other front, however—that of producing new plays to challenge the existing tradition—he was experiencing mixed results. By the time he had reached the end of his "Plays Pleasant" sequence with *You Never Can Tell* and the beginning of the next group of plays with *The Devil's Disciple* (1896), he began to adopt a strategy of writing plays that outwardly conformed to the conventions of popular nineteenth-century theatrical genres yet possessed a very distinctive Shavian style and subject matter, casting a critical light on the popular forms themselves. In *You Never Can Tell* he created a fashionable comedy for West End theaters that was like no other of its kind that had ever been seen there. In *The Devil's Disciple* he wrote a play that employed the stock conventions of Victorian melodrama but was nevertheless quite unlike other plays in this genre.

Shaw was only partially successful in this new, Fabian strategy for the theater. The plays that followed *Arms and the Man* in the Shavian canon did not maintain the momentum of theatrical success that had been briefly gained by that work at the Avenue Theatre in early 1894. *The Man of Destiny* languished unperformed while in the keeping of Sir Henry Irving. *Candida*, the writing of which was completed in 1895, was given some provincial performances beginning in 1897 but did not reach London until 1 July 1900, when it was produced by the Stage Society. In America Richard Mansfield, having hired Janet Achurch at a salary of two hundred and fifty dollars a week to play the role of Candida, had a major falling out with Shaw when he decided that he didn't like either the play or Achurch. In a brutally frank letter to Shaw written during April 1895, Mansfield said that the work was "charming" but not a play. It was all "talk—talk—talk," with Shaw trying to build a play out of "a mere incident." He was even more insulting about Shaw's beloved Janet: "I never fall in love with fuzzy-haired persons who purr. . . . I detest an aroma of stale tobacco and gin. . . . I don't like women who comb their tawny locks with their fingers, and claw their necks and scratch the air with their chins. . . . The stage is for romance and love and truth and honor," wrote Mansfield, obviously seeing himself as a kind of theatrical *preux chevalier.*[45] *You Never Can Tell,* which Shaw later said was deliberately cast in the mold of "fashionable comedies for West End theatres,"[46] was completed in 1896 but was not publicly performed until 1900.

As was often also the case with William Archer's astonishingly insulting comments to Shaw about his plays and his career, Mansfield's ferocious assault on *Candida* and Janet Achurch did not bring his relationship with Shaw to an end. During 1896, partly through Shaw's cordial correspondence with Mansfield's wife, Beatrice, the relationship was sustained. By September 1897 Shaw was successfully driving a hard bargain about his royalties for a forthcoming production by Mansfield of his uniquely Shavian version of a melodrama, *The Devil's Disciple.* The play opened at the Fifth Avenue Theater in New York City on 4 October and ran for sixty-four performances, which constituted Mansfield's greatest success since his season of directing and playing the lead in Clyde Fitch's rags-to-riches historical drama *Beau Brummel.* Shaw's royalties from the New York season of *The Devil's Disciple* amounted to seven hundred pounds, and he received another thirteen hundred when Mansfield toured with the play in the Midwest early the following year.[47]

On 4 November 1897, as the first royalties were coming in, Shaw was reporting the "sensational success" of the play to Charlotte Payne-Townshend, then on a visit to Paris, saying he was richer than he had ever been in his life before and that he had £314 to his credit in the bank.[48] Set in Puritan New Hampshire during the American War of Independence—with a well-knit plot leading to a last-minute rescue of its hero from the gallows and a victory for the revolutionary townsfolk, who march off at the end to the cheeky tune of "Yankee Doodle"—*The Devil's Disciple* struck a sympathetic chord with American audiences. Its portrayal of the rigidly puritanical and repressive New Hampshire society of the 1770s gave the play interesting cultural resonances with Nathaniel Hawthorne's portrayal of a similar society in his 1850 novel *The Scarlet Letter.*

* * *

Both *The Devil's Disciple* and its immediate predecessor have clear autobiographical dimensions. In *You Never Can Tell,* a comedy with surprising depths of theme and characterization, Shaw created a fantasy in which all the members of his own family are represented in one way or another, and in which an uneasy form of family reunion is achieved, as it never was in real life—although Shaw does say that his sister Lucy was in Dublin and was on "affectionate terms" with her father when he died.[49] Like Bessie Shaw, Mrs. Clandon is estranged from her husband and has three children, two girls and a boy. The husband, Mr. Crampton, has not seen his children for many years, their mother having changed her name and moved to Madeira. There is a strong hint in the play that Mr. Crampton has—or did have—a drinking problem. There are thus parallels with Shaw's own father, or at least with the Shavian account of him. But here the similarity ends. Mr. Crampton is irascible and cantankerous, and was apparently capable of violence toward his own children in the past, which does not match what we know of the character of Shaw's father.[50]

Two of the children, Dolly and Phil, are twins, whose bantering good-humored mockery of their mother, and chirpy transgression of the ordinary social decorum of conversation seem very likely to have been based on the behavior of Shaw and his sister Lucy in relation to one another and to their mother. Shaw probably gave the older daughter—the "proud, opinionated,"[51] and attractive Gloria—traces of his own superior and authoritative bearing in his family relations during his boyhood and early manhood.

The progression from the pain experienced in the dentist's chair during the opening scene of *You Never Can Tell* to the revelry of the fancy-dress ball—held at the Marine Hotel "for the benefit of the Life-boat"—at the end of the play is a rich dramatic experience. But it was to be some time before the play's virtues began to be appreciated, and before the role of the Shakespearean Waiter, William, began to attract leading actors, such as Louis Calvert in the early twentieth century and, later, Ralph Richardson and Cyril Cusack. An aborted production by manager Frederick Harrison and actor-manager Cyril Maude (who was to play the Waiter) at the Haymarket Theatre in the spring of 1897 ended in disarray and led to the withdrawal of the work. Shaw wrote a burlesque, self-mocking account of the disastrous rehearsals for this aborted production—written from the point of view of Maude himself, and sweetly depicting the impossible and absurdly incompetent playwright as being entirely responsible for the fiasco—that was published anonymously as a chapter in Maude's book *The Haymarket Theatre* (1903).

Shaw's opinions about *You Never Can Tell* vacillated wildly. Writing to Florence Farr on 8 September 1897, he described it as "the dullest trash I ever revised,"[52] and on the same day he told Ellen Terry that it was "a frightful example of the result of trying to write for the theatre de nos jours."[53] By 1906, however, he did much more justice to the work—one of the sunniest and most delightful of all his early plays—when he described it in a letter to William Archer with the words: "The thing is a poem and a document, a sermon and a festival, all in one."[54]

Set in a hotel by the seaside, where members of a bitterly divided family accidentally come together, *You Never Can Tell* becomes a celebration—with feasting, music, and dance as accompaniments—of life's contradiction of expectation, system and reason and of the possibilities it always holds out of fruitful change and development. More clearly than any of the early plays, *You Never Can Tell* gives the lie to views of Shaw as archrationalist and trumpeter of the intellect as a means of solving the problems of human relations: "Don't think. I want you to feel: that's the only thing that can help us," cries the estranged husband and father to his daughter.

Throughout the play settled prejudices are undermined by the contrariness of experience and by unpredictable shifts in perspective and feeling. The spirit of the title reigns over the action. Seemingly inviolable principles and decisions become irrelevant. The poised intellectuality of the young lovers—Gloria and her talkative dentist-suitor Valentine (also a partial self-portrait of Shaw)—is seen to conceal vast gaps in their emotional experience, and to create unnatural barriers to the fulfillment of their real needs and desires. The class structure turns out to be less rigid than it at first appears. Outrageous coincidences are the essence of both plot and theme. Although the realities of pain, bitterness, and discord are not underestimated, the emphasis falls on hopeful possibilities: life and chance appear in their benign aspects. The inclusion of the twins in the cast is but one reminder of playful and exuberant benignity in the workings of the Life Force in which the play invites us to rejoice.

* * *

Shaw began writing *The Devil's Disciple* on 10 September 1896 and completed it on 30 December. At the beginning of the year he had published an essay entitled "On Going to Church." The writing of this essay brought back memories of the narrow, puritanical Irish Protestantism to which he had been unwillingly exposed in his childhood. The more prosperous Dublin Shaw relatives, such as Sir Frederick Shaw, the Recorder of Dublin, and Shaw's uncle, Richard Frederick Shaw, head of the Dublin Valuation Office, were pillars of the Protestant Church of Ireland, and the Carr Shaw family owed at least outward allegiance to it. Shaw's attendance at a suburban Protestant church in his youth left the indelible memory of the "unnaturally motionless figures of the congregation in their Sunday clothes and bonnets, and their set faces, pale with the malignant rigidity produced by the suppression of all expression" quoted earlier in the present book.[55] It was from one of the pillars of the church, his uncle Richard Frederick Shaw, that GBS received the 1885 letter of stern disapproval about the "Socialist and Atheistic views" that had been reported to him by George Carr Shaw.[56]

Shaw's description of the Protestant church congregation of his youth could well be applied to the pharisaical Dudgeon family to which we are introduced in the first act of *The Devil's Disciple,* and especially to the embittered and malignant "*hard, driving, wrathful woman*" Mrs. Dudgeon, with her tight-lipped, suppressed anger. Mrs. Dudgeon was acknowledged by Shaw in the preface to *Three Plays for Puritans* to be practically a replica of Mrs Clennam in Dickens's *Little Dorrit.* In creating Richard Dudgeon—his blasphemous, uncle-baiting renegade, with his satirical attacks on the pious Dudgeon clan in the opening act of the play—Shaw seems to be taking comic revenge against the narrow Protestant churchgoers of his youth and the Shaw relatives in Dublin. Perhaps he was even taking a dig at his uncle by giving his "devil's disciple" the same first name as that of the man himself, Richard Frederick Shaw.

In the course of his letter to Shaw in 1885, his uncle had conceded to his errant nephew that "no one who knows you either personally, or by report, through your Father, ever doubted that in all the relations of private life and habits you are not otherwise than you ought to be—in fact I have no doubt myself that in these respects you are [an] example to many of very decided Christian profession." This thought also anticipates the play in that during the course of the action, it is the atheistic Richard Dudgeon who displays the most christian conduct when he bravely risks his life at the hands of the English authorities in order to save that of the Presbyterian minister Anderson. The minister, for his part, matches this role reversal when he decides, at the end of the play, that he is much more suited to being a military commander than a minister.

The theme of "you never can tell" runs through *The Devil's Disciple* in a different key from that of its predecessor. Good and evil and hero and villain are by no means as easy to tell apart as they were in the old Adelphi Theatre melodramas. Shaw nevertheless frankly admitted to plundering Victorian melodramas for familiar standbys of plot and action in his play. "Every old patron of the Adelphi pit," he wrote, would "recognize the reading of the will, the arrest, the heroic sacrifice, the court martial, the scaffold, the reprieve at the last moment, as he recognizes beefsteak pudding on the bill of fare at his restaurant."[57]

Another, very different influence behind the creation of *The Devil's Disciple* was that of William Blake, particularly *The Marriage of Heaven and Hell.* Shaw also mentions Nietszche's *Beyond Good and Evil* as part of the intellectual ethos of the period when his play was being written. His diary records a reading of a reprint of *The Marriage of Heaven and Hell* in the arts-and-crafts quarterly *The Hobby Horse* on New Year's Day 1888. In addition, while on a journey from Leeds to London on 27 October 1890 (after lecturing on "Socialism" in Bradford) he records that he "read a lot of Blake's poems in the train."[58] These readings seem to mark the beginning of the powerful influence that Blake would exert on Shaw's thought and imagination, making the poet one among a handful of writers whose "peculiar view of the world" he recognized as "more or less akin" to his own.[59] Shaw probably knew about Nietzsche's *Beyond Good and Evil* at least as early as 1894, when he met Miss Sophie Borchardt, a German mathematician, who mistakenly thought he must have read Nietzsche's book before writing *The Quintessence of Ibsenism.*[60] *Beyond Good and Evil* was not available in English translation until 1907, but Shaw seems to have been aware of the main thrust of its arguments well before that.

In the section "On Diabolonian Ethics" in his 1901 preface to *Three Plays for Puritans,* Shaw brought Blake and Nietzsche together in his account of the intellectual lineage of ideas in *The Devil's Disciple,* preceding this comment with a mention of Bunyan as opening up the notion of easy passages from heaven to hell: "A century ago William Blake was, like Dick Dudgeon, an avowed Diabolonian: he called his angels devils and his devils angels. His devil is a redeemer. Let those who have praised my originality in conceiving Dick Dudgeon's strange religion read Blake's Marriage of Heaven and Hell, and I shall be fortunate if they do not rail at me for a plagiarist. But they need not go back to Blake and Bunyan. Have they not heard the recent fuss about Nietzsche and his Good and Evil Turned Inside Out?"[61]

Shaw's inversion of conventional ideas about good and evil in *The Devil's Disciple* and its preface was to have far-reaching echoes in his work, especially in such plays as *Major Barbara.* His refusal to divide the world into the clear-cut heroes and villains of melodrama was to become one of the hallmarks of his oeuvre.

* * *

A first experience of cycling for Shaw occurred on 27 February 1885 when he took a two-hour ride on a tandem bicycle with fellow music critic and Socialist Belfort Bax.[62] Unfortunately, no pictorial record of this event exists. Shaw made his first attempt at riding solo on 24 April 1891. Then, two years later, on 1 May 1893, he "went to Praed St. [London], and carried out a resolution which had been half formed for some time, by taking a lesson in bicycle riding at Goya's school." It proved to be a "most humiliating experience," he reported, "but I paid for a dozen lessons, feeling that I must not retreat a beaten man."[63] It became a favorite recreation, both for Shaw and his friends Beatrice and Sidney Webb. On regular midyear retreats in the 1890s and early 1900s, either to attend Fabian summer schools or to thrash out matters connected with the Fabian Society's policy, planning, and publications, the cycling Fabians rode up hill and down dale in the English countryside.

Shaw was an unusually accident-prone cyclist, as he was later to be in his careers as a motorcyclist and car driver. In July 1896 he was run down by a bolting horse drawing a railway van in the Haymarket. Although he escaped with just bruises, his bicycle was mangled into "an amazing iron spider with twisted legs and umbrella-blown-inside-out wings."[64] This was one incident in a series of disasters the occasions of which he came to refer to in his correspondence as his "annual bicycle accident." In September of the previous year, while on a working holiday with the Webbs in South Wales, he had a spectacular collision with the philosopher Bertrand Russell on the way to visiting Tintern Abbey. As Shaw placed his feet on the footrest of his bicycle and surrendered himself "to the enjoyment of a headlong toboggan" down a long hill, Russell unexpectedly stopped in front of him. The future author of *The Analysis of Mind* and *The History of Western Philosophy* had paused to get his bearings.

> Imagine my feelings [Shaw later wrote to Janet Achurch, who liked his cycling stories] when I saw Russell jump off and turn his machine right across my path to read a signpost! Or rather imagine what I would have felt if I had had time for speculation. I rang my bell and swerved desperately to the right; he looked round and backed with his machine to the right—my right also. Then—smash. In the last second I managed to make a twist to the left which prevented my going into him absolutely at right angles. . . . Russell, fortunately, was not even scratched; but his knickerbockers were demolished—how I don't know.[65]

Shaw was shaken but survived. After jumping on a wheel to make it "moderately round," he resumed his journey.

Shaw's collision with Russell, with whom he later formed a quite close friendship, occurred on 12 September 1895. During the following year a new member of the Fabian bicycling set, Charlotte Payne-Townshend, would open another chapter in Shaw's philandering history and become increasingly important to him in both his professional and personal life.

12 An Irish Courtship

"I want to tell you lies face to face—close." Shaw's famous declaration to the woman who was later to become his wife, Charlotte Payne-Townshend, is contained in a letter dated 4 November 1896 from 29 Fitzroy Square that, significantly, begins with a discussion of Ireland. Charlotte was staying at her family's home at Rosscarbery, Derry, and had been writing to Shaw about the miseries of Ireland, quoting Joseph Sheridan Le Fanu, the Irish novelist and editor of various periodicals. The fact that Charlotte enclosed photographs of the Rosscarbery estate with her letter drew a teasing comment from Shaw: "Now was there ever so sentimental a woman as this! You quote Lefanu [*sic*] on the miseries of your country and then send me 'photographs of the palatial splendors in which you weep.'" He nevertheless continued: "I wish I were with you among those hills: there are two laps in which I could rest my fagged head just now—Nature's and yours." He went on to declare that he would have liked to travel directly to Derry by sea or balloon—no doubt to avoid the Dublin he disliked—just to spend one evening with her.[1] A desire to visit rural Ireland—he was later to make numerous visits to the west and enjoy long stays there—and his affection for the new friend he had met at the beginning of 1896 are interestingly combined in this letter.

The importance of Charlotte's Irish background and outlook in her relations with Shaw—apparent from his early letters to her—is sometimes overlooked. Like Shaw, she viewed the world from an Irish rather than an English perspective. When an occasion for doing so arose in 1935–36, they both formally declared their Irish citizenship.[2] Early in 1896 Charlotte had taken an apartment with "delightful rooms overlooking the river [Thames]"[3] at 10 Adelphi Terrace, W.C., above the new London School of Economics. This became for Shaw his Ireland of the imagination in London: "The address of *my* Ireland at present is 10 Adelphi Terrace," he told her in his letter of 4 November. In a letter to Ellen Terry Shaw referred to Charlotte as "Irish, shrewd & green eyed." In another summary description of Charlotte for Ellen he wrote:

"Miss P.T. is a restful person, plain, greeneyed, very ladylike, completely demoralized by contact with my ideas, forty, with nice rooms on a solid basis of £4000 a year, independent & unencumbered, and not so very plain either when you are in her confidence."[4]

In a way, the relationship with the "restful" Charlotte seems to have represented a form of Irish homecoming for Shaw, a spiritual reunion with his country, free of the unhappy associations with Dublin, and without the problematic aspects of his relationship with his previous Irish lady friend, Jenny Patterson. It is noteworthy that two of Shaw's most fully committed female relationships—those with Jenny and Charlotte–were with Irishwomen.

Charlotte was not, as Malcolm Muggeridge archly pointed out in his otherwise rather misleading account of the lead-up to the Shaw–Payne-Townshend marriage, one of Shaw's "luscious actresses."[5] As Beatrice Webb wrote in her diary, partly echoing Shaw's observations to Ellen Terry, Charlotte could appear as alternately attractive and rather plain. When she met Charlotte Payne-Townshend, then in her late thirties, Webb created in her diary an evocative cameo of the wealthy young woman who was becoming an important new member of the Fabian circle: "In person she is attractive—a large graceful woman with masses of chocolate brown hair, pleasant grey eyes, matte complexion which sometimes looks muddy, at other times forms a picturesquely pale background to her brilliant hair and bright eyes. She dresses well—in her flowing white evening robe she approaches beauty. At moments she is plain. By temperament she is an anarchist—feeling any regulation or rule intolerable."[6]

Although Charlotte was intelligent, well read, and of high social rank, she remained unpretentious and without the acute sense of class consciousness and snobbery that in English society often accompanies social position of the kind she occupied. As her own correspondence and several accounts by others testify, she had a graceful, natural courtesy and warmth and an underlying strength of character and perspicacity. There is, of course, a good deal of Shaw's characteristic blarney and gaiety in his letters to her. But there is also in some of them a tone of directness and plain-speaking, a matter-of-fact reporting of events and affectionate familiarity that contrasts with the ostentatious gallantry he frequently displayed with other women. Their shared national, social, and cultural background—albeit different in material circumstances—may have combined with the special qualities in Charlotte's character to create this relaxed atmosphere in his letters to her.

The characteristics Charlotte had inherited from her father—a love of serious reading and foreign languages and an interest in public affairs—were not particularly appreciated in the social whirl of London, Dublin, and the counties of Ireland and England that occupied a great part of her life as a young woman. The family had a house in London at 21 Queen's Gate, near Hyde Park, as well as the estate in Derry. These provided the base for what Charlotte's biographer, Janet Dunbar, has described as the "variegated treadmill"[7] of Charlotte's social life, involving attendance at balls, the opera (including Wagner), riding and hunting, the season in London, and travels to the Continent. Such activities did not fulfill her inner need for purpose and direction in life—different from the more common path for a woman in her situation of a suitable marriage and motherhood—or square with her emerging feminist inclinations. Like Shaw, she was a born nonconformist.

Throughout her life Charlotte—who was known as "Lottie" in the family circle—was a careful recorder of her activities and kept numerous diaries. She had an orderly, practical side to her character, which was reflected in the keeping of these records, in the detailed packing lists she drew up for her travels, and in her exceptional skills as a household manager. One of the diaries—a blue, lined writing pad totaling 106 pages—contains annual summaries from 1876 to 1919. The early sections provide a broad picture of her life before marriage. In 1880, when she was twenty-three, she "saw much of Lord Aranmore," a very eligible young Irish bachelor. This was one of the first of several relationships with men that did not result in marriage. On 18 June that same year she records "our first large London ball"; the Payne-Townshends hosted another ball in London in June of the following year. In 1882, "at dinner at Lord Tollemaches," she met her future brother-in-law, Colonel (later Brigadier General) Hugh Cholmondeley, who married Charlotte's sister, Mary, in March 1885. In February 1882 her father died, and with the death of her mother, Mary Susanna Townshend, in September 1893, she and her sister came into their full inheritance.[8]

Charlotte's numerous suitors prior to meeting Shaw included: Count Frederick Wilhelm Sponnek, secretary to the Danish legation in London; Arthur Smith Barry, a wealthy MP; David Finch Hatton, a young Irish adventurer who made a fortune in America and sent Charlotte a bearskin from Wyoming; a Major Hutton, who proposed to her precipitously in Hyde Park; and a General Clery, a sensitive and intelligent man with whom she had a serious but inconclusive relationship. During the course of these affairs she traveled extensively and in great style. In the northern winter of 1892–93 (when Shaw's career as a playwright was beginning) she visited India, where she attended a state ball in Calcutta, a garden party at Government House, dinners and dances, and joined a hunting party, shooting panthers.

During 1893, while on a visit to his house at Aldershot, Charlotte and General Clery had a long, passionate, and apparently rather meaningful kiss in the drawing room. The moment presented Charlotte with a serious challenge concerning the future course of her life. The general was an eminently eligible suitor and wanted to marry her, but she was not ready to give up her personal freedom. He wrote: "If I kissed you too passionately my kiss was as pure and sacred as your own. . . . I never saw your eyes so soft before."[9] Charlotte retreated to Yorkshire to stay with Hugh and Sissy and think things over. In a long letter to Clery she explained her feelings. She wanted to do something useful in life, and marriage was not the answer to her needs. He wrote back generously: "You are free, as free as if that night had never been. The only one tied to that is *me*. Whatever step you may take, even if the saddest for me . . . I still remain your debtor for a debt nothing in this world could enable me to repay."[10]

On 5 January 1894, leaving behind the Clery affair and a recently established London residence at Walsingham House, the thirty-seven year-old Charlotte traveled to Egypt on the steamer *Khedive*. In Egypt she was invited by Lord and Lady Waterford to join them aboard their yacht and had lunch with General (later Earl) Horatio Herbert Kitchener, then commander in chief of the British forces in the Sudan, who served as the model for Shaw's character General Mitchener in *Press Cuttings* (1909), his one-act comedy about the woman suffrage movement. Having toured in Egypt, Charlotte decided to journey to Rome via Naples, reaching her destination on 31 March. Upon arrival, she dined at the Grand Hotel with Edmund Yates (presumably the editor who had employed Shaw as art critic for his periodical the *World* from 1886 to 1889) and his wife.[11] It was on this occasion that Charlotte met Axel Martin Fredrik Munthe—the person with whom she would have the last of her serious involvements before meeting Shaw—a Swedish doctor and psychiatrist who was later to become physician to the Swedish royal family and an acclaimed author.

The handsome Dr. Munthe, who was born in 1857 (the same year as Charlotte), was a charismatic figure, an unusual mixture of dedicated medical man, world traveler and raconteur, animal and bird lover, and romantic nature-mystic. He fulfilled his dream of building a villa on the isle of Capri, and subsequently wrote an autobiographical bestseller entitled *The Story of San Michele* about that and his earlier career. The book, the writing of which he claimed was suggested by Henry James, includes his account of his studies at Salpêtrière in Paris under the famous French neurologist Jean-Martin Charcot. Munthe was critical of Charcot's use of hypnosis in his treatment of female patients and of his theories concerning hysteria, which interested Freud. Munthe's patients included the poor and destitute in Naples, Rome, and Paris as well as the very rich. When Charlotte met him in Rome, he had an *ambu-*

latorio, a clinic in one of the poor quarters, in addition to looking after his wealthy—mainly female—patients. While still in his early twenties he had married a Swedish girl, Ultima Hornberg, whom he divorced after eight years.

Upon arrival in Rome, Charlotte stayed briefly in a flat at 25 Via Gregoriana, a fashionable area near the center of the city, and then moved to the Hôtel de l'Europe. She continued to see more of Dr. Munthe in Rome, and by 8 May she "started for Venice," where Dr. Munthe was also staying. On her side at least the relationship had turned into a love affair, but Munthe evidently did not want it to go beyond a friendship. Meetings and a desultory correspondence between them continued. In 1895, while on another visit to Rome, Charlotte had a pastel portrait of herself done by the Italian painter Giulio Aristide Sartorio, which she subsequently gave to Munthe. He wrote back to say "I cannot and will not accept it."[12] The portrait was returned to Charlotte and later became one of the objets d'art in Charlotte and Bernard Shaw's houses.

Charlotte was clearly deeply impressed by Munthe, and their meetings and correspondence continued until nearly the end of 1895. When Shaw later told Ellen Terry that Charlotte had "picked up a broken heart somewhere a few years ago," he was almost certainly referring to the outcome of the Munthe affair.[13] Munthe subsequently married his second wife, Hilda Pennington-Mellor, and built his villa on the site of one previously established (according to tradition) by the Roman emperor Tiberius on a promontory, on the isle of Capri, with a spectacular view of the Bay of Naples.

* * *

Charlotte returned to Rome late in 1894 and stayed there for several months without meeting Munthe, sitting for her Sartorio portrait during the early months of the following year. Back in London in the summer of 1895, she "learned to bicycle" a few months after Shaw had learned the same accomplishment, in his case "with a desperate struggle."[14] The two were still personally unacquainted. It was during the late summer of 1895 that she began to make contact with the Fabian circle. She heard the Canadian-born, somewhat wayward, Fabian Society member Grant Allen lecture at William Morris's Kelmscott House on 4 August.[15] Around this time she also met Sidney and Beatrice Webb and became interested in their work, as well as in the founding of the new London School of Economics, to which she made a handsome gift of one thousand pounds to its library.[16] Charlotte records a "luncheon with the Sidney Webbs" on 10 October 1895, in the company of her sister, Mary.[17]

Charlotte's meeting with Shaw occurred at another luncheon with the Webbs on 29 January 1896. The brief statement in her annual summary for 1896—"met G.B.S. first time at Webbs"—is the only record we have of this occasion.[18] It was at about this time that Charlotte began leasing the apartment at 10 Adelphi Terrace that was to become their London home following their marriage. On 21 March Shaw was invited to an at home hosted by Charlotte at Adelphi Terrace in connection with one of a series of lectures on German Social Democracy being presented by Bertrand Russell for the London School of Economics during its first year of operation.[19] Shaw's diary indicates that he did not attend this at home, his main occupation for the day being to "meet Archer in British Museum Reading Room at 12 and go to see bicycle." William Archer had succumbed to the new craze and Shaw was going to show him the Elswick and Osmond models available in London bicycle shops.[20]

The friendship between Shaw and Charlotte began to flourish during the late summer and early autumn of 1896. From 1 August to 17 September of that year Charlotte and the Webbs rented the Stratford St. Andrew Rectory, near Saxmundham, in Suffolk. They invited Shaw and Graham Wallas—the Fabian political scientist who was now a lecturer in the London School of Economics—to join them as house guests. According to the ever-watchful Beatrice Webb, very early in this working holiday Shaw and Charlotte became "constant companions . . . scouring the country together and sitting up late at night."[21]

The period of courtship—the term itself is something of a misnomer since Shaw spent considerable effort early on trying to persuade Charlotte *not* to fall in love with him—was protracted and complicated. Shaw had never been busier, and his hectic work schedule was destined to lead, by the summer of 1898, to a serious breakdown in his health, which was to be a precipitating event in his and Charlotte's decision to marry. In 1896 and 1897 his Fabian meetings and his lecture schedule continued unabated, along with the production of his weekly articles on the theater for the *Saturday Review*. At the end of 1896 he completed *The Devil's Disciple*, and in the following year he was involved in the abortive production of *You Never Can Tell* at the Haymarket Theatre, as well as in the considerable task of preparing his *Plays Pleasant and Unpleasant* for publication in two volumes by Grant Richards in April 1898.

As if all this were not enough, he decided to become actively involved in local government. In 1894 he had run unsuccessfully for the St. Pancras Vestry, the predecessor of the St. Pancras Metropolitan Borough Council. He stood again in 1897 and was elected unopposed, attending his first Vestry meeting on 26 May 1897 and continuing to serve as an effective and reformist Vestryman and Borough Councillor in St. Pancras until 1903.[22] Shaw was not a man interested in the pursuit of power for its own sake. He searched for and found in the local government work a way of doing something practical about the conditions of life referred to in his first play, *Widowers' Houses.*

* * *

In the meantime, there was also the problem of Bertha Newcombe, the last in a long line of disappointed Fabian ladies Shaw left in his wake on his journey toward marriage. In the letter of 24 August 1895 in which he had told Janet Achurch that "everybody seems bent on recommending me to marry Bertha," he made it clear that he himself was quite averse to the idea, but that this resolve only had the effect of further encouraging Bertha's feelings toward him. He complained that "she has no idea with regard to me except that she would like to tie me like a pet dog to the leg of her easel & have me always to make love to her when she is tired of painting."[23]

More than thirty years later, when she reread this letter in connection with a proposal for a publication that did not materialize, Bertha wrote a sad, still bitter account of her side of the story of her unrequited love, which remained unpublished until it was included in the first volume of Shaw's *Collected Letters.* Bertha acknowledged that Shaw was not really in love with her, but that on her side there was "a deep feeling most injudiciously displayed." She claimed—perhaps with some justification, considering the affair with Jenny Patterson—that while admitting the "power & pleasure" of passion, Shaw had come to fear it because of experiences he had undergone.[24] Bertha may have been partly taking her cue for her description of Shaw in this 1928 "note" from his own melodramatic representation of himself as an unfeeling, satanic monster. "I am a fiend, delighting in vivisectional cruelties, as indicated by the corners of my mouth," he told her sardonically in a letter dated 31 March 1896. This followed his telling Bertha that her sex only liked him "as children like wedding cake, for the sake of the sugar on top. If they taste by an accident a bit of crumb or citron, it is all over."[25]

Beatrice Webb was almost certainly one of those who had been encouraging Shaw to marry Bertha: on at least two occasions in 1894–95 she had arranged for them to join her holiday parties. On 9 March 1897 she visited the heartbroken Bertha, a petite woman with jet-black hair, at her studio in Cheyne Walk and was greeted coldly. Bertha, "a sad soul full of bitterness and loneliness" and looking physically shrunken, poured out her tale of five years' devotion to Shaw and his "cold philandering" with some resentment toward her visitor, who, she had been told, was now encouraging Shaw to marry Miss Townshend. Beatrice told Bertha gently that she was well out of the relationship with Shaw, that she herself admired him enormously as a critic and literary worker, but that in his relations with women he was vulgar, cruel, and vain. After this imperious judgment, as she was about to make her way out of the uncomfortable meeting with Bertha, they both looked up at her portrait of the subject of their conversation, seeing "his red-gold hair and laughing blue eyes and his mouth slightly open as if scoffing at us both." As she made her escape down the stairs, Beatrice's thoughts turned to Bertha's rival, Charlotte: "And then I thought of that other woman with her loving easygoing nature and anarchic luxurious ways, her well-bred manners and well-made clothes, her leisure, wealth and knowledge of the world. Would she succeed in taming the philanderer?"[26] "Taming the philanderer" was a difficult task, and one that was never, in fact, fully accomplished, but Charlotte was to prove more successful than others.

* * *

Beatrice Webb's view of the—to her—"disturbing" friendship between Shaw and Charlotte as it developed from 1896 through the first half of 1898 was clearly colored by her own deeply—and self-admittedly—ambivalent attitude toward Shaw himself: "Whether I like him, admire him or despise him most I do not know," she wrote in her diary on 8 May 1897. Soon afterward she was praising his "extraordinary good nature" in spending days going over work written by herself and Sidney and saying that "an astute reader will quickly divine those chapters which Shaw has corrected and those which he has not—there is a conciseness and crispness in parts subjected to his pruning-knife lacking elsewhere."[27]

On a personal level Beatrice and Shaw had a strained relationship, probably not unconnected with sexual tension. She was a strikingly attractive woman.[28] In a revealing letter Shaw wrote to Janet Achurch in 1895 from the Webbs' retreat at The Argoed, in the Wye Valley, he provided a detailed account of his relationship with Beatrice, contrasting it with his much more easygoing friendship with Sidney. He and Beatrice got on one another's nerves and were embarrassed when left alone without some distracting subject of keen interest to them both to discuss. She disliked his "silly . . . philanderings" and vanity.[29] He felt himself temperamentally at odds with her and found the Webbs' constant physical expressions of their affection for one another, "their incorrigible spooning over their industrial and political science," distasteful.[30] The Fabian trio appears to have had extraordinarily frank discussions about one another's characters and foibles during their numerous stays in the country.

Beatrice Webb's sharply critical view of Shaw's behavior toward Charlotte in the years preceding his marriage is greatly modified by a reading of Shaw's letters to this new woman in his life during the same period. The letters not only indicate Shaw's growing fondness for Charlotte—even the hypercritical Beatrice acknowledged a "sort of affectionateness"[31] in his character—but also show a real concern on his part about the danger for her of falling in love with him and, more generally, about her emotional well-being. Shaw was thirty-nine when he met Charlotte, and by this time—if not earlier—must have entertained serious doubts at to whether "the irrational knot" (as he called marriage in the title of his early novel) was one he ever wanted to tie, or whether this was a state for which he was personally suited. The institution of marriage had been viewed very critically by Shaw in his writing's, from the early novels to *Candida*.

Charlotte appears to have experienced times of deep unhappiness—as well as great enjoyment of her newfound friends and interests—during this period before mid 1898. Whether this was caused by the uncertainty about her relations with Shaw, lingering sadness about the failure of previous affairs, or a combination of both is difficult to determine. Shaw tried to rally her from her depressions: "You look as if you had returned to your old amusement of eating your heart," he observed in an undated note to her written sometime in late 1896 or early 1897.[32] After her return from Stratford St. Andrews in September 1896, Charlotte continued staying with the Webbs—who were now back at their London house in Grosvenor Road—before setting off with Beatrice on 26 October to attend a conference of the National Union of Women Workers in Manchester. She was experiencing some illness and pain (possibly neuralgia, from which she frequently suffered at this time) when Shaw wrote her on the twenty-seventh, "unspeakably hurried and worried," and saying: "Oh for ten minutes peace in the moonlight at Stratford! Keep me advised of your address; keep me deep in your heart; write me two lines whenever you love me; and be happy and blessed and out of pain for my sake."[33]

This letter gave the first clear indication that the constant companionship at Stratford St. Andrew had become a love relationship. On 4 November—by which time Charlotte had moved to Derry—he wrote his letter expressing his wish to be with her, telling her "lies face to face." Two days later the "heart-wise" Ellen Terry was called upon like an agony columnist for advice about his situation with the green-eyed lady, who had become fond of him and who, before she met Shaw, had read *The Quintessence of Ibsenism*, "in which she found, as she thought, gospel, salvation, freedom, emancipation, self-respect & so on."[34] Terry's reply was forthright, sensitive, and sensible: "'Plainly and bluntly' you are a great silly Dear. . . . If *she* does not dote upon the quintessence of *you*, she'd better marry your book! . . . How very silly you clever people are. Fancy not knowing! Fancy not being sure! Do *you* know you love her? 'Cos if so, that would be safe enough to marry on. . . . One thing I am clever enough to know. . . . You'd be all bad, and no good in you, if you marry anyone unless you know you love her."[35] She advised Shaw to ask for Charlotte's hand in marriage.

Things had become serious, with the Shavian Uranian liberty under threat once again. Two days later, on Saturday, 7 November, he was trying to talk Charlotte out of being in love with him: "No: you don't love me one little bit. All that is nature, instinct, sex: it proves nothing beyond itself. Don't fall in love: be your own, not mine or anyone else's. From the moment that you can't do without me, you're lost, like Bertha."[36] But the following Monday, in the midst of preparations to go to Paris to see a Lugné-Poë production of *Peer Gynt,* he wrote: "I will contrive to see you somehow, at all hazards: I *must;* and that 'must,' which rather alarms you, TERRIFIES me." He wanted to run away—if that would help—fearful that his "ingrained treachery and levity" with women would make her miserable when what he wanted was to make her "strong and self possessed and tranquil." He continued with the words: "Bless me! How I should like to see you again for pure *liking;* for there is something between us aside and apart from all my villainy."[37]

The affair was to drag on for another eighteen months before its resolution in June 1898. Charlotte joined the Fabian Society toward the end of 1896 and began attending meetings and Shaw's lectures. He regularly visited Adelphi Terrace and the two attended plays together. From April to June 1897 Charlotte and the Webbs took a cottage at Tower Hill on the North Downs, near Dorking, in Surrey. Shaw commuted between there and London, where he was still reviewing, attending meetings, and overseeing rehearsals for the eventually abandoned production of *You Never Can Tell* at the Haymarket. By this time Charlotte had begun to act as his secretary. Beatrice Webb's diary for May provides a glimpse of the morning activities of Shaw and his "secretary" at the cottage: "Charlotte sits upstairs typewriting Shaw's plays. Shaw wanders about the garden with his writing-book and pencil, writing the *Saturday* article, correcting his plays for press or reading through one of our chapters."[38]

But also down in Surrey there occurred an incident in the relationship, which Shaw described to Ellen Terry as "a sort of earthquake"—when Charlotte took the initiative of making a proposal of marriage. Shaw's later description of this event to Ellen Terry in August makes his response sound frivolous: "When I received that golden moment with shuddering horror & wildly asked the fare to Australia, she was inexpressibly taken aback, and her pride, which is considerable, was much startled."[39] Nearer the time of the proposal, however, he wrote a remorseful letter to Charlotte about the pain his rejection of it had caused her. In this letter the idea of a flight to Australia takes on an entirely different complexion: “I have an iron ring round my chest, which tightens and grips my heart when I remember that you are perhaps still tormented. Loosen it, oh ever dear to me, by a word to say you slept well and have never been better than today. Or else lend me my fare to Australia, to Siberia, to the mountains of the moon, to any place where I can torment nobody but myself. I am sorry—not vainly sorry; for I have done a good morning's work, but painfully, wistfully, affectionately sorry that you were hurt.”[40]

In this letter Shaw's rhetorical idea of self-banishment to a remote place is part of his way of expressing what seems to be a quite genuine concern about his capacity for causing pain to Charlotte. The way he put it in the letter to Ellen Terry—presenting himself as a man desperately wanting to bolt from the clutches of a woman bent on his capture in marriage—had more potential for use in comedy. It was to find just such a use in Shaw's depiction of the reverse love-chase at the center of the action in his early-twentieth-century play *Man and Superman.* Here the voluble and amusing gentleman Socialist Jack Tanner is a highly intelligent talker but sublimely ignorant about affairs of the heart and the wiles of the opposite sex. When his shrewd chauffeur, Straker, finally gets him to realize that it is he, Tanner, and not the conventionally romantic young poet Octavius, who is the “marked down victim, the destined prey” in the heiress Ann Whitefield's plans for a husband, Tanner immediately orders Straker to break the land speed record from London to Biskra and get to “any port from which we can sail to a Mahometan country where men are protected from women.”

Further echoes in Shaw's dramatic writings of his relation with Charlotte and his general situation in the days before their marriage can be found in *John Bull's Other Island* (1904), the successor to *Man and Superman* in the Shavian canon. The John Bull figure in this play is Tom Broadbent, an ebullient, unquenchably optimistic, sentimental, gullible, and rather stupid yet amiable Englishman. One of his numerous triumphs while on a visit to the small town of Rosscullen is to win the hand of Nora Reilly, a local Irish lady. Nora is a sensible and perceptive woman with a delightful Irish accent, but she carries a heavy burden of sadness caused by the heartbreak of her failed relation with Broadbent's partner, Larry Doyle, over whom she has been pining for eighteen years. Broadbent offers her his broad (“not less than forty-two inches”) chest to cry on and a large silk handkerchief to wipe her tears with. After confessing to several previous dalliances with other women (“mostly married already”), he succeeds in buoying Nora's spirits. Instead of offering her a love affair ("love affairs always end in rows"), he offers her a solid marriage, "a four-square home: man and wife: comfort and common sense. And plenty of affection." She accepts.

Autobiographical strains in *John Bull's Other Island* are more commonly traced to the portrayal of Larry Doyle—Broadbent's cynical and unromantic partner, expatriate Irishman, and scathing critic of "romantic" Ireland—and the visionary defrocked priest Keegan. However, beneath the splendid satirical portrait of Broadbent there are echoes of Shaw's situation in the years immediately preceding his marriage and his relationship with Charlotte: his numerous dalliances with other women "mostly married"; his love affairs ending in rows; his attempts to cheer Charlotte out of her fits of melancholy and "eating [her] heart" and to get her to look forward to a future of useful activity rather than back upon a past of broken dreams. Even Broadbent's image of the kind of marriage he envisages for Nora and himself— of "comfort and common sense . . . and plenty of affection"—is not so very different from the actual marriage that Shaw finally gladly settled for—much to his sister Lucy's disgust—with Charlotte.

If an impulse to take flight, however motivated, was one response by Shaw to the prospect of marriage with Charlotte, there were also needs within him that—combined with his "pure *liking*" for her and the accidental circumstances that arose in relation to his health—were to point Shaw in the opposite direction.

* * *

In December 1897 Shaw declined an invitation from Charlotte to join her and her friend Mrs. Lucy ("Lion") Phillimore—a social worker and wife of Fabian Society member and St. Pancras Vestryman Robert Charles Phillimore—on a short trip to Dieppe. Probably annoyed by Shaw's response, Charlotte departed for Dieppe on 5 December without informing him. Still unaware that she had left the country on the seventh, Shaw dispatched a curt note: "Secretary required tomorrow, not later than eleven."[41] He had become heavily dependent on Charlotte's help. She, however, was to make a much longer visit to the Continent, again in the company of Lion Phillimore, from March to May 1898, obliging Shaw to call on Kate Salt as a substitute secretary.

Perhaps influenced by her association with the Webbs and Shaw's work with the St. Pancras Vestry—he was later to write a book called *The Common Sense of Municipal Trading*—Charlotte had conceived the idea of researching and writing a book about the Roman municipality. She traveled to Rome and collected "a gigantic quantity of documents."[42] In her absence Shaw kept a diary of his activities, written on the leaves of his desk calendar, posting them off to Charlotte with covering letters. The installment recording her departure on 12 March 1898 reads:

> Charlotte deserts me at 11.
> Divide the rest of the day between tears and answering letters.
> Digestion wholly ceases.
> Try to sing "Egypt was glad when they departed," by Handel.
> Failure.
> No exercise today.[43]

Charlotte's departure for Rome almost coincided with that of the Webbs, on 23 March 1898, for a tour of America and Australasia that lasted until the following December. Shaw was left feeling "detestably deserted" in London, with only his mother and the St. Pancras Vestry people to talk to.[44] He was not eating properly and was working furiously at all hours of the day and night.

His detailed reports of his days to Charlotte show an underlying wish to keep closely in touch with her. But there were many notes of querulousness—and even melancholy—especially in early April, when he heard about Eleanor Marx's suicide, which had occurred on 31 March 1898, after she had found out about her common-law husband Edward Aveling's secret marriage to Eva Frye the previous year.

The day before this event Shaw gave vent to some extraordinarily ferocious feelings about Charlotte in a letter. Shaw the vivisectional fiend erupted, with Charlotte as the subject-victim. He revived his old rhetorical practice of dividing his close women friends into split personalities. It was quite good that she had departed, he wrote, because it left him with just the Charlotte who fitted his "dreamland," the woman with "die schöne grüne Augen" and not "the other Charlotte, the terrible Charlotte, the lier-in-wait, the soul hypochondriac, always watching and dragging me into bondage, always planning nice sensible, comfortable, selfish destruction for me . . . with the absorbing passion of the spider for the fly."[45] The Lawrentian ferocity of this letter was only slightly modified by its half-comic ending—containing an orthographic representation of an extended growl—and by the tone of the next installment of news, in the course of which he admitted that Kate Salt was complaining of his "irritability and savagery." Charlotte, the rival secretary, was probably pleased to hear that Shaw's mother thought Kate "a dense divil."[46] Shaw was finding Kate, his old pianoforte duet partner and admirer, exasperating and was irritated by her habit of producing a comb and titivating herself in his mirror before the beginning of every work session.[47]

He missed Charlotte physically. It was "frightful not to be able to kiss your secretary occasionally."[48] He needed hugs, a characteristic he gave to Tom

Broadbent in *John Bull's Other Island*. On 12 April, having finally received a letter from Charlotte ("the vindictive Irishwoman") after a break in their correspondence—which aroused his suspicion that some Italian doctor (a Munthe substitute, perhaps) was distracting her—he exclaims triumphantly: "Ha! Ha! If only I had her here in these arms: all her ribs would crack."[49]

April 1898 was to prove a cruel month for Shaw. His teeth had been giving him trouble for some time, providing him with material for the opening scene in a dental clinic in *You Never Can Tell*. On the 7 April he gave Charlotte a graphic account of a dental operation that day involving general anesthesia. He was feeling exhausted as well as deserted. "Oh Charlotte, Charlotte," he wrote, "is this a time to be gadding about in Rome!"[50] Then there followed another medical problem. For no reason apparent to him other than that he had pinched his instep while doing up his shoelaces, Shaw's left foot began to swell to an enormous size. With characteristically lively exaggeration he reported to Charlotte on 19 April that the foot was "the size of a leg of mutton." By the twenty-first it had become "as large as the Albert Hall."[51]

His cycling having aggravated the original condition, he was now suffering excruciating pain and was barely able to get about. He was "a fearful wreck."[52] The following day he wrote to her saying he had hopped to a Fabian business meeting on one leg, and that she had been elected to the executive of the society, of which she had become a member in late 1896. He also told her that he had resolved to consult Dr. Salisbury Sharpe, who by this time had married Shaw's old flame Alice Lockett. When Sharpe visited on the twenty-third, he was accompanied by Alice, who, without revealing her presence, sat in an adjacent room during the consultation. Another ghost from the past who had appeared during Charlotte's absence was Jenny Patterson. On his return to 29 Fitzroy Square one day, Shaw was amazed to discover "BILLY" (a nickname for Jenny) brazenly visiting his mother. Making a hasty escape, Shaw bolted into his study like a rabbit.[53]

Sharpe recommended a hot-water treatment plus rest. Shaw took the opportunity, on 23 April, to begin the writing of a new play entitled *Caesar and Cleopatra* (1898). Against Sharpe's advice, he was still hopping around London and attending meetings. By the end of the month Charlotte's return was imminent. On the 1 May he made his way round to Adelphi Terrace to welcome her home at 8 p.m., only to discover to his dismay that, owing to some missed train connection, she had not yet arrived. An apologetic and concerned letter from Charlotte came to Fitzroy Square the following morning. She had had a dreadful journey and had herself been rather ill in Rome: "Well, here I am anyway now! Yes: I *might* have telegraphed: it was horrid of me. I am a wreck, mental & physical. Such a journey it was! . . . My dear—& your foot? Shall I go up to you, or will you come here, & when? Only tell me what you would prefer. Of course I am quite free—Charlotte."[54]

The foot problem, definitely not helped by Shaw's refusal to take sufficient rest, was worse than originally thought, and on the ninth of May he was operated upon under chloroform. A bone in his foot was found to be "*carious*," he wrote to Janet Achurch. Some form of necrosis had developed.[55]

One of the immediate consequences of his deteriorating health was to hasten his resignation from the *Saturday Review*. He had earlier given notice of his intention to quit at the end of the season, a decision partly based on his improving fortunes as a playwright and partly on a feeling that he was holding down a position that should go to somebody from the younger generation. His valedictory notice, written with great panache despite his disabled state, was published on 21 May 1898. He announced his successor to the post, Max Beerbohm, with a fine salutation: "The younger generation is knocking at the door; and as I open it there steps spritely in the incomparable Max."[56] The last of his weekly notices may have been concluded, but Shaw had by no means laid down his arms in the battle against the contemporary London theater. In a spirited opening passage of his preface to *Three Plays for Puritans* he elaborated on an idea foreshadowed in his last notice in the *Saturday Review*, namely, that his breakdown in health had actually been *caused* by the inanity of the nineteenth-century English theater: "The theatre struck me down like the veriest weakling. I sank under it like a baby fed on starch. My very bones began to perish, so that I had to get them planed and gouged by accomplished surgeons. . . . The doctors said: This man has not eaten meat for twenty years: he must eat it or die. I said: This man has been going to the London theatres for three years; and the soul of him has become inane and is feeding unnaturally on his body."[57] The valedictory notice in the *Saturday Review* marked the end of his regular theater-reviewing activities and employment as a journalist. The curtain was about to rise on an entirely new phase of his life.

13 Marriage

The question about the future of Shaw's relations with Charlotte was resolved at almost the same time as the publication, on 21 May 1898, of his "Valedictory" as theater critic in the *Saturday Review*, with events unfolding rapidly thereafter. On 20 May he casually asked Henry Arthur Jones—in the last sentence of a letter concerning Tolstoy's essay "What Is Art?"—whether he would advise him to get married.[1] Jones replied with a qualified "yes," referring Shaw to François Rabelais, whose character Panurge (*Pantagruel*, bk. 3, chap. 35) famously receives extensive advice on the subject, much of it ribald and completely self-contradictory. When Panurge asks Trouillogan, "Should Panurge, pray you, marry, yea or no?," he receives the perplexing answer: "He should do both." On 23 May Shaw wrote to his publisher Grant Richards: "I am going to get married. . . . Keep this dark until I have done it."[2]

Shaw's health problems were serious and would not get better for some time. He needed looking after and proper nursing in a comfortable household environment. He also needed to get away from London and committee work. In the letters he wrote Charlotte during her absence in Rome—aside from the fierce outburst contained in his letter of 30 March 1898—there were strong undercurrents of dependency and affection, not to mention his unreasonable expostulations about her desertion of the post of "secretary." He had grown accustomed to having this unusual and intelligent Irishwoman around, and this was one relationship he was not about to sever. They had both shown themselves to be wary of and skeptical about marriage as an institution; moreover, Charlotte can hardly have forgotten the painful rebuff she received when she previously overcame her doubts and proposed to Shaw. Nevertheless, a combination of mutual need and the circumstance that life had created in the form of Shaw's health troubles was sufficient to override the questionings of reason. They needed one another—and they needed to live together. To fulfill the latter aim without marriage would, in 1898, have caused serious damage to their reputations and, collaterally, to the Fabian Society and their whole social circle.

Once the decision had been made, Charlotte's organizational skills were tested. Because of Shaw's immobile condition, it was she who had to make the appointment at a registry office for the marriage ceremony, to go to a West End jeweler to buy her own wedding ring, and to seek out for rental the house in Haslemere, Surrey, to which the couple would retreat after the marriage, in addition to having to make numerous other arrangements necessary for Shaw's convalescence. In a letter written on 26 May to Graham Wallas, who, with Henry Salt, was to serve as one of the two witnesses at the ceremony, Shaw described Charlotte's ring—her "symbol of slavery," as he called it—as "a modern article of such portentous weight and thickness, that it is impossible for anyone but a professional pianist to wear it; so my mother has presented her with my grandmother's wedding ring for general use."[3]

William Albert Samuel Hewins, the first director of the London School of Economics, met Charlotte a few days before the wedding and—with a reference to Tennyson's description of the happy isle to which the dying King Arthur travels to "heal his grievous wound" at the end of *Idylls of the King*—reported to Sidney Webb on May 30 that "Miss P.T. is very busy nursing Shaw and looking for some 'bowery hollow crowned with summer seas' where he can recover his strength." According to Hewins, Charlotte had really gone to Rome because she "couldn't make up her mind to marry Shaw."[4]

The wedding took place at 11:30 a.m. on Wednesday, 1 June 1898, at a registry office situated at 15 Henrietta Street, Covent Garden, close to where people take shelter from torrents of rain and where Eliza Doolittle sells her flowers in the opening scene of *Pygmalion*. Shaw's comic inventiveness was apparent in several accounts of the wedding. In a version supplied much later to Archibald Henderson, Shaw said that he was "altogether a wreck on crutches and in an old jacket which the crutches had worn to rags," whereas his two witnesses, Henry Salt and Graham Wallas, had put on their best clothes. "The registrar" he continued, "never imagined I could possibly be the bridegroom; he took me for the inevitable beggar who completes all wedding processions. Wallas, who is considerably over six feet high, seemed to him to be the hero of the occasion, and he was proceeding to marry him calmly to my betrothed, when Wallas, thinking the formula rather strong for a mere witness, hesitated at the last moment and left the prize to me."[5]

Just as heavy summer rain accidentally initiates the action in Shaw's 1912 play *Pygmalion*, so it does in the miniature comedy, with a distinctly Irish flavor, that Shaw created in the form of a newspaper report of his wedding. On

2 June 1898, the day after the event, his report was published anonymously in the *Star*, his old hunting ground, as the music critic "Corno di Bassetto":

> As a lady and gentleman were out driving in Henrietta-st., Covent-garden yesterday, a heavy shower drove them to take shelter in the office of the Superintendant Registrar there, and in the confusion of the moment he married them. The lady was an Irish lady Miss Payne-Townshend, and the gentleman was George Bernard Shaw.
>
> Mr. Graham Wallas and Mr. H. S. Salt were also driven by stress of weather into the registrar's, and the latter being secretary of the Humanitarian League would naturally have remonstrated against the proceedings had there been time, but there wasn't. Mr. Bernard Shaw means to go off to the country next week to recuperate, and this is the second operation he has undergone lately, the first being conducted, not by a registrar, but by a surgeon.[6]

Shaw slipped into the final paragraph of this story references to Charlotte's wealth and his own frugal habits as a vegetarian: "Miss Payne-Townshend is an Irish lady with an income many times the volume of that which 'Corno di Bassetto' used to earn, but to that happy man, being a vegetarian, the circumstance is of no moment." The subject was, of course, quite delicate, especially for someone as scrupulous and honorable about money as Shaw. He didn't want to be seen as a fortune hunter or "adventurer," the charge he had unkindly leveled at his father.

At the time of the marriage—largely owing to the success in America of *The Devil's Disciple* and the modest but steady income he had been receiving from journalism—Shaw had banked quite a lot of money and had even begun to make a few investments in stocks.[7] Nevertheless, he was still far from wealthy and fully secure financially. He could not justly be accused of marrying her for money, although in fact he virtually was so by Charlotte's relatives; but the marriage did nevertheless provide him with substantial financial support. Genteel poverty was no longer his lot. On 24 May 1899 two trust funds (to be administered by Sidney Webb and Stage Society founder and Fabian Frederick Whelen) were established in a settlement drawn up by Charlotte's solicitors, according to the terms of which Shaw was guaranteed an annual income. The settlement provided "about £750 a year" for Shaw, of which he gave his mother £300 a year. He also paid for extensive renovations to 29 Fitzroy Square to make it "decent and healthy."[8] In the following century he was to become a relatively wealthy man in his own right.

Following the marriage, the newlyweds remained for a week in London, with Shaw not yet having made the move to Charlotte's apartment at 10 Adelphi Terrace. As though to prove that the philanderer had not been tamed, Shaw wrote a playfully flirtatious note to the actress Lena Ashwell (née Pocock, later Dame Lena Ashwell) on the very afternoon of his wedding day. In this communication Shaw told Lena that after he had "hopped into a registrar's office and got married" that morning, he had found a letter from her awaiting him when he returned to 29 Fitzroy Square. Had the letter arrived by an earlier post, he continued, "I think I should have waited on the chance of something fatal happening to Mr Playfair [Lena's first husband, Arthur Playfair] in the course of the next forty years or so."[9] Lena was to play an important part in Shaw's later career as a playwright, as well as to become a close friend of Charlotte's.

The marriage had its critics from both the bride and bridegroom's side. Eventually a cordial friendship developed between Shaw and Charlotte's sister Mary Cholmondeley. The Shaws later took holidays with the Cholmondeleys, and Mary accompanied them on numerous automobile tours. She made a ballooning ascent with Shaw in 1906, and it was a request from her in the 1920s that prompted Shaw to write *The Intelligent Woman's Guide to Socialism and Capitalism.* But at the time of the courtship and marriage, Shaw was decidedly a persona non grata to Mary. He referred to her disparagingly as "The Infant" and was sometimes prevented from visiting Charlotte at Adelphi Terrace before the marriage because of "The Infant's" presence. When the marriage came about, Mary thought it a dangerous misalliance. She wrote to Charlotte, stating: "Do not ask me to meet This Man. And as a last kindness to me, & for my sake, I ask you to secure your money."[10]

Expressing opinions about Shaw that she was later to revise, Charlotte's cousin Edith Somerville (coauthor of *Some Experiences of an Irish RM,* a series of comic stories set in Skebawn, County Cork) wrote letters following the marriage that clearly showed her disapproval. In one she stated: "He is distinctly somebody in a literary way, but he can't be a gentleman and he is too clever to be really in love with Lottie, who is nearly clever, but not quite," adding that "Charlotte seems perfectly happy and delighted with her cad, for cad he is in spite of his talent."[11] Somerville did not have the advantage of Hilaire Belloc's insight that "Shaw was a gentleman pretending to be a cad."

Shaw's sister Lucy later presented the other side of the case. She disliked Charlotte, to whom she referred flippantly as "Carlotta," and thought her brother had made a mistake in settling for what she saw as a disappointingly unromantic match. In a forthright letter to her friend Janey Drysdale dated 24

July 1901, in which she reports a confidential conversation she had with her brother in London, Lucy says: "I gave it to him about the 'Comfortable Marriage' and he said it was the only compromise he could make, and it satisfied Carlotta."[12]

A large number of incautious inferences, exaggerations, and unsupportable assertions have accumulated in Shavian biography concerning Charlotte's attitude toward her in-laws and her relationship with them. Shaw did tell St. John Ervine that "there was no love lost" between Charlotte and his mother and sister, and that "Charlotte dreaded and disliked my very unconventional family; and I took care not to force them on her."[13]

What has developed from the seed of this statement forms a small pattern of Orwellian historical revisionism in Shavian biography. As H. G. Farmer has pointed out, St. John Ervine raised the temperature of Shaw's statement by adding the word *despised* to *disliked* when he came to describing Charlotte's attitude toward Lucy. A further palimpsest was supplied by Michael Holroyd, who described Charlotte's attitude toward both Bessie and Lucy as one of "hatred." Charlotte is supposed by Hesketh Pearson to have been "horrified" at the state Shaw was living in at 29 Fitzroy Square when she returned home in May 1898 following her visit to Rome.[14] This notion is echoed and elaborated upon in Holroyd's description of the supposed scene that took place when Charlotte visited Fitzroy Square to discover the allegedly dreadful state in which Shaw had been living: "Charlotte's horror turned to a hatred of his mother and sister."[15] There is no documentary evidence either for the scene itself or for the "horror" and "hatred." Lucy, now at the height of her career as a musical-comedy star, spent most of 1897 and 1898 on tour in America and Britain, with only occasional visits home; she therefore can have had little or no influence on the state of things at Fitzroy Square.

The basis of the story of Charlotte's "horror" at the state of Shaw's living quarters when she returned from Rome in May is traceable to a graphic description, written over twelve months earlier in a letter to Ellen Terry, of the untidy state into which Shaw habitually let his study and bedroom slide. Shaw describes his habit of leaving piles of open books on his table, building up a "mountain of buried books, all wide open," which became covered in dust and soot.[16] Shaw the health fiend always kept his windows open both in winter and summer, and over half a century was to elapse before clean air legislation was passed in Britain to prevent domestic use of coal fires for heating. Before this, the air in large English cities—especially in cold weather—was laden with soot, which drifted into rooms through windows. In December 1897 Shaw told Ellen that "the curse of London is its dirt. . . . I have long resigned myself to dust & dirt & squalor in external matters: if seven maids with seven mops swept my den for half a century they would make no impression on it."[17] It was London in general, not 29 Fitzroy Square in particular, which was dirty. Although it was in need of renovation, there is no evidence that the house was unusually squalid. On the contrary, when Janey Drysdale visited the Shaw apartment in 1898 she found it "a tidy, well furnished, and very pleasant abode."[18] Besides, Charlotte had visited the house in Fitzroy Square on numerous occasions before May 1898 and knew very well what it was like and how Shaw lived there.

From out of the clouds of storytelling that surround the subject of Charlotte's relations with her in-laws, a few seemingly solid pieces of evidence have emerged. As is evident from more than one of her letters, Lucy Shaw did seem to nurse an inexplicable dislike of Charlotte. Shaw mentions his mother's gift to Charlotte of his grandmother's wedding ring for everyday wear, a gesture that seems to show a reasonably kindly disposition toward the marriage on Bessie's part. Charlotte and Shaw did make visits to Fitzroy Square following their marriage. While admitting that Charlotte made herself "externally . . . charming and agreeable," Lucy referred to these as "duty visits."[19]

Underlying the whole situation was the fact that Charlotte was indirectly a major contributor to the generous care that Shaw was able to extend to his mother—and to his sister—in the years immediately following the marriage. Although Bessie continued to teach at the North London Collegiate School for Girls until well into her seventies,[20] the three-hundred-pound annuity that Shaw was able to give her thanks to the settlement agreed to by Charlotte in 1899 must have made an enormous difference to her comfort and well-being in old age. There is, however, no evidence of any close friendship between Charlotte and Bessie following the marriage. More than likely the relationship was maintained on a level of ordinary politeness.

* * *

As the anonymous "reporter" of the story about his wedding in the *Star*, Shaw concluded his merry piece with best wishes to the happy couple: "Years of married bliss to them." In its early years at least, this wish seems to have been largely fulfilled. Despite Shaw's painful health problems—which he was to compound on 17 June by breaking his left arm in a fall down a flight of stairs that he had rashly ascended on his crutches—in the early years of the marriage the two seem to have experienced what may have been one of the most contented periods of their lives up to that point.

In December 1898, after returning from their travels, Beatrice and Sidney Webb immediately went down to stay with the Shaws in Surrey. Beatrice found that Charlotte, "under pressure of anxiety for the man she loves, has broadened out into a motherly woman and lost her anarchic determination to live according to her momentary desires." By October the following year Beatrice noted that Shaw and Charlotte had "settled down into the most devoted married couple, she gentle and refined, with happiness added thereto, and he showing no sign of breaking loose from her dominion."[21]

* * *

The "bowery hollow" that Charlotte had found for Shaw's recuperation was a converted farmhouse called "Pitfold," near Haslemere, an attractive small town flanked by wooded hills in southwest Surrey, about forty-five miles from London—and accessible by rail by the late nineteenth century. They moved down to Haslemere on 10 June 1898. Shaw either hobbled about on his crutches or used a large chair fitted with wheels and a swivel footrest. They engaged a live-in nurse—Dorothy Kreyer, who was trained at the City of London Hospital—to dress, wash, and massage Shaw. It was just as well, wrote Shaw to Sidney Webb in October, that the nurse was "not of an ardent temperament," as she was "a rather goodlooking young woman."[22] Among the equipment the Shaws took to Surrey was a new Kodak camera, with which several snapshots were taken by Dorothy Kreyer of scenes from the unusual honeymoon, including Shaw clowning in the pose of a beggar on crutches and sitting, Jaeger-suited, in the wheeled chair. A photograph of Shaw reclining in the chair was sent for publication in the *Academy* on 15 October, with a caption supplied by Shaw: "The Dying Vegetarian."[23] He was infuriated at the way in which all his problems were traced by the medical profession to his vegetarianism.

With his painful foot problem, his broken arm, and generally run-down condition, it was a situation not very conducive to the dalliance usually associated with honeymoons. In the correspondence before the marriage there were clear indications of physical intimacy, at least in the form of hugs and kisses, between Shaw and Charlotte. It is difficult to say with any certainty what happened to the sexual relationship following the marriage, the only accounts being those of the not always reliable Shaw. There are significant differences between the original letter Shaw addressed to Frank Harris in June 1930 concerning his sex life and the version published in 1949 in *Sixteen Self Sketches*. In the letter Shaw does not actually say that his marriage was unconsummated, instead writing that "I found sex hopeless as a basis for permanent relations, and never dreamt of marriage in connection with it. . . . In permanence and seriousness my consummated love affairs count for nothing besides the ones that were either unconsummated or ended by discarding that relation."[24] In 1949 this was changed to a more decisive statement about his marriage: "As man and wife we found a new relation in which sex had no part. It ended the old gallantries, flirtations, and philanderings for both of us. Even of these it was the ones that were never consummated that left the longest and kindliest memories."[25]

It is not true in Shaw's case—though it was almost certainly so in Charlotte's—that the marriage "ended the old gallantries, flirtations and philanderings." Among the omissions and revisions Shaw made to the Frank Harris letter in *Sixteen Self Sketches* was the dropping of the words *that were either unconsummated or ended by discarding that relation* and their replacement with *never consummated.* The earlier wording "or ended by discarding it" could be a reference to the fact that Shaw remained on reasonably friendly terms with Florence Farr following the end of his sexual relationship with her. But it could also be a veiled indication that he and Charlotte did consummate the marriage but later abandoned the sexual side of it. The only statements that can be made with confidence are that the marriage was without issue and appears to have been mainly one of companionship.

As Charlotte had written in her letter to T. E. Lawrence of 17 May 1927, her own family life had fostered in her a firm resolve not to become a mother. She was forty-one and Shaw was nearly forty-two at the time of their marriage. Not only did she not want to have children, but a pregnancy at her age would have been medically risky. Shaw made this point in his statement to Harris, describing Charlotte and himself as "middle-aged people who have passed the age at which the bride can safely bear a first child."[26]

* * *

During the first six months of the lengthy honeymoon Shaw completed the writing of two major works upon which he had embarked before the wedding, a major essay entitled *The Perfect Wagnerite* and his new play *Caesar and Cleopatra*. The manuscript of the first was dispatched to Grant Richards on 20 August 1898 and was published on 1 December. Shaw had early struggled with the composition of *Caesar and Cleopatra*, finding difficulty in giving the work sufficient narrative drive, but it was finished by 9 December.

The Perfect Wagnerite is an interpretative commentary on *The Ring of the Nibelung*, Richard Wagner's immensely complex four-part music-drama based on mythological narratives deriving from the Old Norse *Völsunga Saga*. Shaw was very much alive to the musical and dramatic qualities of this work, often evoking its mood and imaginative effects in lively and accessible ways. In the essay Shaw views Wagner as a revolutionary figure not only in the history of Western music and opera but also in political and philosophical terms. He makes a convincing case for seeing parallels between the *Ring* and Shelley's *Prometheus Unbound*, another dramatic poem involving cosmic conflict. Despite his great admiration for both works, he was critical of the way in which Wagner and Shelley ultimately proffer love as a panacea for the human ills they portray. He also criticized Wagner's anti-Semitism, saying that for Wagner the Jew had become "the whipping boy for all modern humanity."[27]

To Shaw the *Ring* is a "world-poem," having as its subject no less than "the whole tragedy of human history," and in particular the horrors of late-nineteenth-century capitalism.[28] In this account, Nibelheim—the underworld kingdom ruled over by the dwarf Alberich, whose dwarf-slaves toil miserably at their clinking anvils to pile up more and more treasure for their master—becomes an allegorical image of exploitative nineteenth-century factories: match factories, like Bryant & May, where girls on wretched wages get "phossy jaw" from exposure to yellow phosphorus; or whitelead factories, such as the one Kitty Warren speaks of in *Mrs. Warren's Profession*, in which one of her sisters slaved for nine shillings a week before dying of lead poisoning.[29]

Idiosyncratic as it may seem from certain perspectives—some admirers of the tetralogy may prefer to have its giants, dwarfs, gods, heroes, and heroines remain as they are rather than being turned into allegorical representations—*The Perfect Wagnerite* is a deeply thoughtful and impressive political reading of Wagner's *Ring*. In its various revisions the essay also became a significant articulation of Shaw's ideas about creative evolution. It is tempting to link Shaw's close engagement with Wagner with his reading of Goethe's *Faust* as being among the experiences that prompted him to try his hand at the larger philosophical and historical canvases he experimented with in *Caesar and Cleopatra* and *Man and Superman*. Henrik Ibsen's poetic dramas *Emperor and Galilean* and *Peer Gynt*—he saw a Lugné-Poë production of the latter in Paris in November 1896, during the early period of his courtship of Charlotte—should also be counted as important influences in this regard.

* * *

By the time he reached the end of his career as a regular theater critic, Shaw had become fed up with "love," both in its nineteenth-century literary, dramatic, and operatic formulations—in which it reappeared monotonously as the mainspring of prurient and sentimental narratives—and in real-life relationships centered on sexual passion, with its attendant problems of possessiveness, jealousy, and threats to personal freedom and creative activity, such as he had experienced with the "sexually insatiable" Jenny Patterson.[30] Jenny had surrendered herself to him "body and soul," but he did not want to surrender himself in return. She had been his Cleopatra, from whose "fetters" of love he needed to escape. Even Florence Farr had begun to show the same kind of possessiveness.

It was particularly appropriate that the play Shaw was writing at the time of his marriage—he began the work on 23 April 1898 and continued writing it during his convalescence in Surrey—was *Caesar and Cleopatra*, the middle work in his *Three Plays for Puritans* sequence. *Caesar and Cleopatra* enters into a playful critical dialogue with both Shakespearean works in which Caesar appears, namely, *Julius Caesar* and *Antony and Cleopatra*. In Shaw's play Shakespeare's doomed amorist Antony is almost completely displaced in the narrative by the powerful realist Caesar, who at the end of the play says farewell to Cleopatra and Egypt.

Through his portrayal of Caesar and downgrading of Antony in Cleopatra's story, Shaw seems to be imaginatively saying farewell—at least for the time being—to what he may have seen as the potentially doomed amorist in himself, the "incorrigible philanderer" with whom he became impatient—even disgusted—when reading over his letters to Annie Besant. There are several features of his portrayal of Caesar's character and outlook with which Shaw could identify. He makes his Caesar a Carlylean hero whose principal heroic attributes are not those of the *preux chevalier*, the gallant warrior-lover of romance, but superhuman clear-sightedness, magnanimity, and generosity of spirit. Caesar is also a humorist, a lover of music, an admirer of "wit and imagination," and a critic of dull "doers and drudgers." He is the opposite of his unimaginative secretary-slave Britannus—a butt of Shavian satire targeting stodgy British moralism and the insistence on the importance of keeping up appearances—who supplies the memorable explanation of the ancient Britons' custom of staining their bodies with woad, which he declares is their way of preserving, even if stripped of clothing and life by their enemies, their respectability. Among other features in Caesar's characterization—reflecting Shaw's deep respect for feminine insight—is the fact that his spiritual power is associated with the female aspect of the Sphinx, before whom the Roman conqueror stands contemplatively near the beginning of the action, saying: "I am he, of whose genius you are the symbol: part brute, part woman and part god." Caesar is a fusion of anti-masks, man of action and man of sensibility.

Even the usually severe critic of Shavian drama W. B. Yeats—who saw *Caesar and Cleopatra* twice, with Forbes-Robertson in the role of Caesar—told Florence Farr of his admiration for the play's "gay heroic delight in the serviceable man," perhaps discerning in its themes parallels with those he had explored in the characters of Cuchulain and Conchubor in his 1904 play *On Baile's Strand*. Yeats also told Florence he was convinced "the whole play is half of you in your Egyptian period."[31]

"The gay heroic delight" in the play derives, in part, from the several exuberant reflections of Shaw's own persona in its challenging portrayal of Caesar. In a comic and almost preposterous way, the Caesar that Shaw was creating at the time of his marriage was one of his numerous fantastical self-portraits: Bernard Shaw in particularly illustrious historical garb. A new Caesar of Irish extraction was on his way toward making a second conquest of Britannia, directing operations, for the time being, from an early-model wheelchair in Surrey.

Although he does not seem to have had any clear realization of this possibility in the early days of his marriage, another "Cleopatra" in Shaw's personal life, in the comely form of Mrs. Patrick (Stella) Campbell, was waiting in the wings as a serious new temptress. Fourteen years were to pass before his love affair with her began, although references to Stella in his 1890s theater criticism show that he greatly admired both her acting abilities and her physical charms—and he had already become personally acquainted with her. In March 1899 Stella played the role of Cleopatra in a copyright performance of *Caesar and Cleopatra* at the Theatre Royal, Newcastle-upon-Tyne, opposite Nutcombe Gould as Caesar. On 12 April Shaw wrote his first letter to Stella, inviting her to "bring Caesar [Gould] down to lunch" in Surrey. "Mrs Shaw," he wrote with words whose irony would become apparent in the light of future events, "will be delighted to see you."[32]

* * *

When this invitation to Stella Campbell was made in April 1899, Charlotte and Shaw had taken a six-month lease on another house in Surrey, "Blen-Cathra," in nearby Hindhead. They had found the Haslemere house too small and "stuffy," and "Blen-Cathra," which they moved into on or about Saturday, 12 November 1898, was better situated and had "lofty, airy rooms."[33] Shaw's foot was still in such a bad state that he told Pakenham Beatty: "I am clamouring to have my toe off and make an end of it, but the specialist prefers to try a little Christian Science first."[34] The specialist was Dr. Bowlby, who had operated on him in July and whom they went up to see in London on 3 November. In September they had visited Freshwater, at the western end of the Isle of Wight, where W.A.S. Hewins had visited them during a bicycling tour; he thought Shaw's health had deteriorated since he had seen the couple in Haslemere.[35]

By the end of 1898, with the Webbs still staying with the Shaws at "Blen-Cathra," his foot continued to cause trouble. However, on 28 January he was fit enough to appear with Grant Allen as one of the two principal speakers at a peace conference held in the Hindhead Hall and chaired by Sherlock

Holmes's creator, Sir Arthur Conan Doyle. The conference was held in the wake of a call by Czar Nicholas of Russia for "a pause in the development of European armament." In a letter to Conan Doyle, Shaw said that what was wanted was not "a string of rubbish about disarmament" but rather "a combination of the leading powers to police the world and put down international war just as private war is put down."[36]

His next public appearance in Hindhead was on 26 May at a tiny schoolhouse, where a teacher—"an accomplished lady . . . with a pretty wit"—had invited him to address a natural history club she had organized among her charges. Taking his cue from a notice at the school about closed periods for game-hunting in the district, Shaw pointed out that the real reason why adults put up such notices was not because of their love of wild things and horror at the idea of killing them but rather in order that there be more game left for them to shoot. Raising "peals of laughter" among the students, Shaw expatiated on the generally fraudulent nature of rules devised by grown-ups for children, and instructed them—to their joy—that their first duty in life was to disobey their parents. The teacher with the "pretty wit" gave a spirited reply, saying that it was all very well for Mr. Shaw to give such subversive advice during a single visit, but that it would take her weeks to restore law and order. The poet Richard Le Gallienne, a Hindhead neighbor, accompanied Shaw on this occasion of his first talk to children, and left a lively account.[37]

* * *

Before giving this talk, on 3 May 1899 Shaw had begun to draft the scenario of what was to become *Captain Brassbound's Conversion*, his creative tribute to the "heartwise" Ellen Terry, on whom he modeled one of the principals of the play, Lady Ciceley Waynflete. He began writing the dialogue on 14 May and completed the play on 7 July.

Drawing on material he had found in an 1898 travel book by Scottish writer and politician Robert Bontine Cunninghame Graham,[38] Shaw fashioned a dramatic narrative of adventure set in the wilds of Morocco, near the Atlas Mountains, in which several English tourists fall into a trap set by their supposed travel guide, the saturnine freebooter Captain Brassbound. With her qualities of shrewdness, magnanimity, and clemency, Shaw's Lady Ciceley resembles his Caesar: she is an all-conquering female in a world of males. With the tourists trapped in a remote Moorish castle, a power struggle develops between the unfailingly tactful and polite Lady Ciceley and the surly and melodramatic social rebel Brassbound. Whereas he keeps his gang of ruffians in line through aggressiveness, kicks, and threats, she constantly displays a combination of firmness of character, motherly considerateness, tact, and sensitivity, gently mocking Brassbound's melodramatic poses of villainy and vindictiveness. Disarmed by her "real cleverness," Brassbound finally acknowledges her superiority and even makes a surprising proposal of marriage in the final scene.

From a biographical viewpoint *Captain Brassbound's Conversion* is interesting not only for its reflection of Shaw's relationship with and deep respect for Ellen Terry as a friend but, more generally, for what it reveals about his appreciation of her kind of emotional intelligence, a quality he clearly felt was most commonly displayed in women.

* * *

In August 1899 the Shaws left the house in Hindhead for a month's holiday in Cornwall, where Shaw continued to get himself back to full health by regular swimming. According to the account he provided in a letter to Graham Wallas, he spent half the time swimming on the surface of the water for his own amusement and the other half "underneath in the capacity of life preserver for Charlotte, who is learning to swim with nothing between her and death but a firm grip on my neck."[39]

If Charlotte had commenced a reign as a kind of substitute mother in Surrey, the swimming instructor in Cornwall played a parallel role as a father figure for her. Shaw gave Charlotte's life a purpose and direction that it might otherwise not have had. There was little or no future for her in the writing of Webb-like blue books, such as the projected tome on Roman municipal governance. As her letters show, she could write elegantly and interestingly, but she was not a born creative writer. She believed in Shaw's genius and in his causes, some of which she had been drawn to herself before her meeting with him. He, for his part, had found a solicitous, perceptive, and loyal companion under whose sway he found contentment but against which he was to have some serious rebellion in the future.

On 30 August Shaw provided Wallas with another installment of news, this time concerning the death of his maternal uncle, Walter John Gurly, which left him with an unwanted legacy consisting of the Gurly family estate in Carlow. Apparently his former tolerance of and even liking for his "Rabelaisian" Uncle Walter—who had entertained the family with his outrageous limericks and stories in Shaw's youth, and at whose house he had recuperated from his illnesses in 1881 and 1882—had given way to impatience and dislike: "My infernal uncle has died," he wrote to Wallas, "and the Carlow estate has descended on me like an avalanche."[40]

Another family event that occurred at about the same time, (late August 1899) was the revelation that Shaw's sister Lucy was diagnosed as having tuberculosis, a calamity that brought her singing career to an abrupt end.[41] In 1897 she had experienced great success in the role of Kitty in Villiers Stanford's *Shamus O'Brien* at the Broadway Theater in New York, and in the following year she had triumphed while on tour in England as Honor Luxmore in S. Baring Gould and Learmont Drysdale's comic opera *The Red Spider*. After more than one hundred performances, the production finally closed on 27 November 1898. Lucy was as yet unaware that this was to be her last performance as a professional singer.[42]

Following their holiday in Cornwall, on 21 September 1899 Charlotte and Shaw continued their peregrinations by embarking on a six-week Mediterranean cruise aboard an Orient Line steamer with the same name as the Cunard liner SS *Lusitania*, which was torpedoed by a U-boat in 1915.[43] For a number of reasons the cruise was not a success. They were accompanied by Beatrice Webb's sister, Margaret (Maggie) Hobhouse, about whose behavior aboard ship Shaw penned a hilarious account in a letter to Beatrice written off Malaga, along the southern coast of Spain. She annoyed Charlotte, flirted with Shaw, alarmingly seemed to be discovering a gypsy self at Granada, dressing accordingly, and exasperated the ship's officers through numerous complaints and demands—with the result, according to Shaw, that "the ship rapidly became conscious of a Reign of Terror, with Maggie as Robespierre."[44] There was also bad weather to contend with.

As they entered the Straits of Gibraltar, Shaw described the experience to playwright Edward Rose as "a godless cruise, with godless people" aboard "a floating pleasure machine"; to Sidney Cockerell, from somewhere between Crete and Malta, he wrote that it was "a guzzling, lounging, gambling, dog's life."[45] Such idle pursuit of pleasure for its own sake was Shaw's idea of Hell. Indeed, this experience in late 1899 is likely to have contributed to his portrayal of that region in the "Don Juan in Hell" dream scene of *Man and Superman*, his first play in the new century. In that scene Hell is described as "the home of the unreal and of the seekers for happiness."

In a letter to Ida Beatty written from Haslemere during the early days of the marriage, Shaw had mentioned that he and Charlotte proposed to remain in separate houses when they returned to London. The context was his solemn warning to Pakenham Beatty not to send any wedding presents: "If Paquito sends me any Venice glasses or anything else of the sort I will stick them on the lawn and shy bricks at them with my unbroken arm. Relics, idols and presents drive me out of my senses. Besides, wedding presents are supposed to belong to the joint establishment; and my wife and I are going to keep up our separate domiciles in London just as before. Pawn them promptly."[46]

The message about wedding presents was to be echoed in the vehement tirade on the same subject by the newly engaged Jack Tanner at the end of *Man and Superman*. However, the idea of "separate domiciles" for the recently married Shaws did not materialize. On their return from the cruise on 30 October 1899, Shaw moved his belongings from Fitzroy Square and took up residence with Charlotte at 10 Adelphi Terrace.

2.1. Shaw in 1898.

2.2. Beatrice Webb.

2.3. Sidney Webb, Baron Passfield. Chalk portrait by Jessie Holliday, c. 1909.

2.4. Graham Wallas.

2.5. William Archer (photograph by Shaw).

2.6. Alice Lockett.

2.7. May Morris (detail), pastel on paper by Dante Gabriel Rossetti, 1872.

2.8. Mrs. Jane Patterson.

2.9. Florence Farr as Amaryllis in John Todhunter's play *A Sicilian Idyll*, 1890.

2.10. Ellen Terry.

2.11. Janet Achurch.

2.12. Annie Besant.

2.13. Eleanor Marx.

2.14. Sir Arthur Wing Pinero and Shaw. Caricature by Max Beerbohm.

2.15. GBS, *Platform Spellbinder*. Photo of lost painting by Bertha Newcombe executed in 1892.

14 New Century, "New Religion"

"I rather think I shall start a new religion." Shaw made this startling declaration while still at school, according to a memoir published by his friend Matthew Edward McNulty in 1901, when the two of them were discussing their life ambitions. McNulty had just suggested "literature" as a possible vocation for his precocious friend. "I don't care much about that" was the alleged reply from Shaw.[1] Like many of McNulty's anecdotes about Shaw as a boy, this has a fanciful air. Yet it gains plausibility from the fact that Shaw—who read aloud *The Pilgrim's Progress* on his father's knee as a child—was deeply interested in religion. His first publication—in the form of a letter to the press—was about religion, and his first attempt at writing a play—*Passion Play* (*Household of Joseph*)—was on a religious subject. Moreover, he made a very similar declaration about wanting to start a new religion in an 1895 letter to the London bookseller, bibliophile, and amateur photographer F. H. Evans, who was discussing publishing possibilities with him: "I want to write a big book of devotion for modern people, bringing all the truths latent in the old religious dogmas into contact with real life—a gospel of Shawianity in fact."[2]

Early in the twentieth century Shaw greeted the new age with the first major expression of this "gospel"—a system of ideas to which he later gave the name creative evolution—in the form of *Man and Superman: A Comedy and a Philosophy*, which was published in 1903 with a prefatory "Epistle Dedicatory" addressed to the theater critic A. B. Walkley plus an appended "Revolutionist's Handbook." In May 1900 he drew up a scenario for the "Don Juan in Hell" scene—a dreamlike philosophical conversation between the Devil and Shavian transformations of principal characters in Mozart's *Don Giovanni*—which occurs in the third act of his comedy. The work was completed in the latter half of 1902, and in January 1903, over the course of three evenings, Shaw gave a first reading to Beatrice and Sidney Webb, Graham Wallas and his wife Ada, and Charlotte, who were all spending a week by the sea at Overstrand, near Cromer, in Norfolk. "To me it seems a great work, quite the biggest thing he has done," Beatrice wrote of the play in her diary on 16 January 1903.[3]

The leading character in the play is the amiable revolutionary gentleman-Socialist Jack Tanner—self-confessed Member of the Idle Rich Class but enemy of the capitalist system to which he belongs, in which the rich live by "robbing the poor"—who is finally captured in marriage (an institution described by his counterpart in the Dream as "a mantrap baited with simulated accomplishments and delusive idealizations") by a rich heiress. The elite audience of Fabians who heard the first reading of the play in Norfolk could hardly have failed to be amused at the reflections of Shaw himself in the portrayal of Tanner: a revolutionary Socialist; a critic of marriage who had recently married a rich heiress; and a gentleman who at this time was largely living on the unearned income from skillful investments in nineteenth-century capitalist enterprises made by his bride's father, Horace Payne-Townshend.

* * *

Shaw described *Man and Superman* as "a dramatic parable of Creative Evolution"[4] and frequently referred to the third act, "Don Juan in Hell," as a statement of his creed. He developed his ideas concerning creative evolution in *The Perfect Wagnerite* and in various speeches on religion delivered in the first two decades of the twentieth century. He produced his most extensive exploration of evolutionary themes at the end of that period, in the preface and five plays of *Back to Methuselah: A Metabiological Pentateuch* (1921). The later prose tale *The Adventures of the Black Girl in her Search for God* (1933) is also primarily concerned with evolutionary themes in relation to religion.[5]

In all of the major publications where they are expressed, Shaw's ideas about creative evolution appeared in contexts that radically qualify—and at times even threaten to completely undermine—his position. The main thrust of his ideas about religion, however, was that the godhead is not a perfect, complete, and unchanging entity but rather an evolving phenomenon. The universe is driven by an intelligent, purposive force, the Life Force, which strives toward higher forms of life and consciousness through the processes of evolution. In one of his religious speeches Shaw explicitly identifies God with the evolutionary process itself. In this gospel according to Shaw, the purpose of human life is to *contribute* to the evolution of the godhead, of which we indeed are a part. God is will and we are the hands and brains of God: "We and our father are one. . . . The kingdom of heaven is within us."[6]

The teleological goal of the evolutionary process—and human cooperation with it—is variously described by Shaw. In the third act of *Man and Superman*

Don Juan speaks of the "working within [him] of Life's incessant aspiration to higher organization, wider, deeper, intenser self-consciousness, and clearer self-understanding." Elsewhere in the same act he declares: "I sing not arms and the hero, but the philosophic man who seeks in contemplation to discover the inner will of the world, in invention, to discover the means of fulfilling that will, and in action to do that will by the so-discovered means." The Shavian Superman, in other words, is similar to Plato's philosopher-king, the contemplative man of action.

* * *

While Shaw is often thought of and described as a meliorist, a world betterer, his "new religion" is actually grounded in deeply pessimistic and skeptical ideas about human society and the possibility of its improvement. Like the love in Andrew Marvell's poem "The Definition of Love," it is "begotten of despair, upon impossibility." One of the sections of "The Revolutionist's Handbook"—the fiery essay and set of witty maxims that Shaw appended to the text of *Man and Superman*—is entitled "Progress an Illusion." This echoes a statement Shaw made to A. B. Walkley in the Epistle Dedicatory: "I do not know whether you have any illusions left on the subject of education, progress, and so forth. I have none."[7] These words set the tone of much of the writing to be found there, as well as in two other sections of *Man and Superman* most relevant to the theme of creative evolution, namely, the third act and "The Revolutionist's Handbook." As Shaw wrote in the latter, "Let the Reformer, the Progressive, the Meliorist . . . reconsider himself and his eternal ifs and ans which never become pots and pans."[8]

The Epistle Dedicatory and "Revolutionist's Handbook" present a view of democracy as a completely failed political system. Edmund Burke's "swinish multitude" has displaced the old selectively bred ruling aristocracy and the land is now misruled by "college passmen . . . well groomed monocular Algys and Bobbies . . . cricketers to whom age brings golf instead of wisdom."[9]

In "The Revolutionist's Handbook" the invective against mankind becomes more severe. Man in his present state of evolution is seen as incapable of progress. Each attempt at civilization is followed by a rapid and disastrous backward slide into destructive savagery, and each high point of civilization is "but a pinnacle to which a few people cling in giddy terror above an abyss of squalor." The spirit of the author of *Gulliver's Travels* and "A Modest Proposal" seems close at hand when, at the end of this diatribe, Shaw's revolutionary declares that one must eliminate the Yahoo and goes on to make extravagant proposals for the creation of either a State Department of Evolution or perhaps a private society or chartered company "for the improvement of the human live stock." The true function of the modest proposals at the end of "The Revolutionist's Handbook" seems to be as much a rhetorical amplification of the preceding expressions of despair about and condemnation of man in his present state as a serious advocacy of creative evolution.

The Swiftian invective of the "Epistle Dedicatory" and "The Revolutionist's Handbook" is paralleled in various speeches in the third act of *Man and Superman.* Although Shaw uses Don Juan and the Devil interchangeably as critics of human folly, he nevertheless gives to the Devil what is probably the most sustained condemnation of the human species in all of his works. "Is Man any the less destroying himself for all this boasted brain of his?" asks the devil before going on to argue that man's inventive energies have been most successfully deployed not in the service of life but in the service of death. In the evolutionary scale he is the most successful of all predators, the cruellest of the animals and "the most destructive of the destroyers."

Skepticism and satire attend every step of Shaw's expression of the idea of creative evolution. Even the core idea—namely, that the human race in its present state is so hopeless that it needs to evolve into a superior form of being—is as much a form of satirical rhetoric as it is of meliorist philosophy. Man is so degenerate that he needs to be replaced altogether. When, in *Back to Methuselah,* Shaw actually creates fictional images of highly evolved human beings of the future, they are endowed with many more repellent than attractive features, providing a foretaste of the horrors of such later futuristic fiction as Huxley's *Brave New World.* In other words, *Back to Methuselah* can be seen as quite as much a dystopian as a utopian work. The old dialectic between Shaw's Mephistophelean and Bunyanesque selves runs right through the artistic expressions of his "religion" of creative evolution. The more positive aspects of Shaw's ideas concerning creative evolution rest precariously on a powerful undercurrent of pessimism and skepticism.

* * *

The most important sources of Shaw's ideas about creative evolution were the anti-Darwinian writings on evolution of Samuel Butler—one of whose diatribes (*Luck, or Cunning?*) Shaw reviewed in the *Pall Mall Gazette* on 31 May 1887[10]—and the evolutionary theory of the pre-Darwinian naturalist Jean-Baptiste de Monet de Lamarck. These debts are clearly acknowledged in Shaw's preface to *Back to Methuselah* (1921). During the early years of the twentieth century Shaw associated his ideas with those of the French philosopher Henri Bergson, whose important work *L'Évolution Créatrice* was published in French in 1907 and in an English translation as *Creative Evolution* in 1911. Shaw's term *creative evolution,* which he uses as one of the headings in the preface to *Back to Methuselah*, is probably an adoption of Bergson's title. Shaw invented the term *Life Force* in *Man and Superman* and later linked it with Bergson's "élan vital."[11]

Although there are certainly strong similarities between Shaw's ideas and those of the French philosopher, Bergson was evidently not very happy with the way in which Shaw identified the two. Bertrand Russell provides an entertaining account of a luncheon held in honor of Bergson in London (probably in October 1911) at which Shaw "set to work to expound Bergson's philosophy in the style of the [later] Preface to *Back to Methuselah*." Of Shaw's exposition and Bergson's response Russell wrote: "In [Shaw's] version the philosophy was hardly one to recommend itself to professionals, and Bergson mildly interjected, 'Ah, no-o! It is not qvite zat!' But Shaw was quite unabashed, 'Oh, my dear fellow, I understand your philosophy much better than you do.' Bergson clenched his fists and nearly exploded with rage; but with a great effort, he controlled himself, and Shaw's expository monologue continued."[12]

The idea of the "Superman," another key element in Shaw's synthesis of concepts concerning creative evolution, had several conceptual antecedents in his own writings—for example, in *The Quintessence of Ibsenism, The Perfect Wagnerite*, and *Caesar and Cleopatra*. Shaw was also at pains to point out that neither he nor Nietzsche originated the notion: "The cry for the Superman did not begin with Nietzsche, nor will it end with his vogue." The term *Superman* itself, however, was invented by Shaw, undoubtedly with Nietzsche's *Übermensch* in mind.[13] The Shavian coinage had a zing and lasting quality lacking in literal translations of the Nietzschean term as *overman*. (What Shaw thought of the embodiment of the term in the alter-ego of Clark Kent in the late 1930s is, to the best of my knowledge, not recorded.)

The wider context of Shaw's "new religion" of creative evolution can be found in the broad tradition of Romantic and post-Romantic responses to the undermining of religion by, on the one hand, the perception of intellectual weaknesses, naïve credulity and absurdities in orthodox religious teachings, and, on the other hand, by mechanistic philosophical systems and scientific materialism. In the Romantic period William Blake characterized the conventional image of the Christian God as "Nobodaddy," ridiculed the idea of Christ as meek and mild, and railed against the philosophical writings of Bacon, Locke, and Newton. Shelley's rejection of orthodox Christianity influenced Shaw's conception of God as an immanent power in the universe. Schopenhauer's concept of the will in *The World as Will and Idea* (1818)—which Shaw read in 1887, the same year in which he reviewed Butler's work—contributed substantially to the Shavian synthesis. Shaw was also almost certainly influenced by Auguste Comte and the religion of humanity developed in his

Système de Politique Positive (1851–54) as well as by John Stuart Mill's utilitarian arguments in *Three Essays on Religion* (1874).

All of the major Victorian creative writers sought in different ways to reaffirm religious and spiritual values in the later nineteenth-century "darkling plain" of disintegrating creeds, secularist philosophical thought, the dissemination of Darwinian theory, and the advance of scientific explanations of natural phenomena. Shaw's ideas on religion clearly belong to the zeitgeist in this respect, however much his style and accent may differ from writers such as Carlyle, Arnold, Ruskin, and Tennyson. In *Sartor Resartus,* when Carlyle's Teufelsdröckh speaks of embodying "the divine Spirit of . . . Religion in a new Mythus [*sic*], in a new vehicle and vesture,"[14] he might very well have been describing Shaw's design in developing his "new religion" of creative evolution. Shaw's strategy was an attempt to marry a *mythos* of science with a *mythos* of religion. What was needed, in Shaw's view, was "the revival of religion on a scientific basis."[15] Although Nietzsche and Bergson influenced Shaw's writing on creative evolution, the essential shape of his ideas on the subject had been formed in the matrices of nineteenth-century debates on evolution and religion well before he came into contact with these later writers.

Shaw was quite circumspect in his treatment of Darwin, describing the basic Darwinian theory as "not finally refutable."[16] Yet he also sympathized with Darwin's opponents. Butler declared that Darwin had "banished mind from the universe," and could not accept the way in which Darwinian theory seemed to reduce evolution to a process determined by a series of accidental events, whereby some variations in individual species gave them an advantage in the struggle for existence within particular ecological niches, thus contributing, through the operation of natural selection, to evolutionary development.[17] In Butler's view this amounted to a view of evolution as nothing but "a chapter of accidents" in which "beauty, design, steadfastness of purpose, intelligence, courage" and other human qualities had no role to play.[18] Shaw closely echoes this view in a comparison of Lamarckian and Darwinian theories: "As compared to the open-eyed intelligent wanting and trying of Lamarck, the Darwinian process may be described as a chapter of accidents. There is a hideous fatalism about it, a ghastly and damnable reduction of beauty and intelligence, of strength and purpose, of honor and aspiration, to such casually picturesque changes as an avalanche may make in a mountain landscape, or a railway accident in a human figure."[19]

By acknowledging Darwin and, at the same time, backing Lamarck and Butler, Shaw was, strictly speaking, supporting two scientifically incompatible theories. Lamarck's account of the process by which evolutionary change occurs is now generally regarded as invalid in two main respects. His most often quoted example of evolutionary change is his account of the way in which the giraffe gained its long neck. In the wild, the giraffe feeds mainly on the foliage of trees. Lamarck assumed that over a long period of time, an originally short-necked species of mammal developed a long neck because of its constant need to strain upward in order to reach the foliage. This theory was later memorably—if not quite correctly—summarized in verse by Lord Neaves:

A deer with a neck that was longer by half
Than the rest of its family's (try not to laugh)
By stretching and stretching became a Giraffe
Which nobody can deny.

Lamarck's theory rests on an assumption (accepted by Shaw and now known to be false) that characteristics acquired by a parent—for example, unusual muscular development resulting from a particular activity, such as weight lifting—can be inherited by its offspring. Lamarck also falsely assumed that the pattern of evolutionary change was always from simpler to more complex organisms. It is now known that although evolution does sometimes follow that pattern, by far the most common evolutionary events are what C. L. Stebbins describes as "adaptive radiations at one particular level of complexity."[20]

Darwin's account, modified and developed by Mendel's understanding of genetics, is the basis of currently accepted, mainstream scientific theory. Nevertheless, the possibility of human intervention in evolutionary and genetic processes has—without contradicting Darwinian concepts—introduced a new dimension into the argument. It is well within the bounds of possibility that dramatic modifications to human life expectancy and genetic and physical composition are attainable.

There are deep contradictions in Shaw's expression of his creed. The railer against the idea of progress sometimes appears to undermine the whole card pack of creative evolution. How can we evolve creatively if progress is "an illusion"? A further problem is that, unlike other religions, the Shavian creed does not come with a built-in code of ethical social conduct: in Shaw's view, codes of conduct needed to be accommodated to the realities of life, not the other way round. (Shaw's demolition of conventional codes of conduct can be disarming: the first of his "Maxims for Revolutionists" reads: "Do not do unto others as you would that they should do unto you. Their tastes may not be the same.") Nevertheless, the idea that the divine is immanent in the universe and in us, that we are an expression of a mysterious Life Force that it is possible to serve in ways that could possibly ameliorate the human condition, and the notion of self-dedication to a cause that one recognizes as mightier than oneself—rather than, say, happiness—as the goal of human life provided Shaw with a framework of faith that, however shakily it was adhered to, was to influence the whole of the rest of his creative career.

* * *

Much as he disliked the Mediterranean cruise he took with Charlotte aboard the SS *Lusitania* in September–October 1899, like subsequent sea voyages she persuaded him to embark upon, it had significant results in Shaw's creative and intellectual life. As has been suggested in the previous chapter, his experience on this "floating pleasure machine"—observing at first hand the idle rich engaged in a "guzzling, lounging, gambling, dog's life"—almost certainly contributed to the creation of the unusual portrayal of Hell in *Man and Superman*. In addition, his wanderings around the sites of ancient civilizations in the Mediterranean prompted reflections on the history of human empires that found expression in nondramatic writings composed at the same time as he was beginning work on *Man and Superman*, in particular his essay entitled "Civilisation and the Soldier," which was published in the *Humane Review* in January 1901.

The fantastic vision of Hell that Shaw presented in the "Don Juan in Hell" dream sequence of *Man and Superman* is populated by strange creatures; his conception of both the hellish and heavenly states is like no other that has ever been dreamed up. The scene is too long for most modern tastes, and the play is impossible to stage in its entirety without entering into a special arrangement, such as starting at a late-afternoon hour and including a dinner break. However, the imaginative force of the "Don Juan in Hell" dream sequence—its symphonic sweep of ideas, creative exuberance, and subtle interrelationships with both the comic aspects of the play proper and Mozart's *Don Giovanni*—remains impressive.

The four characters in the "Don Juan in Hell" scene appear as supernatural manifestations of dramatis personae in the play. The "*very Mephistophelean*" Devil, introduced by a theme from Gounod's *Faust* (Shaw's childhood favorite), turns out to be none other than Mendoza, the chief bandit-cum-author of dreadful sentimental love poetry and ex-waiter at the Savoy Hotel, London. Don Juan Tenorio, the extraordinarily loquacious philosophical expositor of creative evolution, represents a recasting of the play's Jack Tanner. Donna Anna is a dream version of his pursuer in the play's reverse love chase, Ann Whitefield. And, most surprisingly, among the creatures rather enjoying themselves in the Shavian Hell is the Commendatore/Statue, the literal pillar of respectability in Mozart's opera, who also strongly resembles Ramsden, the deeply conservative liberal in Shaw's play.

In Shaw's fantasia there are no restrictions of movement between Heaven and Hell. "People" are at liberty to come and go as they choose, according to their tastes. It's just that those in Hell would find Heaven—the home of the serious-minded realists, philosophers, poets, and visionaries; the seekers through contemplation of "the inner will of the world"—boring. Hell is the natural home of the seekers of pleasure, happiness, and romance; the shunners of reality; the bon vivants; the celebrators (like Mozart's Don Juan) of wine, women, and song; the connoisseurs of the fine arts and good taste; and the lovers of music, here described (in a work written by one of the great music lovers) as "the brandy of the damned." It is a place "where you have nothing to do but amuse yourself." In other words, Hell is like a perpetual Mediterranean cruise, with rich English pleasure seekers on the SS *Lusitania*, listening to the ship's band playing waltzes, selections from musical farces, sentimental love songs, and "God Save the Queen."

The voyage on the SS *Lusitania* in late 1899 also provided the setting for the essay "Civilisation and the Soldier," which Shaw contributed to the *Humane Review* in January 1901.[21] Sitting in his deck chair aboard the vessel (which was somewhere between Athens—where he would walk the next day among the ruins of the ancient civilization of Greece—and Syracuse, which he had visited the day before), Shaw was in a reflective mood about his fellow passengers and the fate of empires, such as the one to which most of the passengers belonged. The second war conducted by the British imperium against the rebel Boers in South Africa broke out on 11 October, during the cruise. Shaw dates the recollection of his shipboard musings to a morning just before that event: "In the last days before the war, I fell a-musing . . . rocked into reverie in my deck chair on the bosom, gently heaving, of the Ionian Sea. . . . I am surrounded by respectable English people. It is a fine morning; and for the moment the bosom, gently heaving, soothes them into a peaceful contentment with their guide books."

The "respectable English people" were not at all a bad lot, these "moneyed, travelled substantial Englishmen of good credit and standing" enjoying themselves on the "bosom, gently heaving." The only shots they were firing in this location—"the cradle and grave of many civilisations"—were harmless ones with their Kodak cameras. Occasionally some savagery appeared in the form of "nocturnal rompings" on the dance floor, when the veil of gentility sometimes dropped off altogether. Perhaps Beatrice Webb's sister was not the only one discovering her gypsy self aboard the SS *Lusitania*. For the most part, however, their entertainments would seem fairly innocent from ordinary points of view.

The "respectable English people" were content not only with their guidebooks but even more with the fact that they were English, that they belonged to a nation of wealth and prosperity and, as Shaw satirically pictured them imagining, to an "Empire growing ever greater, until the Last Judgement shall be enacted—probably in Westminster Abbey—and the millennium inaugurated by the extension of British rule to the entire universe." In two months' time, with the dawning of the new century, England would wallow in self-congratulation on its magnificent achievements in the previous century and look forward to a continuation of magnificence for the next hundred years. The London *Times* editorial on 1 January 1900 reviewed the glory of the nation's past and proclaimed its future prospects as follows: "We enter upon the new century with a heritage of achievement and of glory older, more continuous, and not less splendid than that of any other nation in the world." The auguries for a continuation of Britannia's glorious rule, the paper opined modestly, were "not unpropitious."[22]

However, to the man sitting on his deck chair on the SS *Lusitania* two months earlier, the prospects for England and the English looked very different. He was "an Irishman, looking at [the English] with the completest detachment of national sentiment." It was from that perspective he concluded: "Nothing is more clear to me than that English civilisation is at the end of its tether, and that the tether can only be lengthened by the substitution for these artless grown-up children of a quite different sort of Englishman."

England was at the "imperialist stage of democratic capitalism." Shaw maintained that no civilization had ever survived that stage. He was only partly right. While he did predict the future of the British Empire correctly—it was to last only another half century—"English civilisation" did not exactly expire with the gaining of independence by its colonies, and it could hardly be argued that "democratic capitalism"—which has proven to be the most resilient and relatively stable of all the major political and economic systems in operation since 1900—was the cause of the decline of the empire. However, Shaw was writing his essay at the end of a century in which capitalism displayed what was perhaps its worst face ever of exploitation and ruthless treatment of people in the lower socioeconomic sections of society. Shaw wanted a new order—and he wasn't alone. There were many battles to be fought and won. In the England of 1901 Labour had not yet gained control in Parliament and women were still judged as unfit to vote in the democratic political system to which they belonged.

* * *

Shaw returned from his cruise on the SS *Lusitania* to find the Fabian Society in turmoil about the Boer War, which represented a resumption of an earlier struggle between the British regime in South Africa and the Boer settlers in the Transvaal—with land, diamonds, and gold at stake. The war had created deep differences of opinion among members as to how the organization should react, resulting in a crisis. Some members were in favor of a sweeping denunciation of England's involvement in this imperialistic and capitalistic struggle. Others, including Webb, wanted the Fabian Society to exclude it from its political agenda. Historian Patricia Pugh summarized the situation as follows: "When war with the Boers became inevitable, [Sidney] Olivier and Shaw realized that if Fabians confined themselves to studies and statements on Webb's beloved 'gas and water' socialism, the Society would cease to be regarded as a political think tank."[23] The Fabian Society could not afford to remain aloof.

Together with other members of the "Old Gang" of the Fabian Society, Shaw succeeded in fending off a strident pro-Boer motion calling for an expression of "deep indignation" at the British "conspiracy against the independence of the Transvaal."[24] He thought that the British regime was, in fact, the lesser of two evils in South Africa and favored an approach more consistent with the Fabian style. The triumph of "Afrikanderdom," Shaw thought, would be the "triumph of [Cecil] Rhodes" and rampant capitalism in South Africa, like that in America.[25] Given the existence of the empire, he wanted the Fabian Society to attempt to influence the ways in which the former conducted itself and advocated controlled devolution of power in the colonies, as was happening in Commonwealth countries such as Australia.

Feelings ran high among the Fabians. Shaw was a principal speaker at the largest ever meeting, held at Clifford's Inn, London, on 23 February 1900, where he spoke on "Imperialism." Part of Shaw's provocative—and, in a sense, truthful—argument was that the Socialist movement was also "imperialistic" in its aims in that it sought to spread its sphere of influence beyond national boundaries. Later, of course, with such developments as the formation of the USSR, the parallels with imperialism became obvious. Shaw was the editorial supervisor of *Fabianism and the Empire*, the election manifesto published later in the year. The Fabian Society had survived the war within its ranks, but not without casualties in the form of resignations, which included the future Labour prime minister Ramsay MacDonald, who by then had other quarrels with the organization, and Sylvia Pankhurst.

Charlotte and Shaw had a close personal interest in the Boer War since Charlotte's brother-in-law, Colonel Hugh Cholmondeley, had been posted to the Transvaal to command the City Imperial Volunteers Mounted Infantry. Writing at Charlotte's request—she was grappling with "a troublesome influenza cold"—Shaw reported her anxiety about Cholmondeley in a letter to

Mary Cholmondeley dated 30 December 1899: "Personally our patriotism covers a natural anxiety to see him safely back again, which Charlotte feels doubly—on your account as well as on his own."[26] Cholmondeley served with great distinction in the war and was awarded the honor of being made Companion of the Order of the Bath.

* * *

Charlotte's decision, following the Shaws' marriage in June 1898, to lease the house at Haslemere while still retaining 10 Adelphi Terrace as a London base established a pattern of living arrangements that was to last for the rest of their lives. They always had a London home (with only one move—from Adelphi Terrace into a serviced apartment at 4 Whitehall Court—in 1927) and another residence within easy reach of London in a semirural area in the southern counties.

From 1900 to 1906 the Shaws led a curiously nomadic existence, renting a succession of houses in the country and going on frequent tours to various parts of the United Kingdom and Europe. From May to October 1900 they rented "Blackdown Cottage" in Haslemere, which was succeeded as their country residence by "Piccard's Cottage," St. Catherine's, Guildford, Surrey, which they occupied periodically from early November 1900 to April 1902. When the lease on "Piccard's Cottage" expired, they moved to Maybury Knoll, Woking, which they continued leasing until 25 April 1904. It was from there that the wanderers moved again on 2 July 1904 to "The Old House," in Harmer Green, Welwyn, which was to bring them close to their final choice of country residence at Ayot St Lawrence. Before they moved into "The Old House" at Harmer Green, Shaw described it—in a letter dated 13 May 1904 to Lady Stanley from Rome, where he and Charlotte were holidaying—as having "walls 9 feet thick, and doors like the gates of a canal lock."[27]

In November 1906 the Shaws finally adopted as their permanent country residence a large red-brick Edwardian villa on a corner of a narrow lane in Ayot St Lawrence, a tiny village north of London, in Hertfordshire. Shaw concluded that the village must be a healthy place to live when he noticed a tombstone inscription in the churchyard that said of one Mary Ann South, who lived for nearly seventy years (from 1825 to 1895): "HER TIME WAS

SHORT."[28] He liked the seclusion of the place. "Civilisation took a jump over Ayot St Lawrence," Shaw told a visiting journalist. "We are two miles from the main road. We get no dust from motor cars. People do not come this way unless they want to, and so we are left undisturbed and happy."[29] Set in a garden consisting of roughly three acres, the house had originally been built in 1902 as the New Rectory for the village, but the size of the parish was found not to justify the presence of a resident minister. In 1920, having leased it until then, the Shaws purchased the house for £6326.10s.[30] This was the house—now managed by the National Trust—that was to become famous as "Shaw's Corner."

* * *

It was between the summer and autumn of 1900, when the Shaws were commuting between "Blackdown Cottage" in Haslemere and London, that Shaw discovered the genius of the then twenty-three-year-old actor Harley Granville-Barker, who was to become a close friend and associate in the future course of Shaw's career as a playwright. On 10 June 1900 Shaw had come up to London to see a Stage Society presentation of Gerhart Hauptmann's play *Das Friedensfest* (translated as *The Coming of Peace*) by Janet Achurch and Dr. C. E. Wheeler. Granville-Barker was a member of the cast, and Shaw was very impressed with his acting, immediately seeing him as the right choice, as Charles Charrington had suggested, for the role of the poet Marchbanks in *Candida*.

Shaw's meeting with Granville-Barker was an extraordinarily serendipitous throw of the dice that the Life Force had produced at the precise moment when Shaw was evolving his "new religion," as well as trying to secure a foothold as a playwright in the London professional theater. Granville-Barker was young, good-looking, intelligent, imaginative—and keenly responsive to the new kind of drama Shaw was creating. As well as being a fine interpreter of Shavian roles—including that of Tanner in *Man and Superman*—he went on to become a playwright of considerable achievement in his own right. He also left his mark as a distinguished Shakespeare scholar and director who broke with the style of many Shakespearean productions of the late nineteenth century, characterized by elaborate settings and mauling of the texts in order to give prominence to the roles played by actor-managers such as Irving. The Granville-Barker return to the Elizabethan and Jacobean style of Shakespearean production, with spare sets and free-flowing action, was exactly in tune with the ideas Shaw had been expressing in his criticism and correspondence of the 1890s. In April 1906 Granville-Barker married the vibrant and attractive actress Lillah McCarthy, who had already become a figure of major importance in the Shavian universe as both friend and leading lady in his plays.

The peregrinations of the Shaws during the early 1900s, far-ranging though they were, did not include a visit to Ireland until July 1905. However, the subject of Ireland was never far from Shaw's thoughts, and in his next play, *John Bull's Other Island*, he "returned to the country," so to speak, in a powerful act of creative imagination. Granville-Barker played the role of Father Keegan, the eccentric seer, philosopher, and ex-priest. This play represented Shaw's first new contribution to the repertoire of the Vedrenne-Barker 1904–7 seasons at the Royal Court Theatre, London, and greatly increased public recognition of his rising star as a professional playwright in London.

When Granville-Barker first became involved with it in 1904, the Court Theatre had recently been taken over and renovated by an amateur actor named J. H. Leigh, whom Shaw described as "a gentleman with a fancy for playing Shakespearean parts, and money enough to gratify it."[31] Leigh engaged John E. Vedrenne as his associate business manager. In 1904 Granville-Barker was approached to direct and act in *The Two Gentlemen of Verona*. He agreed on condition that he would be allowed to present at the Court six matinee performances of *Candida*, in which he would play the poet Marchbanks. Thus, as he and Shaw simultaneously gained entrée into the theater in Sloane Square in which both their careers were to advance, an important new chapter in the history of English drama was being written.

15 Eternal Irishman

The decision of the Corporation of Dublin in 1946 to offer Shaw the Honorary Freedom of the City was not arrived at unanimously. One councillor declared Shaw to be not a fit mentor for either the youth or the adults of Ireland. Another complained that all he could find that Shaw had done for Ireland was to send "an occasional long-distance wise-crack."[1] Other compatriots were more generous in their recognition of his achievement and more discerning in their understanding of his relations with Ireland. Nevertheless, perceptions of Shaw as having almost completely abandoned his Irish identity when he migrated to England—and that he was "not very Irish," as one critic put it—have lingered despite a great deal of evidence to the contrary.[2]

Shaw's attitude toward Ireland was complex, ambivalent, and often astringently critical. He once described himself as "a Supernationalist," and in the preface to *John Bull's Other Island* he declared that "nationalism stands between Ireland and the light of the world."[3] He detested the religious bigotry, political fanaticism, provincialism, and squalor of the nineteenth-century Dublin in which he spent his first twenty years. He wrote satirically about the late-nineteenth-century literary revival and cultural nationalism. However, counterbalancing these critical notes in his writings are images of another Ireland, a place sanctified by its ancient religious traditions and populated by people with unique gifts of warmth and wit. He also had a deep sense of the beauty of its landscapes and seacoasts, its western islands and its skies. It was with this other Ireland that Shaw identified, even to the point of describing himself in a public lecture as "a patriotic Irishman."[4] In a 1948 essay entitled "Ireland Eternal and External" he remarked that, despite reason and common sense, he shared the conviction of the Irish that they are "The Chosen Race." In the same essay he described his country and his connections with it as follows: "Eternal is the fact that the human creature born in Ireland and brought up in its air is Irish. . . . I have lived for twenty years in Ireland and for seventy-two in England; but the twenty came first, and in Britain I am still a foreigner and shall die one."[5] In a letter dated 27 December 1941 Shaw told Lord Alfred Douglas—with whom he had a lively late correspondence—"Nothing will erase the native stamp of an Irishman."[6]

Shaw deployed his Irishness—and his situation in England as a semi-foreigner and outsider—in a variety of ways in the construction of his public persona and dealings with others. From his "Supernationalist" ideological stance he berated the Irish for their hopeless dreaming, their constant revival of ancient hatreds and useless causes, and their hotheaded use of violence in politics. He ended his statement (made in Ireland) about being a "Supernationalist" by saying he had to "hurry back to London" since "the lunatics there are comparatively harmless." However, when in London—or surrounded by the English as he was on his SS *Lusitania* voyage—he represented himself as the sane, clear-sighted Irishman objectively reflecting on the complacency, density, and stodginess of John Bullish Englishmen. A complex alternation of self-distancing from and self-identification with Ireland is evident in Shaw's various formulations of his Irish identity.

In a description of his method of settling quarrels in the Fabian Society Shaw mentions one way in which he deployed his Irish identity. He recalled that his approach on those occasions was to infuriate everybody by lucidly explaining their positions in the most exaggerated terms, thus diverting their anger onto the impossible Irishman in their midst: "Result: both sides agreed that it was all my fault. I was denounced on all hands as a reckless mischief-maker, but forgiven as a privileged Irish lunatic." As Shaw coolly went on to explain in this passage from *Sixteen Self Sketches*, the "unique survival" of the Fabian Society among the wrecks of its rivals in its early days was owing to "the one Irish element in its management."[7] Irish lunacy, his story suggests, is a disguised form of sanity.

Apart from the fact already noted that two of Shaw's most fully committed relationships with women—those with Jenny Patterson, his lover of the 1880s and 1890s, and his wife, Charlotte—Shaw's connections with Ireland (even in easily quantifiable ways) were far more extensive than the 1946 councillor apparently realized. He treats Ireland and includes Irish characters in a number of his creative writings, often in ways that have autobiographical dimensions. He had culturally and historically significant associations and friendships with Irish contemporaries. He was centrally involved in a 1909 episode of great moment in the early history of the Abbey Theatre, with Shaw's plays subsequently becoming an important part of the Abbey's repertory. He was constantly in touch with Irish affairs and made penetrating comments on them. Having left Ireland in 1876, he first returned in 1905 and thereafter made quite frequent visits, especially enjoying stays in the west, where parts of some of his plays were written. Moreover, he never lost his delightful—and much commented upon—Irish accent.

* * *

Shaw's most extensive and searching engagement with Ireland in his creative writings is found in the 1904 play *John Bull's Other Island*, which marked the first real step on the ladder in his ascent to real success and fame in the professional theater in England. However, several lesser-known treatments of Irish subjects and characters in his works also deserve examination. The fact that the matter of Ireland is not regularly featured in Shaw's plays does not diminish its significance. Some of the defining qualities of his outlook and sensibility are shown in his imaginative explorations of Ireland and its relations with England.

The earliest engagement with Ireland in Shaw's creative writings occurs in his novel *Immaturity*. At first glance the novel might be seen as Shaw's way of turning his back on the country he had recently left. He not only gave his central character the quintessentially ordinary English name of Smith but also underscored his Englishness in various ways in the narrative. An Irish grandmother Smith possessed in an earlier version of the novel was done away with in the published version. Moreover, Smith looks at Ireland and Irish characters from an English perspective. Nicholas Grene suggests that there is some ground for thinking that in this novel Shaw was creating a de-Hibernicized version of himself, "allowing him to escape from his provincial status as Irishman."[8] Yet the eradication of Irish connections from the central character does not extend to the novel as a whole, which includes a number of Irish characters and a complex range of references to Ireland.

Immaturity initiates a pattern of ambivalence in Shaw's treatment of Ireland that constantly recurs in his work. The passionate denunciation of Ireland by one of the characters is immediately balanced by an exclamation from another character: "Dear me! I get on very well with Irish people." The character who denounces Ireland is the flighty, Irish-born Isabella, who declares that she will never revisit the country of her birth. Yet in the course of the novel she does return. Moreover, on different occasions she gives completely contradictory accounts of it to Smith. In a letter written to him from Ireland, she speaks of a visit to a village, the ugliness of which "would make Mr Ruskin cry," and gives an equally unflattering account of Newry, the town Shaw visited when his childhood friend Edward McNulty was involuntarily transferred there by the bank that employed him. However, when Isabella returns to London, her opinion of the two countries is reversed. She claims to have enjoyed the beauty of rural Ireland—in particular Rosstrevor, "a darling place"—and now it is London that is horrid: "I think London a detestable place. After the mountains, the sea, and the beautiful fresh air, it seems intolerable to breathe in this prison of a city."

Apart from Isabella, the cast of Irish characters in *Immaturity* includes: her indulgent father, Foley Woodward, a kindly gentleman reminiscent of Mr. Allworthy in Henry Fielding's *Tom Jones*; Mr. Woodward's housekeeper, Mrs. Daly; and his manservant, Cornelius Hamlet. Mrs. Daly has an Irish brogue that Smith hates. Her opinion of Smith as a rather silly individual is significant in terms of the novel's comic exploration of whether it is Smith or the out-of-joint society in which he is placed that is immature. Like Mrs. Daly, the manservant has a very thick accent that at times becomes almost incomprehensible, as when he announces at breakfast that "bruckhust" is ready. Both the eccentric Hamlet and Mrs. Daly exhibit a down-to-earth shrewdness that complicates and enriches the portrayal of Ireland and its inhabitants.

Two noteworthy examples of Shaw's dramatic treatment of the Irish are presented in the one-act plays *O'Flaherty VC* and *Press Cuttings*. The most fervent nationalist in all of Shaw's works is Mrs. O'Flaherty, the mother of the hero of *O'Flaherty VC*, whose Hiberno-centric outlook on life includes the beliefs that Shakespeare was born in Cork, that Venus arose out of the sea in Killiney Bay, and that Lazarus was buried in Glasnevin.

O'Flaherty is in trouble with his mother because she was tricked into believing that he was going to fight against rather than with the English in World War I. The son's report of his mother's ecstatic response to this deception reads: "And sure the poor woman kissed me and went about the house singing in her old cracky voice that the French was on the sea, and theyd be here without delay, and the Orange will decay, says the Shan van Vocht." *O'Flaherty VC* carries the ironic subtitle *A Recruiting Pamphlet*, and in the play Irish nationalist fervor is one component of the general satire on patriotism and protest against war. In the middle of the play O'Flaherty, a reluctant and skeptical instrument of the recruiting campaign in Ireland, declares—no doubt thinking of his own kith and kin as much as anything else—"youll never have a quiet world until you knock the patriotism out of the human race." He decides that it will be more peaceful going back to the front in France than staying at home in Ireland with his mother and family.

Press Cuttings is a topical sketch on what is described in its subtitle as "the Women's War in 1909." In a letter to Bertha Newcombe dated 14 May 1909, Shaw confessed that "the only really sympathetic woman in [the play] is a charwoman."[9] He was referring to Mrs. Farrell, whose only female rivals for sympathy are the dangerous, pistol-toting soprano Lady Corinthia Fanshawe and Mrs. Banger, the militant and distinctly masculine secretary of the "Anti-Suffraget League." Mrs. Farrell, the survivor of an Irish marriage that produced eight children (her husband used to argue that controlling himself was against his religion), is now in the employ of the play's principal male character, General Mitchener.

Although it is only a minor role in a minor, albeit delightful, play, Mrs. Farrell presents a very positive image of the Irish character. She is canny, sharply observant, verbally resourceful, and a natural wit, a woman of both common and uncommon sense. She knows what goes on beneath the exterior of male pomposity and pretentiousness as well as "the seamy side o General Sandstone's uniform, where his [whisky] flask rubs agen the buckle of his braces." Defeated in verbal combat with Mrs. Farrell over the relative risks of bearing "livin people into the world" and "blow[ing] dhem out of it," General Mitchener is forced to acknowledge her as being "a woman of very powerful mind." In a typical example of upward social mobility in Shavian comedy, Mrs. Farrell eventually condescends to accept his offer of marriage.

Entitled *Tragedy of an Elderly Gentleman*, the fourth part of *Back to Methuselah* (Shaw's post–World War I five-play cycle) begins on a fine summer day in a.d. 3000. The opening scene is set on Burren Pier, on the southern shore of Galway Bay, on the west coast of Ireland, where the Elderly Gentleman of the play's title is discovered sitting on a stone bollard used to secure vessels to the shore. As though jokingly to suggest a certain identification with the old buffer in his play, a photograph of Shaw as an "elderly gentleman" sitting on such a bollard in Galway Bay was taken during one of his visits to Ireland.

Despite its futuristic setting, the play has some sharply topical references to an Ireland in the throes of political conflict and violence leading up to the 1922–23 civil war. Included among a raft of extinct concepts in this Shavian vision of the future is the idea of nationalistic movements. All struggles for national independence have long ago been fought and won: "The claims of nationality were so universally conceded that there was no longer a single country on the face of the earth with a national grievance or a national movement." In the speech in which this is reported, the Elderly Gentleman becomes Shaw's instrument for satire aimed at the plight of Ireland after being thus robbed of a principal occupation and source of interest: "Think of the position of the Irish, who had lost all their political faculties by disuse except that of nationalist agitation, and who owed their position as the most interesting race on earth solely to their sufferings! The very countries they had helped to set free boycotted them as intolerable bores. The communities which had once idolized them as the incarnation of all that is adorable in the warm heart and witty brain, fled from them as from a pestilence."

The astringent mockery in the Elderly Gentleman's summary history of Ireland is balanced by some very positive notes. A land of mystery, beauty, and holiness peopled by a race adored for its "warm heart and witty brain"—this image of Ireland's past is an essential part of the argument directed against the soulless, humorless, and ruthless materialism of the brave new world of the Elderly Gentleman's custodians, Zoo and Zozim, which is also, as the dialogue conveys, the brave new world of post–World War I Europe. Shaw permits Zoo to proffer one pithy piece of advice to the Elderly Gentleman, which is undoubtedly also directed at contemporary Ireland: "How often must I tell you that we are made wise not by the recollections of our past, but by the responsibilities of our future."

Shaw frequently lamented the constant revival of old sectarian and political animosities in Ireland—and the way in which parents encouraged their children to maintain them. *Tragedy of An Elderly Gentleman* echoes other Shavian statements on this theme. In December 1914 Shaw wrote an interesting letter to Mabel Fitzgerald, wife of the Sinn Féin MP Desmond Fitzgerald, who was involved in the 1916 Easter Rising in Dublin. Under her maiden name McConnell, Mabel had briefly substituted for Georgina "Judy" Gillmore as Shaw's secretary in 1909. The letter is generally friendly in tone, suggesting that Shaw liked his Irish Catholic friend—and found her attractive. Nevertheless, he gave her a very stern lecture about her anti-Protestant and anti-English passions and the fact that she was instilling the same bigotry in her son: "As an Ulsterwoman, you must be aware that if you bring up your son to hate anyone except a Papist, you will go to hell. Just you see what I have said in my letter to the Irish press about people who have no positive nationality and are only anti-English instead of being Irish. You must be a wicked devil to load a child's innocent soul with a burden of old hatreds and rancors that Ireland is sick of."[10] The letter continues in a much gentler vein and includes a compliment and a reference to other aspects of Shaw's feelings about Ireland: "I will certainly call on you next time to see whether you have kept your good looks. The magic of Ireland is very strong for me when I see a beehive dwelling. Did you ever make the pilgrimage to Skellig Michael? If not, you have not yet seen Ireland."

One of a group of rocky island pinnacles off the coast of County Kerry, in southwest Ireland, Skellig Michael is famous for its early Christian monastery, built around the seventh century a.d. and perched about six hundred feet above the water. Shaw and Charlotte visited the island on 17 September 1910 during a rather dangerous journey by rowboat. (The island is only accessible in favorable weather and they had failed to get there by yacht the previous day.) The experience left an indelible impression on Shaw, who provided a vivid description of the island—still quoted in tourist information—in a letter to his retired solicitor friend Frederick Jackson, written from the Parknasilla Hotel the following day: "An incredible, impossible, mad place," he wrote in the course of his description. "I tell you the thing does not belong to any world that you and I have lived and worked in; it is part of our dream world."[11] This "dream world" of ancient religious traditions and haunting beauty was an essential component in the multifaceted Shavian image of Ireland.

* * *

On 23 June 1904 Shaw wrote to W. B. Yeats: "I have it quite seriously in my head to write an Irish play (frightfully modern—no banshees nor leprechauns) when I have finished a book I now have in hand on the succulent subject of Municipal Trading."[12] The play to which he was referring was *John Bull's Other Island*, which he had, in fact, already begun writing on 17 June under the working title "Rule Britannia."[13] A letter from Yeats to Lady Gregory dated 12 March 1900 shows that the idea of "a play on the contrast between Irish and English character" had been in Shaw's mind for several years before his letter to Yeats in 1904.[14] In August and September 1904 the Shaws visited Scotland, where the first draft of *John Bull's Other Island* was completed at Alness, Rosemarkie (near Inverness), on 23 August. The play was first produced the following November by the Vedrenne-Barker company at the Royal Court Theatre in Sloane Square, Chelsea, London.

John Bull's Other Island is a work of major importance in the Shavian canon. Although it had a mixed reception from the critics, who mistook its lack of conventional plot complications for a lack of structure, it attracted a great deal of notice. The then prime minister, Arthur J. Balfour, who was first accompanied to a performance by Beatrice Webb, saw the play no fewer than five times, bringing with him two leaders of the Liberal opposition, Sir Henry Campbell-Bannerman and Herbert Henry Asquith. On 11 March 1905 a special performance was held for King Edward VII, who, according to legend, laughed so heartily that he broke the chair he was sitting on.[15] The play had 121 performances at the Royal Court during the Vedrenne-Barker seasons and was later hugely appreciated by audiences in Dublin, where it was first presented in 1907 at the Theatre Royal.

Had negotiations not broken down (like King Edward VII's chair), the play could conceivably have become the first work to be presented in the newly founded Abbey Theatre in 1904. In his 1907 preface to *John Bull's Other Island*, Shaw wrote that the play had been written "at the request of Mr William Butler Yeats, as a patriotic contribution to the repertory of the Irish Literary Theatre," and suggested that it had been turned down because it was "uncongenial to the whole spirit of the neo-Gaelic movement, which is bent on creating a new Ireland after its own ideal, whereas my play is a very uncompromising presentment of the real old Ireland."[16]

Shaw's statements are misleading. Yeats does not seem to have invited him to write the play, and although it did contain material that was "uncongenial to . . . the spirit of the neo-Gaelic movement"—Shaw was well aware that his satirical reference to Kathleen ni Hoolihan might raise a laugh "at Yeats's expense"[17]—this was not the main reason why the Irish National Theatre Society did not go ahead with a production. The major problems were the scale of the work, its technical demands, and the difficulty of casting it with the resources available to the fledgling company. In fact, it was quite warmly commented on by the Abbey people. The actor W. G. Fay, though worried about the casting, thought it "a wonderful piece of work."[18] J. M. Synge thought it would "hold a Dublin audience," an understatement when considered in the light of later events.[19] In a three-page letter to Shaw written in 1904, W. B. Yeats was highly complimentary: "You have said things in this play which are entirely true about Ireland, things which nobody has ever said before. . . . You show your wonderful knowledge of the country. You have laughed at the things that are ripe for laughter, and not where the ear is still green."[20]

However, Yeats gave a very different-sounding report to Lady Gregory after seeing the production in London. "It acts very much better than one could have foreseen . . . [and] certainly keeps everybody amused," he began on a positive note, but then went on to say: "I didn't really like it. It is fundamentally ugly and shapeless."[21] Yeats's judgment may not have been entirely uninfluenced by the fact that some of the play's satire came close to the bone of his own projects and constructions of "romantic Ireland." Shaw's play nevertheless moves beyond satire; in its final act in particular there are striking parallels with central concepts in Yeats's philosophical writings.

Considered as a whole, *John Bull's Other Island* is a trenchant satire about England and Ireland that subverts stereotypical views of the national identities of both countries. It is also an imaginative expression of Shaw's vision of an ideal society in which socially constructed obstacles standing between different forms of human activity, and between the human and divine states, are dissolved. The play can ultimately be seen as presenting a Shavian version of what Yeats calls Unity of Culture.[22]

The assault on national stereotypes in the play begins with the bold comic stroke of introducing a fake Irishman (who is later discovered to have been born in Glasgow) in the form of the scruffy, small-time confidence man Tim Haffigan. Shaw provides Haffigan with all the clichés associated with the stage Irishman. His blarney is larded with a generous sprinkling of all the linguistic identifiers of the type. The grasping and alcoholic Haffigan—Shaw uses the joke he made about his own father by turning this character into a teetotaler in principle but not in practice—is seen by the gullible John Bullish Englishman Tom Broadbent as epitomizing the Irish character: "Rash and improvident but brave and goodnatured; not likely to succeed in business on your own account perhaps, but eloquent, humorous, a lover of freedom, and a true follower of that great Englishman Gladstone." The trap is set both for Broadbent and the audience. It is left to a real Irishman, Larry Doyle, Broadbent's partner in the engineering firm, to reveal the truth about Haffigan and his Glasgow origins. In response to Broadbent's protest following the revelation ("But he spoke—he behaved just like an Irishman"), Doyle explodes: "Like an Irishman!! Man alive, don't you know that all this top-o-the-morning and broth-of-a-boy and more-power-to-your-elbow business is got up in England to fool you. . . . No Irishman ever speaks like that in Ireland, or ever did, or ever will."

As Shaw was well aware, the stage Irishman not only bears little or no relation to actual Irish people but is also a way for the English not to take the race seriously.[23] A high-culture version of this put-down was Matthew Arnold's collection of lectures *On The Study of Celtic Literature*. Broadbent's epitome of the Irish national character echoes the Arnoldian doctrine that "the Celtic genius [has] sentiment as its main basis, with love of beauty, charm, and spirituality for its excellence, ineffectualness and self-will for its defect."[24] As Declan Kiberd has suggested, Arnold was articulating a late-Victorian view of Ireland as representing a suppressed, feminine side of England: "If John Bull was industrious and reliable, Paddy was held to be indolent and contrary; if the former was mature and rational, the latter must be unstable and emotional; if the English were adult and manly, the Irish must be childish and feminine."[25] In the preface to *John Bull's Other Island* Shaw specifically reverses this dichotomy by saying that the Englishman is "wholly at the mercy of his imagination," whereas the Irishman "always has one eye on things as they are."[26] In the play it is not the Irish characters but the John Bullish Englishman who is most given to sentimentality and seeing the world through rose-colored glasses.

No doubt partly drawing on his journeys as a young man out of Dublin on business for the Uniacke Townshend real estate firm and his visit (in the summer of 1872) to McNulty in Newry, in this play Shaw provides a deft, knowledgeable portrait in miniature of Irish village life in his presentation of the local inhabitants of Rosscullen. A far cry from sentimentally idealized Irish men and women in works such as Dion Boucicault's *The Colleen Bawn*—and some of the musical comedies his sister Lucy performed in—are Shaw's seedy former land agent Cornelius Doyle; the disgruntled and quarrelsome small-time landlord farmer Matt Haffigan; the sturdy but unimaginative and limited local priest Father Dempsey; the superstition-ridden Patsy Farrell; the redheaded, loutish Doran; the commonsensical Aunt Judy; and the wan, emotionally starved Nora. As with James Joyce, Shaw did not need to be in Ireland physically to recover it creatively. It was inside his mind and imagination.

Autobiographical elements in the play are distributed among several characters. As we have seen, even in the absurd Broadbent there are touches of Shaw, especially the echoes in Broadbent's cheerful wooing of Nora of his courtship with the frequently unhappy and pining Charlotte. More obvious reflections of Shaw are evident in the portrayal of the self-exiled Irishman Doyle. Like the young Shaw, Doyle has left Ireland—and a father of whom he is very critical—for the larger horizons of London in order to be "made a man of" in the "world that belongs to the big Powers." Doyle's embracing of this solid cosmopolitan ambience and rejection of Irish parochialism is certainly conveyed with a force that suggests close authorial involvement. Much of the play's most searching and trenchant criticism of Ireland and English attitudes toward Ireland comes from him. The picture of Ireland that Doyle evokes for Broadbent is of a squalid "hell of littleness and monotony." With a strongly critical glance at Yeats and the Irish nationalist movement, Shaw has Doyle deliver the play's fiercest denunciation of Irish religious and political attitudes:

> [The Irishman] cant be religious. The inspired Churchman that teaches him the sanctity of life and the importance of conduct is sent away empty; while the poor village priest that gives him a miracle or a sentimental story of a saint, has cathedrals built for him out of the pennies of the poor. He cant be intelligently political: he dreams of what the Shan Van Vocht said in ninetyeight. If you want to interest him in Ireland youve got to call the unfortunate island Kathleen ni Hoolihan and pretend she's a little old woman. It saves thinking.

However, like some of the characters in Shaw's novels, Doyle seems partly to function in a self-critical way, representing the kind of heartlessness that Shaw knew he was sometimes capable of himself, particularly in relation to women. Doyle may long for a country where "the dreams are not unreal," but he is presented throughout the play as a rather negative—even callous—figure whose contribution to change would likely be no more than that of a critic on the sidelines. The morally authoritative yet similarly ineffectual Keegan describes him late in the play as "foolish in his cleverness," holding him and his kind responsible for turning Ireland into "a Land of Derision," thus making Doyle seem partly responsible for the very conditions he despises. By showing Broadbent to be—despite his stupidity—a much more kindly soul than Doyle, it was as though Shaw were playing off two sides of himself in the characters of his two partners in the engineering firm.

The third figure in the play's complex trinity of partly autobiographical shadows is Keegan, a defrocked priest whose loyalties lie with a broader conception of religion than that represented by the village's unimaginative Father Dempsey, and whose spiritual and philosophical vision counterbalances the relentless materialism of Broadbent. It is Keegan who, at the end of the play, not only provides a reminder of Ireland as a land sanctified by its ancient religious traditions but also presents a supranational vision of unified culture. Echoing ideas found in the positivist religious system of Auguste Comte and some of the writings of William Morris, Keegan presents a philosophical vision in which conceptual divisions between human and divine, church and state, work and play are all dissolved. It is this dream that he opposes to the "foolish dream of efficiency" that Broadbent represents. However, all is grist to the all-conquering Broadbent mill. In the grand scenario Broadbent has in mind for Rosscullen—a combination of golf course and theme park—Keegan will come in handy. As the local eccentric, "almost equal to Ruskin and Carlyle," the Irish visionary will take his place, along with the round tower, as a tourist attraction.

* * *

The intellectual and imaginative limitations of John Bullish Englishmen had also been the target of satire and complaint for Shaw's compatriot Oscar Wilde in the 1890s. In February 1893, in a letter sent with a copy of his new play *Salomé* (which had just been published in its purple binding), Wilde wrote to Shaw: "England is the land of intellectual fogs but you have done much to clear the air: we are both Celtic, and I like to think that we are friends: for these and many other reasons Salome presents herself to you in purple raiment. Pray accept her with my best wishes."[27]

In the same letter Wilde praised Shaw for his writings on "the ridiculous institution of a stage censorship," adding "your little book on Ibsenism and Ibsen is such a delight to me that I constantly take it up." Wilde thought of Shaw and himself as forming a small "Hibernian School" of writers in England: they were Celtic allies united in their witty opposition to the thick-witted and complacently philistine John Bulls and censorious moralists of fin-de-siècle English society. When he sent Shaw a copy of *Lady Windermere's Fan* in 1893, Wilde dubbed his play "Op. 1 of the Hibernian School." Later in the same year he referred to Shaw's *Widowers' Houses* as "Op. 2 of the great Celtic school," continuing this playful reference system up to Opus 5, which was his own play *An Ideal Husband*.[28]

Wilde's present of *Salomé* was held up in the mail. Shaw wrote: "Salome is still wandering in her purple raiment in search of me; and I expect her to arrive a perfect outcast, branded with inky stamps, bruised by flinging from hard hands into red prison [i.e. postal] vans."[29] In this letter Shaw likewise presented himself as being allied with his fellow Hibernian in a common cause against English puritanism and censorship. He included Wilde, William Morris, and himself in a triumvirate of writers on the periphery of English society who had assumed a special combative and educative role in relation to these forces: "We have to half fight down, half educate up, if we are to get rid of Censorships, official and unofficial. And when I say we, I mean Morris the Welshman and Wilde and Shaw the Irishmen."[30]

In 1893 both Shaw and Wilde confronted the absurdity of the English system of stage censorship. In the summer of that year a planned production of Wilde's *Salomé* was banned by E. Smyth Piggott, the Lord Chamberlain's Licenser of Stage Plays, a gentleman described by Shaw as "a walking compendium of vulgar insular prejudice."[31] Apart from Wilde himself, only Shaw and William Archer publically criticized this action. Wilde threatened to leave the country and become a naturalized Frenchman. "I shall not consent to call myself a citizen of a country that shows such narrowness in artistic judgement. I am not English. I am Irish, which is quite another thing," he declared in an interview published in the *Pall Mall Budget*.[32] In November 1893 Shaw completed his controversial play *Mrs. Warren's Profession*, but the idea of a production by J. T. Grein's Independent Theatre was not pursued: it was a foregone conclusion that Piggott would not grant a license for public performance.

Despite the mutual respect evident in their 1890s correspondence as fellow Hibernians, friends, and allies, Shaw and Wilde did not have much social contact. The fairly obvious reflections of Wilde in Shaw's satirical portrait of the dandy-poet Hawkshaw in *Immaturity* (which remained in its mice-nibbled manuscript state until long after Wilde's death) suggests some of the reasons why the two never became close friends. "Oscar, as you know, was a snob to the marrow of his bones, having been brought up in Merrion Square, Dublin," Shaw wrote to Frank Harris in 1908.[33] Apart from the poorly documented story about Sir William Wilde's unsuccessful operation on George Carr Shaw's squint, there is no direct evidence of contact in Dublin between the rather indigent Shaws of Synge and Hatch Streets and the wealthy and socially prominent Wildes of Merrion Square. However, previous social contact between the families is perhaps suggested by Shaw's invitations to the house of Lady Wilde in his early London days.

After her husband's death, Lady Wilde, the ardent Irish patriot, littérateur, and grande dame who gave herself the exotic pen name "Speranza," moved with her elder son Willie—who, when asked what he worked at, is said to have replied "at intervals"[34]—to London, where she held at homes at 116 Park Street, off Grosvenor Square, that were attended by writers and artists. Beginning in November 1879, when his diary records his first visit, Shaw attended some of these at homes, to which W. B. Yeats was also invited. The shy young Shaw's entrée to this salon may have been helped by the fact that both Willie and Oscar Wilde were fond of his vivacious sister, Lucinda Frances Shaw.

At the time of their "Hibernian School" correspondence in 1893, Shaw and Wilde were both Irish allies and rivals, though Wilde had outstripped his compatriot in terms of literary and theatrical fame. Wilde was launched on the upward path of his meteoric career as dramatist, wit, critic, and dandy, while being simultaneously on the road to the ruin and imprisonment that followed his trials in the summer of 1895. Shaw was hardly known as a dramatist in 1893: even the partial triumph of *Arms and the Man*—after the memorable opening of which Yeats declared him "the most formidable man in modern letters"—was still to come in April 1894. Nevertheless, by 1893 Shaw had made a very considerable mark as critic, polemicist, and wit—and Wilde generously acknowledged this fact. Shaw enjoyed and admired Wilde's celebrated epigram: "Shaw has not an enemy in the world; and none of his friends like him."[35]

Despite obvious differences in their outlook, Shaw and Wilde were both witty subverters of conventional ideas and assumptions and wrote with a crispness and point that often makes their writings and bons mots indistinguishable. The similarity caused confusion about the authorship of unsigned reviews they contributed to the *Pall Mall Gazette*. All those "of a distinctly Irish quality during the 1885–1888 period," Shaw wrote, "may, I think, be set down to either me or to Oscar Wilde, whose reviews were sometimes credited to me."[36]

Shaw was present in 1895 at one of the regular Monday lunches at the Café Royale, which were organized by Frank Harris, when Wilde and "young Douglas" arrived. The Queensberry trial was imminent and Wilde was attempting to persuade Harris to appear as a "literary expert witness" for the defense and vouch for the high artistic merit of his novel *Dorian Gray*. According to Shaw's recollection, Harris's advice to Wilde was to forget about literary matters—"it is not going to be a matter of clever talk about your books"—and leave for

France that night. Harris knew what was going to happen: "I know what evidence they have got. You must go." Wilde and Douglas left in dudgeon—but not for France. Like a victim of tragic hubris, Wilde remained in England to face the sequence of events that ultimately led to Reading Gaol.[37]

Although Shaw drafted a petition to the home secretary for Wilde's release, after discussing the matter with Willie Wilde he decided not to submit it since his own and the other signatures he could obtain would carry no weight and possibly do more harm than good. Shaw continued to "defend" Wilde by inserting laudatory remarks about his work in theater reviews, even—after Wilde's release and exile in disgrace in France—boldly suggesting (in correspondence) that his name be added to a list of possible candidates for election to a British Academy of Letters: "The only dramatist, besides Mr Henry James, whose nomination could be justified, is Mr Oscar Wilde."[38]

* * *

Running through W. B. Yeats's recollections of his association with Shaw in the Florence Farr and Avenue Theatre days of the 1890s is a strain of ambivalence that characterizes most of the poet's comments concerning his fellow Irishman and his works:

> I listened to *Arms and the Man* with admiration and hatred. It seemed to me inorganic, logical straightness and not the crooked road of life, yet I stood aghast at its energy. . . . Presently I had a nightmare that I was haunted by a sewing-machine, that clicked and shone, but the incredible thing was that the machine smiled, smiled perpetually. Yet I delighted in Shaw, the formidable man. He could hit my enemies and the enemies of all I loved, as I could never hit, as no living author that was dear to me could ever hit.
>
> Florence Farr's way home was mine also for a part of the way, and it was often of this that we talked, and sometimes, though not always, she would share my hesitations, and for years to come I was to wonder, whenever Shaw became my topic, whether the cock crowed for my blame or praise.[39]

While the positive notes in this passage tend to be forgotten, the negative ones have contributed to persistent shibboleths about Shaw. Yeats's characterization of Shaw as some kind of mechanistic logician does not stand up under serious scrutiny. "Logical straightness" is neither a characteristic of *Arms and the Man* nor of any other of Shaw's works. It is a misreading to view it simply as an attack on romance. Shaw's outwardly pragmatic hero Bluntschli is actually a self-confessed romantic, and it is really the pseudoromance of operatic tradition that the play satirizes. More generally, in Shavian drama intellectual theory and mechanistic system are swept aside by instinct, passion, and vitality. His plays invariably conclude in a state of irreducible complexity that indeed corresponds to "the crooked road of life." Two of the most potent influences on Shaw were the Romantic poets Shelley and Blake, who were also among Yeats's major mentors.

Shaw did not sympathize with the Yeatsian "Cuchulanoid"[40] vision, nor did Synge, Wilde, Joyce, and others who were nevertheless deeply committed to Ireland and its causes and whose personal identities were strongly shaped by their nationality. Nevertheless, the marked differences between the thoroughly modern ("no banshees, no leprechauns") Shaw and the "Cuchulanoid" Yeats tend to obscure some important intellectual and imaginative similarities, as well as objectives and antipathies they had in common. As his statement in *Autobiographies* shows, Yeats viewed Shaw as a powerful ally in causes that were dear to him. Whatever their differences, his fellow Irishman clearly thought of Shaw as one member of a small circle of Hibernian opponents to philistinism and intellectual narrowness and illiberality. In this respect the relationship echoed that between Wilde and Shaw.

Apart from the striking parallel between Father Keegan's dream and Yeats's ideal of Unity of Culture, another similarity between Shaw and Yeats lay in their shared hostility toward the domination of Irish life by the Catholic Church and its priesthood. The anticlerical strain in Yeats's writing is strikingly illustrated in a draft of a play he wrote about a young shepherdess, accused of witchcraft and heresy, who is arraigned by a Bishop and other churchmen.[41] Although Shaw could not have seen this early fragment, it bears striking similarities to his *Saint Joan*, especially the ways in which Shaw's heroine—who is also called a "shepherd girl"[42]—challenges the authority of the church and asserts her own religious vision. When he saw it in London in 1924, Yeats gave *Saint Joan* a mixed review typical of his response to Shaw's plays. He "liked all the ecclesiastical parts, thought it even noble, but hated Joan and the actress. . . . I thought Joan half cockney slut and half nonconformist preacher."[43] Nevertheless, Yeats's experimental early fragment—with its own nonconformist, banshee "Saint Joan"—shares multiple parallels with Shaw's work.

Yeats's play is set in a courthouse. Seated on a large chair, the Bishop is surrounded by monks and a few laypersons. A rough pyre is visible at the back of the stage. Yeats gives the Bishop the same kind of sincere but ill-motivated magnanimity and charity that Shaw gives his Inquisitor in *Saint Joan*. The Bishop wants the shepherdess, who has turned from the church and communed with the unseen, to repent. She obstinately refuses, declaring that she is not a part of his church. As it turns out, this Yeatsian Saint Joan is a woman of the Sidhe, the Irish fairy world. In the course of the trial, the accused removes her gray shroud and appears "dressed in a long clinging robe of peacock feathers; her arms & neck are bare, with gold ornaments." The fragment ends before the reader discovers if she was sent to the pyre like her Shavian counterpart. Underlying this curious meeting of mind and imagination between Shaw and Yeats is a form of Protestantism, a mutual dislike of priestly control over religious impulses and social life. They both lived to see the Protestant Ascendancy in Ireland become the Protestant minority. By the time Yeats became a senator in the Irish Free State, the tables had been turned with respect to the balance of power that had existed between Catholics and Protestants. In a speech he delivered to the Senate on 11 June 1925, in which he attacked the prohibition of divorce in the Irish Free State as disadvantageous to Protestants, Yeats included a eulogy of the Protestant Irish. Shaw sent a message of congratulations through Lady Gregory: "Remember us favourably to W.B.Y. and his missus. I greatly like him in the Senate upholding the flag of modern civilisation as the Protestant Boy who carries the Drum."[44]

* * *

"Come over & help us to stir things up," Yeats wrote to Shaw from Dublin on 19 October 1901 during preparations for the third season of the Irish Literary Theatre.[45] Shaw did not act on this suggestion, but many years later an opportunity arose for him, in collaboration with Yeats and Lady Gregory, to "stir things up" in Dublin in a sensational manner.

In 1909 Shaw again encountered stage censorship in England with the banning of two of his one-act plays, *Press Cuttings* and *The Shewing-up of Blanco Posnet*. Shaw, Lady Gregory, and Yeats sensed an opportunity: Why not have the first showing of a play by a son of Erin that had been banned in England at Dublin's Abbey Theatre? *The Shewing-up of Blanco Posnet* was the play chosen for the challenge.

Set in the courthouse of a pioneering settlement in America, *The Shewing-up of Blanco Posnet* is about a social rebel (cast in the mold of such earlier Shavian renegades as Dick Dudgeon of *The Devil's Disciple* and the blackguard Captain Brassbound) who is on trial for stealing a horse, a hanging offense made worse by the fact that the horse in question belonged to the local sheriff. During the trial it is revealed that despite his determination to be a godless tough guy, Blanco finds himself overwhelmed at a crucial moment by a mysterious and irresistible sense of compassion when he is confronted by a poor woman whose child is dying of croup. Against his better judgment Blanco had given her the horse to get the child to the hospital, an act of involuntary self-sacrifice that leads to his capture and trial.

During his trial Blanco asks difficult questions. "What is justice?" he truculently inquires of the sheriff, who promptly cuts to the chase with the answer: "Hanging horse thieves is justice; so now you know." More worrying to Mr. George Alexander Redford, the Lord Chamberlain's licenser of plays in London, was the fact that Blanco also raises the old question concerning the existence of evil by asking why God made the croup. Blanco also uses the word *immoral* with reference to the promiscuous behavior of one of his accusers, Feemy Evans, a Carmen-like young woman who has gained notoriety in the town for her sexual promiscuity. These were the trivial grounds for censorship.

Blanco Posnet is subtitled "A Sermon in Crude Melodrama." Although its "sermon" is rather obliquely expressed, the work can be viewed as a partial exception to the rule of ambiguity and complexity in the patterns of meaning in Shavian drama. The play is, in fact, an expression of Shaw's creed of creative evolution, here couched in a mixture of wild comedy and melodramatic action. The God presented in the play accords with the Shavian conception of an incomplete, evolving, experimental force in the universe: creating the croup was one of His mistakes. The mysterious force that prompts Blanco to perform his noble deed is an example of the way in which the divine works through human agency, which serves as the hands and brain of God. Viewed in this light, the play has a quite serious if unconventional religious theme. Shaw's friends Gilbert Murray, a professor of Greek and translator of Euripides, and his wife Lady Murray concurred that the banning of the play was "one of the most utterly unintelligent things in Redford's record."[46]

The problem was that many of the same kinds of guardians of other peoples' moral and spiritual welfare who held sway in London were also active in Dublin. A more particular problem was the fact that the vice-regal authorities in Dublin Castle—Lord Lieutenant John Campbell Gordon, 7th Earl of Aberdeen, and his under-secretary, the Right Honorable Sir James Dougherty—were placed in an embarrassing position by the prospect of a performance of a play in Dublin that had been banned by the Lord Chamberlain's office in London. In the final analysis, Dublin Castle had the whip hand: as the issuer of the Abbey Theatre's patent (the patentee being Lady Gregory), it also had the power to withdraw its license.

As the play went into rehearsal, with leading Abbey actress Sara Allgood—sister of Molly, J. M. Synge's great love—playing the disreputable Feemy Evans and Fred O'Donovan in the title role, what has rightly been described as "a wonderful social and political comedy"[47] was unfolding in the background, in the form of a war of words between Lady Gregory, Yeats, and Shaw, on the one hand, and the Dublin Castle authorities, on the other. Shaw's play was at the center of a larger struggle involving the independence of the Irish theater from English censorship, as well as broader issues relating to stage censorship in both England and Ireland. The controversy was an important moment in the history of censorship and attracted intense press interest in England, Ireland, and elsewhere. Lord Aberdeen did not actually ban the production, instead sending an admonitory letter to the company that, in effect, suggested that if the play caused riot or offense, the Abbey's licence might be withdrawn. Under this sword of Damocles, the company bravely decided to go ahead.

Shaw was in western Ireland, staying at the grand Parknasilla Hotel on the Ring of Kerry, when the play opened on 25 August 1909. He deliberately refrained from coming up to Dublin, but Charlotte and her sister, Mary Chomondeley, were among those who attended the sold-out premiere of the play, which was presented in a triple bill with Yeats's *Kathleen Ní Houlihan* and Lady Gregory's *Workhouse Ward*. Representatives from virtually all the major newspapers in England, plus those from Frankfurt and Milan, were present. James Joyce, who was in Dublin at the time, attended and reviewed the play for Trieste's *Piccolo della Sera*. As one commentator put it, "an event of a lifetime was taking place."[48]

The audience was not disappointed: the play proved a triumph. Near the end of the play Blanco leaps onto a table and gives an impromptu sermon concerning the choice people have in their lives of either playing the "great game" of generosity of spirit and altruism or the "rotten game" of mean-spiritedness and small-mindedness. For many in the Dublin audience on 25 August 1909 the words must have had a resonance far beyond the immediate context of the play. A telegram sent that night from Yeats and Lady Gregory to Shaw read: GLORIOUS RECEPTION SPLENDID VICTORY WHERE IS THE CENSOR NOW.

At midnight Lady Gregory followed up the telegram with a letter, in which she wrote: "The shouts are still in our ears! Never was such a victory. From first line to last of the play sustained and intense attention, and applause—and much applause at the end." She reported that the police, who had been stationed outside the theater to carry the Abbey people and/or rioters off to prison, "went home like fishermen with nets empty."[49]

The triumph of 25 August 1909 at the Abbey Theatre must have done much to enhance the alliance between Yeats and Shaw. They never became close friends, but Yeats was a frequent lunch guest at the Shaws' apartment in London and once at Ayot St Lawrence; in August 1910, the year after the

Blanco Posnet affair, both were guests of Lady Gregory at Coole Park. In a letter written in 1940, Shaw said of his relationship with Yeats: "I was always on very good terms with him personally; but I was not on literary terms with him; did not read enough of him to pontificate about his work; and did not get into his movement at all."[50]

It was during his stay at Coole Park in 1910 that Shaw began properly to appreciate Yeats's intellectual strengths. In the 1890s he had thought of him rather than Wilde (on whom the character of Bunthorne in *Patience* was supposedly based) as the true incarnation of the precious young man at the center of Gilbert and Sullivan's satire on the Aesthetic movement. However, in his 1940 recollection he went on to say: "Not until I spent some time in the house with him at Lady Gregory's . . . did I learn what a penetrating critic and good talker he was; for he played none of his Bunthorne games, and saw no green elephants at Coole." Shaw was even touched by Yeats's ultranationalistic play *Kathleen Ní Houlihan* and wrote that Charlotte filled their theater box with tears during a performance of it.[51] In 1932 Yeats and Shaw joined forces in the creation of the Irish Academy of Letters, to which Shaw was elected president and Yeats vice-president. Yeats served as president from 1935 until his death in 1939, when Shaw served another year in the office.[52]

There is apparently no record of any discussion between Yeats and Shaw concerning their flirtations with Fascism in the late 1920s and early 1930s. That shared late folly is yet another example of the strange concord that sometimes manifested itself between the two great Irishmen whose literary works and aims were outwardly so different in character.

* * *

If Shaw's personal relations with Yeats were cordial and mutually respectful, those with Lady Gregory were much more those of a warm friendship. Lady Gregory admired Shaw tremendously and got on very well with both him and Charlotte. On 16 April 1915 she records in her journal: "The Shaws are here. They are very easy to entertain, he is so extraordinarily light in hand, a sort of kindly joyousness about him." She dedicated her play *The Golden Apple* to Shaw, referring to him as "the gentlest of my friends." The Shaws visited her at Coole Park on motoring tours in 1910, 1915, and 1918, while she accepted frequent overnight and weekend stays at Ayot St Lawrence and lunches at Adelphi Terrace and Whitehall Court. One of her journal entries in November 1916 provides a glimpse of the Shaws' hospitality at Ayot St Lawrence: "We came on here in snow, but the house is warm and bright with fires in every room and pots of chrysanthemums."[53]

Shaw told her stories about his childhood—in particular one about a dream he had had in which God appeared to him in the form of the statue of William III in College Green, Dublin—and gave her private readings of his work-in-progress on *Heartbreak House, Back to Methuselah* (including the scene on Burren Pier in Galway Bay), and *Saint Joan*. It was Lady Gregory's suggestion that the long-awaited change of wind that alters the fortunes of the combatants at the battle of Orléans (in the third scene of *Saint Joan*) should be signaled by a sneeze from the page attending Dunois.[54] Lady Gregory's work at the Abbey was tireless and multifaceted. Thinking it could be perceived as an insult, Shaw refrained from publishing a joking description of her, contained in a speech, as "the charwoman of the Abbey," but she liked the title and enjoyed using it herself.[55]

It was not an easy task to enlist Shaw into the cause of promoting the Cuchulanoid mythology in which Lady Gregory had steeped herself, but she did say that Shaw reminded her of the Great Jester in the history of the ancient Irish gods, who, "for all his quips and mischief . . . came when he was needed to the help of Finn and Fianna, and gave good teaching to the boy-hero Cuchulain."[56] She may well have been thinking of the *Blanco Posnet* affair, among other things, which occurred at a critical time in the financial and political history of the Abbey Theatre. On the other hand, when she invited Shaw to deliver a lecture in Ireland in 1917—presumably on some subject having to do with Irish nationality—in his letter of reply he gave one of his most vehement denunciations of nationalism and patriotism: "As to the lecture, NO. The very words nation, nationality, our country, patriotism, fill me with loathing. Why do you want to stimulate a self-consciousness which is already morbidly excessive in our wretched island, and is deluging Europe with blood?"[57]

Seven weeks later Lady Gregory's son, airman Major Robert Gregory, became a victim of the European conflict when his plane was shot down over northern Italy. Shaw, who had recently been infuriated by the death (from a German shell) of Mrs. Patrick Campbell's son, wrote a kindly letter to the "maimed" Lady Gregory, to which she replied: "I was hoping for a letter from you. I knew it would be helpful."[58]

* * *

The primary orientation of Shaw's attitude toward Irish nationalism was established in a book review published in 1888, in which he wrote, "Nationalism is surely an incident of organic growth, not an invention. A man discusses whether he shall introduce a roasting jack into his kitchen but not whether he shall introduce an eye tooth into his son's mouth or lengthen him as he grows older."[59] Shaw saw Ireland's self-determination as a "natural right," part of an "inevitable order of social growth."[60] He described the gaining of national liberty as the second phase in an ultimately unstoppable process that begins with the gaining of personal liberty from feudal systems and slave-holding oligarchies and ends with the formation of international federations. While insisting, in his pre-1923 comments on nationalism in Ireland, on the need for national self-determination, Shaw simultaneously expressed a strongly critical view of nationalism as a cultural and social phenomenon.

In a section of the preface to *John Bull's Other Island* entitled "The Curse of Nationalism," Shaw describes nationalistic movements in general as "the agonizing symptoms of a suppressed natural function."[61] A country without national self-determination is like a man with a broken bone who can think of nothing else until the bone is set. In Shaw's view rabid nationalism, as distinct from naturally assumed national identity, is a manifestation of a fundamental disorder in the body politic. Until that disorder is righted, all the evils of nationalism—the windbaggery and tub-thumping, the callousness and rancor, the stifling parochialism, the false sentimentality—will flourish. This sharply critical attitude toward Irish nationalism needs to be seen in the context of other aspects of Shaw's commentary on Irish affairs, such as his defense of Parnell (at the time of his fall) and of Roger Casement, his passionate protest at the summary execution of the leaders of the Easter Rising, and his trenchant arguments (in 1919) against the policy of devolution. He wanted the relationship between England and Ireland to be one of free and politically independent states, with acknowledgment of mutual obligations established by treaty.

Shaw the supernationalist and Shaw the Irish patriot are not totally irreconcilable entities. Yet his Irish selves and Irish nations tend to be mercurial states, like his different personae as the Mephistophelean skeptic and derider versus the Bunyanesque religious pilgrim and reformer. As we have seen, his Irish self ranged from that of the "privileged . . . lunatic" and jester who employed mischievous irresponsibility as his strategy in the Fabian Society to the clear-eyed man of sanity and reason observing the sentimental and deluded Englishmen aboard the SS *Lusitania*.

Shaw's view of national stereotypes at times exhibited a postmodernist fluidity. He delighted in turning the Arnoldian formula about the supposed differences between the Celtic and English racial characteristics on its head, as well as destroying the mythic persona of the stage Irishman, both of which he does so effectively in *John Bull's Other Island*. In a 1946 interview he even denied the existence of the Irish race altogether: "for heaven's sake, don't talk to me about that hackneyed myth, the Irish race. There is no Irish race. We are a parcel of mongrels: Spanish, Scottish, Welsh, English, and even a Jew or two."[62]

Nevertheless, some essentialist features in his vision of Ireland remain. In both his dramatic and nondramatic writings there are recurrent strains of image and thought that point to a deep attachment to his native land. Landscapes and seascapes such as those of Dalkey and the west coast haunted his imagination. The Elderly Gentleman's phrase about the Irish as "the incarnation of all that is adorable in the warm heart and witty brain" is tinged with sentimentality, as befits the character, but it lingers in the mind and is reflected in some of Shaw's characterizations of Irish people in the plays.

Through Father Keegan (at the end of *John Bull's Other Island*) Shaw creates an image of the Ireland that Broadbent, with his "foolish dream of efficiency," will destroy. Despite his good nature and good intentions, Broadbent is for Father Keegan the ass of Mammon, "mighty in mischief, skilful in ruin, heroic in destruction," who has come to browse in Ireland "without knowing that the soil his hoof touches is holy ground." Through Keegan's eyes Ireland is viewed as a place sanctified by its ancient religious traditions but betrayed in its finer aspirations by its own servants of Mammon. His alternative vision of a unified social, religious, and political dispensation may be the "dream of a madman," but he asserts the value of dreams in the same play where Larry Doyle has described dreaming as a primary cause of paralysis of the will in Ireland. Father Keegan's reinstatement of the dream occurs in a memorable utterance that the speaker and dramatic context associate with Ireland: "Every dream is a prophecy: every jest is an earnest in the womb of time." Keegan's "dream of a madman" conveys the belief that in an ideal self-realization or self-recovery "the Holy Land of Ireland," as the medieval lyric calls it, could provide a counter to the foolish and destructive "dream of efficiency" and service of Mammon that motivate John Bull.

16 Edwardian Summers

Adroit as he was at playing the role of the strategically impossible Irishman in the Fabian Society, Shaw had less success with a venture he made into a new political arena when he ran as a Progressive candidate in the London County Council elections of 1904. He had resigned from his position as a St. Pancras borough councillor in November of the previous year. Encouraged by Charlotte—who thought his talent for public work should not go to waste—and supported by Sidney Webb, Shaw entered the lists for the County Council elections with a vigorous and a basically serious policy platform, one element of which was his support for the important new Education Acts of 1902 and 1903, which were being resisted by nonconformists in the St. Pancras electorate.[1]

On the day of the election Shaw declared in the pages of the *St. James's Gazette* that he and his Progressive partner, Sir William Geary, would win easily "if the intelligent people in the constituency can be induced to vote. But 3,000 of them sat at home last time—reading my books, I suppose."[2] Shaw enjoyed his campaign, but Beatrice Webb wrote with asperity about its provocative character: "He . . . refused to adopt any orthodox devices . . . insisted that he was an Atheist, that though a teetotaller he would force every citizen to imbibe a quartern of rum to cure any tendency to intoxication, laughed at the Nonconformist conscience and chaffed the Catholics about Transubstantiation, abused the Liberals and contemptuously patronised the Conservatives—until nearly every section was equally disgruntled."[3] This was an exaggeration. Although Shaw was unsuccessful, he polled quite well, scoring 1,460 votes compared to the 1,808 and 1,927 of the successful Moderates.[4]

To what extent county politics would have hindered Shaw's creative career is a matter of speculation. In all likelihood his loss in the elections was a gain for the Edwardian theater, where his comedic impulses would be an advantage rather than a drawback. His 1904 comedy *John Bull's Other Island* probably attracted more attention from national leaders as well as other quarters than he was ever likely to achieve in a political career; and his plays of the Edwardian period almost certainly wielded far more influence in the shaping of social attitudes than he could have achieved in politics. He became a force in the land, widely recognized as someone who was sweeping away the cobwebs of Victorian attitudes and taboos in manifold areas of social life. The spirit of the age had created an appetite for a new, post-Ibsen drama that could make people both laugh and think, able to see society and its institutions and assumptions in new ways. Shaw produced a series of plays in the Edwardian and early Georgian era that answered that need.

* * *

"Marvellous weather and the view's marvellous."[5] Helen Schlegel's words to her sister, Margaret—which occur in one of her happy letters from "Howards End" at the beginning of E. M. Forster's 1910 novel of the same title—could well stand as a metaphor for conventional ideas—both at the time and later—of the social climate, outlook, and prospects of Edwardian England. For some people the Edwardian years still conjure up images of sunny tranquility, prosperity, and national self-confidence and optimism. As we have seen, the optimism was not shared by Bernard Shaw in his 1901 essay "Civilisation and the Soldier." Indeed, there are many reasons for not viewing the Edwardian years as the golden age it is sometimes remembered as being. Nevertheless, from some perspectives (as, for example, in the poignant hindsight of writers like Siegfried Sassoon, whose *Memoirs of a Fox Hunting Man* was written after he had experienced the horrors of the front in France) the period seemed a time of endless summers and pleasant pastimes. It became legendary as a time of long days of cricket and croquet, lawn tennis, and garden parties replete with cucumber sandwiches; of delightful motoring in the country, such as that enjoyed by the portly, sports-loving Edward VII, and later by Bertie Wooster and his impeccable manservant Jeeves in the novels of P. G. Wodehouse; of adventures in the increasingly popular sports of flying and ballooning. The period saw the rise to fame of the great English composer Edward Elgar, whom Shaw championed and befriended and who was later to be coupled with Shaw as one of the two main attractions of the Malvern Festival. The tune of Elgar's *Pomp and Circumstance* Overture (no. 1) was adapted as the musical setting of an ode written by Arthur Christopher Benson for the coronation of Edward VII in 1901. Entitled "Land of Hope and Glory," the song captured the national mood and became the unofficial second national anthem. Elgar disliked the jingoistic sentiments his serene music inevitably came to arouse.

For Shaw further fame and recognition were to follow in the 1920s and beyond, but the Edwardian years—together with those immediately following them, under George V, before the outbreak of World War I—were in many ways the heyday of his career. Creatively it was an extraordinarily productive period. After the completion of his first Edwardian play, *Man and Superman*, in 1903, he produced a steady stream of full-length works—virtually at the rate of one each year—until 1912, as well as a number of playlets. By 1909 his fame and achievement as a playwright had grown to the point where he could be described as "the most famous of living dramatists"[6] in a public statement issued by W. B. Yeats and Lady Gregory at the height of the *Blanco Posnet* controversy in Dublin.

In 1905 the first book-length critical study of Shaw, *George Bernard Shaw: His Plays*, by H. L. Mencken was published, and by 1912 no fewer than nine books about his work—including the best early critical study by G. K. Chesterton—had followed, some of them in languages other than English. The first authorized biography, begun in 1904 by the young American mathematician Archibald Henderson, was published in 1911. Shaw's works were then being translated into seven foreign languages and performed in numerous countries outside England. The English portrait artist Sir William Rothenstein painted a study of Shaw in 1903, having previously included him in a monthly series of lithograph drawings called *English Portraits*, published in a bound volume in 1898. The first of numerous sculptures of Shaw was created by Auguste Rodin at his Meudon studio, outside Paris, during several sittings in 1906, with the poet Rainer Maria Rilke, Rodin's secretary at the time, in attendance.

Throughout the Edwardian period Shaw remained a caustic satirist and critic of the complacent and still very hidebound, class-ridden, inequitable and, in many ways, deeply troubled society in which he was achieving fame. He was "the gadfly of the commonwealth," as T. S. Eliot described him in 1921.[7] "Socialist—London" was the address he chose for himself in the new age of telegraphic communications, and a Socialist critic of society he remained—at least in his nondramatic writings and activities, if less clearly in his plays. Yet in some respects he fitted into the Edwardian age as comfortably as into his Jaeger suits. In many of its outward trappings his life was that of a prosperous Edwardian gentleman. The Adelphi Terrace apartment the Shaws maintained in London was well situated, overlooking the Thames and located just off the Strand, within a few minutes' walk from Piccadilly, and from the Royal Automobile Club, of which Shaw became a member during the Edwardian years. After the club moved to new quarters in Pall Mall in 1911, when he was in town Shaw enjoyed daily swims before breakfast in a pool situated in the basement of the club's building.[8]

The move to their country residence at Ayot St Lawrence in November 1906 added a further dimension to the image of Shaw as outwardly leading the life of an Edwardian gentleman. The County of Hertfordshire to which Ayot belongs is a main focus of E. M. Forster's elegiac[9] descriptions in *Howards End* of a vanishing way of life, with rural landscapes threatened by twentieth-century progress. At Ayot the Shaws employed several servants, a cook/housekeeper, a maidservant, two gardeners, and (beginning in 1909) a chauffeur.

The Shaws continued their regular routine of taking long working holidays and tours in the summer months, with the automobile replacing the bicycle as a principal form of recreational transport. Unlike Forster and other early modern writers, Shaw took a boyish delight in the new technologies that were emerging in the twentieth century. Beginning with the Kodak box camera he had on his honeymoon in 1898–99, he graduated to more sophisticated photographic equipment in the Edwardian period, becoming a very keen and knowledgeable photographer. In 1906 Shaw—accompanied by his sister-in-law, Mary Cholmondeley, Harley Granville-Barker, and the actor and World War I airman Robert Loraine—departed from Wandsworth Gas Works in a balloon piloted by Percival Spencer and ascended to nine thousand feet before landing in the field of an angry farmer.[10] (The pilot's first name was employed in Shaw's 1909 play *Misalliance* as the surname of the aviator Joey Percival, who crashes his airplane into the greenhouse belonging to the underwear manufacturer Tarleton.)

Shaw bought his first motorcar, a magnificent double cabriolet de Dietrich, in 1908 and sent Harry Higgs, one of the gardeners, to the Royal Automobile Club for driving lessons. The Shaws were both erratic drivers themselves: Charlotte damaged the de Dietrich on the day of its delivery and Shaw later had several motoring accidents. As had happened on previous occasions and in other ways, Shaw's life was imitating his art when in 1909 Albert J. Kilsby was employed as the Shaws' full-time chauffeur, which echoed the fiction of *Man and Superman* in which the gentleman-Socialist Tanner has a chauffeur, named Henry Straker. Motoring tours in England, Scotland, Ireland, and Europe became a new part of the Shaws' lives. In 1913 Shaw bought a green Lea & Francis motorcycle, on which he was also accident-prone. He joined the Aeronautical Society of Great Britain in 1909, the year in which he began writing *Misalliance*.[11] "All my life I've wanted to fly," says Mr. Tarleton in that play, perhaps reflecting the author's feelings. Shaw took his first flight on 20 May 1916 as a joyride from a flying school at Hendon in a two-seater biplane piloted by the distinguished aviator Henri Charles Biard. As he climbed out of his seat at the end of the flight, he remarked to the pilot concerning his impression of flying upside down in a loop: "The world is like that young man."[12] During the following year he endured a very rough ride in an army tank at the front in France "with a smile of perfect happiness on his face."[13]

* * *

Early on in the Edwardian period 10 Adelphi Terrace became the port of call for an extraordinary number and variety of visitors. Newspaper and magazine journalists in search of interviews and feature stories, writers, artists, intellectuals, theater people, aspiring translators of Shaw's works, his first biographer Archibald Henderson, overseas visitors (including Mark Twain), politicians (including Winston Churchill), and diplomats were among the throng who either visited on business or were entertained at the Shaws' frequent luncheon parties.[14]

A glimpse of the interior of 10 Adelphi Terrace, and of the outlook from its windows, at the beginning of the century is provided in a feature article "Celebrities at Home . . . Mr George Bernard Shaw in Adelphi Terrace, Strand," which was published in the *World* on 18 July 1900. When a westerly wind cleared the city haze, the apartment commanded a splendid view: "The fair green hills of Kent and Surrey, the latter jewelled with the sunlit Crystal Palace, demarcate the horizon; and the flowing Thames, flanked east and west by St Paul's and the Houses of Parliament, agreeably fill the middle distance; while at your feet the fresh verdure of the Embankment Gardens vividly contrast with the grey antiquity of Cleopatra's needle." Shaw insisted that he was never greatly concerned about where he resided: "Any place that will hold a bed and writing table is as characteristic of me as any other. . . . I have no more home instinct than a milk-can at a railway station." It was not surprising, the article continued, that Shaw was content in his Adelphi Terrace surroundings. In the drawing room:

> Delicate landscapes by the Italian pastellist, Sartorio, decorate the sage-green walls which the white furniture charmingly relieves; and one *chef d'oeuvre* has been deftly inserted in the setting over the overmantel. This is the camping ground of a crowd of knickknacks—carved ivories, bronzes and curios mostly collected by Mrs Shaw during a tour in India [in 1892]; indeed, the spoils of the east are as much a feature of this artistic room as the great bookcase which monopolises one side of it, and which is the repository of such heterogeneous strains of thought as are indicated by mention of the names of Ruskin, Nietzsche, Balzac, Sidney Webb, Stanley Jevons, William Morris—a miscellany of literary labour which is well reflected on the facets of your host's mind as dramatist,

novelist, journalist, economist, critic and political pamphleteer. He is, however, impatient of books, and declares that the only author from whom a dramatist can learn anything is Bunyan, for whom he has an unbounded and somewhat unexpected admiration.[15]

A Bechstein piano was among the other items of furniture in the room. As Mrs. Shaw explained, on this instrument Shaw—with "a remarkable power of making extraordinary noises with his throat"—performed multiple roles as pianist, symphony orchestra, and male and female operatic stars. The chef-d'oeuvre above the mantelpiece was the Sartorio pastel drawing of Charlotte, which she had unsuccessfully offered to Axel Munthe as a present during their one-sided love affair in the 1890s. The style of the lively, unsigned piece about 10 Adelphi Terrace, reminiscent of his famous stage directions, suggests extensive Shavian involvement in its creation.

* * *

An early visitor to Adelphi Terrace during this period was the young Austrian novelist, playwright, and journalist Siegfried Trebitsch. He called on Shaw in November 1901, carrying a letter of introduction from William Archer, who had told him about Shaw and his work the previous spring. Trebitsch had done his homework before this interview and came armed with a very good knowledge of Shaw's work. He told the latter that he was "determined to translate his plays into German," that he had set himself "the aim of conquering the German stage for him." Trebitsch described Shaw's appearance at the time of their first meeting as that of "an amiably mirthful giant."[16] The meeting turned out to be the beginning of a lifelong, mutually advantageous friendship, the course of which is recorded in a very extensive correspondence that often sheds light on Shaw's works and opinions, as well as on domestic matters. Charlotte was fond of Trebitsch, whose wife, Tina, was also drawn into the circle of friendship.

Aided by some diplomatic intervention by Charlotte, who seems to have quickly summed up Trebitsch's qualities and potential, the "mirthful giant" granted the young Viennese Jew sole rights to the German translation of his works and to the agency of German and Austrian productions of the plays. As Shaw's German translator and trumpeter, Trebitsch had great success despite some ridicule from German Anglicists about the English of several of his early translations. It was in translations by Trebitsch that two of Shaw's outstanding works of the early twentieth century, *Androcles and the Lion* and *Pygmalion*, had their first productions in German-speaking countries, the former at the Kleines Theater, Berlin, in November 1912 and the latter at the

Hofburg Theater, Vienna, in October 1913. By the time of the outbreak of World War I, Shaw was at least as famous in Germany as he had become in England.

Another visitor to Adelphi Terrace during the Edwardian years who was to become an important new associate and close friend was the actress Lillah McCarthy. A decade before her initial visit early in 1905, Shaw had seen Lillah as a nineteen-year-old girl playing Lady Macbeth in a production at St. George's Hall in London. He had given her performance a mixed notice in the *Saturday Review*: she was too "immature" for the part, he wrote, and she evidently viewed the tragic depths of the play as "delicious excitements of the imagination" to be conveyed by "strenuous pose, and flashing eye, and indomitable bearing." Shaw nevertheless confessed that some of the acting was "very nearly thrilling." He sensed her promise and predicted that "some years of hard work would make her a valuable recruit to the London stage."[17]

The spirit if not the letter of Shaw's 1895 review had evidently lodged itself firmly in Lillah's memory. Having heard about the Stage Society production of *Man and Superman* that was to be mounted in May 1905, she wrote to Shaw, saying that she had served the years—she remembered it as *ten*—of hard work he had prescribed and asking if she might come and see him. A "summons" to Adelphi Terrace soon followed. The "gorgeously goodlooking young lady in a green dress and huge picture hat . . . with the figure and gait of a Diana" who appeared at the door was greeted by a smiling Shaw, who said: "Why, here's Ann Whitefield."[18] It took her a little time to realize that this was the name of the leading lady in *Man and Superman*, presented in the play as an attractive and forceful character and described in Shaw's stage direction preceding her entry as "*one of the vital geniuses.*"

The spirited young lady whose "instinct and courage" Shaw had admired in the immature Lady Macbeth of 1895 was found to have just the right qualities not only for the beguiling schemer Ann Whitefield in *Man and Superman* but also for other principal roles in Shavian drama of the Edwardian age, including: Jennifer Dubedat, the artist's wife, in *The Doctor's Dilemma*; the rebellious Margaret Knox in *Fanny's First Play*; and the captive Christian heroine Lavinia (written especially for her) in *Androcles and the Lion*. In some ways Lillah McCarthy was an incarnation of the Diana-like Harriet Russell in Shaw's first novel *Immaturity*. Like Harriet, Lillah was a skillful rower.

In his prefatorial "Aside" to Lillah McCarthy's 1933 autobiographical book *Myself and My Friends*, Shaw conveyed a sense of the way in which Lillah McCarthy's outlook and acting skills chimed with his own aims in the Edwardian theater. He argued that changes in theater history come about through a mysterious creative impulse in the zeitgeist, the outward signs of which, he said without false modesty, are playwrights and actors of genius. Having shattered the Victorian drama, the "tornado" of Ibsen had left a vacuum in its wake. "Everybody wanted a new drama of Ibsenian novelty and importance," Shaw wrote, "but pleasant and with plenty of laughs at the right side of the mouth."[19] Both his own moment and Lillah's had arrived during the Edwardian years. Lillah was imaginative and intelligent. She combined a declamatory acting style harking back to the grand school of Mrs. Siddons with what Shaw called "a natural impulse to murder the Victorian womanly woman," a concept he described as an "impudent sham . . . manufactured by men for men."[20] Shaw had already begun "murdering" the Victorian womanly woman in the Victorian age; now he was finishing the job in a series of striking dramatic portraits of women in the Edwardian age. Shaw thought Lillah performed some of these roles in ways that will "probably never be surpassed."[21] Shaw, Harley Granville-Barker, and Lillah McCarthy formed a powerful trio that played a major part in the revolution taking place in the English theater during the Edwardian period.

Just under a year after they had played opposite one another as Tanner and Ann Whitefield in the Stage Society production of *Man and Superman*, Harley Granville-Barker and Lillah McCarthy converted the projected marriage at the end of Shaw's comedy into a real one: they married on 6 April 1906. Harley and Lillah both became very close to the Shaws, frequently holidaying, touring, and staying at Ayot St Lawrence with them. On one of Lillah's prewar summer holidays by the sea with the Shaws, Violet Asquith (later Lady Bonham Carter)—daughter of Herbert Henry Asquith, the Liberal prime minister who served from 1908 to 1916—was also a member of the party. Lillah's account provides an Edwardian snapshot. She and Violet were sunbathing and reading while Shaw worked on a manuscript when a wave unexpectedly broke over them. "What a helter-skelter!," Lillah recalled. "I, laughing at Shaw grabbing in the water for his manuscript, and Violet Asquith grabbing for her floating rug."[22]

Shaw, whose father had taught him to swim at an early age, gave Lillah lessons. In the course of these she discovered another, more tranquil side of the man than the one he presented to people on land. He underwent what she describes as "a sea change." Recalling the lessons in the pre–World War I period, she wrote:

> Shaw is a very strong swimmer. I am not. Many times he would give me lessons. When he is teaching some exercises or art, away from the theatre, he is both patient and kind. He would tell me to put one hand upon his shoulder and just swim, on and on. We would find ourselves well out

> to sea. Then a change would come over Shaw, a sea change. He is vigorous on land but when he is swimming in the sea, he becomes for once tranquil. He would say to me as we swam: "We are in another world." If I were afraid when I saw the land skipping farther and farther away, he would say: "Have no fear, Lillah, gently and slowly does it."[23]

Mixed bathing was frowned upon in Edwardian society and not permitted in many places. That fact, combined with Shaw's seemingly asexual marriage and his avowed appreciation of Lillah's physical attractiveness, leads one to conjecture that there may well have been an element of eroticism in these swimming lessons. Lillah's account of them also provides an interesting insight into Shaw's less public persona.

A reminder of the close interest Shaw took in every aspect of the production of his plays is supplied by Lillah's recollection of his instructions about her costume as Jennifer in *The Doctor's Dilemma* for the scene in which she appears after the death of her husband, Louis Dubedat. As was previously noted, Shaw hated the trappings of Victorian mourning, thinking that the death of a loved one should be an occasion of celebration rather than one of darkness and gloom. As Lillah recorded the scene, when Dubedat dies his wife leaves the room while the doctors bend over him. "She returns, not in black and sombre clothes, but in a lovely flaming gown, and a jewelled head-dress. London is shocked."[24]

Shaw was very conscious of the significant difference in age between himself and his young friend and collaborator Harley Granville-Barker; at the beginning of the Edwardian era, when their association began, Shaw was in his mid forties, while Granville-Barker was only in his early twenties. In a letter to Charles Charrington written about a year after his first encounter with Granville-Barker, Shaw made a joking reference to Lewis Carroll's poem: "We are old Father William. Barker regards me as a vulgar old buffer, devilish clever, and with a sympathetic wife."[25] Despite the age difference, the "vulgar old buffer" and the stylish young actor, director, and playwright got on extraordinarily well. Given their sharp minds, interest in Shakespeare, and in all aspects of the theater, Shaw and Granville-Barker had much in common, enjoying a friendship that was relaxed and—like Shaw's interest in new inventions—almost boyish in nature.

The latter quality was observed by Shaw's cousin and secretary Judy Gillmore when she was a member of a motoring tour of England in April and May 1912, which included Shaw, his chauffeur Albert Kilsby, and Granville-Barker, who joined them at York. Years later Judy (who was then Mrs. Judy Musters) recalled that she had "sat in the back, with Barker riding alongside Shaw, who was driving. All through the journey the two men chatted and joked and giggled like schoolboys. Then Shaw suddenly threw a Shakespeare quotation at Barker, who threw one back, and they kept shouting quotations rhetorically back and forth, laughing uproariously all the while."[26]

During this journey Shaw wrote letters to Charlotte. Although he was mostly in good spirits, he complained bitterly of lumbago, the pain of which he described as "beyond expression," and migraine. At one point in the journey, with Shaw and Kilsby both involved in reversing the direction of the car after taking a wrong fork in the road, it accidentally slipped over an embankment in the Lake District and, as Shaw told Charlotte, "slid down gracefully like the elephant on the chute at the Hippodrome—backwards without the slightest shock, except one of surprise to Kilsby."[27]

Much to the distress of Charlotte, for whom Granville-Barker became almost like a son, his marriage with Lillah broke up in 1915 when he fell in love with an American, Helen Huntington, wife of millionaire Archer M. Huntington. Shaw was a very gentle and helpful counselor to Lillah at this time.[28] Granville-Barker married Helen in 1918, and four years later Lillah married Professor (later Sir) Frederick Keeble, a botanist and fellow of Magdalen College, Oxford. In what was to be his final letter to William Archer, Shaw asked his old friend: "Do you ever see anything of Harley now; or has he dropped you as he has dropped me? " In the same letter he continued: "I take it that under Helen's influence he [Granville-Barker] has relapsed into his natural Henry Jamesism, and found that Henry Jamesism, which was always nine tenths naïve American worship of English high life, is a hopeless no-thoroughfare."[29]

Another man of the theater whose success during the Edwardian period was closely bound up with Shaw's was Robert Loraine, who first met Shaw in the summer of 1905 at a matinee performance of *Man and Superman* at the Royal Court Theatre, following this meeting up with a visit to Ayot St Lawrence. Playing the role of Tanner himself, he produced *Man and Superman* in New York in the autumn of 1905 and successfully toured America with the production. He subsequently played several other Shavian roles, became a close friend of Shaw, and named him as his next of kin when he joined the Royal Flying Corps in 1914. When Loraine was seriously wounded on 22 November 1914, Shaw was the first person to be officially informed.[30]

Loraine left accounts in his diary of meetings and adventures with Shaw, including the balloon ride in July 1906. On 12 August the following year they had a more serious adventure when a swim they took together in rough Welsh seas nearly became a double drowning. The two had been swept out to sea by a current and had become exhausted after diving through countless large waves. Adopting his usual style in relating such incidents, Shaw provided a vivid and elaborate account of the episode in a letter to H. G. Wells dated 14 August 1907: "For five hours (probably minutes) I swam without the slightest hope of escape, solely to put off the disagreeableness of drowning as long as possible." As he thought of his "obsolete will" and Charlotte's plight in having to deal with his complicated business affairs, he saw Loraine "swirling like a tub in the suds, not gaining an inch." After they had finally scrambled to shore, both men, like heroes of a *Boys' Own* adventure story, pretended to be calm: "A bit of a shave that," Shaw remarked casually to Loraine, to which the other replied "Yes." "We kept up appearances to the last."[31] During a visit to the French front in 1917, Shaw made a special effort to see Loraine at Treizennes, where he was stationed as an airman. Loraine's personality and war experiences inspired certain aspects of Shaw's characterization of Aubrey Bagot, the ex–flying ace-turned-clergyman/burglar, in his 1931–32 play *Too True to Be Good.*

A love of adventure and risk-taking characterized many of Shaw's recreational activities, such as swimming, cycling, motoring, motorcycling, and occasional flying in airplanes. Perhaps this is reflected in the characterization of the fiery Captain Shotover in *Heartbreak House*—who likes to court danger so that he can, as he puts it, "feel the life in me more intensely"—and in the reaction of the characters at the end of the play, who hope that the bombers who carry out a terrifying aerial raid will "come again" the following night. "The ice of life is slippery" forms part of the motto Shaw invented for the Cambridge Fabian Society in *Fanny's First Play*. "You cant live without running risks" declares the daring Polish acrobat Lina Szczepanowska in *Misalliance.*

* * *

In one of her recollections of talks with Shaw, Lillah McCarthy mentions that the conversation turned to "the vagaries"[32] of a new member of the Fabian Society, namely, H. G. Wells. As a student Wells attended William Morris's Sunday-evening meetings at Hammersmith, where Shaw often spoke, but did not meet Shaw personally until 5 January 1895 at the premiere of Henry James's *Guy Domville* at the St. James's Theatre. They subsequently met only intermittently until 1903, when Wells joined the Fabian Society. In February 1906 Wells delivered a lecture entitled "Faults of the Fabian" to a closed meeting, in which he represented the organization as feeble, inadequate, and "arrested" in its attempts to enact its stated objectives. The executive appointed a committee chaired by Wells to consider ways of extending the Fabian Society's influence, financial viability, and social effectiveness. However, when Shaw perceived that Wells's agenda could likely result in the (destabilizing) removal from power of the "Old Gang," the battle lines were drawn. Wells conducted himself badly in the whole affair, and at a meeting held on 7 November to consider his committee's report, he moved an amendment that virtually demanded that the executive resign and deliver up the Fabian Society to him.[33]

Showing his usual disarming courtesy in debate, Shaw demolished Wells at a meeting held on 14 December 1906, an eyewitness report of which has been left by Samuel George Hobson, Fabian author and promoter of Guild Socialism:

> At the final meeting Shaw blew up the wearisome business with a characteristic joke. "Ladies and gentlemen," he said, "Mr Wells in his speech complained of the long delay by the 'Old Gang' in replying to his report. But we took no longer than he. During his Committee's deliberations he produced a book on America. And a very good book too. But whilst I was drafting our reply I produced a play."[34] Here he paused, his eyes vacantly glancing round the ceiling. It really seemed that he had lost his train of thought. When we were all thoroughly uncomfortable, he resumed: "Ladies and gentleman: I paused there to enable Mr Wells to say: 'And a very good play too!'"[35]

At this point, according to Hobson's account, the meeting dissolved into laughter, with Wells smiling sheepishly and self-consciously on the platform before withdrawing his amendment. Wells ultimately resigned from the Fabian Society in 1908. Looking back on the affair, he later wrote: "No part of my career rankles so acutely in my memory with the conviction of bad judgement, gusty impulse and real inexcusable vanity, as that storm in the Fabian teacup."[36]

The friendship between Wells and Shaw endured, this despite the fact that in 1909 they had another serious confrontation over Wells's scandalous affairs with two young Fabians, Rosamund Bland, secretary of a section called the Fabian Nursery, which was created for the education of young Fabians, and Amber Reeves.

Like Rosamund Bland—illegitimate daughter of Fabian treasurer Hubert Bland, and wife of Clifford Sharp, the first editor of the *New Statesman*—Amber Reeves had very close connections with the Fabian circle. Her father was the director of the London School of Economics and her mother was a member of the executive of the Fabian Society. Amber herself was treasurer of the Cambridge University Fabian Society (for which Shaw invented his amusing motto) and belonged to the younger generation of Fabians who, led by Wells, were beginning to influence the direction of the Society during the Edwardian period. Her affair with Wells, conducted during his marriage to

Jane Wells, resulted in a pregnancy. Shaw was drawn into the scandal by a "torrent of abuse" from Wells, as he explained in a letter to Beatrice Webb dated 30 September 1909.[37] The "torrent of abuse" was presumably along the lines of an angry letter Wells had previously directed to Shaw in relation to the Bland affair, in which he described the advanced Edwardian playwright as "an unmitigated middle-Victorian ass" who had intruded his "maiden judgement" into something he didn't understand.[38]

Amber extricated herself from the scandal by marrying a young barrister named George R. Blanco White in July 1909. The child was born in December. According to Shaw, Amber boasted about her conquest of Wells, who "held out against his determined assailant for a whole year."[39] After Amber Reeves's marriage, Wells changed his mind about Shaw's interventions, which had, in fact, been skillfully diplomatic and not in the least prudish. He wrote to Shaw in August 1909 "in a gust of violent friendliness": "Occasionally you don't simply rise to a difficult situation but soar above it and I withdraw anything you would like withdrawn from our correspondence of the last two years or so."[40] The Reeves affair is recalled in the themes and narrative of Wells's novel *Ann Veronica*, which was published in October 1909, and is also reflected in Shaw's *Misalliance*, the writing of which was completed the following month.

* * *

Five years before the publication of *Howards End* (1910) Shaw had written *Major Barbara*, a play that explores some of the central conflicts presented in Forster's novel, which centers on the lives of two English families, the Schlegels and the Wilcoxes. Forster makes the Schlegels—whose name recalls that of August Wilhelm von Schlegel, the German Romantic and translator of the plays of Shakespeare—representatives of a class of civilized, middle-class English people who are devoted to literature and the arts and believe in the supreme importance of personal relations, the latter being described as "the important thing for ever and ever" by one of the Schlegel sisters. The male Wilcoxes are philistines who belong to the materialistic "real" world of high finance, "telegrams and anger," and practicality.

Late in *Howards End* there is a passing reference to Shaw by Henry Wilcox, the father of the family. In an interesting anticipation of mid twentieth-century adverse criticism of the playwright from the direction of Forster's alma mater, Cambridge University, he claims: "I am not one of your Bernard Shaws who consider nothing sacred."[41] Wilcox's assumption about Shaw—who, as we have seen, had a strong religious sense and a reverence for life and its recurring miracles of change and growth—can, of course, be challenged. The remark given to Wilcox provides the only occasion on which Shaw is mentioned in *Howards End*. However, the influence of Shavian ideas can be felt earlier in Forster's novel, especially in the recognition that the social superstructure within which the Schlegel life of art and culture can flourish has as its essential underpinning the solid wealth created by people such as Henry Wilcox himself. Henry Wilcox's opinion that "one sound man of business did more good to the world than a dozen of your social reformers" seems to be echoing the philosophy of Andrew Undershaft, the business tycoon and munitions manufacturer in Shaw's play.

The Schlegel-like idealists and believers in culture and civilized values in *Major Barbara* include the title character herself and her fiancé, Adolphus Cusins, a professor of Greek. Their philosophies of life are challenged by Undershaft, who employs Wilcox-like arguments about wealth as the creator of moral values and social well-being. When Cusins asks Undershaft if there is any place in his religion of "money and gunpowder" for "honor, justice, truth, love, mercy and so forth," he receives the reply: "Yes: they are the graces and luxuries of a rich, strong and safe life."

* * *

During the writing of *Major Barbara* in 1905, Shaw was justifiably excited about the creation of his new character, Andrew Undershaft, who, he sensed, was becoming "more and more formidable" as the play developed.[42] The role was to be created by Louis Calvert, the actor who had recently successfully played the John Bullish Englishman in *John Bull's Other Island*. Writing to Calvert from Charlotte's estate in Rosscarbery, where the Shaws were staying at the time, he began by asking the actor if he could play the trombone, a brass instrument that Undershaft surprisingly reveals himself to be both fond of and capable of playing with reasonable skill early in the play.* With a playful misspelling, Shaw told Calvert that the dramatic effect of this trombone-playing plutocrat was going to be "TREMENJOUS." Shaw's description of the character in this letter shows that he thought of Undershaft as a combination of the all-conquering John Bullish Englishman and the visionary defrocked priest in his previous play, together with his own childhood hero, Mephistopheles. Undershaft was turning out to be "Broadbent and Keegan rolled into one, with Mephistopheles thrown in." Taking up music would be a good thing, Shaw counseled Calvert, since it would help him give up "those con-

*Shaw's choice of this musical instrument for Undershaft is an amusing recollection of his Irish childhood. A fondness for brass instruments such as the trombone ran in the Shaw family (see chap. 1). Shaw himself took up the cornet briefly in 1873 while still a teenager in Dublin; see CL2:542.

founded cigars" and save his voice. As Calvert and later actors must surely have discovered, a good voice was essential for playing the prodigiously eloquent and witty persona Shaw had created in his new play.

Under the direction of Granville-Barker (who played Adolphus Cusins) and Shaw, and with Annie Russell in the title role and Calvert as Undershaft, *Major Barbara* opened at the Court Theatre on Tuesday, 28 November 1905. According to Alfred Sutro, playwright and translator of Maeterlinck, "all the intelligentsia of London were there."[43] Beatrice Webb attended the first night in the company of retiring prime minister Arthur J. Balfour. She had recently recorded in her diary that "all the smart world is tumbling over one another in the worship of GBS," and that "his egotism and vanity are not declining; he is increasing his deftness of wit and phrase, but becoming every day more completely iconoclastic, the ideal derider."[44] The audience also included a group of uniformed members of the Salvation Army, many of whom were attending a theater for the first time in their lives. Sutro reported that the first two acts were received with "rapturous enthusiasm," but that the final act did not go down well. A major problem, for which Shaw castigated him severely the next day, was that Calvert kept fluffing his lines. Shaw vowed that he had taken a box at the theater for the Friday performance with "a hundredweight of cabbages, dead cats, eggs and gingerbeer bottles stacked in it" to fling at Calvert if he repeated his offenses.[45]

Major Barbara has remained a deservedly popular and frequently performed play. It is a robust, challenging work that memorably defines the dilemmas perennially confronting reforming idealists when they come to grips with the realities of power in society. Like Saint Joan, her successor in Shaw's work, Major Barbara has achieved iconic status as an image of a courageous individual woman pitting her will and faith against the hostile forces of society. Equally impressive and enduring as a dramatic image is Shaw's portrait of the munitions manufacturer Andrew Undershaft. Few other writers have so impressively represented onstage the type of the unrepentantly successful, engaging, yet ruthless modern business tycoon. Shaw aptly summed up the character of Undershaft when he described him to Calvert as "diabolically subtle, gentle, self-possessed, powerful, stupendous, as well as amusing and interesting."[46]

The action of the play embodies an imaginatively conceived allegory about different forms of power, bringing into dynamic confrontation the brute force of "money and gunpowder," the spiritual energies of religious idealism, and the civilizing agencies of humanistic culture and philosophy. The intellectual debate in the work is firmly anchored in a human drama involving family loyalties and division, a love affair put to the test in the crucible of ideological conflict, and an intricate pattern of coercive power play that appears in many guises throughout the action, including a subtly connected subplot about the pugnacious Bill Walker. The whole work is enlivened by searching humor, comic inventiveness, and complex, richly ambiguous characterization.

In some ways the play revisits the old Shavian clash between Bunyanesque religious idealism and Mephistophelean skepticism and mockery: "Mephistopheles" is one of several nicknames applied to Undershaft in the play. Apart from Shaw's lifelong preoccupation with these two contrasting figures first encountered in his childhood, other influences that lie behind the shaping of *Major Barbara* include Blake's *Marriage of Heaven and Hell* and Nietzsche's *Beyond Good and Evil.* Both these works subverted simplistic categorizations of good and evil, such as those endorsed by Lady Britomart and her son, Stephen, in Shaw's play. Blake recognized that the divine forces of creativity in the universe included the "fearful symmetry" of the tiger as well as the gentleness of the lamb; he also felt that Milton's magnificent rebel Satan was the real hero of *Paradise Lost.* Blake's radical subversion of conventional ideas about good and evil were echoed in the writings of Nietzsche. Decrying the Christian virtues of humility and self-abasement, Nietzsche exalted the splendid Dionysian energies of joy and passion. Like Blake, he attacked simplistic dichotomizing of good and evil. Although Shaw disavowed the influence of Nietzsche in the preface to *Major Barbara,* Nietzschean ideas are certainly paralleled in the play.

Shortly before he wrote *Major Barbara,* Shaw read, and was deeply impressed by the translation of Euripides' play *The Bacchae* by his friend the Australian-born professor of Greek, Gilbert Murray. The *Bacchae* dramatizes the conflict in ancient Thebes between the forces of authority and order, represented by King Pentheus, and the god-man Dionysus, leader of a disruptive religious mystery cult.[47] The maenads, female followers of Dionysus, engaged in wildly joyous and ecstatic rituals in the forests outside the city, dancing to the accompaniment of cymbals and tambourines and often becoming demented and tearing apart the limbs of animals. Displaying a brilliant leap of imagination, Shaw perceived a link between these Dionysian rituals and the way in which the women of the Salvation Army were transported out of themselves in their joyous singing, music making, and tambourine shaking. He used this insight as a way of suggesting mysterious links between the "religion" of "Dionysos Undershaft," as the insightful Cusins calls him, and the Salvationists.

Shaw's play moves toward a synthesis of the opposing forces presented in the first two acts. By finally assenting to the belief that "life is all one," and that "the way of life lies through the factory of death," Barbara and Cusins imaginatively create a Shavian marriage of heaven and hell. In recognizing that, despite its virtues, Undershaft's model village of Perivale St. Andrews does not answer all the needs of the human spirit, Barbara rediscovers her faith and sense of purpose. There is work to be done among the well-fed, snobbish creatures in her father's materialistic dream town. Yet even as Shaw was writing his play, Undershaft's counterparts in real life were busily manufacturing the weapons that within the space of a few years were to be deployed in one of the worst wars in human history. By 1905 the German and English arms race that preceded that war was well under way. The prospect held out in *Major Barbara* of a union of intelligence, spiritual enlightenment, and power—a type of Schlegel-Wilcox marriage—was shattered in 1914. Shaw's wartime work *Heartbreak House* grimly reflects that fact.

Calvert's fluffing of Undershaft's lines was not the only thing that worried some contemporaries about the last act of *Major Barbara*. The setting of the scene in Undershaft's munitions factory—with a huge cannon center stage—and its associated model village makes a powerful visual and metaphorical statement. The well-appointed library in Lady Britomart's Wilton Crescent home and the scenes of abject poverty in the Salvation Army Center are suddenly placed in the context of (and dwarfed by) the image of immense power, fueled by "money and gunpowder," which is represented by Undershaft's kingdom of Perivale St. Andrews. "Ask anyone in Europe" is Undershaft's reply when asked about his address. The 1905 play conveys an uncanny sense of the forces that were already threatening the tranquillity of Edwardian summers and made local political issues and power systems appear trivial by comparison. "I am the government of your country," says Undershaft to his conservative son, Stephen, who clings to the notion of a completely stable national and world order, providentially overseen by Westminster and democratically minded, decent Englishmen.

The creation of Undershaft represents a new and, in some ways, disturbing element in Shaw's worldview. To borrow a metaphor from munitions making, the character was something of a loose cannon in Shaw's politico-philosophical universe. It was not that Shaw was not previously fully conscious—as a result of his own thinking and the influence of Blake, Ibsen, Wagner and, more recently, Nietzsche and Gilbert Murray—of the kind of Dionysian energies in the universe that Undershaft clearly and quite explicitly represents in *Major Barbara*. Yet how could this monstrously successful, amoral capitalist be reconciled with Socialism?

The question troubled Shaw's friends. After seeing the play, Beatrice Webb commented in her diary that "GBS is gambling with ideas and emotions in a way that distresses slow-minded prigs like Sidney and I."[48] She spoke frankly to Shaw about "the triumph of the unmoral purpose" that she saw as the final import of the work.[49] During the writing of the play, Gilbert Murray also expressed concern about the ending and the danger it presented of suggesting "a simple defeat of the Barbara principles by the Undershaft principles."[50] Murray sent some passages of dialogue to Shaw in order to illustrate his view that Cusins and Barbara should emerge more strongly in the denouement of the work. Shaw's adoption of several of Murray's hints did not entirely bring the cannon under control, but it did allow a more critical view of Undershaft to emerge. The ending of the play also reasserts the power of Shaw's Lady Britomart, a Lady Bracknell-like character and one of his most successful comic creations, who dominates some of the earlier scenes thanks to a combination of epigram, imperious dogmatism, and common sense, and whose authority is reasserted in the final scene.

* * *

Before the death of King Edward VII in May 1910, Shaw had followed *Major Barbara* with three more full-length plays—*The Doctor's Dilemma* (1906), *Getting Married* (1908), and *Misalliance* (1909)—in addition to the one-acter *The Shewing-up of Blanco Posnet*, which, after being banned in London by the censor, was at the center of the Abbey Theatre battle with Dublin Castle in 1909.

Shortly after the beginning of *The Doctor's Dilemma* a procession of his friends and associates arrive at the rooms of the distinguished medical scientist Sir Colenso Ridgeon to congratulate him on his newly awarded knighthood. The character and professional interests of Ridgeon were based on that of a man described by Charlotte as "a great friend"[51] of the Shaws, namely, Sir Almroth Wright, who was knighted in 1906, the year in which the play was written. An Irishman and graduate of Trinity College, Dublin, Wright rose to eminence as a medical researcher and practitioner in the fields of bacteriology and immunology. At the time of the writing of *The Doctor's Dilemma* he was principal of the Institute of Pathology and Research at St. Mary's Hospital, Praed Street, London. The title of a fairly recent biographical study of Wright refers to him as "The Plato of Praed Street."[52]

The system of antityphoid inoculation that Wright developed is estimated to have saved thousands of lives thanks to its use on troops in World War I. His method of measuring opsonins (protective substances in human blood) forms the basis of the great discovery made by Ridgeon in *The Doctor's Dilemma*. During his officially sponsored visit to the French front in 1917, Shaw drove to Boulogne (in a car lent him by Robert Loraine), where he stayed briefly as a guest of Wright, who had established a large hospital there.[53]

Shaw's friendship with Wright continued into the 1940s, surviving a fierce clash in 1912 over the question of woman suffrage.[54] Even by the standards of the day, Wright was an extraordinarily bigoted male chauvinist. A fierce opponent of the women's suffrage movement, he was the author of a book called *The Unexpurgated Case Against Woman Suffrage* (1913).

The Doctor's Dilemma is subtitled *A Tragedy*. In fact, the play is for the most part a wildly funny satirical attack on the medical profession, a symphony of laughter about medical hobbyhorses, cant, and humbug, the unscrupulous promotion of faddish and dubiously useful—but, for the doctors money-generating—operations and nostrums (for which read, in the late twentieth and twenty-first centuries, liposuction and other forms of cosmetic surgery, not to mention multitudinous cures and prophylactics promoted by "health" and drug companies). However, behind the provocative subtitle lies the story of an argument Shaw had with William Archer in 1906 about Ibsen and the handling of death in his plays.

Shaw's obituary on the occasion of Ibsen's own death on 23 May 1906 opens with the sentence: "The greatest dramatic genius of the nineteenth century is dead."[55] Among the many interesting things Shaw said about the Norwegian playwright and his followers, he dared to include some critical remarks about the master occasionally resorting to "Scribish artificiality" (as in the Scribe-like melodramatic plotting of *A Doll's House*) and made some well-judged comments about Ibsen's frequent exploitation of death as a dramatic motif in the plays—his *morbidezza*, as he called it. William Archer took the bait and solemnly attacked Shaw in the *Tribune*, of which he was a chief columnist, as a dramatist "fatally at the mercy of his impish sense of humour" and shrinking from "that affirmation and confirmation of destiny which only death can bring."[56] Shaw replied in the form of a press release to the same newspaper, which he entitled "Mr G. B. Shaw's Next Play: Mr Archer's Challenge and Its Sequel": "Stung by this reproach from his old friend, Mr Shaw is writing a play all about Death, which he declares will be the most amusing play ever written."[57]

Both the retort to Archer and the play to which he was referring (*The Doctor's Dilemma*) can be seen as statements of the Shavian credo concerning comedy. What Archer perceived as a fatal flaw in his friend, namely, his impish humor, was in fact the essence of his genius, the Shavian form of seriousness. Shaw regarded humor as an instrument of truth and prophecy. "When a thing is funny, search it for a hidden truth," says the He-Ancient in *Back to Methuselah*. "Every jest is an earnest in the womb of Time," says Keegan in *John Bull's Other Island*. For Shaw the sacred resides not in the solemnities of death but in the holy gift (the "splendid torch") of life; it is the latter that comedy as a form fundamentally affirms. Shaw's aim as a comic dramatist can be partly defined as a form of redefinition of the sacred, an emphasis on the rituals associated with a celebration of life rather on those associated with the accommodation of death and loss in the human imagination. *The Doctor's Dilemma* deliberately confronts tragedy with the spirit of comedy. The play also illustrates the idea of comedy as a dramatic form in which the world is turned upside down by a carnivalesque dethroning of figures of authority and order in the social hierarchy, such as doctors, judges, professors, and so forth.[58]

Within an overall framework of satirical comedy, *The Doctor's Dilemma* is a generic hybrid. It turns the "tragic" material of the artist's death scene into anticlimactic, parodic farce. At times—as when the chorus of doctors descant on the virtues of their various medical hobbyhorses—it seems a mixture of comic opera and Aristophanic satire. The plot surrounding the "dilemma" of the title takes the form of a murder mystery. Ridgeon has limited resources at his hospital and has to decide between saving a dull but worthy old medical friend and a brilliant but morally unscrupulous young artist. Although his choice appears to be based on moral grounds, his motives in electing to save the worthy old friend instead of the artist are mixed in that (as is ultimately revealed in an epilogue) he is actually in love with the artist's wife. At the end of the play Ridgeon is devastated to find that Jennifer Dubedat has remarried. In the play's revelation of the illustrious Sir Colenso Ridgeon's susceptibility to female charm and his hypocrisy, Shaw may well have been taking a sly dig at Sir Almroth Wright, who, despite his views regarding the opposite sex, was quite the ladies' man and was popular with the nurses at St. Mary's Hospital.

In the fourth act of *The Doctor's Dilemma* Shaw employs an image and a Shakespearean allusion that are both linked to a memorable statement he made not long after writing the play concerning his idea of life and its purpose. As Dubedat lies dying, Jennifer recalls an occasion when the couple lit a fire in her home in Cornwall and were delighted to see in the window a reflection of the flames, which seemed to be dancing in a bush in the garden. The image appeared as a miraculous burning bush unconsumed by the flames. Dubedat wants to be like the flame both literally and metaphorically. He wants to be cremated, to become the flame, yet he also wants to live as the flame in Jennifer's imagination. Shaw brilliantly manages the transition from this level of solemnity to its final descent into bathos by presenting a pastiche of mangled quotations from Shakespeare's tragedies and *The Tempest*, all of which are delivered by Sir Ralph Bloomfield Bonington, the prototypical medical humbug—and probable immediate cause of Dubedat's death—a character Shaw manages to make at once absurd and engaging.

“Out, out, brief candle,” Bonington intones to round off his medley of Shakespearean epitaphs for the dying artist. In a lecture delivered in Brighton in March 1907, shortly after the completion and first performances of *The Doctor's Dilemma*, Shaw alluded to this precise quotation from *Macbeth* in a memorable statement about his own outlook on life, one that also recalls the image of the burning bush in his play: “I rejoice in life for its own sake. Life is no ‘brief candle’ to me. It is a sort of splendid torch which I have got hold of for the moment; and I want to make it burn as brightly as possible before handing it on to future generations.”[59]

By turning his “tragedy” into a comedy, in *The Doctor's Dilemma* Shaw was creating what might be described as a performance of his life's philosophy, enacting, as it were, a subversion and rejection of the tragic vision and an affirmation of the “splendid torch” of life.

* * *

The final two Shavian plays of the Edwardian period, *Getting Married* (1908) and *Misalliance* (1909), touched on more intimate areas of Shaw's experience, in which the restlessness over his married state—which would finally erupt in 1912 in the full-blown affair with Stella Campbell—was already becoming apparent. In the opening scene of *Getting Married*, the sagacious and philosophically inclined greengrocer Mr. Collins offers some remarks on the married state that may well be an oblique reflection of some of his creator's own thoughts about his (by now) decade-long marriage to Charlotte. In the course of his remarks, Collins echoes thoughts about marriage and its restrictive effect on other relationships that also occurred to Shaw and to the poet who strongly influenced him in his younger days, Percy Bysshe Shelley.

In Shelley's poem *Episychidion* the poet-speaker refers to marriage in disparaging terms as “the dreariest and the longest journey,”[60] declaring that he is not of “that great sect / Whose doctrine is, that each one should select / Out of the crowd a mistress or a friend, / And all the rest, though fair and wise, commend / To cold oblivion.” In his confidential discourse to Mrs. Bridgenorth, the bishop's wife, concerning marriage, which occurs near the beginning of *Getting Married*, Collins talks about how he has had to curb his impulses to run away from his wife because he knew how deeply it would hurt her to think he didn't care about her. He has, as it were, been broken into marriage and has abandoned the idea of escape. Nevertheless, in a colloquial echo of Shelley he remarks that “it cut me off from all my old friends something dreadful, maam: especially the women, maam.”[61] He then goes on to talk about “Mrs George,” the clairvoyant wife of his brother, George; she solves the problem of the constraints of marriage by simply running off from time to time with men she falls in love with. There may have been some authorial wishful thinking in Collins's stories. In all likelihood he was acting as a spokesman for his author concerning the ways in which marriage placed constraints on relations with others.

* * *

The first clear sign of restlessness on Shaw's part in his marriage during the Edwardian years dates from the proverbial seventh year following the marriage. Ironically—and with some degree of hypocrisy—while engaged in castigating Wells about his affairs Shaw himself had been involved in a dangerous flirtation with Erica May Cotterill, a young devotee of himself and Socialism. A letter from Shaw to her dated 13 October 1909 indicates that she was aware of the Wells–Amber Reeves affair and wanted to write to Wells about it, an impulse Shaw discouraged.[62] In September 1905, after seeing one of his plays, the intelligent, attractive, and impetuous twenty-four-year-old Erica became infatuated with Shaw. Signing herself seductively as "Miss Charmer," she began a correspondence with him by sending along some of her writings for comment. Shaw was obviously flattered by the advances and adulation of this interesting young woman and clearly encouraged an association that eventually seriously threatened his marriage. The charms of "Emerica" (the nickname Shaw employed in his letters to her) were not lost on the fifty-year-old playwright.

Erica Cotterill was a cousin of the poet Rupert Brooke and daughter of an undistinguished Fabian schoolmaster named Charles Clement Cotterill—author of a book called *Human Justice for Those at the Bottom* (1907)—with whom she was locked in a state of fierce rebellion. She herself had considerable literary talent. She wrote an engaging comedy entitled *A Professional Socialist* (1908) and published a series of epistolary confessions, most of which were addressed to Shaw. Her autobiographical works—*An Account* (1916), which is dedicated to Shaw, and *Form of Diary* (1939)—reveal her creative intelligence and sensitivity as well as her self-absorption. Shaw knew Erica had real literary talent. He had read an unfinished draft of *A Professional Socialist* in 1907 and made suggestions about how to end it. In 1910 he told her: "You will either die a lunatic before you are 33 or be the greatest English woman writer—indeed one of the greatest of English writers."[63] Although she did not fulfill either of these prophecies, she was unusually gifted.

On 24 October 1906 Shaw wrote to Erica: "You are certainly a clever young devil; and I suppose I shall have to treat you as a friend."[64] Partly encouraged by Shaw, Erica wanted a great deal more than friendship. It was as though a vibrant young Hilde Wangel had stepped out of the pages of Ibsen's play *The*

Master Builder and had arrived at the Shaw household, demanding not only a great deal of attention from the master builder of English plays and master exponent of Fabian Socialism but also love and marriage.[65]

On 12 June 1907 Shaw invited Erica to the Court Theatre to see the Charles Ricketts production of the "Don Juan in Hell" scene from *Man and Superman*. The following month he wrote to her while on a train journey to Margate, taking her to task about her carelessness in dress, which he said carried over into her writing ("You don't want to be bothered with stops and paragraphs"), yet also paying her some very handsome compliments: "You are a woman of exceptional strength, well bred, refined, and of altogether superior quality. Even your appearance is extraordinary: you are like the edge of a knife."[66] By the following year Erica had taken to making frequent visits to Adelphi Terrace and (by motorbike) to Ayot St Lawrence at all hours of the day and night. Proferring more than friendly caresses, she behaved as though she, rather than Charlotte, were the true wife of Bernard Shaw. The boldness of Erica's physical advances toward Shaw can be deduced from one of his numerous—apparently ineffectual—lectures to her on the matter:

> In brief, if you enter my wife's house, you enter it on the understanding that you don't make love to her husband. If I introduce you to Mrs. [Granville-] Barker, I shall do so on the understanding that you don't make love to *her* husband. You may admire & dream & worship & adore until you are black in the face; but you are not to sit and hold their hands, nor kiss them, nor cuddle them, nor nestle in their manly bosoms—oh, so sweetly, so innocently, so heavenlikely [*sic*]—because if you do the Life Force will suddenly leap out and gobble you up.[67]

In a letter written in 1942, Shaw gave a further graphic glimpse of Erica's behavior: "If a man interested her she would walk into his house at any hour: mostly in the middle of the night; take possession of him as if his astonished and outraged wife did not exist; and be quite unconscious of any reason why she should not sleep with him and live in the house as long as she wanted to."[68] She had begun to behave toward Shaw in ways, he said, that he "would not stand . . . from Cleopatra herself."[69]

The bold advances of this young woman in her mid twenties toward the "elderly gentleman" (as Shaw, far from his dotage at this time, was describing himself to Erica)[70] could hardly have failed to produce some powerful fantasies in Shaw's mind. The relationship clearly seems to be reflected in the portrayal of that between Ellie Dunn and Captain Shotover in *Heartbreak House*. The idea of a marriage between an elderly man and an attractive and imaginative young woman had been firmly lodged in Shaw's mind in a very personal way in the pre–World War I years. When, in November 1907, a proposal of such a marriage was put to him by Erica in the form of a declaration of love, Shaw replied with a long, platonic letter of refusal that may be seen to adumbrate the idea of the spiritual marriage of Ellie and Shotover: "As for me, I have taken declarations of love all in the day's work, as it were. They are not all illusion: there is really a divine spark in me to which the divine spark in the woman yearns: the ultimate goal of the impulse is holy."[71]

Though it has its own logic in Ellie's development in the play, the odd moment in the third act of *Heartbreak House* when Ellie precipitously announces that she has given herself to Shotover as her "spiritual husband and second father" is partly explicable as a sanitized fictional echo of the Shaw-Cotterill relationship. The correspondence shows that, apart from being an object of adoration in a romantic and erotic way, Shaw was clearly a "second father" to Erica Cotterill. She had what Shaw described much later as "a terrible hate fixation"[72] against her real father. Several of Shaw's letters take the form of counseling concerning her oppressive family situation and her need to escape its effects. In one letter he described the "hideously unnatural situation" of adolescents and older children being locked up in a house with their middle-aged parents.[73] Parent-child relationships had always been a strong interest of Shaw's. In the Edwardian and early Georgian period of his career, this interest spilled over into the enormously long preface to his play *Misalliance*, which he entitled "Parents and Children" (1910); into *Misalliance* itself, where the father, Tarleton, speaks of "the impassable, eternal gulf" between parents and children and despairingly advises himself to read *King Lear*; into *Fanny's First Play* (1911), where the daughter, Margaret Knox, says of her emancipation from her family, "I've been set free from this silly little hole of a house and all its pretences. I know now that I am stronger than you and papa"; and, finally, into *Heartbreak House*, where it becomes entangled—in more complicated ways than in *Misalliance*—with Shakespeare's treatment of the theme in *King Lear*.

By 1909 Shaw had tired of Erica: "Miss Charmer" had turned into what he described as "a quite disgustingly ill behaved young devil, grossly abusing the privilege of my acquaintance."[74] The following year a plan was devised by Shaw and Charlotte to put a stop to any further development of intimacy and future visits by Erica. Shaw drafted a letter for Charlotte to send to Erica stating that although she did not dislike the young woman—and, in fact, found her "in some ways rather fine and sensitive"—she strongly disapproved of her presence in the house and was "determined to put a stop at once and for ever to any personal intimacy between us," that is, between the three of them. Her husband, the letter said, had allowed Erica to become "far more attracted to him" than he should, and she, Charlotte, did not intend to let Erica "drift any further into an impossible position." Interestingly, Charlotte restored a deleted sentence in her ghostwriter's letter: "I could not trust him to keep you at a distance."[75]

Thus ended the intimacy. Erica, however, was not merely a sexually challenging figure in Shaw's life, eventually becoming a serious and threatening nuisance; she also exerted an important—and critically underestimated—influence on his creative life. She provided a striking, firsthand example of a young, uninhibited rebel against the constraints of the Edwardian nuclear family and its codes of conduct, which is clearly reflected in plays of the period and beyond. The wild and sexually aggressive Hypatia Tarleton in *Misalliance* is one example of that influence. Hypatia "wants adventures to drop out of the sky," flirts tauntingly with a man twice her age, and breaks all the rules concerning the reverence due parents from their children. Lina Szczepanowska, another character in the same play, matches Hypatia's contempt for the dullness of Edwardian respectability and domesticity. Margaret Knox, in *Fanny's First Play*, follows these examples of young females in revolt. Lastly, Shaw's relationship with Erica Cotterill left its imprint on the relations of Ellie Dunn with much older men, including Mangan as well as Shotover, in *Heartbreak House*.

* * *

Shaw's last two Edwardian plays and their immediate successor, *Fanny's First Play*, questioned the two cornerstones of Victorian and Edwardian social life—marriage and the nuclear family—and their overarching principles of duty, obedience, respectability, and conformity. Contrary to some accounts, the plays are not overtly didactic or political. Rather, they present a positive maelstrom of conflicting, unresolved opinion. The most direct reference to Socialism occurs in connection with the surprising discovery of an incompetent burglar with Socialist opinions—a kind of Shavian Leonard Bast—in the portable Turkish bath of the amazingly well read and genial capitalist Mr. Tarleton. On this occasion Tarleton calms his alarmed wife with an assurance concerning the burglar's strident discourse: "All right chickabiddy: it's not bad language: it's only Socialism." With an echo of Charlotte Shaw's thoughts about Erica Cotterill, Mrs. Tarleton replies by saying that she won't have any of that in the house.

Within a general framework of witty dialogue and subtly unfolding action, punctuated by an occasional spectacular incident, these plays present potent images of revolt against the respectable world of Edwardian society. The Englishman's castle is seen not as a sanctuary of order and hallowed values but as a little hell of stifling constraint of the free expression of the human spirit—especially, although not exclusively, that of women. The Edwardian bourgeois marriage and family are seen as institutions that enslave men and prevent women from taking a full part in the social, professional, economic, and political life of the human species. Both in his private life and in his plays, the clouds in Shaw's Edwardian summer skies were quite threatening; as far as his private life was concerned, they would soon bring a storm. Nothing, however, interrupted the progress of his ebullient creativity.

Guthrie Memorial Library
Hanover's Public Library
Hanover, PA 17331-2283

17 Votes for Women

During the later Edwardian and early Georgian period in England agitation for woman suffrage had reached unprecedented levels of intensity and public attention. One of the characters in Elizabeth Robins's topical play *Votes for Women!*—first presented at the Royal Court Theatre under the direction of Harley Granville-Barker on 9 April 1907*—says that the more militant suffragettes had "waked up interest in the Woman Question so that it's advertised in every paper and discussed in every house from Land's End to John O'Groats."[1]

This was close to what was happening in the real world. Not only in London but throughout England the question of woman suffrage had become a burning political and social issue. The dialogue in the first act of *Votes for Women!* reflects the fact that there was a considerable split within the suffragette movement as a whole between the moderates, who wanted to pursue gentler strategies of reason and persuasion, and the more militant agitators, who were heckling politicians, staging mass demonstrations, chaining themselves to the railings outside public buildings, committing acts of civil disobedience, and getting themselves arrested and thrown into prison.

Living up to his self-description as being "up to the chin in the life of his own time,"[2] Shaw was very much involved in this cause. In fact, as early as 26 April 1892 he had delivered a speech in favor of woman suffrage at a stormy meeting held in St. James's Hall, London.[3] *The Quintessence of Ibsenism*, published the previous year, contained a lively attack on the Victorian conception of the womanly woman. Shaw made a very strong statement about the subject of votes for women in March 1906 in an interview with Mrs. Maud Churton Braby, the popular novelist, writer on marriage, and suffragette, with whom he occasionally corresponded. (Some of Mrs. Braby's rather unconventional

---

*Shaw was touring in France with Charlotte at the time of the first production of *Votes for Women!*

and liberal views on marriage are paralleled in Shaw's 1908 play *Getting Married.*) In the interview Shaw presented himself as being decidedly in favor of militant action, even to the point of violent revolution. Going well beyond the "sex strike" plan adopted by the women in Aristophanes' *Lysistrata*, Shaw recommended that "if I were a woman, I'd simply refuse to speak to any man or do anything for men until I'd got the vote. I'd make my husband's life a burden and everybody miserable generally. Women should have a revolution—they should shoot, kill, maim, destroy—until they are given a vote."[4]

In March 1907—the same month in which he made the speech at Brighton that included his declaration about the "splendid torch" of life—Shaw spoke in favor of woman suffrage at a meeting in Queens Hall, London, under the auspices of the National Union of Women's Suffrage Societies. This speech, verbatim reports of which appeared in periodicals on both sides of the Atlantic, was published in the *New York American* on 21 April under the title "Why All Women Are Peculiarly Fitted to Be Good Voters." His remarks in this speech, more temperate in tone than the statement of the previous year, were directed not only at the question of voting rights but also at the fact that women were ineligible to be members of Parliament.

A main plank of Shaw's argument in his Queens Hall speech was that the exclusion of women from the political process—apart from being a denial of a natural right of citizens in a free society—was a huge waste of resources in the public sphere. Women are "peculiarly fitted" to be good voters because there is a whole range of subjects of vital importance that tend to be left out of account by men but which would "spring into life, and spring into the very front of political warfare if only the influence of women began to be felt directly through the vote." Shaw went on: "Remember that there is in England . . . a very wonderful contingent of women of extraordinary ability who are at present doing first rate work on royal commissions,[5] who in all sorts of social movements have been showing what women can do when they lay their mind to it." This resource was being wasted on agitation over a question "which in any intelligent country ought to have been settled a century ago." By giving women the franchise, he argued, "England will set free an immense and beneficial flood of political and social energy which is now being taken up by this question."[6]

In a deft stroke of rhetorical strategy that must have caused laughter at the time, Shaw used as a prime example of "able public women" Mrs. Humphry Ward, a leading opponent of granting suffrage to women and one of the founders (in 1908) of the Women's National Anti-Suffrage League. Ward, an active participant in public affairs who had originated the idea of after-school play centers and vacation schools in England for the care of children, had just written a letter to the *Times* outlining what she saw as the best arguments for men to use against granting women suffrage. Shaw turned all these arguments—women's ignorance of politics, restricted interests, narrowness of outlook—on their heads by saying that Mrs. Ward must have been talking about men: "She was getting at my sex."[7]

Two other supporters of the cause of woman suffrage in Shaw's own household were his wife Charlotte and his cousin Judy Gillmore, who had become his full-time secretary in 1907. On 13 June 1908 an estimated ten to fifteen thousand women joined a spectacular and well-organized demonstration in support of the suffrage coordinated by the National Union of Women's Suffrage Societies. Led by its president, Mrs. Millicent Fawcett, and bearing banners, women from all over England, from numerous overseas countries, and from many different walks of life marched for two miles through the streets of London, from the Thames Embankment to Hyde Park, where a meeting was held in the Albert Hall. The assembly in the Hall of "women brilliant with summer dresses and the glowing accents of silk banners and university robes,"[8] together with masses of red and white flowers formed a scene described in one newspaper report as "remarkable as any that have been witnessed in that great building. From floor to topmost corner and furthest angle of the huge galleries, the interior was alive with women and bright colour."[9] Charlotte Shaw, Judy Gillmore, and Bernard Shaw were all participants in this demonstration.*

It is unlikely to have escaped Shaw's notice that the figure of Joan of Arc was frequently and prominently deployed during the pre–World War I suffragette demonstrations as a multivalent symbol of feminist rebellion against authority and the conventions of female behavior and dress. Women dressed as Joan of Arc astride white horses led processions of the militant Women's Social and Political Union.[10] We know that an idea for a play about Joan was in Shaw's mind at least as early as 1913, a decade before his *Saint Joan* was written.[11] Shaw's portrayal of Joan was to bear a strong imprint of feminist ideas, as T. S. Eliot recognized when, in an article for the *Criterion*, he complained that Shaw had turned the saint into "a great middle-class reformer, and her place is a little higher than Mrs. Pankhurst."[12]

One of Shaw's most trenchant attacks on anti-suffragist thinking occurs in an essay on *The Unexpurgated Case Against Woman Suffrage*, a book written by his friend Sir Almroth Wright and published in 1913. With a parade of "diacritical judgement," pseudoscientific discussion, and old-fashioned chivalry, the famous medical man and model for Sir Colenso Ridgeon in Shaw's

*Approximately one in ten of those present were men.

Doctor's Dilemma had attempted to elaborate a case against woman suffrage on the grounds that women are normally less capable of objective thought than men. Shaw aptly refers in this essay to Isabella's speech in the second act of Shakespeare's *Measure for Measure,* beginning "but man, proud man, / Drest in a little brief authority, / Most ignorant of what he's most assur'd." In a brilliant display of good-humored, but devastating, ridicule, Shaw brings the house of cards of Wright's arguments to the ground:

> Shakespear, speaking of himself and Sir Almroth and me and the rest of us as glassy essences and angry apes, is bitter, but within his rights, and entitled, alas! to the verdict; but what sort of figure would Shakespear have cut had he added:
>
> You must understand, gentlemen, that these remarks are confined strictly to Ann Hathaway, and that I, the Masculine Male Manly Man, am obviously purely intellectual and aniconic [not human] in appraising statements; am never over-influenced by individual instances; never arrive at conclusions on incomplete evidence; have an absolutely perfect sense of proportion; cannot be tricked into accepting the congenial as true or denying the uncongenial as false; do not believe in things merely because I wish they were true, or ignore things because I wish they did not exist; but live, godlike, in full consciousness of the external world as it really is, unbiased by predilections and aversions; for such, gentlemen, is the happy effect of the physiological attachments of Man's mind.[13]

However, the powerful rhetoric of this essay, one of Shaw's finest pieces of satire, was not enough to shake the prejudices of his friend. In a postscript of a letter to Shaw dated 15 November 1942 the unrepentant Sir Almroth gave his compatriot a further installment of his views about the irrationality of women: "I have been wondering whether our different outlook upon WOMEN is not simply the result of my being outraged at their 'logical abominations.' Things you take quite calmly, I regard as heinous offences. I know that they are—and you are the *only* man I have ever met who is—totally illogical. It is the price you pay for all your other brilliant qualities."[14]

While it suited Shaw's approach in his 1907 Queens Hall speech to talk of the distinctive contributions women could make to public life, in his utterances about gender in nondramatic contexts it was more usual for him to stress the common humanity, the essential sameness and equality, of men and women. In a 1927 essay he described the way in which he created the female characters in his plays: "I have always assumed that a woman was a person exactly like myself, and that is how the trick is done." In the same essay he explained—with an equally beguiling passing over of problems and of a great deal of complicating evidence from his plays—that he always proceeded from the assumption "that a woman is really only a man in petticoats, or, if you like, that a man is a woman without petticoats."[15] In another interview with Mrs. Churton Braby (published the year before the one about women and the vote) for the periodical *The World of Dress,* Shaw applied his principle about the sameness of men and women—a conceptual abolition of sexual difference—to the subject of women's clothing: "A woman is a biped, built like a man; let her dress like a man," he advised.[16]

* * *

The undermining of gender stereotypes carried out by Shaw in early plays such as *The Philanderer, Mrs. Warren's Profession* and *Arms and the Man* and in such statements as his 1891 attack on the Victorian concept of the womanly woman in *The Quintessence of Ibsenism* found new expression in some of his late Edwardian and early Georgian plays. A prime example of the unwomanly woman in the latter group of plays is the splendid Polish acrobat Lina Szczepanowska in *Misalliance* (1909). Shaw introduces Lina by means of a coup de théâtre. Halfway through the action the horrendous sound of glass shattering signals that an airplane has crashed into the greenhouse of the Tarleton residence, in which the action unfolds. After the Aviator has appeared onstage in his flying costume and goggles, we learn that he has been miraculously saved thanks to an extraordinary acrobatic feat on the part of his passenger, who grabbed him in midair, turned him safely in the direction of a flower bed, and "lighted beside [him] like a bird." When the passenger appears, also in flying costume and goggles, it is assumed by all, including the Aviator, to be a man: "Just discussing your prowess my dear sir. Magnificent," says Tarleton. However, as the passenger removes the goggles, she *"stands revealed as a remarkably good-looking woman."*

The destabilizing of gender expectations in this episode—in itself a fine example of the joie de vivre and energy of Shaw's comic inventiveness—is carried into the dialogue, especially in a passionate tirade about marriage and domesticity that Shaw gives to Lina shortly before the end. In her indignant rejection of the idea of a respectable marriage to Tarleton's son, Johnny, and her proud declaration of her independent professional status, Lina can be seen as the rather strident spokesperson for a number of Shavian heroines—and no doubt for many "free-souled" (to use a Shavian term)[17] women of the Edwardian and later ages:

> Oh, your Johnny with his marriage. He will do the straight thing by me. He will give me a home, a position. He tells me I must know that my present position is not one for a nice woman. This to me, Lina Szczepanowska! I am an honest woman: I earn my living. I am a free woman: I live in my own house. I am a woman of the world: I have thousands of friends; every night crowds of people applaud me. . . . I am strong: I am skilful: I am brave: I am independent: I am unbought. . . . And this Englishman! This linen-draper! He dares to ask me to come and live with him in this rrrrrrrabit hutch, and take my bread from his hands, and ask him for pocket money, and wear soft clothes, and be his woman! His wife!

Such is Lina's professional pride that she declares she would sooner stoop to becoming "an actress or an opera singer" than submit her body and soul to the domination of a man—a metatheatrical joke on Shaw's part that helps to relieve the tension created by his character's tirade and modulates the play into its comically irresolute close.

The first speaker of Lina's words on the stage was Lena Ashwell, the actress to whom Shaw addressed his flirtatious note on the day of his marriage. She was one of the marchers in the women's demonstration of 13 June 1908 and represented the Actresses' Franchise League in a Women's Suffrage Deputation to Prime Minister Asquith. When she played Lina at the Duke of York's Theatre in 1910 she did not know that her professional skills were to gain royal acknowledgment in the form of an OBE awarded during World War I. Lena was also to play an important role in the life of the Shaws in the years following her performance in *Misalliance*, a part that included being very supportive of Charlotte during Shaw's affair with Mrs. Patrick Campbell, which began in June 1912.

It would be wrong to suggest too direct a connection between the high-spirited comic and critical explorations of bourgeois marriage in *Getting Married* and *Misalliance* and Shaw's personal feelings. It is equally impossible not to recall, in reading or viewing these plays on stage, Shaw's pronouncement in *Sixteen Self Sketches*: "If a man is a deep writer all his works are confessions."[18] In their treatment of marriage the plays in some ways represent a reversion to the themes of his early novel *The Irrational Knot*. However, in biographical terms the Edwardian plays have the added edge that now Shaw was writing from firsthand experience. Moreover, they do suggest an underlying pattern of restlessness on the part of Shaw—the free-spirited man of the theater and (by now) very well known public figure—with the "rrrrrrrabit hutch" of bourgeois marriage despised by Lina Szcepanawoska.

The dialogue of *Getting Married* supplies a litany of the freedoms normally closed off by the institution that is the subject of the play's title: Mr. Collins's former friendships; Mrs. George's illicit affairs and correspondence with the bishop (recalling Erica Cotterill's with Shaw) as "Appassionata Incognita"; Leo Bridgenorth's desire for a bigamous arrangement that would allow her to enjoy life with Reginald, her present husband, as well as with Hotchkiss, her exciting new admirer; and Lesbia's idea of marriage with the general, "Boxer" Bridgenorth, in which they would maintain separate houses so that she wouldn't have to put up with his obnoxious cigars and other objectionable habits. In an understated way Lesbia's name suggests yet another possible arrangement of human sexual relationships outside the paradigm of heterosexual monogamous marriage, one with which Shaw had been familiar since the days of his association with the bisexual Kate Salt. Lesbianism is not overtly mentioned in the play, but the connotations of the name of this very independent lady could hardly have been lost on an Edwardian audience.

When he is called upon to help in the unsuccessful project of drawing up a template for a rational marriage contract, Mr. Collins, the greengrocer, provides an analytical list of the various categories of people who enter into marriage and their reasons for doing so. This list includes "the people that marry because theyre so much run after by the other sex that they have to put a stop to it somehow." Knowledge of Shaw's remarkable history of being pursued by female admirers before his marriage lends a clear autobiographical dimension to this comic moment.

To some extent Shaw's marriage did serve as a type of protective castle, a philanderer's haven, that imposed some restraints on the advances of female admirers, as well as on his own behavior. As the episode with Erica Cotterill had shown, in emergencies the drawbridge could be pulled up to exclude intruders and besiegers. The castle also provided Shaw with a place of order in which to maintain his extraordinary regimen of creative writing, correspondence, and activities as a public intellectual and controversialist. However, as his late Edwardian plays seem to suggest, the castle could also be a prison. The plays reflect a strong need for men's as well as women's liberation—especially for one particular man's liberation. Part of Shaw's soul, like Lina Szczepanowska's, belonged to the exciting world of professional entertainment and its attendant popular acclaim. As he told Beatrice Webb in a letter, written aboard the SS *Lusitania*, shortly after his marriage to Charlotte, there was a mischievous side to his nature; he and Beatrice's sister, Maggie, who was also onboard, had formed what Shaw described as a "rapscallionly freemasonry, as between a couple of tramps,"[19] during the cruise in 1899. He used the same word, *rapscallionly*, when referring to Stella Campbell,[20] who was to be the next and more successful besieger of the domestic castle after Erica Cotterill.

* * *

Shaw's publicly avowed notion of woman as "really only a man in petticoats," a fellow biped whom he regarded as being exactly the same as man, is not borne out by many of his representations of women, both in real life and in his plays.[21] He thought of some women—the "heartwise" Ellen Terry, for example—as having a particular kind of intuitive wisdom about people and relationships. Some of the female characters in his plays do conform to the "man in petticoats" idea. The female members of the Ibsen Club in *The Philanderer* (1893) stride about in Norfolk tweed jackets and breeches (worn with or without detachable skirts), roll their own cigarettes, and rigorously insist on sexually nondiscriminatory behavior. Vivie Warren, the twenty-two-year-old mathematics graduate in *Mrs. Warren's Profession* (1894), has a "resolute and hearty" handshake that causes a temporary numbness in the hands of recipients. She doesn't accept male help in moving furniture, generally rejects all the usual "chivalrous" courtesies, and is last seen working in what in the 1890s would have been considered a man's world, namely, an actuarial business office in London, where she follows the racy example of the New Women of *The Philanderer* by smoking a cigarette. Principal followers of these early rebels against the conventions of female behavior in Shaw's plays include Major Barbara, Lina Szczepanowska, and Saint Joan.

However, the "man in petticoats" formula covers only a small percentage of Shaw's portrayals of female characters in his plays. In some ways his work and his personal attitudes toward women reflect the madonna/demon duality that characterizes the representation of the female in much Victorian literature and art, which has been the subject of such studies as Nina Auerbach's *Woman and the Demon: The Life of a Victorian Myth.* Auerbach argues that alongside the dominant Victorian mythography about woman as the center of domestic purity, the loving subordinate of the male, and the "Angel in the House" of Coventry Patmore's popular series of poems in celebration of married love there existed a parallel set of myths about her regal powers and connections with the demonic. The idea of woman that haunted the Victorian imagination was, by turns, that of all-powerful queen ("She-Who-Must-Be-Obeyed"),[22] serpent, vampire, destructive mermaid, and demon. In Victorian popular and high-culture representations of the feminine, as Auerbach says, "the angel can modulate almost imperceptibly into a demon."[23]

Despite his advanced views concerning women and unwavering support of female emancipation in political contexts, as well as his frequent representation of different types of the New Woman in his plays, Shaw's ideas about women often reflect this Victorian duality, even though the demonic side of the equation is generally presented in a comic light. Candida, the leading female character in the play that bears her name, is a perfect example of the dual image of woman that sometimes appears in Shavian drama. Her name carries connotations of innocence and purity. She is partly presented as a serene mother figure, strongly associated with the Titian Madonna that dominates the setting. But Candida is also, as Shaw remarked, as "ruthless as Siegfried," an infantilizer of her husband—over whom she has absolute control—and a coquette. Another example of this type of ambiguous female characterization in Shaw is Hesione in *Heartbreak House*, one of the "demon daughters" (as they are called in the play) of Captain Shotover; she presents a dual image of angel in the house and destructively flirtatious femme fatale. Her sister, Ariadne, is equally a manipulator and emotional destroyer of men.

In the Edwardian play *Getting Married* Shaw has his character Hotchkiss provide a fairly comprehensive list of demonic female types in his denunciations of the clairvoyant and sexually magnetic Mrs. George. She is "a harpy, a siren, a mermaid, a vampire." This melodramatic list is immediately undermined by Mrs. George herself. When Hotchkiss begins to address her as "Fatal woman—if woman you are indeed and not a fiend in human form," she cuts him off by asking: "Is this out of a book? Or is it your usual society small talk?" The exchange shows a nice awareness on Shaw's part of the ridiculous and artificial side of the Victorian demonizing of women—and of male posturing about it. The more sinister side of his portrayal of women, however, is by no means always dissolved in laughter.

* * *

Two new forms of influence—the theater and personal experience—came to bear on Shaw's ideas about women in the Edwardian and early Georgian periods. Early in the century Shaw was introduced to the works of August Strindberg and Anton Chekhov. He was enormously impressed with the work of both these dramatists, becoming their champion and advocate before they had gained wide acceptance in England.

By 1905 Shaw had read a translation of Strindberg's play *The Father*,[24] in which Laura, the wife of the "father" of the play's title, is portrayed as having come into her husband's life as his loving "second mother," but who, in the course of the action, torments him, reduces him to impotent childishness, and watches over him as he dies in a straitjacket fastened with maternal solicitude by a nurse. In 1912 the Stage Society in London produced Strindberg's *Creditors*, which Shaw described as "the terrible play with which Strindberg wreaked the revenge of the male for *A Doll's House,*" since in this work "it is the man who is the victim of domesticity, and the woman who is the tyrant and soul destroyer."[25] In a letter to a friend about the mother-wife Tekla in *Creditors,* Strindberg himself had written: "You will find the vampire wife charming, conceited, parasitical . . . loving (two men at once!), tender, falsely maternal, in a phrase, woman as I see her!"[26]

Shaw and Charlotte met Strindberg ("Ibsen's twin giant" was how Shaw dubbed him)[27] in Stockholm in July 1908 during a visit arranged by Shaw's Swedish translator Hugo Vallentin. Accompanied by Strindberg, they attended a special performance of *Miss Julie* at the playwright's Intima Teatern. They were greatly impressed by the play, which was later translated by Shaw's sister Lucy, in collaboration with Maurice Elvey.[28] A strained conversation, conducted in several languages, between the Shaws and Strindberg ended abruptly, according to Shaw's account, when the hypochondriacal Swedish playwright drew out his watch and said "Um zwei Uhr werde ich krank sein!" (at two o'clock I am going to be sick).[29] Shaw's vivid account of the dramatic and peculiar ending to this meeting tends to overshadow the existence of his later kind and friendly letters to Strindberg, which were aimed at trying to get the Swedish playwright's work better known in England. Probably more important than the personal meeting and correspondence, as far as Shaw's creative writing is concerned, were the powerful images of charming but demonic and sadistic females he found in Strindberg's plays. Shaw did not have anything like the misogynistic feelings that possessed the troubled spirit of the Swedish genius with the "sapphire-blue eyes."[30] Nevertheless, in his creation of female characters in his plays, Shaw's imagination often ran along decidedly Strindbergian lines, especially in *Heartbreak House.*

Shaw never met Chekhov, who died in 1904, but he was immensely impressed with his work, famously telling H. G. Wells in 1916 that "everything we write in England seems sawdust after Tchekov and the rest of [the Russians]."[31] Employing one among various spellings he used for the Russian dramatist's name, Shaw declared himself to have been furious when "an exquisite play [*The Cherry Orchard*] by Tchekoff was actually hissed" when it was produced by the Stage Society on 28 May 1911.[32] Chekhov's plays presented several portrayals of women that, like Strindberg's *The Father* and *Creditors,* conform to the Victorian angel-demon pattern. A particularly striking example of this is the character of Yeliena in *Uncle Vanya,* which, at Shaw's urging, was presented by the Stage Society in London in 1914. The powerfully attractive Yeliena—young wife of the irascible old professor Serebriakov and a magnet for male fascination and adoration—is hopelessly courted by both

Uncle Vanya and Doctor Astrov. Her stepdaughter tells her "you must be a witch" and Astrov describes her as "a charming bird of prey." Utterly under her spell, Astrov says: "Here I am, devour me."

The real-life counterpart of these angel-demons of the theater world was to be Mrs. Patrick Campbell, a splendidly attractive, maternalistic, and flirtatious woman who was to cast a spell over Shaw like that of Yeliena on Doctor Astrov and Uncle Vanya.

* * *

An offstage cry of "Votes for Women" is the first utterance heard in Shaw's 1909 one-act play *Press Cuttings*, which contains his most direct dramatic treatment of woman suffrage. The play directly contributed to the suffragette cause in that it was written to be presented at the Court Theatre in support of the London Society for Women's Suffrage; the following year it was performed at the Kingsway Theatre in tandem with Cicely Hamilton and Christopher St. John's pro-suffrage play *How the Vote Was Won*. Bertha Newcombe, the portrait painter and Shaw's rejected admirer of the 1890s (who had remained unmarried), was put in charge of the arrangements for the production at the Court Theatre.[33]

A comic episode of cross-dressing early in *Press Cuttings*— the reverse of that involving the Polish acrobat Lina Szczepanowska in *Misalliance*—is the prelude to a great deal of playful skirmishing with gender stereotypes in the rest of the play. The blustering General Mitchener, in whose room at the War Office the play is set, learns from the unsoldierly and incompetent Orderly[34] that a suffragette has resourcefully chained herself to the door-scraper (a metal fixture for scraping dirt off shoes) outside the building, an item that had been overlooked in the general clearing out of anything that a chain could be passed through. She carries a letter from the prime minister, Mr. Balsquith, instructing Mitchener to have her released with a key provided in the envelope and ushered up to his office at once.

To the dismay and expostulation of the general, the "woman," having arrived at his office, begins to undress, revealing a pair of *"fashionable trousers."* The General protests and is in the process of saying "Not even your letter from the Prime Minister" when the "woman" removes more of "her" outer costume, saying: "My dear Mitchener: I *am* the Prime Minister." The man who now stands revealed as Balsquith—the name is a conflation of those of Balfour and Asquith, both of whom served as prime minister during the Edwardian period—explains that the only way he could safely walk to Mitchener's office through the streets of protesting suffragettes was to disguise himself as one of their kind. Herbert Asquith, the real-life prime minister, was particularly unpopular with the suffragettes because of his strong opposition to their cause.

Shaw's tactic in the play was not to include any actual suffragette figures but rather two satirical portraits of female opponents of woman suffrage in the characters of Lady Corinthia Fanshawe and Mrs. Banger. Lady Corinthia, a highly cultivated egeria and self anointed epitome of the feminine, describes herself as "the highest living soprano" and regards the suffragette movement as "mainly ruled by dowdies." She is, she explains to the General, "one of those women who are accustomed to rule the world through men." She endorses the Salic law, which forbids women from occupying the throne, on the grounds that when women are on the throne countries are actually ruled by men and are therefore ruled badly, "whereas when a man is on the throne the country is ruled by women and therefore ruled well." The New Zealand women have been given the vote and what, she asks rhetorically—in the manner of Harry Lime about Switzerland in the film *The Third Man*—is the result?: "No poet ever makes a New Zealand woman his heroine. One might as well be romantic about New Zealand mutton." During the course of the action Lady Corinthia draws a pistol and threatens to shoot the general if he stirs, an idea that recalls the occasion when Elizabeth Robins threatened to shoot Shaw if he wrote anything about her that she did not approve of for a newspaper article.

A very different type of anti-suffragist visitor to General Mitchener's office is the formidable "man in petticoats," Mrs. Banger, who is described in the stage directions as "*a masculine woman of forty with a powerful voice and great physical strength.*" Mrs. Banger is a more militant type of anti-suffragist who wants to "cast off [her] hampering skirt" and lead a military anti-suffragette campaign with her trusty sabre. She terrifies the Orderly (who refuses to obey the general's orders to have her removed from his office because of his fear of losing out in physical combat with her), and astounds the General himself with her theory that "all the really strong men of history," including Bismarck, "have been disguised women." The suffragette question, according to Mrs. Banger, needs to be "solved by blood and iron." By presenting Mrs. Banger as such a masculine figure, Shaw was turning the tables on satirists of the women's suffrage movement, who often presented the suffragettes as unnaturally mannish.

So appalled is General Mitchener by these two frightful anti-suffragists that he becomes a convert to the women's suffrage movement, before making his proposal of marriage to his shrewd and down-to-earth Irish charwoman, Mrs. Farrell. By making such a laughingstock of the anti-suffragists, Shaw was probably contributing more effectively to the suffragette cause than if he had created any actual exponents of women's liberation. Moreover, he was able to create some very appealing character roles for female actors in a topical work that has proven to be enduringly stageworthy.

* * *

The writing of *Press Cuttings* was begun during a motor tour through Algeria and Tunisia that the Shaws had embarked upon on 16 March 1909 in the company of Charlotte's sister, Mary Cholmondeley. Creating short works such as *Press Cuttings* became the order of the day for Shaw in 1909: like explosions in a fireworks display, *The Shewing-up of Blanco Posnet, The Glimpse of Reality, Press Cuttings,* and *The Fascinating Foundling* all followed one another in rapid succession. It was an extraordinarily eventful year in Shaw's life, his activities in support of woman suffrage forming part of a more general campaign against the restrictive political and social conservatism of the day.

After his return from North Africa, Shaw plunged into battle with the system of censorship in England. In May *The Shewing-up of Blanco Posnet* was refused a license, an action that led to the defiant production in Dublin later in the year. In June the Lord Chamberlain's reader also refused a license to *Press Cuttings* on the grounds that it alluded to "personalities expressed or understood." The name of the prime minister was indeed a combination of Balfour and Asquith, but the mildly presented character was, as Shaw later pointed out with sweet reason, "neither of these statesmen, and cannot in the course of nature be both."[35] A more serious matter was the fact that Mitchener was not only a satirical portrait of Kitchener—the general with whom Charlotte had lunched in Egypt many years earlier and who was soon to become a leading figure in World War I—but also of a "more highly connected commander,"[36] the last Duke of Cambridge, a cousin of Queen Victoria, who had long been a leading opponent of modernization of the army. The truth probably was that Shaw was generally getting on the nerves of the English censors, who no doubt were glad to find excuses to make things awkward for him. The problem of allusions to real-life personalities in the play was overcome in the first production by calling the characters General Bones and Mr. Johnson, black and white minstrel disguises that did not fool the select, invited audiences that attended private performances of the play on 9 and 12 July 1909.

In July 1909 Shaw, armed with an eleven thousand-word submission, appeared before a joint select committee of inquiry into censorship chaired by the Right Honorable Herbert Samuel. Shaw's submission was rejected and the censorship system remained unchanged. The "Rejected Statement" was subsequently incorporated into the preface to *The Shewing-up of Blanco Posnet.*

In August the Shaws went motoring again, this time to Ireland, where Charlotte and her sister enjoyed at first hand the triumphant production of *Blanco Posnet*; Shaw received Lady Gregory's news of it in Parknasilla, on the Ring of Kerry. His main activities for the rest of 1909 included the completion of *Misalliance* and campaigning with Harley Granville-Barker for the establishment of a national theatre. Although it had been a splendid year's work, Shaw had a score to settle with his Edwardian theater critics as well as with the censors. While staying with Lady Gregory at Coole Park, in August 1910 he began writing *Fanny's First Play*, the work that would prove a major weapon of satirical attack in this campaign.

18 Enter Critics, Stage Right

Having reached the pinnacle of his fame as a playwright, and having just been awarded the Nobel Prize in literature, in 1926 Shaw made a wry retrospective comment on the critical reception of his plays in England, compared with other countries, in the early years of the century. His German translator, Siegfried Trebitsch, had made him famous in that country and he was doing well in America and Central Europe. His English critics, however, were still not convinced that he was cut out to be a playwright. Referring to his anomalous situation in England during the Edwardian period, Shaw wrote:

> I presently found myself a successful and respected playwright in the German language whilst the English critics were still explaining laboriously that my plays were not plays, and urging me, in the kindest spirit, to cease my vain efforts to enter a profession for which Nature had utterly unfitted me. In the last decade of the nineteenth century I was deriving a substantial income as a playwright from America and Central Europe. Not until the middle of the first decade of the twentieth could I have lived by my theatrical earnings in London.[1]

Long before he had written these words, Shaw had taken revenge on his early-twentieth-century English critics in his comedy *Fanny's First Play*, the writing of which he completed in March 1911. Shaw described this play in a brief preface as a "pot-boiler." In some respects it can be seen as a reworking of themes he had treated in *Misalliance*, with its heroine, Margaret Knox, rebelling—like Hypatia Tarleton and Lina Szczepanowska—against the Edwardian nuclear family and the "rabbit hutch" of the Edwardian home. "I've been set free from this silly little hole of a house and all its pretences. I've found strength. For good or evil I am set free," Margaret Knox announces to her long-suffering mother. Although it may have been conceived by Shaw as a mere potboiler, judging by the criterion of the length of first run, it was the most successful work of his career. After opening on 19 April 1911 at the Little

Theatre, Adelphi, London, in a production directed by Shaw, the play held the stage for 622 performances. As a joke—and to allow for the guessing game about the identity of the author, which provides much material for satire in the epilogue—the work was presented anonymously in 1911, though its real authorship did not remain a secret for long.

Fanny's First Play is a lively comedy about youthful revolt against parents and the dullness of bourgeois family life. Shaw gave added spice to the work by framing it with an "Induction" and an "Epilogue" in which he presented good-natured satirical portraits of some of the Edwardian theater critics who, to quote his 1926 statement, had been "explaining laboriously that my plays were not plays." The four invited critics who arrive onstage to pontificate over Fanny's play and speculate about its authorship are named Trotter, Vaughan, Gunn, and Flawner Bannal. The first three are caricatures, respectively, of Arthur Bingham Walkley of the *Times,* to whom Shaw had addressed the Epistle Dedicatory of *Man and Superman* and who was previously his colleague on the *Star;* Edward A. Baughan of the *Daily News,* who once called Shaw "an anaemic idealist";[2] and Gilbert Cannan, former critic of the *Star.* The fourth critic, Flawner Bannal, is a composite portrait of hacks from the popular press, with perhaps a glance at Clement Scott, "the sentimentalist of the *Daily Telegraph,*" as Shaw called him.[3] When the magazine *Play Pictorial* devoted a special issue to *Fanny's First Play* during its run, Shaw took the opportunity of writing a letter to the editor, which he signed "Flawner Bannal." In this letter "Flawner" describes himself as a writer for the enormously influential *Matutinal Meddler,* as a representative of the man in the street, and as a "plain straight-forward Englishman" whose firm policy it was never to put forward any original view, "however vaguely," concerning a play he was reviewing.[4]

* * *

Both the frame and main action of *Fanny's First Play* deal with the comic and painful aspects of the vast gaps that often occur between what parents think they know about their offspring—or hope is true about them—and the actual behavior and outlook of the children themselves. The setting is an old-fashioned country house belonging to an Irish aesthete, Count O'Dowda, "*a handsome man of fifty, dressed with studied elegance a hundred years out of date.*" Despising its ugliness and philistinism, he has completely cut himself off from the modern world—which in his case means the post-eighteenth-century world—and surrounded himself with what he calls "beautiful realities." While he lives mainly in Venice, his charming daughter, Fanny, is completing her education at Cambridge University, a place where O'Dowda thinks "the atmosphere of the eighteenth century" has the best chance of still being preserved. As a birthday present for his daughter, he has arranged for her new play to have a professional private performance in the house, with leading London critics in attendance. He imagines the play will be a beautifully dressed harlequinade, "like a Louis Quatorze ballet painted by Watteau."

In most respects the character of the fifty-year-old Irish Count seems completely remote from that of his fifty-four-year-old Irish author. Shaw, of course, disliked escapist worship of culture and art, such as that displayed by the Count, and was a herald and welcomer of change and progress. Yet it is possible to see in Count O'Dowda some facets of Shaw's own outlook. In some manifestations of the complex Shavian self there was a certain eighteenth-century persona. This was especially true in his perception of his own use of language and of his Irish identity. In his 1907 preface to *John Bull's Other Island* he wrote: "I was born in Ireland, and . . . my native language is the English of Swift and not the unspeakable jargon of the mid-XIX century London newspapers."[5] In a lecture to the Fabian Society in 1919, Shaw said that one of the advantages he had as a student of history by being born in Ireland was that he was "literally born in the seventeenth century; that is to say, my father's house from the [candle] snuffers on the drawing room table to the sanitation in the yard was just precisely the sort of house that Samuel Pepys lived in." Moreover, he told his Fabian audience, there were considerable advantages in the pre-nineteenth-century way of life it was still possible to find when visiting Ireland: "If you go from here to Ireland you get back into the seventeenth- and eighteenth-century atmosphere. You find a curious ease of life. It is a country of easy living and easy dying, and it is sometimes a very healthy thing to get back into that sort of atmosphere. The people being poor and not expecting one another to be rich, they have a good deal of time for thinking and a good deal of time for talking."[6]

If the Count can be seen as a comic mask of certain aspects of Shaw's outlook and identity—his eighteenth-century self, so to speak—it is the rebellious Fanny and her play that are more closely aligned with the forward-looking revolutionary playwright, social critic, and new man of the twentieth century.

Unbeknownst to her father, what Fanny has been enjoying at Cambridge is not the "eighteenth-century atmosphere" but rather membership of the University Fabian Society, whose motto concerning the importance of taking risks ("the ice of life is slippery") she quotes to Mr. Trotter, the bemused, old-fashioned critic, before the performance of her play. Fanny has also become a suffragette. The action of her play takes place in the suburban London homes of two respectable bourgeois families, the Gilbeys and the Knoxes, in which the parents are being driven to distraction, and having their lives thrown into disarray, by grown-up children who are in complete revolt against their values and ideas. Both sets of parents find out that their respective children, Bobby and Margaret, have been serving two-week prison sentences for drunkenness and assaulting the police while out on separate sprees in London.

The skillful plotting in Fanny's play—its rapidly developing action and numerous instances of spontaneous and passionate behavior, in which the vitality of youth smashes the constraints of hidebound age—is itself a humorous response by Shaw to his Edwardian critics: the play contained in abundance many of the ingredients they insisted were missing in his work. However, it was in the framing "Induction" and "Epilogue" that Shaw's most pungent and amusing response to his early critics was made.

The first of the walking caricatures of contemporary critics to give expression to his views on drama is Mr. Trotter (alias A. B. Walkley), who has a conversation with Fanny before the curtain goes up on her play. During this Trotter delivers his condemnation of certain plays being performed in London, which he blushes to say are by a friend of his (obviously Bernard Shaw) who calls them "conversations, discussions, and so forth, with the express object of evading criticism," but which he, Trotter, declares "are not plays. Dialogues, if you will. Exhibitions of character perhaps: especially the character of the author. Fictions, possibly, though a little decent reticence as to introducing actual persons, and thus violating the sanctity of private life, might not be amiss. But plays, no. I say NO. Not plays." In Trotter's view, the definition of a play had been settled "exactly and scientifically for two thousand two hundred and sixty years," having been established "for all time by the immortal Stagirite," Aristotle. The new works on the London stage by a certain author of Mr. Trotter's acquaintance were by definition not plays because they did not conform to the Aristotelian rules.

After Fanny's sensational play has been performed, the four critics, "bored and weary," fall to arguing about the authorship. Mr. Bannal, writing for the popular press, says indignantly: "You don't expect me to know what to say about a play when I don't know who the author is, do you?" Mr. Gunn says that since the play is "a rotten old-fashioned domestic melodrama," with a trace of the "hackneyed old Shaw touch," the author must be Granville-Barker. Mr. Vaughan thinks it's Pinero, while Mr. Bannal rashly suggests Shaw, an idea that is immediately discounted by the others since the play has "the note of passion in it," and "Shaw is physiologically incapable of the note of passion." Mr. Bannal, reminded of the correct opinion about Shaw, says, "Yes, I know. . . . A giant brain, if you ask me; but no heart."

* * *

The repeated cry of Shaw's Edwardian critics that his plays were not really plays was partly encouraged by Shaw himself. So fed up had he become with the monotonous conventions and mechanical plotting of Victorian well-made plays and melodramas that he sometimes went out of his way to present his own works as though they were completely devoid of plot. A section of a self-drafted interview about *Candida* by Shaw, published in 1895, ran as follows (with the phantom "interviewer" beginning the line of questioning):

> *And what of the plot?*
>
> If I told you the plot, you would think it the dullest affair you had ever heard. There is a clergyman and his wife—who is Candida, the heroine.
>
> *And who is the villain of the piece?*
>
> I never deal in villainy. The nearest thing I have got to it is a minor poet, who falls in love with the heroine.
>
> *Ah! And then what happens?*
>
> Some conversations. That's all.
>
> *Absolutely nothing more than that?*
>
> No more than that. But such conversations![7]

G. Wilson Knight's description of Shaw's humor as sometimes appearing to be "suicidal" comes to mind during such moments of Shavian discourse about his plays.[8] In fact, what goes on in the "conversations" in Shavian drama, including *Candida,* is usually quite clearly definable as dramatic action, in the sense that the conversations generally impinge closely on the development of the relationships and outcomes of the fortunes of the characters. Although Shaw's plays, like Chekhov's, sometimes end inconclusively or ambiguously, they do not display complete narrative stasis such as that found in Beckett's *Waiting for Godot.* The balance in Shavian drama between relatively static conversation, on the one hand, and verbal exchanges and incidents that are more dynamically and directly related to the outcomes of dramatic narrative, on the other, varies enormously. Even in the Edwardian period there is a great difference, in this respect, between plays such as *Androcles and the Lion,* with its mixture of entertaining pantomime and action-packed historical drama, and more obviously conversational pieces such as *Getting Married,* to which Shaw gave the provocative subtitle "A Disquisitory Play."

Max Beerbohm, Shaw's successor on the *Saturday Review,* was among the first of the Edwardian critics to say of a Shaw play that it was not really a play. Interestingly, however, Beerbohm was converted to a different view when he saw the same play performed on the stage. After reading the published text of Shaw's *Man and Superman: A Comedy and a Philosophy,* Beerbohm wrote an article on the work that was published in the *Saturday Review* in September 1903 under the title "Mr. Shaw's New Dialogues." Both in the wording of the title and in some of the text of this essay, Beerbohm provided Shaw with some of the essential material for the speech, quoted earlier, by Mr. Trotter in *Fanny's First Play,* which was written eight years later. "This peculiar article," wrote Beerbohm in 1903 of *Man and Superman,* "is, of course, not a play at all. It is 'as good as a play'—infinitely better . . . than any play I have ever read or seen enacted. But a play it is not."[9]

In several subsequent reviews of performances of Shaw's Edwardian plays, Beerbohm "climbed down" (as he put it) from his general view about Shaw as a dramatist. In 1905 he categorically retracted what he had said about *Man and Superman*: "When I saw it performed, I determined that I would not be caught tripping again. I found that as a piece of theatrical construction it was perfect."[10] Beerbohm's conversion regarding Shaw's plays began in 1904, after he had seen *John Bull's Other Island.* In a review of the play published in November 1904, he unblushingly defended Shaw against the "usual parrot-cry: 'Not a play'" and remarked on Shaw's effortless dramatic technique: "Mr Shaw evolves his 'situations' with perfect naturalness, and brings his characters off and on, and handles a whole crowd of them simultaneously on the stage, without the least apparent effort."[11] However, it was in a longer essay, written in 1905, that Beerbohm made a fuller retraction of his earlier view of Shaw. A passage in his *Saturday Review* essay entitled "Mr. Shaw's Position" is worth quoting at length since it provides an excellent summary of Edwardian criticism of Shaw and a powerful rebuttal:

> Mr Shaw, it is insisted, cannot draw life: he can only distort it. He has no knowledge of human nature: he is but a theorist. All his characters are but so many incarnations of himself. Above all, he cannot write plays. He has no dramatic instinct, no theatrical technique. And these objections are emphatically reiterated (often with much brilliancy and ingenuity) by the superior critics, while all the time the fact is staring them in the face that Mr. Shaw has created in *Major Barbara* two characters—Barbara and her father—who live with an intense vitality; a crowd of minor characters that are accurately observed (though some are purposely exaggerated) from life; and one act—the second—which is as cunning and closely-

knit a piece of craftsmanship as any conventional playwright could achieve, and a cumulative appeal to emotions which no other living playwright has touched. With all these facts staring them in the face, they still maintain that Mr. Shaw is not a playwright.[12]

In this passage the main battle lines concerning Shaw's plays—not only in the Edwardian period but in much of the later critical discourse on the subject—were drawn. Beerbohm provides a particularly good focus on the issues, and his compliments to the playwright, as well as other acknowledgments of his genius, seem all the more generous when one realizes that he did not very much like Shaw as a person.[13]

* * *

It was ironic that Shaw's most successful dramatic work, judging by the length of first runs, should have been the one in which he lampooned his critics with genial but trenchant satire. This Parthian shot at Edwardian England and his Edwardian critics was followed by *Androcles and the Lion,* which had its premiere in German at the Kleines Theater, Berlin, on 25 November 1912, and was first presented in English on 1 September 1913 in a production directed by Harley Granville-Barker at the St. James's Theatre, London.

In many ways *Androcles and the Lion* was an equally effective, if less direct, retort to Shaw's Edwardian critics than *Fanny's First Play*. The brilliant combination of serious reflection on religious themes with elements drawn from fable, pantomime, and farce in Shaw's parodic version of nineteenth-century plays about Christian martyrdom in Roman times reveals a bravura display of dramatic and comedic skills. From its opening scene, in which Androcles extracts a thorn from the paw of the grateful lion, to the close, in which the same humble animal lover has to step in to rescue the Roman emperor from the lion in "hot pursuit" of him, the play balances on a knife-edge between laughter and horror. The gruesome depravity of the sports in the Colosseum, which include throwing Christians to the lions for the entertainment of the Roman "voluptuaries," is strongly evoked in a work that is nevertheless laced throughout with keen humor and deftly managed farcical action. The lion chasing the emperor around the stage in a moment of vivid dramatic action could almost be emblematic of Shaw in pursuit of his Edwardian critics with the barbs of satire. An even greater artistic success, however, was to follow. Just ahead in Shaw's career lay a dangerous love affair—and a play that has come to be recognized as one of his most outstanding works: *Pygmalion.*

19 A Love Affair, a Death, and a Triumph

On Sunday, 30 June 1912, Shaw wrote to Harley Granville-Barker telling him about two recent meetings with Mrs. Patrick Campbell, during one of which he had read his new play *Pygmalion* to her. He reported that although he had gone to these meetings armed with "insolent confidence in my superiority to a dozen such Dalilas," he nevertheless "fell head over heels in love with her—violently and exquisitely in love. . . . And I am on the verge of 56. There has never been anything so ridiculous, or so delightful, in the history of the world. On Friday we were together for an hour: we visited a lord; we drove in a taxi; we sat on a sofa in Kensington Square; and my years fell from me like a garment. I was in love for very nearly 36 hours; and for that be all her sins forgiven her!"[1]

In a letter to Shaw (undated but postmarked 27 June) Stella—as Shaw would soon be addressing this "Dalila"—thanked him for reading her his play "and for thinking I can be your pretty slut. I wonder if I could please you."[2] The reference was to Shaw's heroine in *Pygmalion*, the cockney flower girl Eliza Doolittle. Stella's remark ("I wonder if I could please you") proved to be an understatement concerning his feelings both about her as a person and her suitability for the role in *Pygmalion*. "There is no other Liza and can be no other Liza," he told her shortly afterward. On the same Sunday he had written to Granville-Barker he also wrote to Stella in terms that—despite his claim to have come down to earth from his heights of rapture—still conveyed his admiration and enchantment: "Many thanks for Friday and for a Saturday of delightful dreams. I did not believe that I had that left in me. I am all right now, down on earth again with all my cymbals and side drums and blaring vulgarities in full blast; but it would be meanly cowardly to pretend that you are not a very wonderful lady, or that the spell did not work most enchantingly on me for fully 12 hours."[3]

Neither "nearly 36" nor "fully 12" hours was anything like correct as a description of the duration of Shaw's enchantment by Stella Campbell's charm.

The meeting and correspondence in June 1912 was the prelude to an affair that lasted until April 1914, when, five days before the opening of *Pygmalion*, Stella precipitously married her second husband, George Cornwallis-West. Even that event did not end the relationship. Stella had lodged herself in Shaw's imagination and affection in a quite unique way, and his emotional ties to her were never quite severed. It was one of the most serious and significant relationships he had formed with women. During the 1912–14 phase it threatened his marriage and became a cause of great distress to Charlotte.

* * *

The future Mrs. Patrick Campbell, Beatrice Rose Stella Tanner, was born of mixed English and Italian parentage on 9 February 1865 at a house known as Forest Hill in the fashionable London suburb of Kensington, opposite the Kensington Palace Gardens. Her father, John Tanner,[4] had met and married her mother, Maria Luigia Giovanna Romanini, in Bombay, where Tanner owned an ordnance factory that supplied arms to the British forces in India. Tanner's restless and adventurous spirit and capacity for making and losing large amounts of money were also characteristics of his famous daughter. Having lost fifty thousand pounds during the Indian Mutiny, which he was unable to recover from the British government, he returned to England and subsequently pursued unsuccessful business ventures in America.[5]

Stella grew up with a love of reading. She once told Shaw that what she knew about her "beloved Blake," whom she had aptly quoted, "would fill a thimble"[6]—but she was in fact well read and highly intelligent. She was a gifted pianist, as Shaw was quick to observe in 1893; her piano master at the Guildhall School of Music, where she studied for a time, wanted her to become a professional musician. At the age of nineteen, without informing her parents, she married the twenty-year-old Patrick Campbell, having become pregnant out of wedlock with his child. The couple settled in London, where she gave piano lessons. She had two children by Campbell, a daughter, also called Stella, and a son, Alan Urquhart ("Beo").

After the birth of the children, Patrick Campbell gave up his job in England and traveled to Australia and South Africa, where, in like manner to his father-in-law in America, he made not very successful attempts to make his fortune. Thrown onto her own resources, with two children to care for, Stella gradually embarked on a career in the theater. After gaining experience with an amateur theater group and a provincial touring company, on 13 March 1890 she made her first appearance on the London stage in Sheridan Knowles's play *The Hunchback* at the Adelphi Theatre. Her rise to fame as one of the leading actresses of her generation began with her highly acclaimed performances as the tragically conceived Paula, the "woman with a past," in Pinero's play *The Second Mrs. Tanqueray* (1893) and as the daringly rebellious though ultimately conformist Agnes in the same playwright's work *The Notorious Mrs. Ebbsmith* (1895). Following these successes, she played Juliet opposite Johnston Forbes-Robertson's Romeo and Ophelia opposite his Hamlet in his celebrated productions of Shakespeare's tragedies at the Lyceum Theatre.

As we have seen, Shaw had been struck by the "perilously bewitching"[7] Stella Campbell's physical attractiveness and skill as an actress long before the fateful reading of *Pygmalion* to her in the summer of 1912. Already in 1893 he had praised her beauty and piano playing in *The Second Mrs. Tanqueray;* he amusingly complained about the "wretched people" on the stage interrupting her expert rendition of a piece by Schubert with distracting dialogue—Pinero's play![8] He was even more complimentary in his mocking review in March 1895 of *The Notorious Mrs. Ebbsmith,* in which he described her as having played the playwright "clean off the stage" with her fascinating acting and presence: "She creates all sorts of illusions, and gives one all sorts of searching sensations. It is impossible not to feel that those haunting eyes are brooding on a momentous past, and the parted lips anticipating a thrilling imminent future, whilst some enigmatic present must no less surely be working underneath all that subtle play of limb and stealthy intensity of tone."[9] There were already in these reviews very strong suggestions of Shaw's feelings about the captivating Stella Campbell. As he confessed in a letter to her dated 4 January 1913, the reviews of the 1890s were thinly veiled love letters. Although he did not know her as "deeply and nearly" then as he did by 1913, his love was not "a new thing," he confessed in the same letter (written six months after the reading of *Pygmalion*). "It shines in every line I wrote about you," he added, recalling his "dithyrambs" to her in the *Saturday Review.*[10]

On one occasion in the 1890s Shaw had met Stella in the company of the English actor-manager Johnston Forbes-Robertson. On 18 February 1897 he read *The Devil's Disciple* to them in the hope that they might be interested in presenting it.[11] It was quite likely this meeting that sowed the seed of an idea in Shaw's mind that, fifteen years later, was to be turned into his play *Pygmalion.* Referring to Mrs. Patrick Campbell and Forbes-Robertson in a letter to Ellen Terry dated 8 September 1897, he said that the work he was currently writing (*Caesar and Cleopatra*) had been driven out of his head by "a play I want to write for them in which he shall be a west end gentleman and she an east end dona in an apron and three orange and red ostrich feathers."[12] Robertson would be the "west end gentleman" and Mrs. Patrick Campbell the "east end dona."*

Another remarkable forecast of things to come in this letter to Ellen Terry is contained in Shaw's reference to Stella as Robertson's "rapscallionly flower girl." Stella was currently playing Ophelia in the long-running season of *Hamlet* at the Lyceum Theatre. Shaw is obviously alluding to the bestowing of flowers by Ophelia in the second of her two mad scenes. Reviewing the production twice, on the first occasion Shaw particularly noted Stella's effective playing of Ophelia. Instead of making her prettily silly and vague, she had made her "really mad" in this performance—to chilling effect, according to Shaw.[13] In the mad scenes Ophelia appears with her hair down, and in one of her songs a sudden bawdiness erupts from beneath the maidenly modesty of the character in the rest of the play.

Stella's rendition of these aspects of the mad Ophelia may have been what inspired Shaw's use of the word *rapscallionly*. Yet the association of Stella with flowers also lingered in his mind. Fifteen years later, she was to play a very different kind of "rapscallionly flower girl" in the form of the cockney Covent Garden flower seller Eliza Doolittle, who is dictated to by a man who possesses in comic form some of the misogynistic feelings Shakespeare gave to his Hamlet. Both the love affair with Stella and the idea of the play she helped to inspire were like long dormant seeds that took a decade and a half to germinate.

* * *

Following Shaw's dramatic declaration to Granville-Barker, in June 1912, about his having fallen in love with Stella, the affair developed rapidly. Playing on two of her first names and practicing his Latin, Shaw (in a letter dated 3 July) addressed her as "Beatricissima" ("most blessed") and "Stella Stellarum" ("star of the stars"). This letter was mostly about "business," and (with a show of complete innocence) Shaw even outrageously said he was going to read it to Charlotte—"my love affairs are her unfailing amusement."[14] Shortly afterward, Stella began a letter in reply to one of his with "Oh darling what a letter," explaining that the address "Dear Mr. Shaw means nothing at all—whilst darling means most dear and most dear means a man and a mind and a speaking—such as you and your mind and your speech!"[15]

*"Woman" (Span. doña). In English use the word had connotations of low social rank; according to a nineteenth-century citation in the OED, a circus man customarily referred to a circus woman as a "dona."

The rapturous beginning of Shaw's affair with Stella was immediately reflected in the one-act comedy *Overruled,* which he wrote in the first three weeks of July 1912. Written in a style of farcical comedy similar to that which was later to characterize some of the works of Noël Coward, *Overruled* is about two marriages in which the husbands and wives enter into amorous and potentially adulterous relationships with the partners in the other marriage.[16] The work was an occasion for playful reflection on Shaw's part about the irresistible forces at work in such relationships and the pangs of guilt they arouse, and contains a good deal of clear autobiographical reference. Notably it is the men in the play who are much more troubled by their consciences than the women, a situation certainly reflected in the Shaw-Stella relationship. First performed as part of a triple bill (the other works being by J. M. Barrie and Arthur Wing Pinero) in October 1912, the play did not have a good reception—and neither did Pinero's. Shaw wrote to the latter afterward, jokingly saying they had both mistaken their profession and should go into "market gardening."[17]

Although he was certainly troubled by his conscience in his relationship with Stella, Shaw was extraordinarily indiscreet about it, as he had been in his affairs with women before his marriage. Apart from Granville-Barker, J. M. Barrie and his and Stella's mutual friend Edith (the Honorable Mrs. Alfred) Lyttelton—who was present at the *Pygmalion* reading on 26 June—were very much aware of the affair since its earliest days. Barrie, also an admirer of Stella, lived opposite the Shaws in Adelphi Terrace. Referring to their alternating fortunes as far as Stella's bestowal of affection was concerned, Barrie compared himself and Shaw to two figures in a toy weather-house, the one coming to the fore while the other disappears, and vice versa.[18]

In the midst of the flurry of letters exchanged between Shaw and Stella during July 1912, Stella was seriously injured, narrowly escaping death, in an accident that occurred when a taxi in which she was a passenger swerved to avoid a bicycle and collided with another taxi. On 30 July, after being laid up at her home in Kensington Square with a severely bruised and aching body, two black eyes, and a swollen jaw, she traveled with her friends Sir Edward and Lady Stracey in their Rolls-Royce and stayed at the Hôtel Mirabeau in Aix-les-Bains, the famous spa resort in the Savoie region of France. On the eve of her departure she sent her hotel address to Shaw together with a song she said reminded her of him, which her daughter, Stella, used to be fond of singing:

He's mad, mad, mad,
He's clean gone off his nut

He cleans his boots with strawberry jam
He eats his hat whenever he can
He's mad, mad, mad—[19]

In reply, Shaw penned a four-stanza nonsense poem in the same style for "Stellinetta" (as he called the young Stella) to sing to the accompaniment of a banjo, with jokes intended for family reading about the Campbell children's opinion of the "silly old man" who thinks the world of their "silly old mam."[20]

Shaw was writing from the Hotel de Russie, Bad Kissingen, another European spa town, in Bavaria. He and Charlotte, in the company of Mary Cholmondeley and the chauffeur Kilsby, had left on a continental tour on 27 July, three days before Stella's departure for France. Charlotte and Mary stayed in Bad Kissingen for expensive therapeutic treatments: "[Charlotte] gasps in rarefied air whilst her sister wallows in mud at five marks per gasp and per wallow," Shaw reported to Stella. Meanwhile he and Kilsby went touring in the de Dietrich, which, in the course of their journey, "ruptured a vital organ" near an isolated alpine village and caused a lengthy delay in their travels while the car was transported by rail for repairs at the de Dietrich motor factory in Luneville.

There was plenty of time for lengthy, diverting, and flattering letters to Stella. He realized, he told her, that he was like the pathetically lovelorn brigand and bad poet Mendoza (in *Man and Superman*) and his adored Louisa—"who was our cook, by the way," Shaw revealed parenthetically—but that he could not restrain his own adoration: "Still, O Stella, I kiss your hands and magnify the Life Force for creating you; for you are a very wonderful person."[21] In mock-schoolmarm fashion Stella promised him that "perhaps someday, if you are very good and behave properly at rehearsal I will write you a love letter."[22]

In September 1912 Stella's health, still affected by the trauma of the accident, deteriorated and she was confined to bed. She spent the rest of the year at her home in Kensington Square, and early in 1913 she was transferred to a nursing home at 12 Hinde Street, Marylebone. Shaw visited her regularly and took a photograph of her lying languorously in bed. Her state of semi-dishabille sharpened his awareness of the physical charms of the "glorious white marble lady," as he addressed her in one of his letters.[23] Passages deleted from the Dent edition (1952) of the correspondence, which was supervised by Stella's daughter, included the lines "O sweet of body and kissable all over" and "I bless your illness for revealing the modelled reality of your beauty—you are really much lovelier than I thought."[24] In a letter to her dated 27 November 1912, he vividly recalled the moment—almost six months earlier—when she first took his hand, making it come into contact with her breast: "Oh, her bosom! I remember now—the jade!—when she first took my hand she shook it so that it touched her bosom, an infamous abandoned trick: it thrilled me through all my brass for hours." With such tricks "the jade" distracted him from his Bunyanesque pilgrimage, the mighty causes in which he was engaged: "I want no Stella," he roundly declared. "I want my brains, my pen, my platform, my audience, my adversary, my mission."[25]

* * *

In truth, even the turmoil of his affair with Stella did nothing to deflect Shaw from the course of his public life, his platforms, and his "mission." In the same letter to her he mentioned a preface and an article he was writing, as well as a big debate that was to take place between himself and his adversary Hilaire Belloc at the Queens Hall on 28 January 1913. This was one of a famous series of debates Shaw had with Belloc and G. K. Chesterton in the years leading up to World War I, in which he did battle with his two conservative Roman Catholic opponents and their attacks on Socialism. The debate on 28 January, the subject of which was "Property or Slavery," was attended by the novelist Arnold Bennett, whose account of it in his diary is one of several reminiscences left by contemporary eyewitnesses. These mighty encounters between formidable minds were like the intellectual equivalent of heavyweight boxing championships. (Bennett makes similar comparisons with a note of disapproval.)

Ironically, Bennett said that Shaw and Charlotte looked rather too "conjugal" when they appeared together at the Queens Hall, which was "crammed, at concert prices":

> Not a seat unsold. Shaw very pale with white hair, and straight. His wife beside him. Effect too conjugal for a man at work. Sidney and Beatrice Webb next to them. Effect also too conjugal here. Maurice Baring supporting Belloc, both very shabby. Maurice with loose brown boots and creased socks. They spoke thus: Belloc thirty minutes, Shaw thirty, Belloc twenty, Shaw twenty, Belloc ten, Shaw ten. Time was kept to three minutes. Belloc's first was pretty good. Shaw's first was a first-class performance, couldn't have been better; the perfection of public speaking (not oratory); not a word wrong. But then afterwards the impression that it was a gladiatorial show or circus performance gained on one, and at

the end was a sense of disappointment, as the affair degenerated into a mere rivalry in scoring. Still I have never seen Shaw emotional before, as he was then.[26]

A similar record of Shaw's prowess as "the best debater in London" was provided by novelist and critic Frank Swinnerton. Audiences, wrote Swinnerton, were "conquered by his voice and his persuasiveness," and by the extraordinary range and variety of his knowledge: "He knew all about municipal politics . . .; he knew all about Shakespeare and the 'Dhrama' because he was a 'dhramatist'; he knew all about economics, 'gahs' [gas], Ibsen, Wagner, Socialism, Chesterton and Belloc, doctors, lawyers, politics, respectability, absurdity, and everything else." It was true, Swinnerton continued, that Shaw's magical words, when printed and subjected to analysis, were themselves occasionally found to be "inflated with 'gahs.'" Nevertheless, he was "the most delightful of speakers."[27]

* * *

Stella showed little interest in the public controversies, social issues, and "blue book" matters that engaged Shaw—a characteristic he gave to the king's mistress—a dramatic persona closely modeled on Stella, in his play *The Apple Cart*. Despite this, she was charmed—as his Edwardian audiences and countless others were—by his Irish voice. She loved his sense of fun, his kindness to her (she later said it had been her salvation during her illness), his mind, and his amazing letters: "Your letters—a carnival of words—how can I answer with my poor whining beggars."[28] Her lack of interest in politics was amusingly reflected in her response when Shaw gave her a copy of one of his essays on Socialism that had just appeared in the *Morning Post* on 13 March 1913: "I tried to read *The Case for Socialism* but I heard a thrush singing all the while." The note of the thrush sometimes sounded to her like his frequent repetitions of her name: "Stella! Stella! Stella!"[29]

She teased him often. At the end of a note written to the loquacious Shaw in November 1912 she appended the comment: "When you were quite a little boy somebody ought to have said 'hush' just once!"[30] Later she nicknamed him "Joey," a generic name for circus clowns, which remained a permanent part of their correspondence.[31] The name, she wrote long afterward, "has a strange significance for me—the tragedy of baffled sincerity."[32] The latter comment was perhaps an acknowledgment of the depth and seriousness of Shaw's love for her despite all the clowning, as well as of the sad state of inconclusiveness and mutual feelings of unfulfilled desire—especially Shaw's, to which her relationship with her beloved "Joey" had finally led. Shaw knew it was a searching nickname. At the end of one of his last letters to her, written in December 1938, he wrote:

> "Joey was the cleverest thing you ever invented, by far, by far, by far——
> —G.B.S."[33]

* * *

Toward the end of 1912 Shaw noted that as she began to recover, the mischievous and even cruel side of the siren Stella was beginning to reemerge. During the early period of her illness Shaw told Edith Lyttelton that Stella had been "half a child and half an angel." However, a partial return to health in December 1912 had brought out all her old "witcheries and devilries": "She plays cat and mouse with me; she teases poor Helen fiendishly: she asks her unlucky brother to play [the piano] for her and then rolls him in the mud because she has used me to make him nervous."[34] Helen was the American daughter-in-law of Stella (wife of Beo), whose accent she mercilessly mimicked and made fun of.[35] These coquettish, teasing, and cruelly manipulative characteristics of Stella, along with the physical attribute of her magnificent black hair, were later directly translated by Shaw into the portrayal of Captain Shotover's "demon" daughter, Hesione, in *Heartbreak House*. Stella's skill at mimicry would be put to great effect in her portrayal of Eliza in *Pygmalion*, a role that of course entailed the skillful "doing" of different voices.

Stella had begun the relationship with Shaw in the rather naïve hope that she and Charlotte would become friends. However, as time passed she became quite satirical about her, referring to her as Shaw's "Old Dutch" and seeing her as dowdy and as one of the "Suffragets,"[36] which for her was a term of contempt. Shaw's explanation of where the telephone was located at Ayot St Lawrence led to Stella's discovery that the couple had separate bedrooms. This, Shaw reported to Edith Lyttelton, brought out the "Italian savage" in Stella, who proceeded to overwhelm him with scorn and ridicule. His feeble protest that a woman needs to have a room "into which a man had not a right to burst without knocking and throw his boots about"[37] aroused further contempt. Any man who would hesitate to throw his muddy boots around in her room deserved nothing but derision.

It was in one of his letters to Edith Lyttelton in late 1912 that Shaw tried to objectify and focus on his predicament. He was a respectable married man. Charlotte might not be as fascinating as Stella, but she was nonetheless "a part of himself" from which he could not be separated. He wanted to keep all his options open: "I havnt the very faintest intention of breaking with Charlotte, nor of cooling one jot to Stella, nor of risking one atom of your regard."[38] The impossible clarity of this view of the situation would not, however, remain undisturbed.

* * *

On 7 January 1913 Charlotte made a brief entry in her engagement diary: "GBS told me about Mrs. P.C."[39] The diary shows that she had further talks on this unhappy subject in January and February. In a letter to Stella dated 6 February 1913 Shaw reported her sad words to him as they parted that day: "I never know now where you spend your afternoons. Once I never thought about it—never doubted. Now I always imagine." In the same letter he told Stella that following his death an inscription should be placed at 12 Hinde Street, the address of her nursing home, reading: HERE A GREAT MAN FOUND HAPPINESS.[40]

The "great man," however, was causing great unhappiness to Charlotte. Charlotte was deeply angry, jealous, and upset about her feeling of displacement as the most important woman in Shaw's life.[41] She made painful discoveries, such as when she came across reminders of appointments with "Stella" that the latter had mischievously scribbled into Shaw's engagement diary. In one week five such entries appeared. (It was no surprise that Stella once signed herself "la dangereuse" at the end of a letter to Shaw.)[42] On another occasion Charlotte overheard an intimate conversation that Shaw conducted with Stella on the fateful telephone at Ayot St Lawrence.

In the early months of 1913 Shaw's feelings of restlessness and sense of being trapped within the married state—about which he seemed to be throwing out hints in the speeches he gave Collins, the greengrocer, in his 1908 play *Getting Married* and in other Edwardian and early Georgian plays—became chronic. "I am in custody down here," he said in a letter to Stella dated 4 January from Ayot St Lawrence, prior to arranging another clandestine meeting with her in London on the following day.[43] He went through an extraordinary range of feelings about Charlotte, some of them charged with great animosity, others with acute guilt.

In April Shaw reported to Stella that Charlotte had emerged from a state of "sick hatred and fury," but that she had now changed from "a fiend" into a disquietingly cheerful "green eyed mermaid." She was now feeling superior to these two "barefooted playmates" (Shaw's expression), who were behaving so childishly, and her hatred had turned to "boundless contempt . . . almost a joyous contempt."[44] The following month Shaw told Stella that he was feeling "torn to bits," suffering "a sort of angina pectoris" from the whole situation, the pain of which had been reawakened.[45] Charlotte had just overheard the telephone conversation, and Shaw could hardly bear to see her suffer: "I must, it seems, murder myself or else murder her."[46] Just as Jenny Patterson had seen herself as "the weak one" in her relationship with Shaw, he now perceived Charlotte as such in this triangular affair: "It is hard that the weak should suffer the most," he wrote to Stella, clearly underestimating Charlotte's strength.[47]

* * *

Shaw's falling in love with Stella Campbell coincided with another major event in his personal life: the final illness and death of his mother, Lucinda Elizabeth Shaw. His relationship with Stella—a "friend who understands about one's mother, and other feelings"[48] prompted several reflections about his mother on Shaw's part, and their correspondence reveals information about her that is not supplied in other sources. One learns, for example, that his mother played chess with Shaw when he was a child and used to give him the friendly warning "prise to your queen" when he had put that piece, the most valuable in the game, in danger of being captured.[49] He reported to Stella that following her death his sister Lucy discovered among their mother's belongings "the cap I used to wear as a baby."[50] And it was to Stella Campbell that Shaw—in a letter written on 22 February 1913, the day of his mother's funeral—provided the remarkable description of her cremation ("my mother became that beautiful fire") referred to in an earlier chapter.[51]

As she was approaching her eighty-second birthday, and shortly after the beginning of her son's affair with Stella Campbell, Bessie Shaw suffered some serious health setbacks. In a letter to Lady Stanley of 18 May 1903 Shaw mentioned some kind of collapse—probably a mild stroke—that his mother had suffered before that date but from which she had recovered well. In August 1912 she suffered the first of three serious, paralyzing strokes that were to lead to her death on February 19 the following year. Lucy Shaw wrote: "The illness was long and trying for the lookers on, although she did not suffer at all from beginning to end. She was unconscious for 16 weeks and passed out in her sleep so quietly and imperceptibly that I could not believe it when they said she was gone."[52]

* * *

Although there are no signs that Shaw's mother exercised any overt control over Shaw's behavior as an adult in the form of counsel or reproof, there is quite possibly an echo of his mother's influence with respect to the affair with Stella in the portrayal of one of the conscience-stricken husbands in the play

Overruled, which he began on 2 July 1912, six days after the momentous reading of *Pygmalion* at Stella's house. The behavior of Gregory Lunn in his amorous affair with Mrs. Juno makes him seem one of Shaw's most direct comic self-portraits. In his joyous rapture over falling in love with Mrs. Juno, Gregory feels suddenly possessed by ecstatic forces beyond his control—and assailed by guilt: "I'm against this. I have been pushed over a precipice. I'm innocent. This wild joy, this exquisite tenderness, this ascent into heaven can thrill me to the uttermost fibre of my heart [*with a gesture of ecstasy she hides her face on his shoulder*]; but it cant subdue my mind or corrupt my conscience, which still shouts to the skies that I'm not a willing partner to this outrageous conduct. I repudiate the bliss with which you are filling me."

It had previously been revealed that the chief driving force in the workings of Gregory's conscience is a promise he made to his mother "never to make love to a married woman," exacted because she herself had suffered from an extramarital affair engaged in by her husband. In response to Mrs. Juno's contemptuous attitude ("Really! To hear a grown-up man talking about promises to his mother!"), Gregory says: "Yes, yes: I know all about that: It's not romantic: it's not Don Juan: it's not advanced; but we feel it all the same. It's far deeper in our blood and bones than all the romantic stuff."

It is possible that as a result of his mother's death Shaw felt released from a major pressure weighing on his conscience, but the turbulent feelings aroused by his love for Stella nevertheless remained with him during the complex events that unfolded in the next six months. By June 1913 Shaw had discovered that Stella had become romantically involved with and was thinking of marrying Major George Frederick M. Cornwallis-West. Cornwallis-West—a society playboy with a handlebar mustache like the one Shaw gave to the dashing Hector Hushabye in *Heartbreak House*—was about to be divorced from his wife, Jenny (widow of Lord Randolph Churchill and mother of Winston Churchill) on the grounds of his desertion and misconduct. On 9 June Shaw wrote to Stella, begging her to postpone her marriage to the "other George" who had appeared in her life and to permit him to live out his dream, which he promised to "hurry through" as fast as he could.[53]

Outwardly Shaw's life continued quite merrily. On 24 June he had a delightful meeting, probably at a reception at the French embassy, with Mary, the queen consort of George V. The queen, "a dear woman, and frightfully beautiful," Shaw reported to Stella, "just slanged me in the most shocking way for a full hour." He nevertheless adored her and parted with "a little blessing" from her. He drew Stella a picture of his heart surrounded by a halo he felt it had acquired as a result of this blessing.[54] Following this, he went on a brief continental tour with Granville-Barker, visiting the avant-garde Dalcroze music school at Hellerau, Dresden. There they attended a fine performance of Gluck's *Orfée* and watched a line of elderly gentlemen dressed in bathing singlets performing exercises in accordance with the theories of Emile Jaques-Dalcroze, the inventor of eurythmics. In one of a set of postcards addressed to Stella on 30 June from Dresden, Shaw provided an amusing account of the exercises and proposed that, after buying Stella a singlet, he would instruct her how to do them and join her in "public demonstrations of the new art."[55]

After returning to England on 4 July, Shaw wrote a consolatory letter about the recent death of her husband to Edith Lyttelton, who told Stella that of all the letters she received "Mr Shaw's was the one that strengthened my spirit."[56] However, Shaw's feelings of resentment toward Stella over what he called his "jilting" by her came out strongly in a letter beginning "Stella: don't play with me," which he addressed to her on 9 July.[57]

The affair was moving toward a turning point—and a wounding disappointment for Shaw—which would occur in the second week of August 1913. Toward the end of July Shaw went down to Devon to stay with Harley and Lillah Granville-Barker and to pay a visit to the playwright and designer Dion Clayton Calthrop and his wife. He left London on 26 July in a mood of depression. "I am no good just now. I am all in rags," he told Edith Lyttelton.[58]

Down in Devon, however, apart from narrowly escaping drowning (again) when he and Lillah McCarthy were struck by a freak wave, he seems to have regained his normal ebullience. Dion Calthrop, in his autobiography *My Own Trumpet*, provides a vivid account of Shaw in holiday spirits at this time: "Shaw, away from a sycophantic world, was pure joy. He swam, played with the village children, stood on his head, talked seriously, talked wisely, talked wittily to my wife and me . . . took numerous photographs, went to the local flower show and guessed the weight of a pig."[59] While in Devon he began the writing of his little comedy in two scenes, *Great Catherine*. From Devon he wrote to Stella, telling her about the near-drowning with Lillah as well as discussing other matters. Struggling to remember the famous lines of Browning, he affirmed that even if she was unable to "recapture the first something something (Browning) rapture,"* he recaptured it again and again in undiminished form.

What Shaw sensed about Stella's feelings in this letter may have been true. He returned to London on 4 August 1913, and on the 8 August Charlotte traveled alone on the P&O steamship *Morea* to Marseilles for a holiday. Immedi-

*"That's the wise thrush; he sings each song twice over, / Lest you should think he never could recapture / The first fine careless rapture" (Robert Browning, "Home Thoughts From Abroad").

ately after seeing Charlotte off on the boat train at Liverpool Street, Shaw went down to the seaside town of Sandwich in Kent, where Stella was staying at the Guildford Hotel. She had warned him before going down there that it was becoming difficult for her "not to love you more than I ought to love you," and insisted that she wanted to be alone at the seaside.[60] Shaw ignored this request and took a room at the same hotel, but he was not welcome there. On 10 August Stella wrote an abrupt note: "Please will you go back to London today—or go wherever you like but don't stay here—If you wont go I must—. . . Please don't make me despise you."[61]

According to a letter of Shaw's written on 12 August, they had arranged to go bathing together on the morning of the eleventh. But when he called round to her room, the bird had flown—with her entourage of maid, chauffeur, and a pet dog—leaving a note: "Goodbye. I am still tired—you were more fit for a journey than I—Stella."[62]

The letdown aroused remarkably powerful feelings of resentment and anger in Shaw. "Deeply, deeply, deeply wounded," he wrote two letters full of wrath and insults on the eleventh, following those up with a third on the twelfth, in which he said: "I want to hurt you because you hurt me. Infamous, vile, heartless, frivolous, wicked woman! Liar! lying lips, lying eyes, lying hands, promise breaker, cheat, confidence-trickster!"[63]

Although the thought is never clearly articulated in the surviving correspondence, it seems probable that Shaw had hoped to bring his affair to sexual consummation during this meeting. He lacerated himself about his folly in being led on by her: "Fool! Dupe! Dotard! Crybaby!"[64] Stella rallied magnificently from the onslaught of this "blind man" and "weaver of words." He was trying to snuff out her "little flame" with his "egotistical snortings." She softened this thrust by adding: "You elegant charmer—you lady killer—you precious treasure of friendship. . . . Do you think it was nothing to me to hurt my friend."[65] Stella clearly thought her departure was essential to preserve their integrity and respectability, as it no doubt was.

Although the relationship was far from over, the events at the Guildford Hotel in August 1913 must have put to rest any hopes Shaw might have entertained that it could be anything more than a stormy and delightful friendship, though that, too, was to be sorely strained by Stella's later importunities concerning publication of the correspondence. According to one side of her nature, Stella was drawn to a different social world, of champagne and oysters and aristocratic friends—a world that her other George inhabited—rather than to that of her dear "Joey" and his "carnival of words." Her marriage in April 1914 to Cornwallis-West, who was unfaithful to her and got himself into serious financial troubles, ended in failure and they separated in 1919.

A significant side effect of Shaw's relationship with Stella was the bringing about of a friendship between her and Shaw's sister Lucy. The two women shared similar backgrounds, both having begun their careers in the theater performing in amateur and provincial companies, and were much more temperamentally akin than Lucy and Charlotte. After Shaw had introduced the two women in 1913, Stella struck up a warm friendship with Lucy, whose health had seriously deteriorated as a result of the tuberculosis she had contracted in August 1899, and who had long since parted from her husband (another aberrant gentleman who bore the name George). In a letter written after one of the frequent visits Stella and Shaw made to Lucy, he told Stella: "You brought out a nice side of Lucy that I haven't seen since she was a girl."[66] On another visit they took along the Irish actress Sara Allgood, who had played Feemy Evans in the 1909 production of *The Shewing-up of Blanco Posnet* at the Abbey Theatre, Dublin. The three visitors performed a concert, with Stella playing the piano very professionally, Shaw singing "all sorts of things in a 'throaty baritone,' while the pianist made fun of him, and Sara singing 'plaintive old Irish songs in a tearful contralto.' The trio then danced a Scottish reel to the tune of 'Wee Macgregor' on the gramophone."[67]

* * *

Stella Campbell was a highly significant figure in Shaw's creative career as well as in his personal life. The affair with her was strongly reflected in a number of ways in the treatment of the relations of the sexes and the theme of heartbreak in *Heartbreak House*, Shaw's next major work after *Pygmalion*, and it is also echoed in several other works. Her personality seems to have contained practically the whole gamut of male fantasies about and stereotyped images of the feminine, ranging from the Vampire—which was also the title of a well-known painting by Philip Burne-Jones for which Stella was recognizably the model—to the Madonna, or "Mother of Angels," as Shaw calls her in a remarkable letter written on New Year's Eve in 1913.[68] The Burne-Jones painting showed "a beautiful woman with cascading black hair in a clinging nightdress, astride a man collapsed across a bed. The woman's face is intent and joyful; her teeth are long and sharp."[69]

The vampire image is recalled in *Heartbreak House* in Hector's cry about the Shotover daughters ("Vampire women, demon women") and in one of Shaw's letters to Stella, which mentions the characters in his plays for which she was the model: "Why, oh why, do you get nothing out of me, though I get everything out of you? Mrs. Hesione Hushabye in *Heartbreak House*, the Serpent in *Methuselah* whom I always hear speaking with your voice, and Orinthia [in *The Apple Cart*]: all you, to say nothing of Eliza, who was only a joke. You are the Vamp, and I the victim; yet it is I who suck your blood."[70]

The "Vamp," however, had another side to her as a forgiving, tender mother. In his personal life Stella Campbell unlocked emotional depths and acknowledgments of need in Shaw as no other person had been able to do. To the man who prided himself on his immunity to sentimentality and romance, the relationship opened up prospects of emotional permissiveness and gratification that were missing in his ordinary life. In a letter written on 13 March 1913 he provided an acutely perceptive description of his predicament of being in love with this maternal siren:

> To miss the resistance that has become to me what water is to a fish, to hear tones in a human voice that I have never heard before, to have it taken for granted that I am a child and want to be happy, to draw the sword for the duel of sex with cunning confidence in practised skill and a brass breastplate, and suddenly find myself in the arms of a mother—a young mother, and with a child in my own arms who is yet a woman: all this plunges me into the wildest terror as if I were suddenly in the air thousands of feet above the rocks or the sea. . . . Here I am caught up again . . . in an ecstasy which must be delirious and presently end in my falling headlong to destruction.[71]

In this letter the experience of being unmanned and becoming a child again is one of delight mingled with terror, and part of a shared and sophisticated game of Peter Pan and Wendy. After receiving a letter from Shaw in which he signed off with:

> oh loveliest doveliest babiest
> Your gabiest
> G.B.S.[72]

she replied: "Its good for you to be with children—to play in the nursery of my heart."[73] They were both experiencing a kind of second childhood, living out the fantasy of perpetual youth that J. M. Barrie had so memorably deployed in his remarkably successful Edwardian play *Peter Pan and Wendy*, a work that Shaw and Stella both knew very well. It was this aspect of the relationship that Max Beerbohm seized on in a brilliant series of satirical drawings—created after some of the Shaw-Campbell correspondence had been published in Stella's book *My Life and Some Letters* (1922)—showing the two frolicsome, middle-aged lovers playing at being children.[74]

* * *

In some ways the history of Shaw's *Pygmalion* as a literary text, as a text in performance, and as a work that has been subject to major transformations as a result of its adaptation to the media of film and musical comedy, is the story of a lost masterpiece—or, if not lost, substantially altered and obscured. It is one of his finest comedies, and it was a triumphant close to the pre–World War I phase of his career as a dramatist. Yet it is also a fascinating example of the ways in which texts—especially but not exclusively dramatic texts—take on lives and meanings of their own once they are launched into the world. Shaw struggled to maintain authorial control over the meaning of "his" text. However, like the statue of Galatea that Pygmalion creates, according to the classical legend, which the title and dramatic narrative of the play recall, the work sprang into independent life as soon as its creator had finished his work. This process began in the very first production of the play, which had a sensational opening, with Mrs. Patrick Campbell playing Eliza Doolittle and Sir Herbert Beerbohm Tree playing Professor Henry Higgins, at Her Majesty's Theatre, London, on 11 April 1914.

Even the first-night audience played a part in wresting the play from authorial control. Shaw provided a graphic account of the occasion to Charlotte, who, unable to face the publicity that the play—and Mrs. Patrick Campbell's role in it—attracted, had decided to travel to America with Lena Ashwell and Dr. James Porter Mills[75] and his wife. She departed on 8 April, unaware that Stella had become married. For the audience as a whole, the opening night was a huge success. Shaw, however, told Charlotte that for the last two acts he "writhed in hell."

The work he had created was already out of control. First of all, even before the last two acts, the performance was "nearly wrecked" by the audience's laughter at Eliza Doolittle's exclamation, in response to Freddy's inquiry as to whether she intends to walk across the park, "Not bloody likely. I am going in a taxi." The 1914 audience found this Cockney departure from the norm of polite drawing-room conversation excruciatingly funny. "They laughed themselves into such utter abandonment and disorder," wrote Shaw, "that it was really doubtful for some time whether they could recover themselves and let the play go on."[76]

It was not the first time "bloody" had been used as an intensive on the English stage. Examples occur in drama of the Restoration period, when it was fairly commonly used in asseverative senses. By Victorian and Edwardian times, however, it had dropped out of polite use, although it was still being employed by people in the lower ranks of society. What made it particularly sensational in Shaw's play were contextual factors: the polite drawing room setting of Mrs. Higgins's at home in Chelsea; the fact that it sprang spontaneously from the lips of Eliza, who is supposed to be learning to conduct herself and speak in the manner of a duchess; and the broader social context supplied by the audience itself, which would have been mainly made up of people who belonged to much the same social class as Mrs. Higgins. Yet even in advance newspaper publicity the use of a "certain forbidden word" by Mrs. Patrick Campbell—which was going to cause THE BIGGEST THEATRICAL SENSATION FOR MANY YEARS—tended to dwarf other significations the play carried.[77] It came to be known as the play that had *that* word in it.

It was not only the audience reaction to "Not bloody likely" but also what Shaw called in his letter to Charlotte "the raving absurdity of Tree's acting" that tended to run away with the work as the author perceived it. Shaw's perception of the play and of its ending is clearly shown in a number of his statements and his various attempts to clarify the implications of the ending.

In its published forms the original English text of *Pygmalion* was that printed in the first editions of the play, published in 1916 by Brentano's in America and Constable in England, in volumes that also contained *Androcles and the Lion* and *Overruled.* The version of the play published in these volumes has been almost displaced by later editions; the only reasonably accessible text of what can be described as the "original" *Pygmalion* is that found in the large omnibus edition of *The Complete Plays of Bernard Shaw,* first published in 1931 by Constable and later by Odhams Press and associated publishers. According to this first version, the play ends with Higgins ignoring Eliza's "Goodbye" and, serenely confident, casually ordering her to buy ham and cheese, a pair of reindeer gloves, and a new tie. Eliza disdainfully replies "Buy them yourself" and "sweeps out." Higgins is left alone onstage with his mother, still cheerfully ignoring the rebellious signals put out by his former pupil:

> MRS HIGGINS. I'm afraid you've spoilt that girl, Henry. But never mind, dear: I'll buy you the tie and gloves.
>
> HIGGINS. [*sunnily*] Oh, don't bother. She'll buy em all right enough. Goodbye.
>
> *They kiss, Mrs. Higgins runs out. Higgins, left alone, rattles his cash in his pocket; chuckles; and disports himself in a highly self-satisfied manner.*

It is a richly suggestive ending, showing the incorrigible Higgins in a comical state of hubris, with very strong hints that he may be taking one step too far in his serene confidence about Eliza's loyalty. The original ending picks up clear indications, dropped earlier in the play, that Higgins's most comfortable relation with members of the opposite sex is that with his mother or women like her ("my idea of a lovable woman is something as like you as possible");

and the rattling of cash in his pockets recalls the disquieting suggestion of property ownership in his relation with Eliza, which is present as a leitmotif in the dialogue from very early in the play. The final quarrel between Higgins and Eliza suggests that Higgins's confidence of the continuation of his ownership might well be misplaced.

Shaw made numerous attempts to reinforce his idea that the play ultimately shows Eliza's emancipation from Higgins. The first attempt was through his coaching of Stella and Tree in the playing of their roles. Shaw's advice to players always shows his acute perception of the dynamics and nuances of stage performance, the significance of timing, movement and stage positioning, posture and expression, as well as tone of delivery in spoken dialogue. His advice to actors and translators of his works into other languages, as recorded in his letters to them, invariably brings us far closer to the experiential texture of his plays than do the discursive essays of the prefaces, which were generally written long after the plays themselves. His various comments to actors about *Pygmalion* are no exception.

For the first production he coached Stella Campbell quite as assiduously and tyrannically (though humorously) as Higgins does Eliza, issuing, on the eve of the opening, a letter headed "FINAL ORDERS." The orders included specific instructions for Eliza not to behave in a friendly fashion toward Higgins at the end of the play: "When Higgins says 'Oh, by the way, Eliza,' bridle your fatal propensity to run like Georgina [her pet dog] to anyone who calls you and to forget everything in an affectionate tête à tête with him. Imagine that he is the author, and be scornful."[78] At least in the early days of the production Stella responded well to Shaw's coaching, having been very conscientious about getting the part right and wanting the play to be a success for him.

The amiable and forgetful Tree was not so compliant. On 11 April 1914 Tree did exactly what Shaw did not want him to do at the end of the play: "I had particularly coached him at the last rehearsal in the concluding lines, making him occupy himself affectionately with his mother, & throw Eliza the commission to buy the ham &c. over his shoulder. The last thing I saw as I left the house was Higgins shoving his mother rudely out of his way and wooing Eliza with appeals to buy a ham for his lonely home like a bereaved Romeo."

The exasperated Shaw "went straight home to bed and read Shakespear for an hour before going to sleep to settle myself down."[79] Later, the "bereaved Romeo" Tree further sentimentalized the ending by introducing the stage business of tossing a rose to Eliza as she departs.

The unruly behavior of the play had already begun. Shaw had written a play he thought was about, among other things, a young woman finally emancipating herself from the domination of her male mentor. In his view it was a play not about the growth of love between master and pupil but about the pupil's regaining, through struggle, her independent identity, thus echoing the way in which the classical sculptor's creation comes to life. Ironically, from the outset the play itself began to behave independently, like the newly created Galatea of the Pygmalion story.

Further efforts by Shaw to encourage performances and readings of the play in accordance with his own strong view of it as a narrative that leads to a parting of the ways for Eliza and Higgins rather than a future marriage between them took the form of rewritten endings. One of the new endings he created was never incorporated in published editions of the play. Evidence of its existence only came to light in 1995 with the publication of a letter of advice to Stella Campbell about her playing of Eliza that Shaw had written in February 1920 in connection with a forthcoming revival of the play at the Aldwych Theatre. Until that time the letter had remained in a library archive.

The last paragraph of this letter not only reveals that Shaw had written a new ending for the play but also contains perhaps the clearest indication we have of his authorial intentions about the outcome of his dramatic narrative. In the last surviving paragraph of the letter he wrote:

> Now comes the most important point of all. When Eliza emancipates herself—when Galatea comes to life—she must not relapse. She must retain her pride and triumph to the end. When Higgins takes your arm on "consort battleship" you must instantly throw him off with implacable pride; and this is the note until the final "Buy them yourself." He will go out on the balcony to watch your departure; come back triumphantly into the room; exclaim "Galatea!" (meaning that the statue has come to life at last); and—curtain. Thus he gets the last word; and you get it too.[80]

Although this "Galatea" ending was never published, another version was published in a text of the play written for the 1938 film version directed by Gabriel Pascal. Unfortunately, despite the fact that this version introduces structural and artistic flaws, the text has been widely circulated. This version has Higgins laughing uproariously at the suggestion that Eliza might marry Colonel Pickering and saying: "Nonsense: she's going to marry Freddy Ha ha! Freddy! Freddy!! Ha ha ha ha ha !!!!!." A marriage to Freddy Eynsford-Hill was also described as part of Eliza's future destiny in a nondramatic sequel to the play that Shaw added to the 1916 published text.

In the opening paragraph of this sequel-postcript to the play, Shaw declared that in using the term *romance* in the subtitle "A Romance in Five Acts" he was not associating the play with the "ready-mades and reach-me-downs of the ragshop in which Romance keeps its stock of 'happy endings' to misfit all stories," but rather referring to the romance of Eliza's social "transfiguration." Despite his strenuous attempts to counter sentimental interpretations of the work, Shaw was swimming against powerful tides. The latter were partly created by himself, with suggestions in the dialogue of increasing intimacy and familiarity in the Higgins-Eliza relation and of their affectionate feelings—combined with hostility—toward one another.

Generically the play is related to traditions of Cinderella-like stories that carry their own imperatives as far as narrative outcomes are concerned. It was the stereotypical pattern of this kind of "romance," much beloved by Hollywood filmmakers of the day, which won out in the 1938 film and in the 1956 musical comedy based on the play. Both have great charm and appeal, and both achieved great success. Yet there is room for regret that a tougher, more finely drawn, more interesting work has been partly obliterated by these later representations.

* * *

In the creation of *Pygmalion* and its central characters—the lordly, intellectually preoccupied phonetician who displays a strong attachment to his mother and the vibrantly alive, emotionally greedy, funny, and rebellious cockney flower girl—Shaw was touching on deep-seated and perennial subjects of interest and conflict in his own creative career and personal experience. In his preface to the play he made the work sound as if it were an essay on the subject of phonetics. Indeed, it is true that the play is a fascinating reflection on the significance of language in social life and the huge part language plays in the creation of class distinctions. His superb comic creation of Alfred Doolittle, the upwardly mobile dustman-orator and enemy of middle-class morality, adds a further element of fine satire to the play's reflection on the class system. Yet behind these "public" and sociological aspects of the play lie other themes that are more intimately related to Shaw's history as artist and man.

The play reflects aspects of Shaw's history as a creative writer which go back as far as the self-searching about his identity found in his creation of such characters in the early novels as Smith and Connolly and their lively female antagonists. There are echoes in the characterization of Eliza of his first London girlfriend Alice Lockett's scornful mockery of the idiotic young Irishman "George Shaw," with his high and mighty ideas and lack of emotional understanding. Jenny Patterson had slippers made for him (Eliza becomes the custodian of Higgins's slippers), bought things that he liked to eat, and looked after him in countless little ways (as Eliza does for Higgins).

Sometimes she could not believe the blindness of the "man of stone" when it came to understanding her feelings. Ellen Terry had chided him about his lack of ordinary intuitive common sense in his relations with Charlotte. Though Stella Campbell was an inspiration for and creator of the role of Eliza, the character is based on a number of important figures in Shaw's life.

One of the great achievements of the play is the way in which it enters so convincingly into the imagination and attitudes of its two main characters, the creation of which richly reflects both sides of the lifelong dialogue Shaw held with himself and with others about feelings and intellect. Shaw was able to portray the interior world of his cockney flower girl as empathetically and engagingly as that of her mentor. Had he written no other work, *Pygmalion* would have assured its author a permanent and distinguished place in the history of comedy.

3.1. Charlotte Shaw on the beach at the time of her honeymoon in 1898.

3.2. Shaw posing as a beggar while convalescing during his honeymoon in 1898.

3.3. Charlotte in early 1900s.

3.4. Shaw in 1910.

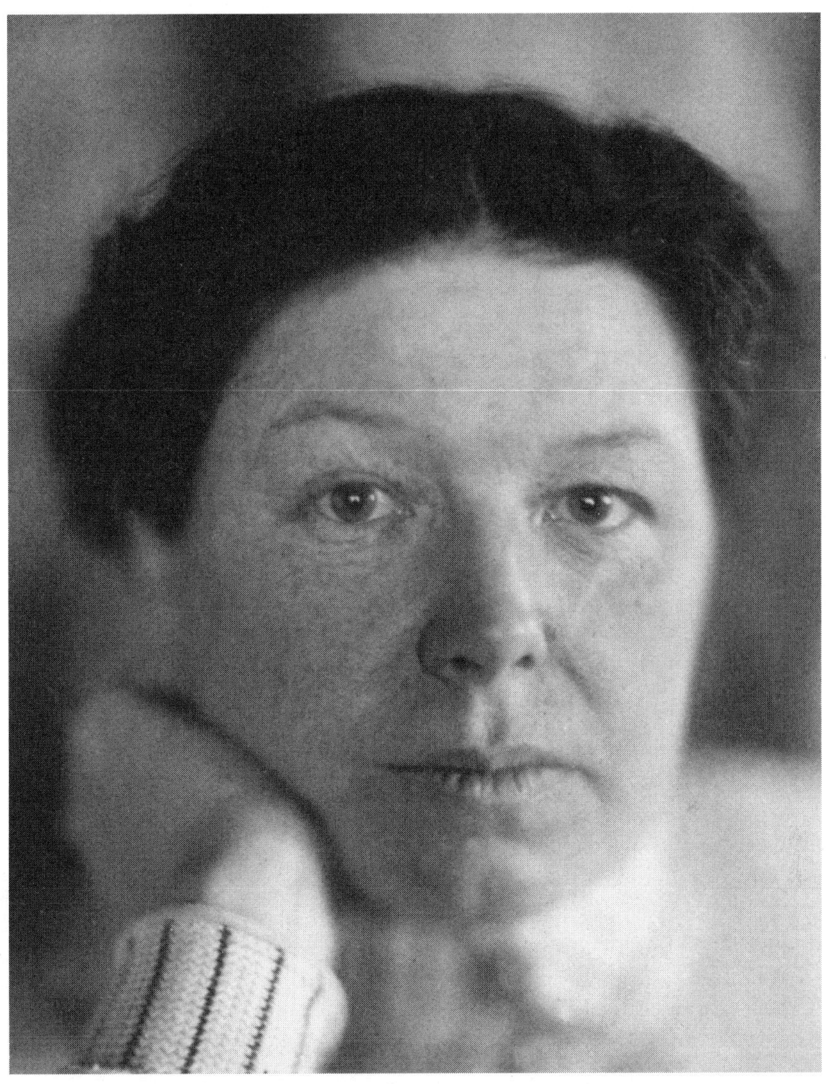

3.5. Charlotte, 24 January 1904.

3.6. Harley Granville-Barker.

3.7. Lillah McCarthy as Ann Whitefield in *Man and Superman*, 1905.

3.8. Erica May Cotterill.

3.9. Mrs. Patrick (Stella) Campbell.

3.10. Shaw at Lady Gregory's estate, Coole Park, Ireland, in 1915 (photo by Lady Gregory).

3.11. Portrait of Shaw by Augustus John, 1915. Oil on canvas.

20 Armageddon, and the "Ruthless Light of Laughter"

Judging by the tone of his letters to her in America written during the week after the opening of *Pygmalion* in London on 11 April 1914, Shaw's relationship with Charlotte appears to have been restored to harmony by this time. She was the one to whom he confided his thoughts about the "raving absurdity" of Tree's acting in the part of Higgins, the huge press attention to "Not bloody likely," and "tomfooleries" that had developed in the production, from which he had absented himself after the first night.

Charlotte attempted to travel incognito in America, but while she was staying with a Mr. and Mrs. W. F. Morgan at their home in the Hotel Tudor, Boston, a journalist from the *Boston Post* managed to obtain an interview with her in the Morgans' drawing room. The result was a six-column article, accompanied by an artist's sketch of the visitor, under the seemingly alarming but actually innocuous headline WIFE REVEALS BERNARD SHAW, which appeared on 29 April 1914.[1] In this interview—apparently the only one she ever gave—Charlotte made statements about the difference between what she saw as her husband's private self and the perceptions of others concerning his public persona, in addition to discussing her own interests and beliefs. There was, of course, no hint, let alone revelation, in this article of the difficulties she had recently been experiencing with the two "barefooted playmates," her husband and the famous actress Mrs. Patrick Campbell. On the contrary, she presented herself in this interview as completely devoted to Shaw and his causes. The *Boston Post* journalist, H. F. Wheeler, described Charlotte as

> a matronly woman of perhaps 45 or 50 years [she was 57], yet appearing younger as keen large grey eyes, their everchanging lights reflecting her moods and feelings, looked straight at one through rimless glasses and from beneath a mass of light brown hair. Then, too, a mobile mouth and features untouched by creases of care or worry were always smiling, and added to the charm of her personality, as did a pleasing dress of brown

matching her hair. Her only ornaments were two rings, one with a diamond and the other a plain gold band wedding ring, and a strip of velvet about her neck.

Her husband, Charlotte informed the citizens of Boston, was an ardent Socialist and a strong supporter of the feminist movement who went so far as to believe that "all government should be by women." She wished to correct popular misconceptions about him: "Few persons . . . understand Mr. Shaw. He is a great man, a dreamer of wonderful dreams, an idealist and an individualist. . . . He is not the blatant, bombastic person of popular conception. He is bashful and retiring, quiet and reserved by nature. But he does not let that part of his nature overrule him. He sweeps it aside by might of will when he must, and when he thinks it is the only way to propagate his ideas and beliefs."

Charlotte went on to describe herself as "a Socialist and a suffragist," mentioning her membership of the boards of governors of the Fabian Society and of the London School of Economics, which she helped to establish. Conservative readers of the *Boston Post*—the article was flanked by a notice of the death of a former chairman of the Boston Stock Exchange and an advertisement for men's shoes ("Wide Toes for the Conservative Man")—could hardly have failed to be struck by the image projected in this article of an elegant, charming, and self-possessed Irish lady who held views that would have been anathema to most of them. It was a very good example of the way in which the Fabian Society lent respectability to Socialism.[2]

Charlotte returned to London on 15 May 1914, and by the twenty-third she had plucked up enough courage to go and see *Pygmalion*. The exclamation points in her diary entry regarding this event bear silent witness to her feelings about seeing her rival in the leading female role: "Pygmalion running at his Majesty's. Saw it on 23rd!!" She saw the play again on 10 June.[3] The play ran for 118 performances before closing on 24 July.

Early the same month Shaw took part in an unusual event—in the form of a farcical cowboy movie—organized by J. M. Barrie and Harley Granville-Barker. On 3 July Barrie had held a "cinema supper" at the Savoy Hotel in which various literary guests, including Shaw, were filmed. Barrie then followed this up by collaborating with Granville-Barker in the creation—at a location in Hertfordshire during the following four days—of a silent movie in which Shaw, William Archer, G. K. Chesterton, and Lord Howard de Walden acted as cowboys and frolicked about in farcical sketches, one of which had Shaw rolling down a hill in a barrel. Another of the sketches required the portly Chesterton, dressed in cowboy gear, to paddle across a river in a canoe.

The Chestertonian frame proved too much for the canoe, which sank, leaving only its occupant's head visible above the water, a plight from which he was rescued by his fellow cast members.[4]

Stella Campbell mentions that she was to introduce a showing of the movie at the Coliseum in London on 9 June 1916, which indicates that it was still in existence then.[5] The film was later discarded; a still photograph of the cast taken at the time is the only thing that has survived. In a letter to William Archer in December 1916, Shaw remarked that the film "wasnt in the least funny," adding that "Chesterton has possibilities as a comic film actor—or had before his illness spoilt his figure—but the rest of us were dismal failures as amateur Charlie Chaplins."[6] Shaw was subsequently to have a few meetings with the latter, the first being on 25 February 1931, when he and Charlotte were invited to a luncheon at Lady Astor's palatial house Cliveden, on the banks of the Thames, to meet Charlie Chaplin and the famous pioneer airwoman Amy Johnson.[7]

* * *

In stark contrast to the mainly lighthearted mood of Shaw's comedy *Pygmalion* and the frolics of the filmmakers in Hertfordshire was the crisis in European politics—unfolding at the same time as the last performances of the play and the shooting of the film—which in late July led to the outbreak of World War I. The precipitating event that led to war—the assassination by a Serbian nationalist of Archduke Francis Ferdinand of Austria and his wife at Sarajevo—had already occurred on 28 June 1914. Armed combat began on 29 July with the bombardment of Belgrade by Austro-Hungarian artillery. Great Britain was formally drawn into the conflict by its treaty obligations to uphold the neutrality of Belgium. On 3 August Germany invaded Belgium, and on the following day Britain declared war against the invader, thus bringing itself and the British Empire into an alliance of world powers—including France, Russia, Italy, Japan, and eventually (by 1917) the United States—against Germany, Austria-Hungary, and Turkey.

Charlotte and Shaw heard of Britain's entry into the war at Salcombe, on the coast of Devon, while on their way to a holiday stay at the Hydro Hotel, Torquay, which they reached the same day as the declaration, 4 August 1914. Shaw's first action upon hearing the news was to send a cable to his German translator, the gentle and mild-mannered Austrian novelist and playwright Siegfried Trebitsch, which included the following exclamations: "WHAT A HIDEOUS SITUATION CIVILISATION TEARING ITSELF TO PIECES . . . YOU AND I AT WAR CAN ABSURDITY GO FURTHER."[8]

Overnight the two friends and intellectual collaborators and their wives had officially become enemy aliens. There could hardly have been a more striking instance of the helplessness of cultivated, intelligent people in the face of the huge groundswell of political and economic forces, imperial rivalries, and international power struggles that led to the eruption of World War I.

In the last months of 1914—as war fever, jingoism, and anti-German feeling mounted in England; as a massive campaign of voluntary recruitment got under way; as women were exhorted on hoardings to encourage their sons to serve king and country; as the air was filling with patriotic songs, such as Ivor Novello's "Keep the Home Fires Burning" (the same tune Randall plays on his flute at the end of Shaw's World War I play *Heartbreak House*); as panic spread, with tens of thousands of Belgian refugees pouring into the country with exaggerated tales of German atrocities; and as thousands of young men were already being slaughtered at the front—Shaw sat down to write a polemical pamphlet that went completely against the grain of the national mood. His thirty-five-thousand-word essay *Common Sense about the War* was published as a Special War Supplement to the left-wing periodical the *New Statesman* on 14 November 1914.

Predictably enough, the essay provoked hostility from all quarters. The public reaction is summed up by the Shavian scholar Dan H. Laurence as follows:

> *Common Sense about the War* shook the nation to its underpinnings, generating a fury of outrage and splenetic derogation from the press. He was denounced as a traitor, an enemy "within our walls." Former friends cut him dead at committee meetings and in the streets. Booksellers and librarians removed his works from their shelves. Socialist colleagues took up the cry, with one of them . . . describing *Common Sense about the War* as "insensate malice and dirty innuendo" and its authorship as "the meanest act of treachery ever perpetrated by an alien enemy residing in generous and long-suffering England."[9]

The official immediate justification for Britain's declaration of war was Germany's violation of Belgian neutrality as its forces trampled over its neighbor in the march toward the campaign against its old enemy France. Although he described the war as "a monstrous crime against civilization and humanity,"[10] Shaw's position was not that of a pacifist, and what he wrote about the war was not a call for the laying down of arms after it had begun. His aim was to uncover the real motivations for the conflict beneath the political and patriotic rhetoric of the day. He saw the violation of Belgian neutrality as a pretext for a war that was essentially a struggle for supremacy between rival European imperial powers, promoted by Junker militarist classes in Britain as well as in Prussia and elsewhere. "This war is a Balance of Power war and nothing else," Shaw had declared on 11 August 1914.[11] In *Common Sense about the War* he was just as critical of British politicians—and what he saw as their devious ways of presenting the issues—as he was of Prussian militarists.

As the war dragged on and its appalling death toll rose, disillusioned and fiercely critical voices were raised—including those of such distinguished British combatants as Siegfried Sassoon and Wilfrid Owen—and Shaw's arguments began to seem more like the "common sense" of his title. However, at the time of its publication the main public reaction was one of outrage. There were a few supporters. Shaw's views were in some respects quite close to those of Bertrand Russell. Arnold Bennett praised Shaw's courageous statements on "recruiting, the treatment of soldiers' and sailors' dependents, secret diplomacy, militarism, Junkerism, the Church, peace terms and disarmament," describing them as "the most magnificent, brilliant and convincing commonsense that could possibly be uttered." Bennett, however, then went on to accuse Shaw of perversity and "disingenuous, dialectical bravura" in his account of the causes of the war.[12]

On the personal front, many of Shaw's close friendships were strained as a result of his stance about the war. In a newspaper exchange in December 1914, H. G. Wells described him as being "an almost unendurable nuisance" at the time.[13] Shaw and the Webbs had stormy discussions and disagreements about the war. Lena Ashwell (who played his Polish acrobat Lina Szczepanowska in *Misalliance,* accompanied Charlotte on her 1914 visit to America, and whose stories about her seafaring father contributed to the creation of Captain Shotover and his unusual abode in *Heartbreak House*) also had a falling out with Shaw over his attitude toward the war. In contrast to the hostility directed toward Shaw, Lena was awarded her OBE for her work in organizing theatrical companies to entertain the troops in numerous countries during and after conflict.

While most of the friendships were mended, one was irreparably damaged—that with Shaw's fellow playwright Henry Arthur Jones. Shaw's views on the war infuriated Jones, who on 1 November 1915 told Shaw that he was harming the British cause with America and neutral countries: "I believe that England's cause is a most righteous one. I am sure that England did not provoke this war. I am sure that Germany did. These are to me, not matters of opinion, but clearly established facts."[14]

Jones went on, in John Bullish manner, to say that Shaw was generally regarded as a man who had kicked his mother when she was on her sickbed in order to demonstrate his agility: "You will say that England is not your mother—well then put it that Englishmen regard you as a man that kicked and defamed *their* mother when she was on a sickbed." On the following day Shaw sent back a spirited (and reasonable) reply, accusing Jones of echoing rubbish from the popular press: "If you think you are going to put ME off with a sheet of notepaper containing extracts from the Daily Express copied with your own fair hand, you have mistaken your man."[15] In a quite hysterical open letter to Shaw, Jones described him as an offspring of the "hag Sedition" begotten by Perversity, a "freakish homunculus, germinated outside of lawful procreation."[16] Shaw would normally have shrugged off this abuse, but he was saddened over the broken friendship, which was beyond repair. Shaw's attempt to renew it when Jones was ill was kindly received but unsuccessful.

Henry Arthur Jones was party to a more general campaign of ostracism by some of Shaw's fellow playwrights following his further statements about the war in 1915, which included a powerful speech entitled "The Illusions of War," delivered to a capacity audience at the King's Hall, Covent Garden (near the setting of the opening scene of *Pygmalion*) on 26 October 1915. The minutes of a meeting of the Dramatists' Club the following day show that there had been some discussion—resulting in the sending of a letter to Shaw—about "the objection of some members to meet Mr. G. B. Shaw on account of his attitude regarding the War, and the Secretary was instructed to inform him of the fact, and to suggest that he should absent himself for the present." Jones was a supporter of this action.[17]

This letter of advice was not an act of formal expulsion; as Shaw rightly pointed out, was an irregular form of club procedure. However, it was the precursor to the severance of his ties not only with the club but also with the Society of Authors and its Dramatic Sub-Committee the following month. In fact, although he enjoyed the lunches and meetings with some members, Shaw was not particularly enamored of the Dramatists' Club. He thought it too cliquish and objected to the fact that it excluded women. In a measured and friendly letter dated 2 November 1915 to the then president of the club, the successful West End playwright R. C. Carton, Shaw indicated that on the previous day he had announced that he was not running for reelection to the Committee of Management of the Society of Authors, and this would mean discontinuation of his membership of the Dramatic Sub-Committee, whose membership overlapped with that of the Dramatists' Club. Two of Shaw's major, interrelated professional associations were thus in the process of being dissolved: "Next year there will be no Shaw on the horizon," he wrote to Carton. "What the devil is to become of you all without your shepherd, God only knows; but the world contrived to get on before I was born (I don't quite know how) and I daresay it will make some sort of lame shift after I am dead."[18]

Shaw had worked hard and successfully to build up the Dramatic Sub-Committee over a number of years, and was well aware that his activities and influence on it would be greatly missed. Having already announced his decision on 1 November 1915 not to run for reelection to the Management Committee of the Society of Authors, he formally tendered his resignation from the Dramatists' Club on 19 November in a letter to its secretary, H. M. Paull, unswayed by a previous letter from Paull expressing the hope—with support from Sir Arthur Wing Pinero—that he would not carry out this intention.[19] There is no doubt that the war and his stance toward it were significant factors in Shaw's severing of these important ties.

During the early years of the war, Shaw—having delighted audiences with his play *Pygmalion* immediately before the catastrophic events of July and August 1914—was an extraordinarily isolated and reviled figure in England. Much of what he said in his forceful and courageous *Common Sense about the War* is convincing. Nevertheless, the reaction of people such as Wells and Henry Arthur Jones, however strident the expression of their views, is certainly understandable. As a result of his Mercutio-like cursing of both warring houses (Prussia and the militaristic elements of British society), his questioning of the motives of Britain's entry into the war at the very outset of the conflict, and his attack on British leaders such as Sir Edward Grey, Shaw was perceived by some as giving comfort to the enemy and as posing a threat to national morale. As a result, he was ostracized by several individuals and groups. There must surely have been a great deal of personal feeling behind the impressive speech Shaw gave his heroine Joan at the end of the fifth scene of his postwar play *Saint Joan*, when she finds that her supporters have one by one abandoned her: "I am alone on earth: I have always been alone."

It was not until 1917—when, surprisingly, Shaw received an official invitation from the British authorities to visit the French front—that he began to return to public favor. Even then he is reported to have joked of this invitation that it was "either a compliment or a design on his life."[20] In the meantime he had written *Heartbreak House*, a remarkable new play that bore the unmistakable imprint of his personal experiences both before and during World War I.

* * *

The scale and horror of the destructiveness of World War I prompted in many people's minds thoughts of Armageddon, the ultimate world conflict predicted in ancient apocalyptic literature.[21] "We lived in the atmosphere of the end of civilisation," wrote the poet Stephen Spender of the experience of living during and immediately after World War I.[22] With the introduction of such instruments of attack as submarine warfare, aerial bombardment of civilian targets, and the use of gas in field combat, the war brought new and nightmarish dimensions to human conflict, with whole societies dislocated and thrown into chaos on a scale never before known.

Several literary works written around the time of the war are infused with apocalyptic themes: the character Birkin's musings about the ultimate destruction of mankind and his expression of the idea that "man is a mistake" and "he must go" in D. H. Lawrence's *Women in Love* (written in 1916 and published in 1921); W. B. Yeats's powerful rhetoric in his poem "The Second Coming" (1919) describing the world being inundated by a "blood-dimmed tide" and given over to "mere anarchy"; and T. S. Eliot's surreal images in *The Waste Land* (1922) of disintegrating cities, "falling towers," and universal conflagration and destruction—all present a pattern of apocalyptic ideas that were obviously provoked by the war. Shaw's *Heartbreak House,* written in 1916–17 and first published in 1919, belongs to this group of works, in which the concept of what Frank Kermode has called "the modern apocalypse" is present as a major theme.[23]

In his 1919 preface to *Heartbreak House* Shaw makes clear allusions to biblical writings about the Apocalypse and its attendant visitations of plague and flood. The war is seen as a form of divine punishment for the "Wicked Half Century" (1850–1900) that saw Darwinism and Capitalism combine to foster a new "religion" in which ethics, human purpose, and moral choice were marginalized in favor of a form of secular Calvinism, a religion that validated aggressive and predatory behavior as part of the natural order of things. The four years' duration of the war that had just ended was a modern and terrible form of divine retribution against this "Wicked Half Century." In the Shavian view of the universe, the Divine resides in and is expressed through Nature. It is Nature to which the pronoun "she" refers in the following passage from the preface to *Heartbreak House,* which is seen as smiting mankind for its wickedness and folly just as the God of both the Old and New Testaments smote the wicked and unprepared with plague, flood, and other disasters: "For four years she [Nature] smote our firstborn and heaped on us plagues of which Egypt never dreamed."[24] Several of Shaw's close friends—including William Archer, Mrs. Patrick Campbell, and Lady Gregory—lost sons in the war. In each case the offspring were not only "firstborn" but only sons.

In *Heartbreak House* there are several ways in which apocalyptic ideas are invoked, the clearest example being the speech of Hector in the nighttime scene in the garden of the Shotover house near the beginning of the third act, in which he attempts to explain the mysterious "splendid drumming in the sky" that Hesione reports having heard, which is, in fact, a prelude to the tremendous explosion that occurs at the end of the play. For Hector this sound is "Heaven's threatening growl of disgust at us futile creatures. [*Fiercely*] I tell you, one of two things must happen. Either out of that darkness some new creature will come to supplant us as we have supplanted the animals, or the heavens will fall in thunder and destroy us."

As the play develops, the shiplike house of Captain Shotover and its inhabitants, leading what the captain calls their "foolish lives of romance and sentiment and snobbery," take on symbolic dimensions. Cultivated and intelligent though they are, the people in Shaw's "house without foundations" represent a society on the brink of doom, playing futile, childish games of flirtation and humiliation of others and being unable to control the drifting ship of state. The capitalist Boss Mangan and the colonial governor Sir Hastings Utterword (an offstage character) provide powerful and threatening contexts for the main action of exploitative capitalism and brutal, imperialistic systems of racial subordination.[25]

Heartbreak House is in some ways a play about large public themes. The "Heartbreak House" of the title, Shaw wrote in the opening paragraph of the preface, is "cultured, leisured Europe before the war." The work presents a society in dangerous disarray that, in his role as satirist and social critic, he lashed with the "the fierce castigation of comedy and the ruthless light of laughter."[26] It is one of his most complex and allusive works, entering as it does into playful dialogue with a number of literary and dramatic texts, ranging from Homer's *Iliad*, through Shakespearean tragedy, to more contemporary works by Tolstoy and Chekhov.[27] The latter connections explain the subtitle "A Fantasia in the Russian Manner on English Themes." Nevertheless, the numerous literary echoes are all modulated in ways that give the play a uniquely Shavian character. Although *Heartbreak House* deals with the grimmest of themes, it essentially remains what Shaw called it, a "comedy." A 1920s reviewer caught some its spirit when he described it as "one of the larkiest" of Shaw's plays.[28]

Apart from its treatment of important public themes and its literary allusions, *Heartbreak House* also reflects in a number of subtle and disguised ways some of Shaw's own painful and comic experiences in the period leading up to World War I, especially his associations with Erica Cotterill and Mrs. Patrick Campbell, who are recalled in the portrayals of Ellie Dunn and Hesione Hushabye, respectively. It is a much more autobiographical play than is commonly recognized. In the preface to the play Shaw places the emphasis on the intellectual and social origins of the malaise that resulted in the catastrophe of World War I.

The preface, however, is more historically specific than the play, where very much in the foreground of dialogue and action are the cruel, manipulative, and often childish games pursued in the duel of sex. It is in this area, which is also related to the apocalyptic themes the play touches on, that Shaw's personal experiences can most clearly be seen to have contributed to the genesis of *Heartbreak House*. In a letter written to his Swedish translator, Hugo Vallentin, shortly after completing the writing of *Heartbreak House*, Shaw recalls a recurrent theme in apocalyptic writings, namely, that of the sexually aberrant behavior of the people to whom divine punishment is to be meted out: "The old Captain [Shotover] is your prophet Jeremiah bawling the judgement of God on all this insanity. And you have the undercurrent of sex continually reproducing quicksand as the welter tries to consolidate itself."[29]

This "undercurrent of sex" is what principally drives the series of fitful meetings, cruel flirtations, discussions, and games of exposure that make up much of the complex, discontinuous, and anticlimactically incomplete action of the play. Also, it is in the treatment of sexual themes and male-female relations that the autobiographical dimensions of *Heartbreak House* are most clearly evident.

* * *

Shaw left contradictory reports concerning the time he actually began to compose *Heartbreak House*, a matter that is relevant to its biographical origins. He often recorded in the manuscript of his plays the date when he began and finished writing. In the case of *Heartbreak House* he noted that he began composition on 4 March 1916 and finished on 12 May 1917, which is supported by references in his correspondence. However, in the preface as well as in other statements Shaw insisted that the play was begun at a time when "not a shot had been fired" in World War I.[30] The most likely explanation of this curiously contradictory evidence is that although he did not physically begin to write it until 1916, the play *was* essentially begun in Shaw's imagination before the war.

When Shaw began writing *Heartbreak House*, he employed the working title "Lena's Father." The reason for this is that his ideas for both the shiplike house in which the play is set and for the character of Captain Shotover were influenced by the stories Lena Ashwell told Shaw in 1913 about her seafaring father, Captain Pocock. During her childhood, Pocock had made his house on a sailing ship moored on the River Tyne, Newcastle, England. The ship became the family home and was fitted out with a nursery, a drawing room, and even (on the upper deck) a greenhouse. Pocock was an imposing and commanding figure, a man of "strong views" who, according to Lena's account, could subjugate his family with his "righteous wrath." She remembered his calling for cheese to go with the bread of the Sacrament when he seemed to be on his deathbed in Lausanne. This seeming blasphemy was explained by the fact that a doctor had put him on a diet that had almost caused him to starve to death.[31]

According to Ashwell, there was no resemblance between Shaw's "quaint old drunkard" Shotover and her father, the "grand old darling with his power of self-control, of self denial."[32] However, there was clearly a great deal in Lena's stories about her unusual father and his shiplike house to stir the dramatic imagination. The resultant character that Shaw created in Shotover—the eccentric, rum-drinking, raging prophet with an acerbic wit—remains a powerful dramatic role that has attracted some of the world's best-known actors throughout the play's stage history.

The most significant influence on the treatment of sexual themes and male-female relations in the play—indeed, on the theme of heartbreak itself—was Shaw's prewar affair with Stella Campbell. As we have seen, Shaw specifically mentions Hesione Hushabye in *Heartbreak House* as one of the characters for whom Stella Campbell served as the model. The qualities that Shaw and others found in Stella—magnificent physical attractiveness and maternal sweetness combined with occasionally fiendish behavior, cruel coquettishness, wit, and a love of teasing—all served as ingredients in the creation of his vividly portrayed and musically named character Hesione, with her "*magnificent black hair . . . white skin and statuesque contour.*"

Much is made in the play of Hesione's hair, and at one point she invites Ellie Dunn to tug on it to prove it is not a wig. This recalls an actual incident in Stella Campbell's acting career. While playing the title role in an adaptation of Sophocles' *Electra* at Southport, her hair was accidentally set on fire by a torch. This caused a great stir; a report in a local newspaper published an article under the headline GREAT ACTRESS ON FIRE, which incorrectly stated that Stella was wearing a wig. Stella's biographer records that Stella was much more put out by this falsehood than by the incident itself: "Stella was rather vain about her magnificent black hair, and the wig charge infuriated her."[33] It will be recalled that in the letter in which he listed the characters (including Hesione) for which he had exploited Stella as the model, Shaw refers to her as a vampire: "You are the Vamp, and I the victim; yet it is I who suck your blood."[34] This playful theme, like that about the wig, is echoed in *Heartbreak House* with Hector's exclamation ("Vampire women, demon women") about the Shotover daughters.

The affair with Stella Campbell, especially the 1913 episode at Sandwich, probably brought Shaw as close to the experience of heartbreak as he would ever come. This relationship cast its spell over the composition of *Heartbreak House* in a number of ways. Critics have often located a Shavian "voice" in the character of Captain Shotover. However, certain elements of Shaw's psychological experience—especially in his relationship with Stella—are reflected and distributed among a number of different male personae in ways that conceal their autobiographical origins—even under such unlikely disguises as the portrayals of Randall, Mangan, and Hector.

In its depiction of male-female relations *Heartbreak House* presents a consistent pattern of female domination involving an initial mutual flirtation and sexual negotiation between male and female figures, followed by exposure, humiliation, and rejection of the male, and his reduction to abject states of frustration and childishness—his infantilization.[35] The two principal victims of this pattern of sexual behavior are Randall and Mangan, with Hector a lesser victim. However, Captain Shotover is also drawn into the web of female seduction and control. When, toward the end of the second act, Ellie takes him for a walk in the garden, Hector remarks to Randall: "She has the Ancient Mariner on a string like a Pekinese dog." This was probably another allusion to Stella Campbell, who was famous for her small pet dogs,[36] and who, Shaw felt, had strung him along in the past. Even the Burglar in the play is discovered to have been the despised and dismissed husband of Nurse Guinness.

In one of his letters to Stella Campbell, Shaw conjures up a comically grotesque image of himself in the role of the howling, spurned, and betrayed suitor: "Have you ever dodged elusively round a room with a weeping, howling, red faced, swollen, aged, distorted-featured man pursuing you with a letter in his hand, pressing on you the documentary evidence in your own writing that you once loved him or pretended to?"[37]

This presents a prefiguring of the sobbing, humiliated, protesting, exposed, and unprepossessing character of Mangan in *Heartbreak House*. As in the case of Randall, the play brings Mangan to a state of complete abjection. He is flirted with, ruthlessly exposed, and casually rejected. "I like him best when he is howling," Ellie remarks of him in the third act. The "low snivelling" that besets him after her naming of the house "Heartbreak House" remains with him until his final departure: "*tearfully, as he disappears*" is the last stage direction accorded him. Mangan is just as surely destroyed by the "mothering tyranny" of the women of Heartbreak House as by the final explosion in the gravel pit. In such manner the repellent capitalist becomes the peculiar fictional *semblable* and *frère* of the author as the desperately disappointed lover of Stella Campbell in 1913. In his treatment of Mangan and the other frustrated and rejected males Shaw seems to have been exorcising in a comic and creative way his own painful experiences.

Another prewar association Shaw had with a member of the opposite sex that is clearly reflected in *Heartbreak House* is that with Erica Cotterill, the fair-haired, attractive, and intelligent young woman who became infatuated with him in 1905 and whose bold advances to him included a proposal of marriage. As we have seen, although he was only in his late forties and early fifties at the time, Shaw was describing himself to her as an "elderly gentleman." Among the developments of action in *Heartbreak House* is the strange announcement by the young Ellie Dunn that the ancient Captain Shotover has become her "spiritual husband."

Earlier in the play Ellie has made the heartbreaking discovery that the handsome man (Hector) with whom she has fallen in love is the husband of Hesione, her friend and hostess in the Shotover household. Beginning as an ingénue who listens to Hector's stories of adventure in much the same way the spellbound Desdemona does to Othello's stories in Shakespeare's play, Ellie develops into a much tougher "hard as nails" character who, passing through a phase more like Goneril and Regan in *King Lear*, is quite merciless in her treatment of Mangan, who has become her suitor. In her final transformation she appears as a kind of knowing Cordelia, devoted to the Lear-like character Shotover. In presenting this portrait of a fair-haired, attractive young woman (whom Hesione mockingly calls "Goldilocks") as initially an innocent visitor and later as the person who takes possession of the father bear himself in the Shotover household, Shaw can hardly have failed to be recollecting the young Erica Cotterill, who in real life tried to take him over as her husband in the years before World War I.[38]

* * *

After commencing writing in March 1916, Shaw took an unusually long time (by his standards) over the composition of *Heartbreak House*. On 14 May 1916 he wrote to Stella Campbell: "I who once wrote whole plays *d'un seul trait*, am creeping through a new one (to prevent myself crying) at odd moments, two or three speeches at a time. I don't know what its about."[39] In contrast to *Pygmalion*, which was written in the remarkably short space of three months, *Heartbreak House* took more than a year to complete. During this period events occurred in Shaw's life that provided him with more material for the play. In particular, two episodes in his life in 1916—his presence at a country house party in Sussex and his witnessing a German zeppelin being shot down near his home—added to the biographical matrix that helped shape *Heartbreak House*.

* * *

In June 1916 Shaw went on a walking tour with the Webbs, which concluded with a stay at Wyndham Croft, a house near Crawley, in West Sussex, about midway between London and Brighton, where they were joined in the middle of the month by Charlotte. From the seventeenth to the nineteenth the house party was enlarged by a visit from Virginia and Leonard Woolf. This gathering in Sussex was recalled by Shaw in a remarkable concluding paragraph of a letter to Virginia Woolf dated 10 May 1940, which refers to *Heartbreak House*:

> There is a play of mine called Heartbreak House which I always connect with you because I conceived it in that house somewhere in Sussex where I first met you and, of course, fell in love with you. I suppose every man did.
>
> always yours, consequently
>
> G. Bernard Shaw[40]

Earlier in the letter Shaw had provided Woolf with some lively recollections of his association with the artist Roger Fry, whose biography she was writing. In a letter to Shaw dated 15 May 1940, Woolf replied: "Your letter reduced me to two days silence from sheer pleasure. You wont be surprised to hear that I lifted some paragraphs and inserted them in my proofs." She then went on to say: "As for the falling in love, it was not, let me confess, one-sided. . . . Indeed you have acted a lover's part in my life for the past thirty years; and though I daresay it's not much to boast of, I should have been a worser woman without Bernard Shaw."[41]

In a postscript to this letter Woolf added: "Heartbreak House, by the way, is my favourite of all your works." Woolf's reply to Shaw's remark about his having fallen in love with her balances some sharply critical comments she made about him, along with complimentary ones, in her diary entries concerning meetings with him. Quite apart from the intriguing revelations of the two writers of their feelings toward one another, the 1940 exchange of letters is of considerable interest because of what Shaw says about his association of *Heartbreak House* with Woolf.

We know, of course, that many ideas for the play were planted in Shaw's mind before the meeting with Virginia Woolf in June 1916—indeed, that he had already begun some of the writing. Although one can only guess at how, exactly, Shaw connected the play with her, the fact remains that the 1916 house party in Sussex brought together a small group of some of the most highly intelligent and cultivated people in England. On the other side of the English Channel the war in France raged. Given Shaw's interests—and reading this situation in the light of the play—it is very likely that he was struck by the complete impotence of the group he was with in relation to the terrifying forces that had been unleashed in the conflict. Several of the characters in the house party in his play are in many ways like those down in Sussex. At one point he has his character Mazzini Dunn respond to Hector's description of them as "heartbroken imbeciles" by protesting: "Oh no. Surely, if I may say so, rather a favourable specimen of what is best in our English culture. You are very charming people, most advanced, unprejudiced, frank, humane, unconventional, democratic, free-thinking, and everything that is delightful to thoughtful people."

Every one of these epithets would have been appropriate to the real-life group that was gathered at Wyndham Croft in Sussex in June 1916, two of whom were important members of the Bloomsbury circle. To Shotover, however, the people whom Dunn describes so flatteringly have become dangerously dissociated from the real sources of power and are thus completely vulnerable to forces such as those represented by Boss Mangan. In his role as an inventor, the angry old man Shotover is busy creating weapons to "kill fellows like Mangan." The house party of "delightful" and "advanced" people in Sussex must have seemed to Shaw just as desperately in need of some way of combating what was happening in the world outside as the one depicted in his play.

At the end of the play several characters seem bent on self-destruction. There is a distinct note of *schadenfreude* in some of the dialogue in the final scene, as though anything, no matter how catastrophic, would be welcome to break the stifling and tormenting hothouse atmosphere. The end expresses an unfulfilled desire for an ending. Hesione and Ellie are thrilled by the "Beethoven" music of the bombers in the sky as the first of several bombs explode around them; Ellie seems to want a second Troy to burn when she tells Hector to "set fire to the house." The two "burglars"—Billy Dunn, the actual burglar, and the capitalist Mangan, the socially sanctioned one—have died after trying to seek shelter in the gravel pit. However, the promise of a cleansing apocalypse fades on the ambiguous, anticlimactic notes that are heard as Randall finally succeeds in playing "Keep the Home Fires Burning" on his flute. The dialogue ends with a richly charged, partly metatheatrical joke as Ellie ("*radiant at the prospect*") concurs with Hesione's wish that the bombers will return the following night: "Oh, I hope so."

The Shaw house at Ayot St Lawrence in Hertfordshire was close to the flight paths of the zeppelins, the cigar-shaped, hydrogen-filled airships the Germans had begun to employ in bombing raids on English towns and cities since December 1914. The zeppelins were capable of a maximum speed of only twenty miles an hour; the drumming of their engines must have lingered in the air for considerable periods of time. On the night of 1 October 1916 an L31 zeppelin bound for London flew directly over Shaw's house, "with the nicest precision . . . straight along our ridge tiles," as Shaw put it in a letter to

Sidney and Beatrice Webb written a few days later.[42] The zeppelin was successfully attacked from below by a fighter plane and slowly descended to the ground like a huge fireball, landing near Potters Bar, a village ten miles to the south of Ayot St Lawrence. Shaw witnessed the spectacle and traveled by motorbike to Potters Bar to view the wreckage.

As was first pointed out in 1966,[43] a passage in Shaw's letter to the Webbs directly anticipates the extraordinary mood of exhilaration that accompanies the violent close of *Heartbreak House*. It also contains the seed for the idea of Nurse Guinness's "hideous triumph" at the annihilation of Billy Dunn and Mangan in the gravel pit:

> What is hardly credible, but true, is that the sound of the Zepp's engines was so fine, and its voyage through the stars so enchanting, that I positively caught myself hoping next night that there would be another raid. I grieve to add that after seeing the Zepp fall like a burning newspaper, with its human contents roasting for some minutes (it was frightfully slow) I went to bed and was comfortably asleep in ten minutes. One is so pleased at having seen the show that the destruction of a dozen people or so in hideous terror and torment does not count. "I didnt half cheer, I tell you" said a damsel at the wreck. Pretty lot of animals we are.[44]

In this candid account Shaw's response to immediate wartime events came into very close touch with some of the imaginative depths and psychological insights of *Heartbreak House*.

* * *

Although it was completed in 1917, *Heartbreak House* was not produced until 1920, when it had its world premiere at the Garrick Theater in New York. It was first presented in London at the Court Theatre in 1920, having originally been published (with its preface) in 1919. The period of the war was not, Shaw pointed out in the preface, a time when serious theater flourished. The men in khaki were not seasoned theatergoers, and they and their "damsels (called flappers) . . . crowded the theatres to their doors."[45] What they attended were music-hall variety shows and lightweight, old-fashioned farcical comedies. The final section of the June 1919 preface is entitled "How War Muzzles the Dramatic Poet," which Shaw explained as follows: "You cannot make war on war and on your neighbor at the same time. War cannot bear the terrible castigation of comedy, the ruthless light of laughter that glares on the stage." When men were "heroically dying for their country," it wasn't the time to tell their loved ones about the follies that produced the war.[46] He concluded the preface by saying that he withheld the play from production during the war because "the Germans might on any night have turned the last act from play into earnest, and even then might not have waited for their cue."[47] When the play was presented in 1943, during the air raids on London in World War II, a special program note was provided for the audience to explain the procedures in case a real air raid occurred.

Though it was destined to become one of Shaw's most frequently revived plays, *Heartbreak House* had a very mixed reception during its early history on the stage. When the play came to be presented in New York and London, newspaper critics greeted it with some bewilderment and a considerable amount of hostility. This does not seem to have altogether discouraged audiences, for the play had 125 performances in New York and 63 in London. The early reviews frequently complained about its length—because of a technical problem the play ran for nearly four hours at its London premiere—and verbosity.

Yet among the early reviews there were clear signs that at least some of the critics were aware of the play's importance. Desmond MacCarthy, a penetrating early commentator on Shaw, remarked that *Heartbreak House* needed only a blue pencil and a pair of scissors to turn it into "a masterpiece."[48] This was the first of many occasions upon which theater critics applied the term to the work. More than twenty years later MacCarthy saw a very good production of the play and wrote: "When *Heartbreak House* is as well performed as it is at the Cambridge Theatre, it is one of the most excitingly amusing and interesting of Shaw's plays."[49] Since the 1920s major revivals of the play have been staged in England and America in each decade, and there have been important productions in many other parts of the world. A recurring feature of reviews has been the comment that the play "always seems to have something new to say to the generation seeing it."[50] The play still divides critics, but its relevance, stageworthiness, and appeal for actors and audiences have been repeatedly demonstrated.

* * *

Apart from *Heartbreak House*, Shaw's only other dramatic writings during World War I were three one-act plays, the amusing *O'Flaherty V.C.: A Recruiting Pamphlet* (1915) and the not very memorable sketches *The Inca of Perusalem: An Almost Historical Comedietta* (also 1915) and *Augustus Does His Bit: A True-to-Life Farce* (1916).

Shaw's decision to make his loquacious and philosophical private, Dennis O'Flaherty, a winner of the Victoria Cross, Britain's highest decoration for military valor, was a nice way of lending moral authority to his hero's tart remarks in *O'Flaherty V.C.* about war and patriotism: "You'll never have a quiet world til you knock the patriotism out of the human race," he tells the patriotic general Sir Pearce Madigan. O'Flaherty's confession that he found life quieter and more peaceful at the front than at home with his Irish relatives shows that Shaw's merry spirit and comic invention had not been dampened by the outcry over *Common Sense*. However, this comment was not regarded by individuals such as the authorities in Dublin Castle as a strong argument for going to war in a work that put itself forward as a "A Recruiting Pamphlet." Even less calculated to please those in power was the idea (which is given an airing in the play) that the Irish would be much keener to enroll if they were told they were going to war against the English rather than the Germans.

Threatening noises from the Dublin authorities before a planned production at the Abbey Theatre had their desired effect on this occasion (in contrast to the attempts to stop *Blanco Posnet* in 1909) and the play was withdrawn. Although it remained unperformed in the professional theater during the war, on 21 February 1917 an amateur production (probably directed by Robert Loraine) was mounted by officers of the Fortieth Squadron, Royal Flying Corps, on the Western Front at Treizennes, France, in a building christened the Theatre Royal.[51]

* * *

Shaw continued to voice his opinions about the troubled course of Irish affairs during World War I—for example, making public his views about the 1916 Easter Rising and the trial of Sir Roger Casement—and made several visits to the country. From 13 April to 9 May 1915 he and Charlotte stayed with Lady Gregory at Coole Park, where they learned of the torpedoing of the *Lusitania*, which resulted in the death of Lady Gregory's nephew, Sir Hugh Lane, founder before the war of the Dublin Municipal Gallery of Modern Art. During this stay Augustus John, also a house guest, completed three portraits of Shaw, two of which are generally regarded as being among the finest of the many studies made of him by artists. Shaw fell asleep during one of the sittings, but John became fascinated by the wrinkles around the shut eyes and continued painting, with the result, Shaw told Stella Campbell, that the painting was dubbed "Shaw Listening to Somebody Else Talking."[52] Although John thought Shaw a "Prince of the Spirit" and greatly enjoyed his piano playing and singing in his "gentle baritone" in the evenings, he complained that the Shavian "monologues, unenlivened by opposition, gained only in length what they lost in piquancy."[53]

Before going down to Coole Park, the Shaws had been staying for a fortnight with Sir Horace Plunkett, founder of the Agricultural Co-operative movement in Ireland, whose advocacy of agricultural reform in Ireland Shaw strongly supported, even mentioning it in the dialogue of *O'Flaherty V.C.* Horace Plunkett, an enlightened and widely respected man whom Shaw greatly admired, was chairman of the Irish Convention set up in 1917 by the Lloyd George government in an attempt to resolve the Home Rule question with the drafting of a constitution for Ireland that would be acceptable to the various contesting factions. Shaw made unsuccessful attempts to be nominated as one of the eminent Irishmen appointed to this convention, which also was not successful in its aims.

Sir Horace lived at Foxrock, on the outskirts of Dublin and close to Dalkey, the scene of Shaw's greatest moments of happiness during his childhood. Before its destruction by nationalists during the Irish Civil War, Kilteragh, Plunkett's splendid house at Foxrock, became Shaw's base whenever he visited Dublin; his friendship with his host, begun in 1908, was strengthened during World War I. During a stay at Kilteragh, Shaw met Sir John Pentland Mahaffy, the famous provost of Trinity College, Dublin, and mentor of Oscar Wilde, and took a photograph of him in the garden.[54]

* * *

By the time of the amateur production in France of *O'Flaherty V.C.*, Shaw had already taken up his unexpected invitation to visit the French front and, in fact, saw a rehearsal of the play on 3 February 1917. He received the invitation from Field Marshal Sir Douglas (later Earl) Haig, commander-in-chief of the Western Front, on 6 January in the same year and traveled to France on the twenty-eighth, remaining there for a week.

The journalist, war correspondent, and author Philip (later Sir Philip) Gibbs, who had initially suggested Shaw's visit, provides one of the several accounts of Shaw's visit to the front in his book *The Pageant of the Years: An Autobiography* (1946). According to Gibbs, Shaw revealed a "well-kept secret" on this visit, namely, that "he was a lover of England, and deeply anxious for our victory." As they were going up to the Vimy Ridge, Shaw remarked: "One's thoughts about this war run on parallel lines which can never meet. The first is that all this is a degradation of humanity, a great insanity, and a crime against civilisation. It ought never to have happened. It's dirty business for which we all ought to be ashamed. That's the first line of thought: and the second is that *We've got to beat the Boche.*"[55] The second line of thought chimes with other statements Shaw made about the importance of ending "Junker rule" in Germany.[56] Shaw's official host, Field Marshal Haig, left a succinct account in his journals of his lunch on 1 February with "Mr Bernard Shaw (the Author and Playwriter)." Haig found his visitor "an interesting man of original views. A great talker!" Poached eggs, spinach, and macaroni were miraculously produced when it was discovered that the guest was a vegetarian.[57] Shaw's own graphic journalistic account of his visit to France was provided in a three-part article, the flippant tone of parts of which was signaled, as Sir Philip Gibbs says, by its title: "Joy Riding at the Front."[58]

* * *

In 1918 sad events occurred in the lives of three of Shaw's closest women friends: Stella Campbell, Lady Gregory, and Lillah McCarthy. On 3 January Stella received the news that her "beloved Beo," her son Lieutenant-Commander Alan Hugh Campbell, had been killed by a German shell. Shaw wrote to her on 7 January expressing a mixture of great sympathy and fury at this event.[59] Close on the heels of this event came the news of the death at the north Italian front of Lady Gregory's son. In June Shaw was in touch with Lillah McCarthy as the final event in the saga of her breakup with Harley Granville-Barker was about to take place. The Shaws met Granville-Barker's new bride-to-be, the American Helen Huntington, on 21 June, after Shaw had written to Lillah saying that "the guilty pair are not yet married."[60] The said "guilty pair" were married on 31 July.

Charlotte Shaw was particularly upset about Granville-Barker's parting with Lillah, and it caused a permanent rift in her relationship with him, which had been very close. She took to deliberately reducing his name to Harley Barker and ordered his portrait to be removed from the wall of Shaw's bedroom. Granville-Barker had almost become one of the sons that Charlotte never had (the other being T. E. Lawrence). According to Judy Gillmore, Shaw's cousin and secretary, Charlotte's affection for him "turned to hatred."[61]

Until the armistice was declared on 11 November 1918, the war continued to take its terrible toll. On 22 May 1918 Shaw wrote a letter to his future biographer, the Belfast-born journalist, novelist, playwright and critic St. John Ervine, whom he had met before the war. Shaw had just been informed that as a result of shell-inflicted wounds Ervine had to have a leg amputated. In his letter Shaw recalled that he himself had nearly lost a limb in 1898 because of the necrosis in his foot, that he had thought at the time that he would be far better off without it, and that it had been a nuisance having to "feed and nurse the useless leg." Making the best of things with a vengeance for Ervine, he cheerfully told him that "for a man of your profession two legs are an extravagance." Ervine would get a pension, and the more the matter was gone into, "the more it appears that you are an exceptionally happy and fortunate man, relieved of a limb to which you owed none of your fame."[62] Considering the circumstances, the jocularity of this letter may well have been more heartening than any expressions of sorrow and sympathy. Ervine himself knew that Shaw wrote with kindly intent: "It was his way of telling me not to dwell too much on my troubles," he later told playwright and theater director Lawrence Langner.[63]

The Shaws spent Armistice Day at Ayot St Lawrence. Long before the final laying down of arms in the fields of destruction, in March 1918 Shaw had already embarked on his major new creative work about evolution, the five-play cycle *Back to Methuselah.*

21 Sages, Saints, and Flappers

Between 1918 and the mid 1920s Shaw completed two major new dramatic works, the five-play cycle *Back to Methuselah* and *Saint Joan*. Although he was now in his early sixties, this period was also marked by further episodes in his career as self-confessed "incorrigible philanderer." Other significant events included the parting of the last surviving member (besides himself) of the Carr Shaw family of Dublin and his acquisition of a new secretary, the formidable Blanche Patch, who remained with him for the rest of his life.

After his visit to the front in 1917, Shaw entered into a phase of reflection about human history and civilization reminiscent of that prompted by his travels among the ruins of classical empires on the SS *Lusitania* cruise at around the time of the outbreak of the second Boer War in 1899. The visit in 1917 had brought him very close to the scenes of action. On one occasion a shell exploded directly in the path of a car he was traveling in and on another he saw a headless man lying beside the road. In one of his letters to Charlotte he gave a vivid account of seeing a regiment of men coming back from the trenches, mouths wide open, in a state of extreme exhaustion.[1] Once again a war seemed to be the trigger in Shaw's mind for very wide-ranging thoughts about the history of humanity.

As though in reaction to what he had seen at first hand of the follies of humanity in its present state, the plays he wrote immediately after World War I were peopled with superhuman figures, such as the He-Ancient and She-Ancient sages in *Back to Methuselah* and the heroine of *Saint Joan*. Shaw does not withdraw from contemporary history in these plays; in fact, he directly confronts it in different ways in both plays. However, the present is placed in the context of very wide historical perspectives. In his imaginative world in the post–World War I period, Shaw made journeys through time like those of the central character in *The Time Machine*, the classic work of science fiction written by his friend H. G. Wells in 1895. The first part of the *Back to Methuselah* cycle, entitled "In the Beginning," is set in the Garden of Eden, where the ancient female Serpent relates the story of the creation of Adam and Eve from the primal androgynous being Lilith. The fifth part, "As Far as Thought Can Reach," is set in the year a.d. 31,920, and concludes with a glimpse into the eternal "beyond" in a speech by Lilith. In *Saint Joan* again the action encompasses widely separated periods of time. The main play takes us back to the early fifteenth century and the life and death of the saint; but in the epilogue Shaw makes Joan herself a time traveler by introducing her to "*a clerical-looking gentleman in black frock-coat and trousers, and tall hat, in the fashion of the year 1920,*" who has come bearing the news of her belated canonization.

Among the elderly gentlemen and sages presented in *Back to Methuselah*, there appear obvious reflections of the new type of brazenly unconventional young women—the flappers—who had begun to emerge during World War I and whom Shaw had mentioned in his 1919 preface to *Heartbreak House.* Typical of these is Cynthia, who is nicknamed Savvy ("short for Savage") in the second part of *Back to Methuselah.* She is described in an introductory stage direction as "*a vigorous sunburnt young lady with hazel hair cut to the level of her neck [who] seems to have nothing on but her short skirt, her blouse, her stockings, and a pair of Norwegian shoes.*" Her father, one of the Brothers Barnabas in the play, complains that she is totally lacking in manners. Some of the characteristics of the flappers of the 1920s were also reflected in Shaw's portrayal of Saint Joan, in the early scenes of the play, as a pert and unconventional young woman with strongly feminist leanings and short-cut hair.

* * *

In a journal entry for early March 1919 Lady Gregory records that on the evening of Sunday, 2 March, during a weekend stay with the Shaws at Ayot St Lawrence, they went over to Lamer Park, the estate of the Shaws' friend and neighbor retired explorer Apsley Cherry-Garrard. On that occasion, she reports, Shaw gave an account of "a wonderful and fantastic play he is writing beginning in the Garden of Eden."[2] The play was *Back to Methuselah*, and on the occasion described by Lady Gregory Shaw read a scene from the fourth part, "Tragedy of an Elderly Gentleman." The writing of the huge work was completed by September 1920. Although Shaw thought it his masterpiece and chose it as the one play of his to be included in the Oxford World's Classics series, *Back to Methuselah* has had mixed fortunes in its own travels through time on the stage. It was first produced in two three-week cycles by the Theater Guild at the Garrick Theater, New York, in February and March

1922. The first British production was presented by the Birmingham Repertory Theatre in October 1923, with a cast that included Edith (later Dame Edith) Evans, then in her mid thirties, as the Serpent and the She-Ancient.

A production of *Back to Methuselah* by the Royal Shakespeare Company at the turn of the twentieth and twenty-first centuries at least showed that it was still stageable, almost a century after its first productions, even if it had to be heavily cut. The lively reviews that this production provoked reflected both the fascinating and problematic aspects of Shaw's daunting creation. The reviewer for the London *Independent* described the work as a "behemoth" but reported that the production had, "against all odds," managed to turn the monster into "a fairly frisky beast." Another reviewer caustically expressed his annoyance at the length of the work and hoped he wouldn't have to see another production until the year of its final scene, a.d. 31,920.[3]

The friskiness that the *Independent* reviewer found in the work is perhaps partly attributable to the fact that although it ultimately presents a vision of humanity that has evolved to a state where sex and other fleshly pleasures have been superseded by contemplation as the principal enjoyment of humans, *Back to Methuselah* is charged with a surprising amount of erotic imagery. Scantily clad young women, of differing racial origins, make an appearance in several of the plays. In one scene a "negress,"* having accidentally left her televisual messaging device running, is discovered in her bedroom dressed only in her underwear, a fact about which she is unembarrassed. Viviparous childbirth having become obsolete, in the fifth part a fully developed seventeen-year-old girl, Amaryllis, is hatched out of a huge egg, clad only in strands of egg-white filament. The Newly-Born joins a group of other young flappers and youths among whom the He-Ancient and She-Ancient wander, uttering their sometimes memorable Shavian aphorisms, such as the former's "when a thing is funny, search it for a hidden truth."[4]

It is difficult to gauge to what extent, if at all, Shaw meant his idea of going "back to Methuselah" to be taken seriously. The idea is perhaps most satisfactorily explicable as a Swiftian satirical device that highlights the shortcomings of the human race in its present stage of evolution. In any event, despite their sagacity Shaw's sexless, hairless, ultra-ascetic Ancients have understandably won few admirers. Strephon, one of the characters in the fifth part, probably speaks for many when he asks, apropos the state attained by the Ancients: "What is the use of being born if we have to decay into unnatural, heartless,

*This term, now generally considered racially offensive, was widely accepted in the first half of the twentieth century.

loveless, joyless monsters . . . ?" In George Gershwin's opera *Porgy and Bess* the character Sporting Life poses the question more pungently in his verse about Methuselah when he asks "But who calls dat livin' / When no gal'll give in, / To no man what's nine hundred years?" Shaw himself was not at all enthusiastic about the idea of living forever. "What man is capable of the insane self-conceit of believing that an eternity of himself would be tolerable even to himself?," he asked in the preface to *Misalliance*.[5] When, aged seventy, Shaw was asked in an interview if he thought he himself would become an example of the idea, expressed in *Back to Methuselah,* of enormous extensions of the human life span, he replied: "I can imagine nothing more dreadful than an eternity of Bernard Shaw. . . . If I were like Ahasuerus I could think of nothing else except my tragic fate."[6]

* * *

However we view them, the Ancients in the fifth part of *Back to Methuselah* belong to a recurrent pattern of imagery in which elderly people are surrounded by youthful communities from which they are radically estranged. The "Elderly Gentleman" who gives his name to the title of the fourth part is confronted by a threatening future society of ruthless creatures, represented by a young woman called Zoo (an evolved version of Savvy) and others to whom conventional human value systems and the language used to describe them have become completely foreign. Primitive marital and parental relations have disappeared, words such as "father," "Miss" and "Mrs." have fallen out of polite use, and blushing is unknown. A "landlord" is an extinct creature.

To what extent Shaw himself identified with the elderly creatures of his imagination while composing the work is at once an intriguing and difficult biographical question. According to the theater director Lawrence Langner, Shaw was highly indignant when he discovered that the actor playing the Elderly Gentleman in the New York production had been made up to look like the playwright himself, declaring that the character was "an old duffer."[7] It was in some ways a gross production mistake. Yet there are several scenes in the cycle that seem to reflect a sense of bemusement on Shaw's part at the way in which World War I appeared to have created a new generation of young people who had lost touch even with ordinary bourgeois codes of conduct and value systems. These were the morally disoriented flappers and young men of the jazz age whose fictional counterparts people the work of F. Scott Fitzgerald. The twenty-four-year-old novelist published his collection of short stories entitled *Flappers and Philosophers* in 1920, the same year in which Shaw completed *Back to Methuselah*. The two writers were extraordinarily quick to sense and chart the social revolution represented by these young creatures of the zeitgeist in the post–World War I era.

Unlike his central character in the fourth part of *Back to Methuselah*, Shaw was the least stuffy and hidebound of elderly gentlemen. The evidence suggests that he got on famously with at least the young Fabian representatives of the flapper generation. Moreover, "frisky" seems to be a fair description of the behavior of the elderly author of *Back to Methuselah* as well as of parts of the work itself.

Beginning in 1907, the Fabian Society had established summer schools to provide opportunities for Fabians of all ages to meet, debate, exchange ideas, and hear lectures. Naturally the sage GBS was a much sought after speaker. He was also involved in a good deal of flirtation with the Fabian flappers. Before attending one of the schools in August–September 1918, Shaw wrote to Charles Charrington asking him if he had "ever tried the Fabian Summer School, with Miss Hankinson [hostess of the schools] to Swedish drill you and plenty of dancing." Characteristically presenting himself as the victim rather than initiator of flirtation, he then went on to say: "There is no remedy for the fact that a saintly old age makes man the sport of every flapper. Women lose all shame when their prey is over 60."[8]

Shaw provided other views of his flirtations with the flappers at the Fabian summer schools in letters to Henry S. Salt and Lillah McCarthy, in which he referred to twelve dancing lessons he took at one of the schools in 1917. The problem of what to do in the evenings at these gatherings had evidently prompted Shaw to make belated amends for the social deficiency—his inability to dance—that had caused him to turn down the invitation to an at home that was to include dancing and to which he had been invited by Mrs. Elizabeth Lawson during his very early days in London. In 1917, now aged sixty-one, the man who had turned down Mrs. Lawson's invitation in 1880 because he felt he would be a "gloomy wallflower"[9] was "going through a sort of retrograde juvenility" and "learning to dance and tomfool like a youth." As he told Henry Salt:

> I was received as a sort of bishop, as became my 61 years. . . . But I soon perceived that intellect was useless after 8.30 p.m. without social accomplishments, and that . . . I should have to go to bed at that hour, or else be a failure, unless I could respond to the repeated applications for the pleasure of a waltz with me which showered on me from the fairest Fabians. The funniest part of it was that I was found to possess a senile and lum-

bering diable au corps which made my King Davidlike gambols amusing to myself and not so utterly unbearable for my unfortunate partners as might have been expected.[10]

"My flirtations are scandalous," he confessed to Lillah McCarthy after reporting these "gambols" with the "fairest Fabians" to her from the school in Godalming.[11] Given the social constraints under which these flirtations occurred, it can reasonably be assumed that they were fairly harmless. However, in 1921 Shaw met Molly Tompkins, a lively and attractive twenty-four-year-old American actress, with whom he established a relationship that was to develop into a serious affair later in the 1920s.

* * *

On 27 March 1920, the day after her sixty-seventh birthday, Shaw's sister Lucy, finally succumbed to her long illness from tuberculosis and died at her home, Champion Cottage, in southeast London. A statement about her health, contained in a letter she wrote in 1915 to her friend Janey Drysdale, epitomizes the courageous spirit she showed during the gradual decline and suffering that led up to this event: "I am bobbing up serenely again, being as hard to kill as 50 cats."[12]

Although she held on for a remarkably long period after contracting tuberculosis in 1899, the last two decades of her life were fraught with health troubles, with much of her time being spent in unsuccessful searches for a cure. In 1901, on Shaw's advice and with his financial assistance, she moved to a health resort in Germany, where she resided until 1908, making regular visits to England in the summer to stay with her mother and her mother-in-law, Mrs. Robert Butterfield. In Germany she met and formed a friendship with the Schneider family, one of whose daughters, Eva Maria Schneider, was to become a nurse-companion first to Bessie Shaw in her final illness and then to Lucy herself.

The strain of the final illness and death in 1913 of Bessie Shaw, for whom Lucy felt great love and admiration, brought on a major breakdown in health for the daughter. "My lung has been galloping to perdition," she wrote to Janey Drysdale in April 1913, "and a halt had to be called if I did not want to follow Mama, which I certainly did."[13] Shaw engaged a leading chest specialist, Dr. Harold des Vouex, to attend to his sister, but his treatment failed to effect a cure. Unable to continue her career as a singer and actor, the former musical-comedy star was deprived of some of her major interests in life. Nevertheless she did have plenty of mental resources; her letters show that she maintained her spirits bravely. She continued to take a keen interest in the doings of the "Super-One" (her brother) and longed for his visits, which were too few and far between for her liking.

During World War I Lucy's troubles were exacerbated by the horror of the zeppelin raids and antiaircraft guns, both of which were in close proximity to where she was living. In fact, one of the antiaircraft guns was located next to her garden. "The din of the guns is horrid, they are all round us," she wrote to Janey in July 1915.[14] In the same letter she reported the sudden death of her ex-husband, the faithless but charming Charles Robert Butterfield, with whom she remained on surprisingly good terms following their divorce in 1909. "Although divorced, we were the best of friends . . . he lived with his rich brother quite near here and was a constant and regular visitor which was a source of never ending amazement to our relations and friends." In "very jolly and happy" spirits, he visited Lucy the day before his death, the result of a stroke in 1915.[15]

Shaw was visiting Lucy when she died in the early evening of 27 March 1920. He recalled this event in a letter to Charles MacMahon Shaw:

> One afternoon when her health was giving some special anxiety I called at her house and found her in bed. When I had sat with her a little while she said "I am dying." I took her hand and said, rather conventionally, "Oh no: it will be all right presently." We were silent then; and there was no sound except from somebody playing the piano in the nearest house (it was a fine evening and all the windows were open) until there was a very faint flutter in her throat. She was still holding my hand. Then her thumb straightened, and she was dead.[16]

When a doctor arrived, Shaw asked what cause of death should be registered, assuming that it was tuberculosis. The doctor replied that the cause of death was starvation, explaining that since the war began they had never been able to make her eat enough.

During the funeral service in the chapel at the Golders Green crematorium, which was "crowded with her adorers," Shaw delivered a funeral oration. Considering the way in which the war had shattered his sister's nerves, he aptly concluded the oration with a recital of the funeral dirge from Shakespeare's *Cymbeline,* which, as he mentioned to Charles MacMahon Shaw in the 1937 letter, includes the lines:

> Fear no more the lightning flash
> Nor the all dreaded thunder stone.

* * *

The same day that Shaw attended Lucy's funeral he also attended the wedding of his secretary, Ann M. Elder, a woman with whom Lucy had been on very good terms, who was now marrying a certain Mr. Jackson and moving with him to India. The huge scale of Shaw's theatrical and other business affairs was such that a full-time secretary was essential. After a temporary replacement for Ann Elder had been found, Blanche Patch was invited to take on the task in a letter from Shaw dated 3 June 1920, which is misquoted in the opening sentence of her book *Thirty Years With G.B.S.* "Would you care to be my secretary?" Shaw wrote. "My own has gone and got married on me."[17]

Blanche Patch had been introduced to Shaw in 1917 at a garden party held by nieces of Beatrice Webb at Presteign, a town in Radnorshire, Wales. She had obtained a certificate of qualification from the Apothecaries' Hall in London as a dispenser of medicines (pharmacist), and was employed as such by a doctor in Presteign. In his letter of invitation Shaw advised Blanche to call on Ann Elder at Adelphi Terrace so that she could see the "horribly poky place" in which she would work "and learn the worst."[18] After some hesitation, Blanche accepted the post at a salary of £3.10s a week and commenced her duties toward the end of July 1920. At the beginning of her book she quotes verses written by Geoffrey Dearmer in praise of her service to "the Sage," which conclude:

. . . I sing
As our undying creditor
As much as Shaw—his editor
Miss Patch—the doyen of her age
Amanuensis to the Sage—
Tell me Miss Patch, how does one start
To Learn to drive an Apple Cart?

Not everyone was as enthusiastic as this versifier about Miss Patch, who became quite a dragon at the Sage's door. Shaw's relations with her were perfectly cordial, but there is evidence to suggest that she was not a warm-spirited person, and that she was rather critical of both Shaw and Charlotte. She was, however, a capable and efficient secretary and practically ran the business side of Shaw's affairs. Throughout her career Patch made a point of declaring how uninterested she was in Shaw and his works, although the book of memoirs published under her name does express admiration for her famous employer as a writer, social critic, and satirical exposer of hypocrisy and sham. The final sentence salutes the man who worked in the little hut he had built as his study in the garden at Ayot St Lawrence as "the patriarch toiling down there at the end of the garden in the hut from which so many shams went up in laughter."[19]

* * *

The idea for a play about Saint Joan had been germinating in Shaw's mind for many years before he began the composition of the work in April 1923. Shaw declared his intention to "do a Joan play some day" in a letter written from Orléans to Mrs. Patrick Campbell on 8 September 1913:

> Strangely enough I have never been in Orleans before, though I have been all over the Joan of Arc country. . . . I shall do a Joan play some day, beginning with the sweeping up of the cinders and orange peel after her martyrdom, and going on with Joan's arrival in heaven. I should have God about to damn the English for their share in her betrayal and Joan producing an end of burnt stick in arrest of Judgement. "What's that? Is it one of the faggots?" says God. "No," says Joan "it's what is left of the two sticks a common English soldier tied together and gave me as I went to the stake; for they wouldn't even give me a crucifix; and you cannot damn the common people of England, represented by that soldier[,] because a poor cowardly riff raff of barons and bishops were too futile to resist the devil."[20]

Shaw considered the soldier to be "the only redeeming figure in the whole business" of the fifteenth-century warrior saint's martyrdom; his fastening on this detail in the letter to Stella Campbell provides an interesting insight into the way in which he viewed the Joan story. The soldier was not forgotten in Shaw's play. His action is mentioned in the dialogue of the final scene, and he is introduced as a character ("*a ruffianly English soldier*") in the epilogue, where he enters singing a song he says comes "straight out of the heart of the people." These words partially echo those in speeches Shaw gives Joan at the end of the fifth scene in the play. Betrayed and deserted by the courtiers and bishops, she asserts that her true friends are to be found among the "common folks," who understand things that their social betters do not. Turning her back on the court, she declares: "I will go out now to the common people and let the love in their eyes comfort me for the hate in yours." In short, the soldier provided an important part of Shaw's strategy in accommodating the story of a heroic individual to a social and religious vision in which the common people have spiritual sovereignty over the dominions and powers of the political and ecclesiastical hierarchies of worldly institutions.

Both in *Saint Joan* itself and in the preface that accompanied publication of the play in 1924, Shaw explicitly associated Joan's history with the dawning of European Protestantism. The point, of course, is debatable. Nevertheless Joan of Arc has proven to be a multivalent icon. Some salient ingredients of the legend—such as the "Voices" she hears in the fields, her claims about direct guidance from God, and her revolt against the ecclesiastical authorities—do lend support to the Shavian interpretation of her significance. In some ways she is at one in spirit with the Puritans of the Reformation period in England and the Continent, who turned their backs on priest, bishop, and church and held meetings in the fields and villages in search of direct communication with God, unmediated by sacerdotal and institutional agencies. *Saint Joan* is a work created in accord with a Puritan temper in religion—represented by such figures as Bunyan, Milton, and Paine—with which Shaw had strong sympathies. He once declared: "I am more nearly a Quaker than anything else that has a denomination,"[21] a self-description clarified by his description of Quakers as people who have "no use for institutional worship because their churches are their own souls."[22]

Since the early fifteenth century Saint Joan can be said to have both created and been created by history. Apart from the fact that she left a powerful imprint on the actual history of late medieval France and of the Roman Catholic Church, she has also been drawn into the service of numerous causes, such as that of French nationalism and the campaign for woman suffrage in the early years of the twentieth century, a cultural phenomenon that coincided with the process leading up to her beatification in 1909. The times made her a feminist, just as the later times of World War II made her a French Resistance fighter. Shaw's treatment of her reflects her role as protofeminist and also echoes his own ideas about gender stereotypes and the ways in which they restrict women's actions and behavior. The warrior saint who disliked having to "drag about in a skirt" was in some ways the archetypal Shavian heroine.

Shaw carried out a great deal of research for the writing of *Saint Joan* and conducted an interesting correspondence concerning the history of the saint with a Catholic priest, Father Joseph Leonard, C.M., a member of the Vincentian order, whom he had met at Parknasilla during the composition of the play. Shaw read—and closely followed in some of the dialogue of the play—records of the trial of Saint Joan in T. Douglas Murray's 1902 book *Jeanne d'Arc: The Story of Her Life*, which supplied a fairly full translation of Jules Quicherat's five-volume *Procès de Jeanne d'Arc* (1841–49). The play was finished in a remarkably short period of time. Having begun writing on 29 April 1923, Shaw completed the first draft the following August while staying at the Great Southern Hotel, Parknasilla.

* * *

Among early responses to *Saint Joan* that have survived is that of Sybil (later Dame Sybil) Thorndike, the first English actress to create the lead role, and her husband, Lewis Casson. In the winter of 1923 Shaw read the play to a small group of people assembled at Apsley Cherry-Garrard's home at Ayot St Lawrence. "We simply could not believe our ears," Dame Sybil recalled. "It seemed to me the most wonderful first scene that I had ever heard. . . . It was extraordinary—and then the way he developed the mystery in that first scene. So daring and true, with that girl who was exactly as I had imagined her. When that first scene came to an end Lewis and I didn't say a word to one another. We both just felt, 'Oh, wonderful.'"[23]

First produced in New York at the Garrick Theater on 28 December 1923 and in London at the New Theatre on 26 March the following year, *Saint Joan* was greeted with wide acclaim. In a notice of the first production in New York, the Italian dramatist Luigi Pirandello declared it to be "a work of poetry from beginning to end."[24] Shaw's old friend and frequent critic A. B. Walkley, reviewing the London production in the *Times*, judged it to be "one of Mr Shaw's finest achievements"[25] and G. H. Mair in the *Evening Standard* declared it to be "Mr Shaw's best play."[26] English critic J. I. M. Stewart later described *Saint Joan* as "certainly Shaw's outstanding play, conceivably the finest and most moving English drama since *The Winter's Tale* or *The Tempest*."[27] Dissenting voices in the 1920s included that of T. S. Eliot, who, however, subsequently admitted that he may have been influenced by Shaw in the writing of *Murder in the Cathedral*.

* * *

Saint Joan and Shaw's play about her were the subject of early correspondence between Shaw and Margaret McLachlan, a Benedictine prioress who was known in her order as Sister Laurentia. A woman of great distinction, she was made Mother Abbess of Stanbrook Abbey, near Malvern, in 1931 and later became Dame Laurentia. Shaw was introduced to her in April 1924 by Shaw's old friend Sir Sydney Cockerell, director of the Fitzwilliam Museum at Cambridge University, who had known her for many years. Kept alive by letters and occasional visits to the abbey by Shaw, the friendship lasted until Shaw was in his nineties. He sometimes expressed envy of her cloistered life and was always grateful to be remembered in her prayers. As the Shaws were setting off for a holiday in Madeira in December 1924, he concluded a letter to Sister Laurentia about Saint Joan and other subjects with the following promise: "When we are next touring in your neighbourhood I shall again shake your bars and look longingly at the freedom at the other side of them."[28]

The friendship was strained at times by Dame Laurentia's disapproval of some of Shaw's later writings on religious subjects, such as his 1932 tale *The Adventures of the Black Girl in Her Search for God*. However, it generally remained a most cordial and mutually respectful relationship, providing interesting insights into Shaw's thinking about religion and the religious life. At the end of a letter written in his eighty-eighth year, Shaw confessed to Dame Laurentia: "I count my days at Stanbrook among my happiest."[29]

* * *

The great success of *Saint Joan* and the international acclaim accorded it must have contributed significantly to the decision made by the Swedish Academy in 1926 to award Shaw the Nobel Prize in literature for 1925. Judgments in the 1920s in such influential organs as the periodical the *Bookman* varied as to whether Shaw or Thomas Hardy, who was widely expected to be awarded the Nobel Prize, deserved to be ranked as the preeminent literary figure of the day. In the December 1924 issue of the *Bookman* William Archer decided in favor of Shaw, saying that "the death of Anatole France leaves Bernard Shaw the Grand Old Man of literary Europe. Thomas Hardy, indeed, is an older man; but his fame is comparatively insular." On this occasion Archer took the opportunity to deliver a characteristic chiding of Shaw for his "greatest moral failing . . . a certain impishness, a Puck-like *Schadenfreude*."[30] In a tribute to Shaw, the chairman of the Nobel Committee for the Swedish Academy, Dr. Per Hallström, took a more positive view of the "impishness" when he spoke of Shaw's uniting of ideas with "a ready wit, a complete absence of respect for any kind of convention, and the merriest humour—all gathered together in an extravagance which has scarcely ever before appeared in literature."[31]

Shaw joked to Archibald Henderson that he had been awarded the Nobel Prize "as a token of gratitude for a sense of world relief—as he had published nothing in 1925."[32] He did not covet honors and was only persuaded to accept the Nobel Prize by Charlotte on the grounds that it was a tribute to Ireland. He did not attend the presentation ceremony in Stockholm and imaginatively arranged for the prize money of about £6,500 to be used "to encourage intercourse and understanding in literature and art between Sweden and the British Isles" through support of translations into English of neglected Swedish works.[33] The Swedish writer who was uppermost in Shaw's mind was August Strindberg, for whom he had great respect. His impulse to reject public honors was exercised on several occasions. In February 1926 he declined the offer of an honorary doctorate from Edinburgh University and rebuked the university for "making a tomfoolery of its graduations."[34] Later he turned down the offer of a knighthood from Labour Prime Minister James Ramsay MacDonald and discouraged a move to offer him the Order of Merit.

Although he wanted to remain Bernard Shaw and to be judged by his works, the tide of fame—and its attendant nuisances—was irresistible. In England the much reviled figure of 1914 had become a national institution, a venerable sage, albeit a clown as well. The baffling character of his public persona was partly captured in the title of a laudatory article Winston Churchill published about him in 1930 under the heading "Bernard Shaw—Saint, Sage and Clown." From being one of his "earliest antipathies," Churchill wrote, Shaw had come to be regarded by him as one of the greatest masters of English prose. He described him as a "bright, nimble, fierce and comprehending being, Jack Frost dancing bespangled in the sunshine, which I should be very sorry to lose."[35]

Meanwhile the price of fame was being paid by Shaw in the form of countless importunities for aid of various kinds and mountains of mail that poured into Adelphi Terrace and Ayot St Lawrence. "The Nobel Prize was a hideous calamity for me," he told his French translator, Augustin Hamon. "All Europe wrote to me for loans, mostly of the entire sum, when the news was announced. When the further news came that I had refused it another million or so wrote to say that if I was rich enough to throw away money like that, I could afford to adopt their children, or pay off their mortgages on their houses . . . or let them have £xxxx to be repaid punctually next May, or to publish a priceless book explaining the mystery of the universe."[36]

Blanche Patch recalled that letters reached him no matter how vague the address: "'George Bernard Shaw, Man of letters, Writer, Statesman, Politician, etc., London' was sufficient; one from a US Army Lieutenant simply had 'Mr George Bernard Shaw, Great Britain.'"[37] Although Shaw was extraordinarily generous in his support of innumerable deserving causes and individuals, some limits had to be set. Since 1906 he had resorted to the practice of having politely but firmly worded postcards printed to deal with requests for autographs, financial assistance, reading literary manuscripts, opening exhibitions, speaking at dinners, contributing to periodicals, and similar favors, as well as to provide standard answers to requests for his opinions on various subjects. Copies of the cards are scattered round the world and have become collectors' items. A typical card, dated copies of which survive from around 1927, reads:

> Mr. Bernard Shaw, who is not and never has been a professional lecturer,* is now obliged to restrict his appearances as a public speaker to special and exceptional occasions, mostly of a political kind. He therefore begs secretaries of societies to strike his name from their lists of available speakers. Mr. Shaw does not open exhibitions or bazaars, take the chair, speak at public dinners, give his name as vice-president or patron, nor do any ceremonial public work; and he begs his correspondents to excuse him accordingly.[38]

Before the end of the 1920s, other forms of media apart from the print variety were contributing to the spread of Shaw's international fame. What appears to be his first radio broadcast—relayed from Savoy Hill, London, by the British Broadcasting Corporation on 20 November 1924—involved a reading of his play *O'Flaherty, V.C.*, during which he sang a couple of verses of the famous wartime song "Tipperary." Several broadcasts of talks given by Shaw and debates in which he participated were created during the late 1920s. On 28 October 1930 his toast to Albert Einstein—in a speech given at a dinner at the Savoy Hotel, London, to promote the welfare of East European Jewry—was shortwaved to the CBS in America, becoming the first of numerous Shaw broadcasts to that country. In 1934 he broadcast an address from Wellington, New Zealand, that bore the resounding title "GBS Speaks to the Universe."[39] Few educated people in the world at the time would have needed an explanation of the initials "GBS."

The actor and clown in Shaw's personality were put to good use in his ventures with the medium of sound film. Invited by Movietone News in 1928 to make a talking film appearance at his home at Ayot St Lawrence, he organized matters so that he would step from behind a shrub in the garden and pretend to be surprised that a camera had appeared. After a few wisecracks, he gave a comic impersonation of the self-important Italian Duce, Benito Mussolini.[40] This was the first surviving example of several Shavian capers on sound film that were enabling people around the world to become familiar with the unusual and amusing Irishman "in person."

* * *

A perceptive aside in A. B. Walkley's 1924 review of the first English production of *Saint Joan* in the *Times* drew attention to a feature of the play that has attracted a great deal of critical comment, namely, the sympathetic—even fa-

*Shaw always refused payment of fees for any lectures he delivered.

vorable—treatment by Shaw of the church authorities in charge of her trial. After mentioning the character of Cauchon, the bishop of Beauvais, Walkley placed within brackets the words *whom, by the way, Mr Shaw is inclined to whitewash.* As later commentators have suggested, this was probably an understatement. It has been argued that "The 'Shavianisation' of Cauchon" (to quote the title of a later essay)[41] represents the most significant example of the poetic license Shaw took with historical fact in creating his play. While this is not a major problem in the play when considered as a work of art, the very sympathetic treatment of Cauchon unfortunately parallels Shaw's attitude toward several sinister real-life political figures who emerged on the stage of world politics in the late 1920s and early 1930s and who turned out to be unquestionably villainous.

One of Shaw's strengths as a dramatist was the way in which he could enter imaginatively into the minds of the kinds of people against whom much of the animus of his social criticism and satire was directed. *Saint Joan* represents, among other things, a fascinating exploration of the self-justifying strategies of human systems of authority. From very early in his career Shaw had criticized and rejected simplistic, melodramatic classifications of characters as heroes and villains. In his plays characters who would normally be regarded as out-and-out villains are explored in ways that show their mind-set and the way the world appears from their point of view. The burglars who appear in several of his works are entertainingly vocal in defense of themselves and their profession; in some cases (as in *Heartbreak House*) attention is drawn to the fact that there is no real difference between the burglars who are judged to be criminals by the legal system and the socially sanctioned burglars of capitalism. As I have noted elsewhere, Shaw was fond of quoting Proudhon's dictum "Property is theft."

Even in the plays, however, Shaw's genial and generally sympathetic views of "villains" can be problematic. His treatment of Undershaft in *Major Barbara*, for example, has been fairly criticized by one commentator as "giving the devil more than his due."[42] Some of Shaw's early responses to the emerging forces of fascism and the so-called strong men of Europe in the late 1920s and early 1930s provide examples of the danger into which his willingness to see the other side of a case could lead Shaw. Shaw's attitude toward Mussolini, who had risen to supreme power in Italy after he and his Fascist Blackshirts marched on Rome in 1922, is a prime example of these dangers.

* * *

On 26 December 1924 Shaw and Charlotte set off for a six-week holiday in Madeira, where they stayed in Reid's Palace Hotel, Funchal. Before they left,

William Archer wrote what was to be his last letter to Shaw. Archer was about to enter the hospital to have a cancerous tumor removed. Although he thought his chances of surviving the operation were "pretty good," he took advantage of the occasion to write to Shaw: "Though I may sometimes have played the part of the all-too-candid mentor, I have never wavered in my admiration and affection for you, or ceased to feel that the Fates had treated me kindly in making me your contemporary and friend. I thank you from my heart for forty years of good comradeship."[43]

Three days after their arrival in Madeira, the Shaw's received the news that Archer did not survive the operation and had died on 27 December. In his preface to a posthumous edition of Archer's *Three Plays* (1927) Shaw wrote that the news had thrown him into a "transport of fury," which he admitted was probably unjustly directed at the doctors who had performed the operation, but which helped carry him over his "first sense of bereavement." He recalls that he returned from Madeira to an "Archerless London," feeling "that the place had entered on a new age in which I was lagging superfluous."[44]

* * *

After *Saint Joan* there followed an unusually long period of silence from Shaw as a playwright, which was not broken until 1929, when *The Apple Cart* had its world premiere in Warsaw. As far as literary activities were concerned, his main preoccupation in the intervening years was the writing of *The Intelligent Woman's Guide to Socialism and Capitalism*, a work that he called on the title page of the first American edition in 1928 "*My Last Will and Testament to Humanity*." The work had an occasional origin in that Shaw embarked upon it in response to a request from Mary Cholmondeley for some ideas on Socialism she could present to a women's meeting in Shropshire. From that beginning it grew into Shaw's major exposition of his political ideas.

Whereas Shaw's plays sometimes present a picture of almost baffling complexity in their political implications, *The Intelligent Woman's Guide* follows fairly consistently in the paths of socialistic thought mapped out by Shaw and his fellow Fabians in the 1880s and 1890s. The title of the work now seems condescending. But it needs to be seen in the light of the facts that its writing was inspired by a woman seeking ideas about Socialism, and that it was written at a time when political decision-making was almost exclusively in the hands of men. The title was a way of rhetorically wresting ownership of the territory from male possession. In its tone and style the guide once again displays the remarkable gifts of communication seen in Shaw's early Fabian tracts, such as *The Fabian Society: What It Has Done & How It Has Done It* (1892). The "voice" is not that of a doctrinaire Socialist, such as Trefusis in *An*

Unsocial Socialist, or an expert speaking in professional jargon. Rather, it is that of a human being entering into a dialogue with other human beings in a rational discussion concerning the organization of society. In a time of great political confusion in the world and when the first Labour prime minister in Britain, the former Fabian Ramsay MacDonald, had come to assume office, as he did in 1924, there was clearly a demand for enlightenment about the still widely discredited and reviled philosophy of Socialism. Shaw's book was seen as answering that need. It was a publishing success on both sides of the Atlantic. Nearly sixteen thousand copies of the first English edition and seventy-five thousand copies of the first American edition were printed in 1928, and further editions followed in the 1930s.

The arguments in *The Intelligent Woman's Guide* are conducted with exemplary good humor and fair-mindedness. The teaching of Fabian Socialism is offered as an *opinion* as to how wealth should be distributed "in a respectable civilized country."[45] Shaw's method is to open the subject up and invite his readers to join him in exploring it. His diagnosis of the ills of capitalism is incisive—and not at all easy to refute. Capitalism, he argues, may be thoroughly benevolent—even visionary—in intention. The major problem, however, is that there is no way of *guaranteeing* that its motives will be altruistic. In two central chapters ("Capitalism in Perpetual Motion" and "The Runaway Car of Capitalism") Shaw describes the ungovernable forces of capitalism in terms that still ring true:

> Capitalism leads us into enterprises of all sorts, at home and abroad, over which we have no control, and for which we have no desire. The enterprises are not necessarily bad: some of them have turned out well; but the point is that Capitalism does not care whether they turn out well or ill for us provided they promise to bring in money to the shareholders. We never know what Capitalism will be up to next; and we never can believe a word its newspapers tell us about its doings when the truth seems likely to be unpopular.[46]

Apart from its creation of social divisiveness and alienation, Shaw argues, one of the chief moral flaws in the capitalist system is that it destroys belief in "any effective power but that of self-interest backed by force."

Shaw arrives at what he describes as the central tenet of Socialism after a careful analysis of various plans for the distribution of wealth. Formulas such as "To Each What She Produces," "To Each What She Deserves," and "To Each What She Can Grab" are shown to contain serious pitfalls and insoluble problems of equity. The "true diagnostic" of Socialism, as distinct from other ideologies—radical, philanthropic, liberal, or syndicalist—that appear to have similar aims, is equality of income. To achieve this aim the government must become "the national landlord, the national financier, and the national employer."[47]

Although Shaw was sometimes equivocal concerning the use of violence in bringing about social and political change, in this work he was clear. In the chapter on revolutions he argues against the use of violence. "Socialists who understand their business," he writes, "are always against bloodshed."[48] Violence does not create Socialism, only waste, leaving the basic work of constitutional and economic planning still to be done. It is necessary to be aware of the possibility of violent revolutions. Even after such revolutions, however, the problems still remain to be solved, and the bloodshed might just as well not have occurred: "In the long run (which nowadays is a very short run) you must have your parliament and your settled constitution back again; and the risings and *coups d'état*, with all their bloodshed and burnings and executions, might as well have been cut out as far as the positive constructive work of Socialism is concerned."[49]

There is a poignant quality in *The Intelligent Woman's Guide* that has largely been created by history. In some ways it seems a work worthy of a sage and a voice of sweet reason in the midst of the political and social turmoil that was to lead to World War II. Yet in the late 1920s and early 1930s variations of its philosophy formed part of the rationale of thoroughly evil political movements. As was quite often the case, the analysis and critique Shaw provides of existing systems now seem more convincing than the solutions offered. In the light of history and the appalling totalitarian regimes created in the name of hard-line Socialist principles in the twentieth century, the Shavian-Socialist nostrums of equality of income and the idea of making government "the national landlord, the national financier, and the national employer" have quite fallen out of favor. Although its positive proposals now seem unsatisfactory, the spirit of the work—its search for ways to promote a fairer and more just social dispensation than that which commonly results from laissez-faire capitalism—remains admirable.

22 The Road to Baveno

Dangerous Flirtations

"Old men are dangerous: they no longer care what will happen to the world." The pithy pronouncement Shaw gave to Captain Shotover in *Heartbreak House* is only partly true of the playwright himself in old age. Despite increasing feelings of despair about man as a political animal, Shaw did go on caring about what happened to the world. Nevertheless, during the later 1920s and early 1930s he was involved in some dangerous flirtations, one in his personal life and several in the political sphere. Two of these had strong connections with Lake Maggiore in Italy, where the Shaws stayed for long periods in the summers of 1926 and 1927. It was there that Shaw's flirtation with the young American actress Molly Tompkins became more intense, and it was in the same location that he appears to have developed sympathetic attitudes toward Mussolini and Italian Fascism, the expression of which justifiably attracted fierce criticism and alarmed his friends. Shaw's responses in the period between the world wars to the two other major leaders of totalitarian regimes, Hitler and Stalin, were equally misguided and remain difficult to reconcile with the more admirable aspects of his career as a critic of society and with the engaging and humane spirit that informs his best comedies.

* * *

Inspired by her admiration for Shaw's works, Molly Arthur Tompkins, aged twenty-three, arrived in London in 1921 accompanied by her artist husband, Laurence, and her infant son, Peter. Her dual ambitions were to establish a Shavian theater and to advance her fledgling career as an actress.[1] The main source of information about Shaw's relationship with Molly Tompkins remains a collection consisting of about 150 letters and postcards he wrote to her from December 1921 to January 1949, the year before his death. Very few of Molly's letters to Shaw (estimated by her son to have numbered close to a thousand) have survived, and she burned all the notebooks containing her recollections.[2] Shaw's letters to Molly were gathered together in a handsome illustrated volume, edited by Peter Tompkins and published by Constable in 1960 under the title *To a Young Actress: The Letters of Bernard Shaw to Molly Tompkins.*

Peter Tompkins's edition of the letters was followed in 1961 with the publication of a second book edited by him called *Shaw and Molly Tompkins in Their Own Words.* Pieced together by her son from tape recordings of Molly's recollections of her association with Shaw, news clippings, and other sources, this work of semifiction is cast in the form of an "autobiography" written by her. While the main outline of the narrative is plausible enough and is often corroborated by other evidence (such as Shaw's letters), the conversations and novelistic scene settings with which the work is embroidered are another matter. On the reverse side of the title page is a note from the executor and trustee of the Shaw estate (at that time the Public Trustee) stating that the estate "disclaims all responsibility for the accuracy of the purported conversations with Mr Shaw in this book, based, as they are, only upon recollections dating from some thirty years previously."[3] Thus, the story of Shaw's last significant romantic association with a woman has to be gleaned from rather mixed sources.

Molly and Laurence Tompkins presented themselves at 10 Adelphi Terrace in late summer 1921 with the intention of introducing themselves to Shaw, their idol, and telling him of their plans. Put off by a not very welcoming maid, Laurence retreated to a nearby coffee shop, but Molly waited and introduced herself to Shaw in the street as he was returning home. She was invited into the Shaw apartment, where she explained her mission. Judging by Shaw's first surviving letter to her (21 December 1921), she was "really pretty," blessed with natural "grace and a fine shape." However, in the conclusion to the same letter he wrote: "Give my regards to poor Tompkins: he has taken on a fine handfull."[4]

The couple belonged to well-to-do families in America and evidently enjoyed a considerable income from investments at the time. The Shaw theater they envisioned, in which Molly was to act, had been designed by Laurence. It was to have "a Romanesque façade with the story of Creative Evolution carved into sandstone." Laurence, a painter and sculptor, had executed a work called "Lilith," the mythical being Shaw had introduced as a character in *Back to Methuselah.* The drawing depicted a voluptuous female nude, with luxuriant pubic hair, reclining on her back with one knee raised. The model was apparently a Piccadilly chorus girl, but the Peter Tompkins narrative suggests that many people thought it to be a drawing of Molly herself; as the narrator of "her story," Molly notes: "Laurence always seemed to put a little of me in everything he did."[5] (Though she clearly possessed many vivacious and appealing attributes, Molly apparently was not blessed with a strong sense of humor.) It was intended that the drawing of Lilith, as the keystone of the Creative Evolution story, would lie across the main entrance of the planned theater. Perhaps fortunately, the idea of this thespian temple to Shaw and his "religion" never went beyond a small-scale model that Laurence created in a borrowed London studio.

Following their arrival in England, Shaw took the young Yankees under his wing, inviting Laurence to the Royal Automobile Club in Pall Mall for morning swims, driving them both on tours around England, and introducing them to a Fabian summer school, where they were photographed with Shaw in 1922.[6] His first advice to Molly was that she should enroll in the Royal Academy of Dramatic Art, of which Shaw had been a very active council member and supporter since 1911. Her first teacher there was Claude Rains, who formed an instant dislike of her—which was reciprocated.

Next, in order to overcome "provincialisms" in her speech, such as the pronunciation of "butter" as "budder," Shaw advised her to take lessons from his friend Daniel Jones, a Welsh professor of phonetics at London University, who may have served as one of Shaw's models for Henry Higgins in *Pygmalion*. She persevered with her acting career, and had some modest success; but she later found a better outlet for her creative impulses in painting. Shaw advised her not to try comic parts: "You have not a laugh catching note in your voice," he wrote from Parknasilla on 27 August 1923, "and must succeed for the present as a woman of sorrows, with eyes like muscatel grapes, drowning the stage with unshed tears instead of setting the table in a roar."[7]

Shaw's relations with Molly in the early stages of their association were very much like those of Pygmalion-Higgins with his Galatea–Eliza Doolittle. He lectured his "Mollytompkins" (as he addressed her) on pronunciation, elocution, handwriting, social etiquette, and diet ("I have been giving you warnings about your vowels and consonants when I should have been giving you warnings about your meals"), and tried to persuade her not to wear makeup (her face would look "much better unbuttered").[8] An early letter expressed outrage when she addressed an envelope "Mister Bernard Shaw." With echoes of his own upbringing in the household of the gentleman corn merchant George Carr Shaw, Esq., he explained that "Mister" was for tradesmen. He was "G. Bernard Shaw, Esquire." This advice was fairly clearly given more to save her from making social gaffes than to snobbishly assert his social rank, or put on side, as the English say.[9] Having begun as Higgins to her Eliza, he later often sounded more like Captain Shotover angrily denouncing his amorously inclined demon daughters in *Heartbreak House*. Shaw soon discovered a predatorily amorous side to his brash but appealing young friend.

The correspondence from 1922 to 1924 was largely taken up with advice from Shaw about various theatrical matters relating to Molly's acting career. However, it was interspersed with discussions of love, which the contexts clearly indicate were prompted by declarations on her part about her feelings toward Shaw. Love is discussed in letters from Shaw to Molly on 10 February and 10 June 1924 in ways that suggest Shaw was fending off the subject with the appearance of nonchalance and detachment he had shown in earlier relationships. In February he quoted a maxim by La Rochefoucauld, one of his favorite authors: "The very old and the very young should not speak of love: it makes them ridiculous."[10] In the letter of 10 June, addressed to "My dear Mollytomps," he asked: "Is it not delightful to be in love? I will pose for you to your heart's content. You will find it described in Heartbreak House as far as it can be described. . . . It does not last, because it does not belong to the earth; and when you clasp the idol it turns out to be a rag doll like yourself."[11]

At about the time of this second letter, Molly decided that she did not want to be an actress. According to her son, "what she wanted was to live."[12] She chose Italy as the place where this was to be accomplished, and by August she was traveling with Laurence in that country, where several Shaw letters reached her. Early in 1925 she angered Shaw—who had been spending the 1924–25 winter in Madeira with Charlotte—by telling him about a flirtation she had experienced with the husband of an Italian lady. On 22 February, after the Shaws had returned from their holiday, he wrote fiercely to her:

> Dont you try to humbug me: you may do these things automatically; but you don't do them unconsciously. You are a coquette according to the classical definition: that is, a woman who deliberately excites passions she has no intention of gratifying. If you stole that unhappy padrona's husband because you wanted him it would have been at least a reasonable proceeding; but to steal him for the mere pleasure of stealing, and throw him away, is a wanton exercise of power. . . . I suppose it is no use telling you to be careful. Coquettes and philanderers are incorrigible.[13]

In the incorrigible coquette the "incorrigible philanderer" had found his match. Shaw went on in this letter to recall Edith Nesbit's complaint to him when he refused her advances ("You had no right to write the preface if you were not going to write the book"), accusing Molly of doing exactly the same thing with the "prefaces" she was going about the world writing without any intention of following through with "the book." This letter itself, however, was one of Shaw's own philandering "prefaces," and in a lengthy postscript he confessed: "I am very nearly as bad as you."

* * *

It was during the summers of 1926 and 1927, by the shores of Lake Maggiore in Piedmont, Italy, that the most intense—and sexually consummated—phase of the relationship between Shaw and Molly Tompkins occurred. The Tompkins' travels to Italy in the summer of 1925 had taken them to Baveno, a picturesque village on the southwest shore of the lake, about two miles from the larger lakeside resort of Stresa. While staying at the Hotel Bellevue in Baveno, Molly and Laurence conceived the idea of renting a villa on one of the Borromean islands on the lake. They met Vitaliano Borromeo, a member of the aristocratic family that owned the islands, and negotiated a greatly reduced rent for one of them, Isola San Giovanni, and its villa. However, they did not take up residence there until 1927,* after renovations had been completed to the villa; in the meantime, during the winter of 1925–26, they moved to Paris, where Laurence established a studio.

In January 1926 Shaw wrote to Molly one evening from Ayot St Lawrence while Charlotte had decided to go up to town. It was a mild evening, with Shaw sitting with his typewriter on his knees "like a sailor with his lass" listening to Mozart's "A Little Night Music" on the wireless. Having established an air of clandestine communication in this letter, Shaw broached the subject of the physical side of their relationship. He wrote about his resistance in old age to being kissed and fondled by women, as well as his reluctance to take advantage of his fame and assume that young female admirers would like themselves to be "pawed" by him. "There is a shyness of age as well as of youth," he wrote, "and that is the only reason why a man, especially an old man, does not always devour his natural prey." Her romance with him had lasted a long time without being spoiled, and there were times when she wanted to "consummate it." He went on, somewhat enigmatically: "But these things do not fit into words and arguments. They belong to the Elysian fields . . . into which we both want to escape to meet each other, and in which we shall never meet except in imagination. But we shall do as well on this solid earth as we need; for next time you will not be so tongue tied to say the least."[14]

---

*Beginning in 1927, the Tompkins made the villa their permanent home until their losses in the Wall Street crash of 1929 forced them to give it up in 1931. See *To a Young Actress*, 96.

In late summer 1926 the Shaws traveled to Stresa for a holiday, departing on 4 August (shortly after his seventieth birthday) and making their way to the grand Regina Palace Hotel overlooking Lake Maggiore. Shaw arrived in a state of exhaustion ("I left London stupid with fatigue," he told Molly), a condition exacerbated by a feverish malady he contracted in Italy itself.[15] His health and spirits soon recovered thanks to boating, bathing, enjoyable conversations about music with the conductor Albert Coates (who had a villa on the lake), and socializing with his circle, which included the English writer Cecil Lewis and his Russian wife, "Dooshka." Part of his time was occupied in sitting for a small seated figure and a bust of him by the sculptor Prince Paul Troubetskoy, creator of the statue of Shaw now in the National Gallery of Ireland.[16] Troubetskoy, Charlotte told Beatrice Webb in a letter from Stresa, had "a villa on the Lake, a big studio & an astonishing wife."[17]

Both Shaws immediately became interested in identifying "Molly's" island on the lake, sending postcards to her in Paris depicting several of the islands with which the lake is studded. Molly must have set them right by 8 August, when Shaw sent a letter saying that he had exchanged his "poetic" feelings about the idea of leasing one of the islands to those of a "house agent" upon discovering that the tiny Isola San Giovanni was directly off Pallanza, on the opposite side of the lake from Baveno, and practically part of the garden of a huge hotel. Practical questions from the former employee at an estate agency in Dublin, and borough councillor in London with an interest in drains, followed. Did she realize that the "Grand Hotel Pallanza, with its jazzings, is right on top of you?" Had she found out about the drainage in Pallanza, "to say nothing of the drainage of S. Giovanni?"[18] Charlotte sent her a postcard of the island on 22 August, followed by a friendly and kindly letter on 10 September.[19]

During the weekend of 18–19 September 1926, Molly, having sent a telegram announcing her visit, arrived at Lake Maggiore from Paris. For reasons which can only be surmised but which involved what Shaw perceived as poor behavior ("tomfoolery") on Molly's part, the visit began badly: a stormy exchange of letters and notes immediately erupted between Shaw and the "little beast," who, at one point, had left a curt note saying she was returning immediately to Paris.[20] After this, however, things appear to have settled down, and it was during the fortnight immediately following her arrival at the lake—before the Shaws returned to England on 4 October—that the first period of happiness between the two occurred. A principal location of those times was the lakeside road to Baveno from Stresa, along which Shaw accompanied Molly back to the Hotel Bellevue after dinners at the Regina Palace. In the words given to Molly in her son's book of her reminiscences: "There were sun-filled days and quiet evenings, and every night Shaw would walk me to Baveno and then I would walk back with him halfway to Stresa and then he would return again to leave me at Baveno on the steps of the Bellevue, striding off into the night."[21] The phrase "the road to Baveno" was to become a shorthand expression in Shaw's and Molly's later correspondence about what transpired between them in Italy.

Shaw and Charlotte returned to Stresa in 1927 for another lengthy stay that lasted from late July to early October, by which time Molly and her family had taken up residence in the villa on Isola San Giovanni. The Tompkins narrative records regular visits there by the Shaws by boat from the Regina Palace in the mornings for swimming and picnics. In the afternoons, while Laurence worked and Charlotte read, Shaw and Molly explored the hills and townships surrounding the lake in her Renault. A passage of the Molly Tompkins "autobiography" created by her son conjures up a romantic scene where she and Shaw are said to have parked the car in a secluded copse along the banks of the Toce River. As they lay on a sandy bank by the river, she says that Shaw suggested she write his biography. She replied that she didn't know anything about him except what he was to her, and they "talked and talked about his relations with women." Her narrative continues: "At the end I stretched and said: 'I'm so full of you, and the river, and trees, and sweetness, but still I couldn't write your life. I would make a fool of you and myself.'"[22]

It was not until 2004 that Peter Tompkins released a 1944 letter from Shaw to Molly that unequivocally confirms what some commentators (including the present writer) had assumed to be the case, that the affair was sexually consummated. In this letter, written after the death of Charlotte, Shaw inquired about the fortunes of Molly's now-divorced husband and went on to ask: "Did any of your numerous Sunday husbands, of whom I was certainly the most eminent, really fail to respect Lawrence's [*sic*] conjugal rights as we did. I hope he never suspected me of 'betraying' him. Yet no consummated love affair ever gave me greater pleasure."[23]

Several references to their experiences on the road to Baveno in Shaw's previously published correspondence with Molly clearly suggest that more than mere conversation occurred between the two there and elsewhere at Lake Maggiore. In a letter dated 2 February 1929 from London to his "Dearest Mollikins" Shaw wrote: "You desire to know whether I am Thru with you. At my age one is thru with everybody, and can only beg for a little charitable tolerance from young persons. I hoarded my bodily possessions so penuriously that even at seventy I had some left; but that remnant was stolen from me on the road to Baveno and on other roads to paradise through the same district."[24]

In a letter written 12 January 1927 he recalled "the road to Baveno at night" as one of the places and times on the shores of Lake Maggiore about which she could have sweet dreams, and on 2 March 1928 he told her that "his restless hands sometimes tire of the pen and remember the road to Baveno."[25] On a postcard dated 10 January 1927 he asked, in reference to her lease of Isola San Giovanni, when she was going to "the Isle of the Ever Blessed Many Times Kissed."[26] Among the works included in Molly's successful exhibition of her paintings at the Leicester Galleries in London in 1934 was one called "The Road to Stresa." According to the Tompkins account, Shaw purchased it and insisted that its title should be "The Road to Baveno."[27] During one of her stays at Lake Maggiore, Molly traveled to Milan to have an abortion. According to her son, the baby was fathered by Shaw, who was reported in the Molly Tompkins narrative to have been very upset about the abortion.[28]

In one surviving letter from Molly to Shaw, written in 1945, she confessed that at the time of their Lake Maggiore meetings she had been "dazed by the violence of my passion for you," and referred to him as "the B. Shaw that gave my body and my mind and my heart peace when I lay by the side of a river or a lake, with him in Italy, or walked the Baveno road with him."[29] She was writing from New York in response to a letter from Shaw in which he had expressed dismay at a proposal from her that she should come and visit him. In this letter she insisted that she was not thinking of renewing their sexual relationship:

> I don't want the Baveno Road in fact again. I will have it always deep & sweet in my heart As to Charlotte I considered that too. I didn't like Charlotte—she didn't give me much chance to and I never seem to have time to get to know women well enough to know whether I liked them or not. But I do know how very much you cared for Charlotte, and also the slight sense of guilt the man who is loved more than he loves has and could not have done anything that would hurt her. If I had thought that my visit might by any chance have been mistaken for a re-adventure I would not have dreampt [*sic*] of coming.[30]

When, in his June 1930 letter to Frank Harris, Shaw wrote that he "liked sexual intercourse because of its amazing power of producing a celestial flood of emotion and exaltation of existence," he must clearly have had in mind much more recent experiences than has previously been supposed.[31]

* * *

Shaw's affair with Molly Tompkins followed in the wake of the publication in 1922 of Mrs. Patrick Campbell's *My Life and Some Letters*, a major selling-point of which was that it contained a selection of Shaw's letters to her. Shaw had great—and justified—misgivings about this book because of the hurt it would cause Charlotte and the embarrassment it would cause him. However, Stella was able to refer to a letter he had written her on 2 December 1921 giving her copyright ownership and was adamant about going ahead: "Start saying your prayers,"[32] she wrote to him in the course of the lengthy and sometimes acrimonious correspondence concerning the plans for her book. The publication duly appeared with the selected letters fairly heavily cut.

For Charlotte the Molly Tompkins affair must have seemed an exasperating repetition of the dalliance with a "barefooted playmate"[33] her wayward husband had engaged in with Stella. However, the letters from Charlotte to Molly that are included in the Peter Tompkins collection (1960) show her perfect manners and graciousness, as well as a quite friendly disposition toward the young American woman, who by 1926 had largely displaced Stella as the most immediately absorbing and troublesome enchantress in Shaw's life. In Molly's reminiscences, Charlotte is presented in a very unflattering light. She irritates Molly with her allegedly starchy manner and reverential and possessive attitude toward her Great Man husband "GBS." Catty observations are made. According to the Tompkins account, Charlotte—then in her late sixties—did not do much swimming in the lake, but appeared in a black taffeta bathing costume with a stuffed canary on her shoulder, "its mouth slightly open as if it were about to sing."[34] It is insinuated that a pair of powerful binoculars spotted on the balcony of the Shaw suite at the Regina Palace was used by Charlotte to spy on the behavior of Shaw and Molly.[35] How much of this is unfounded gossip is impossible to tell. There is a persuasive particularity about some of the observations, but the spirit in which Charlotte is treated in this narrative seems unjust in the light of her kind letters.[36]

There must have been tensions resulting from the situation at Lake Maggiore. However, Charlotte does not seem to have taken any steps to prevent the relationship between Shaw and Molly from developing; perhaps by this time she had become more or less resigned to Shaw's philandering ways. She was probably also reasonably confident that Shaw would not commit himself to any kind of relationship with Molly that would involve scandal or cause the breakup of his marriage. For Shaw—still a very physically fit man in whose marriage sex either played no part or had been discontinued early—the attractive and ardent young American must have presented an enormous temptation. Charlotte—who may well have guessed what was going on during Shaw's walks with Molly on the road to Baveno and drives with her around "other roads to paradise in the same district"—decided on forbearance.

* * *

The relationship with Molly Tompkins produced symptoms of a familiar and deep-seated conflict in Shaw's emotions regarding sexual experience. At times she appears in his letters as a person with whom he enjoyed extraordinary bliss, while at other times she is cast in the role of a wicked enchantress, like the nymphs in *The Odyssey* who ensnare sailors on their islands. In a letter to her dated 31 May 1928 Shaw invoked the legend of Calypso and Odysseus, which had been part of the language he employed in his love relations since the time of his very early poem about the "bewitching Calypso" from whom he had escaped, as well as the sketch entitled "Calypso" that he drew as a teenager in Dublin, depicting a nude female figure reclining by the sea. In this letter—which is affectionately addressed to his dear "Mollikins" and ends romantically with the operatic salute "a te, O cara"*—he takes her to task for being "a fiend Vamp" who goes prowling round the lake, making men's wives miserable. Mephistopheles whispered in his ear, he told her, that she was not the first siren who had tried to seduce him: "Before you were born I have had to do with sirens as seductive as you." He then went on to accuse her of trying to be a Calypso to him on her island in Italy: "You thought that when you had secured your Ogygia and lured me to its shores you could play Calypso to my Odysseus and make a hog of me. Arn't you glad you didn't succeed: after all you have some brains in your upper half. This erotic-romantic attitude to life doesn't make you happy."[37]

It is difficult to think of a letter of his that more clearly encapsulates Shaw's conflicting impulses about sex than this one, in which he tenderly addresses his "Mollikins" in the language of Italian opera as "O, cara" and at the same time brands her a destructive vamp.

The conflict aroused in Shaw as a result of his relations with Molly Tompkins provides another reminder of his spiritual links with the traditions of English Puritanism. In some ways his attitude is reminiscent of that expressed in the work of the great Puritan poets of the English Renaissance, Edmund Spenser and John Milton. In Spenser's *Faerie Queene* sex is frequently presented as sensual bait that distracts the knights-errant of Gloriana from their spiritual quests and lures them into delusive bowers of bliss, rob-

*This is an allusion to the aria from the third act of Bellini's opera *I Puritani*, the opening lines of which are:

"A te, o cara, amor talora / Mi guidò furtivo e in pianto; / Or mi guida a te d'accanto / Tra la gioia e l'esultar." (To you, oh dear one, love at times / Led me furtively and in tears; / Now it guides me to your side / In joy and exultation.)

bing them of manly integrity, strength, and noble purpose—just as Odysseus and his sailors are seduced and waylaid in Homer's poem. In Milton's early poem *Lycidas* the shepherd-poet struggles to decide between his proper calling and the temptation to "sport with Amaryllis in the shade / Or with the tangles of Neæra's hair." (Shaw was possibly remembering this passage when he named the Newly-Born damsel Amaryllis in *Back to Methuselah.*)[38] As we have seen, the story of Samson—the biblical hero who is robbed of his strength by Delilah—which Milton powerfully explores in *Samson Agonistes* was recalled by Shaw in his account of his first meeting with Stella Campbell. Molly was the last in a long line of women Shaw found irresistibly attractive but whom he also puritanically perceived as distracting him from his life's mission as creative artist and social reformer.

Shaw never resolved his mixed feelings about Molly Tompkins, and remained fond of her till the end of his life. He helped her through troubled times in the 1930s and also generously assisted with the education in England of her son, Peter. A picture postcard sent to Molly on 3 January 1949 showing Shaw standing behind his gate at Shaw's Corner, Ayot St Lawrence, carries the following message:

> The Old Man at his gate
> As he was in fortyeight
> And still is at ninety three
> Awaiting news of thee
>
> Molly Bawn[39]

* * *

Shaw's experiences with the two enchantresses, Stella Campbell and Molly Tompkins, were reflected in *The Apple Cart,* which had its premiere at the Teatr Polski, Warsaw, on 14 June 1929 and was one of the works by Shaw presented at the first Malvern Festival the following August. Molly Tompkins probably also influenced Shaw in his creation of the unabashedly lustful nurse, Sweetie, in his play *Too True to Be Good,* which had its British premiere at Malvern in 1932. In that work Aubrey, a clergyman-turned-burglar with whom Sweetie runs away, declares: "I . . . was madly in love with her. She was not my intellectual equal; and I had to teach her table manners. But there was an extraordinary sympathy between our lower centres." Sweetie is seen by Aubrey as representing, in the wake of World War I, a new articulation of the human passions, of the "lower centres" of consciousness that were formerly kept dumb and hidden as "a sort of guilty secret."[40] Sweetie is remarkable because "her lower centres speak." Molly Tompkins, the ardent young woman to whom Shaw had to teach manners but with whom he seems to have found great rapport physically seems very likely to have been in Shaw's mind when he wrote these passages in the play.

The Apple Cart is a virtuoso piece in the discussion play form. In this work, as in most of the late plays, Shaw takes jester's license to dispense almost completely with conventional plot material. The structure of the play resembles that of a musical composition, falling somewhere between symphony and light opera. A constitutional crisis arises from the clash between King Magnus and his cabinet caused by the former's refusal to remain silent concerning political issues and an ultimatum by the cabinet designed to gag him. This crisis, together with the subjects of the king's relations with his exotic mistress and plain wife and the American Ambassador's proposal for the amalgamation of the British Empire with the United States, provide the slender—too much so, for some tastes—narrative props upon which the debates of the play are mounted.

In the creation of the alluring and troublesome mistress Orinthia, who endeavors to prise the king away from his absorption in boring politics and his loyalty to his faithful and calming "old Dutch" wife, Jemima, Shaw made bold use of his personal experiences with Stella Campbell and Molly Tompkins in relation to his marriage with Charlotte. The "Interlude" between the King and his mistress ends farcically, with the two locked in combat and rolling across the floor as a result of King Magnus's attempts to extricate himself from Orinthia's embraces in order to go and deal with the cabinet crisis. This was founded on an actual scene that occurred at Stella Campbell's home in Kensington when she and Shaw were discovered by a servant in a similar situation.[41] Stella Campbell strenuously objected to Shaw's "vulgar" use of their relationship in this way and Shaw responded by modifying the dialogue to some extent.[42] However, the wrestling match, halted by the arrival of a servant, remained in place as a joyously indecorous ending to the scene.

The Apple Cart continues to have point and relevance as a satirical portrait of democracy in disarray. Reflecting the chaotic state of democratic societies in the late 1920s and early 1930s, democracy is shown in the play to be a dysfunctional system. It is seen not as government of the people, by the people, and for the people, but rather as a pawn in the power play of large corporations, busily engaged in creating goods with built-in obsolescence to enhance profits and commandeering public utilities in the service of private greed. Democracies, in other words, are a front behind which the real power is wielded by plutocracies. With its presentation of a hopelessly divided, quarrelsome cabinet whose conflicts result in a stalemate, the play is reminiscent of the bon mot Shaw gives to Lord Summerhays in *Misalliance*: "Democracy reads well; but it doesn't act well, like some people's plays." Equally memorable is Shaw's Swiftian image of democracy, in the preface to *The Apple Cart*, as a hot-air balloon containing a tiny number of incompetent politicians that descends to earth every five years or so at election time and, after a scramble among a few contestants to get aboard, "goes up again with much the same lot in it and leaves you where you were before."[43]

In its treatment of capitalism, the play echoes some of the same critiques in *The Intelligent Woman's Guide*. To the bewilderment of some, however, *The Apple Cart* seemed to be finally endorsing entirely different political solutions from those offered by Socialism. When the play was first performed, it seemed to many people to represent a complete volte-face in Shaw's political attitude. In its portrait of the polite, genial, and intelligent King Magnus and his triumph over the politicians in his cabinet, Shaw was understandably considered guilty of "political apostasy" and presenting a "triumph of autocracy over democracy."[44] He attempted to counter this idea in the preface that was published with the play in 1930. In the page proofs of the play itself he added the following lines to one of King Magnus's speeches: "Do not misunderstand me: I do not want the old governing class back. It governed so selfishly that the people would have perished if democracy had not swept it out of politics. But evil as it was in many ways, at least it stood above the tyranny of popular ignorance and popular poverty. Today only the king stands above that tyranny."

But people did "misunderstand," and this addition was not sufficient to cancel the impression that Shaw was somewhat attracted to the idea of intelligent and far-sighted autocracy as one possible road out of the morass of democracy. His King Magnus—a witty ironist who runs rings around the blustering politicians in the cabinet and outfoxes Proteus, the cunning prime minister—is an engaging and amusing creation, who bears a family resemblance to such other portraits of powerful and intelligent individuals in the Shavian canon as Caesar in *Caesar and Cleopatra* and Undershaft in *Major Barbara*. King Magnus is one of the most benign of these Shavian creations. The problem was simply that in the real world of international politics Shaw seemed to be showing far more sympathy for the autocratic figures then emerging on both sides of the political spectrum than history has shown they deserved.

It would be easy to use history and the later revelations concerning the regimes of Mussolini, Hitler, and Stalin as sticks to beat Shaw for his statements about them in the 1920s and 1930s. Shaw was one among many people at the time who thought that Hitler and Stalin were responsible for many positive reforms in their respective countries. It is, of course, well known that many Western intellectuals—including such leading literary figures as George Orwell, Kingsley Amis, and Iris Murdoch—were strongly attracted to Communism.[45] Although the totalitarian states that developed under Mussolini, Hitler, and Stalin are now thoroughly discredited, Shaw's favorable comments concerning their beginnings were by no means unique among Western intellectuals, and they form part of his story that needs to be told.

* * *

The most significant phase of Shaw's controversial interventions in the English and European debates about Mussolini and Fascism began a few months after his first stay at Lake Maggiore in late summer and early autumn 1926. On 24 January 1927 the *Daily News* (London) published a sympathetic letter with the caption "Bernard Shaw on Mussolini: A Defence." Shaw pointed out to Graham Wallas that the subheading "A Defence" was not provided by him.[46] The letter drew attacks from many Socialists and Italians in exile, including Dr. Friedrich Adler, leader of the Austrian Labor Party and secretary of the Labour and Socialist International. The controversy was reawakened when the *Daily News* published an extensive correspondence on the subject between Shaw and Adler in October 1927.[47]

The affair prompted one of Beatrice Webb's most severe comments on Shaw in her diary. After the October 1927 exchange between Shaw and Adler, she wrote: "GBS has created a sensation: he has gone out of his way to testify to the excellence of Mussolini's dictatorship—to its superiority over political democracy as experienced in Great Britain and other countries." Had the matter not been revived by Shaw in October, it would have remained at rest. "But," Beatrice Webb went on to write:

> GBS fortified his admiration of Mussolini by spending eight weeks and £600 in a luxurious hotel at Stresa in continuous and flattering interviews with Fascist officials of charming personality and considerable attainments; [he] handed to the Italian Press, in the middle of October, a deliberately provocative answer to Adler's February letter, this letter being broadcast, considerably garbled, throughout Italy. From the published correspondence in the English press and still more from a private correspondence with Adler, it appears that GBS puts forward the Mussolini régime as the New Model that all other countries ought to follow! His argument seems to be that either the Haves or the Have Nots must seize power and *compel* all to come under the Fascist or the Communist plough. It is a crude and flippant attempt at reconstruction, bred

of conceit, impatience and ignorance. It will injure GBS's reputation far more than it will the democratic institutions in Great Britain. But it reinforces the Italian tyranny. It is only fair to add that this naïve faith in a superman, before whose energy and genius all must bow down is not a new feature in the Shaw mentality. What is new and deplorable is the absence of any kind of sympathetic appreciation of the agony that the best and wisest Italians are today going through, any appreciation of the mental degradation as implied in the suppression of all liberty of act, of thought and of speech.[48]

Although there is some truth in the general thrust of this criticism, two assertions are questionable. The idea that Shaw's views on Fascism were influenced by "continuous and flattering interviews with Fascist officials of charming personality and considerable attainments" is contradicted by a statement contained in a letter written by Shaw to James Ramsay MacDonald on 21 October 1927, in which he says: "In Italy I discussed Fascism with only *one* Fascist, to whom I took my letter [to Adler] *after* writing it."[49] In other words, Shaw appears to have developed his own thoughts about Mussolini independently of any discussions he had in Italy.

Shaw was, however, introduced to some very high-ranking Italians at Stresa, several of whom may well have had connections with Fascism—and one of whom definitely did. In August 1926 Shaw told Molly Tompkins about an incident when the hotel porter at the Regina Palace dashed in and—to the dismay of Shaw and Charlotte—announced the unexpected arrival of a party of distinguished visitors who had come to pay court to the famous English playwright. They included, Shaw told Molly, "the Princess Borromeo, the governor of the provinzia of Novara, half a dozen mayors and ex-mayors, and countless marchesane, principesse, baronesse d'ogni grado nobile."[50]

One member of this illustrious group, "the governor of the provinzia of Novara," was the "*one* Fascist" referred to in Shaw's letter to Ramsay MacDonald. His name was Carlo Emanuele Basile, author of the book *Discorsi Fascisti* (1930), among other works, and a leading figure in the Mussolini regime. Basile, then in his early forties, and his wife—to whom Shaw refers as "the Baronessa" and who evidently had a better command of written English than her husband—had become part of the circle of friends formed by Molly and Laurence Tompkins.[51] In a letter to Molly dated 2 February 1927 Shaw requests that if she meets Basile she should "tell him that I have got into hot water with the Liberals for defending Mussolini";[52] in the same letter he describes the Italian as "the best talker I know."[53] When Molly wrote a play about the triangular relationship between her, Shaw, and Charlotte—to which Shaw contributed a revised third act—he advised her (with a view to publication in Italy) that "Basile must translate it, using the Baronessa as his dictionary."[54] In an open letter to Adler dated 11 October 1927 Shaw refers to Basile as "a distinguished Italian friend of mine."[55]

About eighteen years after Shaw wrote this letter, at the end of World War II, Basile was tried as a war criminal and sentenced to life imprisonment in 1945. He died in prison the following year. During the war he had risen to high office in Mussolini's government as under-secretary of state for the army. In 1944 he became prefect of the province of Genoa after the Nazis assumed control of northern Italy. In this position he was responsible for the suppression by executions and deportations of anti-Fascist forces that had taken industrial and military action against the Nazis.

The other matter in Beatrice Webb's tirade that is open to debate is that Shaw's sympathy with Fascism was based on a "naïve faith in a superman." The Fascist movements in European politics developed during a period of profound and widespread social unrest and economic instability. Governments operating within the constraints of democratic parliamentary institutions seemed to be failing disastrously to come to terms with these problems. In the metaphor of the title of Shaw's 1933 political play, democracy seemed to be "on the rocks," leaving the way open for dictators such as Mussolini and Hitler to make their appeal and solidify their power. Like many other public figures in Britain, Europe, and the United States, Shaw was impressed by Mussolini's success in achieving stable government in Italy in the 1920s and in bringing about various social and economic reforms.

In Shaw's view the Fascist movements, led by such figures as Mussolini and Hitler, owed their existence to the failure of parliamentary democracy. He expressed this view in relation to Hitler in a 1931 interview published in the *Daily Telegraph* as part of his response to a question about the political difficulties in Germany: "The Third Reich (the Hitlerites' name for their proposed State) owes its existence and its vogue solely to the futility of liberal parliamentarism on the English model." Because of their inefficiency, he went on to argue, democracies were being "swept into the dustbin by Steel Helmets, Fascists, Dictators, military councils, and anything else that represents a disgusted reaction against our obsolescence and uselessness." Shaw insisted that if we repair our political institutions and set to work on social problems (along Socialist lines, of course) "the steel Helmets will melt in the sun."[56] Ironically, during the time when the "Helmets" were being forcibly removed in World War II, and afterward, when the Attlee Labour government was swept into power in England, Shaw was to become a rather querulous victim of ruthlessly high taxes, in the imposing of which Socialist principles could be seen to be operating even though they were first brought in under the Churchill administration.

Unfortunately, in the case of Mussolini Shaw had a tendency seriously to underestimate—or to treat blandly and theoretically as a necessary part of political reform—the ruthlessly repressive character of the dictator's regime. Events such as the murder in 1924 of the anti-Fascist Italian Socialist Giacomo Matteoti, as well as other "revolting incidents of the Fascist terror,"[57] as Shaw himself called them, tended to be viewed by him with a sort of historical relativism that placed them alongside other examples of the use of violence in the interest of effecting necessary social and political change. As an Irishman he was able to point with some conviction to the fact that brutal methods of repressing dissent had been quite recently employed under the British system of parliamentary democracy. But this *tu quoque* line of argument—which Shaw directed at England and declared that Mussolini was entitled to employ—looks feeble in the light of history and full knowledge of the scale and horror of repression in Mussolini's Italy. In October 1927 Shaw was severely taken to task by Professor Gaetano Salvemini, an anti-Fascist Italian historian in exile, for "delivering judgements about matters of which he is wholly ignorant, and his callous ridicule of hardships and sufferings which his intelligence ought to understand even if his moral sensitiveness is unequal to appreciating them."[58]

Although he came to be very critical of Adolf Hitler— indeed, he thought him a madman long before the outbreak of World War II—some of Shaw's comments about the German dictator during the 1930s now seem embarrassingly sympathetic, though Shaw was certainly not the only prominent individual in England to have been impressed by the positive achievements of Hitler and his National Socialist Party.[59] He viewed Hitler, like Mussolini (who was a Socialist journalist early in his career), as a reformer. In an interview in 1933 he said: "The Nazi movement is in many respects one which has my warmest sympathy." It is some relief to find that he followed this statement with one about his "dismay when at the most critical moment Herr Hitler and the Nazis went mad on the Jewish question" and described anti-Semitism as a form of insanity: "Judophobia is as pathological as hydrophobia." The Germans were not acting as Socialists or Fascists, he declared, "but simply running amuck in the indulgence of a pure phobia: that is acting like madmen."[60] Shaw was not really condemning Hitler *as* a fascistic dictator but rather as an insane anti-Semite. Fascism and other "dictatorial tactics," he claimed, "had the sympathy of the vast mass of public opinion which has turned angrily away from the delays, the evasions, the windy impotence and anarchistic negations of our pseudo-democratic parliamentary system."[61]

In these flirtations with Fascism in the late 1920s and early 1930s there can be discerned a sort of "apostasy" on Shaw's part. The Fabian advocate of gradualism and opponent of radical Marxist Socialism and violent revolution seems often to have given way in his later years to a man displaying the impatience of age and an atypical and disquieting recklessness. Many of his later pronouncements on international politics—in letters to the editor, published interviews, and the preface to his play *On The Rocks*—seem to constitute a betrayal of the fundamental warmth, benevolence, and humanity of his comic muse as a dramatist and the continued geniality, humor, and liveliness of the later correspondence. Mrs. Patrick Campbell's witty remark contained in an early letter to Shaw ("When you were quite a little boy somebody ought to have said 'hush' just once!")[62] often comes to mind when reading Shaw's later polemical writings. That, however, was an injunction he was constitutionally incapable of obeying. The later polemical writings do not, of course, negate the worth of Shaw's earlier penetrating and effective commentary on social, cultural, and political issues. In retrospect, the late 1920s and early 1930s do not appear as Shaw's finest hour as a critic of society.

* * *

The balance of Shaw's earlier comments on Hitler and Mussolini was partly redressed by the portraits he created of them in *Geneva*, his 1938 play about the League of Nations, in which they are represented, respectively, as the bombastic and verbose orators Battler and Bombardone. Here, in a dramatized representation of an international court of justice, the two leaders are lampooned in cartoonlike satirical caricatures. But, significantly, in the same play the Russian commissar Posky is portrayed very sympathetically. The positive portrayal of the commissar and of Russia in *Geneva* obviously reflected Shaw's hope that the new order being established in that country represented a way out of the mess created by capitalism. In the West, the Dutch judge who presides over the court of justice in the play says, "We despair of human nature, whereas Russia has hopes that have carried her through the most appalling sufferings to the forefront of civilisation."

It was to Russia—with admiration, and in the remarkable company of Lady Nancy Astor, a capitalist Tory politician who became the first woman member of Parliament in English history—that Shaw was to travel in 1931 on the first of a series of world travels upon which he embarked in the 1930s. As the road to Baveno was slipping into memory, the road to Moscow replaced it as a principal focal point of interest in Shaw's career.

23 World Traveler and Village Squire

During the early 1930s Shaw became a world traveler on a grand scale. From 1931 to 1936 he and Charlotte spent a very large part of their life aboard ocean liners, traveling in great style to far-flung corners of the earth, with Shaw being treated rather in the manner of a visiting head of state in many of their ports of call. To recall the expression employed by Irish poet, playwright, and essayist Oliver Goldsmith in the title of one of his works, Shaw had truly become a "Citizen of the World."

Shaw's visits attracted huge media attention, and with his wit, provocative statements, and ready turn of phrase, he often obliged with headline-grabbing statements and pieces of advice. The South Africans were prescribed "less surf-bathing and more thinking" and told to fix up their "slums."[1] The anglophile New Zealanders were told to be less subservient to the "mother" country and not to make the mistake of thinking that the English were greatly concerned about New Zealand—or were even aware that it is a different country from Australia.* (An English lady who heard Shaw was going to New Zealand hoped he would stay with her daughter, who "had a very nice house in Sydney").[2] The students in Hong Kong were counseled to be "revolutionaries at twenty" or risk being hidebound in middle age, advice that was duly reported as "Incitement to Revolution" in the local press.[3]

The eyes of travel agents in the Strand in London must have lit up when they heard of yet another proposed excursion in the 1930s of Mr. and Mrs. Bernard Shaw of flat no. 130, 4 Whitehall Court, which by this time had become their London home.[4] Because of the custom they had adopted since the beginning of their marriage—which drew such scorn from Mrs. Patrick Campbell—of always maintaining separate bedrooms, the Shaws required separate first-class staterooms on ocean liners and separate suites in the large

---

* New Zealand is separated from Australia by the Tasman Sea and lies about two thousand kilometers—roughly three quarters the width of the Atlantic Ocean—from Sydney.

hotels they stayed in. There was also Mr. Shaw's vegetarian diet to be carefully attended to, though he was not a particularly fussy traveler. What he wanted most was to be left alone by conversation-seeking fellow passengers on deck so that he could read and write, both of which he did to a prodigious extent on his voyages.

A two-page document written in Charlotte's hand and headed "Packing List" provides some insight into the remarkably elaborate arrangements that lay behind these Shavian safaris. Charlotte's "Packing List" reflects a world and style of travel largely forgotten in the age of jet planes. Conjuring up images of porters staggering beneath trunks and suitcases, hatboxes, and holdalls, Charlotte's list omits none of the paraphernalia necessary for the continuation of ordinary life. Under the heading "General" are sheets, boots and shoes, books, underclothes, hair nets, a comb cleaner, washing things, pincushion, hairpins, eyecup, foot-ease, a muslin shoulder cape, jewel box, toilet instruments, steel mirror, work things (for needlework?), watches, bath brush, and cotton. A "Night Bag" held caps (silk) "shade/eye" and other items, and into the "Hat Box" went—in addition to hats—gloves, scarves, and spectacles. In the "Hold-All": umbrella, stick, maps, and guidebooks. The "Pen Box" had to contain, apart from all the necessities for writing, the "dressing table silver." Not forgotten were goggles (presumably for motoring or flying), eye glasses, and prescriptions. A veritable pharmacist's shop of unguents and medicines appears on the second page: five different kinds of lotion (soothing, emollient, tonic, spot, eye), clinical thermometer, and numerous other items, including (mysteriously) "Animal wool" and "New Skin."[5] Could a polar explorer have packed more carefully?

The cycle of journeys—mostly taken at times chosen to get away from the English winter—began on 3 March 1931, when the Shaws traveled to Marseilles to join the Hellenic Travellers' Club tour of the Mediterranean and the Holy Land. In a letter written on this first journey—bearing as date and place of dispatch "St Patrick's Day in Damascus"—Shaw sent a lively and evocative account of his travels in the Holy Land to his friend the prioress of Stanbrook Abbey, Dame Laurentia McLachlan. She had asked him to "bring her something from Calvary." Rejecting the trashy souvenirs available, he picked up two little stones from Bethlehem, one to be thrown "blindfold" among the other stones at Stanbrook to provide a permanent link with Calvary, the other to be furnished with a "setting or mounting" and presented to the prioress as a relic.[6] At the end of his long letter to Dame Laurentia, Shaw suggested she sell the manuscript of it to Sydney Cockerell—their mutual friend and director of the Fitzwilliam Museum, Cambridge—and "endow a chapel to St Bernard at Stanbrook with the proceeds."[7]

Charlotte did not accompany Shaw on his visit to Russia, which occurred in July 1931. Thereafter the schedule of their travels together included: South Africa, from December 1931 to April 1932; a world cruise aboard the SS *Empress of Britain* in the same period the following winter, taking in countries in the Mediterranean, Asia, and America (including New York, where Shaw gave a celebrated address at the Metropolitan Opera House in April 1933); a journey to New Zealand on the SS *Rangitane* in the early months of 1934; a voyage around South Africa on the *Llangibby Castle*, from March to May 1935; and a cruise to the Pacific on the *Arandora Star* in 1936, which included a visit to Honolulu, where the Shaws had lunch with Charlie Chaplin, and to the Grand Canyon, where they met the novelist J. B. Priestley.[8]

Back in England, the Shaws became regular visitors to the annual summer festival—of which Shaw was the secular patron saint—held at the Worcestershire spa town of Malvern. The Malvern Festival was cofounded and managed by Sir Barry Jackson, the enterprising founder and director of the Birmingham Repertory Theatre, and fellow producer and theater manager Roy Limbert.[9] With its steep streets leading up to a backdrop of hills, Malvern has something of the character of an alpine village. The town has many literary and cultural associations: it was in the hills of Malvern that the narrator in a work by the medieval poet William Langland—a much earlier moralist and visionary world-betterer—says he had the dream that serves as the subject of the fourteenth-century allegorical alliterative poem *Piers Plowman*. The same hills overlook the lovely countryside that inspired the music of Edward Elgar and the poetry of A. E. Housman. The Shaws stayed in the Malvern Hotel in Abbey Road, a short walk from the Festival Theatre where several of Shaw's plays had their English and, in some cases, world premieres. All of the following had their first English productions at Malvern: *The Apple Cart* (1929), *Too True to Be Good* (1932), *The Simpleton of the Unexpected Isles* (1934), *Geneva* (1938), and *In Good King Charles's Golden Days* (1938–39).

At Malvern the tall playwright, dressed in tweed Norfolk jacket, knickerbockers, and cloth cap, striding across the hills like a man a quarter of his age, chatting at afternoon teas with Elgar and the poet John Drinkwater and others, taking snapshots and sitting in the front of the theater dress circle watching his plays—which, Barry Jackson recalls, "he appeared to enjoy as much as the most loyal Shavian"[10]—was a familiar and (except possibly to the more conservative townsfolk) much-liked figure. He wrote some sprightly introductions to the elaborate and well-illustrated programs for the festivals. One year when he was in Malvern an arresting bust portrait entitled *Bernard Shaw Writing* was executed by Malvern artist Victor Hume Moody.[11]

The playwright, novelist, composer, and dramatic critic Beverley Nichols has provided a memorable account of Shaw and Charlotte at the Malvern Hotel (where Nichols was a fellow guest) in his book of recollections entitled *All I Could Never Be*. There seemed to be an unwritten convention among the patrons of the hotel—a place of "stunning respectability" in which "female hypochondriacs" sipped the Malvern spa water through "pruney-prismy lips"—not to stare at the celebrity within their midst. Shaw and Charlotte dined in complete and contented silence, with books propped up against bottles of water. Nichols thought Shaw himself a delight to behold. What particularly struck him was "the cleanliness of the man! He was like snow and new linen sheets and cotton wool and red apples with rain on them. One felt that he must even smell delicious, like hay or pears."[12]

When he was not "peacocking" (Charlotte's nice expression) as an international and national celebrity abroad and at places such as Malvern, Shaw's life at Ayot St Lawrence was hardly distinguishable from that of an ordinary English village gentleman. When Francis Hopkins, a journalist from the *Lady's Realm*, visited him at Ayot St Lawrence in 1909, he discovered that Shaw was locally known as the "village squire."[13] All accounts suggest that the Shaws were good neighbors and were liked and respected by the villagers, their children, and by the servants at their residence, which was known as Shaw's Corner.

Thus, in the early 1930s Shaw led a double life as celebrated world traveler and as a member of a small community in a tiny village in the county of Hertfordshire. This alternation between contrasting scenes of life was reflected in one of Shaw's most delightful short comedies, *Village Wooing*. Written during the 1932–33 world cruise, the play comprises three "conversations" between a man and a woman, the first of which takes place on the deck of an ocean liner—where the last thing the man wants is conversation. He is an author and is trying to concentrate on writing. Nevertheless his fellow passenger, the woman, cheerfully persists. The other two scenes are set in an English village shop, where the woman doubles as a shopkeeper and postmistress and where the man turns up by chance in the second scene. In one of her speeches back at home, the woman, disappointed by all the sights she had imagined in her daydreams and had now seen in reality on her travels, declares: "Travelling just destroyed the world for me as I imagined it. Give me this village all the time." The man becomes her contented employee at the village shop, and by the end of the play, after taking an order over the telephone from the local rectory for artichokes, the woman asks to speak to the rector about banns for a wedding.

Village Wooing contains numerous autobiographical touches, being partly inspired by Shaw's own friendship with one of the villagers in Ayot St Lawrence, Mrs. Jisbella ("Jessie") Lyth, who served as the shopkeeper and postmistress there. Shaw the world traveler—who did a great deal of writing on the decks of ocean liners and had to develop strategies to avoid conversations while doing so—was also deeply fond of "his" village of Ayot St Lawrence and had regular chats with Mrs. Lyth when he was there. The shop-cum-post office, a half-timbered fifteenth-century cottage that also served as Jessie Lyth's home, was a short stroll from Shaw's Corner. Before settling there, Jessie had experienced an "adventurous life of travel," as she described it, to distant parts of the world. (Her husband died shortly after the couple arrived at Ayot St Lawrence in 1931.) Shaw inscribed a copy of *The Adventures of the Black Girl* to Jessie Lyth with the words "good friend and neighbor" and sent a copy of *Pygmalion* to her with the message "For a Good Girl," which was probably a playful allusion to Eliza Doolittle's protestation about her moral character ("I'm a good girl, I am") in the opening scene of the play.[14]

* * *

Shaw set off on his journey to Russia from Victoria Station, London, on 18 July 1931 with a touring party that included, in addition to Nancy Astor, her husband, Viscount Astor; their son, the Honorable Francis David Astor (then a student at Balliol College, Oxford); Philip Henry Kerr (11th Marquess of Lothian), a newspaper editor, Liberal statesman, and secretary of the Rhodes Trustees; and Charles Tennant, a Christian Scientist. According to Shaw, the reason for the journey was that "the Astors took it into their heads to see for themselves whether Russia is really the earthly paradise I had declared it to be; and they challenged me to go with them."[15] Aptly evoking theatrical imagery of the commedia dell'arte, Winston Churchill described the political odd couple of Shaw and Nancy (on the occasion of their visit to Russia) as "the World's most famous intellectual Clown and Pantaloon in one, and the charming Columbine of the capitalist pantomime."[16]

The "Columbine" traveled under the cloud of devastating news about her beloved son Bobbie, a handsome officer in the Royal Horse Guards. Five days before the commencement of the Russian tour she was informed that he had been warned by the police that he was about to be arrested for homosexual offenses, and on the day before the tourists left London he was sentenced to four months' imprisonment in Wormwood Scrubs. Shaw promptly wrote a sympathetic letter to Nancy about this incident that gives a clear indication both of his thoughtful, uncensorious views of and personal distance from homosexuality. On 15 July he wrote:

Dearest Nancy,

Why is Providence so jealous of your high spirits that it deals you these terrible BIFFS at your most hopeful moments? What can one do to comfort you? . . . In his case I think I should plead technically Guilty, admitting the facts but not the delinquency. The natural affections of many men, including some very eminent ones (Plato and Michael Angelo, for instance) take that perverse turn; and in many countries adults are held to be entitled to their satisfaction in spite of the prejudices and bigoted normality of Virginians and Irishmen like our two selves. Bobbie can claim that he has to suffer by a convention of British law, not by Nature's law.[17]

In a second letter to Nancy in 1932 he made the general observation about homosexuality that "the Bible, with its rubbish about Lot's wife, is positively dangerous. . . . A man may suffer acutely and lose his self-respect very dangerously if he mistakes for a frightful delinquency on his part a condition for which he is no more morally responsible than for color blindness."[18] Possibly helped by these sensible letters, the "columbine" seems to have recovered her usual lively spirits on the journey with the "pantaloon."

Shaw once wrote to Nancy Astor that Charlotte "is very fond of you. So am I. I don't know why."[19] It was indeed a strange friendship. In their publicly declared political affiliations Shaw and Astor were poles apart. Nevertheless the friendship can be seen to reflect the heady mix of political impulses and leanings within Shaw's own mind at this time of his life, as shown, for example, in his favorable comments about Mussolini. Beginning in 1927, when the Shaws accepted an invitation to spend Christmas with the Astors at their famous Thames-side country estate of Cliveden,[20] Nancy Astor and Shaw enjoyed an affectionate, bantering relationship. Shaw obviously responded to Nancy's vitality, wit, and public-spiritedness. He took an interest in the Christian Science beliefs in which she became increasingly absorbed as she grew older and (according to more than one witness) crankier. Nancy was one of the last people to visit Shaw before his death in 1950. Knowing Molly Tompkins would probably be jealous of her new, rich and famous, American rival for his friendship, Shaw teasingly headed one of his 1928 letters to Molly with the address and exclamation: "chez Lady Astor . . . (O gelosia!)."[21] Nancy was forty-eight when she first met Shaw, and, given his disposition, there was very likely to have been an element of flirtatiousness in his relationship with her.[22] For Charlotte, however, Nancy was one of her rivals for Shaw's affections with whom she apparently felt quite safe, and the two women enjoyed a warm friendship.

As the first woman member of Parliament in England, Nancy Astor was the Conservative Party member for the Sutton division of Plymouth from 1919 to 1945. She was born in 1879 in Danville, Virginia, one of five daughters of Chiswell Dabney Langhorne, a wealthy businessman who made his fortune in railway development. The Langhorne sisters were a bevy of horse-riding, tennis-playing Southern belles who moved in the highest social circles and who all went on to lead remarkable lives.[23] After an unsuccessful marriage to Robert Gould Shaw, by whom she had her son Bobbie, Nancy met the immensely wealthy Waldorf Astor, whom she married in 1904. Waldorf was the son of the 1st Viscount Astor, whose title and seat in the House of Lords Waldorf inherited following his father's death in 1919.

Shaw was at first hesitant to respond to Nancy's overtures, which apparently began in 1926, about getting him to visit her at Cliveden and be introduced to people ("She thinks I want to meet people: I don't. But Charlotte sometimes does").[24] However, after accepting the invitation for Christmas 1927 Shaw and Charlotte enjoyed regular stays at Cliveden until 1942 (the year before Charlotte's death), by which time a section of the house had been turned into a military hospital for the second time, the first being during World War I. Under Nancy's regime as mistress of the house, it was visited by a remarkable number of famous people, including President Franklin D. Roosevelt and his wife, Eleanor, Winston Churchill, Charlie Chaplin, and Helen Keller. The Shaw-Astor friendship itself became famous. A. E. Johnson, an American academic, has left a record of his memories of a reception Lady Astor gave for Shaw at the Astor town house, at which someone quoted the definition of England as "an island lying off the east coast of the Irish Free State entirely inhabited by Bernard Shaw and Lady Astor," to which Shaw is reported to have replied: "*Why drag in Lady Astor?*"[25]

* * *

Shaw's visit to Russia in 1931 was attended by extraordinary fanfare. When the train carrying the visiting party pulled into the Alexandrovsky station in Moscow, he was amazed to be met by a brass band, a military guard of honor, banners emblazoned with his name and portrait, cheering crowds of workers ("a monstrous mobbery" is how Shaw described the scene to Charlotte in one of his almost daily and sweetly affectionate letters to her),[26] flashing cameras, journalists, and dignitaries representing the Communist government and the Society of Soviet Writers.

In Moscow Shaw and the other visitors were ensconced in the Hotel Metropole, where Shaw found himself well accommodated: "Food splendid for me. Hotel sitting, bath, and bedroom en suite, couldn't be bettered. . . . Health uproarious. Envy me," he wrote in a postscript to a letter addressed to Charlotte.[27] Upon arriving at the Metropole, the "desperately mothering" Nancy insisted Shaw be allowed to rest. (A couple of days later Shaw reported that Nancy wanted to wash his hair with Lux, a task she said she could do better than the Bond Street hair stylist Bertha Hammond—and later did perform.)[28] Her indefatigable charge was not to be controlled, however, and he immediately set off to see Lenin's tomb, the Kremlin, and "the three churches where the Tsars were christened, married, & buried."[29] The following days and evenings were crowded with an extraordinary series of meetings, receptions, and theatrical events, which included meetings with the great director and drama theorist Konstantin Stanislavsky, plus visits to a huge electrical works factory (where they were mobbed by workers at lunchtime), a penal settlement for homeless boys, a collective farm, and to the Kamerny Theater, where Shaw witnessed an adaptation of the Bertolt Brecht and Kurt Weill work *Die Dreigroschenoper* (*The Threepenny Opera*), which he described to Charlotte as "an amazing and at points disgusting perversion of [John Gay's] the Beggar's Opera."[30]

From Moscow the travelers made an excursion to Leningrad, where they were accommodated in the Grand Ducal suites of the Hotel de l'Europe. Returning to Moscow on his seventy-fifth birthday (26 July), Shaw was taken to a racetrack where the events included a special "Bernard Shaw Handicap," about which he remarked: "I suppose there will be only one horse in the race since there's no competition in a Socialist state."[31] In the evening of the same day he was taken to the Trade Union Central Hall, formerly the Hall of Nobles, where, before an audience of some two thousand people, he was lauded in a marathon birthday celebration speech by Anatoly Lunacharsky, a former Soviet commissar responsible for education and the fine arts and one of Shaw's principal hosts in Russia. Both the speech and Shaw's complimentary reply about Russia were greeted with thunderous applause. Three days later, on 29 July 1931, the crowning event of the whole visit took place when Shaw, Lady Astor, and Lord Lothian were granted the rare privilege of an informal interview with Joseph Stalin, the general secretary of the Central Committee of the Communist Party. The interview lasted two hours and twenty minutes—far beyond the standard twenty minutes usually allotted.

Shaw's visit to Russia was at times comically stage-managed. On 22 July, after visiting the penal settlement for homeless boys, the tourists were taken to a big theater where a film about the penal settlement was being shown. "We were late," Shaw wrote to Charlotte, "but the film was stopped and begun over again when the audience had been instructed to receive me with tumultuous applause, which I acknowledged in Chaliapin's* best manner."[32] Every effort was made to impress and flatter Shaw, and everywhere he was shown what the Russians wanted him to see—which was also what he wanted to see. In Shaw's eyes Russia seemed to be fulfilling many of the hopes he had cherished since his early days as a young Socialist firebrand in London.

The Stalin who greeted Shaw on 29 July 1931 was a mask, the same smiling and apparently benevolent figure who was known as "Uncle Joe" in America, western Europe, and the British colonies throughout World War II and beyond. An American lecturer and author with the imposingly literary name of Henry Wadsworth Longfellow Dana, who had been spending six months in Russia working on a book about Soviet drama at the time of the touring party's visit, records that Shaw said of Stalin: "I expected to see a Russian working man and I found a Georgian gentleman. He was not only at ease himself, but he had the art of setting us at our ease. He was charmingly good humoured. There was no malice in him, but also no credulity."[33]

There was, alas, a great deal of uncharacteristic credulity in Shaw's assessment of both Stalin and Russia. There was less, apparently, in the reactions of Nancy Astor, who evidently asked awkward questions and, according to Shaw, maintained a critical stance toward the Communist officials and workers. "Nancy jollies them all until they do not know whether they are head up or heels," Shaw reported after one round of visits; and at the electrical works factory she "got on a dray and schoolmarmed them in a manner utterly unconceivable by the Communist mind."[34]

Eugene Lyons, a journalist representing the American United Press agency in Russia, who was responsible for covering the visit, took a very dim view of what he summed up from the point of view of himself and his staff as "a fortnight of clowning that ran us ragged." Shaw, he says, was completely taken in by appearances: "He judged food conditions by the Metropole menu, collectivisation by the model farm, the GPU by the model colony at Bolshevo, socialism by the twittering of attendant sycophants."[35] By the time of Shaw's visit, the Stalinist reign of terror—which comprised forced labor camps for political prisoners, compulsory collectivization, and a ruthless process of suppression, which involved the murder of millions of people—was well under way.

In the early 1930s a few Westerners—including people who began by being quite well disposed toward Communism, such as Malcolm Muggeridge,

*Fyodor Ivanovich Chaliapin (1873–1938) was a famous Russian opera singer whom Shaw had heard at Drury Lane in 1914 (SM3:541). He is said to have excelled in the role of Mephistopheles (Shaw's childhood hero) in Gounod's *Faust*.

and Shaw's great friend, the heavyweight boxing champion Gene Tunney—were denouncing the brutally repressive regime in Russia.[36] Nevertheless Shaw's faith in the Russian experiment not only remained unshaken but was strengthened by his visit; upon returning to England, he wrote very favorable reports of what was happening in that country. According to Charlotte Shaw, he came back to Ayot St Lawrence looking bronzed and fit, having had "the time of his life" and saying that the visit seemed like "a splendid, sunny dream."[37]

Although Shaw never joined the Communist Party, his overall admiration for "the great Communist experiment,"[38] as he called it in his reply to Lunacharsky's encomium in Moscow, was repeatedly expressed. In many ways his endorsement of the "Communist experiment" seems completely at odds with the spirit of Shavian comedy, in which, so often, attempts to impose system and theory on life and experimentations with living beings—the word *experiment* is placed in a very critical light in the dialogue of *Pygmalion*—are swept away by laughter and the unexpected ways in which life itself behaves. In the case of Russia, Shaw seems almost to have been trapped in the web of his own earlier ideas. Those ideas were fashioned in response to the tyrannies and injustices of nineteenth-century capitalism. Shaw, however, never seems to have realized that "solutions" such as the kind of state that was being created in a sea of blood in twentieth-century Russia involved far worse forms of tyranny than those that had been overthrown.

* * *

The pattern established in the Moscow visit of 1931—huge publicity, the besieging of Shaw by journalists and paparazzi, public receptions and welcomes by high-ranking officials—was repeated in his subsequent world travels over the next five years. During his South African tour in 1932, he met Prime Minister James Hertzog, General Jan Christiaan Smuts, and millionaire I. W. Schlesinger. He also addressed an audience numbering three thousand in the Cape Town City Hall for three hours—without using notes. During his meeting with Smuts he confused the general (who thought he was talking about Lawrence of Arabia, not D. H. Lawrence), by telling him that "every schoolgirl of sixteen should read [D. H. Lawrence's] *Lady Chatterley's Lover*."[39] On the world cruise in 1933 the Shaws dined with the governor of Manila and Theodore Roosevelt Jr., the son of the former president. In Shanghai they were introduced to Soong Chingling, widow of the Chinese revolutionary leader Sun Yatsen and sister of Madame Chiang Kai-shek, before taking a train to Beijing and flying over the Great Wall of China in an airplane. In Japan they met the prime minister, Admiral Makoto Saito, and had a two-hour talk with the minister of war, General Sadao Azaki, before witnessing a performance of a Noh play in Shaw's honor.

In the United States, where they concluded their world tour in 1933, they mingled with celebrities from the media and entertainment worlds rather than with political leaders. After a daylong bombardment by journalists in San Francisco, the next day they flew to newspaper magnate William Randolph Hearst's "ranch" at San Simeon, where they were the guests of Hearst and his mistress, stage actress and film star Marion Davies. During their four-day stay, Shaw swam in the Hearst swimming pools and no doubt enjoyed being surrounded by a number of "Hollywood starlets and intimate friends of Davies."[40] (One female observer in Moscow noted that "even at seventy-six . . . he had an eye for the ladies.")[41] From the Hearst ranch the Shaws headed for Santa Monica. Following an alarming forced landing in their airplane, they visited the MGM Studios at Culver City, where they were entertained at a luncheon hosted by Davies; the other guests included Louis B. Mayer, Charlie Chaplin, Clark Gable, and John Barrymore.

From Culver City the Shaws rejoined the *Empress of Britain* and sailed via Los Angeles and the Panama Canal to the Caribbean, and then north to New York. They arrived at Pier 61, on West Twenty-first Street, on 11 April 1933 and were greeted by the usual flurry of journalists and photographers. Shaw's main engagement in New York was an address at the Metropolitan Opera House under the auspices of the American Academy of Political Science. The lecture, which lasted one hour and forty minutes, was entitled "The Future of Political Science in America." Shaw roundly criticized American capitalism and culture, which was not exactly music to the ears of most of the thirty-five hundred audience members in the opera house; nor was it to many of those who listened to a live broadcast on national radio, several hundred of whom sent in complaints during the speech. Quite early in his speech, in the context of criticizing the excessive worship of individual freedom as an ideal (at the expense of social responsibility) and what he described as the anarchistic forces of laissez-faire capitalism, Shaw described the Statue of Liberty as a "monstrous idol" and suggested that all the monument needed for completion was to carry on its pedestal "the inscription written by Dante on the gate of Hell: 'All hope abandon, ye who enter here.'"[42]

According to the American critic Edmund Wilson, who was present, Shaw's Irish voice and graceful stage manner had not lost their charm. However, although he received an enthusiastic response from a few radicals in the dollar seats in the gallery, he was addressing a mostly unsympathetic, stony-faced audience. In Wilson's colorful description, Shaw was speaking in a depressingly unfriendly environment, supplied by the "ugly and stale magnificence" of the huge auditorium, to a "vast dumb audience," a "demoralizing aquarium of blind deep-sea creatures." Among the "shirt-fronts" in the five-dollar seats, according to Wilson, not a hand stirred in applause during the speech.[43] Shaw was unaware at the time that sitting behind him onstage was a group of financial tycoons of the kind he was criticizing in his speech, members of the board of directors of the Academy of Political Science.[44] It is possible that Wilson may have exaggerated the poor reception of the speech. However, it was mostly very pugnacious in substance—albeit tempered by some complimentary remarks about the sponsoring organization for which the lecture was, in fact, intended as a fund-raiser and for which Shaw, as usual, claimed no fee. When it was published in an British edition later in 1933, it appeared under the title *The Political Madhouse in America and Nearer Home.*

The most distant journey for these world travelers was that to New Zealand in 1934, for which they embarked on the SS *Rangitane* on 8 February, a round-trip voyage that was not concluded until 17 May. Both Shaws greatly enjoyed New Zealand and felt they could quite happily have settled there. They were, in turn, warmly greeted and much feted. In Auckland they were welcomed at a viceregal garden-party luncheon at Government House by Viscount Bledisloe, the governor-general, and his wife. Later in their visit they called on the prime minister, George Forbes. There were other public occasions, including addresses to the Auckland and Wellington Fabians, and a meeting with Sir Truby King, founder of the Karitane hospitals and clinics for infants. As was normally the case, Shaw's career as a creative writer was not at all interrupted by this voyage. During his travels to New Zealand he began and completed his new play, *The Simpleton of the Unexpected Isles,* and immediately afterward began composing another full-length play entitled *The Millionairess,* the first draft of which was completed before the SS *Rangitane* docked at Plymouth in May.

* * *

One of the most marked effects his world travels—particularly those to Africa, India, and the Pacific—had on Shaw's creative writing and his world outlook was the way in which it stimulated a new interest in non-European religions, cultures, and peoples. The action of the later plays frequently involves a journey to exotic settings and locales, including the Middle East, the Pacific, and, finally, the place where the twain of East and West do meet: Panama. Black Africans, Chinese, Indians, and island natives perform major roles in the narrative and thematic developments of the plays; it is significant that Shaw chose a young African woman as the protagonist of his 1933 fable *The Adven-*

tures of the Black Girl in Her Search for God. In the final act of Shaw's last full-length play, *Buoyant Billions: A Comedy of No Manners,* the eastward journey comes full circle, and the drawing room of English comedy undergoes a radical transformation. The setting for the last two acts of *Buoyant Billions* is "*a drawing room in Belgrave Square, London, converted into a Chinese temple on a domestic scale.*" Members of colored races in the late works are often presented as physically beautiful and spiritually dignified people against whom decadent and unhealthy whites compare very unfavorably.

Shaw was particularly impressed by the beauty of the people and the sights he saw in Ceylon (now Sri Lanka), India, and China. In April 1933, upon returning from a world cruise, he had a chance meeting in Hyde Park with Virginia Woolf, who on this occasion recorded—among other samples of Shaw's "great spurt of ideas"—his comments on the Sinhalese and Chinese people: "The Ceylon people are the original human beings—we are smudged copies. I caught the Chinese looking at us with horror—that we should be human beings!"[45] His comment on the people of "Ceylon" was directly reflected in a speech given to Sir Jafna Pandranath, the elderly Sinhalese gentleman in the play *On the Rocks* (1933), who, having denounced the English as barbarians, goes on to say: "Look at your faces and look at the faces of my people in Ceylon, the cradle of the human race. There you see Man as he came from the hand of God, who has left on every feature the unmistakeable stamp of the great original artist. There you see Woman with eyes in her head that mirror the universe."

In Bombay Shaw was entertained by "three exquisite dancers (sisters) from Nepal" who "gave their best performance before Bernard Shaw" in a ceremony lasting three hours.[46] In the Walkeshwar Hills, outside Bombay, he was delighted by a panoramic view from a Jain marble temple on a hilltop; once inside the temple, he became intensely interested in the small images of various gods and goddesses that had been placed in individual niches in the walls. "When the people see these sculptured images," he asked his guide, "do they accept them in, in their beliefs and in their thoughts, conceived as such, in concrete form and shape?" "I affirmed this," the guide reported. The same guide gave Shaw a detailed explanation of the posture of meditation portrayed in the "huge central marble image of Tirthankara," a prophet in the Jain religion, in the inner sanctum of the temple.[47]

The visit to the temple and other experiences in India and Sri Lanka are likely to have been in Shaw's mind when he conceived the setting of the first act of his play *The Simpleton of the Unexpected Isles,* the writing of which he commenced on 16 February 1934 en route to New Zealand. The setting includes a "raised flower garden" in which four shrines contain living figures of two girl-goddesses and two youthful gods sitting cross-legged. Aged somewhere between seventeen and twenty, at this point in the play they appear "magically beautiful in their Indian dresses, softly brilliant. . . . Their expressions are intent, grave, and inscrutable."

His visits to the East left a powerful imprint on Shaw's mind and imagination. The perceptions of non-European civilizations, religions, and cultures he had formed during the course of his travels in the early 1930s now began to vie with Russia as touchstones against which the West was weighted and found wanting. The Orient became for him something of an ideal place—a pastoral world, so to speak—in which humanity survives in its unspoiled state and in whose religious cultures great physical beauty is combined with contemplative stillness. Shaw's preoccupation with religious subjects was particularly pronounced—and took off in new directions—during this period of his life. At the end of a long letter, written in December 1934, to Sir Francis Younghusband—explorer, soldier, and religious mystic who, two years later, was to become the founder of the World Congress of Faiths—Shaw referred to his play *The Simpleton* and said that it would show Younghusband that "I too have found in the east a quality of religion which is lacking in these islands [England and Ireland]."[48]

* * *

The erotic figures of young Indian gods and goddesses in *The Simpleton* (who, in a characteristic Shavian twist, eventually turn out to be completely vapid and quite dangerous) belong to a vein of sexual fantasy that runs through the later works of Shaw and is closely related to his interest in nonwhite peoples and cultures. Fictional marriages between dark-skinned women and white male characters convey the impression of being projections of Shaw's own fantasy life that have clear autobiographical reference. In *Heartbreak House* we learn that Captain Shotover has a "black" wife "somewhere in Jamaica." After being frustrated in her extensive search, the heroine of *The Adventures of the Black Girl in Her Search for God* ends up marrying a bearded, red-headed Irish Socialist who likes gardening, has homespun ideas about Creative Evolution, and who, in John Farleigh's authorized illustrations to the story, looks very much like Shaw. The nubile "black girl" herself is represented in the illustrations as a strongly eroticized naked figure who carries a phallic-looking knobkerry for smashing idols; she is described in the story as "a fine creature, whose satin skin and shining muscles made the white missionary folk seem like ashen ghosts by contrast." Physically she recalls the "handsome negress" with "black satin skin" in *Back to Methuselah*, who is discovered in her underwear when she accidentally forgets to switch off her visual communication device, and who talks about the "ashy faces" of "white beauties."

The Adventures of the Black Girl in Her Search for God was written in Africa in 1932 during an enforced stay brought about by a motorcar accident, with Shaw at the wheel, which resulted in extensive injuries to Charlotte. The Shaws had set out from Cape Town in a hired car, heading for Cape Elizabeth, where they planned to embark for Durban and the return voyage to England. Having successfully negotiated some mountain ranges "in a masterly manner," as he jokingly reported in a letter to his friend Lady Rhondda—a feminist and founding editor of *Time and Tide*—Shaw had increased his speed on a straight stretch of road, and put the car into a spin, which he overcorrected. "I got out of it," Shaw wrote, "by jumping a fence, crashing through a bunker with 5 strands of barbed wire snapping one after another in a vain attempt to restrain me, and plunging madly down a steep place until I had the happy thought of shifting my straining foot from the accelerator to the brake." He himself escaped lightly, with a crack on the chin and a clip on the knee. Drawing on a medley of Shakespearean allusions, he gave a vivid description of his passenger's very different fate: "But Charlotte!! I can't describe it. Broken head, two black eyes, sprained left arm, bruised back, and a hole in her shin not so deep as a well nor so wide as a church door but—let me not think on't." Charlotte, he added ruefully, had been "so happy and well in the sunshine."[49]

The accident occurred on 10 February and it was not until 17 March that Charlotte had recuperated sufficiently at Knysna—an attractive seaside town on the South Cape, between Port Elizabeth and Cape Town—to be able to travel to the town of George, where there was a substantial airport. There the Shaws chartered a Union Airways Junker to take them back to Cape Town, where they joined their ship, the *Warwick Castle*.

The tale Shaw wrote in less than three weeks during his stay in South Africa in early 1932 is a remarkable work. Drawing on narrative models such as Voltaire's *Candide* and Samuel Johnson's *Rasselas*, Shaw has the lively protagonist of *The Adventures of the Black Girl in Her Search for God* undertake a picaresque journey, in the course of which she encounters and interrogates representatives of most of the world's major religions, beginning with the vengeful God of the Old Testament, who demands human and animal sacrifices. The quizzical and independent-minded young woman finds fault with each religion she encounters during her search and wields her trusty knobkerry to smash numerous idols.

Eventually the Black Girl meets an old philosopher, who, in both his opinions and in John Farleigh's illustrations to the tale, is clearly meant to represent Voltaire. The philosopher tells her that "the best place to seek God in is a garden." It is in the garden of this philosopher that she meets and captures in marriage another philosophical gardener, the red-headed Irish Socialist. Shaw had a strong tendency to identify himself with Voltaire, and the closing pages of *Black Girl* provide a very clear instance of this.[50] The two gardeners are both potential marriage partners for the Black Girl, but the Voltaire-like candidate says he is too old and that she had "better marry that Irishman."

The Irishman provides for his charming captor a rustic version of the idea of God—according to Shaw's theory of Creative Evolution—as an evolving, incomplete phenomenon immanent in the universe. His comic account of God, delivered during a pause while digging up "podatoes" in "Voltaire's" garden, in fact provides one of the most succinct expositions of the Shavian credo: "My own belief is that he's not all that he sets up to be. He's not properly made and finished yet. There's somethin in us that's dhrivin at him, and somethin out of us that's dhrivin at him: that's certain; and the only other thing that's certain is that the somethin makes plenty of mistakes in thryin to get there. We'v got to find out its way for it as best we can, you and I; for there's a hell of a lot of other people thinkin of nothin but their own bellies."

Following this speech, the narrator of the tale delivers an even more succinct account of the Irishman's conception of God as "an eternal but as yet unfulfilled purpose." *The Adventures of the Black Girl in Her Search for God,* written during a brief pause in one of the world traveler's own adventures, was a daring and risky story; for a time it seriously imperiled the friendship between Shaw and Dame Laurentia McLachlan and aroused the anger of some religious groups. But, it was a great publishing success. The tale was published in a print run of twenty-five thousand copies in December 1932 and there were five additional printings of that edition, totaling fifty-seven thousand copies, and another nine from 1933 to 1936, totaling forty-eight thousand copies.

* * *

It was on their second journey to South Africa in 1935 that the Shaws received news in Durban of the death in a motorcycle accident of T. E. Lawrence (Lawrence of Arabia). Lawrence was first introduced to the Shaws on 25 March 1922 by Sydney Cockerell. Five months later he sent one of the eight privately printed copies of his book *Seven Pillars of Wisdom* to Shaw, asking him if he would read it and give his opinion as to its worth. Both Shaws were enormously impressed with the work and greatly assisted Lawrence with revisions and the production of an abridged version for general circulation, which was published in 1927 under the title *Revolt in the Desert.* Lawrence had an almost filial relationship with the Shaws and developed a particularly close friendship with Charlotte, who, as we have seen, conducted an extensive and often self-revelatory correspondence with him. Lawrence was a frequent guest at Ayot St Lawrence. While he was in military camp, Charlotte sent him hampers of food from the London store Fortnum & Mason. Seeking anonymity after his discharge from the Royal Air Force in 1923, Lawrence sought to reshape his identity by joining the Royal Tank Corps as a private soldier, adopting the name Private T. E. Shaw.[51]

Lawrence was a keen motorcyclist, and the machine on which he had his fatal fall on 14 May 1935—a Brough SS-100, which he named "Boanerges"—was a gift to him from Charlotte and several other friends.[52] Charlotte felt his loss keenly. "I somehow cannot feel he is really gone," she wrote to Emery Walker's daughter, Dorothy, from Ayot St Lawrence. "He seems to be here in this little house he came to so often." Later she told Dorothy that her association with Lawrence was "the strangest contact of my life."[53] In Shaw's 1932 play *Too True to Be Good* the character of Private Meek—whose knowledge of local dialects and customs and strategic brilliance astound his superior officers in an outpost of the British empire where the later acts of the play are set—was closely modeled on Lawrence of Arabia. Private Meek makes his first appearance in the play on a rather noisy motorcycle.

* * *

Two other literary associations of Shaw's that flourished in the 1930s and early 1940s were those with fellow playwright Sean O'Casey and Oscar Wilde's former lover Lord Alfred ("Bosie") Douglas.

Sean O'Casey's plays portrayed with intimacy, humor, and trenchant criticism a Dublin world of tenement houses and slums that Shaw had acquired some knowledge of in his childhood—and from which he recoiled. Perhaps no playwright has ever captured so powerfully as O'Casey the tragicomedy of fanatical and self-destructive patriotism in Ireland. Shaw had a great respect for O'Casey's work and paid him a generous tribute in a 1934 letter to Nancy Astor, in which he wrote that his plays "are wonderfully impressive and *reproachful* without being irritating like mine."[54]

After early successes in Dublin at the Abbey Theatre in the 1920s, O'Casey felt profoundly disappointed and let down when Yeats rejected his play *The Silver Tassie* in 1928. Before this he had become unhappy about the new Irish state, and had moved to London where he met his wife, Eileen. They were great admirers of Shaw's work and became very fond of him and Charlotte, often lunching with them at Adelphi Terrace and Whitehall Court. Shaw read all of O'Casey's plays and attended London productions of a number of them.

In 1932 O'Casey declined the invitation (drafted by Shaw) to join the Irish Academy of Letters, founded by Yeats and Shaw. Shaw was delighted when Eileen visited him at Ayot St Lawrence in January 1950 and had framed the photograph she presented him of the O'Casey family. Like Nancy Astor, Eileen was one of the last people to see Shaw alive; she provides a moving account of her visit to Shaw on his deathbed in her book *Sean* (1971).

Shaw met Oscar Wilde's "Bosie," Lord Alfred Douglas, once in 1895 and thought him a "brat" on account of his behavior toward Wilde. In the 1930s, however, a friendly and lively correspondence was conducted between the two, in the course of which Douglas began calling Shaw, who was very helpful to him in a number of ways, "St. Christopher"—Shaw responded by addressing Douglas as "Childe Alfred."[55] A main subject of the early letters was Frank Harris's controversial biography of Oscar Wilde. Shaw was indirectly associated with the second edition of Harris's biography (1918) through having some of the annotations he made on the work in page proof announced (without his permission) on the cover of the published book as a promotional strategy. A hostile critique of the biography by Robert H. Sherard, published in 1937, was endorsed in a preface by Lord Alfred Douglas, who thought he had been misrepresented by Harris.

The Shaw-Douglas correspondence thus began under tricky circumstances. Shaw admired the Harris biography of Wilde. By the time of the controversy, which surfaced in the Sherard book, he was urging Constable to bring out an English edition of the biography in order to help Harris's widow, Helen O'Hara ("Nellie") Harris, who was living in straitened circumstances in France and depended on what little income she derived from her former husband's publications. Shaw was extremely generous with his time and advice to Nellie, but the stumbling block with respect to Harris's biography of Wilde was the opposition and likely litigation from Douglas. As a result of the correspondence—and not without further contretemps—a new edition of the biography, with emendations and revisions carried out by Shaw with Douglas's aid, was published in 1938 and bore a lengthy preface by Shaw.

From this base, the Shaw-Douglas correspondence widened into other subjects, including religion (Douglas had become a Catholic and a teetotaler by this time), Douglas's poetry (about which Shaw was quite complimentary), and English and Irish politics. With regard to the latter, a principal point at issue in the correspondence was De Valera's declaration in 1940 of Irish neutrality and his refusal to allow Allied use of Irish ports, which had aroused the fury of Douglas, who had published a violently anti-Irish pamphlet on the subject entitled *Ireland and the War against Hitler*. Shaw had a very clear grasp of the political complexity of the "Irish ports" question and understood the grave threat to Ireland (as well as England) posed by its neutrality. He thought Douglas's approach was inflammatory and unwise and on 14 November 1940 wrote:

> Childe, Childe
> Politically you have the brains of a grasshopper; and you have far too much courage. If the Douglases had less courage and more commonsense they would now be the royal house of Scotland. . . . Your notion of dealing with the situation is to rake up old dirt to set the Irish by the ears again.[56]

In a letter written a few days earlier, Shaw told Douglas that the situation was "dangerous, but has the advantage that it offers for the first time to unite Ireland, not in support of England, but against Hitler, which comes to the same thing."[57]

* * *

In 1961 a book was published in London entitled *Shaw the Villager and Human Being: A Biographical Symposium.* The editor was the author, photographer, and Shavian enthusiast Allan Chappelow, who—apart from compiling this work and a large companion volume entitled *Shaw: "The Chucker-Out"* (1969)—made a number of fine photographic studies of Shaw in the last year of his life. One of the great merits of *Shaw the Villager* is that Chappelow was able to include recollections of Shaw—and often also of Charlotte—from quite humble village folk and servants in the Shaw household that would otherwise almost certainly have been lost. The overall impression left by the reports recorded in Chappelow's book is that Shaw was highly respected and well liked as a neighbor in his village and employer in his household, and that Charlotte was also well regarded.

As with all recollections, those of the villagers and servants at Ayot St Lawrence need to be treated with circumspection as biographical evidence. Can one really believe the report of Mrs. Edith Reeves—who, with her husband, ran a farm that adjoined the Shaw property—that "Mrs Shaw told me once that she would very much like to have children"?[58] This is contradicted by what Charlotte told T. E. Lawrence in her letter to him dated 17 May 1927. On the other hand, it is hard to reject Mrs. Reeves's other statements about her neighbors, including the comment that Shaw used to toss the mown grass from the extensive lawn at "Shaw's Corner" over the fence as fodder for his neighbors' cows and livestock, and that although he gave them cabbages and other vegetables free of charge from his garden, he always paid for the raspberries and cherries he got from the Reeves (especially the White Hart cherries he was particularly fond of). As Mrs. Reeves explained, "I think his view was that fruit and vegetable growing was part of our business as farmers, but only a hobby for him."[59] Her husband made up for this arrangement by helping the Shaws' gardener, Henry ("Harry") Higgs, with mowing of the lawn. Harry Higgs was the Shaws' head gardener from 1901 to 1943, and his wife, Clara Rebecca Higgs, was his housekeeper for the same period.

"I was very fond of him. During all the 16 years I was with him, he never said one cross word to me, nor I to him." This testimony from Margaret ("Maggie") Cashin, an Irish parlor maid who served Shaw for the last sixteen years of his life, was typical of most of those coming from the servants in Shaw's household. Maggie Cashin summed up a remarkable quality in Shaw, noted by many others who have left recollections of him that: "He never bore malice to anybody. If an article or play of his was criticised he'd only laugh at it. He didn't care—he was too big a person—very charitable and good-natured and charming."[60] He was a very tidy man, she reported, and no trouble to look after.

In 1938 Maggie Cashin was joined by a housemaid, the seventeen-year-old Violet Pond, who was later to serve Winston Churchill and Clement Attlee in the British prime ministerial residences of Chequers and No. 10 Downing Street. According to an interview about her career published in the *Times* (London) in 2001, what Violet liked best about Shaw was "his invariable courtesy to her and the way he said her name." As she recalled: "I used to plan to be dusting the telephone when he came down the stairs. He would come down and he would say: 'Good morning, Vi-o-let.' It was like music. Nobody has said my name like Mr Shaw."[61]

Violet loved music and "the highlight of her day was standing discreetly on the landing and listening to Shaw play the piano. It stood in the hall, and he played every evening for his own benefit and also for Charlotte." Shaw took a photograph of Violet, an incident that created a frosty atmosphere in the kitchen when Mrs. Higgs found out; she did not think "a maid should push herself forward." In 1943 Violet was called up to serve in the Auxiliary Territorial Service (ATS). After some horrifying experiences in the London Blitz, she was suddenly summoned to Watford, where an army car took her to a destination she only later discovered was Chequers, the country retreat of British prime ministers. She served there in the household of Winston Churchill and, later, under the postwar prime ministership of Clement Attlee, at No. 10 Downing Street. The strict training of Mrs. Higgs stood her in good stead for such posts. Later on she married a Mr. Fred Liddle.[62]

At the time of the appointment in 1938 of Violet Pond as housemaid, the Shaw staff included (in addition to her): Blanche Patch, secretary; Clara and

Henry Higgs, housekeeper and head gardener; Maggie Cashin, parlor maid; Frederick William Day, chauffeur; and Frederick Thomas Drury; assistant gardener. Following the retirement in 1943 (after forty-two years of service with the Shaws) of Clara and Henry Higgs, Fred Drury became head gardener and Mrs. Alice Laden was appointed housekeeper.

Charlotte Shaw inspired a similar loyalty and respect from servants to that accorded her husband. "Mrs Shaw *made* Mr Shaw," declared Fred Drury. "She was a real helpmate and constant companion in all aspects of his life." Drury made this declaration after evoking some memorable images of the Shaws in their garden at Ayot St Lawrence: "Mr and Mrs Shaw used to walk around the garden together quite often. . . . They used to put stones in a heap in a certain spot to mark every mile. They had a special route round the garden which was just about a mile, and they put one stone down every time they passed it. Both their initials were engraved on the glass of the greenhouse, framed around with shamrocks."[63]

Drury was one of several people who commented on Shaw's generous support of local activities, including sizable donations to the local football club (of which Drury was honorary secretary), the provision of Christmas boxes for all the children in the village, and other examples of the squire's bounty. Drury summed up his two employers with the words: "Mr. Shaw was a very nice gentleman—all bark and no bite. And Mrs. Shaw was one of the best."

One of the liveliest of the Shaw servants was the Scottish cook-housekeeper Mrs. Alice Laden. A trained nurse from Aberdeen, she was first employed by the Shaws to look after Charlotte at Whitehall Court during her final illness. Following Charlotte's death in 1943, she stayed on with Shaw at Ayot St Lawrence and "guarded and protected him with the ferocity of a lioness."[64] Although she clearly had great admiration for Shaw, from the outset she made no bones about what she thought of his Socialist ideas and her own politics. Shaw had explained that he didn't want a housekeeper who was a Shaw fan, but rather one who was a good housekeeper. "Well," said Mrs. Laden, "I am a rank Tory and I heartily disagree with all Socialist views."[65] During the British election campaign in 1950, she cheekily pinned a photograph of Winston Churchill to the gate of Shaw's Corner. The magnificent and varied feasts that resulted from Alice Laden's repertoire of vegetarian cooking for Shaw are described in *The George Bernard Shaw Vegetarian Cookbook*, which she wrote and published in 1972. During his later years, she says, Shaw "lived on soups, eggs, milk, honey, cheese, fruit, cream and lemon juice."[66] Although she thought him "queer and cantankerous at times," she described him—in her Aberdonian burr—as "a vur-r-r-ee nice man . . . so generous and kind, and a charming man to the last."[67]

* * *

It is difficult not be impressed by the almost complete uniformity of positive remarks about Shaw from the Ayot St Lawrence villagers and his servants. Except for Mrs. Laden, who became quite bossy—perhaps necessarily—toward Shaw during his last years, a respectful distance was maintained between the servants and their employers. However, both Shaws were obviously unusually kind and considerate in their dealings with the people who worked for them. Their relations with them is in sharp contrast to the often contemptuous and snobbish attitudes many people of similar social rank at the time—such as Virginia Woolf and other members of the Bloomsbury circle—adopted toward servants. Clive Bell referred to them as "one's body slaves."[68]

After reading some of Shaw's later political writings, which dealt with society in the abstract (or semiabstract), it is quite a relief to turn to these accounts of the almost unfailingly kindly and friendly way in which he engaged with people with whom he actually came into close contact in his house and village. In these accounts we see a side of Shaw that was also displayed in his unusual capacity for forming and sustaining meaningful friendships and his generosity with his time and money in helping people with their personal problems. Works such as the preface to *On the Rocks*, in which Shaw conducts the extended bad joke of a "scientific" discussion of extermination, and some of his writings about Mussolini show a callousness that is curiously out of keeping with this aspect of his personality. Fred Drury's comment about Shaw ("all bark and no bite") was no doubt true in some respects. But the bark could sometimes be quite chilling, representing a side of Shaw that cannot simply be dismissed as not being the "real" person. Fortunately we possess a host of other images of him, in his more private dealings with fellow human beings, that show him in a very engaging light.

4.1. Shaw seated on a stone bollard at Burren Pier on the southern shore of Galway Bay, 1922.

4.2. Shaw in AC Motor Car, December 1921.

4.3. Shaw on diving platform at Casa Estella, Cap d'Antibes.

4.4. Shaw at Pompeii, 1932.

4.5. Shaw diving at Madeira, aged sixty-nine, in 1925.

4.6. Shaw in the Strand, London, May 1927.

4.7. Shaw at work in his revolving hut in the garden at Ayot St Lawrence, 1929.

4.8. Sir Edward Elgar, conducting his "Nursery Suite," flanked by the Duke and Duchess of York (later King George VI and Queen Elizabeth, the Queen Mother) on his right and Shaw on his left, 4 June 1931.

4.9. Maggie Cashin, the Shaws' Irish housemaid, receiving mail at Ayot St Lawrence.

4.10. Villa leased by Molly Tompkins on Isola San Giovanni, Lake Maggiore, Italy.

4.11. Molly Tompkins at her exhibition in the Leicester Galleries, London, in 1934.

4.12. Shaw, aged eighty-nine, in the garden at Shaw's Corner, Ayot St. Lawrence, 20 July 1946.

4.13. The house viewed from the garden, with Shaw in foreground.

4.14. Shaw with Danny Kaye at Ayot St Lawrence, 3 May 1949.

4.15. Shaw with Robert Morley and Gabriel Pascal. Publicity photo for the film version of *Major Barbara*, 1941.

4.16. The unreliable caption, written by the ninety-four-year-old Shaw in his own hand, reads: "This is John Graham's latest photograph of me at 96. G. Bernard Shaw 15/8/1950."

24 Last Flourishes and the Call of the Silver Screen

A good deal is conveyed about the spirit of the plays created by Shaw in the last phase of his career as a playwright in a letter he wrote to Leonora (Nora) Ervine, the wife of his future biographer St. John Ervine, in 1934 while returning from New Zealand: "My bolt is shot as far as any definite target is concerned and now, as my playwright faculty still goes on with the impetus of 30 years vital activity, I shoot into the air more and more extravagantly without any premeditation whatever—*advienne que pourra* [come what may]."[1]

The exuberant, freewheeling spontaneity of many of the late flourishes of Shaw's creative genius is well captured in these words. His immediate points of reference in the letter were two works he was composing "mostly in the tropics" on board ship during the cruise: *The Simpleton of the Unexpected Isles* and *The Millionairess*. The first of these two plays—both of which were completed in draft during the 1934 cruise—he described in the letter as "openly oriental, hieratic and insane," and the second as "quite commonplace in form: three acts in the metropolitan area, and the theme quite stuffily matrimonial; but the dialogue is raving lunacy from beginning to end."

Extravagance, in various senses, became a hallmark of the style of the late plays. Exotic settings and fantastical incidents and characters, with frequent complete departures from the conventions of naturalism, became the norm in most of these works. In the opening scene of *Too True to Be Good* (1931) a Monster Microbe, which resembles a human in shape but "*seems to be made of a luminous jelly with a visible skeleton of short black rods,*" reclines on an easy chair next to the bed of a patient in a suburban villa. (The role of the Monster was first played—in a spectacular outfit—by Ernest Thesiger, who had created the role of the Dauphin in the English premiere of *Saint Joan*.) In *The Simpleton* an Angel descends after the sounding of a Last Trump to deliver a selective Last Judgment on various useless specimens of the human race. The Angel is equipped with a comically inefficient flying mechanism, for nothing is perfect in the constantly evolving Shavian universe: "There is always something better," the Angel explains as he asks directions to some convenient "parapet" from which to do a takeoff.

The last trumpetings of Shaw's dramatic career take us into strange worlds of the imagination, with characterizations and narratives often resembling those of allegorical fable. Not surprisingly, *Farfetched Fables* was the title Shaw gave to one of the very last of his works, a series of thematically linked dramatic sketches he wrote in 1948, in which the characters are given generic names such as "Young Man" and "Young Woman."* At times the dramatic techniques in the late works seem to present distinctly Shavian versions of expressionism and surrealism, placing them at a far remove from the basically naturalistic form typical of the works of the 1890s belonging to the "Plays Unpleasant" group, which prompted Oscar Wilde's praise of Shaw's "superb confidence in the dramatic value of the mere facts of life" and "the horrible flesh and blood of [his] creatures."[2]

Although they often express despair, the late plays are still dominated by the comic muse. It was in the course of a discussion of the late works that the American critic Edmund Wilson said: "It is interesting to note—what bears out the idea that Shaw is at his best as an artist—that the last thing he is to lose, apparently, is his gift for pure comic invention, which has survived, not much dimmed, though we may tire of it, since the days of *You Never Can Tell*."[3] The late works have a strong advocate in Martin Meisel, who described them as being "among Shaw's most noteworthy and least noted achievements for the modern theater." Other qualities Meisel praises in these works include "their invention of non-Euclidean worlds for philosophical purposes" and their "use of open allegory and frankly symbolic action and setting."[4]

Although the works written between 1930 and 1950 often exhibit a remarkable continuation of Shaw's creative energy, comic inventiveness, and original way of viewing the world, they also suffer from an excessive profusion of character and incident and too many different focal points of dramatic interest. They are also uneven in quality, a fact Shaw himself perhaps recognized when he remarked to Molly Tompkins in 1935 that "my plays, though not so heavy as they used to be, have still bits and scraps of fine stuff in them."[5] As a group, the late plays have not proven to be enduringly successful on the stage. Among the full-length works, only *The Apple Cart* has had a reasonably strong record of theatrical revival. Other plays in the group had successful revivals in

*Under the direction of Esmé Percy, *Farfetched Fables* was given thirty performances by a private theater club commencing on 6 September 1950, about two months before Shaw's death in November of that year.

the late twentieth century at venues such as the annual Shaw Festival in Canada. Generally they have not become part of the staple repertory of Shavian productions in the theater. On the whole, the last plays received a very mixed reception by contemporary reviewers, who often found them to be eccentric and difficult to fathom.

One of the late plays that has had an unusually interesting life in the theater and on screen is *The Millionairess* (1935), the work mentioned in Shaw's letter to Nora Ervine, whose lead role has attracted such stars as Edith Evans, Katherine Hepburn, Sophia Loren, and Penelope Keith. (A proposal for a film of the play starring Marlene Dietrich did not come to fruition, but a film based on the play and starring Sophia Loren and Peter Sellers was made in 1960.) One of the things Shaw no doubt had in mind when he referred to "the raving lunacy" of the dialogue in *The Millionairess* would have been the manic quality of many of the speeches of the central character—the pugnacious, volatile, tantrum-throwing millionairess—to whom he gave the resounding name of Epifania Ognisanti di Parerga, and who is finally tamed by the gentle, religiously minded Egyptian Doctor. The play is in some ways reminiscent of *The Taming of the Shrew*.

The role of Epifania was well suited to the talents of Katherine Hepburn, who was a great hit in the play during its first West End production in 1952, with Robert Helpmann playing the Doctor. The English theater critic Kenneth Tynan described Hepburn in a Coventry performance of this production as "bang[ing] through the play like a battering ram, living at the top of her lungs, and barking orders like a games mistress run amok."[6] (Unfortunately Hepburn did not encounter the same success on Broadway, where the play flopped.) In the next decade *The Millionairess* gained a new lease on life with the film version, directed by Anthony Asquith, in which Sophia Loren played Epifania and Peter Sellers the Egyptian Doctor, who in this version is Indian.

As a consequence of the fame of the two leading players and the unusual combination of talents, a great deal of media hype surrounded this film. As a biographer of Sellers put it, the production brought about a meeting of "Europe's most voluptuous star and Britain's funniest comic." In the course of making this film, Sellers fell wildly in love with Loren, a feeling brought on, according to more than one account, by the fact that the gentle Doctor Kabir was required to apply lotion to the screen goddess's naked back. Ironically, this passion, openly discussed with his wife, Anne, precipitated serious problems in Sellers's own marriage that echoed those dealt with in the early scenes of Shaw's play.[7]

* * *

The fantastical and extravagant form of the late plays did not prevent some of them from having a pointed relevance to what was happening in the contemporary world, as well as being of interest biographically. Particularly significant in these respects were *Too True to Be Good* and *The Simpleton of the Unexpected Isles.*

As we have seen, *Too True to Be Good* appears to contain clear reflections of Shaw's affair with Molly Tompkins in the portrayal of Aubrey, the ex–flying-ace-and-clergyman-turned-burglar, and Sweetie, the Nurse. In the second act of the play, the born preacher Aubrey philosophizes about Sweetie's unabashed and frank attitude toward erotic desire in ways that clearly link her to the revolutionary new openness toward the "guilty secret" of human sexuality with which D. H. Lawrence was shocking the world in works such as *Lady Chatterley's Lover* (1928) and the paintings, which the police seized as indecent, during his exhibition at the Warren Gallery in London.

Aubrey sees Sweetie as part of an "earthquake" in human discourse, institutions, and our understanding of the world that had occurred in the wake of World War I, blasting old certainties and decorums out of existence. In the second act of *Too True to Be Good* Aubrey likens Sweetie and her articulation of what goes on in the "lower centres" of human consciousness, to Balaam's ass—an allusion to the Old Testament story in which the beast proves wiser than its master after miraculously hearing the will of God through the voice of an angel.[8] In reply to Sweetie's understandable but ignorant objection to being called "Balaam's ass," Aubrey springs to his feet and says:

> Woman: I am paying you a compliment: Balaam's ass was wiser than Balaam. . . . That is what makes Sweetie almost superhuman. Her lower centres speak. Since the war the lower centres have become vocal. And the effect is that of an earthquake. For they speak truths that have never been spoken before—truths that the makers of our domestic institutions have tried to ignore. And now that Sweetie goes shouting them all over the place, the institutions are rocking and splitting and sundering. They leave us no place to live, no certainties, no workable morality, no heaven, no hell, no commandments, and no God.

This is not only an oblique Shavian compliment to D. H. Lawrence and the way in which he courageously smashed the taboos surrounding the subject and celebration of human sexuality. It is also an instance of the way in which *Too True to Be Good* reflects with sharp insight on the contemporary world.

Aubrey's succinct description of the world between the two wars as a place of physical and spiritual disorientation—where there were "no certainties, no workable morality, no heaven, no hell, no commandments, and no God"—is linked to speeches by the philosophical character The Elder in the third act. The Elder tells an audience consisting of Sweetie and the handsome Sergeant she has taken a fancy to that the stable universe of Isaac Newton "has crumbled like the walls of Jericho before the criticism of Einstein . . . all is caprice: the calculable world has become incalculable."

The Sergeant provides another autobiographical link in the play apart from Aubrey. He is an avid reader of Shaw's favorite childhood author, John Bunyan, whose *Pilgrim's Progress* he is discovered reading in a grotto called The Abode of Love. After listening to a reading (with commentary) by the Sergeant of Bunyan's opening words of doom concerning the certain destruction of this world by fire from heaven, Sweetie reveals her familiarity with *The Pilgrim's Progress,* having seen copies of it—in jail, where she has spent some time.

Beneath its fantastical and extravagant surfaces, *The Simpleton of the Unexpected Isles* also demonstrates its relevance to the contemporary world, albeit in ways different from those of *Too True to Be Good.* It, too, conveys a sense of shifting, unstable realities, as suggested in the second part of its title. The work may, as Shaw described it to Nora Ervine, be "openly oriental" and "hieratic," but it is far from being "insane." Both the name of the Canadian liner on which the Shaws were traveling at the time he was writing the play (*The Empress of Britain*) and its early port of call (India) have important resonances in the play. Among other things, *The Simpleton of the Unexpected Isles* is a play about Empire, colonialism, and the uses of religious missionary work as a front for imperialistic exploitation. The "Simpleton" of the title, a Church of England clergyman named Iddy Hammingtap, has been kidnapped at Weston Super Mare by a group of pirates. The "pirates"—clearly a satirical metaphor for commercial entrepreneurs in colonial lands—employ the gentle and naïve Iddy to lend respectability to their activities as "crooks, racketeers, smugglers . . . anything that pays them." In recounting his story, Iddy reports the pirates' remark at the time of his capture: "'You look so innocent and respectable' they said. 'Just what we want!'" Wilks, a suicidal British colonial officer in the play, wishes he were Cecil Rhodes and has fantasies about transforming the whole world into England.

The term *postcolonial* had not, of course, come into currency when *The Simpleton* was composed. Yet in its themes and form the play can lay fair claim to being regarded as anticipating postcolonial preoccupations. Seen from the vantage point of the late-twentieth-century critique of imperialism and colonialism, *The Simpleton* emerges as a strikingly original work, a prescient commentary on eurocentric presumptions about the other worlds over which Britain and Europe held sway.

Although Shaw engaged in notorious flirtations with Fascism in the late 1920s and 1930s, *The Simpleton* remains highly critical of authoritarianism and creates a counterdiscourse to Shaw's nondramatic utterances concerning Fascist leaders. An experiment involving miscegenation between Western and Oriental races in the play ends disastrously, producing four beautiful but mindless and conscienceless children who appear as goddesses and gods at the beginning. As the play develops, the children become progressively more dangerous, finally chanting their masochistic desire to subordinate themselves to Prola as their empress and declaring that "obedience is freedom from the intolerable fatigue of thought." In his treatment of the children, Shaw satirically reflects on both the rise of authoritarianism in Europe and the hysterical jingoism and cultural and political subservience of the British colonies. The abstractions the children finally turn into (when they vanish like the beautiful child of Goethe's Faust and Helen)—Love, Pride, Heroism, and Empire—are treated very critically in the play. Western imperialism is implicitly likened to a Faustian quest for power, ending in empty but dangerous mantras.

A new development in Shaw's thinking about Creative Evolution can be seen in *The Simpleton*. The emphasis here is less on the will and intellect as agents in the evolutionary process and more on Eastern ideas of acquiescence and acceptance, the need to remain open to what life might have in store for us rather than to approach it with preconceived theories. "Let life come," says the spirited young woman in the opening scenes, an injunction that has numerous echoes in the unfolding of the play's singular stories. The end of the play, presided over by the Priest and Priestess of life, Pra and Prola, returns us—albeit in a very different key—to the theme summed up in the title of Shaw's early work *You Never Can Tell*. "There is no Country of the Expected. The Unexpected Isles are the whole world," says Prola, declaring that the future belongs to those "who prefer surprise and wonder to security." The play ends with a ritualistic hailing by Pra and Prola of the "life to come," as "they pat hands, eastern fashion."

The "Irish Methuselah to whom debating and writing are the elixir of life" (as Shaw was described in a 1948 review of *Buoyant Billions*, his last full-length play)[9] still had plenty of playwriting activity in him following the completion of *Too True to Be Good* and *The Simpleton of the Unexpected Isles*. He was still writing a play entitled *Why She Would Not* (disparagingly described by the author as "a pitiable little old man's drivel")[10] as he was turning ninety-four in July 1950, only a few months before his death. However, none of the other late works have quite the same edge, and interest from a biographical viewpoint, for what they reveal about Shaw and his changing perspectives on life in his later years as the two extravaganzas, *Too True* and *The Simpleton*. His farewells to the theater, in the form of public performances, took place in August 1949 at the Malvern Festival, which had been revived after its closure during World War II. The 1949 program included productions of the two final works of Shaw to be staged during his lifetime, *Buoyant Billions: A Comedy of No Manners*, a wild mixture of fablelike narrative and philosophical discussion, and the puppet play *Shakes versus Shav*, in which Shav engages in a war of words and fisticuffs with a figure of the Bard who had been such a potent influence in Shaw's writing from beginning to end.

* * *

The range of Shaw's interests, activities, and associations during the last two decades of his life was greatly extended by his involvement during that time in the film world. With his characteristic zestful interest in such developments, Shaw had become fascinated with film and its possibilities as a medium early in the century, having been a keen photographer. As Bernard F. Dukore points out, as early as 1908 Shaw had confided to Arthur Wing Pinero that he found films irresistible. In a letter dated 19 August 1912 he told Mrs. Patrick Campbell that "I who go to an ordinary theatre with effort and reluctance cannot keep away from the cinema."[11] In the same letter he showed himself to be a very well informed moviegoer. In short, he was, as he declared in 1927, "a movie fan."[12]

From quite early in the century many overtures were made to Shaw about having his plays turned into movies, and large offers were made for the film rights. Shaw's own creative engagement with film as a writer of screenplays occurred during the 1930s and early 1940s. It was during this period—specifically in February 1939—that Shaw's screenplay for *Pygmalion* was awarded an Oscar at the Academy Awards ceremony. Such baubles did not greatly matter to Shaw, though the trophy was displayed on the mantelpiece in his drawing room at Ayot St Lawrence, near a crockery Staffordshire figurine of Shakespeare, shown leaning on a pile of books on a pedestal in a pose somewhat resembling that in the marble statue in Westminster Abbey. The figurine, which he described as his "favourite image" of Shakespeare, was bought by Shaw and Charlotte at the outbreak of World War II in a curio shop at Frinton-on-Sea for twenty-three shillings.[13] Shaw is said to have used the academy trophy for cracking nuts.

During the years he was involved in producing screenplays of his works and collaborating in theatrical productions, Shaw came into contact with many people, the list of whose names now reads like a small roll call of legendary figures in the history of the film at the time: Leslie Howard, Wendy

Hiller, Rex Harrison, Robert Morley, Claude Rains, Vivien Leigh, and Stewart Granger—all of whom played leading roles in film versions of Shaw plays during his lifetime. Almost buried in the cast lists are the names of Deborah Kerr, who debuted in films by playing the part of Jenny Hill, the Salvation Army victim of Bill Walker's bullying ways in *Major Barbara*; Jean Simmons, who appears as a slave girl who plays the harp in *Caesar and Cleopatra;* and Anthony (later Sir Anthony) Quayle, who played the part of Eliza's hairdresser in the British film version of *Pygmalion*.

Shaw also had personal meetings and some associations with Clark Gable, Charlie Chaplin, Louis B. Mayer, and Arthur Rank. A very late entry in Shaw's diaries (10 March 1950) practically jumps off the page when encountered for the first time: "Arthur Rank to pay me £83,705."[14] Looking at the history of Shaw's connections with the film industry, one is reminded again of his remark to Archibald Henderson that he was "up to the chin" in the life of his times.

The major interpreter of Shaw's plays on the screen during the 1930s and 1940s was a flamboyant Hungarian-born film director and producer who went by the name of Gabriel Pascal, his real name being Gabor Lehöl. Pascal says he first met Shaw in 1925 during a nude swim at dawn on the French Riviera. Ten years later he arrived penniless in London, where he requested and was granted the film rights to *Pygmalion*. Pascal produced film versions of *Pygmalion* (starring Wendy Hiller as Eliza and Leslie Howard as Higgins) in 1938, *Major Barbara* (starring Wendy Hiller as Major Barbara, Rex Harrison as Cusins, and Robert Morley as Undershaft) in 1941, and *Caesar and Cleopatra* (starring Claude Raines as Caesar and Vivien Leigh as Cleopatra) in 1945, each with the addition of new scenes devised in collaboration with Shaw. On 18 October 1947 Pascal visited Ayot St Lawrence to introduce Shaw to Valerie Hidveghy, whom he had recently married.

Throughout the 1940s the friendship between Shaw and Pascal deepened and their collaborative Shavian projects continued apace. Some months before his death (which he sensed was near) Shaw wrote a touching, fatherly letter in which he encouraged Pascal to seek out "a young Shaw" for the second half of his career. "You must live in your own generation, not in mine," Shaw told Pascal. "Devotion to an old crock like me is sentimental folly."[15] Pascal died in 1954, a few years after the playwright who had made his name.

Leaving aside the question of their relation to the plays, there is much to admire in the films. In *Major Barbara* a portly and magisterial Robert Morley created a superb rendition of Undershaft. Wendy Hiller, Leslie Howard, Claude Rains, and Vivien Leigh all give excellent performances that linger in the memory in the films in which they appear. However, in some ways the films were a very mixed blessing in the textual history of Shaw's plays. It would not be such a problem if the original play texts had the same accessibility and currency as the screenplays. In the cases of *Pygmalion* and *Major Barbara* in particular the wide circulation of the screenplay versions has meant that the original play texts have tended to be pushed aside and neglected.

There are solid grounds for arguing that the screenplays represent the plays in artistically inferior forms. This is not only evident in a general way—for example, things that are lightly and deftly suggested in the dialogue and left to the reader's or audience's imagination in the plays are often represented in the films in tedious and heavy-handed visual form—but also in terms of major structural and interpretative changes that crudify and sentimentalize the original works.

There is, of course, no way in which critical or biographical commentary can control the multiple lives of cultural texts. To everyone his or her *Pygmalion*. Who can resist *My Fair Lady*, a delightful and engaging work in its own right? Yet it is a matter for concern that the original play version of *Pygmalion* has almost been lost. The play has become rather like a masterpiece hidden away in the vaults of an art gallery, while gaudy and much-altered copies of it are on public view.

25 "A man all light"

Last Years

"What life, what vitality! What immense nervous spring!" This exclamation about Shaw in his mid seventies occurs toward the end of one of several sharply evocative diary entries Virginia Woolf made about her meetings with him.[1] She was not the only person to be struck by Shaw's astonishing energy in the later years of his life. The occasion that inspired this particular comment was a lunch party that she, together with her husband Leonard and the Shaws, attended at the home of economist Maynard Keynes on 2 June 1932, when Shaw was approaching his seventy-sixth birthday.

On 28 April the following year Virginia Woolf had the previously mentioned meeting with Shaw in Kensington Gardens during which he described, in "a great spurt of ideas," his recent world cruise and identified the Sinhalese people as "the original human beings." It was during Woolf's walk with Leonard on that summer evening in 1933, with "chestnuts in their crinolines, bearing tapers," that Shaw suddenly appeared: "There was Shaw, dwindled shanks, white beard; striding along. We talked, by a railing, for fifteen mins. He stood with his arms folded, very upright, leaning back; teeth gold tipped. Just come from the dentist, & "lured" out for a walk by the weather. Very friendly. That is his art, to make one think he likes one. A great spurt of ideas."[2]

Virginia's account of this meeting makes it seem as though Leonard had moved away from her before Shaw appeared and was not present during the conversation. If he had moved away, he evidently returned to her side since he also left an account of the occasion. In a 1964 autobiographical work Leonard recalled that "Shaw stood in front of us in 'the characteristic GBS attitude,' very erect with folded arms, his beard wagging as he talked, and gave us a brilliant unflagging monologue."[3] A small crowd of about twenty strangers gathered around to gape.

It was not only Shaw's astonishing vitality the Woolfs noticed. Leonard singled out a characteristic of Shaw's that was also noticed by Virginia and by

E. M. Forster. "One of the strangest things about Shaw," Leonard wrote, "was that he was personally the kindest, most friendly, most charming of men, yet personally he was almost the most impersonal person I have ever known." When Shaw spoke to you, Leonard recalled, it was as if you were the "one person in Europe" he most wanted to speak to at the time. But when you looked into "that slightly fishy, ice blue eye of his, you got a shock. It was not looking at you; you were nowhere in its orbit; it was looking through you or over you into a distant world or universe inhabited almost entirely by GBS."[4] Reflecting the elusive quality of such memories, Virginia Woolf recalled his eyes being "sea-green like a sailors or a cockatoos." Yet she also commented that "he doesn't much notice who's there."

Shaw was not in the least selfish or inconsiderate in the ordinary senses of the term. "But aren't I keeping you and making you cold," Virginia Woolf recalls him saying during the Kensington Park meeting; he was always doing things for and concerned about other people. However, as he grew older and more famous, Shaw seems to have become rather like a living version of those inscrutable fictional artifacts of the Romantic imagination explored by Frank Kermode in *Romantic Image*: a self-contained, self-sufficient, and self-delighting figure. In Leonard Woolf's arresting, oxymoronic phrase, he seemed an "impersonal person." No doubt in conversations in his younger days Shaw always did plenty of talking, but the impression gained from accounts in his early diaries and letters about tête-à-têtes with people such as May Morris, Florence Farr, and others is that these exchanges were interactive dialogues. Later these often seem to have been replaced by effortless cascades of brilliant monologue by a man with whom it must have been very difficult to compete in conversation. Of course, the thought sometimes occurred to people—as it did to Augustus John when he was painting his portrait of Shaw at Lady Gregory's Coole Park—that the monologues went on too long, however lively and entertaining they may have been. In his private life at home Shaw was not a particularly talkative person.

* * *

The erect carriage, extraordinary vitality, and "dwindled shanks" are three impressions of Shaw in the Woolf accounts that stand out as belonging to a key set of images of him in his later years. The seventy-six-year-old man the Woolfs met in Kensington Gardens on 28 April 1933 still had seventeen years and another world war to live through. Although he did have some serious bouts of ill health during his later years, on the whole he remained extraordinarily active and vigorous. His singing voice remained strong and his wits sharp despite occasional memory lapses. A visitor to Shaw shortly before his eighty-eighth birthday found him a little frail and unsteady, but "erect as an exclamation point."[5] A visitor the day before the same birthday was told by the Irish maid, Maggie Smith, that Shaw was in the garden chopping wood. The visitor found him "under the apple trees, wearing an amazing style of headgear with a talc eyeshield,* sawing away vigorously, surrounded by a pile of logs."[6]

Even photographs taken in his nineties show Shaw with only a slight stoop, though by then he regularly used a walking stick. The onset of his final illness, when he was ninety-four, was caused by a fall that occurred while he was out pruning a tree in the garden.

In his eighties and nineties Shaw became increasingly ethereal in his physical appearance. In March 1938, when Shaw was eighty-one, theater critic James Agate visited Ayot St Lawrence bearing a basket of spring flowers for Charlotte. Catching a glimpse of Shaw with his back to a window, bathed in a shaft of brilliant sunshine, Agate thought: "He has become so insubstantial that even in ordinary light he looks like a figure in stained glass."[7] Agate was prompted to think of saints and an image of translucent seraphic figures in Coleridge's "Rime of the Ancient Mariner": "The point about the shaft of sunshine is that it stressed the unreality of one who is rapidly turning into a saint. Which I expect will make it very uncomfortable for other saints. The sun streaming through the white hair made a halo of it, and I thought of Coleridge's 'a man all light.'"†

Three years later, in February 1941, Shaw wrote in a letter to Beatrice Webb: "I am losing weight so fast that I shall presently have totally disappeared. . . . I am still six feet high; but I weigh only nine stone, my old weight having been between 10 stone 8lbs and 11 stone." When stripped, he said, he looked like "an imperfectly concealed skeleton."[8]

* * *

World War II was, of course, a major overshadowing event in the final years of Shaw's life. Amid speculation in 1939 about the possibility of war with Germany, Shaw was at one with Prime Minister Neville Chamberlain and others in making a wrong call. In an interview published on his eighty-third birthday (26 July 1939), Shaw predicted that mutual fear ("funk") among the European powers would prevent the outbreak of war. He acknowledged his mistake in a

*The amazing headgear was a miner's helmet Shaw wore to keep wood chips out of his eyes.

†A reference to the Ancient Mariner's vision of angelic figures standing over each of the dead bodies on board his ship: "A man all light, a seraph-man/On every corse there stood." ("The Rime of the Ancient Mariner," ll. 490–1.)

long letter to the *New Statesman* on 5 July 1941.[9] A little over a month after this interview (31 August) Hitler invaded Poland. World War II had officially begun. Recalling his criticism of British attitudes at the outbreak of World War I, Shaw wrote an article entitled "Uncommon Sense about the War" that was published on October 7 in the *New Statesman*. Shaw called for "an immediate truce and a world conference to make a constructive peace."[10] His comments again invited attack and controversy, but not nearly to the same extent as they had in 1914.

Whatever else he may have thought about the war, Shaw—who in 1933 had already condemned the "insanity" of Hitler's anti-Semitic policies and ideas about the Aryan as the chosen race—had no doubt that Hitler had to be brought under control somehow. On 28 September 1939, shortly before the publication of "Uncommon Sense about the War," he wrote to Nancy Astor as a member of the House of Commons, saying that "we should announce our intention of lodging a complaint with the International court against Hitler as being unfitted for State control, as he is obsessed by a Jewish complex: that of the Chosen Race, which has led him into wholesale persecution and robbery."[11] However, it was too late for complaints to international courts, and by May 1940 Shaw was writing in almost Churchillian tones to the *Manchester Guardian* about the need to resist Germany to the last: "When Germany made its move to conquer the world . . . someone had to bell the cat. We took on the job, and now for one or both of us the hour has come. We're in a very tight corner, but what can we do? We can either practically surrender or we can die in the last ditch. I think we should die in the last ditch."[12]

The onset of war—especially the German air raids over London—meant that the Shaws' old routine of spending part of the week at Whitehall Court and part at Ayot St Lawrence had to be abandoned. "Slept every night this year in Ayot St Lawrence," Shaw wrote in his diary in December 1941.[13] Even Ayot St Lawrence was not safe from bombing attacks. Since an antiaircraft searchlight had been placed in the district, it briefly became a target. "Grand bombardment of Ayot at night," Shaw recorded in his diary on 15 November 1940, and in a letter to Nancy Astor the following January he said there had been eight bombs "within a stone's throw" of the house in the November raid.[14] With the removal of the antiaircraft battery at Ayot St Lawrence, things improved, but London had become extremely hazardous, especially for residences as close to the center of the city as Whitehall Court. Blanche Patch had to be evacuated from Whitehall Court and lodged in the guest room at Ayot St Lawrence. During a temporary lull in the bombing in 1943, Blanche returned to London. However, the following year the blast from a V-bomb that landed near Charing Cross blew in the study window of the Whitehall Court apartment and shattered a grandfather clock, a terrifying event that caused Blanche to retrace her steps to Ayot St Lawrence.[15]

* * *

The British declaration of war against Germany virtually coincided with a serious deterioration in Charlotte Shaw's health. On 29 August 1939, practically on the eve of Hitler's invasion of Poland, the Shaws had gone on holiday to Frinton-on-Sea in Essex. (Coincidentally, they had also been on holiday by the sea at Torquay when World War I broke out.) On 5 September 1939, two days after the declaration of war, Charlotte became bedridden with what was thought to be "lumbago" but was actually a condition most likely associated with a bone disease, the invasions of which were to cause her great suffering up to the time of her death in 1943. The period of suffering in September 1939 was the prelude to others Charlotte was to endure. As Shaw wrote to Beatrice Webb on 30 January 1941, "She has a bad return of her lumbago and has been bedridden for weeks, well enough except for the dread of bringing on the pain by moving about, and raging because of the confinement and helplessness," adding that "her nerves are all in rags."[16]

It was during the Shaws' final stay with Nancy Astor at Cliveden in July and August 1942 that a Canadian doctor diagnosed Charlotte's complaint as *osteitis deformans*, or Paget's disease, the symptoms of which are abnormal growth and occasionally curvature in bone structures, which in advanced cases can involve severe pain. In Charlotte's case, according to Shaw, the disease also caused breathlessness, as the *osteitis* impinged on her lungs. In the last three years of her life she became increasingly incapacitated.

The end came at two-thirty in the morning on Sunday, 12 September 1943 at Shaw's Corner, with Charlotte dying at the age of eighty-six after double pneumonia had set in. In many ways it was a relief. As Shaw told H. G. Wells in a letter written on the day of her death, Charlotte had become "an old woman bowed and crippled, furrowed and wrinkled, and greatly distressed by hallucinations of crowds in the rooms, evil persons, and animals." (Shaw told Lady Murray that he tried to pacify Charlotte by telling her that she had become clairvoyant and that all the dreadful people she imagined seeing "were really in Australia or elsewhere.")[17] In an account he repeated, with variations, to other correspondents, Shaw told H. G. Wells that a remarkable change had come over Charlotte in her last thirty hours of life: "But on Friday evening a miracle began. Her troubles vanished. Her visions ceased. Her furrows and wrinkles smoothed out. Forty years fell off her like a garment. She had thirty hours of happiness and heaven. Even after her last breath she shed another twenty years, and now lies young and incredibly beautiful. I have to go in and look at her and talk affectionately to her. I did not know I could be so moved."[18]

In accordance with Charlotte's will, the funeral ceremony held at Golders Green Crematorium on 15 September was simple, with "no flowers; no black clothes; no service," only the music of Handel, her favorite composer. Shaw rebelliously wore a black suit that Charlotte liked. The only other mourners were Nancy Astor and Blanche Patch. According to the latter, when the organ played Handel's aria "I know that my redeemer liveth" during the cremation, "Shaw, standing with his hands slightly outstretched, sang the words softly, as though to himself."[19]

As is often the case when people die after a great deal of suffering, Shaw's reaction to Charlotte's death reflected a mixture of moods. In a letter to Molly Tompkins he wrote that he was "not in the least grieved; for she was only a year younger than I and it was time for her to go; but I was very deeply moved."[20] In a letter to Ada Tyrrell, a childhood friend with whom Shaw corresponded from time to time in his later years, he said: "People who cry and grieve never remember. I never grieve and never forget."[21] St. John Ervine's report that Shaw was completely "desolate" and lost after her death tells only part of the story.[22] It was a blessed release not only for Charlotte but for all those in the household—including Shaw, whose own health began to improve markedly after the strain imposed by her illness had been lifted. He told Molly Tompkins what he had told others, namely, that it was only after Charlotte's death that he realized what an enormous strain her illness had been to everybody: "My own health improved so much that I realized that if she had lived another year she would have killed us all, though we were not conscious of the strain while we were under it."[23]

There was also another dimension to Shaw's feelings after Charlotte had died. In the first act of Shakespeare's *Tempest* Prospero asks of his usually ebullient but now apparently "moody" servant-spirit Ariel, "What is't thou canst demand?" In his first reference to the ruling passion that drives him throughout the play, Ariel promptly replies: "My liberty." Shaw possessed an Ariel-like passion for freedom, a need to preserve what he called his "Uranian liberty" to an unusual degree. It was precisely this need that had caused such tensions in all his relations with women, both before and after his marriage. Without wishing to convey any disrespect for or ingratitude toward Charlotte, he told Sidney Webb (and others) that he enjoyed the resumption of his bachelor state. "This bachelor life," he wrote to Webb in October 1945, "with nobody to consult but myself—eat when I like, go to bed when I like, work when I like, order the house and garden as I fancy, and be solitary (or social) all to myself—suits me very well; it actually develops me at 90!"[24] The previous year he had said much the same thing to Molly Tompkins—with a noteworthy comparison of himself to his mother—concerning his liking for solitude: "I have had enough of marriage, and am quite happy alone, as I inherit from my mother a great capacity for solitude in my own company."[25]

Yet in a letter written in 1946, on the subject of Shaw's own possible funeral arrangements, there was also a touching reminder of the marriage of companionship with Charlotte, and his walks in the garden with her at Ayot St Lawrence. As he wrote to Sydney Cockerell, who had raised the matter of the funeral arrangements, "My ghost would be bored by big buildings like the Abbey or St Patrick's Cathedral (next Swift) in Dublin. I need seasons: trees and birds. What I should really like would be a beautifully designed urn on a little pedestal in the garden here in Ayot with Charlotte and myself inside listening for the first cuckoo and the nightingale and scenting the big cherry tree."[26]

Despite the apparent harmony of their spirits, there were things about Charlotte's inner life that Shaw did not learn about until after her death. From reading a diary of hers and "some letters which she wrote to T. E. Lawrence," he realized that "there were many parts of her character that even I did not know, for she poured out her soul to Lawrence."[27]

In addition to legacies—such as the one totaling one thousand pounds to Sidney Webb—and provisions for servants, Charlotte's will left Shaw a life interest in her estate, stipulating that after his death the money was to be used for public causes in Ireland. The first provision in the latter category was "to make grants to foundations or institutions having as their object the bringing of masterpieces of fine art within the reach of the Irish people." The second two provisions, though well-intentioned, invited ridicule and anger. They were designed to encourage education in Ireland in the arts of self-presentation in social, business, and professional life. The trouble was that when reduced, as it was in the media, to the bald idea that Charlotte had left a large amount of money to the cause of teaching the Irish manners, her will inevitably created a bad impression.

The first item in the list of accomplishments the second provision was designed to promote must have seemed especially provocative. Funds were to be directed toward the teaching of "self-control, elocution, oratory and deportment, the arts of personal contact and social intercourse, and the other arts of private, professional and business life to Irish men and women." A third provision concerned the establishment of a chair or readership in an Irish university to provide instruction in those subjects. "The Eliza Doolittle bequest"[28] was one of the satirical descriptions given to the will—a reference of course to the education of the "guttersnipe" cockney flower girl by Professor Higgins in *Pygmalion*.

* * *

By the end of 1943 most of the early leading players on the stage of Shaw's remarkable life in London had made their exit. The man who strategically played the role of the "privileged Irish lunatic" in the early years of the Fabian Society eventually outlasted all the "Old Gang" in the group, proving to be not only the most famous of them all but also an exceptionally hardy plant. The two witnesses at Shaw and Charlotte's wedding, Henry Salt and Graham Wallas, died in the 1930s, and both Sidney Olivier and Beatrice Webb died early in 1943, the same year as Charlotte. (In a letter to Sidney Webb dated 29 April 1943, Shaw reported that Olivier had written to him sometime before his death the previous February to say he agreed with the view of the defrocked priest in *John Bull's Other Island* that "this world is hell.")[29] Shaw had not heard from Beatrice Webb for some time and was unaware that she would die the day after he had written his letter to Sidney. Shaw and Sidney Webb were, as Shaw said, "the sole surviving Essayists" from among the early Fabians, and Webb had only another three years to live.[30]

Shaw's principal women friends and lovers of the 1880s and 1890s all predeceased him. The spirited Alice Lockett—who, following her affair with Shaw, had married Dr. William Sharpe in 1890 and assisted her husband when he operated on Shaw's foot—died in 1942. Jenny Patterson and her rivals, Florence Farr and Annie Besant, had died long before the 1940s, as had Janet Achurch and Ellen Terry. Edith Nesbit died in 1924, and Shaw's other disappointed admirer and would-be wife, Bertha Newcombe, died in 1947. (Shaw was still getting "an occasional line" of correspondence from Bertha in 1944.)[31] May Morris—she of the so-called Mystic Betrothal with Shaw in the 1880s—died in 1938.

Stella Campbell's last letter to Shaw was written from the Hôtel Calais, rue des Capucines, Paris, on 28 June 1939. By this time she was living in seriously straitened circumstances. She was, she wrote, "getting used to poverty and discomfort." She had no maid "to take a few of the little daily cares from me, and give me an arm when I cross the road carrying 'Moonbeam' [the last of her little dogs, a Pekingese] through the terrifying tearing traffic."[32] She was in her mid seventies and an old knee injury—a compound fracture she incurred in Philadelphia in 1905 when she slipped on ice while boarding a brougham—was causing problems with mobility. In 1938 she had to be carried off the ferry by three men when she arrived at Boulogne on her way to Paris.[33] Her career had gone downhill during the 1930s and included some not very successful ventures into film acting.

In August 1937 Shaw had—"with infinite labour and a little heartbreak," as he told Stella—packed all her letters to him and sent them back to her in six envelopes.[34] He assigned the copyright of his letters to her but continued to deny permission to publish the correspondence for fear of the hurt it would cause Charlotte. Stella was naturally very angry and frustrated about this decision but did not live long enough to be able to publish the correspondence and thereby help repair her waning fortunes.

Not long after writing to Shaw in June 1939, she was forced to leave Paris because of the gathering clouds of war. Carrying Moonbeam and—among numerous other items of luggage—a black hatbox containing the letters between Shaw and herself, she traveled down to Antibes. Forced to move on from there as well due to the possibility that it might become the center of a military evacuation plan, she finally arrived at the resort village of Pau, at the foot of the Pyrenees. Some time before this, while staying in Italy at Sirmione, on Lake Garda, Stella had met a woman in her late thirties called Agnes Claudius, who became one of her devotees. Because she thought Agnes had a face like that of a pharaoh, Stella called her "Egypt." In the winter of 1939–40, lonely and almost destitute in Pau, Stella invited Egypt to join her in the Hôtel Pavillon de Navarre, where she was staying. Egypt managed to persuade the authorities at the passport office in England to allow her to travel. She became Stella's companion during the last few months of her life. In the early spring of 1940, while driving in the country, Stella caught a chill from an icy wind blowing in from the Pyrenees and developed pneumonia. She died in the hotel at Pau on 9 April, aged seventy-five.

Molly Tompkins and Nancy Astor, the two American women friends with whom Shaw had become associated in the late 1920s, both survived him, living on until 1960 and 1964, respectively. To Shaw's astonishment, after the breakup of her marriage and other troubles, in the 1940s Molly Tompkins became "a shop assistant" in a bookshop in New York belonging to the publisher Brentano's, a firm with whose publishing department Shaw had a long association. "You a shop assistant!," he wrote in December 1946, "and in Brentanos whom I helped to bankrupt years ago."[35] Nancy Astor, probably seeking consolation for her unhappy and broken marriage with Waldorf, went on "mothering" Shaw till the end.

* * *

Shaw was practically silent as a playwright during World War II. In May 1939 he had completed *In Good King Charles's Golden Days*, a discussion play in two acts dealing with topics ranging from Newtonian physics and Quakerism to love and marriage, and set in the Restoration period in England. It had its premiere at the New Theatre, London, on 9 May 1940, but lasted only twenty-nine performances. The outbreak of the war immediately prompted the writing of a new scene—marking "the arrival of the news of Battler's [Hitler's] attack"—for *Geneva*, his much-revised play about the League of Nations.[36] However, no new dramatic works came from his pen during the war, and he did not return to his career as a playwright until August 1945, when he resumed work on *Buoyant Billions*, a play he had started but abandoned in 1936 under the title *The World Betterer*.

Shaw's principal literary work during the war years, *Everybody's Political What's What?* (1944), was intended as a sequel to his 1929 political treatise *The Intelligent Woman's Guide*. Written in a mood of optimism mingled with despair about the future, it is a rather diffuse work, often digressing from politics into sociological and cultural topics. As a statement of Shaw's political ideas, it does not add a great deal to what was said in the 1929 treatise, except for some modification of his utopian ideas about equality of income. In this work Shaw seems to have settled on the term *democratic Socialism* as the core institutional system of his creed. He does, however, say that "the British Party System should be scrapped ruthlessly," an idea that has had strong supporters among later political commentators.[37] The work also contains quite a few—perhaps best forgotten—laudatory remarks about Stalin.

* * *

For someone who declared that "all autobiographies are lies" and said that everything that was of any interest about him was contained in his novels, plays, and other works, Shaw did a remarkable amount of tinkering with and recycling of his autobiographical writings. After World War II the principal successor to *Everybody's Political What's What?* among the nondramatic writings was his collection of autobiographical essays *Sixteen Self Sketches*. This book, totaling about 140 pages, was published in 1949 by Constable in the handsome format used for the publisher's Standard Edition of Shaw's works, with a print run of 50,000 copies. An American edition by Dodd, Mead was published simultaneously in a printing totaling 10,500 copies.

With its attractive illustrations and short, lively chapters, *Sixteen Self Sketches* was a seductively accessible work, and has been greatly influential in the shaping of biographical accounts of Shaw. The majority of the "Sketches" (of which there are, in fact, seventeen) were revised versions of autobiographical essays that Shaw had written earlier in various literary formats. Some of them were originally written and published half a century before the appearance of *Sixteen Self Sketches* and then republished, in revised form, in a 1939 book entitled *Shaw Gives Himself Away*. Other chapters began life in the form of lengthy letters to various correspondents.

As a biographical source, *Sixteen Self Sketches* must be taken for what it declares itself to be in the title: a series of sketches rather than a continuous and coherent narrative. It leaves out of account altogether large areas of Shaw's experiences and (as we have seen) presents highly suspect accounts of some of the experiences it does treat. The book certainly has its appeal, and in the early chapters at least has the stamp of a short classic of autobiographical writing. However, the numerous and heterogeneous origins of the various chapters inevitably lead to a distinct quality of scrappiness in the book as a whole. Nevertheless, the work does show that the man who prepared it for publication in 1949 had his wits very much about him and was still very keen to maintain control over the story of his life—and to correct accounts written by others, as he did with the five authors admonished in the chapter entitled "Biographers' Blunders Corrected."

* * *

A good deal of Shaw's time during the period stretching from the last years of World War II to 1950 was spent in a grand tidying up of his affairs. It was also a period marked by further recognition of his achievements and standing. Numerous celebrities from various walks of life came down to visit the "man all light" at his home in Ayot St Lawrence.

On the literary side of the tidying-up process, Shaw was not very ably assisted by Dr. F. E. (Fritz) Loewenstein, a Jewish refugee from Hitler's Germany and a graduate of the University of Würzburg, who became a Shaw acolyte and the founder in 1941 of the Shaw Society. Loewenstein had contacted Shaw in 1936, hoping to obtain his assistance in compiling a bibliography of the master's works. Although he described Loewenstein in a letter dated 31 December 1943 as "an unholy terror: a man to be avoided beyond any other fellow creature,"[38] Shaw felt sorry for him and, following Charlotte's death, was persuaded to allow him to work on a regular basis in an upstairs sitting room of the house at Ayot St Lawrence, with access to all his files. By this time a rival acolyte had appeared on the scene in the form of a young Scottish journalist, John Wardrop, who during the war assisted Shaw with the proofreading of *Everybody's Political What's What?* prior to its publication in 1944. Tensions in Shaw's domestic world created by the rivalry between

Loewenstein and Wardrop—who both considered themselves pretenders to the throne as Shaw's literary executor—were compounded by the presence of Blanche Patch, who couldn't stand "the non-stop smoking German Jew,"[39] as she called Loewenstein, and who felt that her own position was threatened by the two men.

Eventually Loewenstein displaced Wardrop as Shaw's literary assistant and was made his "authorised bibliographer and remembrancer." According to Shaw scholar and bibliographer Dan H. Laurence, Loewenstein quietly raided the Shaviana that he was being paid to catalogue and added it to his own collection, which was sold in 1953. Fortunately most of the items in his collection have made their way into American university libraries and archives. A massive quantity of material escaped Loewenstein's predations. The great majority of Shaw's personal files (including vast numbers of letters from others he had saved throughout his adult life) were bequeathed to the British Library, where they are now held in a multivolume collection. His diaries, account books, and papers were bequeathed to the library of the London School of Economics, which, as a consequence of the school having changed its name, is now the British Library of Political and Economic Science. Loewenstein's dream of becoming curator of Shaw's Corner following the playwright's death in 1950 was rudely shattered. On the day of Shaw's death the public trustee instructed him to leave the house, with the position of curator going to the forceful and capable Scottish housekeeper Alice Laden.

The grand tidying up also included a continuation of arrangements for the disposal of Shaw's properties. Shaw's offer of the house at Ayot St Lawrence to the National Trust in January 1944 was accepted by James Lees-Milne, the acting secretary at the time. With a view to completing his plan to hand over the properties he owned in Carlow to the Urban Council of the city, in 1945 Shaw wrote to Eamon De Valera, the prime minister of the Irish Republic, requesting the introduction of legislation establishing local civic improvement funds to which private individuals could make gifts or bequests. This was effected in June, with the legal conveyance of the property executed in August 1945.

Shaw's last will and testament—which he signed on 12 June 1950 and jokingly referred to as "my crowning masterpiece"—was the final testamentary instrument in a series that began with the drawing up of his first will in July 1901.[40] This 1901 will was revoked by another in August 1913. Among provisions of the 1913 will were legacies of £104 each to Florence Farr and Jane Patterson, the latter being described as one "whose kindness to me from One thousand eight hundred and eighty six to One thousand eight hundred and ninety two has been of enduring service to me and has always been held in affectionate remembrance and honor by me." As both women predeceased Shaw, neither inherited these legacies. The 1913 will also provided for the endowment of "a combined Institute of Phonetics and School of Rhetoric, Oratory, Dress Manners and the Arts of Public Life (whether so entitled or not)."[41] The proposed "Institute of Phonetics"—a subject very much on Shaw's mind at the time because of his writing of *Pygmalion* the previous year—was a foretaste of what was to become a controversial feature of the final will. Subsequent wills and numerous codicils were created in 1921 and 1937.

The last will and testament of 1950 provided that Shaw was to be cremated and that the ashes were to be "inseparably mixed with those of my late wife now in the custody of the Golders Green Crematorium and in this condition inurned or scattered in the garden of the house in Ayot St Lawrence where we lived together for thirty five years unless some other disposal of them should be in the opinion of the Trustee more eligible. Personally I prefer the garden to the cloister." (In accordance with this wish, Shaw's ashes were mingled with those of Charlotte and scattered in the garden at Ayot St Lawrence on 23 November 1950.) Declaring himself a believer in Creative Evolution, he stipulated that there should be no ritual suggesting he accepted the tenets of any established church or denomination, "nor take the form of a cross or any other instrument of torture or symbol of blood sacrifice."[42]

Legacies and annuities went to numerous servants as well as to other individuals, such as Eva Maria Schneider, "in remembrance of her devoted services to my late sister Lucy."[43] The major institutional beneficiaries of the will were the British Museum ("in acknowledgement of the incalculable value to me of my daily resort to the Reading Room of that Institution at the beginning of my career"), the National Gallery of Ireland, and the Royal Academy of Dramatic Art.[44]

A singular and controversial provision in the will was Shaw's wish to have funds directed toward the creation of a new British alphabet. Shaw supported the creation of a phonetic alphabet containing "at least 40 letters," which would "enable the [English] language to be written without indicating single sounds by groups of letters . . . instead of by one symbol for each sound." An effect of this change would have been to do away with unsounded letters in words such as "though," which would become "tho" in a phonetic representation. A problematic associated provision was for funding to support a statistical inquiry to determine how many writers of English there are and how much time would be saved by using the Proposed British Alphabet. Another wish—which was, in fact, carried out—was for his play *Androcles and the Lion* to be "transliterated" into phonetic spelling and have it published with a standard spelling text running parallel with it. In 1957 a challenge to the Alphabet

Trusts in the will was mounted by other major beneficiaries, including the British Museum, the Royal Academy of Dramatic Art, and the National Gallery of Ireland. In an elegantly worded but dubious judgment made in the High Court of Justice in February of that year, Mr. Justice Harman held the Alphabet Trusts to be invalid.

Strangely enough, as a result of evolutionary processes in language communication and technology, part of the basic principle behind Shaw's idea is now being put into practice by millions of people in various media, such as text messaging and chat rooms, where the use of phonetic abbreviations ("I luv u," "wd u plz") is the normal, time-saving form of spelling. There are, of course, grounds for concern about these (to many people) distasteful forms of language and the adverse effects they can have on systems of linguistic communication, not to mention the erosion of etymological history they involve. For good or ill, the Shaw Proposed British Alphabet has in a very real sense come into being through a de facto process. Unbeknownst to the majority—if not all—the users of electronic language systems, they are effectively fulfilling part of the underlying wish expressed in a major clause of the last will and testament of Bernard Shaw, signed on 12 June 1950.

* * *

In 1946 Shaw accepted an offer from the Council of the City to be made a Freeman of Dublin—more than a decade after he had been made a Freeman of the City of London.[45] An illuminated scroll commemorating the Dublin honor was presented to Shaw at Ayot St Lawrence in August, with the "Roll of Freedom" being conveyed to him for his signature by officials from the Dublin council. In April that same year he had handed over several weighty volumes containing the manuscripts of his early novels to John W. Dulanty, high commissioner for Eire, for transfer to the National Library of Ireland. In October he made what was to be his last visit to London in order to attend a ceremony, where he was to be awarded the Honorary Freedom of the Metropolitan Borough of St. Pancras. On his way to this ceremony he fell, injuring his leg, and the BBC recorded his acceptance speech from his bed at Whitehall Court. "I wasn't there; but the mike spoke for me," he wrote to Lord Latham, leader of the London County Council.[46]

The year 1946, of course, also marked his ninetieth birthday, an occasion for much celebration that was not at all welcome to Shaw, who became increasingly angry at the fuss made over his birthdays in his last years. "Throw away all the birthday ones. They make me sick," was his curt instruction to Loewenstein about the hundreds of cards he received at Whitehall Court and Ayot St Lawrence.[47] The National Book League presented a Shaw Ninetieth

Birthday Exhibition that ran from 26 July to 24 August. Stephen Winsten, his neighbor in Ayot St Lawrence, edited a festschrift, published in 1946, under the title *G.B.S. 90: Aspects of Bernard Shaw's Life and Work*. It contained a eulogy by poet laureate John Masefield—in which Shaw was described as the possessor of "the bright mind ever young, / The glorious great heart, the witty tongue"—and contributions by numerous well known writers and public figures, including J. B. Priestley, H. G. Wells, James Bridie, Aldous Huxley, Gilbert Murray, Max Beerbohm, and Dean Inge. Sir William Haley, the director-general of the BBC, wrote about Shaw's long and distinguished association with the corporation; referring to Shaw's frequent fiery letters of admonishment about its programs, Sir Haley concluded: "The B.B.C. on his ninetieth birthday salutes its Grandest Inquisitor."[48]

* * *

"The Saint of Ayot,"[49] as Shaw was nicknamed by some, became more and more inclined to refuse visits by "pilgrims" in the last years of his life. He wanted to be left alone. Even old friends and associates sometimes received extraordinarily fierce letters of refusal when they proposed visits. "I do not want to see you. I do not want to see ANYBODY . . . Keep away Gabriel," he wrote to Pascal in September 1947.[50] Poor Siegfried Trebitsch, who had his final meeting with Shaw in 1948, received an even more emphatic version of this message when he proposed another visit the following year. Many visitors were kept at bay by the jealously protective Alice Laden, who became known as St. George's Dragon. A Palestinian visitor in 1947 managed to get through and wrote a newspaper account of the occasion under the title "Pilgrimage to Bernard Shaw," which described Shaw as resembling "an idol . . . or a very old and rather dangerous bird, ready to jump out and peck."[51] The writer noticed that the idol engaged in "a veritable flirtation" with the girlfriend he had brought with him. (Women visitors seemed to be rather more welcome than men.) Shaw gave the title "The Chucker-Out" to a striking photograph of himself, taken by Allan Chappelow in 1950, which showed him standing with his walking stick on the doorstep of his house in a distinctly threatening pose.

However, the bark was still worse than the bite (or peck), and Shaw did receive a number of visitors, albeit reluctantly at times, in his final years. Even Gabriel Pascal came down to Ayot St Lawrence despite the forbidding letter. The people from the entertainment world who visited Shaw included Vivien Leigh (when she was playing Cleopatra in the film version of *Caesar and Cleopatra*), Danny Kaye, Gertrude Lawrence, Frances Day, and Lilli Palmer. The visit by actress, dancer, and revue artist Gertrude Lawrence occurred in February 1949. In the course of a discussion about pantomime, she and

Shaw—singing loud and clear in what Blanche Patch described as an "astonishing" duet—sang one of the songs from *Aladdin* beginning "Come, little girl, for a sail with me, / Up in my bonny balloon."[52] In the same year Shaw was present in the garden of his neighbor Stephen Winsten when Esmé Percy conducted a rehearsal of *Buoyant Billions,* the cast of which included the revue star Frances Day and stage and screen actor Denholm Elliott.

One of the most memorable recollections of visits to Shaw at Ayot St Lawrence in his last years was that of Kingsley Martin, editor of the *New Statesman and Nation,* who called sometime toward the end of 1946, after Shaw's ninetieth year. At the end of the visit, during which Shaw talked about his enjoyment of singing grand opera, which he had learned to do in his teens, Martin relates:

> He walked out with us to the car in the road and found in it our marmalade cat which he called "Pussykins" and with whom he conversed as he always did with cats and other animals, finding, as he said, that they apparently enjoyed the conversation as much as he did, even though they might not fully grasp its content. And then as I turned the car round, I heard a surprising sound. I stopped to see Shaw standing in the middle of the lane and singing, at the top of his bell-like voice, an aria from Verdi. He turned round and said: "My voice is no penny whistle now!"[53]

On 29 April 1949 Shaw was visited by Jawaharlal Nehru, the first prime minister of India following independence, who was a graduate of Cambridge University, where he heard Shaw lecture and became a longtime admirer of his work.[54] Writing to Nehru before a proposed visit in 1948, which circumstances at the time had prevented, Shaw said he was able to view India "objectively because I am not English but Irish, and I have lived through the long struggle for liberation from English rule, and the partition of the country into Eire and Northern Ireland, the Western equivalent of Hindustan and Pakistan. I am as much a foreigner in England as you were in Cambridge."[55] Shaw refused a proposed visit from the prime minister of Burma in May 1950 on the grounds of his age and the lumbago from which he was suffering at the time.

* * *

Despite his generally good health—he told Kingsley Martin during his 1946 visit that now that he didn't have to go to bed at ten o'clock, as Charlotte had made him do for the good of his health, he had never felt better in his life—Shaw did have some serious bouts of illness in his later years. In the summer of 1938, as he was turning eighty-two, he collapsed and was diagnosed as suffering from pernicious anemia, following which he underwent a prolonged course of injections of liver hormone and was confined to Whitehall Court for six weeks. In December the same year the single word *FLOP* in his diary referred to a fainting spell he had experienced at the home of Edith, Lady Londonderry, which he attributed to a hormone injection he had received that morning. Prior to this episode, he had a minor heart attack in 1934, after which he slept for sixty hours and was confined to his bed for several days. He had had a number of falls before the one that led to his final illness in 1950, and in April 1947 he had undergone daily heat treatment for muscular rheumatism as an outpatient at the nearby Welwyn Victoria Hospital. (Keeping up with the times, however, at the beginning of 1947 he joined the British Interplanetary Society as a life member.) In May 1950, as his ninety-fourth birthday was approaching, Shaw made another eleven visits to the Welwyn Victoria Hospital to receive further treatment for his troublesome rheumatism. He wrote the first draft of his last play, *Why She Would Not*, from 17 to 23 July 1950 and completed the work on the thirty-first.

The fuss made over his ninety-fourth birthday—which fell on Wednesday, 26 July 1950—annoyed Shaw even more than those made on previous occasions. In a letter written to Sydney Cockerell the following day, he described the situation at Ayot St Lawrence that Wednesday as "simple hell": "The Times statement that I was 'resting' elicited a yell of rage from me. The telephone and door bell never stopped. The lane was blocked with photographers all day. None of them would take NO for an answer. Fortnum & Mason made huge profits on giant cakes, gorgeous and uneatable. The Post & Telegraph services staggered under their burdens."[56]

Shaw's penultimate press interview was published on 6 August 1950. The subject was the atom bomb. Asked if he thought the use of it was ever justified, Shaw replied that although "in war the word justifiable has no meaning"—the only rule of conduct being to kill the enemy or be killed by him—"the bomb is a boomerang, fatal alike to the bomber and his victim." He deplored the Korean War as a crusade against Russian Communism.[57]

* * *

The beginning of the end occurred on Sunday, 10 September 1950 when, late in the afternoon, Shaw fell while pruning a tree in the garden at Ayot St Lawrence and fractured his thigh. By this time Shaw, like Captain Shotover in *Heartbreak House*, carried a whistle to signal emergencies. He used it on this occasion, and the first to answer his summons was the Irish maid Maggie Cashin, who, having married and become Mrs. Smith on June 12 1950, returned to Ayot St Lawrence as a temporary replacement for Mrs. Laden. (Alice Laden had gone to Inverness on holiday but was recalled after the accident.) Maggie held Shaw on her knees for fifteen minutes until he instructed her to put him down and fetch someone. Not wanting to put him on the wet grass, she used the whistle to summon her husband, who came and helped Shaw into the house. Dr. Thomas C. Probyn was called and gave instructions for a radiologist to be brought in. An X ray taken with a portable machine revealed that Shaw had fractured his thigh. On the following day he was taken by ambulance to the Luton and Dunstable General Hospital, where he underwent surgery on his thigh in the evening. The hospital was inundated with telephone calls and a second operator had to be employed to help deal with them. Newspaper reporters crowded the anterooms and were given a hospital boardroom to receive bulletins. Press photographers made unsuccessful offers of very large amounts of money to be allowed to photograph Shaw in his room.

Shaw appeared to be making a good recovery, but on 21 September he had to be operated on again for a kidney and bladder condition. On 4 October, after visits from a few people, including Nancy Astor and Frances Day, he was transported back to Ayot St Lawrence, having refused a further kidney operation. A bed was set up in the downstairs drawing room of the house, where Shaw was nursed by Sisters Gwendoline Howell and Florence Horan.

F. G. Prince-White, a journalist on the editorial staff of the *Daily Mail*, visited Shaw's Corner on 12 October. An interview published the following day reported that Shaw had requested to be taken out into the garden in a wheelchair to enjoy the autumn sunshine. Prince-White saw "a gentleness on his face now, a softness in his once-piercing glance."[58] There were gleams of humor from Shaw in the last days. He told the hospital staff at Luton that it was pointless trying to repair an "Ancient Monument." Nancy Astor relates a joke she says he told her during the last hours she was with him.[59] Eileen O'Casey says that he gave her "one of his lovely smiles" and asked her if she would stroke his forehead for him. Of her last moments with him she recalled that "when I said 'Goodbye and God bless you' he answered in his old quick manner, 'He has blessed you already.'"[60]

Shaw was running high temperatures because of his kidney dysfunction. Toward the end of October his condition deteriorated, and on 1 November he lapsed into a coma after saying, "I am going to die."[61] He died in the early morning of Thursday, 2 November 1950. The following announcement was written by F. G. Prince-White and was affixed to the wrought iron gates of Shaw's Corner: "Mr Bernard Shaw passed peacefully away at one minute to five o'clock this morning November 2. From the coffers of his genius he enriched the world."

Shaw's death attracted worldwide media attention. The lights on Broadway in New York were dimmed for several minutes, theater audiences in Australia stood for two minutes of silence, and tributes to Shaw poured in from all around the world.

A brief funeral service was conducted in the West Chapel of the Golders Green Crematorium at 4 p.m. on 6 November. The music, chosen by Shaw, included the "Libere me" from Verdi's *Requiem* and extracts from Elgar's *The Music Makers* (a setting of Arthur William Edgar O'Shaughnessy's poem "We Are the Music Makers"), and the Nimrod variation from his *Enigma Variations.* Instead of a funeral oration, Sydney Cockerell read the final speech of Mr. Valiant for Truth from Bunyan's *The Pilgrim's Progress*, which contains the words "my sword, I give to him that shall succeed me in my pilgrimage, and my courage and skill, to him that can get it," followed by the sentence: "So he passed over, and the trumpets sounded for him on the other side."

Although he was—and has remained—a controversial figure, many thought that a great light had been extinguished in the world with Shaw's death. Several of the accounts of her employer his Scottish housekeeper, Alice Laden, gave after his death contained inaccuracies. However, about one thing she said—recorded in a written form that attempted to convey her Aberdeen accent—there can be little disagreement: "There'll never be another Ber-r-r-nard Shaw."[62]

Notes

Abbreviations

Agits	Bernard Shaw, *Agitations: Letters to the Press 1875–1950*, ed. Dan H. Laurence and James Rambeau (New York: Frederick Ungar, 1985)
Auto1, 2	*Shaw: An Autobiography*, 2 vols., ed. Stanley Weintraub (New York: Weybright & Talley, 1969–70; London: Max Reinhardt, 1970–1971)
AutoMisc	*Shaw Gives Himself Away: An Autobiographical Miscellany* (Newtown, Montgomeryshire: The Gregynog Press, 1939)
BB	Charles MacMahon Shaw, *Bernard's Brethren, with comments by Bernard Shaw* (London: Constable, 1939)
BL	British Library, Department of Manuscripts
BLPES	British Library of Political and Economic Science
Chron	A. M. Gibbs, *A Bernard Shaw Chronology* (London: Palgrave, 2001)
CL1, 2, 3, 4	Bernard Shaw, *Collected Letters*, 4 vols., ed. Dan H. Laurence (London: Max Reinhardt, 1965–88)
Cornell	Rare Manuscripts Collection, Kroch Library, Cornell University, Ithaca, New York
D1, 2	*Bernard Shaw: The Diaries*, 2 vols., ed. Stanley Weintraub (University Park: Pennsylvania State University Press, 1986)
DBW1, 2, 3, 4	*The Diary of Beatrice Webb*, ed. Norman and Jeanne Mackenzie, 4 vols. (London: Virago/London School of Economics and Political Science, 1982–85)
Dent	*Bernard Shaw and Mrs. Patrick Campbell: Their Correspondence*, ed. Alan Dent (London: Victor Gollancz, 1952)
Drama1, 2, 3, 4	*The Drama Observed*, 4 vols., ed. Bernard F. Dukore (University Park: Pennsylvania State University Press, 1993)
Farmer	Henry George Farmer, *Bernard Shaw's Sister and Her Friends* (Leiden: E. J. Brill, 1959)
Guelph	Dan H. Laurence Collection, University of Guelph, Ontario, Can.
Harvard	Houghton Library, Harvard University, Cambridge, Mass.
Hend1	Archibald Henderson, *George Bernard Shaw: His Life and Works* (London: Hurst & Blackett, 1911)
Hend2	Archibald Henderson, *Bernard Shaw: Playboy and Prophet* (New York: D. Appleton & Co., 1932)

Hend3	Archibald Henderson, *George Bernard Shaw: Man of the Century* (New York: Appleton-Century-Crofts, 1956)
Heritage	*Shaw: The Critical Heritage*, ed. T. F. Evans (London: Routledge & Kegan Paul, 1976)
I&R	*Shaw: Interviews and Recollections*, ed. A. M. Gibbs (London: Macmillan, 1990). In references to quotations the abbreviation I&R indicates that the passage quoted can also be found in this volume, together with its immediate context.
Imm	Bernard Shaw, Preface to *Immaturity* (London: Constable, 1930)
L&G	*Shaw, Lady Gregory and the Abbey: A Correspondence and a Record*, ed. Dan H. Laurence and Nicholas Grene (Gerrards Cross: Colin Smythe, 1993)
Lbib1, 2	Dan H. Laurence, *Bernard Shaw: A Bibliography*, 2 vols. (Oxford: Clarendon Press, 1983)
Lgen	Dan H. Laurence, "The Shaws and the Gurlys: A Genealogical Study," in *SHAW: The Annual of Bernard Shaw Studies*, vol. 18 (University Park: Pennsylvania State University Press, 1998), 1–31
McNulty	Matthew Edward McNulty, "Memoirs of G.B.S.," ed. Dan H. Laurence, in *SHAW: The Annual of Bernard Shaw Studies*, vol. 12, ed. Fred D. Crawford (University Park: Pennsylvania State University Press, 1992), 1–46
Matter	Bernard Shaw, *The Matter with Ireland*, ed. David H. Greene and Dan H. Laurence (London: Rupert Hart-Davis, 1962)
OTN1, 2, 3	Bernard Shaw, *Our Theatres in the Nineties*, 3 vols. (London: Constable, 1954)
Patch	Blanche Patch, *Thirty Years With G.B.S.* (London: Victor Gollancz, 1951)
Prefs1, 2, 3	Bernard Shaw, *The Complete Prefaces*, 3 vols., ed. Dan. H. Laurence and Daniel J. Leary (London: Allen Lane, Penguin Press, 1993–97)
Quintessence	Bernard Shaw, *Shaw and Ibsen: Bernard Shaw's "The Quintessence of Ibsenism" and Related Writings*, ed. J. L. Wisenthal (Toronto: University of Toronto Press, 1979)
Reviews1, 2	*Bernard Shaw's Book Reviews*, 2 vols., ed. Brian Tyson (University Park: Pennsylvania State University Press, 1991–96)
Ross	B. C. Rosset, *Shaw of Dublin: The Formative Years* (University Park: Pennsylvania State University Press, 1964)
SCG	John O'Donovan, *Shaw and the Charlatan Genius: A Memoir* (Dublin: Dolmen Press, 1965)
SM1, 2, 3	*Shaw's Music: The Complete Musical Criticism of Bernard Shaw*, 3 vols., 2nd rev. ed., ed. Dan H. Laurence (London: Bodley Head, 1989)
SSS	Bernard Shaw, *Sixteen Self Sketches* (London: Constable, 1949)
Texas	Harry Ransom Humanities Research Center, University of Texas, Austin
Theatrics	*Theatrics* (Selected Correspondence of Bernard Shaw series), ed. Dan H. Laurence (Toronto: University of Toronto Press, 1995)
Villager	*Shaw the Villager and Human Being: A Biographical Symposium*, ed. Allan Chappelow (London: Charles Skilton, 1961)

Introduction

1. Shaw to Archibald Henderson, 30 June 1904; CL2:427.

2. The full-length biographies of Shaw produced in the course of the twentieth century have not, on the whole, served their subject well. While they are not without their merits—this book is occasionally gratefully indebted to them—they all have serious shortcomings in their portrayal of Shaw's life and career. (For a detailed critique, see my articles: "'Giant brain . . . no heart': Bernard Shaw's Reception in Criticism and Biography," *Irish University Review* 26, no. 1 [Spring-Summer 1996]: 15–35; and "Bernard Shaw's Family Skeletons: A New Look," *Bullán: An Irish Studies Journal* 3, no. 1 [Spring 1997]: 57–74). The earlier works (by Henderson, Pearson, and St. John Ervine) have now been rendered largely out of date by later developments in Shavian scholarship, though they still contain material—much of it supplied to the writers by Shaw himself—that is not easily accessible elsewhere. These biographies shared the weakness of being quite inadequate in their treatment of Shaw's creative writing. At a time when Shaw's reputation was coming under attack from such influential critics as T. S. Eliot, F. R. Leavis, and Raymond Williams, they were providing commentary on Shaw's artistic achievement that was out of touch with critical discussion, which (even while their works were being written and published) was having a significant adverse effect on Shaw's reputation in literary and academic circles. The Holroyd study, though lively and entertaining in style, is based on what I regard as a fundamentally flawed thesis about Shaw's emotional makeup and his various life pursuits. I do not see Shaw as "emotionally . . . lame" and as having been engaged in a "search for love" or "the pursuit of power"; nor do I see him as having been finally seduced by "the lure of fantasy." The Holroyd account of Shaw seems to me in many ways reductive, trivializing, and condescending. It also repeatedly misrepresents and distorts primary biographical evidence in vitally significant areas of discussion. An approach to biography that allows the writer frequently to adopt a role akin to that of an omniscient narrator in a novel is not one that I endorse; it is the source of many problems in Holroyd's work.

3. Shaw to Archibald Henderson, 3 Jan. 1905; CL2:506.

4. Shaw to *Vanity Fair* journalist and novelist Tighe Hopkins, 31 Aug. 1889; CL1:222. The holograph of this letter (Cornell Ms. 4617, Box 10) shows that Shaw made the following noteworthy correction to the sentence in which the quoted statement occurs: instead of "the personal raptures of music," he had originally written "the personal raptures of copulation," a correction not recorded in CL1.

Chapter 1. "A Family of Pooh-Bahs": Shaw's Irish Origins

1. The official record of Shaw's birth fell victim to Irish history. In a (still unpublished) letter written in 1938, Shaw said: "I am an Irishman without a birth certificate," explaining that after the abolition of the Parish of St. Bride's in the church of which he had been baptized by his uncle, the Reverend William George Carroll, the records had been transferred to the Four Courts and were lost when the building was destroyed on 30 April 1922 during the Irish Civil War (Shaw to Denis Johnston, 1 April 1938; Trinity

College, Dublin, Library, Ms. 10066/287/2823). The information about Shaw's breech birth and the officiating doctor was supplied to Mrs. Frances McCarthy, founder and curator of the Shaw Museum, located at 33 Synge Street.

2. Shaw to Frank Harris, 12 May 1930; CL4:188–89.

3. The phrase is given to a character called Ignatius Gallaher, who, like the young Shaw, has left Dublin to make a successful career in journalism in London. He appears in James Joyce's story "A Little Cloud." *Dubliners* (Harmondsworth, Eng.: Penguin Books, 1956), 73.

4. W. B. Yeats, "The Lake Isle of Innisfree."

5. Shaw to Charlotte Payne-Townshend, 4 Nov. 1896; CL1:691.

6. The imposing neoclassical building still known as the Four Courts was constructed at the turn of the eighteenth and nineteenth centuries. It contained four legal courts and also served as a public record office. It was gutted by fire in 1922 during the Irish Civil War.

7. Imm ix; Prefs3:6–7.

8. *The Manuscripts of the House of Lords, 1689–1690*, Historical MSS Commission, Twelfth Report, Appendix Part VI, vol. 2, 1889, 183. I am grateful to Ed Wright for locating this record.

9. See C. J. Shaw, *A History of Clan Shaw* (Chichester, Sussex, Eng.: Phillimore, 1983), 219.

10. This occurred at the funeral of Sir Robert Shaw, the 2nd Baronet of Bushy Park.

11. Imm viii; Prefs3:6.

12. Imm viii; Prefs3:5.

13. Imm ix; Prefs3:6.

14. Ibid.

15. This story was evidently communicated by Shaw to his biographer Hesketh Pearson. See the latter's *Bernard Shaw: His Life and Personality* (London: Collins, 1942), 16.

16. Imm ix; Prefs3:6.

17. Shaw, *Nine Answers* (privately printed, 1923); I&R 24.

18. Imm xii; Prefs3:9.

19. See John O'Donovan, *Bernard Shaw* (Dublin: Gill & Macmillan, 1983), 22.

20. CL4:652.

21. Imm xxiv–xxv; Prefs3:19–20.

22. The history of the Shaw family migrants to Australia is discussed more fully in my illustrated essay "Ascendancy Downunder: George Bernard Shaw's Irish and Australian Relations," in Peter Kuch and Julie-Ann Robson, eds., *Irelands in the Asia-Pacific* (Gerrards Cross, Buckinghamshire, Eng.: Colin Smythe, 2003), 213–36.

23. Bernard Shaw, "In the Days of My Youth," in T. P. O'Connor's magazine *M.A.P.* (*Mainly About People*), 17 Sept. 1898, 324–25. This autobiographical essay has been reprinted in revised form; see AutoMisc and SSS (where the quoted passage appears on p. 45).

24. Subsequently the rooms served various uses. In the 1853 valuation the occupier is the "Carlow Reading Club," and the building is called "News and Assembly Rooms," indicating that one of its uses was for newspaper reading. From 1912 to 1915 the build-

ing served as a cinema called the Picture House, and in 1923 it became Carlow Technical College. Later it functioned as the home of the Carlow County Library and Local Studies archives. See the following: "c. 1853 Primary Valuation of Tenements," Act 9 & 10, Vict., Cap. 110, Carlow County Library Local Studies Section; B. O'Neill, "The Old Assembly Rooms," *Carloviana* 1, no. 2 (Jan. 1948); L. D. Bergin and B. O'Neill, "Shaw's Ties with Carlow," *Carloviana*, n.s., 1, no. 4 (Dec. 1956).

25. For details concerning Walter John Gurly's youth and education, see Ross 8.

26. SSS 14–16.

27. Dan H. Laurence notes that "with the single exception of Constance . . . all the Gurly sisters and their offspring received financial assistance from Shaw as long as they lived." Lgen 8.

28. BL Ms. Add. 50710, fol. 25.

29. Imm x; Prefs3:7–8.

30. See chapter 2.

31. SSS 14.

32. The originals are in the art collection of the Harry Ransom Humanities Research Center at the University of Texas, Austin. One of the most striking of the drawings is reproduced as Item 584 in Dan H. Laurence, *Shaw: An Exhibit*, the catalogue of an exhibition (Sept. 1977–Feb. 1978) displaying representative Shaw materials in the Harry Ransom Center.

33. Register of Marriages in St. Peter's Church, Dublin, No. 239; transcribed in Ross 54.

34. CL3:358.

35. McNulty 24. Shaw himself described Agnes's hair as "Highland red" (SSS 105). McNulty's memoirs comprise a forty-nine-page typescript containing recollections of Shaw in his youth, together with descriptions of other members of the Shaw family and some copies of Shaw's letters to McNulty dating from 1891 to 1924. A copy of the typescript is housed in the Archibald Henderson Collection of Bernard Shaw material, Southern Historical Collection and Manuscripts Department, University of North Carolina, Chapel Hill.

36. Thomas Demetrius O'Bolger, an Irish immigrant living in America, wrote a biographical study entitled "The Real Shaw" as his doctoral dissertation, which he completed in 1913 at the University of Pennsylvania. Shaw provided O'Bolger with a great deal of information by correspondence and initially cooperated in O'Bolger's attempt to have the dissertation published as a book. Shaw eventually refused to allow publication of the work because he considered its treatment of members of his family and himself to be tactless and offensive (see CL3:854–55). The typescript is housed in the Houghton Library, Harvard University, together with an extensive correspondence between Shaw and O'Bolger, some of which has been published in CL3. B. C. Rossett is the author of a 1964 study entitled *Shaw of Dublin*.

John O'Donovan, a Dublin author who provides much useful information about Lee and the Shaw family, was decidedly equivocal about the subject of Shaw's parentage in the main text of his 1965 study *Shaw and the Charlatan Genius*. Nevertheless, he added a postscript to the book, making it clear that he did not consider that "Bernard Shaw was anybody's son but George Carr Shaw's," adding that

> the circumstantial evidence points to Shaw's perfect legitimacy. To deny that George Carr Shaw's letters to Bessie about the year-old G.B.S. are the letters of a father who doesn't doubt that it's his own flesh and blood he is writing about, is perverse. To deny the weight of the fact that Lee did not share a house with Bessie until at least seven years after G.B.S.'s conception is hardly less perverse if you know the Dublin of 1964 and can infer what the Dublin of 1864 was like. . . . To maintain that a colourful resident of a sparsely populated district in a small and gossipy city could habitually go to bed with a housewife from around the corner without anybody knowing anything about it, is to strain a Dubliner's credulity beyond breaking-point.

It was unfortunate that O'Donovan chose to defer these convincing statements until the writing of a postscript, which he claims was necessitated by the fact that an English journalist who saw his book at the proof stage announced that the author was "trying to prove that Bernard Shaw was a bastard" (SCG 106–8).

37. Shaw to Edward B. Shaw, 10 Nov. 1947 (private collection, Tasmania).

38. Shaw to Grace Goodliffe, 3 Dec. 1942; CL4:652. Grace Goodliffe was a distant cousin of Shaw's, being the third daughter of Sir Frederick Shaw (5th Baronet of Bushy Park), who married Major Guy V. Goodliffe.

39. CL3:356.

40. The demolition of the Cromwell claim is described in an informative article "Bernard Shaw's Ancestry: No Link with Oliver Cromwell," *Bath & Wilts Chronicle and Herald*, 28 April 1949.

41. CL4:430.

Chapter 2. The Family Skeletons

1. Shaw's autobiographical writings exhibit what critic and theorist David Lloyd has described (in connection with the Irish writer James Clarence Mangan) as "the tension [in autobiography] between the desire for self-origination, to produce oneself as if without a father, and the awkward knowledge of indebtedness to what precedes and influences the subject" (*Nationalism and Minor Literature: James Clarence Mangan and the Emergence of Irish Cultural Nationalism* [Berkeley: University of California Press, 1988], 162; cited in Emer Nolan, *James Joyce and Nationalism* [London: Routledge, 1995, 37]). I am grateful to Professor Terence Brown for drawing my attention to the similarity between Shaw's and Mangan's treatment of their fathers.

2. SSS 13.

3. AutoMisc 93.

4. Imm xxvi; Prefs3:20.

5. Quoted in Farmer 7.

6. SSS 10.

7. CL3:363.

8. Shaw wrote of his mother's situation at the time of her betrothal that, "having never been taught what marriage really means, nor experienced impecuniosity, she might marry any adventurer without knowing how much she was doing" (SSS 10).

9. SSS 11.

10. SSS 12.

11. Ibid.

12. Ibid.

13. Ross 58.

14. Concerning Bessie's feelings for her husband, Hesketh Pearson surmises that "it is doubtful whether she loved him. It is doubtful whether she ever loved any one." (Hesketh Pearson, *Bernard Shaw: His Life and Personality* [London: Collins, 1950], 17). Under the heading "His mother's cold character," St. John Ervine launches an extraordinary denunciation of Bessie as "a cold girl [who] became a cold wife and mother," declaring "it is certain that Bessie did not love her husband." Having decided that there was some "defect inherent in her nature"—Hamlet's "vicious mole of nature" springs to mind—Ervine brings his adverse report to a climax by effacing Bessie's humanity altogether: "She was, in short, devoid of human qualities." Too late, the reader is bound to feel, when the next page but one is headed "His mother's good points" (St. John Ervine, *Bernard Shaw: His Life, Work and Friends* [London: Constable, 1956], 13–19).

15. Two other writers who have commented on this correspondence are Nathaniel Harris (*The Shaws: The Family of George Bernard Shaw* [London: Dent, 1977], 31) and John O'Donovan ("The First Twenty Years," in *The Genius of Shaw*, ed. Michael Holroyd [London: Hodder & Stoughton, 1979], 20). In their brief but useful studies, both Harris and O'Donovan present a more balanced view of the marriage of Bernard Shaw's parents than those of his major biographers.

16. George Carr Shaw to Lucinda Elizabeth Shaw, BL Ms. 50508, fols. 8, 18, 30.

17. Letter of 5 Aug. 1857; BL Ms. Add. 50508, fol. 24.

18. Letter of July 1857; BL Ms. Add. 50508, fol. 4.

19. Letter of 8 Aug. 1857; BL Ms. Add. 50508, fol. 30.

20. Letter of 30 July 1857; BL Ms. Add. 50508, fol. 18v.

21. Letter of 20 July 1857; BL Ms. Add 50508, fol. 4.

22. Letters of 28 July, 2 Aug., and 5 Aug. 1857; BL Ms. Add. 50508, fols. 18v, 23v, 26.

23. Letter of 28 July 1857; BL Ms. Add. 50508, fol. 15v.

24. CL1:35–36.

25. BL Ms. Add. 50710B, fols. 2–3. Shaw sent a copy of this account of his father's and uncles' drinking habits to J. Kingston Barton on 25 October 1879. The note is reprinted in Shaw's diaries under the sweeping editorial title: "The Shaw Family of Dipsomaniacs" (see D1:27–29). Several details of the note have been manipulated to produce extraordinarily unflattering portraits of George Carr Shaw in the biographies by Michael Holroyd and Sally Peters. The former writes: "Shaw was not a romantic figure. It seems possible that even then he was an advanced alcoholic, and with steady diarrhoea . . . he had a weak mouth, one squinting eye and a number of epileptic ways. . . . He was an unconvivial man, with disconcerting quirks of humour and little interest in women. Drink and money were his world" (*Bernard Shaw, Volume I, 1856–1898: The Search for Love* [London: Chatto & Windus, 1988], 11). Sally Peters elaborates on the information in the note to create an even more unpleasant picture of the man: "In that little room where George Carr Shaw changed his clothes and Sonny slept, the boy had smelled the nauseating odor of sickness and seen the miserable creature running out to the privy, unable to hold his liquor or his bowels" (*Bernard Shaw: The Ascent of the*

Superman [New Haven, Conn.: Yale University Press, 1996], 76). With each biographer George Carr Shaw's diarrhea became worse.

26. In his 1879 note Shaw writes: "Eventually he had a fit, and shortly but—to the best of my recollection—not immediately afterwards, he stopped drinking; and for more than ten years has been so rigid a teetotaller that those who know him find it difficult to realise what he formerly was"; BL Ms. Add. 50710B, fol. 2. For another reference to the fit, see SSS 92.

27. Imm xxi; Prefs3:16; Auto1:37.

28. See chap. 3.

29. SSS 48.

30. George Carr Shaw to Bernard Shaw, 28 March 1881: "You are an illnatured cur that you would not once in a while say 6 or 12 months drop me a few lines. . . . What about your second book—I think it will take if it only gets into proper hands—Tell the Mar I got her letter yesterday—"; BL Ms. Add. 50509, fol. 17.

31. George Carr Shaw to Bernard Shaw, 15 Aug. 1884; BL Ms. Add. 50510, fol. 250r–v.

32. George Carr Shaw to Bernard Shaw, 29 Aug. 1884; BL Ms. Add. 50510, fols. 258–59.

33. SSS 91.

34. SSS 92; cf. CL4:479. The word *expiate* in this sentence has been substituted for *soothe* in the original letter.

35. Imm xxii; Prefs3:17.

36. Hend1, 38.

37. Katharine Tynan, *Twenty-Five Years: Reminiscences* (London: Smith Elder, 1913), 313; I&R 262–64.

38. Letter from Lord Olivier to Archibald Henderson, 8 June 1931, quoted in Hend2, 212; I&R 263.

39. Record of conversation between Shaw and his mother in "Notes to *Captain Brassbound*"; CP2:420.

40. Lucinda Elizabeth Shaw to Bernard Shaw, 24 March 1894; BL Ms. Add. 50513, fols. 39–42. Shaw was staying with the Salt family in Surrey when his mother—apparently at his request—provided this account of her musical training. The envelope in which the letter was sent contains the following description by Shaw: "About Logier & ancient history."

41. Lucinda Frances Shaw to Jane Crichton Drysdale, 27 Jan 1908; Texas.

42. Grace Chappelow recollection in Villager 243–46. Mrs. Harris is described in a letter (30 April 1895) from Shaw to Janet Achurch as "our domestic assistant"; CL1:531.

43. Unpublished letter from Shaw to Edith Benigna Isobel ("Ida") Beatty, 19 Oct. 1903 (private collection).

44. Shaw diary entry for 10 Aug. 1889; D1:530.

45. Shaw to Mrs. Patrick Campbell, 22 April 1913; CL3:167.

46. The Australian cousin may have been endowed with a good deal of the Shaw family pride, but not its snobbery. All indications suggest he was a genial and sociable man. Having served as a branch manager in the Australasian Bank in Victoria, he became for many years secretary/manager of the Metropolitan Golf Club in Mel-

bourne. When he retired in 1936, after serving thirteen years as manager, the club's annual report described him as having carried out his duties "with dignity and distinction." He was granted an honorary lifetime membership and was remembered as "one of the personalities of the golf world." See John Kissling, *Seventy Years: A History of the Metropolitan Golf Club* (Melbourne: Macmillan, 1973), 72. (This reference was kindly supplied by Alan Ferguson, the club's archivist.) Charles MacMahon Shaw died on April 15, 1943 (see obituary notice in *Argus*, Melbourne, 16 April).

47. BB, facing pp. 47, 119, 125, 136. The typescript, with Shaw's holograph marginal and interlinear comments, is housed in the Manuscripts Department of the National Library of Ireland. Although nearly all of Shaw's comments were published in the book, some significant remarks were omitted. Among these was a unique Shavian recollection about his childhood passion for painting. Also omitted was one of Shaw's notes about his treatment of his father in his autobiographical writings.

48. BB 127.

49. BB 124.

50. Ms. 16,686, p. 79 (commenting on p. 124 of BB).

51. Imm xi.

52. SSS 14; SM1:39.

53. On the famine, see Joel Mokyr, *Why Ireland Starved: A Quantitative and Analytical History of the Irish Economy, 1800–1850* (London: George Allen & Unwin, 1983), 11, 15.

54. On the extent of Irish poverty, see: Cormac O Grada, *Ireland Before and After the Famine: Explorations in Economic History, 1800–1925*, 2nd ed. (Manchester: Manchester University Press, 1993), 17; Mokyr, *Why Ireland Starved*, 1, 6–29. On illiteracy, see Mary E. Daly, *The Famine in Ireland* (Dundalk, Ire.: Dublin Historical Association by Dundalgan, 1986), who writes that although literacy levels rose during the 1840s, "in 1851 42% of men and 51% of women were completely illiterate" (121).

55. Mary E. Daly, *Dublin, the Deposed Capital: A Social and Economic History, 1860–1914* (Cork, Ire.: Cork University Press, 1984), 270.

56. Daly, *Dublin*, 32.

57. SSS 27. A "thorough-servant" was one who carried out several household tasks, such as washing, cleaning, and cooking. Eight pounds would have been equivalent to about 380 pounds (700 U.S. dollars) in early twenty-first-century currency. Full board and lodging was, of course, provided to household servants.

58. George Carr Shaw to Lucinda Elizabeth Shaw, 24 and 27 July 1857; BL Ms. Add. 50508, fols. 8, 10.

59. Shaw to Frank Harris, 12 May 1930; CL4:189.

60. SM1:43.

61. SCG 69–73, 77–78.

62. SM1:53.

63. Ibid.

64. Bernard Shaw, *Everybody's Political What's What?* (London: Constable, 1944), 75.

65. McNulty 20.

66. The psychoanalytical approach referred to here is extensively deployed by Michael Holroyd in his biographical account of Shaw.

67. For further discussion of this subject, see chaps. 11, 13, 19, and 20.

68. Farmer 7.

69. CL1:7

70. Lucinda Frances Shaw to Bernard Shaw, n.d. [c. 1876]. Texas. (The letter is reprinted in Farmer, with inaccuracies in transcription, on p. 31.) The word *swit* in the opening of the letter is perhaps a jocular form of *sweet*.

71. Texas.

72. Shaw wrote of her: "She had no use for the family pretensions, nor for the country-gentility of her maternal stock. Yet she hated Bohemianism and was ashamed of it"; SSS 94.

73. Mrs. Mabel Dolmetsch to H. G. Farmer, 27 Nov. 1947; reprinted in Farmer 79.

74. Shaw's voice attracted much comment; see chap. 8.

75. Quoted in *Great Acting*, ed. Hal Burton (London: British Broadcasting Corporation, 1967; New York: Hill & Wang, 1968), 68; I&R 375.

76. In an essay first published in 1942, Auden stated that "the present generation, if it is honest, will have to admit that in comparison with its own spokesmen, the 'vulgar old buffer' not only had nicer manners, a kinder heart, and a more courageous will, but also wrote a lot better." W. H. Auden, "The Fabian Figaro," *The Commonweal*, 23 Oct. 1942; reprinted in *George Bernard Shaw: A Critical Survey*, ed. Louis Kronenberger (New York: World, 1953).

77. J. B. Priestley, "Thoughts on Shaw," *New Statesman and Nation*, 28 July 1956; I&R 508–10. Priestley recalls Belloc as having said "that Wells was a cad who didn't pretend to be anything but a cad; that Bennett was a cad pretending to be a gentleman; that Shaw was a gentleman pretending to be a cad."

Chapter 3. Growing Up in Dublin

1. Bernard Shaw, *Everybody's Political What's What?* (London: Constable, 1944), 81. Shaw characterized schools comprehensively as "child prisons" in this work (73).

2. SSS 23.

3. Shaw, *Everybody's Political What's What?* 81.

4. Ibid., 45.

5. Shaw, preface to *London Music in 1888–89* (1937); Prefs3:327; SM1:40.

6. Prefs3:328; SM1:40.

7. Ross 178; CL4:727.

8. SSS 21.

9. Four further attendances for the same fees are recorded for periods through 31 Oct. 1868; Ross 178.

10. SSS 22.

11. Ibid.

12. Ibid.

13. SSS 28; Auto1:58.

14. SSS 20–21.

15. SSS 30.

16. CL2:499; Hend1:18; Theatrics xii.

17. McNulty 18.

18. Harvard bMs Eng 1046.9:9–23. This file consists of typescript questions about

his childhood put to Shaw by Thomas Demetrius O'Bolger in 1915–16, with autograph replies by Shaw. (Shaw's replies are incompletely represented in CL3.)

19. [Bernard Shaw], "The Search for Another Messiah," unsigned notes in the *Dramatic Review*, 29 Aug. 1885; SM1:346.

20. Bernard Shaw, "A Pride of Fausts," *Dramatic Review*, 19 Dec. 1885; SM1:427.

21. Imm xx; Prefs3:15.

22. D1:366.

23. Beerbohm depicted Shaw as Mephistopheles in a cartoon relating to a controversy about translations of Tolstoy in 1922. Shaw supported the claims of the Tolstoy scholar Aylmer Maude in a letter to *The Times* (London) on 8 May 1922.

24. Henry S. Salt, "Reminiscences of G. Bernard Shaw," March 1929, Texas (Shaw, GB, Misc., Hanley).

25. Imm xxi; Prefs3:16.

26. See Wilfrid Blunt, *Cockerell* (London: Hamish Hamilton, 1964), 211.

27. Bernard Shaw, "Better than Shakespear," *Saturday Review*, 2 Jan. 1897; OTN3:2; Drama2:736.

28. Prefs1:161–62.

29. Shaw made this comment in the preface (1947) to his play *Geneva*; Prefs3:461.

30. In the Epistle Dedicatory to *Man and Superman*, Shaw wrote of "Bunyan's perception that righteousness is filthy rags, his scorn for Mr. Legality in the village of Morality, his defiance of the Church as the supplanter of religion, his insistence on courage as the virtue of virtues, his estimate of the career of the conventionally respectable and sensible Worldly Wiseman as no better at bottom than the life and death of Mr Badman," saying that his vision, expressed "in the terms of a tinker's theology," anticipated the revolutionary ideas of Nietzsche, Wagner, and Ibsen; Prefs1:162.

31. Prefs1:159.

32. Lena Ashwell, *Myself a Player* (London: Michael Joseph, 1936), 254.

33. "When the devil appears the opening staves of Le Veau d'Or, the song of Mephistopheles from Gounod's Faust, rattles out." Letter dated 3 Oct. 1946 from Shaw to BBC producer Peter Michael Watts concerning the music in a current broadcast of the play; CL4:779.

34. SSS 9.

35. Katharine Tynan, *Twenty-Five Years: Reminiscences* (London: Smith, Elder, 1913), 313; I&R 264.

36. Imm xxi; Prefs3:16.

37. According to Shaw, when he asked his father what a Unitarian is, he replied that "the Unitarians are people who believe that our Lord was not really crucified at all, but was seen 'running away down the other side of the Hill of Calvary'"; Auto1:36; CL3:372.

38. Auto1:38

39. Richard Frederick Shaw to George Bernard Shaw, 27 May 1885; BL Ms. Add. 50511.

40. Bernard Shaw, "On Going to Church," *The Savoy*, no. 1 (Jan. 1896); Auto1:31.

41. Imm xix; Prefs3:14.

42. SSS 24.

43. Bernard Shaw, "In the Days of My Youth"; AutoMisc 100.

44. Shaw to Grace Goodliffe, n.d. (assigned to 25 Oct. 1949). In this letter Shaw informed Goodliffe that "the concerts of the Amateur Musical Society were rehearsed in our house; and the tenors, baritones, basses, and sopranos[,] as it happened, were all Catholics"; CL4:857.

45. AutoMisc 101; SSS 46.

46. Sir Thomas Browne, *Religio Medici and Other Works*, ed. L. C. Martin (Oxford: Clarendon Press, 1964), 20.

47. See preface to *Buoyant Billions* (1947); Prefs3:489–93.

48. Shaw to Thomas Demetrius O'Bolger, 24 Feb. 1916; CL3:376.

49. SSS 72.

50. Matter 291.

51. I am grateful to curator Adrian Le Harivel of the National Gallery of Ireland for his advice and assistance with research on its history and holdings. Those of the 1860s and 1870s are detailed in various catalogues and histories of the gallery, as well as in several typescript documents Mr. Le Harivel kindly supplied.

52. "On Going to Church"; Auto1:33.

53. CL3:896.

54. SSS 28.

55. National Library of Ireland, Ms. 16, 686, p. 82.

56. The sketchbook is contained in BL Ms. Add. 50719.

57. BL Ms. Add. 50720.

58. CL1:8.

59. Matthew Edward McNulty to Shaw, 18 Feb. 1883 (corrected in Shaw's hand to 17 Feb.); BL Ms. Add. 50510, fol. 21.

60. Shaw to Matthew Edward McNulty, 3 June 1876; CL1:19.

61. SSS 33.

62. "George Bernard Shaw," in *Irish Literary Portraits*, ed. W. R. Rodgers (London: British Broadcasting Corporation, 1972); I&R 3–10.

63. This recollection is included in Frank Harris, *Contemporary Portraits*, 4 vols. (London: Methuen, 1915–24), vol. 2, 42–43; I&R 10.

64. *Irish Literary Portraits*, 122; I&R 6.

65. *Irish Literary Portraits*, 122; I&R 7; see also "Mr. Foy Tells of G.B.S. (Orchard-raider)," *Empire News* (Irish ed.), Manchester, 19 Nov. 1950; I&R 10–11. In what appears to be a typographical error, Foy is called Fry in *Irish Literary Portraits*. He was ninety-three at the time of the *Empire News* article and had only just revealed his childhood friendship with Shaw. I have been unable to identify the children's game of boxing the fox to which Foy refers.

66. This is part of Shaw's reported answer to Patrick O'Reilly, a Dublin garbage collector who organized the erection of a plaque at Shaw's birthplace and asked him (in the late 1940s) if he remembered the Pottle, a narrow alleyway in Dublin (near which Swift lived). Cited in Desmond M. Fisher, "Shaw's Other Dustman," *American Mercury* (March 1954): 121; I&R 11.

67. Bernard Shaw, "Educational Confessions," *The Schoolmistress*, 17 Nov. 1927; I&R 13.

68. SSS 45.

69. Shaw to Thomas Demetrius O'Bolger, 14 Feb. 1916; Harvard bMs Eng 1046.9.

70. Shaw to Thomas Demetrius O'Bolger, 14 Feb. 1916; Harvard bMs Eng 1046.9. Although in his 1937 preface to *London Music in 1888–1889* Shaw provided less detail about the particular works he knew as a child, he added Haydn, Rossini, and Bellini to this list of composers, some of whose leading works he could "sing and whistle from end to end"; Prefs3:328.

71. O'Donovan entitled his memoir of Lee and the Shaw family (to which I am substantially indebted in the following discussion) *Shaw and the Charlatan Genius.*

72. SCG 47–51; Ross 226–27.

73. SCG 142. Although the title page of the first edition bears the date 1870, O'Donovan reproduces Lee's inscription in a presentation copy to the surgeon Dr. Philip Crampton Smyly that is dated December 1869.

74. SCG 145.

75. Prefs3:335; SCG 94–96.

76. Shaw's replies to O'Bolger's inquiries about his Dublin reading were supplied in installments in 1915 and 1916. See Harvard bMs Eng 1046.9.

77. Preface to *Three Plays for Puritans*; Prefs1:67–68.

78. Shaw reply to Thomas Demetrius O'Bolger, n.d. [1915]; Harvard bMs Eng 1046.9.

79. Shaw reply to Thomas Demetrius O'Bolger, 14 Feb. 1916. The remainder of Shaw's previously unpublished account of his early reading is worth recording here:

> In London [Lee] borrowed a large-print Shakespear from me & complained that he could not find The School for Scandal in it. But pupils used to present him with gift books—Travels in the Pyrenees (in French) illustrated by the then hardly known Doré, and Byron, and [Thomas Moore's] Lallah Rookh, with Teniel's [*sic*] illustrations, also Lord Derby's translation of Homer's Iliad, which led me afterwards to despise Pope unduly. We had bound volumes of Household Words & All The Year Round, and a complete Bunyan. My maternal uncle, then a ship surgeon of the Inman Line (now the American line) brought batches of pirated editions of novels, mostly Anthony Trollope's. We had Chamber's Miscellany with stories about Baron Trenck and poems, including the Ancient Mariner & the Faery Queen (selections) & [William Cowper's] John Gilpin. We had Shakespear, with Selors' illustrations. When I became an office boy and had thirty shillings a month, I always bought a batch of Doré illustrated monthly parts, notably Don Quixote. But by that time I subscribed to Marron's [?] Library and always got the Westminster Review (then in its atheistic glory) & Tyndall & George Eliot &c.
>
> Put beside these two arts the National Gallery, and about two dozen volumes of outline engravings of old masters lent me one by one by Joseph Robinson, a well known Dublin musician; and you will see that though academically I was hopelessly uneducated, yet before I was 15 I had more culture than most of our unfortunate Philistines have at 55.
>
> It all fits, too, into the extraordinary beauty of the Killiney & Dalkey hills & the Dublin & Killiney bays. To this I was intensely susceptible; and I wove out of it

all a sort of heaven which made the material squalor of my existence as nothing. (Harvard bMs Eng 1046.9)

80. Martin Meisel's *Shaw and the Nineteenth-Century Theater* (Princeton, N.J.: Princeton University Press, 1963) has not been superseded in its account of the relationship of Shaw's work to the nineteenth-century popular theater.

81. Shaw recalled his early theatergoing in, among other places, an interview article by Roy Nash, "The Theatre Today and Yesterday According to George Bernard Shaw," *Manchester Evening News,* 6 Dec. 1938, from which the above details are drawn. Tom Taylor (1817–80)—dramatist, editor of *Punch,* professor of English, and public servant—wrote more than seventy plays in popular nineteenth-century forms for the London theater. His *Plot and Passion* was first presented at the Olympic Theatre, London, in 1853. *The Corsican Brothers* was adapted in 1848 by Dionysius Lardner Boucicault (1820–90) from a novel by Alexandre Dumas père (1802–70).

82. Theatrics xiv.

83. Imm xx; Prefs3:15.

84. Shaw reply to Thomas Demetrius O'Bolger. "My struggle . . . was to become efficient in real life. It was like learning to act. In fact the real Shaw is the actor, the imaginary Shaw the real one"; Harvard bMs Eng 1046.9.

85. Imm xliii.

86. Shaw to Frank Harris, 20 June 1930; CL4:189.

Chapter 4. The Townshend Connections

1. See *Burke's Irish Family Records* (London: Burke's Peerage, 1976), 1115–19.

2. Shaw to Lord Alfred Douglas, 9 Nov. 1940; CL4:586. I am grateful to Nora Cullinane for her kind welcome to Derry House during a visit I made in 1997, and for providing me with family records about the history of the house and the Payne-Townshend family.

3. Diary of Charlotte Shaw; BL Ms. Add. 63188A. The description of her father appears in her 17 May 1927 letter to T. E. Lawrence (see n. 5).

4. See *Burke's Irish Family Records,* 1119.

5. Charlotte Shaw to T. E. Lawrence, 17 May 1927; BL Ms. Add. 45922. The Shaws had been introduced to Lawrence in March 1922 by their mutual friend Sir Sidney Cockerell, director of the Fitzwilliam Museum, Cambridge.

6. Michael Collins (1890–1922), an Irish revolutionary, became director of intelligence and a leading figure in the Irish Republican Army after his release from internment following his involvement in the 1916 Easter Rising.

7. Charlotte Shaw to T. E. Lawrence, 17 May 1927; BL Ms. Add. 45922. The duke of Leinster is the premier duke, marquess, and earl of Ireland. The assertion that there was no middle class in Ireland has been contested. Roy Foster (*Modern Ireland, 1600–1972* [London: Penguin, 1989]) writes: "Contrary to so many generalizations there *was* an Irish urban middle class, but it was largely comprised of people in service or distribution industries in provincial towns, whose occupations were rurally derived or 'professional'" (379).

8. Charlotte Shaw to T. E. Lawrence, 17 May 1927; BL Ms. Add. 45922. On the subject of her attitude toward children, the letter continues:

> As I grew older I saw many & better, reasons for sticking to my resolution. The idea was physically repulsive to me in the highest degree, & my reason did not consent to any of the arguments brought to bear upon me. I was told it was my duty to contribute my share to the maintenance of the race. I said I was living in what I considered to be an over-populated country, & I saw no immediate prospect of the disappearance of the race: also I did not desire to produce cannon-fodder. Then they said I was a remarkable person & I should hand on my qualities. I said it did not appear that distinguished people had distinguished descendents [*sic*]: great men & women are "sports" usually. And so on."

9. BL Ms. Add. 56525, Charlotte Shaw Papers, vol. XXXVI (ff.i + 101). Undated comment in financial memorandum-book of Horace Payne-Townshend, with additional notes in other hands (1856–87).

10. BL Ms. Add. 56525, fol. 36.

11. SSS 32.

12. SSS 31.

13. SSS 37.

14. Shaw to Matthew Edward McNulty, 22 July 1913; BL Ms. Add. 50516, fol. 38.

15. SSS 32.

16. SSS 31–32.

17. SSS 32.

18. SSS 31.

19. See the entry on Lalor in *The Oxford Companion to Irish Literature*, ed. Robert Welch (Oxford: Oxford University Press, 1996), 295.

20. Foster, *Modern Ireland*, 381.

21. See above, chap. 3.

22. Imm xxxiv; Prefs3:27.

23. CL1:14, 19, 22.

24. Shaw to Matthew Edward McNulty, 3 June 1876. CL1:19.

25. CL1:22.

Chapter 5. Self-Searching: London and the Novels

1. Imm xxxii.

2. The Shaws stayed at 13 Victoria Grove until 23 Dec. 1881, when they moved to first-floor rooms at 37 Fitzroy Street, W. They remained there only until 22 April 1882, when they made a further move, to 36 Osnaburgh Street, N.W., their home for five years. The moves to Fitzroy and Osnaburgh Streets (the latter near Regent's Park) brought Shaw closer to central London and favorite haunts, such as the British Museum. Early Fabian Society meetings were held at 17 Osnaburgh Street, the home of its secretary, Edward Pease.

In an unpublished letter dated 11 July 1911, Shaw gave directions to Archibald Henderson to help him find Shaw's early London houses and to correct mistakes in

Henderson's recently published biography. (A photograph of a ginger-beer shop near Osnaburgh Street had been mistakenly identified in the biography as Shaw's "first" London home.) Shaw began by telling Henderson that to get to Osnaburgh Street he should take the inner-circle underground railway to the nearby Portland Road station. After drawing a little map, he instructed his disciple to "go along Osnaburgh St a little way past the church railings; and on the opposite side you will presently see a highly respectable house with a plate on the door marked *St Catherine's Home*. That, sir, was formerly St Bernard's home, and NOT his first home in London, which was 13 Victoria Grove, Fulham Road (a cul de sac of little semi-detached villas nearly opposite the West Brompton post office, nor his second, which was the last house in Fitzroy Street on the left before you came to the square going north . . . .)" (Harvard bMs Eng 1046.11). The Shaws had the second floor of the house at Osnaburgh Street, with a room on the third in which Shaw slept (D1:52). Victoria Grove was later renamed Netherton Grove, and No. 13 was demolished to make way for "big buildings" (SSS 37).

3. Shaw to Lewis Wynne, 26 Nov. 1928; CL4:120–21. In CL1:18 and CL4:121 Laurence identifies the opera singer as the basso profundo Richard Deck, who numbered among Shaw's circle of friends in his twenties and instructed him in voice control.

4. The photo appears in SSS facing p. 38.

5. CL1:19.

6. BL Ms. Add. 50508.

7. Preface to *The Irrational Knot* (London: Constable, 1931), xv–xvi; Prefs1:181. Shaw here alludes to Milton's portrayal of Comus, the riotous offspring of Bacchus and Circe, in *A Masque Presented at Ludlow Castle, 1634*, who remains contemptuously deaf to the virtuous pleadings of the innocent young virgin he is intending to ravish.

8. Lucy Shaw to Jane Crichton Drysdale, 27 Jan. 1908; Texas.

9. D1:39.

10. D1:30. The person who effected this introduction (referred to simply by the surname Home in Shaw's diary entry) may have been Captain Risden H. Home, a member of the East India United Services Club, St. James's Square, who is occasionally mentioned elsewhere in the diaries as someone Shaw had conversations with; see, e.g., D1:105.

11. CL1:35.

12. D1:33.

13. The standard work of critical reference for the novels is Richard F. Dietrich's *Bernard Shaw's Novels: Portraits of the Artist as Man and Superman*, 2nd rev. ed. (Gainesville: University Press of Florida, 1996). Other studies include: Charles A. Berst, "*The Irrational Knot*: The Art of Shaw as a Young Ibsenite," *Journal of English and Germanic Philology* 85, no. 2 (April 1986): 222–48; Nicholas Grene, "The Maturing of *Immaturity*: Shaw's First Novel," *Irish University Review* (Autumn 1990): 225–38; Robert Hogan, "The Novels of Bernard Shaw," *English Literature in Transition, 1880–1920* 8 (1965): 63–114; Margery M. Morgan, "The Novels," in her book *The Shavian Playground* (London: Methuen, 1972); Stanley Weintraub, "The Embryo Playwright in Shaw's Early Novels," *University of Texas Studies in Literature and Language* 1 (1959): 327–55.

14. This conclusion of a Macmillan reader's report on Shaw's novel *An Unsocial Socialist* was included in correspondence with Shaw dated 22 Jan. 1885: "The story is designedly paradoxical, absurd & impossible—as if it were one of Peacock's. But whoever he may be, the author knows how to write: he is pointed, rapid, forcible, sometimes witty, often funny, & occasionally eloquent. I suppose one must call the book a *trifle*, but it is a clever trifle. Would it be popular? I half fear that it is too clever for the 'general': They would not know whether the writer was serious or was laughing at them"; BL Ms. Add. 50511.

15. Henderson changed the mice to rats in his account of the story (*George Bernard Shaw: His Life and Works* [London: Hurst & Blackett, 1911], 47), but they are "mice" in Shaw's rather detailed description of the state of the parcels in his 1930 preface to *Immaturity;* Imm xxxviii–xxxix.

16. Shaw to Richard Bentley & Son, 15 Jan. 1880; CL1:26.

17. The term is applied to Shaw's last novel in Eileen Sypher's essay "Fabian Anti-Novel: Shaw's *An Unsocial Socialist,*" *Literature and History* 11, no. 2 (Autumn 1985): 241–53. I see the term as being even more appropriate when applied to the first three novels, the last two coming back into line with conventional romance structures in strictly qualified, Shavian ways.

18. Shaw to Macmillan & Co., 1 Feb. 1880; CL1:27. The Macmillan reader's comments are quoted in the editor's headnote to this letter.

19. Dietrich, *Bernard Shaw's Novels*, 60.

20. Elinor Huddart to Shaw, 10 March 1881; BL Ms. Add. 50535.

21. Shaw played the piano for Lee at rehearsals for a proposed production of *Patience* in January 1883.

22. D1:41. The Grosvenor Gallery is also mentioned in the preface to *Immaturity* on p. xli.

23. D1:31.

24. Elinor Huddart to Shaw, 29 May and 2 Oct. 1881; BL Ms. Add. 50535.

25. Elinor Huddart to Shaw, 6 Sept. 1882; BL Ms. Add. 50535.

26. Elinor Huddart to Shaw, 6 Oct. 1881. BL Ms. Add. 50535.

27. Elinor Huddart to Shaw, 2 Sept. 1883. BL Ms. Add. 50536.

28. Elinor Huddart to Shaw, 26 March 1882. BL Ms. Add. 50535.

29. Acts 26:25.

30. Information about Pakenham Beatty's background and marriage is supplied by Dan H. Laurence in an unpublished typescript in the Dan H. Laurence Collection at the University of Guelph. During the writing of the present work I also relied on a book edited and introduced by a great-nephew of Pakenham Beatty, Dr. C.J.P. Beatty, with the double title *Sidelights on GBS and His Friend Pakenham Beatty: The Letters of Lucy Carr Shaw to Ida Beatty* (Dorchester, Eng.: Plush, 2002).

31. Pakenham Thomas Beatty's correspondence with Shaw (1878–89) is housed in the British Library, Ms. Add. 50530. The quotation is from a letter dated 28 March 1882.

32. Pakenham Thomas Beatty to Shaw, 16 Sept. 1881; BL Ms. Add. 50530.

33. Pakenham Thomas Beatty to Shaw, 15 Dec. 1881; BL Ms. Add. 50530.

34. Pakenham Thomas Beatty to Shaw, 12 June 1882; BL Ms. Add. 50530

35. Shaw to Pakenham Thomas Beatty, undated postcard written sometime after 1908 (private collection).

36. Shaw to Pakenham Thomas Beatty, 12 April 1899 and 24 March 1908 (private collection).

37. The formal name Octavius in *Man and Superman* of course primarily derives from Ottavio in Mozart's *Don Giovanni*. Shaw's Octavius resembles Pakenham Beatty in his aim "to count for something as a poet . . . to write a great play." Thus, it was probably Pakenham Beatty himself rather than his younger brother Tavy to whom Shaw was alluding in the creation of Octavius.

38. The review, entitled "Recent Poetry," was written by Shaw under the pseudonym L. O. Streeter and was published in *To-Day* on 1 August 1884; see Reviews2:22–28. Shaw wrote that Beatty's earlier love poetry, "though free from coarseness and from the ineptitude of most first essays in poetry, breathed infatuation rather than love," and complained that in *Marcia* "the tragic truth of Russian history in 1880" had been replaced by "commonplace fiction."

39. D1:611; CL1:250.

40. Laurence notes, Guelph.

41. Imm xliii; Auto1:86.

42. Imm xlii; Auto1:85.

43. CL1:29.

44. BL Ms. Add. 50509.

45. Elinor Huddart to Shaw, 27 March 1881; BL Ms. Add. 50535.

46. Elinor Huddart to Shaw, 6 Sept. 1882; BL Ms. Add. 50535.

47. This was noted by Margery M. Morgan in *The Shavian Playground* (London: Methuen, 1972): 15. Despite what seem like obvious echoes of Austen in his novels, Shaw does not appear to refer to her in any of his autobiographical writings, letters, or major prose works.

48. Prefs1:56.

49. Shaw makes frequent reference to his early reading of John Tyndall and Thomas Henry Huxley, two of the foremost prophets of nineteenth-century materialism and rationalism, and, as noted above, told Thomas Demetrius O'Bolger of his regular reading of the "old Westminster Review" in the days of its "atheistic glory."

50. Shaw, handwritten reply to Thomas Demetrius O'Bolger, March [?] 1915; Harvard bMS Eng 1046.9.

51. D1:31.

52. Shaw acknowledged Shelley's influence on his decision to become a vegetarian—and his general allegiance to Shelley—in a mock examination paper set for him by author Clarence Rook in September 1896: "My attention had been called to the subject [of vegetarianism], first by Shelley (I am an out-and-out Shelleyan) and later by a lecturer" (Bernard Shaw, *Nine Answers* (privately printed for Jerome Kern, 1923), published in interview form in the *Chap-Book* [Chicago], 1 Nov. 1896; I&R 22–29).

53. *The Revolt of Islam*, Canto VIII, xiii.

54. *Nine Answers*; I&R 27.

55. "Notes on Queen Mab."

56. Grenfell's recollection of the visit is related in her *Joyce Grenfell Requests the Pleasure* (London: Macmillan, 1976), 160–61; I&R 518–19.

57. Shaw, "Wagner and Vegetables," *The Academy* 55 (15 Oct. 1898), 79.

58. SSS 58; CL1:145; I&R 45–46; Doris Arthur Jones, *The Life and Letters of Henry Arthur Jones* (London: Victor Gollancz, 1930), 221.

59. Jones, *Life and Letters*, 221; I&R 45. Henry Arthur Jones (1851–1929) became a leading London dramatist in the 1890s.

60. Charles Churchill Osborne, *Philip Bourke Marston* (London: Times Book Club, 1926), 26–27; I&R 46. Marston (1850–87), a poet and son of the dramatist J. W. Marston, was blinded as a result of an accident in childhood. His account of the Shelley Society meeting is contained in a letter to Osborne dated 17 April 1886.

61. Shaw states that he had been vaccinated against smallpox in his childhood. The failure of this prophylactic in his case became one of the weapons in his later anti-vaccination campaigns. See Bernard Shaw, "Smallpox in St. Pancras," letter to the editor, *The Times* (London), 21 Sept. 1901.

62. This is now the London suburb E10.

63. Patch 215. In the same passage she supplies the explanation—that "he could not shave" because of the small pox—as to how "the famous beard was born." Dan H. Laurence states that "the blemishing effects of [the smallpox] led him to cultivate the beard . . ."; CL1:38. As far as I am aware, neither explanation—if any is needed—has other support; nevertheless, the reason supplied by Patch seems convincing.

64. Preface to first American edition of *Love Among the Artists* (1900); Auto1:97.

65. D1:32. This scheme is incorrectly assigned to March 1881 in Chron.

66. Shaw, preface to *The Irrational Knot* (1905); Prefs1:174.

67. The heroine of the opera itself is, of course, not the gypsy girl she appears to be but rather the daughter of an Austrian count. In *Immaturity* Shaw has his character Smith sing to himself one of the count's arias.

68. SSS 94. This section of *Sixteen Self Sketches* is a revised version of a long letter Shaw wrote to Charles MacMahon Shaw on 17 November 1937, in which the phrase "the country-gentility of her maternal stock" appeared as "the Gurly country-gentlemanism"; CL4:481.

69. Lucy's colorful description overlooks the fact that Shaw was the author of a Fabian tract called "The Impossibilities of Anarchism."

70. Lucy Carr Shaw, *Five Letters of the House of Kildonnel* (London: Lawrence & Jellicoe, 1905), 1.

71. CL3:196.

72. Bernard Shaw, preface to 1901 edition of *Cashel Byron's Profession*; Prefs1:90.

73. Robert Louis Stevenson to William Archer, March 1886; cited in D1:152.

74. Quotations are from the second version of *Lady Chatterley's Lover*, in Dieter Mehl and Christa Jansohn, eds., *The First and Second Lady Chatterley Novels* (Cambridge: Cambridge University Press, 1999), 263. Lawrence read many of Shaw's works, and despite some caustic comments on the older writer's work, he had a great respect for him. The echoes of Shaw in *Lady Chatterley's Lover* are noted—with a different reading of Shaw's treatment of the scene in his novel—by Sally Peters in *Bernard Shaw: The Ascent of the Superman* (New Haven, Conn.: Yale University Press, 1996), 83.

75. References to Alice appear in Elinor Huddart's letters to Shaw of 26 March and 17 April, 1882. Shaw began writing *Cashel Byron's Profession* on 12 April. The first surviving letter in the Shaw-Lockett correspondence was written by Shaw on 9 September of the following year.

76. D1:32; SSS 58; Auto1:113; I&R 32; CL2:489; Hend1:47–48.

77. Archer's outline of the beginnings of his friendship is recorded in C. Archer, *William Archer: Life, Work and Friendships* (London: George Allen & Unwin, 1931), 119–35; I&R 87–88.

78. Imm xl.

Chapter 6. A Fabian Don Juan

1. SSS 113. The chapter is entitled "To Frank Harris on Sex in Biography."

2. CL4:190–93.

3. SSS 115.

4. Bernard Shaw, "Carrying on Wagner's Business," *The World*, 15 March 1893; SM2:833.

5. Shaw to Jules Magny, 18 Dec. 1890; CL1:278. Magny had become associated with Shaw when he undertook the translation for *La Revue Socialiste* of Shaw's lecture entitled "The Transition to Social Democracy," which he delivered at Bath before the British Association on 7 September 1888; see CL1:211.

6. Zsa Zsa Gabor, article in *People*, 15 Aug. 1954; I&R 445. In the summer of 1939 Zsa Zsa (Sari) Gabor visited London with her husband, together with a team of Turkish journalists, as guests of the British Council. She won the Miss Hungary pageant in 1936 and is now generally thought to have been born in 1917.

7. CL1:63.

8. Emily Jane Gurly to Shaw, 19 March 1882; BL Ms. Add. 50509.

9. Rhymes employed by Shaw in a poem written in shorthand, "Love lifted to his lips a chalice," transcribed in a typescript performance script of a narrative "G.B.S. in Love" (Oct. 1977), composed by Dan H. Laurence, and housed at the University of Guelph. Another example of Shaw's verses addressed to Alice is in CL1:62–63.

10. CL1:63.

11. CL1:65, 94.

12. CL1:92.

13. CL1:73.

14. Texas; quoted in CL1:71.

15. Alice Mary Lockett to Shaw, Dec. 1884; BL Ms. Add. 50510.

16. CL1:100.

17. CL1:66.

18. CL1:73.

19. Letter from Lord Olivier to Archibald Henderson dated 8 June 1931, quoted in Hend2:144–45. Sydney Haldane Olivier, later Baron Olivier (1859–1943) was one of the earliest members of the Fabian Society; I&R 41.

20. Hend2:144; I&R 41.

21. The formulations of the aims of the Fabian Society quoted here are by Shaw and

are reprinted in Percy L. Parker, "What Is It to Be a Fabian? An Interview with Mr George Bernard Shaw," *Young Man*, April 1896; I&R 65–68.

22. Bernard Shaw, "Some Impressions," preface to *Sydney Olivier: Letters and Selected Writings*, ed. Margaret Olivier (London: Allen & Unwin, 1948), 9; I&R:40–41.

23. DBW1:329–30.

24. Kitty Muggeridge's reminiscence is cited by Richard Ingrams, *Muggeridge: The Biography* (London: HarperCollins, 1995), 34. A different version of this reminiscence appears in the introductory chapter ("My Aunt Bo") in Kitty Muggeridge and Ruth Adam, *Beatrice Webb: A Life* (London: Secker & Warburg, 1967), 13–14.

25. SSS 65. In the chapter entitled "Fruitful Friendships" in *Sixteen Self Sketches* Shaw followed this description of Webb with the words: "Quite the wisest thing I ever did was to force my friendship on him and to keep it; for from that time I was not merely a futile Shaw but a committee of Webb and Shaw."

26. Ingrams, *Muggeridge*, 34.

27. D1:33.

28. This is Dan H. Laurence's description. In 1988 Laurence made contact with a grandson of Katie Samuel, John de Sola Mosely, of Beverly Hills, Calif., who possessed five Shaw letters to Katie and two verses she had inspired. Information about Katie Samuel—together with the entire correspondence between her and Shaw and a reproduction of a photograph of Katie as a young mother—is included in Laurence's article "Katie Samuel: Shaw's Flameless 'Old Flame,'" *SHAW: The Annual of Bernard Shaw Studies* 15 (1995): 3–19. All references to the correspondence are to this article.

29. D1:33.

30. CL1:822.

31. See Margot Peters, *Bernard Shaw and the Actresses* (Garden City, N.Y.: Doubleday, 1980), 32.

32. The precise date of this reading—apparently the first "performance" of *A Doll's House* in England—is difficult to establish. Shaw records in his diary on 5 May 1885 that he "called at Aveling's to discuss a projected reading of Ibsen's *Nora*" (D1:81). In the second volume of her biography of Eleanor Marx, Yvonne Kapp gives the date of the reading as 15 January 1886. However, as Stanley Weintraub, the editor of Shaw's diaries, points out, this is not corroborated by Shaw's diary, which does not record the date of the reading and shows that he was otherwise engaged during the entire day and evening. See Yvonne Kapp, *Eleanor Marx*, 2 vols. (London: Lawrence & Wishart, 1972–76), 2:103.

33. Preface to *The Irrational Knot* (1905); Prefs1:184.

34. CL1:90.

35. This information was supplied to Dan H. Laurence by Mrs. Georgina ("Judy") Musters and communicated to me by Laurence in a letter dated 5 May 2001. Laurence's "Notes made during a talk with Georgina Musters at Folkestone, 7 August 1960" about Jenny Patterson are housed at the University of Guelph. Mrs. Musters was a daughter of Mrs. Arabella Gillmore, Bessie Shaw's half-sister, who lived with Jenny Patterson in later years as a companion.

36. "Masses and masses" of Shaw's letters to Jenny Patterson were burned (following her death in 1924) by Mrs. Arabella Gillmore (Laurence, "Notes," Guelph).

37. May Morris to Shaw, 11 and 14 Feb. 1886. BL Ms. Add. 50541.

38. A copy of Jane Patterson's will was kindly supplied to me by Dan H. Laurence.

39. Mrs. Jane Patterson to Shaw, 28 Dec. 1882 and 6 Jan. 1886; BL Ms. Add. 50544.

40. D1:59, 63, 80.

41. Sidney Webb's description, cited in D1:35, n18.

42. When Shaw published his *Common Sense of Municipal Trading* in 1904, he sent Wicksteed a copy with the inscription: "To my father in economics"; see also I&R 43.

43. CL1:115 provides information about this production and reproduces the program; see also D1:54, 57.

44. CL3:151–52. Desmond MacCarthy, *Shaw* (London: MacGibbon & Kee, 1951), 213–17; I&R 287.

45. D1:78. J. C. Shaw was probably James Cockaine ("Kaffir") Shaw, a cousin of GBS. Shaw later gave very substantial financial assistance to this cousin and his offspring, including a loan of twelve hundred pounds to "Kaffir" to buy a house in Dublin; see Lgen 16; CL2:904.

46. CL1:132.

47. D1:54, 91.

48. G. K. Chesterton, *George Bernard Shaw* (London: John Lane, 1910), 96.

49. D1:94–98.

50. D1:55 (prefatory note), 99 (record of event).

51. D1:101–2.

52. D1:124.

53. Mrs. Jane Patterson to Shaw, 7 Jan. 1887; BL Ms. Add. 50545.

54. D1:415.

55. Mrs. Jane Patterson to Shaw, 12 May 1886; BL Ms. Add. 50545.

56. Mrs. Jane Patterson to Shaw, 14 June 1886; BL Ms. Add. 50545.

57. Mrs. Jane Patterson to Shaw, 22 Feb. 1888; BL Ms. Add. 50545.

58. Mrs. Jane Patterson to Shaw, 12 May and 20 Oct 1886; BL Ms. Add. 50545.

59. Mrs. Jane Patterson to Shaw, 6 Jan. 1886; BL Ms. Add. 50545.

60. Mrs. Jane Patterson to Shaw, 12 May 1886; BL Ms. Add. 50545.

61. SSS 114.

62. Karl Pearson, "The Woman's Question," in *The Ethic of Freethought and Other Addresses and Essays* (London: Adam and Charles Black, 1901), 361–62; this paper was first read and printed for private circulation in 1885.

63. May Morris to Shaw, 5 May 1886; BL Ms. Add. 50541.

64. Lucinda Frances Shaw to Jane Crichton Drysdale, 24 July 1901; Texas.

Chapter 7. Rival Attractions

1. Eleanor Marx and Edward Aveling, "The Woman Question—From a Socialist Point of View," *Westminster Review* (Jan. 1886): 207–22. The essay was later published separately as a pamphlet.

2. Bernard Shaw, "An Explanatory Word from Shaw," introduction to *Florence Farr, Bernard Shaw, W. B. Yeats*, ed. Clifford Bax (Dublin: Cuala, 1941); Auto1:165. For Shaw's first meeting with Florence Farr, see Chron 96.

3. Mrs. Jane Patterson to Shaw, 8 Feb. 1886; BL Ms. Add. 50545. The letter was written on "Black Monday," which witnessed demonstrations and windows being smashed in Pall Mall to draw attention to unemployment. Several of Shaw's friends—including John Burns, H. H. Champion, H. M. Hyndman, and John E. Williams—were arrested and later acquitted; see D1:144–45.

4. Mrs. Jane Patterson to Shaw, 29 June 1886; BL Ms. Add. 50545.

5. Mrs. Jane Patterson to Shaw, 21 Sept. 1886; BL Ms. Add. 50545.

6. Mrs. Jane Patterson to Shaw, 25 Dec. 1887; BL Ms. Add. 50545; D1:326.

7. Mrs. Jane Patterson to Shaw, 29 Jan. 1888; BL Ms. Add. 50545.

8. May Morris to Shaw, 21 July 1885; BL Ms. Add. 50541.

9. May Morris to Shaw, 8 June 1885; BL Ms. Add. 50541.

10. May Morris to Shaw, 25 Nov. 1886; BL Ms. Add. 50541.

11. May Morris to Shaw, 25 Oct. 1885 and 14 Feb. 1886; BL Ms. Add. 50541.

12. Bernard Shaw, *William Morris as I Knew Him* (New York: Dodd, Mead and Co., 1936); originally published as "Morris as I Knew Him" a preface to the second volume of May Morris's *William Morris: Artist, Writer, Socialist* (Oxford: Basil Blackwell, 1936); Prefs3:283–84; Auto1:167.

13. D1:158, 159.

14. D1:57, 348, 352, 403.

15. D1:348.

16. W. B. Yeats to Katharine Tynan, 12 Feb. 1888. *The Collected Letters of W. B. Yeats*, ed. John Kelly and Eric Domville, 2 vols. (Oxford: Clarendon Press, 1986–97) 1:50.

17. G. Wilson Knight, *The Golden Labyrinth: A Study of British Drama* (London: Phoenix House, 1962), 351.

18. This occurred on 22 May 1893; D2:936.

19. D2:867.

20. Prefs3:285–86; Auto1:168.

21. D2:903, 936–37.

22. Shaw to Alice Lockett, 8 Oct. 1885 and 19 Aug. 1886; CL1:142–43, 157–59.

23. D1:416.

24. Bernard Shaw, "Mrs Besant as a Fabian Socialist," *Theosophist* (Oct. 1917); Auto1:138.

25. Bernard Shaw, "Annie Besant and the Secret Doctrine," corrected galley proof intended for the *Freethinker*; Texas; Auto1:142, 320.

26. Annie Besant, *An Autobiography*, 2nd ed. (London: T. Fisher Unwin, 1893), 57. Anticipating Shaw's use of the word *joy*, Besant went on to describe this longing as "not the act of a deliberate and conscious will, forcing self into submission and giving up with pain something the heart desires, but the following it is a joyous springing forward along the easiest path, the 'sacrifice' being the supremely attractive thing, not to make which would be to deny the deepest longings of the soul, and to feel oneself polluted and dishonoured."

27. Besant, *Autobiography*, 337.

28. The main purpose of the demonstration—attended by a large number of Socialists from different organizations, other left-wing radicals, and many Irish people—was to protest against the provisions of the Crimes Bill for Ireland, which was designed to

facilitate summary suppression of dissent and freedom of assembly and speech. The meeting had been banned and was broken up by mounted police wielding batons, as well as military personnel.

29. Shaw to William Morris, 22 Nov. 1887; CL1:177; D1:314–15.

30. Besant, *Autobiography*, 13–14.

31. "Mrs Besant as a Fabian Socialist"; Auto1:139.

32. Besant, *Autobiography*, 303; I&R 161.

33. D1:34, 237, 252, 288, 315, 326, 328.

34. Hesketh Pearson, *Bernard Shaw: His Life and Personality*, 2nd ed. (London: Collins, 1950), 114.

35. "On the 26th June 1886 I discovered that she [Edith] had become passionately attached to me"; D1:34.

36. Doris Langley Moore, *E. Nesbit: A Biography*, rev. ed. (London: Ernest Benn, 1967), 113; I&R 161–62.

37. Shaw to Molly Tompkins, 22 Feb. 1925; CL3:904–5.

38. Bernard Shaw, preface to *Salt and His Circle*, by Stephen Winsten (London: Hutchinson, 1951); Prefs3:534–35; Auto1:123–24.

39. D1:274, 347.

40. Grace Gilchrist to Shaw, 26 March 1888; BL, cited in CL1:105–6.

41. D1:362–63, 365. Another young female Fabian who followed this affair closely was Edward Pease's future wife, a Scots schoolteacher named Marjory G. ("Minnie") Davidson. Her letters to Shaw at the time (one of which included the following request and statement: "Will you write me a profane letter when you have time? You know what interests me—yourself") suggest that she may not have been an entirely disinterested observer of the Gilchrist affair. Marjory G. Davidson to Shaw, 6 May 1888, writing from her parental home The Manse, Kinfanns, Perth, Scotland; BL Ms. Add. 50547.

42. Grace Black to Shaw, 24 and 25 May 1887; BL Ms. Add. 50511.

43. Grace Black to Shaw, 31 March 1889; BL Ms. Add. 50512.

44. D1:289: "finished the tale 'The Truth about Don Giovanni.' Went up to Mrs. Besant's in the evening and played a couple of duets." The tale was first published in 1932 as "Don Giovanni Explains" and was included in the sixth volume of the Constable collected edition of *The Works of Bernard Shaw* under the volume title *Short Stories, Scraps and Shavings*. It was published again in 1934 in the Constable volume *The Black Girl in Search of God and Some Lesser Tales by Bernard Shaw*. Quotations from the tale are taken from the latter volume.

45. Bernard Shaw, "Darwin Denounced," *Pall Mall Gazette*, 31 May 1887; Reviews 1:277–79.

46. A section of the story dealing with Don Giovanni's sexual initiation by a "widow lady" is misleadingly included as actual autobiography in Stanley Weintraub's two-volume collation of Shaw's autobiographical writings; see Auto1:164–65.

47. D1:230.

Chapter 8. "The Coming Man": Critic and Platform Spellbinder

1. Mrs. Jane Patterson to Shaw, 13 April 1886; BL Ms. Add. 50544. It is possible that

Jenny Patterson was referring to some public mention of Shaw as "a coming man" in 1886. I have been unable to identify the reference.

2. Anon., "Coming Men: Mr. G. Bernard Shaw," *London Figaro*, no. 1748 (10 Aug. 1889): 4–5.

3. Shaw to Mrs. T. P. O'Connor, 16 Sept. 1888; CL1:196. This vivid description of how Shaw spent his days furnished the title ("Stump and Inkpot") of one of the chapters in Norman and Jeanne MacKenzie's book *The First Fabians* (London: Weidenfeld & Nicholson, 1977). The MacKenzies incorrectly state (p. 96) that the letter was addressed to Mr. T. P. O'Connor.

4. CL1:106.

5. Ibid.

6. Typescript of Shaw's letter housed at Guelph.

7. Bernard Shaw, "How William Archer Impressed Bernard Shaw," preface to the posthumous publication of William Archer's *Three Plays*, 1927; Prefs2:558. See also Charles Archer, *William Archer: His Life, Work and Friendships* (London: Allen & Unwin, 1931); Martin Quinn, "William Archer," in *Dictionary of Modern Literary Biography*, vol. 10, *Modern British Dramatists* (Detroit, Mich.: Gale, 1982).

8. William Archer to Shaw, 22 June 1921; BL Ms. Add. 50528.

9. William Archer to Shaw, 1 Sept. 1903; BL Ms. Add. 50528.

10. Archer's review of the published text of *Widowers' Houses* appeared in the *World* on 4 May 1893; see CL1:373.

11. Archer's reviews appeared in successive articles entitled "Mr Shaw's Plays," published in the *Daily Chronicle* (London) on 19 and 21 April 1898, copies of which are housed in Guelph.

12. CL1:373. Shaw's insulting description of Archer probably alludes to A. W. Pinero's sentimental comedy *Sweet Lavender* (1888).

13. CL1:427.

14. Reviews1:12.

15. Reviews1:19–20.

16. Reviews1:200.

17. Reviews1:277–81.

18. Reviews1:52–55.

19. CL1:241–42.

20. Bernard Shaw, "How to Become a Musical Critic," *Scottish Musical Monthly*, Dec. 1894; repr. in *New Musical Review*, Oct. 1912; SM3:339–46.

21. Quoted in Hend1:230.

22. Bernard Shaw, "The Captious Frolic," *Star*, 30 March 1889; SM1:593. Corno di Bassetto had recently (23 March 1889) referred to A. B. Walkley's dubbing him "the frolic Bassetto"; SM1:586.

23. CL1:107.

24. SM2:898.

25. SM1:7.

26. SM1:595.

27. SM2:8.

28. SM1:237.

29. This theater, named after the one with which Shakespeare was associated, opened in November 1868 in Newcastle Street, off the Strand. Considered a fire hazard, it was demolished in 1902.

30. SM1:587

31. SM3:72.

32. Shaw to Harley Granville-Barker, 30 June 1912; CL3:95.

33. W. R. Titterton, *So This Is Shaw* (London: Douglas Organ, 1945), 9–11; I&R 63–65.

34. D. J. O'Donoghue, "George Bernard Shaw: Some Recollections," *Irish Independent*, 17 Feb. 1908; I&R 47.

35. Edmund Wilson, "Shaw in the Metropolitan," *New Republic*, 26 April 1933; I&R 337–38.

36. SSS 58–60; For an account of the British Association for Advancement of Science, see A. S. and E. M. Sedgwick, *Henry Sedgwick* (London: Macmillan, 1906), 497–98; I&R 57–58.

37. A section appended to the published version of *Man and Superman* is headed: "The Revolutionist's Handbook and Pocket Companion, by John Tanner, M.I.R.C. (*Member of the Idle Rich Class*)."

38. William Morris, "A King's Lesson," in *Stories in Prose, Stories in Verse, Shorter Poems, Lectures and Essays*, ed. G. D. H. Cole (London: Nonesuch, 1974), 272.

39. Prefs1:71–72.

40. Shaw to Janet Achurch, 6 Jan. 1891; Texas.

41. Shaw to Janet Achurch, 6 Jan. 1891; Texas; D1:644.

42. D1:54, 127.

43. Lucinda Frances Shaw to Jane Crichton Drysdale, 27 Jan. 1908; Texas.

44. D1:537; SM1:778–83.

45. SSS 52–53.

46. CL1:106.

47. D1:229.

Chapter 9. On Stage

1. Shaw to Tighe Hopkins, 2 Sept. 1889; Theatrics 5.

2. Shaw's description of Clement Scott was provided to Archibald Henderson in a 1925 interview. The unpublished typescript of this interview, entitled "Dramatists Self-Revealed," is housed in the Ivo Currall Collection, Royal Academy of Dramatic Art, London. Henderson published an embroidered version entitled "George Bernard Shaw Self-Revealed" in the *Fortnightly Review*, n.s. 119 April–May 1926; I&R 313–16. Shaw kept a copy of Robert Buchanan's article ("Is Ibsen a Zola with a Wooden Leg?," *Pall Mall Gazette*, 11 June 1889), in the course of which the author wrote: "In a word, Ibsen is a very small writer, with very large pretensions, much as I have previously described him—a Zola with a wooden leg, stumping the north in the interests of quasi-scientific realism"; BL Ms. Add. 50740.

3. Shaw to R. Golding Bright, 10 June 1896; CL1:632.

4. Quintessence 8–9; D1:636.

5. Shaw to Ellen Terry, 27 Jan. 1897; CL1:723.

6. Bernard Shaw, "Ibsen Triumphant," *Saturday Review*, 22 May 1897; OTN3:138; Drama3:853.

7. Quintessence 42.

8. BL Ms. Add. 50595 A–B.

9. D1:514.

10. [Bernard Shaw], "A Play by Henrik Ibsen," unsigned review in the *Manchester Guardian*, 7 June 1889.

11. Shaw to Janet Achurch, 21 June 1889; Theatrics 3.

12. Shaw to Janet Achurch, 17 June 1889; CL1: 215–16.

13. Shaw to T. Fisher Unwin, 16 Feb. 1896; CL1:599.

14. Unpublished letter from Shaw to Janet Achurch, 8 Jan. 1895; Texas. Kensington Gore is a section of Kensington Road, flanked by the Albert Memorial and the Royal Albert Hall. Shaw's reference to the "illuminations" suggests the incident he recalled occurred during the Christmas season.

15. Unpublished letter from Shaw to Janet Achurch, 24 April 1894; Texas. The next day Shaw wrote to Janet, telling her to put the 24 April letter "in the fire"; CL1:430.

16. D1:528.

17. D1:33.

18. Archer's account of the genesis of the play is provided in Charles Archer, *William Archer: His Life, Work and Friendships* (London: Allen & Unwin, 1931),136–37.

19. Shaw recounted this scene in his essay "How William Archer Impressed Bernard Shaw," which was published as a preface to William Archer, *Three Plays by William Archer* (London: Constable; New York: Henry Holt, 1927); Prefs2:573.

20. D1:228.

21. D2:839.

22. D2:865.

23. J. T. Grein, "GBS's First Play Revived," *Illustrated London News*, 14 Aug. 1926; I&R 122–24.

24. Quoted in *Lady Gregory's Journals*, ed. Daniel J. Murphy, Coole Edition 14 (Gerrard's Cross, Eng.: Colin Smythe, 1978), 256; I&R 124.

25. *The Autobiography of G. Lowes Dickinson and Other Unpublished Writings*, ed. Dennis Proctor (London: Gerald Duckworth, 1973), 158–59; I&R 124.

26. Shaw had collected examples of "the frantic and indecent vituperation" that Ibsen and his followers provoked, which he presented in the section on *Ghosts* in *The Quintessence of Ibsenism*. See Quintessence 155–57. Ibsen's followers were attacked as "the sexless . . . the unwomanly woman, the unsexed females, the whole army of unprepossessing cranks in petticoats . . . educated and muck-ferreting dogs . . . effeminate men and male women."

27. Bernard Shaw, "The Author's Preface" to *Widowers' Houses*, appendix 1, in *The Complete Prefaces* (London: Paul Hamlyn, 1965), 705–6. The appendixes to the preface are omitted in the Laurence edition.

28. Scott's thoughts on Ibsen, the new problem plays, and morality in the theater were expressed in an article-interview by Raymond Blathwayt, "Does the Theatre Make

for Good?: A Talk with Mr. Clement Scott," published in December 1897 in a periodical entitled *Great Thoughts from Master Minds.* Shaw kept a copy of the article among his papers; BL Ms. Add. 50740.

29. D1:20.

30. SM2:64.

31. D1:668ff.

32. The euphemism was used by Shaw in a 1930 letter to Frank Harris, well known for his numerous sexual exploits. See the letter to Frank Harris dated 18 Sept 1930, reprinted in Frank Harris, *Bernard Shaw* (London: Victor Gollancz, 1931); Auto1:164.

33. Shaw, preface to *Three Plays by William Archer.* Prefs2:573–74; Auto1:261.

34. D2:716.

35. Shaw to Florence Farr, 1 May 1891; CL1:297.

36. Shaw to Florence Farr, 7 Oct. 1891; CL1:313.

37. Shaw to Florence Farr, 28 Jan. 1892; CL1:332.

38. Henderson, "Dramatists Self-Revealed"; I&R 314.

39. D2:902.

40. D2:909.

41. Shaw letter to *Star,* 18 July 1893; Agits 26.

42. Letter signed "E," *Star,* 21 July 1893; D2:960.

43. Shaw letter to *Star,* 25 July 1893; Agits 28–29.

44. The setting and Shaw's transcription of the poem are reproduced in SM1:205–7. The original manuscript is housed in the library of the University of North Carolina, Chapel Hill.

45. Mrs. Jane Patterson to Shaw, 12 and 28 May 1886; BL Ms. Add. 50545.

46. D2:914.

47. D2:918. The spelling "Rickfield Rd." in the Weintraub edition of the diaries appears to be an error.

48. Shaw to Henry Arthur Jones, 11 June 1894; CL1:444. The continuing stage-worthiness of the play was shown by an excellent and well-received production, under the direction of Jim Mezon, during the 1995 season of the Shaw Festival Theater, Niagara-on-the-Lake, Ontario, Canada. The Shaw Festival is the second largest repertory theater in North America.

49. Bernard Shaw, "Mainly About Myself," preface to the first volume of *Plays Pleasant and Unpleasant,* 1898; Prefs1:29.

50. Shaw to J. T. Grein, 12 Dec 1893; CL1:413.

51. D2:961.

52. D2:962–63.

53. D2:963.

54. Shaw to William Archer, 30 Aug. 1893; CL1:403.

55. Shaw to Janet Achurch, 4 Sept. 1893; CL1:403.

56. Shaw to Janet Achurch, 4 Sept. 1893; CL1:404.

57. Shaw included this statement in an account of the play's genesis in a letter published in the *Daily Chronicle* on 30 April 1898; cited in CL1:404.

Chapter 10. A Taste of Success

1. Quoted in R. Page Arnot, *Bernard Shaw and William Morris* (London: William Morris Society, 1957), 14–16; I&R 125–27.

2. D2:989.

3. Shaw to Harley Granville-Barker, 17 Nov. 1907; CL2:725.

4. Shaw attached particular importance to Raina's line "How did you find me out?"—telling Lillah McCarthy (Shaw to Lillah McCarthy, 30 Dec. 1907) during the Savoy Theatre production in 1907 that she was losing the effect of the line by saying it as she was sitting down: "This is quite fatal to the effect. You must sit down, look at him, and then speak." In a letter to Arnold Daly dated 14 May 1911, Shaw described the line as Bluntschli's "1st victory"; Theatrics 87, 111.

5. On 30 March Shaw wrote to Alma Murray, explaining that "the fiasco last night at the Avenue has made it necessary to produce a play of mine with all possible speed." She accepted his invitation in this letter to play the role of Raina; see CL1:422; D2:1023.

6. D2:1023.

7. Shaw to Henry Arthur Jones, 2 Dec. 1894; CL1:462.

8. See W. B. Yeats, *Autobiographies* (London: Macmillan, 1955), 281–84; I&R 127–29. The version of Shaw's response quoted earlier is that supplied by Laurence in CL1:433.

9. Yeats, *Autobiographies*, 281–84; I&R 127–29.

10. CL1:426.

11. Shaw to Henry Arthur Jones, 2 Dec. 1894; CL1:462.

12. D2:1048. The suggestion that Shaw is alluding to Brahms is made by Weintraub; see D1:5; D2:1048.

13. Shaw to Florence Farr, 12 Oct. 1896; CL1:674.

14. Shaw to Florence Farr, 13 Oct. 1896; CL1:679.

15. Shaw describes them thus in letters to others; see CL1:668.

16. Shaw to Florence Farr, 14 Oct. 1896; CL1:679.

17. Josephine Johnson, *Florence Farr: Bernard Shaw's "New Woman"* (Totowa, N.J.: Rowman and Littlefield, 1975), 66.

18. Shaw to Florence Farr, 12 Oct. 1896; CL1:675.

19. Shaw to Janet Achurch, 3 May 1895; CL1:532.

Chapter 11. Wars of the Theaters, Mothers, and Bicycles

1. Shaw's description occurs in a letter to Ellen Terry dated 1 Nov. 1895; see CL1:565.

2. Shaw to Janet Achurch, 24 Aug. 1895; CL1:547.

3. William Archer, *English Dramatists of To-day* (London: Sampson Low, Marston, Searle & Rivington, 1882), 9. Archer's description of the British public echoes Wilkie Collins's famous formula for successful fiction: "Make 'em laugh, make 'em weep, make 'em wait."

4. "The Author's Apology," preface to *Dramatic Opinions and Essays* (New York: Brentano's, 1906); Prefs1:190.

5. Bernard Shaw, preface to *Ellen Terry and Bernard Shaw: A Correspondence* (New York: Fountain Press; London: Constable, 1931); Prefs3:81.

6. Bernard Shaw to Ellen Terry, 8 Sept. 1896; CL1:653.

7. James Redfern, "The Comparable Agate," *Spectator*, 30 June 1944.

8. Bernard Shaw, "Hamlet," *Saturday Review*, 2 Oct. 1897; OTN3:202–7; Drama 3:906–10.

9. Bernard Shaw, "The Echegaray Matinées," *Saturday Review*, 27 Feb. 1897; OTN 3:58; Drama3:789.

10. Shaw used his coinage "Sardoodledom" as the title of a review that included notices of two works, *Fedora* (in Herman Merivale's English version) and *Gismonda*, by Victorien Sardou. See *Saturday Review*, 1 June 1895; OTN1:133–40; Drama2:353–59. In his review of "Madame Sans Gêne" Shaw wrote: "It is rather a nice point whether Miss Ellen Terry should be forgiven for sailing the Lyceum ship into the shallows of Sardoodledom for the sake of [Victorien Sardou's] Madame Sans Gêne" (*Saturday Review*, 17 April 1897; OTN3:105; Drama3:827).

11. Shaw to William Archer, 22 June 1923; CL3:837. The last phrase of this passage is an adaptation of Ben Jonson's famous line about Shakespeare: "He was not of an age, but for all time."

12. Shaw to William Archer, 21 Aug. 1893; CL1:402.

13. A similar final authorial dismissal of the "New Woman" occurs in Henry Arthur Jones's play *The Case of Rebellious Susan*.

14. Bernard Shaw, "Mr Pinero's New Play," *Saturday Review*, 16 March 1895; OTN 1:63; Drama1:285–86.

15. Shaw to William Archer, 3 July 1908; CL2:801.

16. CL2:799, 842–43.

17. Bernard Shaw, "Two New Plays," *Saturday Review*, 12 Jan. 1895; OTN1:9; Drama 1:240.

18. Bernard Shaw, "An Old New Play and a New Old One," *Saturday Review*, 23 Feb. 1895; OTN1:42; Drama1:268.

19. Bernard Shaw, "The Two Latest Comedies," *Saturday Review*, 18 May 1895; OTN 1:123; Drama2:345.

20. Doris Jones's account of the friendship and falling out is contained in her book *The Life and Letters of Henry Arthur Jones* (London: Victor Gollancz, 1930), 310; see also I&R 231.

21. Shaw to Ellen Terry, 28 Nov. 1895; CL1:572.

22. Shaw to Ellen Terry, 9 March 1896; CL1:609.

23. Bernard Shaw, "Why Not Sir Henry Irving?" *Saturday Review*, 9 Feb. 1895; OTN 1:30–36; Drama1:258–62. Irving was the first actor ever to receive a knighthood.

24. Shaw to Ellen Terry, 2 Oct. 1896; CL1:672.

25. Bernard Shaw, "Richard Himself Again," *Saturday Review*, 26 Dec. 1896; OTN 2:290; Drama2:733.

26. Ellen Terry, *The Story of My Life* (London: Hutchinson, 1908), 320–22; I&R 162–63.

27. Shaw reminded Ellen Terry about this incident in a letter dated 6 April 1896; see CL1:342, 623–24, 832.

28. Shaw to Ellen Terry, 16 Nov. 1896; CL1:702. In his preface to *Ellen Terry and*

Bernard Shaw: A Correspondence (1931), Shaw wrote that "her combination of beauty with sensitive intelligence was unique"; Prefs3:70.

29. Shaw provided William Archer with one of his lists of people who "served me as models" for his characters in a letter dated 21 April 1898. Social reformer Laura Ormiston Chant was also mentioned in this list as a third model for Candida; see CL2:34.

30. Shaw to Ellen Terry, 16 July 1897; CL 1: 785. Explorer Henry Morton Stanley was knighted in 1899 and died in 1904. His wife, Dorothy, edited his autobiography in 1909.

31. Shaw to Sidney Webb, 7 May 1898; CL2:41–43.

32. I am grateful to Peter Daerden of the Royal Museum for Central Africa, Tervuren, Belgium, for drawing my attention to this correspondence and to the museum for allowing me to quote from it. A few letters from Lady Stanley to Shaw are held at BL.

33. Shaw to Dorothy Tennant (Lady Stanley), 17 Nov. 1897. Royal Museum for Central Africa, Tervuren, Belgium.

34. Shaw to Dorothy Tennant (Lady Stanley), 18 May 1903. Tervuren.

35. Shaw to Bertha Newcombe, 31 March 1896; CL1:620.

36. Shaw to Ellen Terry, 11 June 1897; CL1:773.

37. Shaw to Ellen Terry, 16 Oct. 1896; CL1:681.

38. Terry, *The Story of My Life*, 320–22; I&R 162–63.

39. Shaw to Ellen Terry, 6 April 1896; CL1:622.

40. Shaw's description is contained in a letter to Janet Achurch dated 4 Sept. 1893; CL1:404.

41. Shaw to Ellen Terry, 6 Aug. 1896; CL1:641.

42. Shaw to Ellen Terry, 6 April 1896; CL1:623.

43. Quoted in James Huneker, "The Truth about *Candida*," *Metropolitan Magazine* 20 (August 1904): 635.

44. Shaw to William Archer, n.d. [assigned to 21 April 1898]; CL2:34.

45. Richard Mansfield to Shaw, April 1895. The full text of this letter is reprinted in CL1:522–24.

46. Bernard Shaw, preface to *Plays Pleasant* (1893); Prefs1:43.

47. CL1:806.

48. Shaw to Charlotte Payne Townshend, 7 Nov. 1897; CL1:821.

49. In *Sixteen Self Sketches* Shaw wrote: "When it happened that my sister was in Dublin when he [George Carr Shaw] died, which he did instantaneously in the happiest manner, they were on affectionate terms"; SSS 93–94. This is a slightly revised version of a passage in Shaw's letter to his cousin Charles MacMahon Shaw of 17 Nov. 1937; see CL4:480.

50. In his diary entry about the drinking habits of his father's family, Shaw does say that his father had eccentricities that occasionally included demonstrations of wild behavior, although never toward people: "I have seen him when drunk seize a small article on the mantelpiece and dash it upon the hearthstone, or throw a newspaper into the air; but though he was very unstable, he never used the slightest violence"; BL Ms. Add. 50710B; D1:29.

51. Shaw to Charles Charrington, 22 Aug. 1896; Theatrics 18.

52. Shaw to Florence Farr, 8 Sept. 1897; CL1:799.

53. Shaw to Ellen Terry, 8 Sept. 1897; CL1:801.

54. Shaw to William Archer, 10 July 1906; quoted in Charles Archer, *William Archer, Life, Work and Friendships* (London: Allen & Unwin, 1931), 295.

55. Bernard Shaw, "On Going to Church," *Savoy*, no. 1 (Jan. 1896); Auto1:31. See above, chap. 3.

56. See above, chap. 3.

57. This is part of a deleted passage from Shaw's preface to *Three Plays for Puritans* (1901); see Prefs1:85–86.

58. D1:334, 662.

59. Shaw, Epistle Dedicatory to *Man and Superman*; Prefs1:159.

60. D2:1009.

61. Shaw, preface to *Three Plays for Puritans*; see Prefs1:74.

62. D1:64.

63. D2:715, 929.

64. Shaw to Florence Farr, c. 13–15 July 1896; CL1:636; D2:1134.

65. Shaw to Janet Achurch, 16 Sept. 1895; CL1:558.

Chapter 12. An Irish Courtship

1. Shaw to Charlotte Payne-Townshend, 4 Nov. 1896; CL1:691–92.

2. The legal status of their nationality did not become an issue until 1935, when the Irish Free State "repudiated the British citizenship of the Irish people." On 3 July 1936 the Shaws registered as citizens of the Irish Free State under the Irish Citizenship and Nationality Act of 1935 at the High Commissioner's Office in London. See "G.B.S. Registers as an Irish Citizen," *Daily Express* (London), 22 July 1936; CL4:396, 725.

3. Shaw to Ellen Terry, 7 Dec. 1896; CL1:711.

4. Shaw to Ellen Terry, 28 May and 24 Dec. 1897; CL1:771, 831.

5. Malcolm Muggeridge, *Chronicles of Wasted Time: The Green Stick* (London: Collins, 1972), 147.

6. Entry for 16 Sept. 1896; DBW2:100.

7. Janet Dunbar, *Mrs G.B.S.: A Biographical Portrait of Charlotte Shaw* (London: George G. Harrap, 1965), 55.

8. Diary of Charlotte Shaw; BL Ms. Add. 56500.

9. Quoted in Dunbar, *Mrs G.B.S.*, 90.

10. Ibid., 91.

11. Apparently due to a misreading of the manuscript, Dunbar says that Charlotte was the guest of a "Mrs Gates" at this luncheon party. The manuscript reads: "Dined at Grand Hotel with Mr & Mrs Edmund Yates and met Dr Munthe"; BL Ms. Add. 56500; Dunbar, *Mrs G.B.S.*, 93, 96. I am assuming that because of his not very common name, the well-known London editor of the *World* and novelist is likely to have been the same Mr Yates to whom Charlotte refers. He died on 14 May 1894.

12. Dunbar, *Mrs G.B.S.*, 104.

13. Shaw to Ellen Terry, 5 Nov. 1896; CL1:696.

14. D2:1074.

15. Diary of Charlotte Shaw; BL Ms. Add. 56500.

16. D1:1; D2:1124.

17. BL Ms. Add. 56500.

18. Ibid.

19. D2:1119, 1124.

20. D2:1124.

21. DBW2:101.

22. An account of Shaw's work as Vestryman and Councillor is provided in the article by A. G. Edwards entitled "GBS Brought Wit, Vigour, and Good By-Laws to St Pancras," *Local Government Service*, May 1947; I&R 68–70.

23. Shaw to Janet Achurch, 24 Aug. 1895; CL1: 547.

24. Bertha Newcombe, note written for Ashley Dukes, 1928; CL1: 546.

25. Shaw to Bertha Newcombe, 31 March 1896; CL1:620.

26. DBW2:110–11.

27. DBW2:116.

28. As photographs of her taken during this period show. Shaw remarked on Beatrice's attractiveness in his foreword to her book *My Apprenticeship* (Harmondsworth, Eng.: Penguin Books, 1938); Prefs3:350.

29. DBW2:114.

30. Shaw to Ellen Terry, 28 May 1897; CL1:771.

31. DBW2:115.

32. Shaw to Charlotte Payne-Townshend, [c. late 1896 or early 1897]; CL1:657.

33. Shaw to Charlotte Payne-Townshend, 27 Oct. 1896; CL1:686.

34. Shaw to Ellen Terry, 5 Nov. 1896; CL1: 696. Shaw addresses her as "heartwise Ellen" in a letter dated 16 Nov. 1896; CL1:702.

35. Ellen Terry to Shaw, 6 Nov. 1896; cited in CL1:696.

36. Shaw to Charlotte Payne-Townshend, 7 Nov. 1896; CL1:697.

37. Shaw to Charlotte Payne-Townshend, 9 Nov. 1896; CL1:699.

38. DBW2:115–16.

39. Shaw to Ellen Terry, 5 Aug. 1897; CL1:792.

40. Shaw to Charlotte Payne-Townshend, 13 July 1897; CL1:783–4.

41. Shaw to Charlotte Payne-Townshend, 6 Dec. 1897; CL1:826.

42. Shaw to Sidney Webb, 7 May 1898; CL2:40.

43. Shaw to Charlotte Payne-Townshend, 12 March 1898; CL2:14.

44. Shaw to Charlotte Payne-Townshend, 5 April 1898; Shaw to Sidney Webb, 11 April 1898; CL2:27, 29.

45. Shaw to Charlotte Payne-Townshend, 30 March 1898; CL2:24.

46. Shaw to Charlotte Payne-Townshend, 31 March 1898; CL2:25.

47. Shaw to Charlotte Payne-Townshend, 19 and 31 March 1898; CL2:21, 25.

48. Shaw to Charlotte Payne-Townshend, 22 March 1898; CL2:21.

49. Shaw to Charlotte Payne-Townshend, 8 and 14 April 1898; CL2:28, 32.

50. Shaw to Charlotte Payne-Townshend, 7 April 1898; CL2:27–28.

51. Shaw to Charlotte Payne-Townshend, 19 and 21 April 1898; CL2:32–33.

52. Shaw to Charlotte Payne-Townshend, 21 April 1898; CL2:33.

53. Shaw to Charlotte Payne-Townshend, 15 March 1898; CL2:16.

54. Charlotte Payne-Townshend to Shaw, 2 May 1898; BL; cited in CL2:38.

55. Shaw to Janet Achurch, 11 May 1898; CL2:42.

56. Bernard Shaw, "Valedictory," *Saturday Review*, 21 May 1898; OTN3:386.

57. Bernard Shaw, preface to *Three Plays for Puritans* (1901); Prefs1:59.

Chapter 13. Marriage

1. Shaw to Henry Arthur Jones, 20 May 1898; CL2:44.

2. Shaw to Grant Richards, 23 May 1898; CL2:44n.

3. Shaw to Graham Wallas, 26 May 1898; CL2:46.

4. W.A.S. Hewins to Sidney Webb, 30 May 1898; BLPES; I&R 171–72.

5. Archibald Henderson, *George Bernard Shaw: Man of the Century* (London: Appleton-Century-Crofts, 1956); cited in CL2:46.

6. CL2:46–47

7. On 13 April 1898 Shaw wrote to Sidney Webb: "You will be relieved to hear that I have made investments. Wilson's firm got me £1000 New Zealand stock for which I paid them £1174." An unpublished letter (now in a private collection) from Shaw to Ida Beatty dated 14 Aug 1907 shows that he had by then gained a good knowledge of the stock market and of the interest rates paid by various companies.

8. CL2:53, 117.

9. Shaw to Lena Ashwell, 1 June 1898; Texas.

10. Mary's remark is quoted by Shaw in a letter to Beatrice Webb dated 21 June 1898; CL2:51.

11. Quoted in Maurice Collis, *Somerville and Ross: A Biography* (London: Faber & Faber, 1968), 127; I&R 171.

12. Lucinda Carr Shaw to Jane Crichton Drysdale, 24 July [1901]; Texas. St. John Ervine cites another letter by Lucy indicating her dislike of Charlotte; see *Bernard Shaw: His Life, Work and Friends* (London: Constable, 1956), 319.

13. Ervine, *Bernard Shaw*, 321.

14. Hesketh Pearson, *Bernard Shaw: His Life and Personality* (London: Collins, 1950), 209.

15. Michael Holroyd, *Bernard Shaw, volume 1, 1856–1898: The Search for Love* (London: Chatto & Windus, 1988), 458.

16. Shaw to Ellen Terry, 5 March 1897; CL1:731.

17. Shaw to Ellen Terry, 31 Dec. 1897; CL1:840.

18. Farmer 96.

19. Undated letter from Lucy Shaw to Constance Shaw; Ervine, *Bernard Shaw*, 319; Farmer 126.

20. Shaw told Archibald Henderson that his mother was still working at the "famous modern school" in a letter dated 3 Jan. 1905, when Bessie was seventy-four; CL2:501.

21. DBW2:154, 166.

22. Shaw to Sidney Webb, 18 Oct. 1898; CL2:67.

23. Ibid.

24. Shaw to Frank Harris, 24 June 1930; CL4:192–93. Shaw had made earlier revi-

sions to this letter for inclusion in Harris's posthumously published *Bernard Shaw: An Unauthorised Biography* (1931).

25. SSS 115.

26. CL4:193; SSS 115.

27. Bernard Shaw, *The Perfect Wagnerite: A Commentary on The Ring of the Niblungs* (London: Grant Richards, 1898); Prefs3:512.

28. Prefs3:441–42, 495.

29. Prefs3:434.

30. This is how he described her, without mentioning her name, in the 1930 letter to Frank Harris.

31. W. B. Yeats to Florence Farr, 7 Oct. 1907. See *The Letters of W. B. Yeats*, ed. Allan Wade (London: Macmillan, 1954), 500.

32. Shaw to Mrs. Patrick Campbell, 12 April 1899; CL2:84.

33. Charlotte Shaw to Beatrice Webb, 6 Nov. 1898; Dunbar 181.

34. Shaw to Pakenham Thomas Beatty, 12 Nov. 1898 (private collection).

35. W.A.S. Hewins to Sidney Webb, 22 Sept. 1898; BLPES.

36. Shaw to Arthur Conan Doyle, 24 Jan. 1899; CL2:73.

37. Richard Le Gallienne, *The Romantic '90s* (London: Putnam's Sons, 1926), 143–46; I&R:280–81.

38. Robert Bontine Cunninghame Graham, *Mogreb-El-Aska: A Journey in Morocco.*

39. Shaw to Graham Wallas, 24 Aug. 1899; CL2:100.

40. Shaw to Graham Wallas, 9 Sept. 1899; BLPES.

41. Farmer 122.

42. Farmer 114.

43. Dunbar 186; CL2:103.

44. Shaw to Beatrice Webb, 29 Sept. 1899; CL2:106.

45. Shaw to Edward Rose, 25 Sept. 1899; Shaw to Sydney C. Cockerell, 17 Oct 1899; CL2:103, 111.

46. Shaw to Edith Benigna Isobel Beatty, 30 June 1898 (private collection).

Chapter 14. New Century, "New Religion"

1. Edward McNulty, "George Bernard Shaw as a Boy," *Candid Friend*, 6 July 1901; I&R 21.

2. Shaw to Frederick H. Evans, 27 Aug. 1895; CL1: 551. Another project announced by Shaw in this letter, though never fulfilled, was for "an erotic book, which would pass for a sort of novel" in the manner of Laurence Sterne's *Sentimental Journey*.

3. DBW2:267.

4. Bernard Shaw, preface to *Back to Methuselah;* Prefs2:429.

5. For a summary discussion of Shaw's ideas, see my essay "Shaw and Creative Evolution," in *Irish Writers and Religion*, ed. Robert Welch (Savage, Md.: Barnes & Noble, 1992), 75–88.

6. Bernard Shaw, preface to *Androcles and the Lion*, alluding to Luke 17:21; Prefs 2:209.

7. Shaw "Epistle Dedicatory to Arthur Bingham Walkley" (*Man and Superman*), 1903; Prefs1:155.

8. Quotations from "The Revolutionist's Handbook" are taken from *Man and Superman: A Comedy and a Philosophy*, ed. Dan H. Laurence (Harmondsworth, Eng.: Penguin Books, 1946).

9. Epistle Dedicatory to *Man and Superman*; Prefs1:154. Edmund Burke's phrase "the hoofs of the swinish multitude," partially quoted by Shaw here, is from *Reflections on the Revolution in France* (1790).

10. Bernard Shaw, "Darwin Denounced," *Pall Mall Gazette*, 31 May 1887; Reviews 1:277–81.

11. The relationship between Shavian and Bergsonian ideas of creative evolution is explored by Michel W. Pharand in his study *Bernard Shaw and the French* (Gainesville: University Press of Florida, 2000), 243–52.

12. Bertrand Russell, *Portraits from Memory and Other Essays* (London: George Allen & Unwin, 1956), 73–74; I&R 278–79.

13. The sentence quoted is from the second paragraph of "The Revolutionist's Handbook." The OED cites Shaw's use of the term *Superman* in the play as the first appearance in English.

14. Thomas Carlyle, *Sartor Resartus* (London: Oxford University Press, 1902), 165.

15. Bernard Shaw, preface to *Back to Methuselah*; Prefs2:425.

16. Ibid., 405.

17. Shaw reports that Butler made the comment about Darwin having "banished mind from the universe" in the courtyard of the British Museum (*Observer*, 26 March 1950). Dan H. Laurence assumes that "the aphorism is a variation and Shavian improvement on a less memorable phrasing in Butler's *Luck, or Cunning?*" However, the Butler phrasing is not, in my view, the passage quoted by Laurence. The more likely printed source of the saying is a passage in *Luck, or Cunning . . . ?* in which Butler asserts that Darwin's theories involved "the pitchforking . . . of mind out of the universe." See Prefs2:300; Samuel Butler, *Luck, or Cunning, as the Main Means of Organic Modification?* (London: A. C. Fifield, 1920), 18.

18. Samuel Butler, *Evolution, Old & New; or the Theories of Buffon, Dr. Erasmus Darwin, and Lamarck, as Compared with that of Charles Darwin*, 3rd ed. (London: Jonathan Cape, 1921), 53.

19. Prefs2:399.

20. Theodosius Dobzhansky et al., *Evolution* (San Francisco: W. H. Freeman, 1977), 8.

21. Bernard Shaw, "Civilisation and the Soldier," *Humane Review* 1 (Jan. 1901): 298–315; repr. (with several errors) in *SHAW: The Annual of Bernard Shaw Studies* 9 (1989): 99–112. In the following discussion I am indebted to Leon Hugo's analysis of the essay and its historical context in his *Edwardian Shaw: The Writer and His Age* (London: Macmillan, 1999), 16–19. Quotations are taken from the *Humane Review* version of the text.

22. Cited in Hugo, *Edwardian Shaw*, 14.

23. Patricia Pugh, "Bernard Shaw, Imperialist," *SHAW: The Annual of Bernard Shaw Studies* 11 (1991): 98.

24. Ibid., 99.

25. Shaw to George Samuel, undated letter [c. 26–30 Dec. 1899]; CL2:124.

26. Shaw to Mary Cholmondeley, 30 Dec. 1899; CL2:127–28.

27. Shaw to Lady Stanley, 13 May 1904. Stanley Archive, Royal Museum for Central Africa, Tervuren, Belgium.

28. Shaw recorded the churchyard inscription on a postcard, a facsimile of which is printed in F. E. Loewenstein, *Bernard Shaw Through the Camera* (London: B & H White Publications, 1948), 36.

29. Francis Hopkins, "'Squire' Shaw: Being an Unconventional Interview with one of the Most Written-about Persons in the Public Eye," *Lady's Realm* (Oct. 1909); I&R 433.

30. A letter to Shaw from the firm Day & Son dated 17 June 1920 acknowledges receipt of £630 as a deposit on the property; a further letter dated 15 Oct. 1920 acknowledges receipt of the balance of £5696.10s. See Shaw Business Papers, sec. 22/1, BLPES.

31. Bernard Shaw, "Granville-Barker: Some Particulars by Shaw," *Drama*, n.s., no. 3 (Winter 1946). Cited in Hugo, *Edwardian Shaw*, 101.

Chapter 15. Eternal Irishman

1. "Shaw Speaks to His Native City," New York *Journal-American*, 17 and 18 March 1946; *Leader Magazine* (London), 23 March 1946; repr. in Matter 292–93.

2. See, e.g., Henry Summerfield, "AE as a Literary Critic," in *Myth and Reality in Irish Literature*, ed. Joseph Ronsley (Ontario, Can.: Wilfrid Laurier University Press, 1977), 58. See also Daniel Corkery's remark concerning expatriate Irish writers in *Synge and Anglo-Irish Literature* (Cork, Ire.: Cork University Press, 1931): "Some of them, of course, have cut away their own land as summarily as Henry James did his. Shaw, Ervine, Munro, others, are of the class" (5).

3. Bernard Shaw, "The Eve of Civil War," *Irish Times* (Dublin), 21 Aug. 1922; repr. in Matter 257; Prefs1:217.

4. "Socialism and Ireland," lecture delivered to the Fabian Society, 28 Nov. 1919; repr. in Matter 15.

5. "Ireland Eternal and External," *New Statesman*, 30 Oct. 1948; *Atlantic Monthly*, Feb. 1949; Matter 294–97.

6. Shaw to Lord Alfred Douglas, 27 Dec. 1941; CL4:622.

7. SSS 68.

8. Nicholas Grene, "The Maturing of *Immaturity*: Shaw's First Novel," *Irish University Review* 20, no. 2 (Autumn 1990): 233.

9. Shaw to Bertha Newcombe, 14 May 1909; CL 2:843.

10. Shaw to Mabel W. Fitzgerald, 1 Dec. 1914; CL3:271. Shaw was replying to a letter from her (now in the Fitzgerald papers at University College, Dublin) urging him to use his "very forcible voice" in nationalistic causes in Ireland. His letter to the Irish press was published in the *Freeman's Journal*, Dublin, on 30 Nov. 1914 under the title "Ireland and the War—the erratic View of Mr. Bernard Shaw."

11. Shaw to Frederick Jackson, 18 Sept. 1910; CL2:942.

12. Shaw to W. B. Yeats, 23 June 1903; Cornell.

13. CL2:423.

14. *The Letters of W. B Yeats*, ed. Allan Wade (London: Rupert Hart-Davis, 1954), 335; repr. in L&G x.

15. See Hesketh Pearson, *Bernard Shaw: His Life and Personality* (London: Collins, 1950),17, 237; see also Theatrics 62 and CL2:519, 522.

16. Bernard Shaw, *Preface for Politicians* (preface to *John Bull's Other Island*), 1907; Prefs1:193.

17. Shaw to J. L. Shine, 29 Oct. 1904; CL2:460.

18. W. G. Fay to W. B. Yeats, 4 Oct. 1904; BL Ms. Add. 50553.

19. J. M. Synge's comment was reported to Shaw by W. B. Yeats in a letter dated 5 Oct. 1901; see note 20.

20. W. B. Yeats to Shaw, 5 Oct. 1901; BL Ms. Add. 50553.

21. W. B. Yeats to Lady Gregory, 7 Nov. 1904, in *Letters of W. B. Yeats*, 442.

22. For a detailed discussion of this, see A. M. Gibbs, "Yeats, Shaw and Unity of Culture," *Southern Review* (Australia) 6, no. 3 (Sept 1973): 189–203.

23. Prefs1:568.

24. Matthew Arnold, *"On the Study of Celtic Literature" and Other Essays* (London: J. M. Dent, [1910]), 91.

25. Declan Kiberd, *Inventing Ireland: The Literature of the Modern Nation* (London: Vintage, 1996), 30. Having skillfully defined these dichotomies, later in his study Kiberd makes the disappointing generalization (which he attributes to unspecified, frustrated post-1900 audiences) that Shaw's plays—including *John Bull's Other Island*—do not provide "a workable prescription" to match their "devastating diagnoses." Although this seems an odd demand to make of a playwright—it is unusual to hear complaints about Shakespeare's failure to provide "a workable prescription" for questions such as those raised in *Hamlet*—it provides a refreshing change from the equally questionable charge that Shaw's plays are too didactic.

26. Prefs1:198.

27. Oscar Wilde to Shaw, 23 Feb. 1893, in *Selected Letters of Oscar Wilde*, ed. Rupert Hart-Davis (Oxford: Oxford University Press, 1962), 109.

28. Ibid., 112. I am indebted to Stanley Weintraub's essay on the Shaw-Wilde relationship entitled "'The Hibernian School': Oscar Wilde and Bernard Shaw," *SHAW: The Annual of Bernard Shaw Studies* 13 (1993): 25–49.

29. Shaw to Oscar Wilde, 28 Feb. 1893; Theatrics 8.

30. Theatrics 9.

31. Bernard Shaw, "Down with the Censorship!," *Saturday Review* 79, no. 2 (March 1892); D2:1067.

32. See Richard Ellmann, *Oscar Wilde* (London: Hamish Hamilton, 1987), 351–52.

33. Shaw to Frank Harris, 7 Oct. 1908; CL2:813.

34. Ellmann, *Oscar Wilde*, 121.

35. This is the wording used by Shaw in a 1911 letter to Archibald Henderson, in which he castigated his biographer for misquoting Wilde's "really witty sally" (Shaw's phrase) and perverting it into "what will be taken for an envious slander" (Shaw to Archibald Henderson, 22 Feb. 1911; CL3:8). A slightly different wording is recalled by Shaw in a letter to Ellen Terry dated 25 Sept. 1896: "Oscar Wilde said of me 'An excellent

man: he has no enemies; and none of his friends like him.' And that's quite true: they don't like me; but they are my friends, and some of them love me": CL1:668.

36. Weintraub, "The Hibernian School," 29.

37. D2:1060; Weintraub, "The Hibernian School," 40–42.

38. Weintraub, "The Hibernian School," 42.

39. W. B. Yeats, *Autobiographies* (London: Macmillan, 1955), 283–84.

40. The term *Cuchulanoid* (deriving, of course, from Cuchulain, the great hero of Irish saga who reappears as a character in the plays of Yeats) was apparently coined by Stephen McKenna. In a letter to McKenna, J. M. Synge wrote: "I do not believe in the possibility of a 'purely fantastic, unmodern, ideal, spring-dayish, Cuchulanoid National Theatre,' because no drama can grow out of anything but the fundamental realities of life which are neither modern or unmodern." Quoted in *The Collected Letters of John Millington Synge*, 2 vols., ed. Ann Saddlemyer (Oxford: Oxford University Press, 1983–84), 1:74.

41. W. B. Yeats, untitled early draft of a play. National Library of Ireland, Ms. 30,060.

42. Shaw introduces some ambiguity about Joan's status. Although she is called "shepherd girl" (sc. 4) and "shepherd's lass" (sc. 6) by the church authorities, Joan rejects the description during the trial scene, saying she has only "helped with the sheep like anyone else" in the village. In the first scene Robert de Baudricourt informs Poulengey that "she's not a farm wench. She's a bourgeoise."

43. W. B. Yeats, note to Lady Gregory; L&G 171–72.

44. Shaw to Lady Gregory, 28 Aug. 1925; Cornell; L&G 177.

45. W. B. Yeats to Shaw, 19 Oct. 1901; BL Ms. Add. 50553.

46. L&G 37.

47. L&G xv. I am indebted in the present discussion of the *Blanco Posnet* affair, and for information about other matters relating to Shaw's connections with Lady Gregory and the Abbey, to the edition of the relevant materials by Laurence and Grene.

48. See Joseph Holloway, "Impressions of a Dublin Playgoer" (Holograph Journal National Liberty Ireland); L&G 48.

49. L&G 48–49.

50. Shaw to Stephen Gwynn, 28 Aug. 1940; CL4:576.

51. CL4:577.

52. CL4:308.

53. Quoted in *Lady Gregory's Journals, 1916–1930*, ed. Lennox Robinson (London: Putnam, 1946), 200.

54. Ibid., 66–67, 202, 204, 215.

55. L&G xxv.

56. Lady Gregory, note to *The Jester*, in *The Collected Plays of Lady Gregory*, 4 vols., ed. Ann Saddlemyer (Gerrards Cross, Eng.: Colin Smythe, 1970), 3:379.

57. Shaw to Lady Gregory, 3 Dec. 1917; Cornell; L&G 136.

58. Lady Gregory to Shaw, 8 Feb. 1918; BL; L&G 138.

59. Bernard Shaw, "A Crib for Home Rulers," *Pall Mall Gazette*, 25 Sept. 1888; Matter 21. Shaw's attitudes toward Irish politics are discussed further in my essay "Bernard Shaw's Other Island," in *Irish Culture and Nationalism, 1750–1950*, ed. Oliver MacDonagh, W. F. Mandle, and Pauric Travers (London: Macmillan, 1983), 122–36.

60. Prefs1:219; Matter 23.

61. Prefs1:218.

62. "Shaw Speaks to His Native City" (1946); Matter 294.

Chapter 16. Edwardian Summers

1. The Education Acts of 1902 and 1903 introduced by the Balfour Conservative government abolished school boards and made education the responsibility of local boroughs or county councils. The effect of these acts was to bring all schools, regardless of their religious affiliation, into a system of state funding, a move offensive to nonconformists. The drafting of the acts was greatly influenced by Sidney Webb's Fabian Tract No. 106, entitled *The Educational Muddle and the Way Out*. See Leon Hugo, *Edwardian Shaw: The Writer and His Age* (London: Macmillan, 1999), 46–47.

2. "Too Many Electors Sit at Home—Reading My Books," *St. James's Gazette*, 5 March 1904; I&R 71.

3. DBW2:318.

4. Hugo, *Edwardian Shaw*, 57.

5. E. M. Forster, *Howards End* (Harmondsworth, Eng.: Penguin Books, 1995), 8.

6. Cited in L&G 43.

7. T. S. Eliot, "London Letter," *Dial* (Oct. 1921): 253–54; cited in Stanley Weintraub's *Bernard Shaw, 1914–1918: Journey to Heartbreak* (London: Routledge & Kegan Paul, 1973), 326.

8. SSS 127.

9. This apt term is used to describe the whole tone of *Howards End* in Nicola Beauman's *Morgan: A Biography of E. M. Forster* (London: Hodder & Stoughton, 1993), 5.

10. Chron 171; I&R 210.

11. CL2:xii.

12. See H. C. Biard, *Wings* (London: Hurst & Blackett, [1934]), 56–57; I&R 211.

13. See C. D. Baker, *From Chauffeur to Brigadier* (London: Ernest Benn, 1930), 209; I&R 247–48.

14. Mark Twain (Samuel Clemens) and Max Beerbohm lunched with the Shaws on 3 July 1907; see CL2:696 and I&R 276, n2. Winston Churchill, his mother, Harley Granville-Barker, and Lillah McCarthy lunched with them on Friday, 26 January 1912; see CL3:73.

15. "Celebrities at Home, no. MCLIII: Mr. George Bernard Shaw in Adelphi Terrace, Strand," *World*, no. 1359 (18 July 1900); I&R 428–30.

16. CL2:277–78; Weiss 3; Siegfried Trebitsch, *Chronicle of a Life*, trans. Eithne Wilkins and Ernst Kaiser (London: Heinemann, 1953), 122–24; I&R 173–74.

17. Bernard Shaw, "A New Lady Macbeth and a New Mrs Ebbsmith," *Saturday Review*, 25 May 1895; OTN1:132–33.

18. The description of Lillah arriving at Adelphi Terrace was supplied by Shaw in "An Aside," a preface he wrote for Lillah's book *Myself and My Friends* (London: Thornton Butterworth, 1933; Prefs3:145). For Lillah's account of the meeting, see *Myself and My Friends* 55–56; I&R 139.

19. "An Aside," Prefs3:143.

20. Ibid., 148.

21. Ibid., 146.

22. McCarthy, *Myself and My Friends,* 87–88; I&R 213–14.

23. Ibid., 88; I&R 198.

24. Ibid., 84–85; I&R 141. Shaw interested himself in the headdress. The painter Neville Lytton modeled it after a style worn by his wife, Judith. It made its first appearance onstage at the Court Theatre on 20 November 1906.

25. Shaw to Charles Charrington, 27 June 1901; CL2:227.

26. This information was supplied by Judy Musters (née Gillmore) to Dan H. Laurence, Guelph.

27. Shaw to Charlotte F. Shaw, 30 April and 2 May 1912; CL3:87–90. The Westminster Hippodrome, originally built as a permanent venue for circuses, had a vast water tank for stunts such as the one Shaw is recalling.

28. See CL3:352.

29. Shaw to William Archer, 14 Dec. 1924; CL3:894.

30. See CL3:278.

31. Shaw to H. G. Wells, 14 Aug. 1907; CL2:709–10.

32. McCarthy, *Myself and My Friends,* 86; I&R 432.

33. See S. G. Hobson, *Pilgrim to the Left: Memoirs of a Modern Revolutionist* (London: Edward Arnold, 1938), 106–7; I&R 74–75; CL2:596; Edward R. Pease, *The History of the Fabian Society* (London: Frank Cass, 1963), 165–67; J. Percy Smith, ed., *Bernard Shaw and H. G. Wells* [correspondence] (Toronto: University of Toronto Press, 1995), 44–45.

34. *The Future in America* (London: Chapman & Hall, 1906) was the Wells book; *The Doctor's Dilemma,* first presented at the Court Theatre on 20 November 1906, was the Shaw play.

35. Hobson, *Pilgrim to the Left,* 106–7; I&R 74–75.

36. H. G. Wells, *Experiment in Autobiography: Discoveries and Conclusions of a Very Ordinary Brain (since 1866),* 2 vols. (London: Victor Gollancz/Cresset Press, 1934), 2:660–61; I&R 74.

37. Shaw to Beatrice Webb, 30 Sept. 1909; see also Laurence headnote to this letter in CL2:868–71.

38. H. G. Wells to Bernard Shaw, n.d. [Summer or Autumn 1907?], reprinted in *Bernard Shaw and H. G. Wells,* 52–53. A portion of the Shaw-Wells correspondence concerning the Bland and Reeves affairs is missing.

39. Shaw to Beatrice Webb, 30 Sept. 1909; CL2:869.

40. H. G. Wells to Bernard Shaw, 24 Aug. 1909 [dated by Shaw]. *Bernard Shaw and H. G. Wells,* 73–74.

41. Forster, *Howards End,* 407–8.

42. Shaw to Louis Calvert, 23 July 1905; CL2:542.

43. Alfred Sutro, *Celebrities and Simple Souls* (London: Duckworth, 1933), 117–18; I&R 148.

44. DBW2:354–55.

45. Shaw to Louis Calvert, 29 Nov. 1905; CL2:584.

46. Shaw to Louis Calvert, 23 July 1905; CL2:543.

47. When *The Bacchae* was presented at the Court Theatre in November 1908, the role of Dionysus was played by Lillah McCarthy, Shaw's leading lady. A reviewer of the

production wrote in *The Times* on 11 November 1908: "It can be imagined how compelling a figure Miss Lillah McCarthy looks with the ivy and the grapes in her hair, and a flame-coloured tunic under her tiger skin—a strange, Eastern god, full of grace and beauty, and of a subtle, perfume-like charm." (Cited in John Culme, "Footlight Notes" for Sat. 21 Sept. 2002 with postcard showing Lillah McCarthy as Dionysus: http://www.gabrielray.150m.com/ArchiveTextM/LillahMcCarthy.html, accessed 2005).

48. DBW3:12–13.

49. DBW3:14; I&R 149.

50. These comments accompanied the suggested passages of dialogue Murray sent to Shaw in October 1905. The document containing the passages and comments is housed at Texas.

51. Charlotte F. Shaw to Mary Cholmondeley, 16 Feb. 1916. I&R 247.

52. Michael Dunhill, *The Plato of Praed Street: The Life and Times of Almroth Wright* (London: Royal Society of Medicine Press, 2000).

53. I&R 247.

54. See chapter 17 for an account of this.

55. Shaw obituary of Ibsen, *Clarion*, 1 June 1906; repr. in Quintessence 239–45.

56. *Tribune* (London), 14 July 1906; repr. in Hugo, *Edwardian Shaw*, 159.

57. *Tribune* (London), 3 Sept. 1906; repr. in Hugo, *Edwardian Shaw*, 159.

58. For an exposition of this idea of comedy see Ian Donaldson, *The World Upside Down: Comedy from Jonson to Fielding* (Oxford: Clarendon Press, 1970).

59. "Mr Bernard Shaw at Brighton." A partial verbatim report of the lecture "Art and Public Money" delivered at Municipal Technical College and School of Art, Brighton, in early March 1907. *Sussex Daily News* (Brighton), 7 March 1907; a fuller report appeared in the *Brighton Herald*, 9 March 1907; see Lbib2:629.

60. Shelley, "Episychidion," l.159. E. M. Forster derived the title of his novel *The Longest Journey* from this passage.

61. Shaw's own feelings about this are perhaps suggested in a letter to Janet Achurch, dated 8 May 1903, in which he explains Charlotte's unease in the company of friends who belonged to his bachelor days; see CL2:323.

62. Shaw to Erica Cotterill 13 Oct. 1909; CL2:871.

63. Shaw to Erica Cotterill, 30 Oct. 1910; CL2:951.

64. Shaw to Erica Cotterill, 24 Oct. 1906; CL2:659.

65. An allusion to *The Master Builder* in a letter dated 11 July 1907 from Shaw to Erica Cotterill indicates that she knew the play; it is therefore reasonable to assume that she would have been aware of this parallel; see CL2:699–700.

66. Shaw to Erica Cotterill, 11 July 1907; CL2:700.

67. Shaw to Erica Cotterill, 27 April 1908; CL2:774–75.

68. Shaw to John Wardrop, 3 Sept. 1942; CL4:637.

69. Shaw to Erica Cotterill, 22 June 1909; CL2:847.

70. Shaw to Erica Cotterill, 27 Nov. 1907; CL2:732.

71. Ibid.

72. Shaw to John Wardrop, 3 Sept. 1942; CL4:638.

73. Shaw to Erica Cotterill, 17 Nov. 1907; CL2:726.

74. Shaw to Erica Cotterill, 22 June 1909; CL2:847.

75. Letter drafted by Shaw and sent to Erica Cotterill by Charlotte F. Shaw, n.d., assigned to 11 Oct. 1910; CL2:943–45.

Chapter 17. Votes for Women

1. Quoted in *How the Vote Was Won and Other Suffragette Plays*, ed. Dale Spender and Carole Hayman (London: Methuen, 1985), 57. *Votes for Women!* was first published by Mills & Boon, London, in 1909. Granville-Barker changed the original title of the play, *The Friend of Women*, to the one it now bears. For an account of the Court production, see Samantha Ellis, "*Votes for Women!*, Royal Court, April 1907," *Guardian* (London), 19 March 2003; see also the website http://www.guardian.co.uk/arts/curtainup/story/0,12830,921772,00.html (accessed July 2005).

2. Shaw to Archibald Henderson, 3 Jan. 1905; CL2:506.

3. Shaw has provided a vivid description of this meeting in a letter to Archibald Henderson dated 3 January 1905; CL2:493.

4. Maud Churton Braby, "GBS and a Suffragist," *Tribune* (London), 12 March 1906; I&R 405.

5. Shaw must certainly have had in mind as an example his friend Beatrice Webb, who was playing a leading part in the work of the Royal Commission on Poor Law, to which she had been appointed by Balfour in 1905.

6. Bernard Shaw, "Why All Women Are Peculiarly fitted to Be Good Voters," *New York American*, 21 April 1907; repr. in *Fabian Feminist: Bernard Shaw and Woman*, ed. Rodelle Weintraub (University Park: Penn State University Press, 1977), 248–54.

7. Ibid., 249.

8. Lisa Tickner, *The Spectacle of Women: Imagery of the Suffrage Campaign, 1907–14* (London: Chatto & Windus, 1987), 86.

9. *Morning Leader* (London), 15 June 1908; cited in *The Spectacle of Women*, 86. Impressive as the 1908 demonstration was, it did not sway the politicians in Westminster. In not granting the suffrage to women until 1918—and then only to women aged thirty or over—England was extraordinarily backward in comparison with other English-speaking nations, especially in the Antipodes. Equal voting rights were granted to women in New Zealand in 1893, and (with some restrictions) women had gained the vote in Australia in 1901.

10. For a detailed discussion and an illustration of Miss Annan Bryce impersonating Joan of Arc on horseback in a 1911 procession, see *The Spectacle of Women*, 209–11.

11. His intention to "do a Joan play some day" was indicated in a letter written from Orléans to Mrs. Patrick Campbell on 8 Sept 1913; CL3:201; see below, chap. 21.

12. "Crites" [T. S. Eliot], "Commentary," *Criterion* (London) 3 Oct. 1924, 4.

13. Shaw's essay was first published as "Sir Almroth Wright's Polemics" in the *New Statesman* (London), 18 Oct 1913; it was subsequently reprinted as "Sir Almroth Wright's Case against Woman Suffrage" in the form of a penny pamphlet issued by the Irishwomen's Suffrage Federation and is reprinted under that title in *Fabian Feminist*, 243–47. Shaw's references are to Isabella's speech in *Measure for Measure* (2.2.110–23).

14. Sir Almroth Wright to Shaw, 15 Nov. 1942; Ms. 9888/2/33. Trinity College, Dublin.

15. "As Bernard Shaw Sees Woman," *New York Times Magazine*, 19 June 1927; repr.

in *Platform and Pulpit: Bernard Shaw*, ed. Dan H. Laurence (New York: Hill and Wang, 1961), 173–78.

16. Maud Churton Braby, "Dress and the Writer: A Talk with Mr George Bernard Shaw," *The World of Dress*, March 1905; I&R 404.

17. In *The Quintessence of Ibsenism*, in the course of drawing an extended analogy between the captive spirit of the womanly woman and various types of caged parrots, Shaw writes: "The only parrot a free-souled person can sympathize with is the one that insists on being let out as the first condition of making itself agreeable"; Quintessence 130.

18. SSS 6.

19. Shaw to Beatrice Webb, 29 Sept. 1899; CL2:106.

20. Referring to Mrs. Campbell's portrayal of Ophelia in a production of *Hamlet* in 1897, Shaw called her "that rapscallionly flower girl." Shaw to Ellen Terry, 8 Sept. 1897; CL1:803.

21. Shaw's departures from the "man in petticoats" idea are discussed by several writers in the *Fabian Feminist* collection of essays. See especially Rhoda B. Nathan, "The Shavian Sphinx" (30–45), and Elsie Adams, "Feminism and Female Stereotypes in Shaw" (156–62).

22. This is the title her subjects use for the sorceress-ruler Ayesha in Rider Haggard's *She*, comically employed by John Mortimer for Rumpole's mutterings about his wife, Hilda, in the BBC television series "Rumpole of the Bailey."

23. Nina Auerbach, *Woman and the Demon: The Life of a Victorian Myth* (Cambridge, Mass.: Harvard University Press, 1982), 107.

24. In his headnote to a Shaw letter addressed to Archibald Henderson and dated 5 September 1905, Dan H. Laurence records that Shaw had by then read Strindberg's "*The Diary of a Madman* and *The Father*, the latter in Nellie Erichsen's translation"; CL2:553.

25. Shaw, preface to the 1913 edition of *The Quintessence of Ibsenism*; Quintessence 101–2.

26. August Strindberg to Charles Casenove, 26 June 1892; cited in Michael Meyer, *Strindberg: A Biography* (Oxford: Oxford University Press, 1987), 246.

27. Shaw, preface to 1913 edition of *The Quintessence of Ibsenism*; Quintessence 102.

28. According to Dan H. Laurence, *Miss Julie* "was first presented in London [at the Little Theatre] in 1912 by the Adelphi Play Society, in a translation by Maurice Elvey and Lucy Carr Shaw"; CL2:907.

29. Shaw provided an account of his meeting with Strindberg to Chicago eccentric Judge Henry Neil; see the article "Bernard Shaw—as Few Know Him," *Pearson's Magazine*, Feb. 1927; I&R 416–17. See also Shaw to William Archer, n.d. [16 July 1908]; CL2:802.

30. Shaw's reported description is cited in Neil, "Bernard Shaw—as Few Know Him"; I&R 417.

31. Shaw to H. G. Wells, 7 Dec. 1916; CL3:439.

32. Shaw to George Moore, n.d. [Oct 1911]; CL3:53.

33. Shaw to Bertha Newcombe, 14 May 1909; CL2:843. Further information about the early stage history of *Press Cuttings* is provided by Stanley Weintraub in the essay

"One-Act Shaw" published in the program for a production of the play, directed by Glynis Leyshon, at the 1991 Shaw Festival, Niagara-on-the-Lake, Ontario, Canada.

34. The relationship between the Orderly and his bullying employer can be seen as an early draft of Shaw's portrayal of Captain Robert de Baudricourt and the abject Steward in the first scene of *Saint Joan*.

35. Bernard Shaw, preface to his collection *Translations and Tomfooleries* (London: Constable, 1926; rev. and repr. 1932 for the Standard Edition), 130.

36. Ibid.

Chapter 18. Enter Critics, Stage Right

1. Bernard Shaw, "Translator's Note" (introducing his translation of Siegfried Trebitsch's play *Jitta's Atonement*) in his *Translations and Tomfooleries* (London: Constable, 1926; rev. and repr. in 1932 for the Standard Edition), 4.

2. E. A. Baughan, signed notice of *Man and Superman, Daily News*, 24 May 1905; repr. in Heritage 108.

3. The idea that Scott may have been one of Shaw's models for Bannal is suggested by Barbara M. Fisher in her article "*Fanny's First Play*: A Critical Potboiler?" in *SHAW: The Annual of Bernard Shaw Studies*, vol. 7 [special issue: The Neglected Plays, ed. Alfred Turco Jr.] (University Park: Pennsylvania State University Press, 1987), 193.

4. See Raymond Mander and Joe Mitchenson, *Theatrical Companion to Shaw* (New York: Pitman, 1954), 143–44; cited in Fisher, "*Fanny's First Play*," 193–94.

5. Bernard Shaw, preface to *John Bull's Other Island*, in *Preface for Politicians* (1907); Prefs1:195.

6. Bernard Shaw, "Socialism and Ireland," lecture to the Fabian Society, 28 Nov. 1919. Supplement to the *New Commonwealth*, 12 Dec. 1919; Matter 218.

7. "*Candida*: A Talk with Mr Bernard Shaw," *Realm*, 5 April 1895; I&R 131.

8. G. Wilson Knight, *The Golden Labyrinth: A Study of British Drama* (London: Phoenix House, 1962), 351.

9. Max Beerbohm, "Mr. Shaw's New Dialogues," *Saturday Review* 12 Sept. 1903; repr. in Heritage 103.

10. Max Beerbohm, "Mr. Shaw's Position," *Saturday Review*, 9 Dec. 1905; repr. in Heritage 159.

11. Max Beerbohm, "Mr. Shaw at His Best," *Saturday Review*, 12 Nov. 1904; repr. in Heritage 131.

12. Max Beerbohm, "Mr. Shaw's Position," *Saturday Review* 9 Dec. 1905; repr. in Heritage 158.

13. Beerbohm's rather uncomplimentary opinions and recollections of the man who had introduced him as "the incomparable Max" to readers of the *Saturday Review* in 1898, when he became Shaw's successor as theater critic, were recorded by the American playwright S. N. Behrman in his *Conversations with Max* (London: Hamish Hamilton, 1960), 19–21, 162; I&R 274–76.

Chapter 19. A Love Affair, A Death, and a Triumph

1. Shaw to Harley Granville-Barker, 30 June 1912; CL3:95.

2. Mrs. Patrick Campbell to Shaw, n.d. [postmarked 27 June 1912]; Dent 19. The

meanings of the term *slut* intended here are probably those covered by the OED (sense 2): "bold or impudent girl; a hussy, jade," but also "in playful use, or without serious imputation of bad qualities."

3. Shaw to Mrs. Patrick Campbell, 30 June 1912; CL3:96–97.

4. The name could possibly have prompted that of Jack Tanner in Shaw's *Man and Superman.*

5. For some of the information in this chapter I am indebted to the extensive and well-researched biography by Margot Peters, *Mrs. Pat: The Life of Mrs. Patrick Campbell* (London: Bodley Head, 1984; repr. London: Hamish Hamilton, 1985).

6. Mrs. Patrick Campbell to Shaw, 8 and 9 Dec. 1912; Dent 60, 64.

7. Bernard Shaw, "Kate Terry," *Saturday Review*, 30 April 1898; OTN3:373.

8. Bernard Shaw, "Mrs. Tanqueray Plays the Piano," *World*, 20 Dec. 1893; SM3:72.

9. Bernard Shaw, "Mr. Pinero's New Play," *Saturday Review*, 16 March 1895; OTN1:61.

10. Shaw to Mrs. Patrick Campbell, 4 Jan. 1913; CL3:145.

11. CL1:684.

12. Shaw to Ellen Terry, 8 Sept. 1897; CL1:803.

13. Bernard Shaw, "Hamlet," *Saturday Review*, 2 Oct. 1897; OTN3:205.

14. Shaw to Mrs. Patrick Campbell, 3 July 1912; Dent 21–25.

15. Mrs. Patrick Campbell to Shaw, n.d. [July 1912]; Dent 27.

16. The anticipation of Coward in *Overruled* is also noted by Michael Holroyd, who rightly sees the play as a forerunner of Coward's 1933 comedy *Private Lives* about a marital "quadrille." (Michael Holroyd, *Bernard Shaw*, 5 vols. (London: Chatto & Windus, 1989), 2:277.

17. Shaw to Sir Arthur Wing Pinero, 15 Oct. 1912; Texas.

18. Peters, *Mrs. Pat*, 329.

19. Mrs. Patrick Campbell to Shaw, n.d. [29 July 1912]; Dent 31.

20. Shaw to Mrs. Patrick Campbell, 9 Aug. 1912; Dent 32–35; CL3:101–5.

21. Shaw to Mrs. Patrick Campbell, 9 Aug. 1912; Dent 34; CL3:103.

22. Mrs. Patrick Campbell to Shaw, 13 Aug. 1912; Dent 36.

23. Shaw to Mrs. Patrick Campbell, 3 Nov. 1912; Dent 52; CL3:119.

24. Quoted in Peters, *Mrs. Pat*, 500.

25. Shaw to Mrs. Patrick Campbell, 27 Nov. 1912; Dent 58; CL3:129.

26. Arnold Bennett, *The Journal of Arnold Bennett* (New York: The Literary Guild, 1933), 471–72; I&R 78–79.

27. Frank Swinnerton, *Swinnerton: An Autobiography* (London: Hutchinson, 1937),84–85; I&R 77–78.

28. Mrs. Patrick Campbell to Shaw, 13 March 1913; Dent 95.

29. Ibid.

30. Mrs. Patrick Campbell to Shaw, 1 Nov. 1912; Dent 52.

31. In a letter to Shaw dated 8 Dec. 1912 Stella wrote: "Did I once call you a clown? I expect it was when you said 'I am God'"; Dent 61. Shaw's declaration was at least consistent with his religion of creative evolution.

32. Mrs. Patrick Campbell to Shaw, 15 Dec. 1938; Dent 328.

33. Shaw to Mrs. Patrick Campbell, 19 Dec. 1938; Dent 329.

34. Shaw to the Hon. Mrs. Alfred Lyttelton, 22 Dec. 1912; CL3:140.
35. See Peters, *Mrs. Pat,* 287.
36. Shaw to the Hon. Mrs. Alfred Lyttelton, 27 Dec. 1912; CL3:141–42.
37. Ibid., 142.
38. Ibid., 140.
39. BL Ms. Add. 56500.
40. Shaw to Mrs. Patrick Campbell, 6 Feb. 1913; CL3:147–48.
41. A firsthand account of Charlotte's reaction to Shaw's affair with Stella Campbell was provided to Dan H. Laurence by Mrs. Ann M. Jackson (née Elder) in 1975, the correspondence of which is housed in the Dan H. Laurence Collection at the University of Guelph.
42. Mrs. Patrick Campbell to Shaw, 12 Dec. 1912; Dent 70.
43. Shaw to Mrs. Patrick Campbell, 4 Jan. 1913; Dent 72; CL3:145.
44. Shaw to Mrs. Patrick Campbell, 2 April 1913; Dent 105; CL3:163–64.
45. Shaw to Mrs. Patrick Campbell, 24 May 1913; Dent 117; CL3:181.
46. Ibid.
47. Ibid.
48. Shaw to Mrs. Patrick Campbell, 22 Feb. 1913; Dent 88; CL3:153.
49. Shaw to Mrs. Patrick Campbell, 29 Jan. 1913; Dent 75.
50. Shaw to Mrs. Patrick Campbell, 22 April 1913; Dent 111; CL3:167.
51. See above, chap. 6.
52. Lucinda Frances Shaw to Jane Crichton Drysdale, 14 April 1913; Farmer 188.
53. Shaw to Mrs. Patrick Campbell, 9 June 1913; CL3:184–85.
54. Shaw to Mrs. Patrick Campbell, 25 June 1913; CL3:187.
55. Shaw to Mrs. Patrick Campbell, 30 June 1913; Dent 126–27.
56. Mrs. Patrick Campbell to Shaw, 5 July 1913; Dent 129.
57. Shaw to Mrs. Patrick Campbell, 9 July 1913; Dent 129–31; CL3:188–90.
58. Shaw to the Hon. Mrs. Alfred Lyttelton, 25 July 1913; CL3:193.
59. Dion Clayton Calthrop, *My Own Trumpet: Being the Story of My Life* (London: Hutchinson, 1935), 210–11.
60. Mrs. Patrick Campbell to Shaw, 7 Aug. 1913; Dent 137.
61. Mrs. Patrick Campbell to Shaw, 10 Aug. 1913; Dent 137.
62. Mrs. Patrick Campbell to Shaw, 11 Aug. 1913; Dent 138.
63. Shaw to Mrs. Patrick Campbell, 12 Aug. 1913; Dent 141; CL3:196.
64. Shaw to Mrs. Patrick Campbell, 13 Aug. 1913; Dent 143; CL3:197.
65. Mrs. Patrick Campbell to Shaw, 13 Aug. 1913; Dent 141–42.
66. Shaw to Mrs. Patrick Campbell, 17 June 1913; Dent 122.
67. Lucinda Frances Shaw to Jane Crichton Drysdale, 4 Sept. 1913; Farmer 200–201; Peters, *Mrs. Pat,* 329.
68. Shaw to Mrs. Patrick Campbell, 31 Dec. 1913; Dent 155; CL3:212.
69. Peters, *Mrs. Pat,* 142.
70. Shaw to Mrs. Patrick Campbell, 28 July 1929; Dent 291; CL4:157.
71. Shaw to Mrs. Patrick Campbell, 13 March 1913; Dent 96; CL3:155–56.
72. Shaw to Mrs. Patrick Campbell, 29 Jan. 1913; Dent 76.
73. Mrs. Patrick Campbell to Shaw, 31 Jan. 1913; Dent 76.

74. The drawings are reproduced in CL3 between pages 760 and 761.

75. Mills was the founder of a religious organization called The Fellowship of the Way, about which Charlotte wrote a pamphlet entitled *Knowledge Is the Door: A Forerunner,* which was published in 1914.

76. Shaw to Charlotte Frances Shaw, 12 April 1914; CL3:227.

77. See CL3:226.

78. Shaw to Mrs. Patrick Campbell, 11 April 1914; Dent 160; CL3:224.

79. Shaw to Charlotte Frances Shaw, 12 April 1914; CL3:227–28.

80. Shaw to Mrs. Patrick Campbell, ca. 5 Feb. 1920; Theatrics 155.

Chapter 20. Armageddon, and the "Ruthless Light of Laughter"

1. As indicated in the *Boston Post* article cited in note 2, the steamship company Charlotte traveled to America with did not honor her request to have her name left off the passenger list.

2. H. F. Wheeler, "Wife Reveals Bernard Shaw: Noted Englishwoman in Her first American Interview. Says Husband Is Ardent Socialist and Feminist," *Boston Post,* 29 April 1914.

3. Diaries of Charlotte Frances Shaw; BL Ms. Add. 56500; BL Ms. Add. 63190.

4. Stanley Weintraub gives an account of the films in his book *Bernard Shaw, 1914–1918: Journey to Heartbreak* (London: Routledge & Kegan Paul, 1971), 16–17.

5. Mrs. Patrick Campbell to Shaw, 8 June 1916; Dent 188.

6. Shaw to William Archer, 30 Dec. 1916; CL3:447–48.

7. See Chron 280.

8. Shaw to Siegfried Trebitsch, 4 Aug. 1914; CL3:243.

9. CL3:239–40.

10. Bernard Shaw, "Is Britain Blameless?" review of Fenner Brockway pamphlet, *Labour Leader* (London), 4 Feb. 1915; repr. in Prefs2:137.

11. Bernard Shaw, "The Peril of Potsdam: Our Business Now," *Daily News,* 11 Aug. 1914; cited in Weintraub, *Bernard Shaw, 1914–1918,* 29.

12. Arnold Bennett, article in *Daily News* (London); repr. in *New York Times,* November 1914. Cited in Weintraub, *Bernard Shaw, 1914–1918,*62.

13. H. G. Wells, *Daily Chronicle* (London), 31 Dec. 1914; cited in Weintraub, *Bernard Shaw, 1914–1918,* 78.

14. Henry Arthur Jones to Shaw, 1 Nov. 1915; CL3:320.

15. Shaw to Henry Arthur Jones, 2 Nov. 1915; CL3:321.

16. Quoted in R. F. Rattray, *Bernard Shaw: A Chronicle* (London: Leagrave, 1951), 197; cited in Weintraub, *Bernard Shaw, 1914–1918,* 60.

17. CL3:315–16, 320.

18. Shaw to R. C. Carton, 2 Nov. 1915; CL3:326.

19. Shaw to H. M. Paull, 19 Nov. 1915; CL3:332.

20. Cited in Weintraub, *Bernard Shaw, 1914–1918,* 213.

21. Armageddon, originally the Hebrew name given to the site of the conflict in Rev. 16:16, has also come to signify the conflict itself.

22. Spender made this comment in the course of a 1988 BBC televised panel discussion entitled "Eliot and After."

23. Frank Kermode, *The Sense of an Ending* (New York: Oxford University Press, 1967), chap. 4.

24. Bernard Shaw, preface to *Heartbreak House* (1919); Prefs2:322.

25. Some of Shaw's letters written during and after World War I indicate that one of the models for Mangan was Lord Devonport, a prominent businessman and former MP who was elevated to the peerage and appointed Food Controller during 1916–17 (CL3:505, 513, 744). The head of a large wholesale grocery firm, he was one of a number of people from the business world (with obvious vested interests in their posts) who, much to some people's disgust, Lloyd George appointed to his wartime government. Devonport's blunders as Food Controller led to his resignation from the post in May 1917, a fact that possibly underlies the laughter created by Mangan among the other characters when he explains that he was appointed to his position because of his credentials "as a practical business man." Mangan's literary forbears among powerful financiers and swindlers include Melmotte in Trollope's novel *The Way We Live Now* and Merdle in Dickens's *Little Dorrit*. Mangan may have been named after the Irish poet James Clarence Mangan, in particular with reference to his poem "The Nameless One." See A. M. Gibbs, *"Heartbreak House": Preludes of Apocalypse* (New York: Twayne, 1994), 95–96.

26. Bernard Shaw, preface to *Heartbreak House*; Prefs2:318, 352.

27. The intertextual relations and apocalyptic themes of the play are explored in Gibbs, *Heartbreak House*.

28. "The New Shaw Play," unsigned review of Theater Guild production of *Heartbreak House* at the Garrick Theater, New York, 1920; in the Billy Rose Theater Collection, Lincoln Center, New York.

29. Shaw to Hugo Vallentin, 27 Oct. 1917; CL3:513.

30. Bernard Shaw, preface to *Heartbreak House*; Prefs2:318. For a discussion of the actual dates of composition, see Bernard Shaw, *Heartbreak House: A Facsimile of the Revised Typescript*, with an intro. by Stanley Weintraub and Anne Wright (New York: Garland, 1981), xiv, xix.

31. Lena Ashwell, *Myself a Player* (London: Michael Joseph, 1936), 65, 67.

32. Ibid., 66.

33. Margot Peters, *Mrs. Pat: The Life of Mrs. Patrick Campbell* (London: Bodley Head, 1984; repr. London: Hamish Hamilton, 1985), 283.

34. Shaw to Mrs. Patrick Campbell, 28 July 1929; Dent 291; CL4:157.

35. Anne Wright notes the way in which the men in *Heartbreak House* are "infantilised" by women in her study *Literature of Crisis, 1910–1922* (London: Methuen, 1984), 93.

36. The names of the dogs, who always accompanied her on her travels, included Pinky Panky Poo, a tiny Brussels griffon presented to her by the king of Belgium, and Georgina, who is mentioned in Shaw's "Final Orders" letter the night before the opening of *Pygmalion* and who was on Stella's lap when she was involved in the 1912 accident in a London taxi.

37. Shaw to Mrs. Patrick Campbell, 9 April 1913; Dent 107; CL3:164–65.

38. Ambiguity surrounding the character of Goldilocks is similarly present in the history of the tale itself. She did not become a pretty young golden-haired girl until early

in the twentieth century. Before this she appeared as a more sinister figure, an intruder variously depicted as a wicked fox and a crone. The transformation occurred during Shaw's lifetime.

39. Shaw to Mrs. Patrick Campbell, 14 May 1916; Dent 186.

40. Shaw to Virginia Woolf, 10 May 1940; CL4:557.

41. Virginia Woolf to Shaw, 15 May 1940; cited in CL4:557–58.

42. Shaw to Beatrice and Sidney Webb, 5 Oct. 1916; CL3:425.

43. See Shavian scholar Arthur H. Nethercot's article "Zeppelins Over Heartbreak House," *Shaw Review* 9 (May 1966): 49–50.

44. CL3:426.

45. Bernard Shaw, preface to *Heartbreak House*; Prefs2:344.

46. Ibid., 352

47. Ibid., 353.

48. Desmond MacCarthy, review in *New Statesman*, 29 Oct. 1921; repr. in his *Shaw* (London: MacGibbon & Kee, 1951).

49. Desmond MacCarthy, review in *New Statesman*, 3 April 1943; repr. in his *Shaw*.

50. Richard Watts Jr., review in *New York Post*, 19 Oct. 1959.

51. A full account of this production, together with photographs of some of the cast members and a reproduction of the program, is supplied by David Gunby, "The First Night of *O'Flaherty, V.C.*," *SHAW: The Annual of Bernard Shaw Studies* 19 [special issue: Shaw and History, ed. Gale K. Larson] (1999): 85–97.

52. The painting now hangs in the Queen's Gallery, Buckingham Palace Road, London, where it carries the title "When Homer Nods." (Shaw reports the title he or somebody else at Coole Park gave it at the time of his stay there in a letter to Mrs. Patrick Campbell dated 15 May 1915; see Dent 175.) The two most striking and engaging of the portraits are now located at Shaw's Corner, Ayot St Lawrence, and the Fitzwilliam Museum, Cambridge.

53. For his account of the meeting with Shaw, see Augustus John, *Chiaroscuro: Fragments of Autobiography* (London: Jonathan Cape, 1952), 69–71; I&R 288–90.

54. This meeting may have taken place in October 1917; Shaw was corresponding with a member of the Mahaffy family on 23 October 1917 (Shaw to Rachel Mahaffy; ms. housed at Trinity College, Dublin). The photograph is reproduced in F. E. Loewenstein, *Bernard Shaw Through the Camera* (London: B&H White, 1948), 91.

55. Sir Philip Gibbs, *The Pageant of the Years: An Autobiography* (London: Heinemann, 1946) 195–97; I&R 244–46

56. See Prefs2:268.

57. Robert Blake, ed., *The Private Papers of Douglas Haig, 1914–1919* (London: Eyre & Spottiswoode, 1952), 194–95.

58. Bernard Shaw, "Joy Riding at the Front," *Daily Chronicle*, 5, 7, and 8 March 1917.

59. Campbell was killed on 30 December 1917. Shaw wrote to Stella immediately after receiving her letter containing the news on 7 January 1918; CL3:525.

60. Shaw to Lillah McCarthy, 19 June 1918; CL3:552.

61. Information about Charlotte's reaction was supplied by Judy Gillmore to Dan H. Laurence in the form of correspondence, housed at Guelph; see also Chron 230.

62. Shaw to St. John Ervine, 22 May 1918; CL3:551.

63. See Lawrence Langner, *G.B.S. and the Lunatic* (New York: Atheneum, 1963), 29; cited in Weintraub, *Bernard Shaw, 1914–1918*, 270.

Chapter 21. Sages, Saints, and Flappers

1. In a letter dated 16 Feb 1917 Charlotte gave a report of Shaw's experiences at the front to her sister, Mary Cholmondeley, who had asked for a full account. The letter is included in Janet Dunbar, *Mrs. GBS: A Biographical Portrait* (London: Harrap, 1963), 253–56; see also I&R 246–47.

2. Lennox Robinson, ed., *Lady Gregory's Journals, 1916–1930* (London: Putnam, 1946), 202; I&R 302.

3. Reviews of the production appear on the Albermarle of London West End Theatre Guide website at http://www.albemarle-london.com/rsc-methuselah.html (accessed July 2005).

4. One of the He-Ancient's sayings ("Life is not meant to be easy") was famously borrowed in 1971 by Australian Prime Minister Malcolm Fraser in a contribution to the Australian Alfred Deakin Lecture Series, and was widely thought to be his own invention. The saying circulated without its rider in the play: "But take comfort: it can be delightful."

5. Bernard Shaw, "Parents and Children" (preface to *Misalliance*, 1914); Prefs2:4.

6. George Sylvester Viereck, "Shaw Looks at Life at 70," *London Magazine*, Dec. 1927; I&R 421–23. Ahasuerus was the name given in a seventeenth-century German version of the legend to the Jew who taunted Christ on his way to the Cross and was doomed to wander the earth until the time of the Second Coming. A comparable figure in classical legend is Tithonus, the subject of Tennyson's poem of the same name, which expresses thoughts similar to those of Shaw about the "tragic fate" of immortality. Another long-lived character in literature who probably influenced *Back to Methuselah* was Regin the dwarf in William Morris's "Sigurd the Volsung."

7. Lawrence Langner, *G.B.S. and the Lunatic* (London: Hutchinson, 1964), 49.

8. Shaw to Charles Charrington, 17 July 1918; CL3:555.

9. Shaw's prediction of what he would be if he accepted the invitation to Mrs. Elizabeth Lawson's dance at her home in Cheyne Walk, Chelsea, in January 1880; CL1:29.

10. Shaw to Henry S. Salt, 30 Oct. 1919; CL3:502.

11. Shaw to Lillah McCarthy, 2 Sept. 1917; CL3:503.

12. Lucinda Frances Shaw to Jane Crichton Drysdale, 2 Nov. 1915; Farmer 226.

13. Lucinda Frances Shaw to Jane Crichton Drysdale, 14 April [1913]; Farmer 189.

14. Lucinda Frances Shaw to Jane Crichton Drysdale, 2 July 1915; Farmer 222.

15. Lucinda Frances Shaw to Jane Crichton Drysdale, 18 July 1915; Farmer 223.

16. Shaw to Charles MacMahon Shaw, 17 Nov. 1937; CL4:481–82. The letter was published with revisions in SSS 91–96.

17. Shaw to Blanche Patch, 3 June 1920; CL3:676. A less graceful form of the invitation—"Will you come and be my secretary?"—appears in Patch 9. Patch's book was already in preparation before Shaw's death in 1950; unbeknownst to Shaw, it was being ghostwritten by his journalist acquaintance Robert Williamson from memoirs and letters supplied by Patch. The book was published in 1951.

18. Shaw to Blanche Patch, 3 June 1920; CL3:678.

19. Patch 248.

20. Shaw to Mrs. Patrick Campbell, 8 Sept. 1913; CL3:201–2.

21. Note accompanying Shaw's donation toward funds for a church dedicated to Saint Joan in 1927: "As I am more nearly a Quaker than anything else that has a denomination, and Joan was the spiritual mother of George Fox, I can hardly refuse an infinitesimal percentage of the money I have made out of her" Harvard (autograph file).

22. Comment made by Shaw in an interview published as "Bernard Shaw on Religion," *St. Martin-in-the-Fields Review*, May 1922; I&R 411.

23. Quoted in Elizabeth Sprigge, *Sybil Thorndike Casson* (London: Victor Gollancz, 1971), 154; I&R 309.

24. Luigi Pirandello, "Pirandello distils Shaw," *New York Times*, 13 Jan. 1924; repr. in Heritage 279–84 and *Bernard Shaw: "Man and Superman" and "Saint Joan": A Casebook*, ed. A. M. Gibbs (London: Macmillan, 1992), 128–31.

25. A. B. Walkley, unsigned notice, *Times*, 27 March 1924; repr. in Heritage 286.

26. G. H. Mair "*Saint Joan*: Mr. Bernard Shaw's Masterpiece," *Evening Standard*, 27 March 1924; repr. in Gibbs, ed., *Casebook*, 134.

27. J.I.M. Stewart, *Eight Modern Writers*, Oxford History of English Literature, vol. 12 (Oxford: Clarendon Press, 1963), 179; repr. in Gibbs, ed., *Casebook*, 162.

28. Shaw to Laurentia McLachlan, 23 Dec. 1924; CL3:898.

29. Shaw to Laurentia McLachlan, 4 Sept. 1944; CL4:723.

30. William Archer, "The Psychology of G.B.S.," *Bookman* 67, no. 399 (Dec. 1924); I&R 291.

31. Cited in CL4:5.

32. Hend3:838.

33. See CL4:32–34.

34. Shaw to Charles Sarolea, 20 Feb. 1926; CL4:13.

35. Winston Churchill, "Bernard Shaw—Saint, Sage and Clown," *Sunday Chronicle*, 13 April 1930; I&R 494.

36. Shaw to Augustin Hamon, 2 Feb. 1927; CL4:39.

37. Patch, *Thirty Years With G.B.S.*, 142.

38. This card is reproduced in Lbib2:841.

39. See Lbib2:866.

40. CL4:5.

41. M. A. Cohen, "The 'Shavianisation' of Cauchon," *Shaw Review* 20 (May 1977): 63–70; repr. in Gibbs, ed., *Casebook*, 203–12.

42. This is the title and theme of Nicholas Grene's chapter on the play in his book *Bernard Shaw: A Critical View* (London: Macmillan, 1984), 84–100.

43. Quoted in Bernard Shaw, "How William Archer Impressed Bernard Shaw" (preface to William Archer's *Three Plays*, 1927); Prefs2:582.

44. Ibid. See also CL3:895.

45. Shaw produced a revised and expanded edition of this work, taking account of developments in Russia and the rise of Fascism, with the title *The Intelligent Woman's Guide to Socialism, Capitalism, Sovietism and Fascism*, 2 vols. (London: Penguin, 1937), 1. All references are to the Constable Standard Edition (1949).

46. *Intelligent Woman's Guide*, 313–14.

47. Ibid., 97.
48. Ibid., 377.
49. Ibid., 379.

Chapter 22. The Road to Baveno: Dangerous Flirtations

1. The account of the Shaw-Tompkins relationship in this chapter is based on a fresh reading of the primary sources of information. It is also indebted to explorations of the relationship by Margot Peters in chapters 22 and 23 of her book *Bernard Shaw and the Actresses* (New York: Doubleday, 1980) and Charles A. Berst in his essay "Passion at Lake Maggiore: Shaw, Molly Tompkins, and Italy, 1921–1950," *SHAW: The Annual of Bernard Shaw Studies*, vol. 5 [special issue: Shaw Abroad, ed. Rodelle Weintraub] (University Park: Pennsylvania State University Press, 1985), 81–114. Important further information about the relationship came to light in two articles published in 2004. See below, note 23.

2. This is recounted in the prologue to *Shaw and Molly Tompkins in Their Own Words*, ed. Peter Tompkins (London: Anthony Blond, 1961).

3. *Shaw and Molly Tompkins*, verso of title page.

4. Shaw to Molly Tompkins, 27 Dec. 1921. *To a Young Actress: The Letters of Bernard Shaw to Molly Tompkins*, ed. Peter Tompkins (London: Constable, 1960), 12.

5. *Shaw and Molly Tompkins*, 37.

6. The photographs are reproduced in *Shaw and Molly Tompkins* between pages 80 and 81; one of them also appears in CL3 between pages 856 and 857.

7. Shaw to Molly Tompkins, 27 Aug. 1923; *To a Young Actress*, 48. Shaw is here alluding to Hamlet's recollections of Yorick's "flashes of merriment, that were wont to set the table on a roar" (5.1.190–91).

8. Shaw to Molly Tompkins, 22 Dec. and 9 Jan. 1922; *To a Young Actress*, 14, 32.

9. Shaw to Molly Tompkins, 9 Jan. 1922; *To a Young Actress*, 13–14.

10. Shaw to Molly Tompkins, 10 Feb. 1924; *To a Young Actress*, 59.

11. Shaw to Molly Tompkins, 10 June 1924; *To a Young Actress*, 71.

12. *Shaw and Molly Tompkins*, 73.

13. Shaw to Molly Tompkins, 22 Feb. 1925; *To a Young Actress*, 82.

14. Shaw to Molly Tompkins, 27 Jan. 1926; *To a Young Actress*, 90–91.

15. Shaw to Molly Tompkins, 8 and 10 Aug. 1926; *To a Young Actress*, 95, 96.

16. Shaw to Molly Tompkins, 14 Sept. 1926; *To a Young Actress*, 103.

17. Charlotte Frances Shaw to Beatrice Webb, Aug.–Sept. 1926; BLPES.

18. Shaw to Molly Tompkins, 8 Aug. 1926; *To a Young Actress*, 96.

19. Charlotte Frances Shaw to Molly Tompkins, 22 Aug. and 10 Sept. 1926; *To a Young Actress*, 97, 100.

20. Shaw to Molly Tompkins, 18 and 19 Sept. 1926; *To a Young Actress*, 105–6, 107.

21. *Shaw and Molly Tompkins*, 142.

22. Ibid., 157.

23. This sentence was edited out of the text of the letter published in *To a Young Actress* (180–81). The unexpurgated text, together with an interview with Peter Tompkins, was published in Patricia M. Carter, "'Until It Was Historical': A Letter And An Interview," *SHAW: The Annual of Bernard Shaw Studies*, vol. 24 [special issue: Dion-

ysian Shaw], ed. Michel W. Pharand (University Park: Pennsylvania State University Press, 2004), 11–37. See also Richard Owen, "Shaw's Secret Fair Lady Revealed at Last," *Times* (London), 14 June 2004.

24. Shaw to Molly Tompkins, 2 Feb. 1929; *To a Young Actress*, 131.

25. Shaw to Molly Tompkins, 12 Jan. 1927 and 2 March 1928; *To a Young Actress*, 111, 124.

26. Shaw to Molly Tompkins, 10 Jan. 1927; *To a Young Actress*, 109.

27. *Shaw and Molly Tompkins*, 221.

28. Peter Tompkins is reported to have stated that Shaw was the father of the baby in the *Times* article cited in note 23.

29. Molly Tompkins to Shaw, Nov. 1945; BL Ms. Add. 50551. The letter is cited, in part, by Margot Peters, *Bernard Shaw and the Actresses*, 408–9; see also Berst, "Passion at Lake Maggiore," 111–12.

30. Ibid.

31. Shaw to Frank Harris, 24 June 1930; CL4:192; SSS 115. Berst draws attention to the letter to Frank Harris and its possible connection with the Tompkins affair in his article "Passion at Lake Maggiore," 109–10. It is usually supposed that Shaw was referring to his experiences of sex before his marriage.

32. Mrs. Patrick Campbell to Shaw, 24 Feb. 1921; Dent 247.

33. See above, chap. 19.

34. *Shaw and Molly Tompkins*, 131. Blanche Patch recalls that Charlotte asked her to find a dealer in canaries "as she wanted to buy one to take to Ayot St. Lawrence, where the gardener bred them." See Patch, *Thirty Years with G.B.S.* (London: Gollancz, 1951), 555.

35. *Shaw and Molly Tompkins*, 133.

36. In her 1945 letter to Shaw, Molly says: "I didn't like Charlotte—she didn't give me much chance to . . ."; BL Ms. Add. 50551.

37. Shaw to Molly Tompkins, 31 May 1928; *To a Young Actress*, 127–28; CL4:99–100. Shaw is here conflating two Homeric stories. Ogygia was the island on which the nymph Calypso detained Odysseus for seven years. The siren who lured Odysseus's sailors to her island and transformed them into swine was Circe.

38. This was also the name of the shepherdess played by Florence Farr in John Todhunter's play *The Sicilian Idyll.*

39. *To a Young Actress*, 190–91. The name Shaw gives Molly here is probably a joking allusion to the heroine of Dion Boucicault's romantic melodrama *The Colleen Bawn*, which is based on an Irish story.

40. Shaw's development of this theme in the play was no doubt influenced by the publication in 1928 of D. H. Lawrence's *Lady Chatterley's Lover*, as well as the sensation caused by the exhibition of his paintings at the Warren Gallery in London, where some of the works were seized as indecent by the police. See below, chap. 24.

41. In a letter to Mrs. Patrick Campbell dated 31 March 1929 Shaw writes of *The Apple Cart*: "I am too shy to read you the only scene in that play that would interest you. Its scandalous climax is a reminiscence of Kensington Square"; Dent 274.

42. Mrs. Patrick Campbell to Shaw, 12 July 1929; Dent, 288.

43. This analogy was developed by Shaw in a 1929 radio broadcast, the text of which was included in the preface to *The Apple Cart* (1930); see Prefs3:48.

44. See Bernard Shaw, preface to *The Apple Cart;* Prefs3:43.

45. All three of the writers mentioned subsequently turned against Communism. But in the decade before he wrote *Animal Farm,* his trenchant satire on Stalinist Communism, Orwell served in the Spanish civil war with the militia of the Marxist revolutionary force POUM (Partido Obrero de Unificación Marxista). Kingsley Amis was attracted to Communism in the 1930s and became a member of the Communist Party in 1941. He remained a member until 1956, after which he developed very conservative political views. Iris Murdoch is reported to have said she had been a Communist since she was thirteen. She joined the Communist Party after arriving at Oxford in 1938. Although she became disillusioned with Communism after World War II, according to Peter J. Conradi "her recorded nostalgia for it lasted until 1953" (*Iris Murdoch: A Life* [London: Harper Collins, 2001], 211).

46. Quoted in CL4:41–43. For the letter to Wallas, see CL4:42.

47. See CL4:67–74.

48. DBW4:131–32.

49. Shaw to J. Ramsay MacDonald, 21 Oct. 1927; CL4:75. MacDonald, a former member of the Fabian Society served a brief period of office as the First Labour Party prime minister in England after the General Election of 1923. From 1929 to 1935 he served a second prime ministerial term as head of the new National Coalition Party.

50. Shaw to Molly Tompkins, 8 Aug. 1926; *To a Young Actress,* 96.

51. This letter suggests that Molly may have had an affair with Basile. See *To a Young Actress,* 131.

52. Shaw to Molly Tompkins, 2 Feb. 1927; *To a Young Actress,* 112.

53. Shaw to Molly Tompkins, 2 Feb. 1927; *To a Young Actress,* 112.

54. Shaw to Molly Tompkins, n.d. [c. May 1928]; *To a Young Actress,* 127. The play, for which Shaw suggested the title "Triangoli Intrecciati—Interlaced Triangles," is lost.

55. Shaw to Friedrich Adler, 11 Oct. 1927; CL4:71.

56. "G. B. Shaw on Fascism," *Daily Telegraph* (London) 25 Feb. 1931; I&R 355.

57. Shaw to W. S. Kennedy, 7 Feb. 1927; CL4:43.

58. Gaetano Salvemini, letter published in the *Manchester Guardian,* 19 Oct. 1927; CL4:67.

59. In the final volume of his edition of Shaw's *Collected Letters,* Dan H. Laurence points out that Lloyd George, the Prince of Wales, and even Winston Churchill made favorable comments about Hitler's achievements; see CL4:456.

60. The opening performance of Shaw's play *Too True to Be Good* in Mannheim, Germany, in February 1933 was disrupted by Nazis shouting "Jew Shaw" and abusing the (non-Jewish) leading actor as a "Jew" until the police intervened; see CL4:336.

61. Hayden Church, "Halt, Hitler! By Bernard Shaw" (interview), *Sunday Dispatch,* 4 June 1933; I&R 355–58. Following Hitler's appointment as chancellor in April 1933, anti-Semitic policies were formally enshrined in the platform and legislation of the Nazi Party.

62. Mrs. Patrick Campbell to Shaw, 1 Nov. 1912; Dent 19.

Chapter 23. World Traveler and Village Squire

1. "The Dangers of a 'Sun-Trap': Mr. Bernard Shaw's Warning to South Africa," *Cape Times* (Cape Town), 8 Feb. 1932; Chron 285–86.

2. Shaw's remarks were reported in the *Auckland Star* (15 May 1934) and the *New Zealand Herald* (15 and 16 March 1934); see Chron 295–96.

3. Ritchie Calder, interview with Shaw in the *Daily Herald* (London), 20 April 1933; I&R 340; see also Chron 290.

4. In July 1927, while the Shaws were at Lake Maggiore, their belongings were shifted to new quarters, a serviced apartment at Whitehall Court in the same locality (near the Thames Embankment and the Strand) as Adelphi Terrace. Whitehall Court remained Shaw's London address until 1950, the year of his death.

5. Charlotte Frances Shaw, "Packing List"; Texas.

6. Shaw to Sydney C. Cockerell, 13 March 1931; CL4:229.

7. Shaw to Dame Laurentia McLachlan, 17 March 1931; CL4:229–35.

8. Shaw's travels abroad are described in a collection of essays by various hands in *SHAW: The Annual of Bernard Shaw Studies*, vol. 5 [special issue: Shaw Abroad, ed. Rodelle Weintraub] (University Park: Pennsylvania State University Press, 1985). See also relevant sections in Chron and I&R, which add further information.

9. The correspondence between Bernard Shaw and Barry Jackson was published for the first time in 2002 in a volume edited by Leonard W. Connoly entitled *Bernard Shaw and Barry Jackson* (Toronto: Toronto University Press, 2002). Recollections of Shaw at Malvern are also included in I&R 185–86, 372–74.

10. Sir Barry Jackson, "Shaw at Malvern," *Drama*, n.s., no. 20 (Spring 1951).

11. The portrait was painted by Victor Hume Moody (1896–1990) in 1938, the year of Shaw's last visit to the festival. I am grateful to the artist's daughter, Catherine Moody, for showing me the original of this portrait in her home at Great Malvern while on a visit in September 2000.

12. Beverley Nichols, *All I Could Never Be: Some Recollections* (London: Jonathan Cape, 1949), 145–47; I&R 185–86.

13. Shaw reported Charlotte's description of his behavior in front of crowds of people in a letter to Molly Tompkins (8 January 1928) written when they were staying with Viscount and Lady Astor at Cliveden: "Externally I 'peacock' here (Charlotte's expression) amid week end crowds of visitors." *To a Young Actress*, 123; repr. in CL4:83.

14. Jisbella Lyth recollection; Villager 94–95.

15. Shaw to Horace Plunkett, 16 July 1931; CL4:242.

16. Winston Churchill, *Great Contemporaries* (London: Thornton Butterworth, 1937), 55.

17. Shaw to Nancy Astor, 15 July 1931. J. P. Wearing, ed. *Bernard Shaw and Nancy Astor* (Toronto: Toronto University Press, 2005), 33. See also James Fox, *The Langhorne Sisters* (London: Granta Books, 1998), 427. Bobbie was Nancy's son by her first marriage to Robert Gould Shaw of Boston. Shaw's two letters to Nancy about Bobbie remained unpublished until 1998, when they were included in James Fox's biographical study of Nancy Astor's family circle.

18. Shaw to Nancy Astor, 15 April 1932. Bernard Shaw and Nancy Astor, 46–47. The curious biblical story—(recounted in *Gen.* 19:26 and recalled in *Luke* 17:32) of Lot's wife being turned into a pillar of salt as a result of her failure to obey the angel's injunction not to look back at the cities of Sodom and Gomorrah as she, her husband, and her family were fleeing those cities of sin—is frequently invoked in fundamentalist religious attacks on homosexuality.

19. Shaw to Nancy Astor, 13 April 1929; CL4:137.

20. The palatial country house was built during the Restoration period as a pleasure resort (and home for his mistress) by the 2nd Duke of Buckingham. The estate takes its name from its location above steep chalk cliffs rising above the river Thames, of which the house and its formal gardens have a commanding view. The Astors also owned a very large townhouse in London, situated between Piccadilly and St. James's Square, that is now the home of the Naval and Military Club. Cliveden has been converted into a five-star hotel and restaurant.

21. Shaw to Molly Tompkins, 31 May 1928; *To a Young Actress*, 127.

22. J. P. Wearing, editor of the Shaw-Astor correspondence in the Toronto University Press series *Selected Correspondence of Bernard Shaw*, has privately expressed the view to me that Nancy Astor's unhappiness in her marriage with Waldorf, with whom (much to his sadness) she eventually broke off relations, may have meant that she was seeking in Shaw "what she was missing elsewhere in her life."

23. For an excellent account of the family and the girls' lives and careers see Fox, *Langhorne Sisters.*

24. Shaw to Dame Edith ("D D") Lyttelton, 8 July 1926. This letter (CHAN 5/19) is housed in the Churchill Archives Centre, Churchill College, Cambridge, UK.

25. A. E. Johnson, "Encounters with GBS," *Dalhousie Review* (Spring 1951); I&R 493.

26. Shaw to Charlotte Frances Shaw, 21 July 1931; CL4:246. Shaw closed his previous letter to Charlotte with the farewell "Bless you, dearest"; CL4:244.

27. Shaw to Charlotte Frances Shaw, 21 July 1931; CL4:247.

28. Shaw to Charlotte Frances Shaw, 23 and 24 July 1931; CL4:250, 252.

29. Shaw to Charlotte Frances Shaw, 21 and 23 July 1931; CL4:246–47, 250

30. Shaw to Charlotte Frances Shaw, 21 July 1931; CL4:247. Brecht's work is, of course, a "translation" of Gay's eighteenth-century world of highwaymen and other rogues into that of twentieth-century American gangsters.

31. CL4:253.

32. Shaw to Charlotte Frances Shaw, 23 July 1931; CL4:249.

33. H.W.L. Dana, "Shaw in Moscow," *American Mercury* (March 1932); I&R 323.

34. Shaw to Charlotte Frances Shaw, 22 and 23 July 1931; CL4:248, 249.

35. Eugene Lyons, *Assignment in Utopia* (London: Harrap, 1938), 429; I&R 325. The GPU was the state secret police, a major instrument in Stalin's suppression of political dissent. The "Bolshevo" was the settlement for homeless boys at Bolshevo, which Shaw visited.

36. See Gene Tunney and Walter Davenport, "So This Is Russia!," *Collier's, The National Weekly*, 3 Oct. 1931 (available at http://www.genetunney.org/bankers.html—accessed July 2005). See also Malcolm Muggeridge, "Russia Revealed, III, Terror of the

G.P.U. Perverted Soul of Bolshevism. Ceaseless Hunt for "Class-Ties," *Morning Post*, 7 June 1933 (available at http://colley.co.uk/garethjones/soviet_articles/morning_post_3.htm—accessed July 2005).

37. Letter from Charlotte Frances Shaw to William Maxwell; cited in CL4:259.

38. The text of Shaw's speech is reprinted in CL4:256–59. The phrase appears on page 258.

39. See St. John Ervine, *Bernard Shaw: His Life, Work and Friends* (London: Constable, 1956), 522.

40. CL4:332.

41. Rhea G. Clyman, letter to the *American Mercury* (May 1945); I&R 323–24. Clyman was an American journalist based in Moscow at the time of Shaw's visit.

42. Bernard Shaw, *The Political Madhouse in America and Nearer Home: A Lecture by Bernard Shaw* (London: Constable, 1933), 19.

43. Edmund Wilson, "Shaw in the Metropolitan," *New Republic* (New York), 26 April 1933; I&R 337–39.

44. See CL4:770.

45. *The Diary of Virginia Woolf*, vol. 4, *1931–35*, ed. Anne Olivier Bell with Andrew McNeillie (Harmondsworth, Eng.: Penguin, 1982), 152; I&R 499.

46. Atiya Begum, "Bernard Shaw at Aiwan-e-Rafat," *Dawn* (Karachi), 5 Nov. 1950; I&R 332.

47. Hiralal Amritlal Shah, "Bernard Shaw in Bombay," *Shaw Bulletin* (Nov. 1956) (first published in Gujarati in *Prabuddha Jain* [Bombay], 15 Nov. 1950); I&R 330–31.

48. Shaw to Sir Francis Younghusband, 28 Dec. 1934; CL4:395.

49. Shaw to Lady Rhondda, 15 Feb. 1932; CL4:276.

50. Shaw's self-identification with Voltaire is discussed by John A. Bertolini, in *The Playwrighting Self of Bernard Shaw* (Carbondale: Southern Illinois University Press, 1991), 153–54, and Michel W. Pharand, in *Bernard Shaw and the French* (Gainesville: University Press of Florida, 2000), 253–59.

51. For a study of the Shaw–T. E. Lawrence association, see Stanley Weintraub, *Private Shaw and Public Shaw* (London: Braziller, 1963). Though it seems symbolic of the quasi-filial relationship between Lawrence and the Shaws, in a 1937 letter to O. A. Forsyth Major Shaw wrote that Lawrence's "assumption of the name Shaw had nothing to do with me" and insisted that the name was chosen at random from a telephone book; see CL4:465.

52. Boanerges, the name given by Jesus to the sons of Zebedee (*Mark* 3:17), is probably derived from a word meaning "sons of thunder." It is applied to loud-voiced preachers and, as Lawrence doubtless knew, was employed by Shaw as the name for his character Bill Boanerges, the trade unionist MP, in *The Apple Cart*.

53. Charlotte Frances Shaw to Dorothy Walker; cited in CL4:412.

54. Shaw to Nancy Astor, 9 Feb. 1934; CL4:365.

55. See Mary Hyde, ed., *Bernard Shaw and Alfred Douglas: A Correspondence* (Oxford: Oxford University Press, 1989), 46, 48. Shaw's name for Douglas is an allusion to the following line in *King Lear*: "Childe Rowland to the dark tower came" (3.4.182).

56. Shaw to Alfred Douglas, 14 Nov. 1940; CL4:587.

57. Shaw to Alfred Douglas, 9 Nov. 1940; CL4:587.

58. Mrs. Edith Reeves recollection; Villager 167.

59. Ibid., 166.

60. Margaret Smith (née Cashin) recollection; Villager 48.

61. Christina Hardyment, "The Maid, the Playwright and the Prime Minister—Interview—Violet Liddle," *Times* (London), 4 Aug. 2001.

62. At the time of the interview, Violet was working as an adviser to film director Robert Altman on "downstairs" life in English houses during the 1930s for the film *Gosford Park*.

63. Fred Drury recollection; Villager 51.

64. This is Chappelow's description; Villager 26.

65. Alice Laden recollection; Villager 27.

66. Ibid., 28.

67. Ibid., 27, 36.

68. Clive Bell to Mary Hutchinson, 14 Jan. 1916; Texas. Cited in Hermione Lee, *Virginia Woolf* (London: Vintage, 1997), 354. Woolf's complex, class-bound relations with servants are skillfully discussed and contextualized in Lee's study.

Chapter 24. Last Flourishes and the Call of the Silver Screen

1. Cited in St. John Ervine, *Bernard Shaw: His Life, Work and Friends* (London: Constable, 1956), 555.

2. Oscar Wilde to Shaw, n.d., postmarked 9 May 1893. *Selected Letters of Oscar Wilde*, ed. Rupert Hart-Davis (Oxford: Oxford University Press, 1979), 112.

3. Edmund Wilson, "Bernard Shaw at Eighty," in his *Triple Thinkers* (London: Oxford University Press, 1938), 265.

4. Martin Meisel, *Shaw and the Nineteenth-Century Theater* (Princeton, N.J.: Princeton University Press, 1963), 427–28.

5. Shaw to Molly Tompkins, 24 Nov. 1935; *To a Young Actress: The Letters of Bernard Shaw to Molly Tompkins*, ed. Peter Tompkins (London: Constable, 1960), 167.

6. Kenneth Tynan review of performance in Coventry in 1952; cited by Margery Morgan, *File on Shaw* (London: Methuen, 1989), 97–98.

7. For accounts of the making of this film—and Sellers's apparently not very seriously reciprocated infatuation with Sophia Loren—see Ed Sikov, *Mr. Strangelove: A Biography of Peter Sellers* (London: Sidgwick and Jackson, 2002), 142–45; and Warren G. Harris, *Sophia Loren: A Biography* (New York: Simon & Schuster, 1998), 145–53.

8. See *Numbers* 22.

9. Jakob Welti, unsigned notice of a production in Zurich of *Buoyant Billions*, *Zürcher Zeitung*, 22 Oct. 1948; repr. in Heritage 375.

10. Bernard Shaw to Siegfried Trebitsch, 31 July 1950; cited in *Bernard Shaw's Letters to Siegfried Trebitsch*, ed. Samuel A. Weiss (Stanford, Calif.: Stanford University Press, 1986), 468.

11. In the following discussion I am indebted to the account of Shaw's association with the film in Bernard F. Dukore's book *The Collected Screenplays of Bernard Shaw* (London: George Prior, 1980), as well as to Dukore's edition of the correspondence of Shaw and the Hungarian film director and producer Gabriel Pascal in the Toronto University Press *Selected Correspondence of Bernard Shaw* series. For Shaw's letter to

Mrs. Patrick Campbell dated 19 Aug 1912, see Dent 36–41. For recollections and interviews relating to Shaw's association with the film world, see I&R 386–93.

12. "Mr Shaw as Movie Fan," report of Shaw speech on "Secrets of Nature" film, *Manchester Guardian*, 19 Nov. 1927; repr. in *Illustrated London News*, 3 Dec. 1927, and *New York Times*, 4 Dec. 1927. See also Dukore, *Collected Screenplays*, 3.

13. See plate and caption facing SSS 122. Information concerning the purchase of the figurine appears in Patch 35.

14. This was a very large sum, equivalent to over 3.5 million U.S. dollars in 2005 values. The record is contained in the last of Shaw's engagement diaries, housed in the British Library of Political and Economic Science archives. Shaw made a fortune out of the film industry, a huge amount of which disappeared as a result of the crippling tax regimes in England in the 1940s.

15. Shaw to Gabriel Pascal, 18 June 1950; CL4:869.

Chapter 25. "A man all light": Last Years

1. *The Diary of Virginia Woolf*, vol. 4, *1931–35*, ed. Anne Olivier Bell assisted by Andrew McNeillie (Harmondsworth, Eng.: Penguin, 1982), 106–7; I&R 497–98.

2. Ibid., 152; I&R 499.

3. Leonard Woolf describes this and two other meetings with Shaw in his *Beginning Again: An Autobiography of the Years 1911–1918* (London: Hogarth Press, 1964), 120–22; I&R 495–97.

4. Ibid.

5. John Mason Brown, "Back to Methuselah: A Visit to an Elderly Gentleman in a World of Arms and the Man," *Saturday Review of Literature*, 22 July 1944; I&R 522.

6. "Bernard Shaw, at 88, Gives His Home to the Nation," *News Chronicle* (London), 26 July 1944.

7. James Agate, *Ego 3: Being Still More of the Autobiography of James Agate* (London: Harrap, 1938), 296.

8. Shaw to Beatrice Webb, 17 Feb. 1941; CL4:596.

9. E. M. Salzer, "Bernard Shaw (Who Is Eighty-three Today) Says We Will Have Peace," *Daily Express*, 26 July 1939; I&R 456.

10. See I&R 456, n1.

11. Shaw to Nancy Astor, 28 Sept. 1939; CL4:540.

12. "Mr. Shaw's Advice," *Manchester Guardian*, 24 May 1940.

13. Shaw diary entry for December 1941; BLPES.

14. Shaw to Nancy Astor, 30 Jan. 1941; CL4:593.

15. Blanche Patch, *Thirty Years with G.B.S.* (London: Victor Gollancz, 1951), 38.

16. Shaw to Beatrice Webb, 30 Jan. 1941; CL4:592.

17. Shaw to Lady Mary Murray, 21 Sept. 1943; CL4:679.

18. Shaw to H. G. Wells, 12 Sept. 1943; CL4:677–78.

19. Patch, *Thirty Years with G.B.S.*, 197.

20. Shaw to Molly Tompkins, 4 Dec. 1944; *To a Young Actress: The Letters of Bernard Shaw to Molly Tompkins*, ed. Peter Tompkins (London: Constable, 1960), 180.

21. Shaw to Ada Tyrrell, 14 July 1949; CL4:851–52.

22. See CL4:691.

23. Shaw to Molly Tompkins, 4 Dec. 1944; *To a Young Actress*, 180.

24. Shaw to Sidney Webb, 26 Oct. 1945; CL4:757.

25. Shaw to Molly Tompkins, 4 Dec. 1944; *To a Young Actress*, 180.

26. Shaw to Sydney C. Cockerell, n.d., assigned to c. 3 May 1946; CL4:767–68.

27. Quoted in Hesketh Pearson, *G.B.S.: A Postscript* (London: Collins, 1951), 104.

28. CL4:702.

29. Shaw to Sidney Webb, 29 April 1943; CL4:668.

30. Ibid.

31. Shaw to Sidney Webb, 2 April 1944; CL4:706.

32. Dent 332–33.

33. See Margot Peters, *Mrs. Pat: The Life of Mrs. Patrick Campbell* (London: Hamish Hamilton, 1985), 442. I am indebted to this source for several details in the following account of Stella's last years.

34. Shaw to Mrs. Patrick Campbell, 14 Aug. 1937; Dent 313.

35. Shaw to Molly Tompkins, 8 Dec. 1946; *To a Young Actress*, 185. Shaw had a long and sometimes quarrelsome association with the publishing firm of Brentano's. When the firm went into bankruptcy in 1933, his contract obliged them to pay 100 percent of the money owed him, whereas others were only paid 35 percent; see CL4:319.

36. Shaw to Roy Limbert, 17 Sept. 1939; Theatrics 208.

37. Bernard Shaw, *Everybody's Political What's What?* (London: Constable, 1953), 353.

38. Shaw to the Sheffield Shaw Society, 31 Dec. 1943; CL4:687.

39. CL4:694.

40. See Allan Chappelow, *Shaw: "The Chucker Out": A Biographical Exposition and Critique* (London: Allen & Unwin, 1969), 473. Chappelow provides a copy of Shaw's last will and testament (473–523), together with excerpts from previous wills and codicils, and a *Times* (London) report of Mr. Justice Harman's judgment in the Proposed British Alphabet case.

41. Ibid., 482.

42. Ibid., 499.

43. Ibid., 507.

44. Ibid., 513.

45. In another ceremony of recognition in Ireland, a plaque honoring Shaw was unveiled in December 1947 at the childhood home of Torca Cottage, Dalkey, which held such happy memories for him.

46. Shaw to Charles Latham, 1st Baron Latham of Hendon, n.d. [c. 9 Oct. 1946]; CL4:781.

47. Shaw to F. E. Loewenstein, n.d. [c. 29 July 1946]; CL4:775.

48. Sir William Haley, "The Stripling and the Sage," in *G.B.S. 90: Aspects of Bernard Shaw's Life and Work*, ed. S. Winsten (London: Hutchinson, 1946), 170. For an excellent analysis of Shaw's early association with the corporation, see L. W. Conolly, "GBS and the BBC: In the Beginning (1923–1928)," *SHAW: The Annual of Bernard Shaw Studies*, vol. 23 (University Park: Penn State University, 2003) 75–116.

49. Alice Laden recollection; Villager 27.

50. Shaw to Gabriel Pascal, 8 Sept. 1947; CL4:801.

51. R. da Costa, "Pilgrimage to Bernard Shaw," *Palestine Post*, 14 Nov. 1947; I&R 523.

52. Cited in Richard Stoddard Aldrich, *Gertrude Lawrence as Mrs. A: An Intimate Biography* (London: Companion Book Club, 1956), 233–34; I&R 394.

53. Kingsley Martin, *Editor* (London: Hutchinson, 1968), 106–7; I&R 224–25.

54. I am grateful to J. P. Wearing for advising me in correspondence about the date of Nehru's visit to Shaw, which corrects that given in CL4:828. An account of the Nehru visit, together with the dating of it to the spring of 1949, is provided in Patch 106–8.

55. Shaw to Jawaharlal Nehru, 18 Sept. 1948; CL4:828.

56. Shaw to Sydney C. Cockerell, 27 July 1950.

57. Hayden Church, "GBS on the A-Bomb," *Reynolds News*, 6 Aug. 1950; I&R 485.

58. F. G. Prince-White, "'I Would Like to Go into My Garden' said Shaw," *Daily Mail*, 13 Oct. 1950; I&R 527.

59. Letter from Nancy Astor to Archibald Henderson, 25 Sept. 1951, in Hend3:874; I&R 531.

60. Eileen O'Casey, *Sean*, ed. J. G. Trewin (London: Macmillan, 1971), 209–10; I&R 530.

61. This is quoted in the account of Shaw's death and subsequent ceremonies provided by Dan H. Laurence in CL4:878–86. For further accounts, see also I&R 531–34.

62. Villager 36.

Acknowledgments

I was first introduced to the work of Bernard Shaw by the late G.F.J. ("Jack") Dart, the headmaster of the then very small Anglican grammar school I attended in Ballarat, Australia. A New Zealander by birth, Jack Dart was a man of exceptional qualities of mind—and a Shaw enthusiast. He produced several of Shaw's plays at the school while I was there; and, since it was not a coeducational institution at that time, boys had to play the female roles, as in Shakespeare's day. Thus, in my early teens I found myself playing—in a green dress borrowed from one of my sisters and a blonde wig hired from a local theater supplier—the role of the imperious Gloria Clandon in Shaw's early play *You Never Can Tell.* In later thespian activities at the school, I played the truculent trade union MP Bill Boanerges in *The Apple Cart* and the equally truculent horse thief Blanco in *The Shewing-Up of Blanco Posnet.* Since those days I have remained grateful to Jack Dart, my Shavian mentor and friend, for introducing me to a writer who has never ceased to fascinate me—even though he occasionally also infuriates me. Shaw has been part of my mental universe for a very long time.

A fairly long break in my reading of Shaw occurred when I went on from school to study successively at two universities. F. R. Leavis was a strong influence in many English departments in my undergraduate days, and Shaw was not a favored author in the Leavisite school of criticism. At my first alma mater, Melbourne University, I don't remember any of Shaw's plays being selected for study, though I did later discover that one of the staunchest supporters of Leavis at Melbourne, S. L. Goldberg, was a keen reader and admirer of Shaw. At my second alma mater, Oxford University, the Anglo-Saxon Chronicle and the eighth-century A.D. poem *Beowulf* tended to be much more fashionable topics of conversation than the works of later authors. Indeed, authors needed to be dead (in the literal sense) for at least fifty years, and their works had to have gained a mellow patina of age and respectability, before they were even considered for study. I seem to recall that Robert Browning was still a bit suspect. Shaw was out, but one of his most supportive critics, J.I.M. Stewart, was a don at Oxford in my time.

Oxford studies had led me down Renaissance paths, and it was not until I joined the staff of the English Department at the University of Leeds some years later that I had a reunion with the subject of the present book. One of the professors during my time at Leeds was the late A. N. ("Derry") Jeffares, the distinguished Yeats scholar and great catalyst of Irish studies, to whom I have been deeply indebted from early in my career. Derry Jeffares happened to be commissioning the last two titles in the *Writers and Critics* series of which he was general editor. He kindly invited me to write one of these, and gave me the choice of either Alexander Pope or Bernard Shaw. My choice of Shaw was the beginning of a very long scholarly association—including the writing and editing of numerous books on various aspects Shaw's life and career—during which I have incurred almost incalculable debts of gratitude to many individuals and institutions.

I am indebted to several people who have provided advice on the present work during its preparation. Professor Richard Dietrich closely followed the project from its very early stages and has been a wise and supportive counselor. My wife Donna has been infinitely patient in carrying out readings of work in progress, and has made astute and unfailingly helpful comments. Two readers appointed by the University Press of Florida supplied, as well as encouragement, expert advice and constructive criticism, which I was very happy to heed in revisions. I have also been grateful for incisive comments on the manuscript by Mary Cunnane. Over many years I have been one of the beneficiaries of Dan H. Laurence's well-known generosity to Shaw scholars, and I wish to record my thanks to him again here.

Research for the work was carried out with the aid of grants from the Australian Research Council and the Macquarie University Research Committee: I am grateful to both bodies for their support. In working on this and other Shavian research projects I have been helped by a number of research assistants at different times over a period of several years, and I express here my warm thanks to: Lyndy Abraham, Marcelle Freiman, Sue Kossew, the late Juliet McLean; Bernadette Masters, Julie-Anne Robson, Liam Semler, Jeremy Steele, Penny van Toorn, Geoffrey Windon, Annette Wong, and Ed Wright. I am grateful to many other people for assistance, information and encouragement, and I would like especially to thank: May-Brit Akerholt, Effy Alexakis, Peter Alexander, Ruth Amos, Tom Amos, Lawrence Aspden, Claudius Beatty, Stephen Bennett, John Bertolini, Janet Birkett, Sister Kathleen Bourne, Ron Bowles, Helen Boyd, Malcolm Brand, Terence Brown, David Lyne Browne, Lorne Bruce, Lucy Burgess, Tony Cousins, Margaret Clunies Ross, Sarah

Cobbold, Caroline Colton, Leonard Conolly, John Cowlie, the late Fred Crawford, the late Janet and Mac Crombie, Jeremy Crow, Brian and Rohma Cummins, Juliet and Phil Cummins, Peter Daerden, Ian Donaldson, Tamsin Donaldson, Sue Donnelly, Ralph Elliott, Roberta Engleman, Tom Evans, Catherine Fahy, Ann Ferguson, Ron Ford, Pat Fox, Adrian Frazier, Sam and James Gibbs, Jill Golzen, Peter Goodall, Eleanor Grene, Nicholas Grene, Jane Harrington, Elizabeth Harrison, Anna Hawker, Eileen Hoare, Richard and Meredith Hooper, Michael Hughes, the late Leon Hugo, Richard Ingrams, Kathryn Johnson, Michael Kenneally, Daniel Kevles, Elizabeth Killeen, Helen Jessup, Noel Kissane, Peter Kuch, Adrian Le Harival, Melo Lenox-Conyngham, Frances McCarthy, the late Oliver MacDonagh, Fred McDowell, Wayne McKenna, Neil McLean, Dawn Melhuish, Leslie Morris, Donald Morse, Simon Moss, Maureen Murphy, Rhoda Nathan, Margaret Nichols, Stuart Ó Seanóir, Norman Page, Paddy Pearl, Carl Peterson, Chris Petter, Graeme Powell, Michael Roe, Christina Rowe, Sally Ryan, Nancy Sadek, Philip Sargeant, Deryck Schreuder, Marion Shaw, Peter and Lee Shrubb, Barbara Smith, Robin Smith, Anne Summers, Ben Stone, John and Jill Stowell, Richard and Elizabeth Tottenham, Judy Truesdale, Eleanor Vallis, Greta Vashinsky, Annemieke Vimal du Monteil, Peter Wearing, Stanley and Rodelle Weintraub, Tara Wenger, Michael Wilding, Michelle Wilson, Melanie Wisener, Ron Withington, Karen Woo, the late Roma Woodnut, Helen Yardley, Giles Yates, and Di Yerbury. It has been a pleasure to work with the staff at the University Press of Florida.

Research for this book has been carried out in a large number of libraries and other archival centers worldwide. I am especially grateful to the staff of the following for assistance: Archives Division, British Library of Political and Economic Science; Archives Office of Tasmania; Auchmuty Library, University of Newcastle, NSW; Auckland Central Library; Australian National Library; Australian National University Library; Barr Smith Library, University of Adelaide; Bibliothèque de l'Arsenal, Paris; Bibliothèque Nationale de France; Billy Rose Theater Collection (NYPL Library for Performing Arts), Lincoln Center; Bodleian Library, Oxford; British Library Newspaper Collection, Colindale; British Library; Carlow County Library, Local Studies Section; Department of Archival and Special Collections, University of Guelph Library; Division of Rare and Manuscript Collections (Carl A. Kroch Library), Cornell University Library; Fitzwilliam Museum; Harry Ransom Humanities Research Center, University of Texas at Austin; Heritage Centre, Carrick-on-Suir, Co. Waterford; Houghton Library, Harvard; Kilkenny County Library; Macquarie University Library; Mander and Mitchenson Theatre Collection; Manuscripts Room, Trinity College Dublin Library; National Gallery of Ireland; National Library of Ireland; National Library of Scotland Manuscripts

Collection; National Portrait Gallery, London; New York Public Library; Nuffield College Library, Oxford; Royal Academy of Dramatic Art; Special Collections, Wheaton College; Shaw Museum, 33 Synge Street, Dublin; Shaw Photograph Room, Great Southern Hotel, Parknasilla; Shaw's Corner, Ayot St Lawrence, Hertfordshire; Special Collections, University College Dublin Library; State Library of New South Wales; State Library of Queensland; State Library of Victoria; The Fisher Library, University of Sydney; Theatre Museum, Covent Garden; Victoria and Albert Museum; Welwyn Garden City Library, Hertfordshire.

I am glad to acknowledge the kind permission of the following for use of the specified materials: The Society of Authors on behalf of the Shaw Estate for extracts from published and unpublished writings and the reproduction of juvenile sketches by Bernard Shaw; The Trustees of the Will of Mrs. Bernard Shaw for extracts from her writings; Time Warner Book Group for extracts from *The Diaries of Beatrice Webb*, edited by Norman and Jeanne MacKenzie; The Random House Group Limited for extracts from *The Diaries of Virginia Woolf*, published by the Hogarth Press; Dr. Claudius Beatty for extracts from letters by Shaw to Pakenham and Ida Beatty; The Royal Museum for Central Africa, Tervuren, for extracts from Shaw letters to Dorothy Tennant (Lady Stanley) in the Stanley Archive; The British Library of Political and Economic Science for reproduction of images from the Shaw collection, as indicated in the list of illustrations; The Dan H. Laurence Collection, University of Guelph Library, for reproduction of images from the collection, as indicated in the list of illustrations; The University of London Library for reproduction of an image of Florence Farr, MS 982; Getty Images for reproduction of images as indicated in the list of illustrations; The National Portrait Gallery for reproduction of the portrait of Sidney Webb, Baron Passfield, by Jessie Holliday, NPG 5938; The Fitzwilliam Museum for reproduction of No. 1071, "Portrait of George Bernard Shaw" by Augustus John; Mrs. Marion Shaw for reproduction of privately owned portraits and photographs in Tasmania. Every effort has been made to secure all necessary permissions. The author and publisher will be glad to recognize any holders of copyright who have not been acknowledged above.

Index

References in italics refer to illustrations.

Abbey Theatre, 246, 251–52; *Blanco Posnet* production, 260, 261–62, 284, 305, 306, 360; Lady Gregory and, 261, 264, 497n47; patent of, 261

Academy Award, Shaw's, 437

Achurch, Janet, *228*; alcoholism of, 157; as Candida, 157, 176, 186; correspondence with Shaw, 3, 176, 177, 500n61; death of, 447; in *A Doll's House*, 156; Richard Mansfield, 188–89; *Mrs Daintree's Daughter*, 168–69; relationship with Shaw, 120, 150, 156–57; and translations by, 243

Actresses' Franchise League, 298

Adelphi Play Society, 502n28

Adelphi Terrace: Max Beerbohm at, 498n14; Churchill at, 271, 498n14; Erica Cotterill at, 289; Granville-Barker at, 498n14; Lady Gregory at, 263; interior of, 271–72; luncheon parties at, 271, 498n14; Lillah McCarthy at, 273, 498nn14,18; move from, 514n4; Sean O'Casey at, 416; Blanche Patch at, 371; Charlotte Shaw at, 195, 200, 242; Shaw's residence at, 224; situation of, 269; Molly Tompkins at, 383; Mark Twain at, 271, 498n14; view from, 271

Adler, Friedrich: correspondence with Shaw, 395, 396, 397

The Adventures of the Black Girl in Her Search for God (Shaw), 404, 412–15; autobiography in, 413; composition of, 414; creative evolution in, 413, 415; Dame Laurentia McLachlan and, 375, 415; Voltaire in, 414–15

Aeronautical Society of Great Britain, 270

Aesthetic movement: in *Immaturity*, 86–87; Wilde in, 86, 263

Agate, James, 179, 442

Ahasuerus, legend of, 367, 509n6

Airplane flights, Shaw's, 270–71, 277

Alcoholism: Janet Achurch's, 157; Shaw on, 23–24; George Carr Shaw's, 19, 21, 23–24, 30, 465n25, 489n50

Allen, Grant, 199; at Hindhead Hall peace conference, 220

Allgood, Sara, 261, 328

Alphabet Trusts, Shaw's bequests for, 452–53, 519n40

Altman, Robert, 517n52

Amis, Kingsley, 395, 513n45

Androcles and the Lion (Shaw): as drama, 311; German productions of, 272; Lillah McCarthy in, 273; Mephistopheles theme in, 42; performances of, 313; phonetic translation of, 452; publication of, 331; religious themes of, 313

Anti-Semitism: Hitler's, 398, 443, 513n61; Shaw on, 398, 443; against *Too True to Be Good*, 513n60; Wagner's, 218

The Apple Cart (Shaw), 392–94; autocracy in, 394; Mrs. Patrick Campbell and, 321, 329, 392, 393, 512n41; democracy in, 393–94, 513n43; at Malvern Festival, 402; performances of, 432; premiere of, 379; Shaw's marriage and, 393; Molly Tompkins and, 392–93

The Arabian Nights, 52–53
Araki, Sadao, 410
Archer, Charles: *William Archer*, 485n18
Archer, Frances, 156
Archer, William, 166, *226*, 477n77; on *Arms and the Man*, 141; on *Back to Methuselah*, 140; bicycling by, 200; on censorship, 256; correspondence with Shaw, 3, 141, 186, 276, 345; in cowboy movie, 344–45; death of, 379; death of son, 350; and Ibsen, 140, 285; and Vandeleur Lee, 139; at *London Figaro*, 139; on *Man and Superman*, 140–41; marriage of, 156; on Nobel Prize, 375; patronage of Shaw, 139, 141; on Shaw's dramas, 179–80, 189, 483n11; Shaw's meeting with, 101; on Shaw's music criticism, 143–44; and Siegfried Trebitsch, 272; and *Widowers' Houses*, 101, 139, 140–41, 158–59, 483n10. Works: *English Dramatists of To-Day*, 178; *The Green Goddess*, 139–40; *The Old Drama and the New*, 140; *Three Plays*, 379
Aristophanes, *Lysistrata*, 294
Armageddon, 349, 506n21
Arms and the Man (Shaw): Archer on, 141; Pakenham Beatty and, 89; composition of, 170; dialogue of, 171–73; Farr and, 170, 171, 173; gender relations in, 121, 172–73, 297; New Woman in, 171–72; in New York, 174; performances of, 173, 174, 487n4; publication of, 152; reception of, 173; romantic conventions in, 98, 170–71, 173–74, 258; success of, 170, 171; Yeats on, 173, 258
Arms race, German-British, 283
Army, British: modernization of, 305
Arnold, Matthew: *On The Study of Celtic Literature*, 253
Arnot, R. Page, 170
"Art and Public Money" (Shaw), 500n59
Ashwell, Lena, 213; and *Heartbreak House*, 352–53; in *Misalliance*, 298; *Myself a Player*, 42; OBE of, 298, 347; and Charlotte Shaw, 298, 330; during World War I, 347
Asquith, Anthony, 433
Asquith, Herbert Henry, 274; at *John Bull's Other Island*, 251; and woman suffrage, 298, 304
Asquith, Margot, 181
Asquith, Violet, 274
Astor, Bobbie, 404–5, 514n17
Astor, Francis David, 404
Astor, Nancy Langhorne: Christian Science of, 405; and Churchill, 404, 406; correspondence with Shaw, 404–5, 416, 443; death of, 448; friendship with Shaw, 345, 404–6; husbands of, 406, 448, 514n17, 515n22; and Charlotte Shaw, 405; at Charlotte's funeral, 445; and Shaw's final illness, 457; Shaw's visits to, 93, 345, 405, 406, 444; trip to Russia, 406, 408
Astor, Waldorf, 406, 515n22
Atheism, Shaw's, 61, 267
Atom bomb, Shaw on, 456
Attlee, Clement, 419; Labour government of, 397
Auden, W. H., 36, 468n76
Auerbach, Nina: *Woman and the Demon*, 300
Augier, Émile, 158
Augustus Does His Bit (Shaw), 359
Austen, Jane: *Pride and Prejudice*, 83; *Sense and Sensibility*, 91
Australia: Shaw family in, 11–12, 462n10; woman suffrage in, 501n9
Autobiography: self-origination in, 464n1; Shaw on, 20. *See also* Shaw, George Bernard, autobiographical writings; *Sixteen Self Sketches*
Aveling, Edward Bibbins, 112–13, 207; theatrical performances by, 115; "The Woman Question," 123–24, 480n1
Aveling, Eleanor Marx, *228*; romance with Shaw, 120; suicide of, 112, 207; theatrical performances by, 115, 479n32; "The Woman Question," 123–24, 480n1
Ayot St Lawrence ("Shaw's Corner," Hertfordshire), 5, *426*, *428*; canaries at, 512n34; Erica Cotterill at, 289; curatorship of, 451; Lady Gregory's visits to, 263, 365; household of, 419–20; T. E. Lawrence at, 416; F. E. Loewenstein at, 450–51; longevity of townspeople, 242–43; in National Trust, 451; newsreels at, 377; Eileen O'Casey at, 417; Gabriel Pascal at, 438; purchase of, 495n30; Shaw's life at, 403–4, 418–21, 454–57; Shaws' move to, 270; Shaw's social position at, 12; John Wardrop at, 450–51; during World War I, 357–58; during World War II, 443–44; Yeats at, 262

Back to Methuselah (Shaw), 364–67, 392; Archer on, 140; Mrs. Patrick Campbell and, 328–30; composition of, 363, 364; dystopia in, 234; Edith Evans in, 366; evolution in, 234; flappers in, 365, 367; Lady Gregory and, 264, 365; humor in, 285; Ireland in, 249–50; landlordism in, 63; mobile phone in, 80; "negress" character in, 366, 413–14; productions of, 365–66; setting of, 365; sex in, 366–67; spiritualism in, 45; *Tragedy of an Elderly Gentleman*, 249–50, 266
Bacon, Francis, 235
Balfe, Michael: *The Bohemian Girl*, 96, 98
Balfour, Arthur J., 251, 281, 501n5; Conservative government of, 498n1
Balloon ascensions, Shaw's, 270
Balzac, Honoré de, 88
Bancroft, Marie, 77
Baring Gould, S.: *The Red Spider*, 223
Barrie, J. M., 318; cowboy movie of, 344–45; *Peter Pan and Wendy*, 329
Barry, Arthur Smith, 197
Barrymore, John, 410
Barton, James Kingston, 23, 80, 116
Basile, Carlo Emanuele, 396–97; Molly Tompkins and, 513n51; war crimes trial, 397
Battle of the Boyne, 8
Baughan, Edward A., 308
Bax, E. Belfort, 111, 143, 193
Bayreuth Festival, Shaw at, 158
BBC, Shaw and, 454, 519n48
Beatty, C.J.P., 475n30
Beatty, Cecilia Olivia, 90
Beatty, Ida, 28, 89; correspondence with Shaw, 3, 492n10
Beatty, Pakenham Thomas, 88–90, 140; background of, 475n30; correspondence with Shaw, 3, 88–89, 475n31; drinking habits of, 90; love poetry of, 476n38; and *Man and Superman*, 476n37; *Marcia*, 89, 476n38; *My Lady, and Other Poems*, 89, 476n38
Beatty, Pakenham William, 88
Beauty and the Beast (pantomime), 96
Beckett, Samuel, 83; *Waiting for Godot*, 311
Bedisloe, Viscount, 411
Beerbohm, Max: at Adelphi Terrace, 498n14; cartoons by, 329; cartoons of Pinero, 181, *229*; cartoons of Shaw, 40, *71*, 181, *229*, 469n23; on *Man and Superman*, 312; "Mr. Shaw's New Dialogues," 312; "Mr. Shaw's Position," 312–13; at *Saturday Review*, 503n13; on Shavian drama, 312–13; in Shaw Festschrift, 454; Shaw on, 209
Behrman, S. N.: *Conversations with Max*, 503n13
Bell, Alexander Graham, 79
Bell, Clive, 421
Bellini, Vincenzo: *I Puritani*, 391n
Belloc, Hilaire, 36, 213, 468n77; debate with Shaw, 320–21
Bennett, Arnold: on *Common Sense about the War*, 347; on Shaw's debates, 320–21
Benson, Arthur Christopher, 268
Bergson, Henri: *Creative Evolution*, 234–35, 236, 494n11; and Shaw, 235
"Bernard Shaw on Mussolini" *(Daily News)*, 395
Berst, Charles A.: "Passion at Lake Maggiore," 511n1, 512n31
Bertolini, John A.: *The Playwrighting Self of Bernard Shaw*, 516n50
Besant, Annie, 154, *228*; autobiography of, 129, 130; in "Bloody Sunday" demonstration, 129–30; correspondence with Shaw, 131, 136, 219; death of, 447; in Fabian Society, 108, 130; Irish identity of, 130; political activism of, 124, 129; relationship with Shaw, 120, 128–31, 133, 136; on sacrifice, 129, 481n26; Theosophy of, 131, 143, 158
Besant, Frank, 124, 131
Biard, Henri Charles, 270–71
Black, Grace, 108, 132
"Blackdown Cottage" (Haslemere), 242, 243
"Black Monday" demonstrations (1886), 481n3
Blake, William: on Christian God, 235; influence on Shaw, 192–93, 259, 283; *The Marriage of Heaven and Hell*, 192, 282
Bland, Hubert, 111, 278
Bland, Rosamund, 278, 279, 499n38
Blathwayt, Raymond, 485n28
Blavatsky, Helena Petrovna, 142; *The Secret Doctrine*, 131, 143.
"Bloody Sunday" demonstration (1887), 129–30, 481n26
Bloomsbury circle, 357
Boanerges (motorcycle), 416, 516n52

Boer War, 239; Hugh Cholmondeley in, 242; Fabian Society during, 241; second, 364; Shaw on, 241, 242
Bohemianism, Lucy's attitude toward, 96–97, 468n72
Bolshevo (Russia), model colony at, 408, 515n35
Borromeo, Princess, 396
Boucicault, Dion: *The Colleen Bawn*, 253, 512n39; *The Corsican Brothers*, 55, 472n81
Bowlby, Dr., 220
Brahms, Johannes, 174, 487n12
Brecht, Bertolt: *Die Dreigroschenoper*, 406
Brennan, Alice Maude, 48
Brentano's (publisher), 448, 519n35
Brett, Reginald Baliol, 181
Bridie, James, 454
Bright, R. Golding, 173
British Alphabet, Proposed, 452–53, 519n40
British Association for the Advancement of Science, 484n36; Shaw's lecture at, 148
British Library of Political and Economic Science, 451. *See also* London School of Economics
British Museum, Shaw's bequest to, 452
Brooke, Emma, 132
Brooke, Rupert, 288
Brough, Fanny, 166
Browning, Robert: "Home Thoughts from Abroad," 326n
Bryant & May (matchstick firm), 218; strike at, 129
Bryce, Annan, 501n10
Buchanan, Robert, 153, 484n2
Bunyan, John, 149; idealism of, 282; *Pilgrim's Progress*, 41–42, 52, 118, 167, 169, 231, 458; Shaw on, 469n30; in *Too True to Be Good*, 435
Buoyant Billions (Shaw), 435; composition of, 449; orientalism in, 53, 412; performance of, 435, 455
Burglary: capitalism as, 378; in Shaw's plays, 148
Burke, Edmund, 233, 494n9
Burne-Jones, Philip, 328
Bushy Park House (Terenure), 9, 10, *69*
Butler, Samuel: *Luck or Cunning?*, 134, 142, 234, 236, 494n17
Butterfield, Charles Robert, 15, 33; death of, 370
Byatt, A. S.: *Possession*, 1
Byron, Lord, 53

Caesar and Cleopatra (Shaw), 219–20; autocracy in, 394; composition of, 208, 217; film of, 438; Vivien Leigh in, 454; publication of, 152; self-portrait in, 220; Yeats on, 219
Calthrop, Dion Clayton, 326
Calvert, Louis, 190; in *Major Barbara*, 280–81, 283
Calypso *(Odyssey)*, 512n37; Molly Tompkins as, 391
"Calypso" (poem, Shaw), 47–48, 121, 391
"Calypso" (sketch, Shaw), *73*, 391
Cambridge, Duke of, 305
Cambridge University, 279; Fabian Society of, 278
Campbell, Alan Hugh ("Beo"), 315; death of, 264, 350, 362, 508n59
Campbell, Lady Colin, 165
Campbell, Helen (Mrs. Alan), 322
Campbell, Mrs. Patrick (Stella), *341*; affair with Shaw, 146, 185, 220, 287, 298, 300, 314–15, 317–29, 353–54; and *The Apple Cart*, 321, 329, 392, 393, 512n41; automobile accident, 318, 507n36; and *Back to Methuselah*, 328–30; as Cleopatra, 220; correspondence with Shaw, 11, 29, 220, 314, 315, 316, 317–19, 321, 322, 323–24, 326–29, 333, 354, 372, 389–90, 399, 447, 448, 501n13, 504n33, 517n11; death of son, 264, 350, 362, 508n59; early life of, 315; as Electra, 353; as Eliza Doolittle, 314, 316–17, 330–31, 332, 335; and *Heartbreak House*, 322, 328, 351, 353; in *The Hunchback*, 315; illnesses of, 319, 321; last years and death, 447–48, 519n33; love of reading, 315; and Lucy, 328; marriage to Cornwallis-West, 315, 325; marriage to Patrick Campbell, 315; maternalism of, 303; mimicry by, 322; as Mrs. Tanqueray, 146, 180, 316; *My Life and Some Letters*, 329; nickname for Shaw, 321–22, 327; in *The Notorious Mrs. Ebbsmith*, 316; as Ophelia, 179, 316, 317; parents of, 315; personality of, 328; pet dogs, 354, 447, 507n36; poverty of, 447; publication of letters, 389–90, 448; and Charlotte Shaw, 322, 390, 448, 505n41; and Shaw's cowboy movie, 345; on suffragettes, 322; teasing

of Shaw, 321; theatrical career, 315–16, 448; as Vampire, 328–29, 353
Campbell, Stella (daughter of Mrs. Patrick), 315, 318
Campbell-Bannerman, Sir Henry, 251
Candida (Shaw): Janet Achurch in, 157, 176, 186; dualism in, 301; marriage in, 203; motherhood in, 186–87; productions of, 176, 244; publication of, 152; romantic triangles in, 131; Shaw's self-interview on, 311; sources for, 489n29
Cannan, Gilbert, 308
Capitalism: American, 410; as burglary, 378; in *Heartbreak House*, 351; in *The Intelligent Woman's Guide*, 394; Shaw on, 41, 240, 350, 380, 409, 410; in South Africa, 241
Captain Brassbound's Conversion (Shaw), 260; cleverness in, 3–4; composition of, 221; mother figures in, 33, 187; publication of, 152; setting of, 53; sources for, 89, 184; Ellen Terry and, 33, 184, 185–86, 221, 222
Carla Rosa Opera Company, 96
Carlisle, Earl of, 45
Carlow (Ireland): Assembly Rooms, 13, 462n24; Shaw's property at, 451
Carlyle, Thomas: *Sartor Resartus*, 236
Carpenter, Edward, 132; *The Intermediate Sex*, 123
Carr, Reverend Edward, 9
Carroll, William George, 15, 461n1; Shaw's lessons with, 37, 39
Carton, R. C., 348
Casement, Sir Roger: Shaw's defense of, 265; trial of, 360
Cashel Byron's Profession (Shaw), 95, 98–100, 101, 138; composition of, 81, 478n75; publication of, 82, 115; romantic conventions in, 98; sexual themes in, 99; sources for, 89, 100; women characters in, 81
Cashin, Margaret ("Maggie" Smith), 419, 420, *426*, 442; and Shaw's last illness, 456
Casson, Lewis, 374
The Cassone (fragment, Shaw), 156
Catholicism: role in Irish life, 259; Shaw's exposure to, 8, 44, 46, 470n44
"Celebrities at Home . . . Mr George Bernard Shaw in Adelphi Terrace" *(World)*, 271
Celibacy: in Shaw's marriage, 216–17, 275, 390; in Shaw's relationships, 121–22
Censorship: English, 260, 261, 262, 305; Irish, 261–62, 284; Shaw's "rejected statement" on, 305; Wilde on, 256. *See also* Abbey Theatre, *Blanco Posnet* production
Central Europe, Shaw's plays in, 307
Central Model Boys' School (Dublin), 38–39, 47
Chaliapin, Fyodor Ivanovich, 406
Chamberlain, Joseph, 111
Chamberlain, Neville, 442
Champion, Henry Hyde, 7, 82; Shaw's meeting with, 101
Chant, Laura Ormiston, 489n29
Chaplin, Charles, 345, 402, 410; at Cliveden, 406
Chappelow, Allan, 27, 418, 454
Chappelow, Grace, 27–28
Charcot, Jean-Martin, 198
Charrington, Charles, 156, 157, 368
Chauffeurs, Shaw's, 270
Chekhov, Anton, 179, 351; *The Cherry Orchard*, 302; influence on Shaw, 301, 302–3; *Uncle Vanya*, 302–3
Cherry-Garrard, Apsley, 365
Chesterton, G. K., 116, 269; in cowboy movie, 344–45; debates with Shaw, 320
Children: Charlotte Shaw on, 59, 188, 217, 418, 473n8; Shaw's talks for, 221
Cholmondeley, Hugh, 197, 198; in Boer War, 242
Cholmondeley, Mary Stewart Payne-Townshend ("Sissy"), 58, 75, *197*, 509n1; balloon ascension of, 270; at *Blanco Posnet* performance, 262, 306; and Boer War, 242; and *The Intelligent Woman's Guide to Socialism*, 379; Charlotte Shaw's visits with, 198; Shaw and, 213; travel with Shaw, 305, 319
Christian Science, Nancy Astor's, 405
Christian Socialist, Shaw's reviews for, 108
Churchill, Jenny, 325
Churchill, Winston, 325; at Adelphi Terrace, 271, 498n14; and Nancy Astor, 404, 406; "Bernard Shaw—Saint, Sage and Clown," 376; on Hitler's achievements, 513n59; and Violet Pond, 419; as prime minister, 398
Churton Braby, Mrs. Maud, 293–94, 297
Citizenship, Irish: Shaw's, 195, 490n2

"Civilisation and the Soldier" (Shaw), 238, 239, 268
Civilization, English: Shaw on, 240
Civilization, non-European: influence on Shaw, 411–13
Class system: Irish, 6, 59; in *Pygmalion*, 25; Shaw on, 34–36
Claudius, Agnes, 448
Clery, General, 197–99
Cleverness, Shaw on, 3–4
Clibborn, George, 15, 50
Clibborn and Shaw (firm), 15
Cliveden, 515n20; Shaw's visits to, 93, 345, 405, 406, 444, 477n56; visitors to, 406
Clyman, Rhea G., 516n41
Coates, Albert, 387
Cobbett, William: *Rural Rides*, 142
Cockerell, Sidney: correspondence with Shaw, 223, 446; and T. E. Lawrence, 472n5; and Dame Laurentia McLachlan, 374, 401; at Shaw's funeral, 41, 458
Coleridge, Samuel Taylor: "Rime of the Ancient Mariner," 53, 442
Collected Letters (Shaw), 201
Collins, Michael, 58, 472n6
Collins, Wilkie, 487n3; *The Evil Genius*, 142
Comedy, Shaw on, 153, 285–86
"Coming Men: Mr. G. Bernard Shaw" (*London Figaro*), 137, 138
Common Sense About the War (Shaw), 1, 182, 346–47, 349; public reaction to, 347, 360
The Common Sense of Municipal Trading (Shaw), 206, 480n42
Communism: among intellectuals, 395, 513n45; disenchantment with, 408–9; Shaw's opinion of, 408, 409
The Complete Plays of Bernard Shaw, 331
Comte, Auguste: positivism of, 255; *Système de Politique Positive*, 235–36
Conolly, Leonard W.: *Bernard Shaw and Barry Jackson*, 514n9; "GBS and the BBC," 519n48
Conradi, Peter J., 513n45
Coole Park, Shaw's visits to, 263, 306, *342*, 360, 441
Corkery, Daniel, 495n2
Corn Laws, repeal of, 31
Corno di Bassetto, Shaw as, 138, 143, 483n22
Cornwallis-West, George Frederick M., 315, 325; financial problems of, 327
Costume, women's: Shaw on, 297
Cotterill, Charles Clement: *Human Justice for Those at the Bottom*, 288
Cotterill, Erica, *340*; autobiographical works, 288; correspondence with Shaw, 288, 290, 299; and *Heartbreak House*, 351, 354–55; *A Professional Socialist*, 288; relationship with father, 290; relationship with Shaw, 288–91, 354–55; Socialism of, 288
Coward, Noel, 318; *Private Lives*, 504n16
Cowper, William: "John Gilpin," 53
Cromwell, Oliver, 17, 18, 463n40
Cuchulain (Irish hero), 497n40
Cunninghame Graham, R. B., 26, 221
Cusack, Cyril, 190
Cymbeline Refinished (Shaw), 185

Dalkey (Ireland): Shaw family at, 7, 38, 40, 43, 45, 47, 361; in Shaw's imagination, 266
Dana, Henry Wadsworth Longfellow, 408
Dancing, Shaw on, 368–69
Davidson, Majory G. ("Minnie," Mrs. Edward Pease), 482n28
Davidson, Thomas, 109
Davies, Marion, 410
Day, Frances, 455
Day, Frederick William, 420
Dearmer, Geoffrey, 371
Death, Shaw on, 115–16
Deck, Richard, 77, 79
Democracy: in *The Apple Cart*, 393–94, 513n43; failure of, 397; in *Misalliance*, 393–94
Derry House (Rosscarbery), 57–58, *69*, 195, 472n2; Shaw at, 280
Des Vouex, Dr. Harold, 369
De Valera, Eamon, 417, 451
The Devil's Disciple (Shaw), 191–93, 200, 260; autobiography in, 189; composition of, 191; Dickensian elements in, 54; Forbes-Robertson and, 316; good and evil in, 193; Mansfield and, 189; melodrama conventions in, 188; in New York, 189; Protestantism in, 192; publication of, 152; sources for, 192–93; success in America, 212
Devolution, Irish. *See* Home Rule
Devonport, Lord, 507n25

De Walden, Lord Howard, 344
Dickens, Charles: education in, 38; influence on Shaw, 54, 192; *Little Dorrit*, 192, 507n25
Dickinson, G. Lowes, 159–60
Dietrich, Richard F., 85; *Bernard Shaw's Novels*, 474n13
Dipsomania, in *The Irrational Knot*, 23. *See also* Alcoholism
The Doctor's Dilemma (Shaw), 116, 284, 285–87; humor in, 286–87; Lillah McCarthy in, 273, 275, 499n24; Shakespearian allusion in, 286–87; sources for, 112
Doheny, Michael, 62
Dolmetsch, Mabel, 33
"Don Giovanni Explains" (Shaw), 133–36, 482nn44,46
Don Juan, Shaw's identification with, 103, 136. *See also Man and Superman*, "Don Juan in Hell"
Donnelly, Ned, 89
Dougherty, Sir James, 261
Douglas, Lord Alfred ("Bosie"), 58, 246; correspondence with Shaw, 417–18; friendship with Shaw, 416, 417; *Ireland and the War Against Hitler*, 417; teetotalling of, 417; and Oscar Wilde, 257–58, 417
Doyle, Arthur Conan, 221
Drama, Shavian: Archer on, 179–80, 189, 483n11; Max Beerbohm on, 312–13; burglary in, 148; in Central Europe, 307; comedy in, 311, 432; conclusions of, 311; critical reception of, 307–13; critical studies of, 269; dialogue in, 311; didacticism of, 496n25; Edwardian, 268–69, 284, 287, 291; effect on Victorian society, 268; films of, 437–39, 506n4; gender roles in, 297–300; German translations of, 272, 307; influence of travel on, 411–13; of last years, 431–37; Mansfield's productions of, 145, 174, 176, 188, 189; mother figures in, 33, 186–87; naturalism in, 431; New Woman in, 300–301; in old age, 431–37; passion in, 259; political influence of, 268; revivals of, 432–33, 437; surrealism in, 431–32; textual history of, 439; in United States, 145, 174, 189, 212, 307, 359; Wilde on, 432; women characters of, 300–301; during World War I, 359–60. *See also titles of individual plays*
Dramatic Review, Shaw's music criticism for, 115
Dramatists' Club: censuring of Shaw, 348; Shaw's resignation from, 349
Drinkwater, John, 402
Drury, Fred, 420, 421
Drury, Thomas, 420
Drysdale, Jane ("Janey") Crichton, 33, 78, 122, 369
Drysdale, Learmont, 223
Dublin, 5–7; Easter Rising, 249, 265, 360, 472n6; English Scientific and Commercial Day School, 39; Four Courts, 8, 14, 462n6; Municipal Gallery of Modern Art, 360; National Library and Art Gallery, 5–6, 45, 452, 470n51, 471n79; poverty in, 30–31; Shaw as Freeman of, 245, 453; Shaw on, 6; Theatre Royal, 54–55
Dublin Castle, censorship by, 261, 262, 284, 360. *See also* Abbey Theatre, *Blanco Posnet* production
Dukore, Bernard F., 435, 517n11
Dulanty, John W., 453
Dumas, Alexandre (fils): *La Dame aux Camélias*, 167–68
Dumas, Alexandre (père), 53
Dunbar, Janet, 197
Dunne, Frank, 39

Easter Rising (Dublin, 1916), 249, 472n6; executions following, 265; Shaw on, 360
Edison, Thomas Alva, 79
Edison Telephone Company, Shaw at, 80, 96
Education Acts (1902–03), 267, 498n1
Edward VII (king of England), 174; coronation of, 268; death of, 284; at *John Bull's Other Island*, 251
Edward VIII (prince of Wales), 513n59
Einstein, Albert, 377, 435
Elder, Ann M., 371
Elgar, Edward, 402, *426*; *Enigma Variations*, 458; *The Music Makers*, 458; *Pomp and Circumstance* Overture, 268
Eliot, T. S.: on *Saint Joan*, 295, 374; on Shaw, 269, 461n2; *The Waste Land*, 350
Elizabeth (queen consort of George VI), *426*
Elliot, Denholm, 455
Ellis, Havelock, 123
Elvey, Maurice, 302, 502n28

Emery, Edward, 150
Emery, Florence. *See* Farr, Florence
Emotions, Shaw's view of, 82–83
Empress of Britain, SS, 401–2, 410, 435
England: arms race with Germany, 283; class system in, 34–35, 108; stage censorship in, 260, 261, 262, 305; woman suffrage in, 501n9
Ervine, Leonora ("Nora"), correspondence with Shaw, 431, 433, 435
Ervine, St. John, 2, 17, 461n2; correspondence with Shaw, 7, 362–63; on Bessie Shaw, 465n14; on Charlotte Shaw's death, 445; on Shaw's marriage, 214; wartime injuries of, 362–63
Esher, Viscount, 181
Evans, Edith: in *Back to Methuselah*, 366; in *The Millionairess*, 433
Everybody's Political What's What? (Shaw), 449, 450
Evolution, creative, 3, 134, 140, 142, 452, 504n31; in *The Adventures of the Black Girl*, 413, 415; Bergson on, 234–35, 236, 494n11; Butler on, 134, 142, 234, 236, 494n17; Life Force in, 232; in *Man and Superman*, 231, 232; Nietzsche's influence on, 236; in *The Perfect Wagnerite*, 232, 235; pessimism in, 234; in *The Shewing-up of Blanco Posnet*, 261; in *The Simpleton of the Unexpected Isles*, 436; Superman in, 235; teleological goal of, 232
Evolution, Darwinian, 134, 234; Butler on, 494n17; Mendelian genetics in, 237; natural selection in, 236; Shaw on, 236, 350

Fabian Feminist (essays), 502n21
Fabianism and the Empire (manifesto), 241
Fabian Society: aims of, 109–10, 478n21; during Boer War, 241; of Cambridge University, 278; formation of, 109; gradualism of, 399; membership of, 36, 108, 110–11, 478n19; of New Zealand, 411; "Old Gang" of, 278, 447; Charlotte Shaw in, 108, 196, 204, 344; Shaw's entrance into, 36, 107; Shaw's lectures at, 107–8, 114–15, 309, 478n5; Shaw's role in, 265, 267; summer school, 368, 384; Wells and, 277–78; women members of, 108, 132–33, 149; younger members, 278, 368
The Fabian Society: What It Has Done & How It Has Done It (Shaw), 379
Fabius Maximus Cunctator, Quintus, 109–10
Fanny's First Play (Shaw), 277, 307–10; autobiography in, 309; composition of, 306; Lillah McCarthy in, 273; parent-child relationships in, 290, 308; performances of, 308; Socialism in, 291; success of, 307–8; theater critics in, 308, 310
Farfetched Fables (Shaw), 432
Farleigh, John, 413
Farmer, H. G., 214
Farr, Florence: acting skills of, 162; affair with Shaw, 119, 120, 127, 128, 133, 149, 150, 160–63, 167, 174–76, 217, 480n2; and *Arms and the Man*, 170, 171, 173; conversations with Shaw, 441; death of, 447; *Egyptian Magic*, 175; meeting with Shaw, 480n2; and May Morris, 150, 163; mysticism of, 162, 175; in Order of the Golden Dawn, 171, 175; and *The Philanderer*, 161, 164; political activism of, 124; possessiveness of, 219; separation from husband, 150; sexuality of, 160; Shaw's disappointment with, 187; in Shaw's will, 451; in *A Sicilian Idyll*, 227, 512n38; in *Widowers' Houses*, 158–59, 160; and Yeats, 162, 258
Fascism: Shaw's attitude toward, 263, 395–99, 436; Yeats and, 263
Fascists, Italian: control of northern Italy, 397; Shaw's meeting with, 395, 396
Fawcett, Millicent, 295
Fay, W. G., 252
Fellowship of the New Life, 109, 123
Fellowship of the Way, 506n75
Fenianism, 62
Fiction, nineteenth-century. *See* Novels, Shaw's
Fielding, Henry: *Tom Jones*, 248
Finch Hatton, David, 197
Fishbourne, Robert Moore, 72
Fisher, Barbara M., 503n3
Fitch, Clyde: *Beau Brummel*, 189
Fitzgerald, Desmond, 249
Fitzgerald, F. Scott: *Flappers and Philosophers*, 367
Fitzgerald, Mabel W.: correspondence with Shaw, 249, 495n10
Fitzroy Square (London), 212, 214–15, 473n2; move to, 77, 151; singing lessons at, 27

Flappers: in *Back to Methuselah*, 365, 367; Fabian, 368
Fleming, George: *Andromeda*, 143
Forbes, George, 411
Forbes-Robertson, Johnston, 179; as Caesar, 219; and *The Devil's Disciple*, 316; as Hamlet, 316; and *Pygmalion*, 316–17
Forster, E. M., 441; *Howards End*, 268, 279–80, 498n9; *The Longest Journey*, 500n60
Foster, Roy, 62, 472n7
Fox, George, 510n21
Fox, James, 514n17
Foy, Joseph, 50, 470n65
France, Anatole, 375
Francis Ferdinand (archduke of Austria), 345
Fraser, Malcolm, 509n4
Fry, Roger, 356
Frye, Eva, 112, 207
"The Future of Political Science in America" (address, Metropolitan Opera House), 147, 402, 410–11

Gable, Clark, 410
Gabor, Zsa Zsa, 104, 478n6
Gambogi, Elvira, 183
Gay, John: *Beggar's Opera*, 149, 406
G.B.S. 90: Aspects of Bernard Shaw's Life and Work (festschrift), 454
"GBS Speaks to the Universe" (broadcast), 377
Geary, Sir William, 267
Gender relations: in *Arms and the Man*, 121, 172–73, 297; in *Heartbreak House*, 328, 352, 353–55, 507n35; in *Mrs. Warren's Profession*, 297; in *The Philanderer*, 121, 297; in Shaw's nondramatic writings, 296–97
Gender roles: in *Press Cuttings*, 303; in Shaw's dramas, 297–300; Victorian, 3, 121, 123–24, 173
Genetics, Mendelian, 237
Geneva (Shaw): League of Nations in, 399, 449; at Malvern Festival, 402; revisions to, 449
George, Henry, 100, 101
George VI (king of England), *426*
Georgina (dog), 332, 354, 507n36
Georgite Land Reform Union, 100
Gershwin, George: *Porgy and Bess*, 367
Getting Married (Shaw), 284, 287–88, 294, 298, 323; as conversation drama, 311; dialogue of, 299; lesbianism in, 299; women characters in, 301
Gibbs, Philip: *The Pageant of the Years*, 361, 362
Gilbert and Sullivan: *The Mikado*, 7; *Patience*, 86, 87, 263
Gilchrist, Grace, 108, 132
Gillmore, Arabella ("Moila") Gurly, 479nn35–36; and Jenny Patterson, 14
Gillmore, Georgina (Mrs. Judy Musters), 14, 249, 362, 479n35; and woman suffrage, 295
Gillmore, John, 14
Girton College (Cambridge), 123
The Glimpse of Reality (Shaw), 305
Globe Theater (Newcastle Street), 145, 484n29
God: Blake on, 235; immanence of, 235, 237, 350; Shaw's conception of, 235, 350
Goethe, Johann Wolfgang von: *Faust*, 218; *Wilhelm Meister's Apprenticeship*, 85
Goldilocks (fairy tale), 507n38
Golding, William: *The Lord of the Flies*, 1–2
Goldsmith, Oliver, 400
Goodliffe, Grace, 464n38
Goodliffe, Guy V., 464n38
Gordon, John Campbell (earl of Aberdeen), 261, 262
Gosford Park (film), 517n52
Gould, Nutcombe, 220
Gounod, Charles: *Faust*, 39–40, 42, 173, 238, 469n33
Gourlay, James, 13–14
Graham, John: portrait of Shaw, *430*
Granger, Stewart, 438
Granville-Barker, Harley, 153, 310, *338*; at Adelphi Terrace, 498n14; balloon ascension of, 270; in *Candida*, 244; correspondence with Shaw, 171, 314; cowboy movie of, 344–45; as Jack Tanner, 243, 274; in *John Bull's Other Island*, 244; in *Major Barbara*, 281; marriage to Helen Huntington, 276, 362; marriage to Lillah McCarthy, 243–44, 274; in *Mrs. Warren's Profession*, 166; national theater campaign, 306; at Royal Court Theatre, 244; Shakespearian scholarship of, 243; and Charlotte Shaw, 362, 508n61; Shaw's meeting with, 243; Shaw's visits to, 326; travels with Shaw, 325–26; and *Votes for Women!*, 295, 501n1

Great Catherine (Shaw), 326
Great Exhibition (London), 6
Great Famine (Ireland, 1845–49), 30, 467n53
Greene, Arthur, 11
Gregory, Lady Augusta, 252, 260; and the Abbey Theatre, 261, 264, 497n47; and *Back to Methuselah*, 264, 365; and *Blanco Posnet* controversy, 262, 264, 269, 306; death of son, 264, 350, 362; Shaw's visits to, 263, 306, 342, 360, 441; visits to Shaw, 263, 365; *Workhouse Ward*, 262
Gregory, Major Robert: death of, 264, 350, 362
Grein, Jacob Thomas, 152, 159, 166, 256
Grene, Nicholas, 247; *Bernard Shaw: A Critical View*, 510n42
Grenfell, Joyce, 93–94
Grey, Sir Edward, 349
Grosvenor Gallery (London), 475n22; Shaw on, 86
Grundy, Sydney, 153
Gurly, Emily Jane Walton, 14; Shaw's correspondence with, 105
Gurly, Georgina ("young Georgie"), 14, 160
Gurly, Lucinda Whitcroft, 14
Gurly, Walter Bagnall, 13, 14
Gurly, Walter John, 13, 14, 67; legacy to Shaw, 222; Shaw on, 19, 43; youth of, 463n25
Gurly family, 13–14, 477n68; Shaw's assistance to, 463n27

Haggard, Rider: *She*, 502n22
Haig, Field Marshal Sir Douglas, 361–62
Haley, Sir William, 454
Hall, Sir Peter, 166
Hallström, Per, 375
Hamilton, Cicely: *How the Vote Was Won*, 303
Hammond, Bertha, 406
Hamon, Augustin, 376
Hanson, Lady Constance Geraldine, 50
Hardy, Thomas, 375
Harlequin Puss in Boots (pantomime), 55
Harman, Justice, 453, 519n40
Harris, Frank: *Bernard Shaw: An Unauthorised Biography*, 103, 493n24; biography of Oscar Wilde, 417; correspondence with Shaw, 6, 56, 103, 256, 389, 493n30, 512n31; *My Life and Loves*, 103; sexual exploits of, 486n32; and Oscar Wilde, 257–58
Harris, Helen O'Hara ("Nellie"), 417
Harris, Mrs. (housekeeper), 27, 466n42
Harris, Nathaniel, 465n14
Harrison, Rex, 438
Hauptmann, Gerhart: *Das Friedensfest*, 243
Hawthorne, Nathaniel: *The Scarlet Letter*, 189
Hearst, William Randolph, 410
Heartbreak House (Shaw), 58, 350–59, 385; allusions in, 351; apocalyptic themes in, 350–51, 352, 357, 507n27; Lena Ashwell and, 352–53; autobiography in, 355, 413; burglary in, 148; Mrs. Patrick Campbell and, 322, 328, 351, 353; capitalism in, 351; composition of, 349, 352, 353, 355, 507n30; Erica Cotterill and, 351, 354–55; dialogue of, 357; Dickensian elements in, 54; gender relations in, 328, 352, 353–55, 507n35; Lady Gregory and, 264; "How War Muzzles the Dramatic Poet," 358–59; imperialism in, 351; mother figures in, 33; nature in, 350; in New York, 359; parent-child relationships in, 291; performances of, 358–59; pessimism of, 283; poverty in, 30; provisional title of, 143; public themes in, 351; reception of, 359; risk-taking in, 277; sources for, 88, 143, 289–90, 352–55; spiritualism in, 45; stage history of, 353; Strindberg's influence on, 302; vampire imagery in, 328, 353; women characters in, 301; Virginia Woolf and, 356
Hellenic Travellers' Club, 401
Helmsley, Charles, 173
Helpmann, Robert, 433
Henderson, Archibald, 2, 82, 162, 375; at Adelphi Terrace, 271; on Bessie, 26; biographies of Shaw, 461n2; correspondence with Shaw, 496n35, 500n63, 502n24; "George Bernard Shaw Self-Revealed," 484n2; on Shaw family, 20; on Shaw's manuscripts, 475n15; and Shaw's residences, 473n2
Hepburn, Katherine, 433
Hewins, William Albert Samuel, 211, 220
Hidveghy, Valerie, 438
Higgs, Henry ("Harry"), 270, 419, 420
Hill, Caroline, 37
Hiller, Wendy, 437–38
Hindhead Hall, peace conference at, 220
Hitler, Adolf: anti-Semitism of, 398, 443,

513n61; Churchill on, 513n59; invasion of Poland, 443; Lloyd George on, 513n59; Shaw's attitude toward, 394, 397, 398
Hoatson, Alice, 111
Hobhouse, Margaret (Maggie), 223, 239, 299
Hobson, Samuel George, 278
Hoey, John Cashel, 12
Hoey, Mrs. Cashel, 12
Hoffmann, E.T.A.: *Don Juan*, 134
Holroyd, Michael, 2, 214, 461n2, 465n15; on George Carr Shaw, 465n25; on *Overruled*, 504n16; psychoanalytical approach of, 467n66
Home, Risden H., 474n10
Homer: *Iliad*, 351
Home Rule, for Ireland, 265, 361, 455
Homosexuality: fundamentalist attacks on, 515n18; Shaw on, 404–5
Hopkins, Frances, 403
Hopkins, T. Tighe, 119–20; correspondence with Shaw, 152–53
Horan, Florence, 457
Hornberg, Ultima, 199
The Hornet (weekly), Shaw's music criticism for, 78, 79
Horniman, Annie Elizabeth Frederika: patronage of Shaw, 171
The Household of Joseph (Shaw), 79, 231
Housman, A. E., 402
Howard, Leslie, 437, 438
Howell, Gwendoline, 457
"How to Become a Music Critic" (Shaw), 143
Huddart, Elinor L., 85; correspondence with Shaw, 106, 478n75; friendship with Shaw, 87–88; on *The Irrational Knot*, 87; novels of, 87; singing lessons of, 87
Hugo, Leon, 494n21
Human, Edwin, 132
Huntington, Helen (Mrs. Granville-Barker), 276, 362
Hutton, Major, 197
Huxley, Aldous, 454; *Brave New World*, 234
Huxley, Thomas Henry, 476n49
Hyndman, Henry Mayers, 36; *England for All*, 109

Ibsen, Henrik, 283, 484n2; attacks on, 485n26; death themes in, 285; influence on Shaw, 153–56; Shaw's obituary for, 285; themes of, 155. Works: *A Doll's House*, 112, 126, 154, 155, 285, 479n32; *Emperor and Galilean*, 218; *Ghosts*, 159–60, 485n26; *The Lady from the Sea*, 150; *The Master Builder*, 162, 288–89; *Peer Gynt*, 154, 155, 218; *The Pillars of Society*, 140; *The Wild Duck*, 154–55. *See also The Quintessence of Ibsenism*
Ibsenism, 153–56, 274; morality in, 155; in *The Philanderer*, 154; Wilde on, 255, 256
"The Illusions of War" (Shaw), 248
Immaturity (Shaw): Aesthetic movement in, 86–87; composition of, 79; emigration to London in, 63–64; *Hamlet* in, 84; Ireland in, 6, 247–48; marriage in, 83–84, 186; Mephistopheles in, 39; publication of, 82; rejection by publishers, 82, 83; reviews of, 82; revisions to, 85; self-portraiture in, 84–86; sources for, 90; Victorian society in, 84; Oscar Wilde in, 256
Imperialism, 240; in *Heartbreak House*, 351; Shaw on, 241; in *The Simpleton of the Unexpected Isles*, 435–36
"The Impossibilities of Anarchism" (Shaw), 477n69
The Inca of Perusalem (Shaw), 359
Incest, and patriarchy, 168
Income: equality of, 381; Shaw's, 151, 212, 215, 222, 418, 492n7
Independent Theatre (London), 152
India: Charlotte Shaw's visits to, 197, 271, 412; Shaw on, 455; Shaw's visit to, 412
Industrial Revolution, 6
Inge, Dean, 454
In Good King Charles's Golden Days (Shaw), 449; at Malvern Festival, 402
The Intelligent Woman's Guide to Socialism, Capitalism, and Fascism (Shaw), 510n45
The Intelligent Woman's Guide to Socialism and Capitalism (Shaw), 213, 279–81, 394, 449; Mary Cholmondeley and, 379; popularity of, 380
International Inventions Exhibition, 115, 117
International Socialist Congress (Zurich), 168
"In the Days of My Youth" (Shaw), 462n23
Ireland: in *Back to Methuselah*, 249–50; civil war (1922–23), 249; class system in, 6, 59; constitutional convention, 361; Crimes Bill for, 481n28; grain industry in, 31; Great Famine, 30, 467n53; Home Rule for, 265,

Ireland—*continued*
361, 455; in *Immaturity*, 6, 247–48; in *John Bull's Other Island*, 247, 251–54, 266; land agency in, 61; landlord-tenant relations in, 62; literacy levels in, 467n54; middle class of, 472n7; national stereotypes, 252–53; nationalism, 245, 248, 264–65, 495n10; parliament (Dáil), 13; parochialism in, 254; poverty in, 6, 30–31, 467n54; religious attitudes in, 254; sectarianism in, 249; Charlotte Shaw's bequests to, 446–47; Shaw's attitude toward, 3, 47; in Shaw's works, 95–96, 247–51; village life in, 253; during World War I, 360; during World War II, 417–18. *See also* Protestant Ascendancy
Irish Academy of Letters, 263, 417
Irish Diaspora, 11–12
Irish Free State, Citizenship and Nationality Act (1935), 490n2
Irish Literary Portraits (BBC), 50
Irish Literary Theatre, 251, 260. *See also* Abbey Theatre
Irish National Theatre Society, 252
Irishwomen's Suffrage Federation, 501n13
The Irrational Knot (Shaw), 78, 79; composition of, 80, 81; dipsomania in, 23; Elinor Huddart on, 87; marriage in, 91, 298; materialism in, 92; publication of, 115, 130; publishers' readers on, 91; rationalism in, 92; self-parody in, 91–92; Shaw on, 92; sources for, 91
Irving, Henry, 179, 243; knighthood of, 488n23; and *The Man of Destiny*, 178, 182–83
Isola San Giovanni (Lake Maggiore), 387, 388, 389, *427*

Jackson, Ann M., 505n41
Jackson, Barry, 402; correspondence with Shaw, 514n9
Jackson, Frederick, 251
Jaeger suits, Shaw's, 79, 116, 117, 137
James, Henry, 198, 258; expatriatism of, 495n2; *Guy Domville*, 181, 277
Jaques-Dalcroze, Emile, 326
Jevons, William Stanley, 115
Joan of Arc: beatification of, 373; church dedicated to, 510n21; and Protestantism, 373; as suffragette symbol, 295, 373, 501n10. *See also Saint Joan*
John, Augustus: meeting with Shaw, 508n53; portraits of Shaw, *342*, 360, 441, 508n52
John Bull, stereotypes of, 253, 255
John Bull's Other Island (Shaw), 46, 447; autobiography in, 205–6, 208, 254, 255; Beerbohm on, 312; Louis Calvert in, 280; Granville-Barker in, 244; humor in, 126, 285; Ireland in, 247, 251–54, 266; Irish characters in, 253–55, 265–66; nationalism in, 245, 265; national leaders and, 267–68; Synge on, 252, 496n19; village life in, 253; Yeats and, 251–52
Johnson, A. E., 406
Johnson, Amy, 345
Johnson, Josephine, 175
Johnston, Denis, 3
Jones, Daniel, 384
Jones, Doris, 182, 488n20
Jones, Henry Arthur, 94, 477n59; *The Case of Rebellious Susan*, 182, 488n20; on the New Woman, 488n10; and Shaw's marriage, 210; Shaw's reviews of, 181, 182; during World War I, 347–48, 349
Jonson, Ben, 488n11
Joyce, James, 7, 254; "A Little Cloud," 462; *Portrait of the Artist as a Young Man*, 85; review of *Blanco Posnet*, 262; and Yeats, 259
Joynes, James Leigh, 100–101; in Fabian Society, 111

Kapp, Yvonne, 479n32
Kaye, Danny, *429*; at Ayot St Lawrence, 454
Kean, Edmund, 183
Keeble, Sir Frederick, 276
Keenan, Henry F.: *Trajan*, 142
Keith, Penelope, 433
Keller, Helen, 406
Kensington Gore (London), 157, 485n14
Kermode, Frank: *Romantic Image*, 441
Kerr, Deborah, 438
Kerr, Philip Henry, 404
Keynes, Maynard, 440
Kibert, Declan, 253, 496n25
Kilgarriff, Malachi J., 52
Kilsby, Albert J., 270, 275, 276, 319
Kilteragh (Foxrock, Ireland), 361
King, Sir Truby, 411

Kirby, Lieutenant Colonel Thomas, 58
Kitchener, Horatio Herbert, 198; Charlotte Shaw and, 305
Knight, G. Wilson, 126, 311
Knowles, Sheridan: *The Hunchback*, 315
Kreyer, Dorothy, 216, 217

Labor: exploitation of, 108; women's, 129
Labour Party, 110, 240; Attlee's government, 397; Ramsay MacDonald's government, 513n49
Laden, Alice, 421, 454, 458; care of Charlotte Shaw, 420; curatorship of Ayot St Lawrence, 451; *The George Bernard Shaw Vegetarian Cookbook*, 420; and Shaw's last illness, 457
Lady Margaret Hall (Oxford), 123
Lake Maggiore, Shaw at, 382, 386–89
Lalor, James Fintan, 62
Lamarck, Jean-Baptiste de Monet de, 234–35, 236–37
Land League (Ireland), 63
Landlordism, 63, 140
Landlord-tenant relations, Shaw's knowledge of, 62
Lane, Sir Hugh, 360
Lanfranco, Giovanni: *Last Supper*, 46
Langhorne, Chiswell Dabney, 406
Langland, William, 402
Langner, Lawrence, 367
La Rochefoucauld, François, 385
Latham, Lord, 453
Latin: Charlotte Shaw's knowledge of, 58; Shaw's knowledge of, 37
Laurence, Dan H., 1, 477n63; "G.B.S. in Love," 478n9; "Katie Samuel: Shaw's Flameless 'Old Flame,'" 479n28; on F. E. Loewenstein, 451; on Shaw's death, 520n61
Lawrence, D. H.: *Lady Chatterley's Lover*, 99, 409, 434, 477n74, 512n40; paintings of, 434, 512n40; reading of Shaw, 477n74; *Women in Love*, 350
Lawrence, Gertrude, 454
Lawrence, T. E., 362; assumption of Shaw name, 516n51; at Ayot St Lawrence, 416; death of, 415, 416; and *Too True to Be Good*, 416; Charlotte Shaw and, 416, 472n5; Charlotte's correspondence with, 58–59, 60, 217, 418, 446
Lawson, Cecil, 90
Lawson, Elizabeth, 90, 368, 509n9
Lawson family, at homes of, 90–91
League of Nations, in *Geneva*, 399, 449
Leavis, F. R., 461n2
Lee, Eliza, 51
Lee, Robert, 51
Lee, Vandeleur: aid to Shaw, 78; concerts of, 51; death of, 52; *Faust* production of, 40; and GBS, 19; influence on Shaw, 45, 52; and Lucy, 15, 32; musical entrepreneurship of, 51, 111, 475n21; reading of, 53–54; residence with Shaw family, 14, 31, 51, 471n71; and Bessie Shaw, 16–17, 19, 32; Shaw on, 32; *The Voice*, 51–52, 471n73; and W. Archer, 139
Le Fanu, Sheridan, 195
Le Gallienne, Richard, 221
The Legg Papers (Shaw), 79
Leigh, J. H., 244
Leigh, Vivien, 438; at Ayot St Lawrence, 454
Leinster, Duke of, 59, 472n7
Leonard, Father Joseph, 373
Lesbianism, in *Getting Married*, 299
Lewes, G. H.: *Life of Goethe*, 53
Lewis, Cecil, 387
Lewis, Dooshka, 387
Lewis, Leopold: *The Bells*, 179
Leyshon, Glynis, 503n33
Liddle, Fred, 419
Life Force, 4; in creative evolution, 232; in *Man and Superman*, 233; Shelley and, 94; in *You Never Can Tell*, 191
Llangibby Castle, SS, 402
Lloyd, David, 464n1
Lloyd, Humphrey, 61
Lloyd George, David: on Hitler, 513n59; wartime government of, 507n25
Locke, John, 235
Lockett, Alice Mary (Mrs. William Sharpe), 227, 334; correspondence with Shaw, 105–7, 128, 478n75; death of, 447; double personality of, 107; marriage of, 127, 208; quarrels with Shaw, 113; romance with Shaw, 100, 105–8, 112, 113, 133, 149, 165; and Bessie Shaw, 105; Shaw on, 183; Shaw's meeting with, 100, 105
Lockett, Jane, 105
Lockett, Walford Charles, 105

Lodge, Thomas, 115
Loewenstein, F. E., 450–51
Logier, Johann Bernhard, 15
Logier family, 26
London School of Economics: Charlotte Shaw's endowment of, 61, 110, 199; Shaw's archives at, 451
London Society for Women's Suffrage, 303–4
Longevity, Shaw on, 367
Loraine, Robert, 360; balloon ascension of, 270; swimming with Shaw, 276–77; as Jack Tanner, 276; in World War I, 276, 277, 284
Lord, Henrietta Frances, 112
Loren, Sophia, 433, 517n7
Lot's Wife, 405, 515n18
Love Among the Artists (Shaw): composition of, 81; materialism in, 98; rationalism in, 98; Shaw on, 92; sources for, 95; theater world in, 96, 178–79; utopianism in, 95
"Love lifted to his lips a chalice" (Shaw), 478n9
Lunacharsky, Anatoly, 407, 409
Lusitania, sinking of, 360
Lusitania (cruise ship), Shaw on, 223, 238, 239–40, 246, 265, 299, 364
Luton and Dunstable General Hospital, Shaw at, 457
Lyne, "Patty" Shaw (Lady Lyne), 11
Lyne, Sir William, 11
Lyons, Eugene, 408
Lyth, Jisbella ("Jessie"), 404
Lyttelton, Alfred, 326
Lyttelton, Edith (the Honorable Mrs. Alfred), 318; correspondence with Shaw, 322, 326
Lytton, Neville, 499n24

MacCarthy, Desmond, 116
MacDonald, James Ramsay, 380; correspondence with Shaw, 396; in Fabian Society, 36, 241; Labour government of, 513n49; offer of knighthood, 376
MacKenzie, Norman and Jeanne: *The First Fabians*, 483n3
MacMullen, George H., 15
Magny, Jules, 478n5
Mahaffy, Sir John Pentland, 361, 508n54
Mahaffy family, 508n54
Mair, G. H., 374
Major Barbara (Shaw), 156, 279–84; autocracy in, 394; characterization in, 312–13; class difference in, 35; composition of, 80, 279; film of, 438; good and evil in, 193, 282; Granville-Barker in, 281; and *Howards End*, 279–80; influences on, 282; Louis Calvert in, 280–81, 283; Mephistopheles theme in, 42, 280, 283; Gilbert Murray and, 284, 500n50; optimism of, 283; points of view in, 56; popularity of, 281; poverty in, 30; power in, 281–82; and Socialism, 283; villains in, 378; Beatrice Webb and, 281, 283–84
Malvern Festival, 268; revivals at, 437; Shaw at, 402–3
Man and Superman (Shaw), 129; Archer on, 140–41; autobiography in, 205; Pakenham Beatty and, 476n37; Beerbohm on, 312; Bunyan in, 41; composition of, 231; creative evolution in, 231, 232; "Don Juan in Hell," 104, 135, 231, 234, 238–39, 289, 469n33; Epistle Dedicatory, 231, 233–34; genesis of, 134; Granville-Barker in, 243, 274; Life Force in, 233; Loraine in, 276; "Maxims for Revolutionists," 237; Lillah McCarthy in, 273–75, *339*; productions of, 289; rationalism in, 92; "Revolutionist's Handbook," 233, 234, 484n37; sources for, 223, 238; Bessie Shaw and, 28; Beatrice Webb and, 231, 232; Sidney Webb and, 231
Manetti, Rutilio: *Victorious Earthly Love*, 46
Mangan, James Clarence, 26, 463n1; "The Nameless One," 507n25
The Man of Destiny (Shaw), 487n1; composition of, 177; publication of, 152; Ellen Terry and, 177–78, 182–83
Mansfield, Beatrice, 189
Mansfield, Richard: and Janet Achurch, 188–89; rift with Shaw, 188–89; Shavian productions of, 145, 174, 176, 188, 189; Shaw's review of, 145
Maratta, Carlo: *Rape of Europa*, 46
Markham, Sir Clements, 17
Markham, Elizabeth, 17
Markham, Mary, 17
Markham, Bishop William, 17
Marriage: in *Candida*, 203; in *Immaturity*, 83–84, 186; in *The Irrational Knot*, 91, 298; in *Misalliance*, 297–98; in *Mrs. Warren's Pro-*

fession, 94; and prostitution, 94; Shaw on, 81; Shelley on, 287. *See also* Shaw, George Bernard: marriage
Marston, Philip Bourke, 94
Martin, Kingsley, 455
Marvell, Andrew: "The Definition of Love," 233
Marx, Eleanor. *See* Aveling, Eleanor Marx
Marx, Karl, 112, 123; *Das Kapital*, 100, 101; Shaw's writings on, 115
Mary (queen consort of George V), 325
Masefield, John: eulogy of Shaw, 454
Materialism: in *The Irrational Knot*, 92; in *Love Among the Artists*, 98; nineteenth century, 476n49
Maude, Aylmer, 469n23
Maupassant, Guy de: *Yvette*, 168–69
Maybury Knoll (Woking), Shaw's residence at, 242
Mayer, Louis B., 410
McCarthy, Lillah, 244; acting style of, 274; at Adelphi Terrace, 273, 498nn14,18; in *Androcles and the Lion*, 273; as Ann Whitefield, 273–75, *339*; correspondence with Shaw, 368, 369, 487n4; as Dionysus, 499n47; divorce of, 362; in *The Doctor's Dilemma*, 273, 275, 499n24; marriage to Frederick Keeble, 276; marriage to Granville-Barker, 243–44, 274; *Myself and My Friends*, 273, 498n18; swimming lessons of, 274–75
McIntosh, Madge, 166
McKenna, Stephen, 497n40
McLachlan, Dame Laurentia, 46; and *The Adventures of the Black Girl*, 375, 415; correspondence with Shaw, 374, 401
McNulty, Matthew Edward, 15, 32, 39; correspondence with Shaw, 78; on the Kildonnel letters, 97; marriage of, 48; "Memoirs of G.B.S.," 40, 49, 463n35; at Newry, 247, 253; portrait with Shaw, *71*; on Shaw's religion, 231; writings of, 48
Meegan, William, 50
Meisel, Martin, 432; *Shaw and the Nineteenth Century*, 472n80
Men and Women's Club (London), 121
Mencken, H. L.: *George Bernard Shaw*, 269
Mephistopheles: in *Major Barbara*, 42, 280, 283; in "Don Juan in Hell," 238, 469n33; Shaw's identification with, 39–40, 42, 55, 61, 107, 149, 280; in Shaw's writings, 39, 42
Merivale, Hermann, 115
MGM Studios, Shaw's visit to, 410
Middle East, in Shaw's plays, 411
Migraines, Shaw's, 276
Mill, John Stuart: *Autobiography*, 53; *Three Essays on Religion*, 236
The Millionairess (Shaw): composition of, 411, 431; film of, 433, 517n7; performances of, 433
Mills, James Porter, 330; and The Fellowship of the Way, 506n75
Milton, John, 391; *Lycidas*, 392; *A Masque Presented at Ludlow Castle*, 474n7; *Paradise Lost*, 282; *Samson Agonistes*, 392
Misalliance (Shaw), 270, 284, 307; Lena Ashwell in, 298; burglary in, 148; class difference in, 35; composition of, 270, 306; democracy in, 393–94; gender in, 297; and the Kildonnel letters, 97; marriage in, 297–98; parent-child relationships in, 290, 291; sources for, 279
Moody, Catherine, 514n11
Moody, Dwight Lyman, 61
Moody, Victor Hume: *Bernard Shaw Writing*, 402, 514n11
Moonbeam (dog), 447, 448
Moore, George: *Hail and Farewell*, 7
Moore, Thomas: *Lalla Rookh*, 53
Moreau, Émile, 183
Morgan, Margery M.: *The Shavian Playground*, 476n47
Morley, John, 138, 143
Morley, Robert, *429*, 438
Morris, May, *227*; death of, 447; divorce of, 122; and Florence Farr, 150, 163; Lucy on, 122; marriage of, 125–26, 127; on Jenny Patterson, 113; political activism of, 124; relationship with Shaw, 109, 115, 117, 120, 121–22, 125–28, 161, 441; theatrical performances by, 115, 126; *William Morris*, 481n12
Morris, William, 82, 255, 481n12; and censorship, 256; "A King's Story," 148; "Sigurd the Volsung," 509n6; in Socialist League, 109
Mosley, John de Sola, 479n28

Mother figures, in Shaw's plays, 33, 186–87
Motherhood: in *Candida*, 186–87; in *Mrs. Warren's Profession*, 186; Charlotte Shaw's dislike of, 59, 188, 217, 418, 473n8
Motorcars, Shaw's: AC, *422*; accident in, 414; de Dietrich, 270, 319
Motorcycling, Shaw's, 270, 277
Mourning, Victorian, 115
Movietone News, 377
Mozart, Wolfgang Amadeus: *Don Giovanni*, 134, 135, 231, 238, 239
Mrs. Warren's Profession (Shaw): censorship concerns for, 256; composition of, 166, 168–69; factories in, 218; gender relations in, 297; genesis of, 486n57; incest in, 168; marriage in, 94; motherhood in, 186; performances of, 166; publication of, 152; self-portrait in, 169; women characters in, 300
Muggeridge, Kitty, 110, 111
Muggeridge, Malcolm, 196, 408
Munthe, Axel Martin Fredrik, 198–99, 272; *The Story of San Michele*, 198
Murdoch, Iris, 395, 513n45
Murray, Alma, 487n5
Murray, Gilbert, 261; *Bacchae* translation, 282, 499n47; influence on Shaw, 283; and *Major Barbara*, 284, 500n50; in Shaw Festschrift, 454
Murray, Lady Mary, 444
Murray, T. Douglas: *Jeanne d'Arc*, 373
Music criticism, academic, 144. *See also* Shaw, George Bernard: music criticism
Mussolini, Benito: Shaw's attitude toward, 378, 394, 395–96, 397–98, 405, 421; Shaw's impersonation of, 377; Beatrice Webb on, 395–96
Musters, Harold Chaworth, 14
Musters, Judy. *See* Gillmore, Georgina
My Dear Dorothea (Shaw), 97
My Fair Lady (Lerner and Lowe), 334, 439

National Book League, 453
National Coalition Party, 513n49
National Gallery of Ireland, 5–6, 45, 470n51; Shaw on, 471n79; Shaw's bequest to, 452
Nationalism: cultural, 245; French, 373; Irish, 245, 248, 264–65, 495n10; romantic, 62; Shaw on, 63, 245–46, 264–65, 395n10
National Union of Women's Suffrage Societies, 295; Shaw's speech to, 294, 296
National Union of Women Workers, Charlotte Shaw and, 203
Naturalism: in Shaw's plays, 431
Nature, Shaw's view of, 350. *See also* Evolution, creative
Nazi movement, Shaw on, 398
Neaves, Lord, 237
Nehru, Jawaharlal: visit to Shaw, 455, 520n54
Neo-Gaelic movement, 252
Nesbit, Edith: death of, 447; in Fabian Society, 108, 111; relationship with Shaw, 131–32, 133, 385
Newcombe, Bertha: correspondence with Shaw, 185, 248, 447; death of, 447; portrait of Shaw, 146–47, *230*; relationship with Shaw, 149, 177, 201–2; and Beatrice Webb, 201–2
Newton, Isaac, 41, 235, 435
Newton, John: *The Return to Nature*, 93
New Woman, 134; in *Arms and the Man*, 171–72; H. A. Jones on, 488n10; in Shaw's plays, 300–301
New York: *Arms and the Man* in, 174; *The Devil's Disciple* in, 189; *Heartbreak House* in, 359; *Saint Joan* in, 374; at Shaw's death, 458; Shaw's visit to, 410; Statue of Liberty, 410–11
New Zealand: Shaw in, 400, 402, 411; woman suffrage in, 501n9
Nichols, Beverley: *All I Could Never Be*, 403
Nietzche, Friedrich: *Beyond Good and Evil*, 192, 193, 282
Nobel Prize, Shaw's, 6, 375, 376
North London Collegiate School for Ladies, Bessie Shaw's teaching at, 150, 215, 492n20
Novello, Ivor: "Keep the Home Fires Burning," 346, 357
Novels, Shaw's, 81–87, 95–96; erotic novel project, 493n2. *See also individual titles*

O'Bolger, Thomas Demetrius, 20, 56, 92; "The Real Shaw," 463n36; on Shaw's paternity, 16, 17; on Shaw's reading, 52, 471n79
O'Brien, Joseph Henry, 15
O'Casey, Eileen, 416, 457
O'Casey, Sean: and Shaw, 416–17; *The Silver Tassie*, 416

O'Connor, T. P., 20, 137, 143
O'Donoghue, David J., 147
O'Donovan, John, 51; *The Genius of Shaw*, 465n14; *Shaw and the Charlatan Genius*, 463n36, 471n71
O'Flaherty VC (Shaw), 359–60, 361; Irish characters in, 248; productions of, 508n51; on radio, 377
"The Old House" (Harmer Green, Welwyn), 242
Olivier, Sydney Haldane, 101; and Boer War, 241; death of, 447; and Fabian Society, 36, 108, 110, 478n19; on Bessie Shaw, 26
"On Going to Church" (Shaw), 43, 46
On the Rocks (Shaw), 399, 412; extermination in, 421
Ophicleide, Barney Shaw's playing of, 10, 11
Order of the Golden Dawn, 171, 175
O'Reilly, Patrick, 470n66
Orientalism, Shaw's use of, 53, 412–13
Orwell, George, 395, 513n45
O'Shaughnessy, Arthur William Edgar: "We Are the Music Makers," 458
Ouija boards, 45
Our Corner (periodical), 130
Overruled (Shaw), 504n16; adultery in, 318, 325; autobiography in, 318; publication of, 331
Overton, Charles, 174
Owen, Wilfrid, 347

Pacific region, in Shaw's plays, 411
Paget's disease, Charlotte Shaw's, 444
Painting, Shaw's knowledge of, 45–46
Pall Mall Budget, Shaw's interview in, 256
The Pall Mall Gazette: Shaw's reviews for, 115, 141–42, 143, 234, 257; Shaw's "Sketch" for, 138–39; Wilde's reviews for, 257
Palmer, Albert Marshman, 174
Palmer, Lilli, 454
Palmezzano, Marco: *Virgin and Child Enthroned*, 46
Pankhurst, Emmeline, 295; in Fabian Society, 108, 241
Parliamentary Socialist Labour Party, 108
Parnell, Charles Stewart: Shaw's defense of, 265
Pascal, Gabriel, *429*, 517n11; correspondence with Shaw, 454; and *Pygmalion*, 438
Passion Play (Household of Joseph, Shaw), 79, 231
Patch, Blanche, 94, 419; and F. E. Loewenstein, 451; at Charlotte Shaw's funeral, 445; on Shaw's correspondents, 376; *Thirty Years with G.B.S.*, 371–72, 509n17; and Beatrice Webb, 371; during World War II, 443–44
Patmore, Coventry: "Angel in the House," 300
Patriarchy, and incest, 168
Patterson, Jane (Jenny), *227*; affair with Shaw, 113–14, 117–21, 127, 128, 130–31, 133, 134, 135, 149, 158, 159, 161–66, 175; correspondence with Shaw, 3, 113–14, 119, 124–25, 137, 479n36; death of, 447; gifts to Shaw, 118, 334; and Arabella Gillmore, 14; and T. Hopkins, 119–20; interest in Socialism, 124; Irish identity of, 196; jealousy of, 118–19, 130–31, 159, 160, 161, 163, 165, 218–19; loyalty to Shaw, 120; May Morris on, 113; as mother figure, 187; and *The Philanderer*, 165; quarrels with Shaw, 119, 161–66; secretarial assistance to Shaw, 159; and Bessie Shaw, 113, 114, 208; in Shaw's will, 451–52; weakness of, 164, 324
Payne, Thomas, of Edstaston, 58
Payne-Townshend, Horace, 57, 59, 75, 472n3; investments of, 232; prosperity of, 60
Payne-Townshend, Mary Susanna Kirby, 58, 59–60; death of, 197
Payne-Townshend family, 472n2
Pearson, Hesketh, 214, 461n2, 465n14
Pearson, Karl, 121; "The Woman's Question," 480n62
Pease, Edward Reynolds, 131, 154, 473n2, 482n41; *The History of the Fabian Society*, 109
Pellegrini, Giovanni Antonio: *Susanna and the Elders*, 46
Pennington-Mello, Hilda, 199
Percy, Esmé, 166, 432n, 455
The Perfect Wagnerite (Shaw), 29, 217–18; creative evolution in, 232, 235
Peters, Margot: *Bernard Shaw and the Actresses*, 511n1; *Mrs. Pat*, 504n5
Peters, Sally, 465n25, 477n74
Pharand, Michel: *Bernard Shaw and the French*, 494n11, 516n50

The Philanderer (Shaw): composition of, 127, 164–65; dialogue in, 172; Farr and, 161, 164; gender relations in, 121, 297; Ibsenism in, 154; performances of, 165, 486n48; publication of, 152; sources for, 153, 161, 162, 163, 165; women characters of, 300

Philandering, Shaw's. *See* Shaw, George Bernard: relations with women

Phillimore, Lucy ("Lion"), 206

Phillimore, Robert Charles, 206

Phonetics: in *Androcles and the Lion*, 452; in *Pygmalion*, 334, 452; in Shaw's will, 452–53

Photography, Shaw's, 270

"Piccard's Cottage" (Guildford, Surrey), 242

Pinero, Arthur Wing, 310, 318; Beerbohm's cartoon of, 181, *229*; correspondence with Shaw, 3, 181; and Dramatists' Club, 349; Shaw and, 180–81; Shaw's reviews of, 316. Works: *The Notorious Mrs. Ebbsmith*, 182, 316; *The Second Mrs. Tanqueray*, 146, 167, 168, 180, 316; *Sweet Lavender*, 483n12

Pinky Panky Poo (dog), 507n36

Pirandello, Luigi: on *Saint Joan*, 374; *Six Characters in Search of an Author*, 26

"Pitfold" (Haslemere), 216, 242

Planchettes (séance apparatuses), 44–45

Plato, *Symposium*, 120

Playfair, Arthur, 210–14

Plays, well-made, 179

Plays Pleasant and Unpleasant (Shaw): Archer on, 141; publication of, 152, 200

Plunkett, Sir Horace, 360–61

Poerson, Charles: *Assumption of the Virgin Mary*, 46

The Political Madhouse in America and Nearer Home (address, Metropolitan Opera House), 147, 402, 410–11

Political violence, Shaw on, 381

Politics, Irish: Shaw's attitude toward, 497n59. *See also* Nationalism, Irish

Pond, Violet, 419, 517n62

Postcards, Shaw's use of, 376–77

Postcolonialism, 435

POUM (Partido Obrero de Unificación Marxista), 513n45

Press Cuttings (Shaw), 79–80, 198, 303–5; censorship of, 260, 305; composition of, 305; gender roles in, 303; Irish characters in, 248–49; performances of, 305, 502n33; woman suffrage in, 303–4

Priestley, J. B., 402, 454, 468n77

Prince-White, F. G., 457

Probyn, Dr. Thomas C., 457

Progress, illusory nature of, 237

"Prophet" (sketch, Shaw), *73*

Prostitution, 167–78; marriage as, 94

Protestant Ascendancy (Ireland), 61; decline of, 260; Shaw family and, 7–9, 35–36, 191

Protestantism: in *The Devil's Disciple*, 192; Joan of Arc and, 373; Shaw and, 12, 191–92, 260; Yeats's, 260

Proudhon, Pierre Joseph, 378

Public Opinion (weekly), Shaw's letter to, 61

Pugh, Patricia, 241

Puritanism: in *Saint Joan*, 373; Shaw and, 373, 391

Pygmalion (Shaw), 211, 313, 404, 409; adaptations of, 330, 333, 334, 439; autobiography in, 334; Mrs. Patrick Campbell in, 314, 316–17, 330, 332, 335; class difference in, 35; film version (1938), 333, 334, 437, 438, 439; Forbes-Robertson and, 316–17; German productions of, 272; as literary text, 330; musical comedy version, 334, 439; Gabriel Pascal and, 438; performances of, 330, 333, 343; phonetics in, 334, 452; rationalism in, 92; screenplay of, 437; sequel-postscript to, 333–34; Charlotte Shaw on, 344; and Shaw's relations with women, 334–35; sources for, 90, 91, 118, 384; success of, 140; textual variants, 331, 333; Tree in, 330, 331, 332, 343

Quakerism, Shaw on, 501n21

Quayle, Sir Anthony, 438

Quicherat, Jules: *Procès de Jeanne d'Arc*, 373

The Quintessence of Ibsenism (Shaw), 153, 193; genesis of, 154; *Ghosts* in, 485n26; Superman in, 235; Wilde on, 255; women in, 293, 297, 502n17

Rabelais, François, 210

Radio broadcasts, Shaw's, 377

Raines, Claude, 384, 438

Rangitane, SS, 402, 411

Rationalism: in *The Irrational Knot*, 92; in *Love Among the Artists*, 98

Redford, George Alexander, 261

Reeves, Amber, 278–79, 288, 499n38
Reeves, Edith, 418–19
Rhodes, Cecil, 241, 435
Rhondda, Lady, 414
Richard Bentley & Son (publisher), 82
Richards, Grant, 210
Richardson, Ralph, 36; in *You Never Can Tell*, 190
Ricketts, Charles, 289
Rilke, Rainer Maria, 269
Ringland, Dr. John, 5
Robertson, Tom: *Ours*, 77–78
Robins, Elizabeth, 162, 304; *Votes for Women!*, 295, 501n1
Rodin, Auguste: sculpture of Shaw, 269
Rook, Clarence, 476n49
Roosevelt, Franklin D., 406
Roosevelt, Theodore, Jr., 409
Rose, Edward, 223
Rosset, B. C., 21; *Shaw of Dublin*, 463n36
Rothenstein, Sir William: portrait of Shaw, 269
Royal Academy of Dramatic Art, 384; Shaw's bequest to, 452
Royal Automobile Club, 384; Shaw's membership in, 269
Royal Commission on Poor Law, 501n5
Royal Shakespeare Company, 366
"Rumpole of the Bailey" (television series), 502n22
Ruskin, John, 247
Russell, Annie, 281
Russell, Bertrand, 235; collision with Shaw's bicycle, 194; lectures of, 200; on World War I, 347
Russia: GPU, 408, 515n35; Shaw's opinion of, 408, 413; Shaw's travel to, 399, 401, 406–9

The sacred, Shaw on, 285–86
Saint Joan (Shaw), 372–74; authority in, 378; composition of, 364, 373; Eliot's review of, 295, 374; genesis of, 372; Lady Gregory and, 264; Joan's status in, 497n42; and Dame Laurentia, 46; Mephistopheles theme in, 42; performances, 374; poetic license in, 378; Puritanism in, 373; reception of, 374, 377–78; research on, 373; settings of, 365; sources for, 349; success of, 375; Sybil Thorndike in, 374; Yeats on, 259
Saito, Makoto, 409
Salt, Henry S., 40, 132; correspondence with Shaw, 368–69; death of, 447; in Fabian Society, 111; at Shaw's wedding, 211, 212
Salt, Katherine Joynes, 207; bisexuality of, 299; relationship with Shaw, 132, 133, 299
Salt family, 466n40
Salvemini, Gaetano, 398
Samuel, Herbert, 305
Samuel, Isaac, 112
Samuel, Katherine, 112, 479n28
Sankey, Ira D., 61
Sardoodledom, 179, 183, 488n10
Sardou, Victorien, 179; *Madame Sans-Gêns*, 183, 186, 488n10; Shaw's reviews of, 488n10
Sartorio, Giulio Aristide, 199, 272
Sassoon, Siegfried, 347; *Memoirs of a Fox Hunting Man*, 268
Saturday Review: Beerbohm at, 503n13; Shaw's contributions to, 152, 177, 200; Shaw's resignation from, 209
Schlesinger, I. W., 409
Schneider, Eva Maria, 369; Shaw's bequest to, 452
Schools, Shaw on, 37, 468n1
Schopenhauer, Arthur: *The World as Will and Idea*, 235
Scott, Clement, 153, 170; on Ibsen, 485n28; Shaw on, 484n2; Shaw's caricature of, 308, 503n3; on *Widowers' Houses*, 160
Scott, Walter, 53
Séances, Bessie Shaw's attendance at, 15, 44–45
Sellers, Anne, 433
Sellers, Peter, 433, 517n7
Sexuality, and personal relations, 103–4; in *Sixteen Self Sketches*, 103, 216, 217; in *Too True to Be Good*, 434. *See also* Shaw, George Bernard, sexuality of
Shakespeare, William: *Antony and Cleopatra*, 219; *Cymbeline*, 185, 370; in *The Doctor's Dilemma*, 286–87; *Hamlet*, 84, 316, 496n25; *Julius Caesar*, 219; *King Lear*, 290, 355; *Measure for Measure*, 296, 501n13; *A Midsummer Night's Dream*, 102; *Othello*, 355; *Richard III*, 145; in *Shakes versus Shav*, 152, 437; Shaw's figurine of, 437, 518n13; *The Tempest*, 286, 445; *The Two Gentlemen of Verona*, 244; *Venus and Adonis*, 118; *The Winter's Tale*, 98

Shakes versus Shav (Shaw), 152, 437
Sharpe, William Salisbury, 127, 208, 447
Shaw, Bernard, of Hobart, 11, *76*
Shaw, Bernard, of Kilkenny, 8, 9–10, *66*
Shaw, Charles MacMahon, 10, 47, *76*, 96, 370; *Bernard's Brethren*, 12, 29–30, 467n47; career of, 466n46
Shaw, Charlotte (Aunt Charlotte), 10, 12
Shaw, Charlotte Frances Payne-Townshend (Mrs. G. B. Shaw), 177; appearance of, 196; and Lena Ashwell, 298, 330; and Nancy Astor, 405; at Ayot St Lawrence, 420; bicycling by, 194, 199; birth of, 57; at *Blanco Posnet* performance, 262, 306; *Boston Post* interview, 343–44; and Mrs. Patrick Campbell, 322, 390, 448, 505n41; canaries of, 512n34; and *Cashel Byron's Profession*, 99; character of, 196; at Cliveden, 406, 444; and Erica Cotterill, 290–91; courtship with Shaw, 200–201, 202–9; death and funeral of, 444–45; diaries of, 3, 197, 446; dislike of motherhood, 59, 188, 217, 418, 473n8; endowment of London School of Economics, 61, 110, 199; in Fabian Society, 108, 196, 204, 344; final illness, 420, 444; financial settlement on Shaw, 212; and Granville-Barker, 362, 508n61; hallucinations of, 444; horsemanship of, 58; Irish citizenship of, 195, 490n2; Irish identity of, 195–96; and *Kathleen Ní Hoolihan*, 263; and Kitchener, 305; *Knowledge Is the Door*, 506n75; and T. E. Lawrence, 416, 472n5; at Malvern Festival, 403; meeting with Shaw, 200; melancholy of, 206, 254; as mother figure, 222; motorcar accident, 414; and Axel Munthe, 198–99; noncomformity of, 197; Paget's disease of, 444; parents of, 58, 59–60; Blanche Patch on, 371; portraits, 75, *336*; on *Pygmalion*, 344; relations with in-laws, 214–15; Sartorio portrait of, 199, 272; and Lucy Shaw, 206, 213–14, 492n12; and Shaw's elective office, 267; and Shaw's friends, 500n61; and Shaw's Nobel Prize, 375; on Shaw's "peacocking," 402, 403, 514n13; on Shaw's Russian trip, 409; as Shaw's secretary, 210; on Shaw's visit to front, 509n1; social life of, 197; strength of, 324; suitors of, 197–99; swimming lessons, 222; and Molly Tompkins, 387, 389, 390, 512n36; and Siegfried Trebitsch, 272; typewriting of Shaw's plays, 204; upbringing of, 57, 58; visit with Webbs, 203; wealth of, 60–61, 212; will of, 445, 446–47; and Beatrice Webb, 196, 200, 199; and woman suffrage, 295, 344; during World War I, 345; on Almroth Wright, 284; as writer, 222
—correspondents: T. E. Lawrence, 58–59, 60, 217, 418, 446; Shaw, 3, 195, 196, 276, 331, 364, 406–7; Molly Tompkins, 390; Dorothy Walker, 416
—marriage, 210–14, 287, 288; asexuality of, 216–17, 275, 390; honeymoon, *336*; proposal to Shaw, 204, 210; and Shaw's infidelity, 202, 290–91, 318, 322–24, 390, 505n41; wedding of, 211–12; wedding ring, 215
—travel, 400–401; Algeria, 305; Bavaria, 319; Egypt, 198; India, 197, 271, 412; Lake Maggiore, 382, 386–89; Madeira, 374, 378–79, 385; Marseilles, 326, 401; New Zealand, 400, 402, 411; "Packing List" for, 401; Rome, 199, 206–8, 210; South Africa, 401; Tunisia, 305; United States, 330, 343–44, 347; walking tours, 356; world cruise, 409–10, 431
Shaw, Edward Carr, 11, 17, *76*
Shaw, Elinor Agnes ("Yuppy"), 15, *70*, 463n35; death of, 15, 20, 64–65; séances invoking, 28
Shaw, Emily (Aunt Emily), 10
Shaw, Frances ("Fanny," Mrs. Arthur Greene), 11
Shaw, Frances Carr, 9, 10; portrait of, 11, *66*
Shaw, Sir Frederick, *66*, 463n38; and George Carr Shaw, 14; Protestantism of, 191; and Queen Victoria, 9
Shaw, George Bernard: airplane flights of, 270–71, 277; anti-vaccination campaigns, 477n61; archives of, 451; artistic development of, 102; assistance to Gurly family, 463n27; balloon ascension of, 270; beard, 477n63; Beerbohm cartoons of, 40, *229*; bicycling: 177, 193–94, 200, 277, accidents during, 184, 194; biographers of, 2, 461n2; in "Bloody Sunday" demonstration, 129; boxing lessons, 89–90, 140; as Citizen of the World, 400; Civil Service studies, 78;

conversation of, 440–41; cornet playing, 280n; engagement with his epoch, 3; Fabian lectures of, 107–8, 114–15, 309, 478n5; as gadfly, 269; generosity of, 62; hairstyle of, 77, 79; at Hindhead Hall peace conference, 220; and Horace Plunkett, 360–61; iconoclasm of, 41; idealism of, 56; in Irish Academy of Letters, 263; Irish citizenship of, 195, 490n2; Jaeger suits of, 79, 116, 117, 137; and T. E. Lawrence, 516n51; London studies of, 79; meeting with Charlotte, 200; as Meliorist, 233; as Mephistopheles, 39–40, 55, 61, 71, 107, 149, 280, 469n23; mother figures of, 33; moviegoing, 437, 517n11; musical settings by, 164; music lessons of, 77; national theater campaign, 306; newsreels of, 377; notebooks of, 47–48; piano playing by, 40, 77, 272, 419, 475n21; politics: candidacies, 200, 267; poverty of, 30, 78–79; radio broadcasts by, 377; Rathmines accent of, 35, 147–48, 247, 321, 410, 468n74; reading of Marx, 100, 101; relations with dramatists, 180; reputation as playwright, 166, 173, 461n2; risk-taking by, 277; role-playing by, 55–56, 472n84; sexuality of, 2, 53, 103–4, 216–17, 389, 391–92, 461n4, 486n32; Shelley's influence on, 85, 93, 259, 287; singing voice, 272, 377, 441, 455; sketches by, 47–48, 73; social criticism of, 36; social manners of, 12, 35–36, 441; stage fright of, 148; taxes paid by, 397; teetotalling of, 24, 267; theatrical performances by, 112, 115, 126; and Siegfried Trebitsch, 272, 307, 345–46; untidiness of, 214; at Ventnor, 77; and Oscar Wilde, 86, 256–58; on woman suffrage, 285, 293–94, 296, 303–5; in World War II, 442–44; and Almroth Wright, 284–85, 296. *See also* Drama, Shavian; Novels, Shaw's; *titles of individual works*

—attitudes and opinions on: alcoholism, 23–24; anti-Semitism, 398, 443; atom bomb, 456; autobiography, 20; Max Beerbohm, 209; Boer War, 241, 242; Bunyan, 469n30; capitalism, 41, 240, 350, 380, 409, 410; class system, 34–36; cleverness, 3–4; comedy, 153, 285–86; communism, 408, 409; dancing, 368–69; Darwinian evolution, 236, 350; death, 115–16; Dublin, 6; Easter Rising, 360; emotions, 82–83; English civilization, 240; Fascism, 263, 395–99, 436; Grosvenor Gallery, 86; Walter John Gurly, 19, 43; Hitler, 394, 397, 398; homosexuality, 404–5; imperialism, 241; India, 455; Vandeleur Lee, 32; longevity, 367; marriage, 81; Mussolini, 394, 395–96, 397–98, 405, 421; National Gallery of Ireland, 471n79; nationalism, 63, 245–46, 264–65, 395n10; Nazi movement, 398; political violence, 381; the sacred, 285–86; schools, 37, 468n1; Clement Scott, 484n2; servants, 419–21; Sinhalese people, 440; South Africa, 400; spiritualism, 45; Stalin, 394, 408, 449; universities, 37; Victorian mourning, 115; woman suffrage, 285, 293–94, 296, 303–5, 501n3; women's costume, 297; World War I, 1, 182, 346–49, 360

—autobiographical writings, 2, 138–39, 449–50, 464n1; accuracy of, 19, 20; correspondence as, 185; family in, 17

—birth: baptism, 461n1; birthplace, 5–6, 50, *68*, 470n66; certificate of, 461n1; delivery, 5, 462n1; paternity rumors, 16–17, 464n36

—celebrity, 137, 138, 150, 173, 376–77; abroad, 403; in Germany, 273

—childhood and youth, 2, 21–23; artistic ambitions during, 47; at Bushy Park House, 9; in cowboy movie, 344–45; in Dalkey, 7, 38, 40, 43, 45, 47, 361; dependence on parents, 78; diaries of, 81, 90, 114; in *Doll's House* reading, 112, 126, 479n32; dreams during, 264; elective offices, 200–201, 206, 267, 491n22; emigration to America (proposed), 96, 477n65; emigration to London, 48, 63–64, 65, 77–78; exposure to Catholicism in, 8, 44, 46, 470n44; friendships during, 48–49, 50; influences on, 39–42, 45–46; musical education during, 51; nicknames of, 15; reading during, 52–55, 167, 231, 471nn75, 79; religious experiences during, 43, 46, 191–92; schooling, 37–39; theatergoing, 51, 54–55, 472n81; theatricals during, 49

—correspondents: Janet Achurch, 3, 176, 177, 500n61; Friedrich Adler, 395, 396, 397; William Archer, 3, 141, 186, 276, 345; Nancy Astor, 404–5, 416, 443; Ida Beatty,

Shaw, correspondents—*continued*
28, 492n10; Pakenham Beatty, 3, 88–89, 475n31; Annie Besant, 131, 136, 219; Mrs. Patrick Campbell, 11, 29, 220, 314, 315, 316, 317–19, 321, 322, 323–24, 326–29, 333, 354, 372, 389–90, 399, 447, 448, 501n13, 504n33, 517n11; R. C. Carton, 348; Henry Hyde Champion, 7; Charles Charrington, 368; Mary Cholmondeley, 242; Sidney Cockerell, 223, 446; Erica Cotterill, 288, 290, 299; Alfred Douglas, 246, 417–18; Leonora Ervine, 431, 433, 435; St. John Ervine, 7, 362–63; Mabel Fitzgerald, 249, 495n10; Harley Granville-Barker, 171, 314; Emily Jane Gurly, 105; Augustin Hamon, 376; Frank Harris, 6, 56, 103, 256, 389, 493n30, 512n31; Archibald Henderson, 496n35, 500n63, 502n24; Tighe Hopkins, 152–53; Elinor Huddart, 106, 478n75; Barry Jackson, 514n9; Frederick Jackson, 251; Lord Latham, 453; Alice Lockett, 105–7, 127, 478n75; Edith Lyttelton, 322, 326; Lillah McCarthy, 368, 369, 487n4; Ramsay MacDonald, 396; Dame Laurentia McLachlan, 374, 401; Matthew McNulty, 64, 78; Lady Mary Murray, 444; Bertha Newcombe, 185, 248, 447; T. P. O'Connor, 137; Gabriel Pascal, 454; Blanche Patch on, 376; Jenny Patterson, 3, 113–14, 119, 124–25, 137, 479n36; Arthur Wing Pinero, 3, 181; Edward Rose, 223; Henry Salt, 368–69; Charles MacMahon Shaw, 370; postcards used for, 376–77; Lady Rhondda, 414; Charlotte Shaw, 195, 196, 276, 331, 364, 406–7; George Carr Shaw, 22, 25–26, 78; Dorothy Stanley, 3; Ellen Terry, 154, 183–87, 190, 195, 203–5, 316–17; Molly Tompkins, 382–83, 385–86, 387–89, 392, 405, 432, 446, 514n13; Ada Tyrrell, 445; Beatrice Webb, 299, 358, 387, 442, 444; Sidney Webb, 358, 445–46, 447, 492n7; H. G. Wells, 277, 279; Oscar Wilde, 255; Virginia Woolf, 356; Almroth Wright, 296; W. B. Yeats, 251, 252; Francis Younghusband, 413
—debates, 40; with Hilaire Belloc, 320–21; with G. K. Chesterton, 320; with H. G. Wells, 36
—drama criticism, 145–46, 218; on Henry James, 181; on H. A. Jones, 181, 182; for *Saturday Review*, 152, 177, 200; on Wilde, 181–82
—employment: at Edison Telephone Company, 80, 96; at Uniacke Townshend office, 12, 39, 55, 57, 61–62, 64, 65, 253
—family: attitude toward, 12–13; grandparents, 9–10; on his father, 25–26, 29–30, 36, 466n26; on his mother, 17, 27; on his parents, 19, 32–33; relations with father, 23–26; relations with Lucy, 33–34, 370; relations with mother, 27–29, 33, 115–16, 324; resemblance to, 17
—health problems, 5, 94; breakdown of 1898, 200–201, 209, 210; broken arm, 215, 216; dental operation, 208; falls, 456; foot necrosis, 208–9, 216, 220, 362; heart attack, 456; hormone injections, 456; lumbago, 276; migraine, 276; in old age, 441–42, 455–56; pernicious anemia, 456; rheumatism, 456; scarlet fever attack, 100; smallpox, 14, 95, 477nn61,63
—honors, 437; Freedom of Dublin, 245, 453; knighthood offer, 376; Nobel Prize, 6, 375, 376
—income: from films, 418, 518n14; from investments, 492n7; from journalism, 151, 212; in *Sixteen Self Sketches*, 151; trust funds, 212, 215; W. J. Gurly's legacy, 222
—Irish identity, 3, 6–7, 17–18, 47, 63, 64, 130; accent, 35, 147–48, 247, 321, 410, 468n74; in *Fanny's First Play*, 309
—last years: at Ayot St Lawrence, 454–57; death and funeral, 5, 41, 90, 452, 457–48, 520n61; estate of, 383; final illness, 456–57; following Charlotte's death, 445–46; health during, 441–42, 455–56; interviews, 455, 456; plays of, 431–37; relations with women in, 382; vitality during, 440, 442; wills of, 451–53
—lectures, 137, 146–50, 377; Fabian, 107–8, 114–15, 309, 478n5. *See also* Shaw, George Bernard: speeches
—literary criticism, 141–43; for *Christian Socialist*, 108; for *The Pall Mall Gazette*, 115, 141–42, 143, 234, 257; for *To-Day*, 108, 115
—marriage, 210–14, 287, 288; in *The Apple Cart*, 393; asexuality of, 216–17, 275, 390; companionship in, 446; courtship of Charlotte, 200–201, 202–9; Ellen Terry on, 335;

honeymoon, 216, 217, *336*; infidelity in, 202, 290–91, 318, 322–24, 390, 505n41; as refuge, 299; restlessness in, 298, 323; wedding, 211–12; wedding presents, 223
—motor vehicles, 270; AC car, *422*; de Dietrich, 270, 319; driving accident, 414; motorcycling by, 270, 277; motoring tours, 275–76
—music criticism, 137, 143–45; Archer on, 143–44; as Corno di Bassetto, 138, 143, 483n22; for the *Dramatic Review*, 115; for *The Hornet*, 78, 79; Lucy in, 150–51; for the *Star*, 138, 143; for *The World*, 5, 143, 144
—novels, 81–87, 95–96; erotic novel project, 493n2. *See also individual titles*
—patrons: Annie Horniman, 171; William Archer, 139, 141
—portraits, *225*, *336*, *337*, *426*; in AC car, *422*; at Ayot St Lawrence, *425*, *428*; Allan Chappelow's, 418, 454; with Robert Moore Fishbourne, *72*; at Galway Bay, *422*; Augustus John's, *342*, 360, 441, 508n52; with Danny Kaye, *429*; with Lucy, *72*; with Matthew McNulty,*71*; Victor Hume Moody's, 402, 514n11; with Robert Morley, *429*; Bertha Newcombe's, 146–47, *230*; at ninety-four, *430*; with Gabriel Pascal, *429*; at Pompeii, *423*; Rodin's sculpture of, 269; Rothenstein's, 269; in the Strand, *424*; at Ventnor, *74*
—relations with women, 2–3, 104–5, 111–36, 388; Janet Achurch, 120, 150, 156–57; Nancy Astor, 345, 404–6; Eleanor Marx Aveling, 120, 133; Annie Besant, 120, 128–31, 133, 136; Grace Black, 132–33; Mrs. Patrick Campbell, 124, 146, 185, 220, 287, 298, 300, 314–15, 317–29, 353–54; celibacy in, 121–22; Erica Cotterill, 288–91, 354–55; Florence Farr, 119, 120, 127, 128, 133, 149, 150, 160–63, 167, 174–76, 217, 480n2; Alice Lockett, 100, 105–8, 112, 113, 133, 149, 165; Lillah McCarthy, 273–75; with married women, 131–32; May Morris, 109, 115, 117, 120, 121–22, 125–28, 161, 441; Edith Nesbit, 131–32, 133, 385; Bertha Newcombe, 146–47, 149, 177, 201–2; in old age, 382; Jenny Patterson, 113–14, 117–21, 127, 128, 130–31, 133, 134, 135, 149, 158, 159, 161–66, 175; *Pygmalion* and, 334–35; Katherine Samuel, 112; Kate Salt, 132, 133, 299; Dorothy Stanley, 184, 188; as "Sunday Husband," 131, 388; Ellen Terry, 183–84; Molly Tompkins, 369, 382–92, 511n1; train journeys in, 134, 289; Beatrice Webb, 202
—religious views, 94, 231–38, 279, 285; on atheism, 61, 267; in childhood, 43, 66, 191–92; on God, 235, 350; on nature, 350; on non-European religions, 411, 413; pessimism in, 233–34; on Protestantism, 12, 191–92, 260; on Puritanism, 373, 391; on Quakerism, 510n21; on the sacred, 285–86; science in, 236; in *The Shewing-up of Blanco Posnet*, 261; speeches on, 232; Victorian milieu of, 236
—residences: Adelphi Terrace, 195, 200, 224, 242, 269, 383, 514n4; Ayot St Lawrence, 5, 12, 242–43, 270, 403–4, 418–21, *425*, 443–44, 495n30; "Blackdown Cottage" (Haslemere), 242, 243; "Blen-Cathra" (Hindhead), 220; Maybury Knoll (Woking), 242; "The Old House" (Harmer Green, Welwyn), 242; Osnaburgh Street, 473n2; "Piccard's Cottage" (Guildford, Surrey), 242; "Pitfold" (Haslemere), 216, 242; Synge Street (Dublin), 5–6, 21, *68*; Torca Cottage (Dalkey), 7, 38, 40, 43, 45, 47, 519n45; Victoria Grove, 77, 474n2; Whitehall Court, 242, 400, 514n4
—speeches: to children, 221; at Metropolitan Opera House, 147, 402, 410–11; on religion, 232; on woman suffrage, 293–94, 296, 501n3. *See also* Shaw, George Bernard: lectures
—swimming habits, 24–25, 269, 384, *423*; with Robert Loraine, 276–77; with Lillah McCarthy, 274–75; with Charlotte Shaw, 222
—travel, 400–401, 514n8; Algeria, 305; Bavaria, 319; Caribbean, 410; Ceylon, 412; China, 409, 412; Cornwall, 221; effect on creativity, 411–13; Germany, 158; with Granville-Barker, 325–26; Holy Land, 401; India, 412; Japan, 409; Lake Maggiore, 382, 386–89; *Lusitania* cruise, 223, 238, 239–40, 246, 265, 299; Madeira, 374, 378–79, 385, *423*; Marseilles, 401; Mediterranean, 401; New Zealand, 400, 402, 411; Russia, 399, 401, 406–9; Skellig Michael,

Shaw, travel—*continued*
250–51; South Africa, 401, 409, 414, 415; Switzerland, 167; Tunisia, 305; United States, 96, 410; walking tours, 355–56; world, 401–2, 403, 404, 409–10
—vegetarianism, 93–94, 212, 216, 362; Shelley and, 476n52; during travels, 400
—visits: to Cliveden, 93, 345, 405, 406, 444, 477n56; to Lady Gregory, 263, 306, *342*, 360, 441; to Lady Wilde, 86
—in World War I, 346–49, 355–58; on Armistice Day, 363; at Ayot St Lawrence, 357–58; censure during, 347–49; at outbreak, 345; visit to French front, 277, 284, 349, 361–62, 509n1. *See also Common Sense About the War*

Shaw, George Carr, 3, *67*; correspondence with Bessie Shaw, 22–23, 464n36; correspondence with Shaw, 22, 25–26, 78; death of, 79, 81, 115, 116, 189, 489n49; drinking habits of, 19, 21, 23–24, 30, 465n25, 489n50; fit suffered by, 24, 466n26; humor of, 22, 30; marital separation of, 20, 31–32, 328; marriage of, 15, 20–23, 30, 463n8, 464nn14–15; musicality of, 10; occupations of, 5, 8, 14–15; pension of, 15; poverty of, 30, 31; Shaw on, 25–26, 29–30, 36, 466n26; Shaw's dependence on, 78; Shaw's relationship with, 23–26; squint of, 10, 256; on Unitarianism, 43, 469n37; on *An Unsocial Socialist*, 25

Shaw, James Cockaine ("Kaffir"), 116, 480n45

Shaw, Lucinda Elizabeth Gurly ("Bessie"), *67*; attendance at séances, 15, 44–45; autobiographical writing, 3, 26; birth of, 14; childhood of, 15, 43; correspondence with husband, 22, 464n36; death of, 324, 325, 369; education of, 15; family of origin, 13–14; in *Faust*, 40; final illness, 369; funeral of, 115–16, 324; health of, 5; Henderson on, 26; humanity of, 465n14; humor of, 26; income of, 78; independence of, 97–98; and Vandeleur Lee, 16–17, 19, 32; and Alice Lockett, 105; London residence of, 32; Lucy on, 27, 29; and *Man and Superman*, 28; marital separation of, 20, 31–32, 328; marriage of, 15, 20–23, 30, 463n8, 465nn14–15; as mother, 19, 26–27; musical career of, 15, 44; musical training of, 466n40; as music teacher, 27, 78, 87; at North London Collegiate School for Ladies, 150, 215, 492n20; as pianist, 26–27; and Jenny Patterson, 113, 114, 208; relationship with Shaw, 27–29, 33, 115–16, 324; on Kate Salt, 207; Shaw on, 17; Shaw's dependence on, 78; singing voice of, 15; "spirit" drawings of, 15, 463n32; spiritualism of, 15, 28, 45; at Ventnor, 65; visit to father, 21–23

Shaw, Lucinda Frances ("Lucy," Mrs. Charles Butterfield): birth of, 11, 21; and Bohemianism, 96–97, 468n72; and Mrs. Patrick Campbell, 328; death of, 369–70; and father's death, 189, 489n49; funeral of, 370; income of, 78; *Kildonnel Letters*, 97; and Vandeleur Lee, 16, 32; marriage of, 15, 33; mental resources of, 370; on May Morris, 122; and mother's death, 324; portraits, *70*, *72*; relationship with Shaw, 33–34, 370; religious beliefs of, 97; on Bessie Shaw, 27, 29; and Charlotte Shaw, 206, 213–14, 492n12; Shaw's characterizations of, 15; and Shaw's marriage, 206, 213–14; stage career of, 15–16, 96–97, 150–51, 214, 223, 253; translations by, 15–16, 302, 502n28; tuberculosis of, 15, 222–23, 328, 369–70; on Uncle Barney, 11; vocal performances of, 51; and Oscar Wilde, 86, 257; during World War I, 370; and *You Never Can Tell*, 190

Shaw, Richard Frederick, *66*; career of, 12; correspondence of, 3; orthodoxy of, 43; Protestantism of, 191

Shaw, Sir Robert, 9; funeral of, 462n10; and Shaw's grandparents, 10

Shaw, Robert (uncle of GBS), 11, 24

Shaw, Robert Gould, 406, 514n17

Shaw: "The Chucker-Out" (Chappelow), 418

Shaw, Walter Stephen, 11–12

Shaw, Captain William, 8

Shaw, William Bernard (Uncle Barney), 10–11, 465n25

Shaw family, 2; Australian branch of, 11–12, 462n22; churchgoing by, 43; class pretensions of, 7–8, 33–34; connection with Cromwell, 17, 18, 463n40; drinking habits, 10, 24; Vandeleur Lee's residence with, 14, 31, 51, 471n71; music-making by, 10; ortho-

doxy in, 42–43; poverty of, 30–31; and Protestant Ascendancy, 7–9, 35–36, 191; resemblances among, 17; Scottish origins of, 8; servants of, 31; Shaw's attitude toward, 12–13; and Shaw's celebrity, 150
Shaw Festival (Ontario, Canada), 433, 486n48, 503n33
Shaw Gives Himself Away, 450
Shaw Museum (Dublin), *68*
Shaw Ninetieth Birthday Exhibition (National Book League), 453–54
Shaw's Corner. *See* Ayot St Lawrence
Shaw the Villager and Human Being (Chappelow), 418
Shelley, Percy Bysshe: atheism of, 235; influence on Shaw, 85, 93, 259, 287; on marriage, 287; vegetarianism of, 93–94, 476n52. Works: *The Cenci*, 94, 168; *Episychidion*, 287; "Notes on Queen Mab," 93–94; *Prometheus Unbound*, 217–18; *Queen Mab*, 93; *A Vindication of Natural Diet*, 94; "When the Lamp Is Shattered," 164, 486n44
Shelley Society, Shaw at, 94
The Shewing-up of Blanco Posnet (Shaw), 260–63; Abbey Theatre production, 260, 261–62, 284, 305, 306, 360; censorship in England, 260, 261, 305; composition of, 305; creative evolution in, 261; Lady Gregory and, 262, 264, 269, 306; Joyce's review of, 262; justice in, 261; statement on censorship in, 305; Yeats and, 269
Simmons, Jean, 438
The Simpleton of the Unexpected Isles (Shaw): angel in, 431–32; authoritarianism in, 436; autobiography in, 431; composition of, 411, 431; creative evolution in, 436; imperialism in, 435–36; at Malvern Festival, 402; orientalism in, 53, 412–13
Simpson, Palgrave: *Alone*, 115, 126
Sinhalese people, Shaw on, 440
Sinnett, A. P.: *Incidents in the Life of Madame Blavatsky*, 142
"Sir Almroth Wright's Polemics" (Shaw), 295, 501n13
Sixteen Self Sketches (Shaw), 2; friendships in, 49; Gurly family in, 14; marriage in, 298; oratory in, 148; parents in, 20–21, 22, 25–26; photographs for, 77; publication of, 449–50; schooling in, 38; sexuality in, 103, 216, 217; Shaw's income in, 151; Sidney Webb in, 479n25
Skellig Michael (Ireland), 250–51
"A Sketch of Mr George Bernard Shaw: By Himself" *(Pall Mall Gazette)*, 138–39
"Slut," connotations of, 504n2
Smallpox, Shaw's illness with, 14, 95, 477nn61,63
Smith, Maud, 163
Smuts, Jan Christiaan, 409
Smyth Piggott, E., 256
Social Democratic Federation (SDF), 36, 109
Socialism: democratic, 449; emergence of, 108–9; *Major Barbara* and, 283; radical, 399; Shaw's publications on, 379–81, 449. *See also* Fabian Society
Society, Edwardian, 268; marriage in, 291, 292; nuclear family in, 291, 292; rebellion against, 291; Shaw's satire on, 269
Society, Victorian: death in, 115; effect of Shaw's plays on, 268; gender roles in, 3, 121, 123–24, 173; in *Immaturity*, 84; in *The Irrational Knot*, 91; marriage in, 291, 292; nuclear family in, 291, 292; women in, 123–34, 300–301
Society of Authors, Dramatic Sub-Committee, 348–49
Society of Soviet Writers, 406
Somerville, Edith, 213
Soong, Chingling, 409
South Africa: Shaw on, 400; Shaw's travel to, 401, 409, 414, 415
Spanish Civil War, 513n45
Sparling, Henry Halliday, 122, 125, 126
Spencer, Percival, 270
Spender, Stephen, 349, 506n22
Spenser, Edmund: *Faerie Queene*, 391–92
Spiritualism: Bessie Shaw's, 15, 28, 44–45, 463n32; Shaw on, 45
Sponnek, Friedrich Wilhelm, 197
Spooner, Geraldine, 40
St. John, Christopher, 303
St. Nicholas's Church (Carrick-on-Suir), 8
St. Pancras Borough, honoring of Shaw, 453
St. Pancras Vestry, Shaw's service on, 200, 206, 267, 491n22

Stalin, Josef, 515n35; Shaw's attitude toward, 394, 408, 449
Stanford, Charles Villiers: *Shamus O'Brien*, 223
Stanislavsky, Konstantin, 406
Stanley, Dorothy Tennant, 184, 188, 489n30; correspondence with Shaw, 3, 489n32
Stanley, Henry Morton, 184–85, 489n30
The Star: Shaw's contributions to, 138, 143, 163; Shaw's wedding notice in, 212
Statue of Liberty, 410–11
Stead, W. T., 129
Stebbins, C. L., 237
Stereotypes: English, 253, 255; gender, 303; Irish, 252–53, 265–66
Sterne, Laurence: *Sentimental Journey*, 493n2
Stevenson, Robert Louis, 98, 101; *Dr. Jekyll and Mr. Hyde*, 106n
Stewart, J.I.M., 374
Stewart, Sir Robert Prescott, 31–32
Stoker, Bram, 183
Stracey, Sir Edward, 318
Strindberg, August: influence on Shaw, 301–2, 502n24; Shaw's meeting with, 302, 502n29. Works: *Creditors*, 301–2; *The Diary of a Madman*, 502n24; *Miss Julie*, 502n28; *The Father*, 186, 301, 302, 502n24
Suffragettes, 295; Mrs. Patrick Campbell on, 322. *See also* Woman suffrage
Sullivan, Sir Arthur, 144–45; *Ivanhoe*, 183; *The Mikado*, 7; *Patience*, 86, 87
Sun Yatsen, 409
Superman, Shaw's use of term, 494n12
Surrealism, in Shaw's plays, 431–32
Sutro, Alfred, 281
Swift, Jonathan, 233
Swimming, Shaw's, 24–25, 269, 384, *423*; with Robert Loraine, 276–77; with Lillah McCarthy, 274–75; with Charlotte Shaw, 222
Swinnerton, Frank, 321
Synge, J. M.: on Cuchulainoid theatre, 497n40; on *John Bull's Other Island*, 252, 496n19; *Playboy of the Western World*, 26, 133; and Yeats, 259
Synge Street (Dublin), 5–6, 21, *68*
Sypher, Eileen: "Fabian Anti-Novel," 475n17
Tanner, John, 315, 504n4
Tanner, Maria Luigia Giovanna Romanini, 315
Tasmania, Shaw family in, 11
Taylor, Tom: *Plot and Passion*, 55, 472n81
Teetotalling: Alfred Douglas's, 417; Shaw's, 24, 267
Telephone, invention of, 79
Tenant League (Ireland), 62
Tennant, Charles, 404
Tennyson, Alfred, 509n6; "The Charge of the Light Brigade," 173; *Idylls of the King*, 211
Terry, Ellen, 77, *228*; and *Captain Brassbound's Conversion*, 33, 184, 185–86, 221, 222; correspondence with Shaw, 154, 183–87, 190, 195, 203–5, 316–17; death of, 447; and Henry Irving, 179; as Imogen, 185; intelligence of, 489n28; intuitiveness of, 300; in Madame Sans-Gêns, 183, 186, 488n10; and *The Man of Destiny*, 177–78, 182–83; meeting with Shaw, 183; and Shaw's courtship, 203–4, 205; on Shaw's marriage, 335; *The Story of My Life*, 183
Thackeray, William, 53
Theater: morality in, 485n28; social role of, 155
Theater, English: comedy in, 153; drawing-room, 179; love in, 218; popular, 178, 472n80. *See also* Drama, Shavian
Theosophy, Besant's, 131, 143, 158
Thesiger, Ernest, 431
The Third Man (film), 304
Thorndike, Sybil: as Saint Joan, 374
Thorough-servants, 31, 467n57
Three Plays for Puritans (Shaw), 209; *Arabian Nights* in, 53; "On Diabolonian Ethics," 193; self-portrait in, 149
"Tipperary" (song), 377
Tithonus, legend of, 509n6
Titian, *Assumption of the Virgin*, 46
Titterton, William Richard, 147
To-Day (periodical), 82; Shaw's contributions to, 108, 115
Todhunter, John, 171; *Comedy of Sighs*, 173; *A Sicilian Idyll*, 160, 512n38
Tolstoy, Leo, 351, 469n23
Tompkins, Laurence, 382; art of, 383–84; Fascist friends of, 396
Tompkins, Molly Arthur, *427*; abortion of, 389, 512n28; acting career, 384, 385; at

Adelphi Terrace, 383; and *The Apple Cart*, 392–93; and C. E. Basile, 513n51; as Calypso, 391; correspondence with Charlotte Shaw, 390; correspondence with Shaw, 382–83, 385–86, 387–89, 392, 405, 432, 446, 514n13; death of, 448; Fascist friends of, 396; flirtatiousness of, 385; at Lake Maggiore, 385–89; memoirs of Shaw, 383, 390; painting exhibition, 389; play of, 396–97, 513n54; provincialisms of, 384; relationship with Shaw, 369, 382–92, 511n1; and Charlotte Shaw, 387, 389, 390, 512n36; Shaw's advice to, 384; and *Too True to Be Good*, 392–93

Tompkins, Peter, 382, 385, 389, 512n28; education of, 392; *Shaw and Molly Tompkins in Their Own Words*, 383, 390; *To a Young Actress*, 383, 511n23

Too True to Be Good (Shaw), 52, 277, 436; autobiography in, 434–35; as discussion play, 393; interwar period in, 434–35; at Malvern Festival, 402; Molly Tompkins and, 392–93; performance in Germany, 513n60; *Pilgrim's Progress* in, 435; sexuality in, 434; surrealism of, 431; T. E. Lawrence and, 416

Torca Cottage (Dalkey), 7, 38, 43, 45, 47; frescoes of, 40; plaque at, 519n45

Totalitarianism, 395

Townsend, Horatio, 57

Townsend, Richard, 57

Townshend, Charles Uniacke, 57, 62; daughters of, 64. *See also* Uniacke Townshend and Co.

"The Transition to Social Democracy" (Shaw), 478n5

Trebitsch, Siegfried, 272, 307, 454; during World War I, 345–46

Trebitsch, Tina, 272

Tree, Sir Herbert Beerbohm: as Henry Higgins, 330, 331, 332, 343

Trollope, Anthony, 53; *The Way We Live Now*, 507n25

Troubetskoy, Prince Paul, 45–46, 387

"The Truth About Don Giovanni" (Shaw), 104

Tunney, Gene, 409

Twain, Mark: at Adelphi Terrace, 271, 498n14

Tynan, Katherine, 126; on Bessie Shaw, 26, 43

Tyndall, John, 476n49

Tyrell, Ada, 50, 445

Tyson, Brian, 141–43

"Uncommon Sense about the War" (Shaw), 443

Uniacke Townshend and Co., Shaw at, 12, 39, 55, 57, 61–62, 64, 65, 253

Unitarianism, George Carr Shaw on, 43, 469n37

United States: Charlotte Shaw's visit to, 330, 343–44, 347; Shaw's plays in, 145, 174, 189, 212, 307, 359; Shaw's visit to, 96, 410

Universities, Shaw on, 37

University College London, women at, 123

An Unsocial Socialist (Shaw), 380; composition of, 81; Elinor Huddart on, 106; publication of, 82, 108; publishers' readers on, 475n14; romance conventions in, 102; self-portrait in, 165; Shaw's father on, 25; sources for, 89, 100, 101; women characters in, 81

Unwin, T. Fisher, 156

Utopianism, in *Love Among the Artists*, 95

Vallentin, Hugo, 302, 352

Vandeleur, Crofton Moore, 51

Vedrenne, J. E., 153, 244

Vegetarianism, Shelley's, 93–94, 476n52

Vegetarianism, Shaw's, 93–94, 212, 216, 362; recipes, 420; Shelley and, 476n52; during travels, 400

Verdi, Guiseppe: *Requiem*, 458; *La Traviata*, 168; *Il Trovatore*, 61–62

Victoria (queen of England), 9, 115

Village Wooing (Shaw), 403; autobiography in, 404

Völsung Saga, 217

Voltaire: in *The Adventures of the Black Girl*, 414–15; Shaw's identification with, 516n50

Wagner, Richard: anti-Semitism of, 218; *The Ring of the Nibelung*, 217–18; *Tristan und Isolde*, 101; *Die Walküre*, 127

Walker, Dorothy, 416

Walker, Emery, 125–26, 127

Walkley, Arthur Bingham, 145; on Corno di Bassetto, 483n22; and *Man and Superman*, 231, 233; on *Saint Joan*, 374, 377–78; Shaw's caricature of, 308, 310

Wallas, Ada, 231
Wallas, Graham, 200, *226*, 395; death of, 447; in Fabian Society, 110; and *Man and Superman*, 231; at Shaw's wedding, 211, 212
Wall Street crash (1929), 386n
War, romanticization of, 173–74
Ward, Mrs. Humphry, 294–95
Wardrop, John, 450–51
Warwick Castle (ship), 414
Waterford, Lord and Lady, 198
Wearing, J. P., 515n22
Webb, Beatrice, 110–11, 169, *226*, 251; attractiveness of, 491n28; and Bertha Newcombe, 201–2; bicycling by, 193, 194; and Blanche Patch, 371; at Blen-Cathra, 220; correspondence with Shaw, 299, 358, 387, 442, 444; death of, 447; in Fabian Society, 108; and *Major Barbara*, 281, 283–84; and *Man and Superman*, 231, 232; on Mussolini, 395–96; on Royal Commission on Poor Law, 501n5; and Charlotte Shaw, 196, 199, 200; and Shaw's courtship, 202–3; at Shaw's debates, 320; and Shaw's marriage, 215–16; and Shaw's political candidacy, 260, 267; walking tour with Shaw, 355–56; world tour of, 207; during World War I, 347
Webb, Sidney, 110–11, 202, *226*; bicycling by, 193, 194; at Blen-Cathra, 220; and Boer War, 241; correspondence with Shaw, 358, 445–46, 447, 492n7; *The Educational Muddle and the Way Out*, 498n1; in Fabian Society, 36; and *Man and Superman*, 231; and Charlotte Shaw, 199; at Shaw's debates, 320; and Shaw's marriage, 215–16; and Shaw's political candidacy, 260, 267; and Shaw's trust fund, 212; and Shaw's wedding, 211; in *Sixteen Self Sketches*, 479n25; walking tour with Shaw, 355–56; world tour of, 207; during World War I, 347
Weill, Kurt: *Die Dreigroschenoper*, 406
Weintraub, Stanley, 479n32, 502n33, 506n4
Welch, James T., 159
Wells, H. G., 104, 302, 468n77; and Amber Reeves, 278–79, 288; correspondence with Shaw, 277, 279; debates with Shaw, 36; in Fabian Society, 277–78; relationship with Shaw, 277–79; and Rosamund Bland, 278, 279; in Shaw Festschrift, 454; during World War I, 347, 349. Works: *Ann Veronica*, 279; "Faults of the Fabian," 277; *The Future in America*, 499n34; *The Time Machine*, 364–65
Wells, Jane, 279
Welwyn Victoria Hospital, Shaw at, 456
Wesleyan Connexional School (Dublin), 38, 39
Westminster Hippodrome, 276, 499n27
Wheeler, C. E., 243
Wheeler, H. F., 343–44
Whelen, Frederick, 212
Whitcroft, Ellen, 15, 20
Whitcroft, John Hamilton, 14, 15
Whitcroft, Lucinda Davis, 14
White, Arnold, 12, 80
White, George R. Blanco, 279
Whitehall Court, 400; Lady Gregory's visits to, 263; move to, 514n4; Sean O'Casey at, 416; Shaw's convalescence at, 456; Shaw's residence at, 242; during World War II, 443–44
"Who I Am, and What I Think" (Shaw), 2
"Why Not Sir Henry Irving?" (Shaw), 182
Why She Would Not (Shaw), 435, 456
Wicksteed, Philip H., 115, 480n42
Widowers' Houses (Shaw), 158–60, 201; Archer and, 101, 139, 140, 158–59, 483n10; Dickensian elements in, 54; Florence Farr in, 158–59, 160; genesis of, 159, 485n18; landlordism in, 63, 140; performances of, 152, 166; reception of, 159–60; Wilde on, 255–56; working titles of, 159
Wilde, Lady: Shaw's visit to, 86, 257; and Yeats, 257
Wilde, Oscar, 149, 361; in Aesthetic movement, 86, 263; and Lord Alfred Douglas, 257–58, 417; censorship of, 256; childhood of, 6; correspondence with Shaw, 255; dialogue of, 172; exile of, 258; and Frank Harris, 257–58; Harris's biography of, 417; on Ibsenism, 255, 256; in *Immaturity*, 256; on Ireland, 255; reviews by, 257; on Shaw, 496n35; on Shaw's plays, 432; Shaw's reviews of, 181–82; Shaw's support for, 86, 258; and Lucy Shaw, 86, 257; trial of, 257–

58; on *Widowers' Houses*, 255–56; and Yeats, 259. Works: *The Decay of Lying*, 7; *Dorian Gray*, 257; *An Ideal Husband*, 181–82, 256; *The Importance of Being Earnest*, 182; *Lady Windemere's Fan*, 255; *Salomé*, 255, 256; *A Woman of No Importance*, 172
Wilde, Sir William Robert, 10, 256
Wilde, Willie, 86, 257, 258
Wilkinson, Abraham, 9
William III (king of England), 7, 264
Williams, Raymond, 149, 461n2
Williamson, Robert, 509n17
Wilson, Charlotte, 115, 132
Wilson, Edmund, 147, 410–11; on Shaw's comedy, 432
Winsten, Stephen, 455
Wisenthal, J. L., 155
Wodehouse, P. G., 268
Wollstonecraft, Mary: *A Vindication of the Rights of Women*, 123
Woman Question, 123–24, 295, 480n1
Woman suffrage, 109, 293–97; Asquith and, 298, 304; demonstrations, 501n9; in Ireland, 501n13; in *Press Cuttings*, 303–4; Charlotte Shaw and, 295, 344; Shaw on, 285; Shaw's speeches on, 293–94, 296, 501n3
Women: dualistic view of, 300–303; Fabians, 108, 132–33, 149; Fallen, 167–68; New, 134, 171–72, 300, 488n10; in *The Quintessence of Ibsenism*, 293, 297, 502n17; sexual commitment of, 121; Shaw's attitude toward, 300–303; in Victorian literature, 300; in Victorian society, 123–24, 300–301; womanly, 297, 502n17. *See also* Shaw, George Bernard: relations with women
Women's National Anti-Suffrage League, 294
Women's Social and Political Union, 295
Woolf, Leonard, 356, 440–41; *Beginning Again*, 519n3
Woolf, Virginia, 77; attitude toward servants, 421, 517n68; correspondence with Shaw, 356; and *Heartbreak House*, 356; and Shaw, 356, 412; on Shaw, 440, 441
Woolwich Working Men's Club, Shaw's lecture at, 148
The World, Shaw's criticism for, 5, 143, 144
The World of Dress (periodical), Shaw's interview in, 297
World War I: apocalyptic aspects of, 349–50; armistice, 362–63; Ayot St Lawrence during, 357–58; Belgian neutrality during, 346; Bertrand Russell on, 347; intellectual/social origins of, 351; Ireland during, 360; jingoism during, 346; literature during, 350; Lucy during, 370; outbreak of, 345–46; Robert Loraine during, 276, 277, 284; Shaw on, 1, 182, 346–49, 360; Shaw's dramas during; Shaw's visit to front during, 277, 284, 349, 361–62, 509n1. *See also Common Sense About the War* (Shaw)
World War II: Ayot St Lawrence during, 443–44; Irish neutrality during, 417–18; Shaw during, 442–44
Wormwood Scrubbs Murder, 163, 167
Wright, Sir Almroth, 284, 286, 501n13; correspondence with Shaw, 296; *The Unexpurgated Case Against Woman Suffrage*, 285, 295–96
Wright, Anne, 507n35
Writers, Irish, 255–60,263–4; expatriate, 495n2
Wyndham Croft (Crawley, West Sussex), house party at, 355–57

Yates, Edmund, 198, 490n11
Yeats, W. B., 6–7; on *Arms and the Man*, 173, 258; at Ayot St Lawrence, 262; and *Blanco Posnet* controversy, 269; on *Caesar and Cleopatra*, 219; correspondence with Shaw, 251, 252; "Cuchulanoid" vision of, 259, 497n40; and Fascism, 263; and Florence Farr, 162, 258; in Irish Academy of Letters, 263; Irish identity of, 7; and James Joyce, 258; and *John Bull's Other Island*, 251–52; meeting with Shaw, 126; in Order of the Golden Dawn, 171; and Oscar Wilde, 259; plays of, 171; Protestantism of, 260; on *Saint Joan*, 259; Saint Joan-like fragment, 259–60; and Shaw, 258–60, 262–63; on Shaw's celebrity, 173, 257; on Unity of Culture, 252, 259, 496n22; and Lady Wilde, 257. Works: *Autobiographies*, 259; *Kathleen Ní Hoolihan*, 252, 262, 263; *The Land of Heart's Desire*, 173; *On Baile's Strand*, 219; "The Second Coming," 350; *The Trembling of the Veil*, 173

You Never Can Tell (Shaw), 189–91; aborted production of, 200, 204; autobiography in, 189, 191; composition of, 177; dental clinic in, 208; Dickensian elements in, 54; humor in, 432; Katie Samuel and, 112; and the *Kildonnel Letters*, 97; Life Force in, 191; melodrama conventions in, 188; mother figures in, 187; Ralph Richardson in, 190; Shaw's opinion of, 190; sources for, 184; Lucy Shaw and, 190
Younghusband, Sir Francis, 413
Young Ireland Movement, 62

Zeppelin raids: Lucy and, 370; Shaw's witnessing of, 355, 357–58
Zetetical (debating society), 80, 148

A. M. Gibbs is Emeritus Professor of English at Macquarie University, Sydney, and a Fellow of the Australian Academy of the Humanities. He is a graduate of the University of Melbourne, and of Oxford University, where he was a Rhodes Scholar and a member of Magdalen College. He held lectureships at the Universities of Adelaide, Leeds, and Stirling before taking up professorial posts, first at the University of Newcastle, New South Wales, and later at Macquarie University. He is known internationally as a leading authority on Shaw, about whom he has published many books and essays, and is a founding member of the Council of the International Shaw Society. His principal publications include: *Shaw*, Writers and Critics Series (Edinburgh: Oliver & Boyd, 1969); *Sir William Davenant: The Shorter Poems, and Songs from the Plays and Masques* (Oxford: Clarendon Press, 1972); *The Art and Mind of Shaw: Essays in Criticism* (London: Macmillan/Dublin: Gill & Macmillan, 1983); *Shaw: Interviews and Recollections* (London: Macmillan, 1990; *"Heartbreak House": Preludes of Apocalypse* (New York: Twayne; Ontario: Maxwell Macmillan, 1994); *A Bernard Shaw Chronology* (Basingstoke, Eng., and New York: Palgrave, 2001).

Titles of Related Interest from the University Press of Florida

Bernard Shaw and the French
Michel W. Pharand

Bernard Shaw's The Black Girl in Search of God
The Story Behind the Story
Leon Hugo

Bernard Shaw's Remarkable Religion
A Faith That Fits the Facts
Stuart E. Baker

The Matter with Ireland, second edition
Dan H. Laurence and David H. Green

Pygmalion's Wordplay
The Postmodern Shaw
Jean Reynolds

Shaw Shadows
Rereading the Texts of Bernard Shaw
Peter Gahan

Shaw's Theatre
Bernard F. Dukore

For more information on these and other books,
visit our Web site at www.upf.com.

AUG 0 8 2006

Guthrie Memorial Library
Hanover's Public Library
Hanover, PA 17331-2283

By
Guthrie Memorial Library
Hanover's Public Library